STUDENT SERVICES

STUDENT SERVICES

A Handbook for the Profession, Third Edition

Susan R. Komives, Dudley B. Woodard, Jr., and Associates

Foreword by Ursula Delworth and Gary R. Hanson

Jossey-Bass Publishers
San Francisco

Published by

JOSSEY-BASS
A Wiley Company
350 Sansome St.
San Francisco, CA 94104

www.josseybass.com

Jossey-Bass books and products are available through most bookstores. To contact Jossey-Bass directly, call (888) 378-2537, fax to (800) 605-2665, or visit our website at www.josseybass.com.

Substantial discounts on bulk quantities of Jossey-Bass books are available to corporations, professional associations, and other organizations. For details and discount information, contact the special sales department at Jossey-Bass.

We at Jossey-Bass strive to use the most environmentally sensitive paper stocks available to us. Our publications are printed on acid-free recycled stock whenever possible, and our paper always meets or exceeds minimum GPO and EPA requirements.

Library of Congress Cataloging-in-Publication Data

Komives, Susan R., date.
    Student services : a handbook for the profession / Susan R.
Komives, Dudley B. Woodard, Jr., and associates. — 3rd ed.
        p.   cm. — (The Jossey-Bass higher and adult education series)
    Includes bibliographical references and indexes.
    ISBN 0-7879-0210-1
    1. Student affairs services—United States—Handbooks, manuals,
etc.   2. College student development programs—United States—
Handbooks, manuals, etc.   3. Counseling in higher education—United
States—Handbooks, manuals, etc.   I. Woodard, Dudley, date.
II. Title.   III. Series.
LB2342.9.K65   1996
378.1'94—dc20

95-25768

HB Printing 10 9 8 7 6 5

FIRST EDITION

THE JOSSEY-BASS HIGHER

AND ADULT EDUCATION SERIES

To
Esther McDonald Lloyd-Jones
and
Melvene Draheim Hardee

CONTENTS

FOREWORD

The first edition of *Student Services: A Handbook for the Profession* was conceived nearly twenty years ago, in 1977. We both lived in Iowa City, Iowa, at the time and had returned from meeting Allen Jossey-Bass, founder and then president of Jossey-Bass, Inc., at the American College Personnel Association national conference in Denver. He asked us to put our heads together and outline a comprehensive handbook for the student affairs profession, one that would present current issues and "get people to think about what it means to be a student affairs professional." The only guidelines he provided were, "Don't make it a textbook. I don't publish college textbooks!" He wanted the book written for the *practicing* student affairs professional. His invitation to outline a handbook gave us a rare opportunity to reflect on the profession: Who were we? What was our history? What were the challenges? What did people need to read? What ideas were important to discuss with one another? What events were shaping the way we thought about ourselves?

Early in our discussion, we rejected the idea of organizing the book around functional student services areas. We did not want one chapter on counseling centers and another on student activities and yet another on student financial aid. Rather, we felt there were generic themes that held our profession together, themes that crossed nearly all functional service areas. As we examined the student affairs profession, we recognized five core concepts or ideas. First, we valued contextual history—a set of ideas, attitudes, and practice that shaped who we were and how we worked. Second, we knew in our hearts that theory was important, even if we did not have much to call our own. (In the preface to the first edition, we alluded to "buying, borrowing and stealing theory from other disciplines.") Third, we knew that many different "models of practice" directed how we conducted our business. We saw these models of practice as general orientations toward what we should be doing in higher education. Fourth, we observed student affairs professionals using a variety of skills and competencies to do their work. We tried to delineate the most important ones. Finally, we appreciated the importance of organizational structures and the "management" of student services. We wanted to help administrators bring about change through an understanding of sound management and organization. To end our first edition, we proposed a graduate preparation curriculum to help prepare future student affairs leaders.

Looking back, we may not have fully appreciated the breadth and scope of change taking place in the student affairs profession in the late 1970s and early 1980s. The years prior to 1975 may have been the lull before the storm, or they may have been a time of quiet reflection. More likely, student affairs professionals were burned out and worn down from the student protests of the Vietnam War era. Whatever the reason, relatively little was being published. In 1976, however, Ted Miller and Judy Prince published *The Future of Student Affairs.* The acceptance and success of that book paved the way for a flood of new work. An excitement returned to student affairs professionals during the 1980s. New issues, new ideas, and new challenges confronted the profession. As coeditors of *Student Services* as well as Jossey-Bass's New Directions for Student Services series, we tried to shape— but were also shaped by—the continued evolution of the profession.

During the 1980s we saw a more diverse student population attend college. More adult students, more women, and a growing number of underrepresented minority students pursued a college education. Consequently, our theories of student growth and development broadened, and we were forced to look beyond the White middle-class male as the prototypic college student.

We also watched the feminization our profession. Women's issues became increasingly focused during this period, and with this increased clarity came new concepts and ideas that helped us understand gender differences among college students and among our professional staff. As a profession, we embraced the different "ways of knowing" and the different "voices" we used to communicate our views of the world.

Another shift that occurred during the 1980s was that the profession's traditional focus on the individual moved into balance with a needed emphasis on the college system or environment. As a profession, we realized we could do much more than "fix students"—we could also "fix institutions." As a result, we broadened our scope of purpose and began working with academic departments, deans, and presidents to change how we delivered our educational product. We sought advice from organizational theory and the campus ecology movement to help us manage increasingly complex organizations. Issues surrounding campus climate and developing campus community became important topics of discussion and sources of student service programming.

The 1980s also brought a change in our modes of inquiry. Naturalistic and constructionist modes of inquiry challenged the traditional scientific and reductionistic way of thinking. Field studies, ethnographic inquiry, and naturalistic evaluation models were adopted as valid and useful tools of inquiry. Today, both the scientific and naturalistic modes of inquiry have much to offer, and we have a better understanding of when and how to use each of them. Our philosophy, theory, and knowledge has gained a depth and richness that we did not have before.

Increasingly, legal issues confronted the profession during the 1980s. Student affairs administrators spent more time in courts talking with lawyers than ever before. Talk of depositions, discovery, and delays became common during staff development meetings and daily lunches. At times it seemed like nearly everyone was involved in one or more legal cases. This, too, changed how we conducted our business. We became more cautious and sought legal counsel before we acted.

Ethical concerns became more of a focus, due partly to increased legal pressures but also as a result of a heightened awareness of the parameters of respect necessary in dealing with colleagues, students, and supervisors. Revised ethics codes for the profession spelled these out in greater detail.

Accountability and assessment of student outcomes were thrust upon us by external forces. Taxpayers insisted on knowing what students had learned (or why they weren't learning) and what role we played in assisting them. Could we provide the evidence that what we did through our services and programs aided what students learned, how they learned, and how successfully they progressed through our institutions? Without solid answers, some student affairs professionals were forced into new careers.

Much has changed in the last twenty years. Many of our goals remain the same, but our means for achieving them are clearer indeed. Some of these changes, notably in the areas of standards and ethics, diversity, and outcomes assessment, were discussed in the 1989 edition.

This edition of *Student Services* continues the tradition we began, but it also pushes forward in much-needed new directions. First, the theory section has been expanded to acknowledge the increased complexity of the field and the emergence of new theories and perspectives. These chapters on the nature and use of theory should aid professional and student readers alike in understanding the essential value of theory in effective practice.

Diversity, in terms of both students and types of institutions, receives greatly needed expanded coverage, both in specific chapters and throughout this volume. All authors make clear, whatever their topic, that they are not speaking of just one type of student or just one type of educational setting.

Management and outcomes are two other topics that receive expanded coverage. Of particular importance is the material summarizing the impact of college on students. It is impressive to read what we now know, and it is challenging to recognize how much we still need to study. Here is a broad and vital research agenda that is important for each of us, whatever our specific concerns and choices of methodology.

Read these pages and you will think more deeply and more broadly about who we are and where we have been. Most importantly, you will think about where we need to go as professionals committed to helping students enter, enjoy, endure, and exit from college.

To Susan and Doug: take pride in a masterful job well done!

Ursula Delworth
Gary R. Hanson

PREFACE

One hundred years after the first dean of students appeared in American higher education, the field of student affairs can claim a proud tradition of supporting and enriching millions of college students' personal and academic lives. In that time, postsecondary institutions have repeatedly affirmed the need for traditional student affairs functions, and they have continually added new challenges to the student affairs portfolio in response to societal shifts as well as institutional and student needs.

This field of study and practice has developed over time to encompass a broad theoretical base, extended graduate-level preparation, a strong commitment to service rather than personal gain, and a community of practitioners with high standards for ethical practice and conduct. The authors of this book are not interested in an extended debate about whether this field is a profession or not. The examination of our field as a profession has merit, but we assert that we are professionals—we must possess a specialized understanding of students, their experience, and how the academic environment can enhance their development and learning. We must continue to professionalize: we must know more next year than we did this year, we must share what we know, and we must expect the highest standards of quality in our colleagues' work.

As members of a broad and diverse professional field, we continue to face the challenge of achieving a common understanding. This book is intended to promote a common language about students and higher education, to help ground our practice and inform the many professionals who work in student services functions.

The "Green Book"

In 1980, Ursula Delworth, Gary Hanson, and their associates provided a great service to our field when they published the first edition of *Student Services*. At that time, no one publication covered the breadth and depth of student affairs practice and the principles that guide it. Scholarship and literature about students and student affairs seemed to expand exponentially in the 1980s, due in great part to the New Directions for Student Affairs series, also edited by Delworth and Hanson. The second edition of *Student Services*, published in 1989, was eagerly awaited and immediately embraced as a valuable update. The "green book," as it was called, quickly became a fixture in the student affairs field, helping scores of master's and doctoral students become oriented to the profession. And the careful design of the book's contents have stood the test of time; the decision to carry *Student Services* into a third edition is a tribute to the visionary thinking of Ursula Delworth, Gary Hanson, and each of their authors.

A Note on the Title

What term best applies to the profession described in this book? Our field has been called many things: student personnel, student services, student development, student affairs. While some find the appellation "student services" too limiting, believing that it describes only a portion of what we do, we have decided to honor the history and tradition of the previous two editions of this book by keeping the same title for the third edition.

Focus of the Third Edition

This edition, like the first two, focuses on enhancing students' experience with postsecondary education through the development of student affairs professionals' knowledge, skills, and attitudes. We hope that as you read this book, you will ask yourself, "How does this information enhance my work with students?" The third edition focuses specifically on the new student affairs professional, calling upon a wealth of strong literature in the field to establish a solid foundation for student affairs practice. It targets graduate students studying to become student affairs professionals as well as individuals entering the field from other professions, such as nurses, campus child-care center directors, and faculty taking on academic advising roles. Other professionals working in postsecondary education will also find numerous sections of interest that apply to their work with students.

This book presents a scholarly review of the foundations of the student affairs profession, including its history, context, values, and theoretical base. The book reviews the core competencies required of student affairs professionals, assesses desired outcomes of student affairs practice, and explores future directions for the field. The content of each chapter is not only updated but also transformed, viewing each topic through multiple lenses or frames reflecting the wide diversity of institutional types, student characteristics, and developmental experiences. Just as the future will benefit from curricular transformation around multiple frames, the study of student affairs must model that practice.

This edition has been designed as a comprehensive text. While many sections and chapters stand alone, the reader will note that many chapters build on and assume knowledge of information presented in previous chapters.

Contents of the Third Edition

This edition is divided into six sections, addressing the historical and philosophical foundations of student affairs, the professional principles underpinning practice in the field, theoretical understandings of student development, professional competencies that facilitate student learning and the broader collegiate experience, organizing and delivering student affairs and educational interventions, and future challenges.

Specifically, Part One explores our historical and philosophical roots and the contemporary context of student affairs. It presents the history of American postsecondary education and the development of the student affairs profession. The section has been expanded in the third edition to provide a foundation for understanding the many different types of institutions and diverse characteristics of college students.

In Chapter One, John Thelin presents a succinct history of American higher education as a whole, tracing the events and movements that have influenced or reflected the student experience in the United States. In Chapter Two, Elizabeth Nuss presents a history of the student affairs field, tracing the evolution of the profession and its key functions. Nuss also addresses the student affairs practitioner's struggle for a professional identity. In Chapter Three, Johnetta Brazzell describes the foundations of the diversity we see today in American postsecondary institutions. She provides a historical overview of these institutions and portrays the current context, emphasizing institutions that have often been overlooked in the literature, such as Black colleges and universities and women's colleges. In Chapter Four, Elaine El-Khawas explores the diversity of college students. She examines the demographic and social trends that have produced the student body of today, investigating how these trends will affect who will go to college in the future.

Part Two presents the professional principles essential to student affairs practice. These chapters build on the history of student affairs and the needs and characteristics of American institutions and students, enumerating the core values of the field, the ethical principles that guide our professional behavior, and the legal foundations that serve as a context for our professional work.

In Chapter Five, Robert Young presents the philosophies and values guiding the profession. He identifies common themes from historical documents, tracing the evolution of these key ideas into the shared professional vision, values, and philosophy of today's student affairs practitioner. Harry Canon has updated his chapter on ethical standards and principles. In Chapter Six, Canon presents ethical and moral guidelines for practice and illustrates how ethical actions provide a foundation for professional behavior. Ethics and standards are such an important aspect of this profession that the entire ethics statements from both the American College Personnel Association (ACPA) and the National Association of Student Personnel Administrators (NASPA) are included in the Resources section at the back of the book. In Chapter Seven, Margaret Barr updates her discussion of the essential legal principles affecting student affairs practice, applying them to such important topics as speech codes, campus safety, and domestic partners.

Part Three examines the theoretical bases essential to the profession. These bases are changing as the field of student affairs becomes more complex. Student affairs is a proudly interdisciplinary field, integrating theories from psychology, sociology, anthropology, and public policy and applying them to the student experience in the academic environment. The theoretical frames are expanded from the second edition to reflect this growing base of theory and perspective. Each of the chapters in this section make intentional theory-to-practice applications for diverse students.

In Chapter Eight, Marylu McEwen discusses the nature of theory in student affairs and how theory can guide practice. In Chapter Nine, Nancy Evans presents an overview of classic domains of student development theory—cognitive structural, psychosocial, typological—reframed around social construction theory and updated with new theoretical material. This chapter also includes career development theory and includes a critique of the limitations of existing theoretical frames, to teach the reader how to use multiple lenses.

In Chapter Ten, McEwen applies new perspectives to understanding identity development. She presents the student's life in a personal context, including the social construction of such frames as race, gender, class, ability, and sexual orientation. Chapter Eleven, by Patricia King, is a new chapter, focusing on student cognition and learning. King emphasizes the responsibility of student development educators to enhance student learning. In Chapter Twelve, Carney Strange presents an understanding of the collegiate environment and discusses theories on interaction between individuals and their environment. Strange traces the history of this theoretical line and addresses limitations on its development. He emphasizes current theories and research, including ecological models and the concepts of student cultures and climate. George Kuh has updated his chapter on organizational theory. In Chapter Thirteen he describes several inclusive, flexible organizational models for times of rapid change.

Part Four presents the essential competencies and techniques for skillful professional practice in student affairs. As the contributors to this section demonstrate, professional practice is informed by theory and research and implemented through key roles (such as administrator, counselor, educator), with each role drawing on the practitioner's knowledge, skills, and attitudes to guide his or her practice.

In Chapter Fourteen, Judy Rogers writes on leadership. This new chapter presents an inclusive, empowerment-based model of leadership. This model represents a paradigm shift in the profession to process-oriented leadership designed to aid effective change in flexible systems. In Chapter Fifteen, Larry Roper discusses teaching and training in support of the student development educator's role with groups and individuals. In Chapter Sixteen, Roger Winston offers an updated version of his discussion of counseling and advising. He continues to emphasize personal counseling, and he has added the related dimensions of career counseling and academic advising. In addition, Winston addresses integrating cross-cultural counseling strategies. In Chapter Seventeen, Clyde Crego develops the principles and skills of consultation, including concepts like mediation. Donna Talbot discusses multicultural and diversity competencies in Chapter Eighteen. This new chapter emphasizes the importance of developing the knowledge, skills, and attitudes required to effectively work with diverse students and to create and sustain multicultural communities on campus. In Chapter Nineteen, Michael Cuyjet covers program development, including advising student organizations that develop their own programs. In Chapter Twenty, Dary Erwin overviews competency in assessment, evaluation, and research. Erwin clarifies quantitative and qualitative paradigms, referencing select techniques or methods.

Part Five addresses how the student affairs professional organizes programs and services to meet student and institutional needs. The contributors to this section focus on functional areas and the key administrative awareness needed to lead student affairs programs and services.

In Chapter Twenty-One, Art Sandeen presents student service organization, functions, and standards of practice. The chapter overviews traditional functional areas and gives special attention to emerging functional areas. In Chapter Twenty-Two, John Schuh offers an updated discussion of planning and finance, with greater emphasis on revenue sources like activity fees and issues such as fee-based structures, downsizing, and outsourcing. In Chapter Twenty-Three, Larry Benedict challenges us to make creative use of technology and information systems to more effectively reach diverse students. Jon Dalton discusses human resources in Chapter Twenty-Four, presenting a practical foundation for selecting, hiring, developing, supervising, and evaluating staff.

Part Six seeks to lay a new foundation for the future by clarifying the impact of student affairs on students. This section also presents issues, trends, and challenges that deserve attention as student affairs professionals continue to enhance the student experience in the future.

In Chapter Twenty-Five, Leonard Baird pulls the previous chapters together, discussing the overall impact of the college experience on students. These outcomes include central, general findings and findings that are salient for diverse specific groups by institutional type. In Chapter Twenty-Six, we wrap up the book with responses to emerging trends and needs in student affairs. We identify trends and developments in higher education, student characteristics and needs, and professional knowledge bases and competencies, and we discuss the conceptualization and delivery of student services for the new millennium.

Meaningful Work

The greatest compliment any professional can pay his or her work is to be able to say, "This is meaningful work, and I would choose this profession again." We both love our work, and we eagerly look forward to the twenty-first century and new challenges ahead. We were student leaders in the 1960s; we worked in residence halls and held other student affairs positions as new professionals; and we were both vice presidents for student affairs, on five campuses between us. Both of us are now professors. We have experience with small and large institutions, public and private governance, and coed and single-sex colleges. We have worked with many wonderful and diverse students. We have found that faculty want their students to learn and value and support the complementary role student affairs staff play in encouraging student learning, development, and persistence. We have encountered many wonderful professionals in our experience with the American College Personnel Association, the National Association of Student Personnel Administrators, and many other national, regional, and state associations. We have both become full-time graduate faculty in the last ten years, and we agree that our learning curves have not yet peaked—they are still climbing steadily!

The student affairs field brings constant change, constant renewal, and a rich opportunity to learn from many scholarly people. In the process of developing this edition of *Student Services*, we have learned from each of our authors, from our graduate students who assisted in reviewing the contributions, and from each other.

Dedication: To Esther McDonald Lloyd-Jones and Melvene Draheim Hardee

We dedicate this book to two women who modeled personal initiative, scholarship, mentoring, and lifelong learning for us in a caring and challenging manner. Esther McDonald Lloyd-Jones was a forerunner in the student affairs field, founding the first graduate program at Teachers College, coauthoring the first edition of *Student Personnel Point of View* in 1937, and mentoring a generation of scholars who have made their own significant contributions. She served as president of the American College Personnel Association and to the end of her life attended professional meetings and warmly developed new friendships with young professionals. Dr. Lloyd-Jones died in 1992. We dedicate the third edition of this book as a tribute to all she built, to the legacy she left, and to our shared future practice, which will aspire to the "deeper teaching" Dr. Lloyd-Jones taught us to pursue. You will see her name on many of the pages in this book. Some of you knew her, others will come to know her as you read these pages. Thank you, Esther.

We also dedicate this book to Melvene Draheim Hardee. The profession lost a champion and a source of intellectual energy when she died in December 1994. At the time of her death, she had recently retired from her longtime teaching position at Florida State University, where she founded the Hardee Center for Women. Her principled stands, her thoughtful teaching, and her ability to integrate diverse sources into a coherent whole are legend. She served as president of the American College Personnel Association, and with Gordon Klopf she initiated such long-lasting contributions as the commission system. Those of us who were her students will miss her elaborate newsletters, her handwritten notes, the flash of her racing down the hallways of conventions, and news of her nine-hundred-acre Georgia farm, "High Noon." Thank you, Melvene.

These two women remain models for generations to come. This book reflects their life and their work, and we are grateful to have known them.

In Appreciation

The authors of all the chapters in this book would like to thank the many friends and colleagues who helped them with their work. We see keenly how a work of this complexity is a true collaborative effort. We hold great admiration and offer thanks to Susan Jones, former dean of students at Trinity College in Vermont and, during the preparation of this book, a doctoral student at the University of Maryland, College Park. Her assistance in all stages of the organizing and completion of this edition has been invaluable. We are also grateful to Sherry Mallory, a doctoral student at the University of Arizona, who read drafts, made invaluable suggestions, and assisted with the final stages of production. Many thanks as well to Mike Rosenberg, a former master's student at the University of Arizona, who was very helpful in editing the first draft. Mike is now a member of the student affairs staff at Albion College. Thanks also to doctoral students at the University of Maryland, College Park, for their editorial assistance: Peter Eckel, Julie Field, John Foubert, Amy Ginther, Steve Grande, Adrienne Hamcke, Kristy Johnson, Lisa Kiely, Nance Lucas, Alice Mitchell, Linda Murphy, Emily Perl, Kathleen Rice, Gardiner Tucker, and Tracy Tyree.

Doug is grateful to his wife, Karen, whose wisdom kept him from making silly mistakes and whose encouragement was motivating during good times as well as difficult ones. He and Karen offer a special thanks to their children, who have enriched their lives and taught them the meaning of life.

Susan is grateful to her husband, Ralph, whose gourmet meals, computer debugging, and parenting of Jeffrey made this project possible. The compilation of this book coincided with wonderful life events like stepdaughter Rachel's graduation from college and wedding in Silver Plume, Colorado, and son Jeffrey's starting high school. Jeffrey was born when Susan was ACPA president-elect in 1981 and will be a first-year student on one of your campuses in 1999. He proudly says his high school graduating class of 1999 will be the "last and best class, not just of this century, but of this whole millennium!"

And a final thank you to all the colleagues who have helped us during the course of our careers. Each one of you contributed something special to our development and understanding of this profession, and we are deeply appreciative.

We hope this book will guide all of us working with students like Jeffrey, who will spend more of their adult life in the next century than in this one, who will face more change than we can now imagine, and who will build a future in a more interconnected world. We also hope this book challenges us to create more flexible and responsive processes in higher education, processes that focus on students. It is hard to imagine anything more important to our shared future than educating and developing college students. This continues to be meaningful work, and we are pleased to be engaged in it with you.

February 1996   Susan R. Komives
                                                        University of Maryland, College Park

                                                        Dudley B. Woodard, Jr.
                                                        University of Arizona

THE AUTHORS

Leonard L. Baird is a professor in the higher education and student affairs program at the Ohio State University and editor of the *Journal of Higher Education*. His B.S. (1962) and M.A. (1964) degrees are in psychology, and his Ed.D. degree (1966) is in higher education and measurement; all were received from the University of California, Los Angeles. He has over twenty-five years' experience assessing students and institutions in higher education, first as a researcher at the American College Testing Program and then at the Education Testing Service, conducting studies on a variety of aspects of higher education. The author of numerous articles and books, his chief research interests are the impact of college on students, college quality, and the social psychology of higher education.

Margaret J. Barr is vice president for student affairs at Northwestern University. She has written more than thirty books, book chapters, and monographs and has served as president of the American College Personnel Association and directed the National Association of Student Personnel Administrators' Richard F. Stevens Institute for two years. She has received awards from both ACPA and NASPA for contributions to the literature and from ACPA for professional service.

Larry G. Benedict is the dean of Homewood student affairs at the Johns Hopkins University. He previously served as the first vice president for student affairs at the University of Southern Maine and associate vice chancellor for student affairs at the University of Massachusetts, Amherst.

Johnetta Cross Brazzell is vice president for student affairs and professor at Spelman College. She was formerly interim dean of students at the University of Arizona, where she taught in the College of Education's Center for the Study of Higher Education.

Harry J. Canon is a senior associate with Aspen Professional Development Associates. He served as vice president for student affairs at Northern Illinois University for nearly a decade and then joined the faculty as a professor of counseling. He has been a member of the American College Personnel Association's executive council and was chair of the ACPA Ethics Committee.

Clyde A. Crego is director of the university counseling center at California State University, Long Beach, and adjunct professor of counseling psychology at the University of Southern California. A fellow in three divisions of the American Psychological Association, including the Division of Consulting Psychology, he is past president of the APA Division of Consulting Psychology.

Michael J. Cuyjet is associate professor of educational and counseling psychology and coordinator of the college student personnel program at the University of Louisville. Previously, he has held a number of student affairs positions at Northern Illinois University and the University of Maryland, College Park.

Jon C. Dalton is vice president for student affairs and associate professor of higher education at Florida State University. He has served as president of the National Association of Student Personnel Administrators and directs the annual Institute on College Student Values held at Florida State University.

Elaine El-Khawas is vice president for policy analysis and research at the American Council on Education. A sociologist, she has conducted many studies on both students and institutions of higher education. Since 1984, she has been responsible for *Campus Trends*, an annual study of changing campus practices published by ACE.

T. Dary Erwin is director of assessment and professor of psychology at James Madison University. He is the author of *Assessing Student Learning and Development: A Guide to the Principles, Goals, and Methods of Determining College Outcomes.*

Nancy J. Evans is associate professor of education and coordinator of the college student personnel option in the Department of Counselor Education, Counseling Psychology, and Rehabilitation Services at the Pennsylvania State University. She previously taught at Western Illinois University and Indiana University.

Patricia M. King is professor and chair of the Department of Higher Education and Student Affairs at Bowling Green State University. She has served as president of the Association for Moral Education and is currently a senior scholar of the American College Personnel Association. Previously, she was assistant vice president for student services at Ohio State University and senior research psychologist at the University of Iowa. She is the coauthor (with Karen Strohm Kitchener) of *Developing Reflective Judgment* (1994).

Susan R. Komives is associate professor of counseling and personnel services and faculty associate for the Division of Student Affairs at the University of Maryland, College Park. She has served as vice president for student development at the University of Tampa, as vice president and dean of student life at Stephens College, and in various student affairs positions at Denison University and the University of Tennessee, Knoxville. She is a former president of the American College Personnel Association and the 1994 recipient of the Esther Lloyd-Jones Professional Service Award. She is publications and research editor of the National Clearinghouse for Leadership Programs.

George D. Kuh is professor of higher education and coordinator of graduate programs in higher education and student affairs in the Department of Educational Leadership and Policy Studies at Indiana University. He also directs the *College Student Experiences Questionnaire* Research and Distribution Program. An American College Personnel Association Senior Scholar Diplomate, he has received awards from ACPA and the National Association of Student Personnel Administrators for contributions to the literature.

Marylu K. McEwen is associate professor and director of the college student personnel program, Department of Counseling and Personnel Services, University of Maryland, College Park. Previously, she was affiliated with Auburn University and Purdue University and serves as associate editor of the *Journal of College Student Development*.

Elizabeth M. Nuss served as executive director of National Association of Student Personnel Administrators from 1987 to 1995. She received her B.A. degree (1967) in Spanish and secondary education from the State University of New York, Albany; her M.Ed. degree (1969) in higher education and student personnel administration from the Pennsylvania State University; and her Ph.D. degree (1981) in education policy, planning, and administration from the University of Maryland, College Park. She is the author of numerous articles and was the recipient of the National Association of Student Personnel Administrators' 1982 Dissertation of the Year Award.

Larry D. Roper is vice provost for student affairs at Oregon State University and professor of ethnic studies. He earlier served for six years as vice president for student affairs and dean of students at St. John Fisher College. He holds an M.A. degree from Bowling Green State University and a Ph.D. degree from the University of Maryland, both in the field of college student personnel.

Judy Lawrence Rogers is an associate professor of college student personnel in the Department of Educational Leadership at Miami University (Ohio). Prior to joining the faculty, she served in student affairs administrative positions at Miami University, George Mason University, Ohio Wesleyan University, and Saint Mary College.

Arthur Sandeen has been vice president for student affairs and professor of educational leadership at the University of Florida since 1973. He is the author of *The Chief Student Affairs Officer: Leader, Manager, Mediator, Educator.* He is a past president of the National Association of Student Personnel Administrators and chaired the committee that wrote the Perspectives document commemorating the fiftieth anniversary of *The Student Personnel Point of View.*

John H. Schuh is associate vice president for student affairs at Wichita State University, where he also holds a faculty appointment. Previously, he held administrative and faculty appointments at Indiana University and Arizona State University. He earned his B.A. degree at the University of Wisconsin, Oshkosh, and his M.C. and Ph.D. degrees at Arizona State. Schuh has received the Contribution to Knowledge Award, the Presidential Service Award, the Annuit Coeptis Award, and the Senior Scholar Award from the American College Personnel Association. He also received the Contribution to Literature or Research Award from the National Association of Student Personnel Administrators and the Leadership and Service Award from the Association of College and University Housing Officers—International. He has served on the governing boards of ACPA, NASPA, and ACUHO-I. The author of more than 120 publications, Schuh received a Fulbright Award to study higher education in Germany in 1994.

C. Carney Strange is professor of education in the Department of Higher Education and Student Affairs at Bowling Green State University.

Donna M. Talbot is an assistant professor in the Counselor Education and Counseling Psychology Department at Western Michigan University; she coordinates the Student Affairs in Higher Education graduate programs. Previously, she has had experience with residence life research, college counseling and HIV counseling, multicultural affairs, leadership development, judicial affairs, the Peace Corps, and teaching high school mathematics.

John R. Thelin is professor of the history of higher education and philanthropy at Indiana University. At The College of William and Mary from 1981 to 1993, he was chancellor, professor, and director of the higher education doctoral program. He was research director for the Association of Independent California Colleges and Universities from 1979 to 1981. The author of five books and numerous articles on higher education, he was keynote speaker at the 1994 conference of the Association for the Study of Higher Education. He was awarded a major research grant from the Spencer Foundation from 1989 to 1992. In 1986, he received the Phi Beta Kappa Award for faculty scholarship at The College of William and Mary. A 1969 alumnus of Brown University, he concentrated in history and was elected to Phi Beta Kappa. He received an M.A. degree (1972) in history and a Ph.D. degree (1973) in educational studies from the University of California, Berkeley.

Roger B. Winston, Jr., is professor in the student personnel in higher education master's program and coordinator of the student affairs administration doctoral program in the Department of Counseling and Human Development Services at the University of Georgia. He is the author or editor of ten books related to student affairs or academic advising.

Dudley B. Woodard, Jr., is professor and director of the Center for the Study of Higher Education at the University of Arizona. He was vice president of student affairs at the State University of New York, Binghamton, and the University of Arizona. He is a past president of National Association of Student Personnel Administrators and chaired the NASPA Foundation Board.

Robert B. Young is professor of higher education and coordinator of educational leadership in the School of Applied Behavioral Sciences and Educational Leadership at Ohio University.

STUDENT SERVICES

PART ONE

HISTORICAL ROOTS AND CONTEMPORARY CONTEXT

Every profession has a history. In student affairs as in all other professions, we have a collective sense of how we came to be what we are—our values, customs, traditions, and beliefs. Our history forms our identity, becomes an anchor, provides direction. The contemporary context of higher education and student affairs is very much influenced by our understanding of historical events and by the meaning we attach to them. An appreciation of history and context helps the student affairs practitioner understand the ideas, values, and events that shape her or his practice. Thus the first two chapters in this part present a history of American postsecondary education and the development of the student affairs profession. The next two chapters describe the diversity of our institutions of higher education today

and from this description extrapolate the characteristics of tomorrow's college students.

American higher education was distinctive from the beginning in that it was based on the belief that the student's character as well as scholarship must be developed. American colleges were patterned after the residential colleges of Oxford and Cambridge. In Chapter One, John Thelin takes us quickly through over three hundred years of higher education history. Throughout this odyssey, he reminds us that the American system was founded on the principle of student learning and character development. He begins with a discussion of colonial colleges, transitioning into the emergence of a distinctive "American Way" in higher education. The remainder of the chapter discusses the development of the modern university and concludes with an excellent description and analysis of higher education during the "Golden Age" and the "Era of Accountability."

The roots of our profession begin with the development of higher education in America. Although formal student affairs roles did not develop until the late nineteenth century, the concept of student development was born in the early days of American higher education. In Chapter Two, Elizabeth Nuss traces the development of the profession, from the university's in loco parentis role to the development of the contemporary student affairs practitioner, a professional role grounded in theory and practice. She reviews the founding years of the profession and discusses the emerging diversification of functions and students. Most of her chapter is devoted to recent developments, including professional preparation and associations, theory and research, standards, and issues influencing the evolution of the profession.

Both Thelin and Nuss set the stage for viewing the historical development of the profession within the broader context of the place of American higher education today. The remaining two chapters in this part are new additions to the book; they describe the breadth of institutions and students in the nineties. In Chapter Three, Johnetta Brazzell focuses on the diversity of postsecondary education. She describes the development and mission of various types of institutions of higher education. Her focus, however, is not a detailed discussion of the entire range of institutions. Rather, she focuses on understanding those institutions that have traditionally been underrepresented in the literature. Elaine El-Khawas concludes this part with an informative discussion of the diversity of today's college students. Her data on who our students are will help the reader gain an appreciation of the present and future diversification of student bodies and the necessity for understanding one of the major founding principles of our profession—each student is unique. She concludes with advice and suggestions on ways to understand who our students will be tomorrow.

After reading Part One, the reader should have an appreciation for the historical roots of the profession and the social and political forces that have influenced its development. Context is a major ingredient in developing knowledge and appreciating contemporary issues and challenges.

CHAPTER ONE

HISTORICAL OVERVIEW OF AMERICAN HIGHER EDUCATION

John R. Thelin

In 1910, an editor researching the growth of American colleges and universities noted during a visit to the Midwest that "the University of Chicago does not look its age. It looks much older. This is because it has been put through an artificial aging process, reminding one of the way furniture is given an 'antique oak finish'" (Slosson, 1910, p. 429). Indeed, American universities' fondness for Gothic spires and Georgian-revival brick quadrangles reveals an essential feature about higher education in the United States: the American public expects its colleges and universities to be historic institutions, with monumental architecture that invokes a sense of continuity and heritage. In fact, a historical profile of U.S. higher education is in large part a story of structures—not just bricks and mortar, but also the legal and administrative frameworks—products of U.S. social and political history—that have made our colleges and universities enduring institutions.

But our concern is with higher education's history, not its archaeology, so we need a theme to bring these skeletal structures to life. The key is provided by historian Frederick Rudolph's account of a Williams College alumni banquet in 1871. James Garfield, later president of the United States, praised his own alma mater and its president by proclaiming that "the ideal college is Mark Hopkins on one end of a log and a student on the other" (Rudolph, 1962, p. 243). His tribute reminds us that despite the proliferation of magnificent buildings and elaborate facilities in American colleges and universities, and the official language of their college charters notwithstanding, ultimately the history of colleges and universities in this country is about teaching and learning. Students and faculty are central characters in the higher education drama, without which the structures are nothing but inanimate stage props. Whether in the eighteenth, nineteenth, or late twentieth century, the American tradition in higher education has been a strong commitment to undergraduate education. Maintaining this tradition requires vigilance, however, since there has been in recent decades a tendency toward benign neglect of undergraduate students. Both established and aspiring universities have emphasized advanced programs, research centers, and other activities far afield from the bachelor's degree curriculum. From time to time highly publicized commentaries, such as the 1993 report of the Johnson Foundation's Wingspread Conference, have urged higher education leaders to reclaim the American education heritage by rediscovering the importance of "putting student learners first" (Wingspread Group on Higher Education, 1993, p. 1).

Structures and Students

A good way to chart the history of higher education in the United States is to keep in mind that quantitative changes have signaled qualitative changes. For example, from 1700 to 1900, only about 1 percent to 5 percent of Americans between the ages of eighteen and twenty-two enrolled in college. Between World Wars I and II this figure increased to about 20 percent, rising to 33 percent in 1960 and dramatically expanding to more than 50 percent in the 1970s. These numbers define the transformation of American higher education from an elite to a mass activity, with the added historical fact that in the past two decades the prospect for universal access to postsecondary education has emerged as part of the American agenda (Trow, 1970). According to one estimate, in 1990 over fourteen million students enrolled in postsecondary education in the United States. This development is discussed in detail in Chapter Four. Furthermore, as shown in Chapter Three, expansion has been characterized by variety, both in the addition of new kinds of institutions and in the changing demographic composition of undergraduates. Hence, tracing the history of American higher education involves no less than the interesting task of interpreting this blend of continuity and change.

To attempt to grasp the three-hundred-year history of American higher education in a single glimpse is both unwieldy and unwise, because the details of each epoch allow us to test and reconsider what was taking place at the time. Therefore, the following pages first consider the legacy of the English influence on colonial colleges. Attention then shifts to how America wrestled with the question of creating a distinctive "American Way" in higher education during the new national period. Next the discussion highlights the emergence of the "university" model from 1880 to 1914, with the reminder that other institutional forms also flourished during this period. After considering higher education in the three decades between World Wars I and II, the historical analysis moves to the problems of abundance and prosperity in the 1960s. Finally, to bring historical research close to the present, the decades 1970 to 1990 are analyzed as an era of adjustment and accountability. Having completed this narrative account, the chapter then aims to bring coherence to the history of American higher education and its student services profession by considering the implications for professional practice and policies of trends in research and scholarship within a variety of related disciplines.

The Colonial Period: Sorting Out the English Legacy

Although the ideal of an intense undergraduate education by which young adults are prepared for leadership and service is a distinctively American tradition, it owes much to the example set by the English universities of Oxford and Cambridge in the sixteenth and seventeenth centuries. These came to be known for their unique practice of arranging several residential colleges within a university structure, all located in a pastoral setting. This so-called Oxbridge model departed from the patterns of academic life and instruction found in the urban universities of the late middle ages at Paris, Salerno, and Bologna, where scholars banded together for protection and in order to set standards for teaching, pay, and tuition but gave little attention to building a permanent campus or supervising student life (Haskins, 1923). In sharp contrast, by the seventeenth century Oxford and Cambridge had developed a formal system of endowed colleges that combined living and learning within quadrangles. This model consisted of an architecturally distinct, landscaped site for an elaborate organizational culture and a pedagogy designed to build character rather than produce expert scholars. The college was an isolated, "total" institution whose responsibilities included guiding the social as well as the academic dimensions of undergraduate life. The Oxford-Cambridge model not only combined these elements, it integrated them within a coherent philosophy of residential education. This approach would come to influence college builders in the New World.

Frederick Rudolph (1962) called this American educational tradition the "collegiate way" (pp. 86–109). Even when the realities of the American wilderness set in or college officials ran out of money for building, it persisted as an aspiration in the national culture. The most telling legacy of the early college founders is the combination of optimism and caution in their quest to create what historian James Axtell (1974) called the "school on a hill." The American colonists built colleges because they believed in and wished to transplant and perfect the English idea of an undergraduate education as a civilizing experience that ensured a progression of responsible leaders. Their plans reflected a deliberate attempt to avoid the problems and mistakes associated with a loss of control of curriculum and governance, problems that sometimes characterized their European counterparts. Ironically, this meant that the two groups most central to their plan—students and teachers—were from the start restricted from holding official authority in matters of external institutional governance. Ultimate power was vested in a college lay board to maintain discipline and accountability, an antidote to the sloth and indulgence attributed to autonomous masters and scholars at the English universities. By incorporating a tight connection between the college board and its host civil government, the colonial colleges fostered both responsible oversight and a source of government revenues from taxes, tolls, and lotteries. The centrality of colleges to colonial life is suggested by their proliferation and protection—starting with Harvard, founded in the Massachusetts Bay Colony in 1636, and followed by The College of William and Mary in Virginia in 1693, Yale in Connecticut in 1745, and six more colleges by the start of the Revolutionary War.

Colonial college life was characterized by tensions between students and faculty. Indeed, the residential college was as much a recipe for conflict as for harmony, with riots and student revolts frequently triggered by numerous consumer complaints, ranging from bad food in the dining commons to dissatisfaction with the curriculum. Although the student body was relatively homogeneous, it was not unaware of the nuances of social class. College rosters listed students by social rank. Furthermore, following the Oxford tradition, academic robes reflected socioeconomic position, delineating the "commoners" (those who dined at college commons) from the "servitors" (those who waited on tables). Religion, of course, was an important part of the fabric of American culture, including its colleges. Yet emphasis on Christian values was not at odds with preparation for secular life. Above all, the colonial colleges were not seminaries, chartered primarily to educate the clergy. They did train future ministers, but this tells only part of the educational story; that purpose was only one of many among the central mission of the undergraduate bachelor of arts curriculum (Handlin & Handlin, 1974).

In reconstructing the colonial curriculum, we have few written records. The best estimate is that oral disputations were often the most rigorous hurdles, subject to the immediate critical evaluation of both masters and fellow undergraduates. The motivation to study classical texts or to solve complex mathematical problems was to avoid the ridicule and jeers from classmates that greeted a student's poor public speaking, flawed logic, or faulty Latin translations. One puzzling characteristic of the colonial colleges is that there was little emphasis on completing degrees. Many students matriculated and then left college after a year or two, apparently with none of the stigma we now associate with dropouts. Enrollments were modest, seldom as much as a hundred students. At William and Mary, so few undergraduates petitioned for graduation that the new governor of Virginia put up commencement prize money as an incentive for students to complete their degree requirements.

American higher education in the eighteenth century did include some precedents for diversity—and the associated challenges. Once in a while colonial colleges ventured on daring missions and usually encountered weak, even disastrous results. For example, attempts to extend collegiate education beyond the white population of the British colonies were high on intentions, low on planning, and even lower on results. Consider the lore passed on by Benjamin Franklin (1784) concerning the education of sons of Indian chiefs at a colonial college: after the Indian students returned from their scholarship studies, their chieftain fathers complained that the sons had become unhealthy, lazy, and unable to make good decisions. Tribal elders politely refused the college's offer to renew the scholarship program, suggesting instead that perhaps the colonial leaders would like to send *their* sons to the Indians for an education that would make the Anglo boys into men who were strong and wise.

The novelty (and high failure rate) of such experiments underscores the fundamental limits of the colonial colleges' scope and constituency. Enrollment in college courses was confined to white males, mostly from established, prosperous families. There was little expectation for college to provide social mobility. Rather, college attendance tended to ratify or confirm existing social standing. The curriculum might provide an analytic or intellectual edge in the discourse and writing associated with public life or the practice of law (Handlin & Handlin, 1974). In plain terms, the college mission was to ensure the preparation and disciplined seasoning of a future leadership cohort. Certainly this was an "elite" student group. This exclusiveness, so contrary to our contemporary notions of equity and social justice, ought not cancel out the important fact that in the eighteenth century a college education served the serious, albeit limited, societal function of transforming a potential indolent, indulgent cohort of privileged young men into a responsible, literate elite committed to serving the colony and, later, the nation.

The aim of the colonial college, then, was the rigorous education of the "gentleman scholar." If the colonial colleges were limited in their constituency and mission, they were at least remarkably effective in their education of an articulate and learned leadership group, as suggested by the extraordinary contribution of their alumni, including Thomas Jefferson and James Madison, to the political and intellectual leadership of the American revolution and the creation of the new United States.

Creating the "American Way" in Higher Education: The New National Period

During the new national period following American independence in 1776 and extending into the mid nineteenth century, the small college persisted as the institutional norm, despite scattered attempts to create a modern comprehensive university. On closer inspection, there were continual curricular innovations and experimentation in American higher education. An undeniable fact of American life well into the late nineteenth century was that going to college was not necessary for "getting ahead" economically, although a college degree did confer some prestige. Colleges had to compete incessantly for the attention of both donors and paying students. Campaigns to create a truly "national" university were unsuccessful. At the same time, state governments showed little inclination to fund higher education, although granting college charters was a popular and easy way for legislators to repay political debts. Although state universities in Georgia, North Carolina, South Carolina, and Michigan were founded in the early nineteenth century, they enjoyed only sparse support from their respective legislatures and often took years to get around to the business of enrolling students and offering instruction.

That the American college was not universally supported—either by legislators, donors, or paying students—did not mean it was unimportant. Letters from fathers corresponding with their college sons in the early 1800s indicate that established families took college education very seriously, because they wanted to make certain their sons were acquiring the values and skills requisite for responsible, effective participation as adults in public affairs and commerce (Wakelyn, 1985). Also, seemingly every religious group wanted to build its own college as a crucible for reinforcing its distinctive orthodoxy among members who were growing from adolescence into adulthood.

College marketing and student recruitment were peculiar during the new national period. The impoverished colleges often scrounged to survive by lowering their charges to attract more students as the start of the autumn term approached. This usually was a disastrous strategy that perpetuated the idea that pursuing a college education was not a worthwhile endeavor. Reforming presidents, including Frances Wayland at Brown University in Rhode Island and Philip Lindsley at the new University of Nashville, urged colleges to offer a modern, useful course of study for which students and their parents would be eager to pay a fair price. However, the quest for an attractive curriculum was slow and uneven. Even the 1862 Morrill Act, which provided federal support to promote advanced study in the mechanical arts and agriculture, was slow to change matters, although it is usually cited for introducing useful fields into the college curriculum. Today's historians, with the benefit of hindsight, emphasize two reasons colleges lacked qualified students during the period 1800 to 1860. First, American education was top-heavy and overextended; there were literally hundreds of colleges, but most of them had inadequate operating funds or endowments. A second reason was the country's lag in providing secondary education, the obvious and necessary source of college applicants. In a display of American ingenuity, colleges responded to this void by creating preparatory programs to serve the dual purpose of providing sources of operating income and eventually a cohort of students who could pass the college entrance examination.

There is a tendency to depict the early nineteenth century as the "false dawn of the state university." The corollary is the notion that the dominant model was what has been called the old-time college, an institution that was at best moribund, locked into an archaic curriculum of classical texts and daily recitations defined by the Yale Report of 1824 and usually tightly connected to a particular religious denomination (Axtell, 1970). A revised interpretation sees the activities within the college campus of the time as varied and substantive. To gain this perspective, historians have looked beyond the formal course of study of these universities to their extracurricular activities, such as literary societies, debating clubs, and service groups. Here one finds the roots of the extensive university library of today, with readings in modern fiction, journalism, and such new fields as political economy and the natural sciences. Even though most college presidents were drawn locally from the ranks of ordained ministers, the scholarly and intellectual life of the faculty and students included some connections with the Scottish Enlightenment, as found in the works of Adam Smith, David Hume, and John Locke, and the philosophical and academic trends found on the continent. Furthermore, analysis of extracurricular activities of the time shows that students exerted great influence on the life of their college and determined which activities and values were emphasized (Rudolph, 1962). This leverage required tenacity and strong fellowship, as college officials, who feared activities that departed from the formal curriculum, often attempted to discourage or even prohibit the various student literary and social groups.

The image of a stagnant campus has also been modified by evidence of considerable curricular innovation at many colleges, as the pragmatic will to survive led some presidents and boards to approve new courses in engineering, the sciences, and modern languages and to experiment with dual-track curricula. The public did not always respond favorably to such useful innovations, however. The result is an erratic record of survival and mortality among new curricula and programs in the first half of the nineteenth century. New programs may not have always succeeded, but to say there were no attempts at innovation is quite incorrect.

Although it was still not feasible for most Americans to go to college, there was a gradual change in the socioeconomic makeup of many student bodies; the established elite of the colonial colleges was replaced by a mix of students from a wide range of family incomes in what was called a convergence of "paupers and scholars." What this meant was that at some of the newly established "hilltop colleges" such as Amherst, Williams, Bowdoin, and Dartmouth, students came from modest farming families; many were older than the customary seventeen to twenty-one years old (Allmendinger, 1975). Typically they worked their way through college, often taking time out to teach elementary school or perform a variety of subsistence jobs. Furthermore, the creation of a number of charitable trusts and scholarship funds helped colleges provide financial aid for able yet poor young men who looked forward to joining the clergy or teaching (Peterson, 1963).

Elsewhere, some colleges innovated by affiliating themselves with freestanding professional schools of medicine, law, and commerce, most of which (contrary to our contemporary assumption) did not require any undergraduate education or a bachelor's degree for admission. Despite the popularity of the new "scientific" course of study at some colleges in the nineteenth century, a certain snobbery attended the traditional curriculum: at daily chapel, for example, students from the "scientific school" were required to sit in the rear pews, conspicuously apart from the liberal arts students.

Between 1860 and 1900, such historically excluded constituencies as women, Blacks, and Native Americans gained some access to higher education. (See Chapter Three for a detailed discussion of the diversification of American higher education.) By the mid nineteenth century, women in particular had become formal participants in advanced studies. One educational innovation was the founding of the "female academies" and "female seminaries"—institutions that often rivaled the academic excellence of the men's colleges and which, over time, became degree-granting colleges in their own right (Horowitz, 1984; Solomon, 1985). In the late nineteenth century a few colleges, (such as Oberlin and, later, Cornell) pioneered coeducation, enrolling both men and women—a policy that would gain a wide following in the Midwest and on the Pacific Coast (Gordon, 1990).

Between 1865 and 1910 some provisions were made for Black students to pursue higher education, with the founding of Black colleges in the South. The first impetus for financial support for these colleges came from philanthropic groups, such as the Peabody Foundation, based in the North, followed by funds from Black churches and finally a mix of federal and state appropriations. An often overlooked fact is that federal funds and private foundations also supported higher education for Native Americans—whether as part of such campuses as Virginia's Hampton Institute or at distinct institutions like Pennsylvania's famous Carlisle School for Indians.

The cumulative impact of the innovations and experiments in American higher education in the nineteenth century was an interesting social change: by 1870, "going to college" had come to capture the American fancy. As one brash, ambitious undergraduate candidly told historian Henry Adams in 1871, "A degree from Harvard is worth money in Chicago" (Adams, 1918, pp. 305–306). More precisely, to be a "college man"—or a "college woman"—lifted one to a social standing that had both prestige and "scarcity value" (Canby, 1936, pp. 23–56). Around 1890, popular national magazines started to run profiles of selected colleges and universities as a regular feature. The growing number and diversity of students and institutions illustrated the variety of American higher education. There were multiple models, ranging from comprehensive institutions with a diverse student body to special-purpose colleges serving a separate, distinct group.

University Building and More: 1880 to 1914

As higher education became more and more popular, the emergence of the modern university in America dominated press coverage. At one extreme, the ideal of advanced, rigorous scholarship and the necessary resources of research libraries, laboratories, and Doctor of Philosophy programs were personified by the great German universities. Emulating and transplanting the German model to the United States became the passion of the Johns Hopkins University in Baltimore, Clark University in Massachusetts, and the new University of Chicago. At the same time, a commitment to applied research and utility gained a following at the emerging land grant institutions, ranging from the University of Wisconsin to the urban Massachusetts Institute of Technology. In the United States between 1870 and 1910, this "university movement" was an American hybrid. It was a dramatic, monumental movement undergirded by large-scale philanthropy and widespread construction of new campus buildings (Veysey, 1965). As Edwin Slosson (1910) wrote, "the essential difference between a college and university is how they look. A college looks backward, a university looks forward" (p. 374). But when historians look at the situation, they see complications and exceptions to Slosson's typology. Although the university was news, the ideal of the undergraduate college also soared in popularity. Even in the age of university building, the undergraduate—not the doctoral student or professor—became the object of praise, even envy. On balance, the prospect of building great universities in America contributed to the cutting edge of advanced scholarship. At the same time, however, this "cutting edge" remained marginal to the central purpose of undergraduate education. So, although the ideals of research and utility were conspicuous, they were tempered to varying degrees by the value traditionally placed upon a liberal education and piety. The best evidence of this claim is that no American university, including the pioneering examples of Johns Hopkins and Clark, was able to survive without offering an undergraduate course of study! Furthermore, in contrast to higher education in the 1990s, American universities of 1910 remained relatively underdeveloped and small. Only a handful of institutions, such as the urban universities of Harvard, Columbia, and Pennsylvania, enrolled more than five thousand students.

Sponsored research and graduate programs were limited in size and resources. One of the more substantial achievements of the university-building era was the annexation of such professional schools as medicine, law, business, theology, pharmacy, and engineering into the academic structure of the university. Equally important was the ingenuity and perseverance American undergraduates showed in creating a robust extracurricular world of athletics, fraternities, sororities, campus newspapers, and clubs, which vied successfully with the official curriculum. Observers likened the student culture to a "primitive brotherhood" or, drawing an analogy from political science, a "city-state within a campus" (Canby, 1936, pp. 23–36). The strength of the undergraduate culture gained added support from a new entity: organized alumni associations, which created an alliance of old and new students who worked tirelessly to ensure that presidents and professors did not encroach upon the precious traditions of undergraduate life. The result was a compromise of sorts, in which the emerging American campus of 1900 tried to minimize conflicts by accommodating a wide array of programs and priorities.

Even thirty years after passage of the 1862 Morrill Land Grant Act, public higher education was still relatively underdeveloped. After 1900, however, legislatures in the Midwest and West started to embrace and financially support the idea of a great university as a symbol of state pride. Applied research, a utilitarian and comprehensive curriculum, not to mention the public appeal of spectator sports and the availability of federal funds for such fields as agriculture and engineering led to the growth and maturation of the state university. Often overlooked is the second land grant act, of 1890, which created the historically Black land grant institutions along with the agricultural extension services (Wright, 1988). And by World War I, the move to increase the accessibility of study beyond high school was signaled by the founding of a distinctive American institution: the junior college (Diener, 1986).

Higher Education Between the World Wars: 1915 to 1945

Historian David Levine (1986) charted the rise of American colleges and the concomitant "culture of aspiration" (p. 13) in the three decades between World Wars

I and II. The most salient feature of this period was the stratification of American higher education into institutional layers, which indicates that distinctions were drawn between prestige and purpose in pursuing a college education. There was, for example, the emergence of public junior colleges, an increase in state normal schools and teachers' colleges, and the creation of new technical institutes (Diener, 1986; Levine, 1986). The great state universities of the West and Midwest finally started to fulfill the promise of the Morrill Act to serve the public, with enrollment at typical large campuses reaching fifteen to twenty-five thousand. On the other hand, depictions of popular access to state universities must be analyzed carefully and not exaggerated. Many institutions regarded today as large state universities were still relatively limited in size and curricular offerings in the first half of the twentieth century. As late as 1940, many state universities had a total enrollment of less than five thousand, with few offerings in the way of advanced programs or doctoral studies.

Enrollments rose during the Great Depression due, in part, to widespread unemployment. Universities received relatively little federal support, although there was some government involvement in selected scientific research programs. A few campuses, especially those with strong scientific and engineering departments, pioneered working relations with corporations and industry in research and development. But these exceptional ventures remained something of a rehearsal; they did not flourish in any sustained way until the emergence of government-sponsored projects during World War II.

Perhaps the greatest puzzle facing American higher education in the early twentieth century is what may be termed the dilemma of diversity. Ironically, the most glaring conflicts and hostilities were encountered at those institutions that were the most heterogeneous. Coeducation, for example, deserves to be hailed as a positive change in promoting equity and access for women. At the same time, however, such celebration needs to be tempered with careful historical analysis of how women students were treated. Lynn Gordon (1990) found that at the University of California, the University of Chicago, and Cornell, women undergraduates encountered discrimination both academically and in student activities. A comparable pattern of discrimination occurred at those universities that enrolled ethnic, racial, and religious minorities. Historian Helen Lefkowitz Horowitz (1987) traced the effects of this discrimination, noting how student subcultures developed over time, with "insider" groups tending to dominate the rewards and prestige of campus life. Horowitz's account of the founding of new women's colleges from 1860 to 1930 suggests that special-purpose colleges provided distinctive educational benefits for their students and alumni (Horowitz, 1984).

In the 1920s some colleges enjoyed the luxury of choice. For the first time they had more applicants than student places, allowing administrators to implement selective admission policies. Unfortunately these were used to exclude some students on the basis of race, ethnicity, gender, or other criteria unrelated to merit. On balance, American higher education's capacity to provide access ran ahead of its ability to foster assimilation and parity within the campus. The result was a complex dilemma for campus officials and policy analysts: how to best serve minority groups and new participants in higher education? The customary American response was to provide no single answer or consistent policy, relying instead on an imperfect laissez-faire arrangement of student choice and institutional autonomy, predicated on the availability of a mixture of comprehensive and special-purpose institutions. More often than not, American higher education achieved diversity through colleges dedicated to serving a special constituency, whether defined by race, ethnicity, gender, or religious affiliation.

Higher Education's "Golden Age": 1945 to 1970

Oscar Wilde has noted that nothing is so permanent as a temporary appointment. Certainly this describes the dramatic changes in student enrollments after 1945. The Servicemen's Readjustment Act, popularly known as the G.I. Bill, was intended to be a short-term measure by which the federal government could mitigate the pressure of loosing scores of returning war veterans on a saturated labor market by making federal scholarships for postsecondary education readily available. But the G.I. Bill had unexpected long-term consequences: it set a precedent for making portable government student aid an entitlement, and it provided a policy tool for increasing the diversity of American universities.

The popularity of the G.I. Bill underscored the importance of higher education to the nation's long-term adjustment to a new economy and postwar democracy. A 1947 report authorized by President Harry S. Truman brought to Congress and the American public the bold proposition of permanently expanding access and affordability to higher education. This egalitarian impulse coincided with effective lobbying for the expansion of government- and foundation-sponsored research grants for university scholars. The convergence of the two trends resulted in what has been called higher education's golden age, marked by an academic revolution in which colleges and universities acquired unprecedented influence in American society (Freeland, 1992; Jencks & Riesman, 1968). Growing states such as California faced the attractive problem of whether they could build sufficient classrooms to accommodate the influx of new students. Some decisions made in these years would have long-term consequences on student learning and retention. For example, in his landmark study *Four Critical Years*, psychologist Alexander Astin (1977) noted that after 1950 most states tended to favor the construction of new commuter institutions such as community colleges and new state colleges; although this approach succeeded in accommodating growing enrollments, the new institutions had little provision for full-time residential education—a significant departure from the traditional notion of "the collegiate way."

A related development was the emergence of the multicampus university system. In place of having one or two flagship universities, many states now joined numerous branches into a centrally administered network. Although the seventy-five great research universities commanded the most attention in this era, equally noteworthy were the growth and curricular changes in numerous branch campuses and normal schools, most of which added master's and graduate professional programs. Public community college systems became partners with the state universities; the community colleges offered the first two years of undergraduate education, with a smooth transfer to the state university for upper-level work. Such were the coalitions and compacts that characterized this era of state coordinating commissions, master plans, and accrediting agencies, with campus officials working to build in a measure of coherence and quality to accompany the system's growth. The most significant change in the 1960s was the large, enduring presence of the federal government through a complex cluster of programs ranging from the 1964 Civil Rights Act to the accompanying funding for student financial aid and the assistance provided by the Higher Education Facilities Act. All institutions, public and private, were cognizant of the growing federal presence of incentives and penalties.

Problems During a Time of Prosperity: The 1960s

What is difficult to imagine in the 1990s—a time of flat funding for higher education—is that in the 1960s prosperity brought problems. Richard Freeland's (1992) study of universities in Massachusetts during the years 1945 to 1970 recounted an era of ruthless competition among colleges and universities in the pursuit of students, research grants, and external funds. Most troubling for those concerned with the quality of undergraduate education was that even among established universities there was a strong temptation to use undergraduate enrollments as a convenient means of subsidizing new graduate programs and research institutes. Policy proposals included discussions between university officials and state legislatures over teaching strategies. For example, should one opt for large lectures and a single great faculty member, or for small sections?

The prestigious institution that symbolized the era was the "multiversity," or what Clark Kerr (1964) called the "federal grant university." These consisted of a flagship campus with advanced degree programs, whose enrollment often exceeded twenty thousand students and whose budget relied heavily on the "soft money" of research and development projects funded by the federal government and private foundations. Important to note, however, is that enrollments in other kinds of institutions—small colleges, religious colleges, private universities, community colleges, regional campuses, and technical institutes—were also healthy, even beyond enrollment capacity. At the same time that the "multiversity" gained prominence, as sociologist Burton Clark (1970) documented, the distinctive liberal arts college flourished, especially in the private sector. Curricular innovations at these institutions included honors programs and freshmen seminars. Testimony to the strength of the historical "collegiate ideal" for American educators of the late twentieth century was that even the large public universities came full circle to ponder ways in which mass higher education might provide a modern equivalent of the old New England hilltop college. Clark Kerr (1964) of the University of California summed up the challenge for undergraduate education in the early 1960s with the rhetorical question, "How do we make the university seem smaller as it grows larger?" He attempted to answer his own question by supporting an interesting innovation known as the "cluster college"—separate residential units within a large university, which restored the colonial ideal of bringing living and learning together within an Oxford-Cambridge model of higher education. But such experiments were exceptional and expensive; Americans still had not resolved the dilemma of how to ensure high retention and close attention in mass higher education.

Expansion of such relatively young institutions as community colleges, state systems, regional campuses, and tribal colleges created the umbrella system of "postsecondary education" in the three decades of growth after World War II. The ledger sheet around 1960 suggests that American postsecondary education demonstrated remarkable success in providing access to higher learning but remained uncertain about perfecting the process and experience of a college education. Ultimately this gap between ideal and reality fanned a growing discontent among undergraduates. A landmark event, both for higher education and for student services, was the publication in 1962 of an interesting volume edited by psychologist Nevitt Sanford, *The American College*. It was a significant work on two counts: first, its research findings by behavioral and social scientists provided a distant early warning of problems that would surface later in the decade; second, it marked the emergence of higher education as an increasingly systematic field of study with implications for campus administrators and planners.

The history of higher education is often the story of unexpected consequences. And for the college and university administrators of the 1960s, the boom in construction and enrollments tended to mask problems and tensions among students that would emerge between 1963 and 1968 and violently erupt between 1968 and 1972. There were two distinct yet related sources of undergraduate discontent. First was the internal stress of the booming campus. This stress was evident in criticisms about large lecture classes, impersonal registration, crowding in student housing, and the psychological distance between faculty and students. Second, student concern about external political events—notably the Vietnam War and the draft—and allegations of U.S. universities' involvement in them kindled a visible and eventually widespread student activism. This activism not only preoccupied but also strained the real and symbolic foundations of higher education, and it affected universities' internal and external conduct. By 1970 the national media was portraying the American campus less as a sanctuary and more as a battleground in a protracted generational war between college students and the established institutions associated with adult society. Outspoken student activists became symbols of a new popular culture and acquired high visibility in both television and newspaper coverage.

An Era of Adjustment and Accountability: 1970 to 1990

Several years of student unrest had several negative effects on American higher education, not the least of which was declining confidence on the part of state governments and other traditional sources of support. No longer did public officials assume that a university president or dean of students could keep his or her house in order. By 1972 there was a transformation in the federal presence in higher education, reflecting an increased commitment to social justice and educational opportunity. This was the emergence of large-scale entitlements for student financial aid—an alphabet soup of Basic Educational Opportunity Grants (BEOG) and Supplementary Educational Opportunity Grants (SEOG) funding, later known as Pell Grants. These generous grant programs embodied the ideal that issues of affordability should not circumscribe students' choice in making college plans. Enactment of further loan programs and work study programs, combined with increased institutional funds for scholarships, created a formidable change in access to higher education from 1972 to 1980. The traditional student images of "Joe College" and "Betty Coed" were supplemented by women, Native Americans, African Americans, Asian Americans, and Hispanics as central members of the undergraduate world. During the same years, new legislation prohibiting discrimination in educational programs (Title IX) allowed women to gradually gain access to extracurricular activities such as intercollegiate athletics and to such academic fields as business, law, medicine, and a host of Ph.D. programs. By 1990, Section 504 of the Vocational Rehabilitation Act had further encouraged diversity and access by providing guidelines for educational institutions to serve students with disabilities.

How did these new programs and policies shape campus life? The best way to approach that question is to fuse historical analysis with sociology and anthropology. Anthropologist Michael Moffatt's (1989) account of undergraduate life at Rutgers in the 1980s, *Coming of Age in New Jersey,* suggested that students had become increasingly resourceful at navigating the complexities of large institutions. But cohesion was an increasingly uncertain dimension of the campus and curriculum. A perennial question was whether academic standards were becoming diluted as the number of students attending college grew. Obviously there were no clear answers to that complex question. However, Moffatt's study included an historical analysis comparing student life in 1880 to that of a century later. His surprising finding was that undergraduates of the earlier era did not necessarily study more hours than the students of 1980. Rather, they simply devoted more entries in their daily logs and journals commenting on their intention to study or expressing their remorse over not having studied more!

The history of higher education in the past two decades has included other puzzles and uncertainties. For example, economists of the early 1970s were timely and accurate in warning college presidents and trustees about a forthcoming "new depression" in funding. By 1978 it was clear that the financial hard times were even worse than had been predicted. Campuses and other nonprofit institutions encountered two headaches: ten consecutive years of double-digit inflation and soaring heating oil prices. Rounding out the gloomy picture, demographers projected a substantial decline in the number of high school graduates. All of this combined to signal a future marked by campus closings and cutbacks. The problems were real, and the concerns were warranted. The unexpected twist was that American higher education demonstrated a great deal of innovation and resiliency. Enrollment declines were muted as colleges recruited new constituencies, including older students and more students from such traditionally underserved constituencies as women and minorities. Campus administration underwent a managerial revolution, in two ways. First, there was increased reliance on systematic data analysis from national and institutional sources, which helped colleges make informed decisions that promoted budget accountability. Second, new government incentive programs prompted colleges to shift resources to marketing, fundraising, and student recruitment in order to seek and retain new student constituencies (and develop new programs to serve them). Thus the period 1979 to 1989, which was supposed to have been a grim winter for American colleges and universities, turned out to be an extended summer of unexpected abundance.

History, however, always includes seasonal change, and ultimately American colleges and universities could not evade financial problems. By 1990, reports from virtually every governor's office in the country indicated severe shortfalls in state revenues, in addition to other sustained indications of a depressed economy. At the same time, federal support for university-based research waned, making even the most prestigious universities vulnerable to cutbacks. If there was an apt motto for the situation facing higher education in the last decade of the twentieth century, it was to "do more with less." Paradoxically, going to college remained a valued experience in American life, with rising enrollment and student demand at the very time that adequate funding for higher education was uncertain. The rub was that the increased demand for higher education coincided with increased government obligations for road construction, health services, and prison reform, all during a period of scarce resources. Parents were concerned that their daughters and sons might not have access to the same quality of higher education that they had enjoyed in the prosperous decades after World War II. By 1990, changing financial and demographic circumstances were prompting educational leaders and critics to consider the need for a fundamental shift in attitudes toward higher education and the collegiate structure in the United States. The optimism of the 1960s had waned; higher education no longer aimed for unlimited diversity and choice. Perhaps one consolation in this current dilemma is the fact that the present still reflects the past—colleges and universities remain integral to the significant issues of American life.

Conclusion

Any attempt to present a brief survey of American higher education over three centuries risks superficiality. A good resolution to carry away is to see the history of American colleges and universities less as a compendium of facts and more as a lively process in which each generation of college officials, students, donors, and legislators has wrestled with the perennial issue of who shall be educated and how. Central to this orientation is the idea of a "useful past," in which the history of higher education is understood as essential and is applied to one's work in campus administration and other professional roles in higher education. In recent years, the most interesting historical research on higher education has incorporated concepts from the related disciplines of sociology, anthropology, economics, and political science (Goodchild & Wechsler, 1989). Sociologist Burton Clark (1970), for example, has developed the notion of a "campus saga" to explain how some colleges have over time acquired a sense of heritage and mission that they effectively transmit to new students and faculty, as well as alumni. Much work remains to be done in order to apply Clark's concept to numerous understudied and unexamined colleges and universities. Intensive case studies of individual institutions are a good way for higher education administrators to make sense out of their own experience and institution in terms of preceding generations and national trends. The great issues of access, accountability, social justice, and excellence are pressing, but they are not new. Higher education professionals also need to recognize that understanding the history of distant eras remains an unfinished task. Today we take for granted readily available statistical data on such aspects of student life as retention and degree completion and for sophisticated analyses of university budgets. Unfortunately this knowledge does not extend back very far; all too often we rely on sparse anecdotes for our estimates of institutional performance in the eighteenth and nineteenth centuries. There is a great need to compile fresh historical data to supplement contemporary information for policy making. Statistics and other compilations from the past, linked with present data, can be integral to thoughtfully analyzing whether colleges are changing—and if so, how much—in matters of efficiency and effectiveness. At the same time, we have not given much attention to the fiction and memoirs of student life from our own era. The ultimate challenge for a lively history of higher education, then, is to be aware of landmark events and to draw from precedents some information and inspiration to consider the complexities of significant issues dealing with student life, university governance, and the all-too-familiar task of trying to fulfill educational ideals with scarce resources.

References

Adams, H. (1918). *The education of Henry Adams: An autobiography.* Boston: Houghton Mifflin.

Allmendinger, D. (1975). *Paupers and scholars: The transformation of student life in nineteenth-century New England.* New York: St. Martin's Press.

Astin, A. W. (1977). *Four critical years.* San Francisco: Jossey-Bass.

Axtell, J. (1970). The death of the liberal arts college. *History of Education Quarterly, 4*(4), 339–352.

Axtell, J. (1974). *The school upon a hill: Education and society in colonial New England.* New Haven, CT: Yale University Press.

Canby, H. S. (1936). *Alma mater: The gothic age of the American university.* New York: Farrar and Rinehart.

Clark, B. R. (1970). *The distinctive college.* Chicago: Aldine.

Diener, T. (1986). *Growth of an American invention: A documentary history of the junior and community college movement.* New York: Greenwood Press.

Franklin, B. (1784). *Remarks concerning the savages of North America.* London.

Freeland, R. (1992). *Academia's golden age: Universities in Massachusetts, 1945–1970.* New York: Oxford University Press.

Goodchild, L., & Wechsler, H. (1989). *ASHE reader on the history of higher education.* Needham, MA: Ginn.

Gordon, L. (1990). *Gender and higher education in the progressive era.* New Haven, CT: Yale University Press.

Handlin, O., & Handlin, M. (1974). *The American college and American culture.* New York: McGraw-Hill.

Haskins, C. (1923). *The rise of the universities*. Ithaca, NY: Cornell University Press.

Horowitz, H. L. (1984). *Alma mater: Design and experience in the women's colleges from their nineteenth-century beginnings to the 1930s*. New York: Knopf.

Horowitz, H. L. (1987). *Campus life: Undergraduate cultures from the end of the eighteenth century to the present*. New York: Knopf.

Jencks, C., & Riesman, D. (1968). *The academic revolution*. New York: Doubleday.

Kerr, C. (1964). *The uses of the university*. Cambridge, MA: Harvard University Press.

Levine, D. (1986). *The American college and the culture of aspiration, 1915–1940*. Ithaca, NY: Cornell University Press.

Moffatt, M. (1989). *Coming of age in New Jersey: College and American culture*. New Brunswick, NJ: Rutgers University Press.

Peterson, G. (1963). *The New England college in the age of the university*. Amherst, MA: Amherst College Press.

Rudolph, F. (1962). *The American college and university: A history*. New York: Knopf.

Sanford, N. (Ed.). (1962). *The American college*. New York: Wiley.

Slosson, E. (1910). *Great American universities*. New York: Macmillan.

Solomon, B. M. (1985). *In the company of educated women*. New Haven, CT: Yale University Press.

Trow, M. (1970). Reflections on the transition from mass to elite higher education. *Daedalus, 99*(1), 1–42.

Veysey, L. R. (1965). *The emergence of the American university*. Chicago: University of Chicago Press.

Wakelyn, J. L. (1985). Antebellum college life and the relations between fathers and sons. In W. J. Fraser, R. F. Sanders, & J. L. Wakelyn (Eds.), *The web of Southern social relations: Women, family, and education* (pp. 107–126). Athens: University of Georgia Press.

Wingspread Group on Higher Education. (1993). *An American imperative: Higher expectations for higher education*. Racine, WI: Johnson Foundation.

Wright, S. (1988). Black colleges and universities: Historical background and future prospects. *Virginia Humanities, 14*, 1–7.

CHAPTER TWO

THE DEVELOPMENT
OF STUDENT AFFAIRS

Elizabeth M. Nuss

The development of student affairs in the United States parallels that of American higher education. Influenced by changing religious, economic, social, and political forces, the practice of student affairs has evolved and developed. An understanding of this evolution provides an essential context for understanding today's student affairs programs, services, events, and tensions.

This chapter traces the evolution of the profession from the faculty role of in loco parentis to the creation of the specialized roles of deans of women and deans of men and finally to the organizational patterns and roles seen in student affairs today. The evolution of key concepts and components such as extracurricular and cocurricular activities, integration of student affairs with the academic mission, student development theory, professional standards, and student learning and assessment are also discussed. Critical historical points are marked and recorded by key documents and events. Examples of key documents include the *Student Personnel Point of View (SPPV)* (American Council on Education, 1937/1994a), the *Joint Statement on Student Rights and Freedoms (JSSRF)* (National Association of Student Personnel Administrators, 1992), *Student Development in Tomorrow's Higher Education* (Brown, 1972), and *A Perspective on Student Affairs* (National Association of Student Personnel Administrators, 1987), among others. (These documents are introduced here for their historical context; their themes and relevance are discussed in detail in Chapter Five.) The establishment and evolution of professional student affairs associations and the roles they played in the history of the profession are also discussed.

As you consider the history of student affairs, please note two enduring and distinctive concepts. The first is the profession's consistent and persistent emphasis on and commitment to the development of the whole person. In spite of the dramatic changes that have occurred in higher education, the profession's adherence to this fundamental principle should not be overlooked or underestimated. Second, student affairs was originally founded to support the academic mission of the college, and one of the characteristic strengths of American higher education is the diversity among the missions of these institutions. Student affairs' sustained commitment to supporting the diversity of institutional and academic missions over time is a hallmark of the history of the profession. The commitment of student affairs to these two fundamental principles should be viewed as a strength and as evidence of the professional nature of student affairs work rather than as a limitation or shortcoming.

Historical Developments

As Cowley and Williams (1991) so aptly put it, "All historic periodizations are, of course, no more than convenient devices employed to marshal facts and ideas dramatically" (p. 131). Various historians of higher education (Brubacher & Rudy, 1976; Cowley & Williams, 1991; Leonard, 1956; Rudolph, 1965) have used slightly different time periods and labels to present facts and ideas. In Chapter One, John Thelin outlined the history of American higher education using seven time periods: the colonial era, the new national period, the university-building period, between the World Wars, the "golden age," the 1960s, and the era of adjustment and accountability. In tracing the history of student affairs, this chapter is organized around the following time frames and labels: the founding and early years, from 1636 to approximately 1850; the period of diversification, which begins just prior to the passage of the Land Grant Act in 1862 and ends in 1900; the emergence of the profession, from 1900 to 1945; and the modern expansion period, from 1945 to today.

The Founding and Early Years: 1636 to 1850

The roots of today's comprehensive student affairs programs in American colleges can be traced to the founding of the colonial colleges (Leonard, 1956). Patterned on the English universities of Oxford and Cambridge, the colonial colleges were residential, religiously affiliated institutions. Their goal was to teach students the precepts of religion, promote their ability to govern, and prepare an educated clergy. Residential facilities in colonial colleges "were designed to bring the faculty and students together in a common life which was both intellectual and moral" (Brubacher & Rudy, 1976, p. 41). They were an essential aspect of collegiate life in the early colonial colleges. Rudolph (1965) described the collegiate way of life as one based on the "notion that a curriculum, a library, a faculty, and students are not enough to make a college" (p. 87). The dormitory made it possible for the faculty to exercise supervision and parental concern for the well-being of the students. Students were viewed as immature adolescents requiring counsel, supervision, vocational guidance, and, frequently, remedial classes (Leonard, 1956). Colonial colleges were empowered to act in loco parentis. The system of discipline was paternalistic, strict, and authoritarian. The early collegiate way of life was "dependent on dormitories, committed to dining halls, and permeated by paternalism" (Rudolph, 1965, p. 87). Unlike their British faculty counterparts, faculty at the colonial colleges were responsible for enforcing all disciplinary regulations (Brubacher & Rudy, 1976). The first personnel officers were members of the boards of trustees, presidents, teaching fellows, and tutors (Leonard, 1956; Rudolph, 1965).

By the middle of the nineteenth century, a somewhat more relaxed view developed, and the concept of the extracurriculum was emerging. Extracurricular activities were a student response to the traditional, strictly classical course of study. They reflected the desire for the development of the whole student—mind, personality, and body. Early activities included literary societies, debate clubs, and campus publications. Thelin (1990) noted that the establishment of literary clubs, debate teams, eating clubs, and athletic teams tended to go through a life cycle of "being founded by and for students outside the formal course of study; successful activities then faced official sanctions or abolition, but persistence as a 'renegade' activity ultimately led to faculty and administrative acquiescence and, ultimately, official adoption" (p. xiii).

Athletics and physical education in the early American colleges were spontaneous and informal. Games were played for recreation and enjoyment. Some colleges, however, particularly the denominational colleges, frowned on sports as a distraction from the spiritual atmosphere of the college (Brubacher & Rudy, 1976).

The first Greek-letter organization, Phi Beta Kappa, was founded in 1776, essentially as a literary society (Brubacher & Rudy, 1976). Social fraternities began in 1825 with the founding of Kappa Alpha. By 1840, the Greek-letter fraternity had been widely introduced in New England colleges. For many students it represented an escape from the monotony of campus housing (Rudolph, 1965). By the 1850s, the first Greek-letter societies for women had been established, and both fraternities and sororities were providing housing for their members (Brubacher & Rudy, 1976). Throughout history, fraternities and sororities have been criticized as antidemocratic, exclusive, and anti-intellectual. They have, however, demonstrated "remarkable resiliency and staying power" (Brubacher & Rudy, 1976, p. 129).

Student rebellions in the late 1700s and early 1800s were usually the result of dissatisfaction with the prevailing methods of teaching, the intrusive forms of discipline imposed by the faculty, and, on occasion, dissatisfaction with the food (Cowley & Williams, 1991).

Mueller (1961) noted that up to this time "personnel work consisted of a persistent emphasis on extracurricular religion and also a considerable snooping into the personal lives of the students" (p. 51).

Increasingly, education was viewed as a means of obtaining social and economic mobility. As the idea of higher education for the common man developed, the country witnessed the introduction of women and, in a few instances, Blacks to American colleges and universities (Leonard, 1956).

Diversification: 1850 to 1900

The first appointments of special personnel to handle student problems coincided with several events. Growing demands on college presidents, changing faculty roles and expectations, and the increase in coeducation and women's colleges are among the reasons most frequently cited (Boyer, 1990b; Leonard, 1956; Rudolph, 1965). By the mid-nineteenth century, "change was in the wind" (Boyer, 1990b, p. 4). American higher education, once devoted primarily to the intellectual and moral development of students, was shifting from the shaping of young lives to the building of a nation (Boyer, 1990b). One of the most significant events was the passage of the Morrill Act of 1862, which created the land grant colleges. Ingrained in the land grant ideal was the concept of a collegiate education for all at public expense—the beginning of the contemporary concept of equal access.

The passage of the second Morrill Act in 1890 led to the establishment of publicly funded, but segregated, Black colleges in seventeen states (Rudolph, 1965). Unfortunately, the legislation continued to sanction the doctrine of "separate but equal." However, it did increase opportunities for Blacks to pursue higher education, at a time when very few opportunities were available.

During this time period, the participation of women in higher education also increased dramatically (Leonard, 1956; Rosenberry, 1915; Rudolph, 1965). The first U.S. woman's college—Georgia Female Seminary—opened in 1836. Mount Holyoke Seminary was founded in 1837. The term *seminary* designated these institutions as teacher colleges. They served as models for other female seminaries and for female departments of coeducational colleges (Horowitz, 1984). The opening of Vassar College in 1865 signaled a new era for American women (Horowitz, 1984; Rudolph, 1965). Vassar offered a full liberal arts curriculum to women and made the "world take notice of the neglect which had long characterized the higher education of women" (Rudolph, 1965, p. 244).

As enrollments of both sexes increased in the mid 1800s, the search for housing accommodations on and off campus intensified. There was also a shift from "the absolute and unquestioning obedience expected of students in Colonial days" (Leonard, 1956, p. 92) to a more positive tone, in which good conduct was expected rather than imposed.

By the 1860s, the German university movement was influencing American student life in many ways. With the introduction of the gymnasium, American colleges and universities saw expanded athletic activities and a new emphasis on health, physical activity, and life adjustment tasks (Leonard, 1956; Rudolph, 1965). In 1869 the first intercollegiate football game—soccer as we know it today—was played between Rutgers and Princeton (Brubacher & Rudy, 1976). Also, physicians began to join college faculties, marking the beginning of health services for students (Leonard, 1956). German university education reinforced a trend away from "the collegiate way of living" (Cowley & Williams, 1991, p. 148). Their responsibility related only to the training of the student's mind. They had little interest in how students spent their time outside of class. Historians noted that by the late 1800s, the paternalism associated with the colonial colleges and the collegiate way of life had given way to almost complete indifference (Cowley & Williams, 1991). Evidence of this was detected in the diminished interest in residence halls, the decline in compulsory chapel, and the reduced involvement of faculty in student discipline.

In 1870 Harvard University appointed Professor Ephraim Gurney its first college dean in higher education. His main task, in addition to teaching, was to release the president from his responsibilities as disciplinarian (Stewart, 1985). With the appointment of Dean LeBaron Briggs at Harvard in 1891, the role of dean was expanded to include personal counseling. Thomas Arkle Clark, commenting on his appointment in 1901 as the first dean of men at the University of Illinois, observed, "I relieved the President of some very unpleasant duties" (Williamson, 1961, p. 6). (For a more detailed description of student life in these early years, see Sheldon, 1901/1969.)

While this period witnessed many significant events in higher education, there were problems that influenced the development of student affairs. Prior to 1900, the principal function of a college was to provide an education that emphasized mental discipline, religious piety, and strict rules governing student behavior (Bok, 1982). A countervailing view developed among some educators after 1900. They warned against departing from the traditional commitment to intellectual, vocational, and moral education and allowing development of the intellect to become the dominant concern (Williamson, 1961). Cowley (1940) noted that three influences—secularism, intensive scholarship and research, and specialization—threatened higher education's previous commitment to preparing young adults for citizenship. Although the intellectualists of the late 1800s and early 1900s were not able to eliminate the early personnel services, they were "put on a starvation ration" (p. 158).

Another aspect of reform influencing the changing role of faculty and the development of student affairs was led by Charles William Eliot, president of Harvard from 1869 to 1909. Eliot advocated a broadly elective course of study to replace the prescribed classical curriculum. A proponent of the psychology of individual differences, he supported the elective system as a way to allow students to follow their "natural preferences and interests" and thus pursue academic study with greater enthusiasm and interest (Rudolph, 1965, p. 293).

Modern Developments: 1900 to 1945

Emergence of the Profession

The student personnel movement is a twentieth-century phenomenon. By the turn of the century, the participation of faculty in student personnel matters (what is now referred to as student affairs) had changed from total involvement to detachment (Fenske, 1980). As the burden of disciplining and regulating students shifted from faculty, there was greater recognition of student responsibility. Student councils and other forms of student government were widespread during the first decade of the twentieth century. By 1915, at least 123 colleges and universities were employing some variant of the honor system. Brubacher and Rudy (1976) concluded that "in the years following 1918 the student personnel movement gained national recognition and professional stature; it was becoming self-conscious, confident, and widely influential" (p. 336). Williamson (1961) observed that the program of student affairs had been evolving slowly for many years. Then, in the latter half of the nineteenth century, accelerated changes in the character of institutions of higher education and their students produced conditions that made the greater development of these services both possible and urgent. Following the first world war, the organizational patterns of modern student affairs evolved, assuming the forms we recognize today (Brubacher & Rudy, 1976; Rentz, 1994; Williamson, 1961). Yoakum (1919/1994) outlined one of the earliest plans for personnel bureaus in educational institutions. Their primary functions were associated with vocational guidance, including obtaining accurate data on each student, codifying the requirements of different professions, and supervising the use of ability and interest inventories.

Distinct student personnel functions had developed by 1925. For example, organized placement bureaus supervised by staff specialists were set up on many large college campuses and were beginning to appear at small and midsized colleges as well (Brubacher & Rudy, 1976). A sufficient number of colleges and universities were providing student health services, leading to the establishment of the American Student Health Association in 1920. The most significant trend in college health work after 1918 was the growing concern with mental health and psychological services (Brubacher & Rudy, 1976).

A variety of professional titles described student personnel workers (Cowley, 1957/1994b; Lloyd-Jones & Smith, 1938): director of personnel, dean of students, social director, and vocational counselor, among others. While such titles were used at different institutions as though the duties involved were synonymous, diversity rather than conformity was the norm for the organization of student affairs (Lloyd-Jones & Smith, 1938). Two factors—the personalities and idiosyncracies of individuals and the unique history and mission of each institution—contributed to the diversity of student affairs organizations and job titles (Williamson, 1961). As Lloyd-Jones and Smith (1938) pointed out, the personnel aspect of the educational program was "not a simple, unitary thing any more than . . . the curriculum [was]" (p. 19).

Professional Preparation

The first preparation program for student affairs practitioners began at Columbia University's Teachers College. The first professional diploma for an "Adviser of Women" was awarded in conjunction with the Master of Arts degree in 1914 (Bashaw, 1992; Gilroy, 1987; Teachers College, 1914). In 1929 Esther Lloyd-Jones was the first recipient of a doctorate in the field, and the program began to admit men in 1932 (C. Johnson, personal correspondence, August 12, 1993). Today, eighty-three master's and doctoral degree programs in student affairs are listed in the *Directory of Graduate Preparation Programs in College Student Personnel* (American College Personnel Association, 1994a). Many more programs exist that are not included in this directory.

Professional Associations

Once student affairs had emerged as a distinct organizational entity and deans of men and women had become more prevalent, professional associations were established to articulate the shared concerns of student affairs practitioners (Bloland, 1985). The fact that student affairs in the early 1900s were organized by gender and race influenced the development of these associations.

The jobs of the early deans of women varied among colleges and regions of the country (Bashaw, 1992; Rosenberry, 1915). At most coeducational colleges, the dean of women was the highest-ranking woman on campus (Bashaw, 1992). There were few other women on campus with whom the dean of women could consult or collaborate. Many found it useful to have an opportunity to gather to discuss issues related to their job (Sturdevant & Hayes, 1930). In 1910 a group of deans of women came together at the American Association of University Women (AAUW) meeting and concluded that it would be useful to have their own organization. The National Association of Deans of Women (NADW) was organized in 1916. Approximately 70 percent of the early membership came from the Northeast and Midwest; only about 14 percent were from southern schools (Bashaw, 1992). Since its founding, the organization has focused on serving the needs of women in education. In 1956 the NADW became the National Association of Women Deans and Counselors (NAWDC). By the early 1970s there were fewer deans of women on campus; advocates for women had assumed new roles and titles (Bashaw, 1992). As a result, in 1972 the organization became the National Association of Women Deans, Administrators, and Counselors (NAWDAC) (Sheeley, 1983). In 1991 the organization's name was changed to the National Association for Women in Education (NAWE), to more accurately reflect its contemporary scope and focus (Hanson, 1995; Nuss, 1993).

In January 1919 a meeting referred to as the Conference of Deans and Advisers of Men was held at the University of Wisconsin. That meeting is now recognized as the founding of the National Association of Deans and Advisers of Men (NADAM). After two earlier attempts (in 1948 and 1949) failed, the organization officially adopted the name National Association of Student Personnel Administrators (NASPA) in 1951. This broadened the association's base, and for the first time NASPA began to recruit members (Rhatigan, 1991).

As NASPA's organizational mission broadened, a few women began to join. The first woman to attend a NADAM/NASPA conference did so in 1926 (Rhatigan, 1991). In 1958 Mary Ethel Ball, acting dean of students at the University of Colorado, became the first female "institutional representative" of NASPA. Not until the period 1965–1975 did women begin to hold office and participate actively in NASPA. K. Patricia Cross, then of Cornell University, was the first woman appointed to the NASPA executive committee, in 1966. In 1971 NASPA established its women's network, and in 1976 it elected its first woman president— Alice Manicur of Frostburg State University. Today women play a significant role in the governance and leadership of NASPA, and approximately half of its membership is women.

The American College Personnel Association (ACPA) traces its founding to 1924, when it began as the National Association of Appointment Secretaries

(NAAS) (Bloland, 1983; Johnson, 1985; Sheeley, 1983). (Appointment secretaries assisted in placing teachers and other college graduates.) The NAAS's first meeting in 1924 was held jointly with the NADW. In 1929 the NAAS's name was changed to the National Association of Placement and Personnel Officers (NAPPO) to reflect its broader professional role. In 1931 the name was changed again, to the ACPA (Bloland, 1983; Johnson, 1985). In 1952 the ACPA helped form the American Personnel and Guidance Association (APGA); Robert H. Shaffer, an ACPA leader, became its first president. Johnson (1985) observed that only a few years later ACPA members were questioning their affiliation and threatening to withdraw. The issue was discussed numerous times until 1991, when the ACPA voted to disaffiliate from what was by then known as the American Association for Counseling and Development (AACD). The ACPA became an independent organization in 1992 (M. Nellenbach, personal communication, May 17, 1995).

By 1945, other professional organizations had been established to address the specialized student affairs roles developing on campus, including the Association of College Unions International (ACUI), established in 1910; the American Association of Collegiate Registrars and Admissions Officers (AACRAO), established in 1910; the American College Health Association (ACHA), established in 1920; and the National Orientation Directors Association (NODA), established in 1937 (Cowley, 1964/1994b; Nuss, 1993). Over time, many regional and state associations developed independently of these national organizations. Examples include the Western Deans and the Pennsylvania Association of Student Personnel Administrators.

Racial barriers and discrimination prevented the full participation of minorities in these professional associations. African American student affairs deans were unable to attend conferences held in segregated hotels or restaurants. In 1954 two minority professional organizations—the Association of Deans of Women and Advisers of Girls in Colored Schools and the National Association of the Deans of Men in Negro Education Institutions—met to plan, organize, and develop the National Association of Personnel Workers (NAPW) (Barrett, 1991). Membership was opened to deans, counselors, and other personnel workers. Founded a few months before the historic Supreme Court decision barring "separate but equal" educational programs, the NAPW's common interests focused on the "hopes, aspirations, and goals of 'Negro' education" (Barrett, 1991, p. 2). Dr. Sadie Yancey, dean of students at Florida A&M and dean of women at Howard University, was the first president. In 1994 the NAPW changed its name to the National Association of Student Affairs Professionals (NASAP) (S. Whittaker, personal communication, May 19, 1995).

Over time, the other student affairs professional associations became more accepting of minorities. Not until 1976, however, did an African American, Anne Pruitt, become president of ACPA, and not until 1985 was an African American, Bob Leach, elected to serve as NASPA president. Elaine Copeland served as the first African American president of the NAWE, from 1988 to 1989.

The *Student Personnel Point of View*

A landmark report, the *Student Personnel Point of View,* was the result of several years of activity, culminating in a committee appointed by the American Council on Education (ACE) to study personnel practices in colleges and universities (American Council on Education, 1937/1994a). The final paper acknowledged that a long and honorable history stood behind the student affairs point of view. The report recommended that "in addition to instruction and business management adapted to the needs of the individual student, an effective educational program [should include]—in one form or another—the following services adapted to the specific aims and objectives of each college and university" (American Council on Education, 1937/1994a, p. 69). The report emphasized the importance of understanding the individual student, the importance of coordinating the major functions of instruction and management, and the notion that student services should be offered and organized in ways that support the unique mission of each college. It included a list of twenty-three specific functions that should be included in a comprehensive student personnel program. In 1949 E. G. Williamson chaired another ACE committee, which revised the 1937 report (American Council on Education, 1949/1994b). "The concept of education is broadened to include attention to the student's well rounded development—physically, socially, emotionally, and spiritually, as well as intellectually" (p. 109). The 1949 *Student Personnel Point of View* outlined conditions and goals for student growth, the fundamental elements for a student personnel program, and the administrative organization and governance. (The report is also discussed in Chapter Five.) The principles outlined in both the 1937 and 1949 *Student Personnel Point of View* influenced the philosophical development of the profession and persist today as guiding assumptions.

Expansion: 1945 to the Present

Several significant events during this period shaped the development of the student affairs profession. These included increased federal support and involvement in higher education, landmark legal challenges resulting in the end of in loco parentis and changing relationships between students and institutions, the beginning of student development research and theory, and the development of professional standards. Rentz (1994) observed that the literature is "rich with a number of critical issues: the struggles the field experienced regarding its own sense of mission and purpose; the effects of an economic crisis or 'steady state'; a new perspective on practice grounded in the application of the developmental stage theories; an emphasis on change; and an enthusiasm for the roles student development educators could play as integral partners in the academy" (p. 257).

Federal Involvement

By the conclusion of World War II, the concept of providing universal access to higher education was firmly established (Cowley & Williams, 1991). Partially motivated by peacetime economic and employment prospects, the Serviceman's Readjustment Act, commonly referred to as the G.I. Bill, was passed in June 1944. This legislation had dramatic consequences for higher education and student affairs. The massive enrollment buildup from the late 1950s through the 1970s was the direct result of the increased interest in higher education generated by the G.I. Bill.

In 1947 the Truman Commission Report—*Higher Education for American Democracy*—called for dramatically expanded access to postsecondary education, increased financial aid, and a broader curriculum emphasizing world perspectives. The report also influenced and stimulated the development of community colleges (Cowley & Williams, 1991).

The passage of Title IV of the Housing Act of 1950 fueled a massive program of housing construction. The act's goal was to house and feed large numbers of returning students in an economical fashion. This led to the construction of many of the high-rise residence halls common on many college campuses today. Increasingly, colleges and universities recognized that a student's academic performance was affected in important ways by his or her surroundings—particularly housing. Student residence halls were viewed as an effective way to reintegrate the curriculum and extracurricular activities (Brubacher & Rudy, 1976).

The 1960s marked the beginning of increased federal support and hence increased federal interest and involvement in higher education. This increased involvement has led over time to volumes of regulations that influence student affairs policies and practices. It is beyond the scope of this chapter to enumerate or analyze the significant federal legislation enacted in the past thirty years that has affected the student affairs profession. However, when one considers just a sample of the major legislation, the impact becomes clear. In 1963 alone, Congress passed the Vocational Education Act, the Higher Education Facilities Act, and the Health Professions Act. In 1965 Congress passed the Higher Education

Act, "aimed at expanding opportunities for higher education" (Fenske, 1980, p. 15). Other examples include Title VI of the Civil Rights Act of 1964, Title IX of the Education Amendments of 1972, Section 504 of the Rehabilitation Act of 1973, The Drug Free Schools and Communities Act, the 1990 Student Right-to-Know and Campus Security Act, the Americans with Disabilities Act of 1990, and the Higher Education Amendments of 1992. Much of this legislation mandated the elimination of discrimination and required equal access and treatment for educational and other programs receiving federal financial assistance. The legislation influenced the development of increasingly specialized roles for student affairs practitioners, particularly in the area of financial aid and special student support services, and it created new expectations for student and institutional relationships. Staff were either retrained or hired to provide support and services in these areas, and new codes of conduct and grievance procedures were developed.

As a result of this legislation and other societal changes, higher education and student affairs began experiencing what was to become a major shift in student demographics, as increasing numbers of previously excluded or underrepresented groups gained access to higher education. Patterns of enrollment also began to change, with increasing numbers of adult and part-time students enrolling in evening and weekend degree programs. (Elaine El-Khawas discusses these and other changes in detail in Chapter Four.)

Legal Challenges and Changing Relationships

The 1960s are often characterized by the following labels: the age of student activism, the downfall of in loco parentis, the sexual revolution, and the years of civil disobedience. Speaking at a NASPA meeting in 1956, W. H. Cowley, former president of Hamilton College and a faculty member at Stanford, warned that the campus was a likely setting for agitation and destruction if social conditions galvanized students (Cowley, 1957/1994a).

The assassinations of President John F. Kennedy and the Reverend Martin Luther King, Jr., urban rioting, concerns about the impersonal military industrial complex, and the civil rights movement were among the signature events of the decade that impacted students. During this period, special rules and regulations for female students were abolished, coed student housing developed, and the nature of the relationship between the student and the institution changed dramatically.

In the late 1950s and early 1960s, questions about the civil liberties of college students were raised, and the long-standing doctrine of in loco parentis was challenged and eventually abolished. In 1961, in *Dixon* v. *Alabama State Board of Education* (294 F.2d 150), the Supreme Court declared that due process requires notice and some opportunity for a hearing before students at a tax-supported college could be expelled for misconduct (Ardiaolo, 1983; Ratliff, 1972). Following *Dixon,* the Supreme Court rendered a series of student-rights decisions that reflected the recognition that, for the most part, persons above the age of eighteen are legally adults and that students at public colleges do not relinquish their fundamental constitutional rights by accepting student status (Bickel & Lake, 1994).

Activist students protested the Vietnam War, racial injustice, and the shortcomings of higher education. Disruptions at Santa Barbara, Kent State, and Jackson State College resulted in injury and death (Cowley & Williams, 1991). Public pressure and impatience increased, and student affairs professionals' skills at conflict resolution and mediation became essential.

The nature of the relationship between students and their colleges and universities changed significantly during this period. After in loco parentis was eliminated, the emphasis on the student affairs professional's role as disciplinarian or authority figure declined and the role of coordinator and educator increased (Garland & Grace, 1993). The role of student participation in institutional governance also changed. Students began to play more influential roles on academic committees, and many institutions appointed student representatives to their governing boards. As Boyer (1990a) lamented, however, "while old rules were abolished, changes were made more out of compromise than conviction, and few colleges had the imagination or the courage to replace abandoned rules with more creative views of campus life" (p. xii).

One way to view the changing relationship between students and institutions in the 1960s is from a rights and responsibilities perspective. In June 1967 a committee composed of representatives from the American Association of University Professors (AAUP), the United States National Student Association (USNSA), the American Association of Colleges (AAC), NASPA, and NAWDAC met in Washington to draft the *Joint Statement on Student Rights and Freedoms.* The statement, endorsed by each of the five national sponsors as well as a number of other higher education associations, outlined the minimal standards of academic freedom necessary for student learning. The principles embodied in the statement have persisted over time and continue to guide student affairs practice. On the occasion of its twenty-fifth anniversary in 1992, "an interassociation task force met in Washington, D.C., to study, interpret, update, and affirm (or reaffirm) the joint statement. Members of the task force agreed that the statement has stood the test of time quite well and continues to provide an excellent set of principles for institutions of higher education" (National Association of Student Personnel Administrators, 1992, p. 1). The 1992 task force also developed interpretive notes to reflect changes in the law and higher education that have occurred since 1967.

Others saw the relationship between students and their institutions as essentially contractual. More recently the relationship has been cast in terms of a consumer model. The consumer model requires colleges and universities to provide a wide range of information to students on subjects such as tuition refund policies, the release of educational records and information, alcohol and substance abuse policies, graduation rates, campus safety and security networks, and sexual assault polices so that the student consumer can make informed decisions. Much of the federal legislation mentioned earlier is based on a consumer view of the student-institution relationship.

Continued expansion of higher education resulted in increased numbers of specialized student affairs professionals and an increased reliance on paraprofessionals and peer advisors. "Student affairs was called upon to provide admissions, financial aid, registration and records, housing and food services, student activities, personal and academic counseling, orientation, and special student support services" (Garland & Grace, 1993, pp. 5–6). As the roles of student affairs professionals became more specialized and the relationship between students and institutions changed, professional names and titles changed as well. Increasingly, the expression "student personnel" was replaced by "student affairs" or "student development."

Student Development Theory and Research

An increasingly diverse and complex student affairs profession sought to establish its theoretical base at a time when many believed the gap between academics and extracurricular activities was widening (Boyer, 1987). The debate over the purpose of higher education intensified, and it appeared to some that the concept of the development of the whole student was in jeopardy (Brown, 1972). The Council of Student Personnel Associations (COSPA) emerged at least partially in response to this diversity and specialization. Established in 1963 to develop cooperation among the student affairs professional associations, COSPA's goal was to initiate programs that would do for all groups what no single association could do for itself (Cowley, 1964/1994b; Rentz, 1994). One of COSPA's most important contributions was the publication in 1975 of *Student Development Services in Postsecondary Education* (1994). The paper noted the "purpose of student development services in postsecondary education was to provide affective and cognitive expertise in the processes involved in education" (Council of Student Personnel Associations, 1975/1994, p. 429). The paper outlined common assumptions of student development specialists; noted that their clientele included the individual, the group, and the organization; and summarized the competencies and functions of student development specialists. The three broad functions of student affairs were described as administration, instruction, and consultation. COSPA dissolved in 1975 (Fenske, 1989).

A significant amount of published research on the impact of college on students began to appear in the late 1950s and 1960s. In 1969 Feldman and Newcomb published *The Impact of College on Students*, which reviewed and synthesized the findings of more than fifteen hundred studies conducted over four decades. In the intervening decades, both the number of empirical studies and the major areas of inquiry have increased dramatically. Prominent examples include Astin, 1977; Chickering, 1969; King and Kitchener, 1994; Knefelkamp, Widick, and Parker, 1978; Parker, 1978; Perry, 1968; and Rest, 1979. The contribution of early theories of student development as well as that of more recent developments are discussed in detail in Part Three. The ACPA launched its response to the prospect of changes in the profession with its Tomorrow's Higher Education (THE) project. Robert Brown (1972) was commissioned to write *Student Development in Tomorrow's Higher Education: A Return to the Academy*. The monograph focused attention on the changing roles of student affairs professionals and noted that having an impact on student development meant having an awareness of and involvement in the "total environment of the student—not just where he lives or what organization he belonged to" (Brown, 1972, p. 38). Brown also called for student affairs staff to work as partners with faculty in the educational process and argued that the concern for student development needed to move from the extracurricular to the curricular.

Since the introduction of the concept of student development, professional leaders have debated whether there is a difference between the concept of student affairs and that of student development (Garland & Grace, 1993; Rhatigan, 1974/1994). Questions about the influence of 1970s student development theory on the profession are also being raised today. Most recently, Bloland, Stamatakos, and Rogers (1994) questioned the premises of the student development movement and its effect upon the field of student affairs. In their critique of student development, they attempted to resolve the question as to whether the *Student Personnel Point of View* or the 1975 COSPA document *Student Development Services in Postsecondary Education* represented a professional philosophy for the student affairs profession. They concluded that the *Student Personnel Point of View* more adequately fulfills the four components of a philosophy and that the purpose of higher education "is not student development per se but the development of the whole person including, of course, intellectual ability and educational achievement" (p. 112). Strange (1994) and Upcraft (1994) also provide useful analysis and critique of student development theory and the difficulties inherent in translating theory into professional practice.

Professional Standards

Over the years, student affairs has gained stature, vision, and recognition as an essential part of higher education's mission. But until 1979 one important element—comprehensive standards for program development, evaluation, self-study, and accreditation—was missing (Mable, 1991; Miller, 1991). A meeting of student affairs professional associations was held in June 1979 to "consider the desirability and feasibility of establishing professional standards and accreditation programs in student affairs" (Mable, 1991, p. 11). Later that year an invitational conference for interested student affairs associations was held. The conference provided strong support for an interassociation entity, which eventually became the Council for the Advancement of Standards in Higher Education (CAS). A consortium of higher education professional associations, the CAS has twenty-three member organizations. The first *CAS Standards and Guidelines* were published in 1986 and addressed nineteen functional areas of higher education programs and services. The CAS standards provide direction and strategy for professional practice in higher education programs and services and for promoting quality services and programs. They enable institutions to assess, study, evaluate, and improve their student services. The standards are periodically updated and revised to reflect professional changes (Council for the Advancement of Standards in Higher Education, 1986/1992).

The Contemporary Scene

Student affairs and higher education have struggled with the need to affirm the fundamental principles and research that guide the profession as well as with the need to integrate in-class and out-of-class activities to strengthen the quality of the collegiate experience. Attention is currently focused on ways in which student affairs professionals and academic planners can collaborate to enhance the overall educational experience for an increasingly diverse student clientele.

The Carnegie Foundation for the Advancement of Teaching issued a report on undergraduate education in America that noted "conflicting priorities and competing interests that diminish the intellectual and social quality of the undergraduate experience" (Boyer, 1987, p. 2). Eight tension points were identified, most notably the "great separation, sometimes to the point of isolation, between academic and social life on campus" (p. 5). Concerns about what some referred to as "an unhealthy separation between in-class and out-of-class activities" (Carnegie Foundation for the Advancement of Teaching, 1990, p. 2) promoted more research, recommendations, and insights into the conditions that facilitate and enhance student learning.

In commemoration of the fiftieth anniversary of the *Student Personnel Point of View*, NASPA appointed a "plan for a new century" committee, which issued *A Perspective on Student Affairs* (National Association of Student Personnel Administrators, 1987). This report presented a perspective on what the higher education community could expect from student affairs. It outlined the profession's fundamental assumptions and beliefs, including the preeminence of the academic mission and the uniqueness, worth, and inherent dignity of each student. It also emphasized that bigotry cannot be tolerated, feelings affect thinking and learning, student involvement enhances learning, personal circumstances affect learning, and out-of-class environments affect learning.

Kuh, Schuh, Whitt, and their associates (1991) described how "institutional factors and conditions work together in different colleges and universities to promote learning and personal development through out-of-class learning experiences" (p. 4). Pascarella and Terenzini's *How College Affects Students* (1991) was a landmark summary of research on the impact of college on individual students. They explored several fundamental questions: Do students change in various ways during the college years? To what extent are their changes attributable to the college experience? What college characteristics and experiences tend to produce desired changes?

Two of the major professional associations—NASPA and ACPA—engaged in studies and projects designed to stimulate discussion on how student affairs professionals can create conditions that will enhance student learning and personal development (American College Personnel Association, 1994b) and what students and institutions can reasonably expect from each other in terms of enhancing learning productivity (Kuh, Lyons, Miller, & Trow, 1995). ACPA published the *Student Learning Imperative* (1994b) and NASPA produced *Reasonable Expectations* (Kuh et al., 1995).

Conclusion

In 1995 we find higher education in the midst of a major transformation. Economic conditions, eroding public confidence, accountability demands, and shifts in population demographics are the most frequently cited reasons (American College Personnel Association, 1994b; Cowley & Williams, 1991; Wingspread Group on Higher Education, 1993). Increasingly there is a sense that as a nation we can no longer afford the wide access to public higher education that we aspired to in the past. Participation in higher education is viewed more and more as a personal benefit rather than a public obligation. We also find that as higher education around the world experiences changes, there is a growing interest in student affairs issues internationally.

Many argue that student affairs is in serious jeopardy. As a result of downsizing, student affairs positions are being eliminated at some institutions. In some cases even the chief student affairs officer has been eliminated. Increasingly many student affairs officers report to the chief academic officer rather than to the president of their college or university. What does this bode for the future of the profession? An understanding of the history of higher education and student affairs enables us to place current events in context.

At the beginning of this chapter, two enduring and distinctive concepts were noted: the development of the whole person and the fact that student affairs was established to support the academic mission of institutions of higher education. Adherence to these principles is expected to continue to play a dominant role in the future evolution of the profession. But just as accelerated changes in higher education made the development of student affairs possible in the late nineteenth century, so will the changes of the late twentieth century influence the profession's future course, both in the United States and throughout the world.

References

American College Personnel Association. (1994a). *Directory of graduate preparation programs in college student personnel.* Alexandria, VA: Author.

American College Personnel Association. (1994b). *The student learning imperative: Implications for student affairs.* Alexandria, VA: Author.

American Council on Education. (1994a). The student personnel point of view. In A. L. Rentz (Ed.), *Student affairs: A profession's heritage* (American College Personnel Association Media Publication No. 40, 2nd ed., pp. 66–77). Lanham, MD: University Press of America. (Original work published 1937)

American Council on Education. (1994b). The student personnel point of view. In A. L. Rentz (Ed.), *Student affairs: A profession's heritage* (American College Personnel Association Media Publication No. 40, 2nd ed., pp. 108–123). Lanham, MD: University Press of America. (Original work published 1949)

Ardiaolo, F. P. (1983). What process is due? In M. J. Barr (Ed.), *Student affairs and the law* (New Directions for Student Services No. 22). San Francisco: Jossey-Bass.

Astin, A. W. (1977). *Four critical years.* San Francisco: Jossey-Bass.

Barrett, B. N. (1991). The presidential issue. *NAPW Journal III, 1,* 1–35.

Bashaw, C. T. (1992). *We who live "off on the edges": Deans of women at Southern coeducation institutions and access to the community of higher education, 1907–1960.* Unpublished doctoral dissertation, University of Georgia, Athens.

Bickel, R. D., & Lake, P. T. (1994). Reconceptualizing the university's duty to provide a safe learning environment: A criticism of the doctrine of *in loco parentis* and the restatement (second) of torts. *Journal of College & University Law, 20*(3), 261–293.

Bloland, H. G. (1985). *Associations in action: The Washington, D.C., higher education community.* ASHE-ERIC Higher Education Report, no. 2. Washington, DC: Association for the Study of Higher Education.

Bloland, P. A. (1983). Ecumenicalism in college student personnel. In B. A. Belson & L. E. Fitzgerald (Eds.), *Thus we spoke: ACPA-NAWDAC, 1958–1975* (pp. 237–254). Alexandria, VA: American College Personnel Association.

Bloland, P. A., Stamatakos, L. C., & Rogers, R. R. (1994). *Reform in student affairs: A critique of student development.* Greensboro, NC: ERIC Counseling and Student Services Clearinghouse.

Bok, D. (1982). *Beyond the ivory tower: Social responsibilities of the modern university.* Cambridge, MA: Harvard University Press.

Boyer, E. L. (1987). *College: The undergraduate experience in America.* New York: Harper & Row.

Boyer, E. L. (1990a). Foreword. In Carnegie Foundation for the Advancement of Teaching, *Campus life: In search of community* (pp. xi–xiii). Princeton, NJ: Princeton University Press.

Boyer, E. L. (1990b). *Scholarship reconsidered: Priorities of the professorate.* Princeton, NJ: Carnegie Foundation for the Advancement of Teaching.

Brown, R. D. (1972). *Student development in tomorrow's higher education: A return to the academy* (Student Personnel Series No. 16). Washington, DC: American Personnel and Guidance Association.

Brubacher, J. S., & Rudy, W. (1976). *Higher education in transition: A history of American colleges and universities, 1636–1976.* New York: Harper & Row.

Carnegie Foundation for the Advancement of Teaching. (1990). *Campus life: In search of community.* Princeton, NJ: Princeton University Press.

Chickering, A. W. (1969). *Education and identity.* San Francisco: Jossey-Bass.

Council for the Advancement of Standards. (1992). *CAS standards and guidelines.* Washington, DC: Author. (Standards originally published 1986)

Council of Student Personnel Associations. (1994). Student development services in postsecondary education. In A. L. Rentz (Ed.), *Student affairs: A profession's heritage* (American College Personnel Association Media Publication No. 40, 2nd ed., pp. 428–437). Lanham, MD: University Press of America. (Original work published 1975)

Cowley, W. H. (1940). The history and philosophy of student personnel work. *Journal of the National Association of Deans of Women, 3*(4), 153–162.

Cowley, W. H. (1994a). Student personnel services in retrospect and prospect. In A. L. Rentz (Ed.), *Student affairs: A profession's heritage* (American College Personnel Association Media Publication No. 40, 2nd ed., pp. 150–155). Lanham, MD: University Press of America. (Original work published 1957)

Cowley, W. H. (1994b). Reflections of a troublesome but hopeful Rip Van Winkle. In A. L. Rentz (Ed.), *Student affairs: A profession's heritage* (American College Personnel Association Media Publication No. 40, 2nd ed., pp. 190–197). Lanham, MD: University Press of America. (Original work published 1964)

Cowley, W. H., & Williams, D. (1991). *International and historical roots of American higher education.* New York: Garland.

Feldman, K., & Newcomb, T. (1969). *The impact of college on students.* San Francisco: Jossey-Bass.

Fenske, R. H. (1980). Historical foundations. In U. Delworth, G. R. Hanson, & Associates (Eds.), *Student services: A handbook for the profession* (1st ed., pp. 3–24). San Francisco: Jossey-Bass.

Fenske, R. H. (1989). Evolution of the student services profession. In U. Delworth, G. R. Hanson, & Associates (Eds.), *Student services: A handbook for the profession* (2nd ed., pp. 25–56). San Francisco: Jossey-Bass.

Garland, P. H., & Grace, T. W. (1993). *New perspectives for student affairs professionals: Evolving realities, responsibilities, and roles* (ASHE-ERIC Higher Education Report No. 7). Washington, DC: George Washington University, School of Education and Human Development.

Gilroy, M. (1987). *The contributions of selected teachers college women to the field of student personnel.* Unpublished doctoral dissertation, Columbia University Teachers College, New York.

Hanson, G. S. (1995). The organizational evolution of NAWE. *Initiatives, 56*(4), 29–36.

Horowitz, H. L. (1984). *Alma mater: Design and experience in the women's colleges from their nineteenth-century beginnings to the 1930s.* New York: Knopf.

James, H. (1930). *Charles W. Eliot.* Boston: Houghton Mifflin.

Johnson, C. S. (1985). The American College Personnel Association. *Journal of Counseling and Development, 63,* 405–410.

King, P. M., & Kitchener, K. S. (1994). *Developing reflective judgment: Understanding and promoting intellectual growth and critical thinking in adolescents and adults.* San Francisco: Jossey-Bass.

Knefelkamp, L. L., Widick, C., & Parker, C. A. (1978). *Applying new developmental findings* (New Directions for Student Services No. 4). San Francisco: Jossey-Bass.

Kuh, G. D., Lyons, J., Miller, T. K., & Trow, J. (1995). *Reasonable expectations.* Washington, DC: National Association of Student Personnel Administrators.

Kuh, G. D., Schuh, J. H., Whitt, E. J., & Associates. (1991). *Involving colleges: Successful approaches to fostering student learning and development outside the classroom.* San Francisco: Jossey-Bass.

Leonard, E. A. (1956). *Origins of personnel services in American higher education.* Minneapolis: University of Minnesota Press.

Lloyd-Jones, E. M., & Smith, M. R. (1938). *A student personnel program for higher education.* New York: McGraw-Hill.

Mable, P. (1991). Professional standards: An introduction and historical perspective. In W. A. Bryan, R. B. Winston, Jr., & T. K. Miller (Eds.), *Using professional standards in student affairs* (New Directions for Student Services No. 53, pp. 5–18). San Francisco: Jossey-Bass.

Miller, T. K. (1991). Using standards in professional preparation. In W. A. Bryan, R. B. Winston, Jr., & T. K. Miller (Eds.), *Using professional standards in student affairs* (New Directions for Student Services No. 53, pp. 45–62). San Francisco: Jossey-Bass.

Mueller, K. H. (1961). *Student personnel work in higher education.* Boston: Houghton Mifflin.

National Association of Student Personnel Administrators. (1987). *A perspective on student affairs.* Washington, DC: Author.

National Association of Student Personnel Administrators. (1992). *Student rights and freedoms: Joint statement on rights and freedoms of students.* Washington, DC: Author.

Nuss, E. M. (1993). The role of professional associations. In M. J. Barr (Ed.), *The handbook of student affairs administration* (pp. 364–377). San Francisco: Jossey-Bass.

Parker, C. A. (1978). *Encouraging development in college students.* Minneapolis: University of Minnesota Press.

Pascarella, E. T., & Terenzini, P. T. (1991). *How college affects students: Findings and insights from twenty years of research.* San Francisco: Jossey-Bass.

Perry, W. G. (1968). *Forms of intellectual and ethical development in the college years: A scheme.* New York: Holt, Rinehart and Winston.

Ratliff, R. C. (1972). *Constitutional rights of college students.* Metuchen, NJ: Scarecrow Press.

Rentz, A. L. (Ed.). (1994). *Student affairs: A profession's heritage* (American College Personnel Association Media Publication No. 40, 2nd ed.). Lanham, MD: University Press of America.

Rest, J. R. (1979). *Development in judging moral issues.* Minneapolis: University of Minnesota Press.

Rhatigan, J. J. (1991). NASPA history. In *NASPA member handbook* (pp. 5–6). Washington, DC: National Association of Student Personnel Administrators.

Rhatigan, J. J. (1994). Student services vs. student development: Is there a difference? In A. L. Rentz (Ed.), *Student affairs: A profession's heritage* (2nd ed., pp. 438–447). Lanham, MD: American College Personnel Association & University Press of America. (Original work published 1974)

Rosenberry, L. M. (1915). *The dean of women.* Boston: Houghton Mifflin.

Rudolph, F. (1965). *The American college and university: A history.* New York: Knopf.

Sheeley, V. L. (1983). NADW and NAAS: 60 years of organizational relationships (NAW-DAC-ACPA: 1923–1983). In B. A. Belson & L. E. Fitzgerald (Eds.), *Thus we spoke: ACPA-NAWDAC, 1958–1975* (pp. 179–189). Alexandria, VA: American College Personnel Association.

Sheldon, H. D. (1969). Student life and customs. In L. A. Cremin (Ed.), *American education: Its men, ideas, and institutions.* New York: Arno Press. (Original work published 1901)

Stewart, G. M. (1985). *College and university discipline: A moment of reflection, a time for new direction.* Unpublished manuscript, Catholic University of America, Washington, DC.

Strange, C. C. (1994). Student development: The evolution and status of an essential idea. *Journal of College Student Development, 35*(6), 399–412.

Sturdevant, S. M., & Hayes, H. (1930). *Deans at work: Discussion by eight women deans of various phases of their work.* New York: Harper.

Teachers College. (1914). *Columbia University School of Education Announcement.* New York: Author.

Thelin, J. R. (1990). Rudolph rediscovered. In F. Rudolph, *The American college and university: A history* (pp. i–xiii). Athens: University of Georgia Press.

Upcraft, M. L. (1994). The dilemmas of translating theory to practice. *Journal of College Student Development, 35*(6), 438–443.

Williamson, E. G. (1961). *Student personnel services in colleges and universities.* New York: McGraw-Hill.

Wingspread Group on Higher Education. (1993). *An American imperative: Higher expectations for higher education.* Racine, WI: Johnson Foundation.

Yoakum, C. S. (1994). Plan for a personnel bureau in educational institutions. In A. L. Rentz (Ed.), *Student affairs: A profession's heritage* (American College Personnel Association Media Publication No. 40, 2nd ed., pp. 4–8). Lanham, MD: University Press of America. (Original work published 1919)

CHAPTER THREE

DIVERSIFICATION OF POSTSECONDARY INSTITUTIONS

Johnetta Cross Brazzell

Our educational system is the most diverse and developed in the world. Different educational institutions are available for a wide variety of individuals. Among the range of choices are colleges and universities for African Americans, Hispanic Americans, women, and Native Americans; two-year colleges; and proprietary schools.

Inherent assumptions about the nature of American culture define how we think about our institutions, what we write about them, how we construct the history of their formation, and who gets to participate in them. First among these assumptions is the notion that we are a pluralistic nation with a multiplicity of ideas, cultures, and beliefs. This characteristic uniquely distinguishes us from other nations and is felt to be a major cultural strength. A second cultural assumption is that we manage our affairs through democratic processes that work relatively well. A third assumption is that in the midst of this multiplicity of cultures, dissent is cherished and the right of others to express their views is embraced.

This chapter offers an exploration of the liberal arts tradition out of which American institutions of higher education arose. When one looks at the landscape of American postsecondary education, one can observe a variety of types, including military academies, corporate schools, "campuses without walls," upper-division institutions, professional and graduate schools, foreign institutions located within the United States, and American schools located abroad. It is not the intent here to look at the entire range of institutional types. Rather, the focus is on

a thorough understanding of those postsecondary institutions that are often ignored, marginalized, or misrepresented.

An examination of the unique contributions of these institutions begins with
their historical origins. Such an understanding will provide the context for analyzing their unique educational approaches and the special problems that challenge their continued existence. Their contributions include a student-centered
approach, fueled by their special missions and philosophies. The challenges they
face include both legal and financial constraints. This chapter also explores the
lessons these institutions can offer the mainstream educational community.

Why is there such variety in American institutions of higher education? Perhaps one can look at our cultural assumptions and proclaim that this variety is a
positive reflection of our pluralistic character and that it reflects the right of any
group to create what best personifies its definition of the American dream. Conversely, such variety may mirror the hollowness and inaccuracy of these cultural
assumptions. That these institutions can exist is a testament to the tolerance and
uniqueness of American society. That they *must* exist is a reflection of the intolerance and often exclusionary reality that defines the same society.

The need for this variety was rooted in the founding of Harvard College in
1636. It duplicated the English college, which meant that there were immutable
restrictions with regard to class, sex, and race. Even when we fast-forward to the
creation of the land grant college in 1862, these colleges were not open to minorities, offered few opportunities for women, and were inaccessible to a majority of individuals simply because of their location. A brief historical overview of
American colleges and universities is important to understand these institutions.

Historical Overview

Early American institutions of higher education were firmly grounded in the
liberal arts tradition—four years of study, an emphasis on a classical curriculum,
resident fellows, and the awarding of baccalaureate degrees. This structure personified American higher education from the 1640s to the 1800s. For example, at
the outbreak of the American Revolution there were only nine colleges in America (Cardozier, 1987). And, as John Thelin pointed out in Chapter One, "the small
college persisted as the institutional norm, despite scattered attempts to create a
modern comprehensive university."

Change comes slowly, but criticism of the classical curriculum began to set
the stage for the development of modern universities and colleges. There were
three events during the nineteenth century that fundamentally altered the character of the higher education landscape and set the stage for the diversification of
higher education.

The Yale Report of 1828 represented the first major systematic effort to construct a curriculum. It defined the role of the curriculum as a stimulus for students' individual efforts; it saw the curriculum as a tool to assist students in using their minds. The document became the classic frame of reference for refining liberal education. Nevertheless, it is often characterized as a reactionary document that stagnated higher education reforms well into the nineteenth century (Brubacher & Rudy, 1976).

The second event was the passage of the Morrill Act in 1862. This occurred at a time when the country was in one of its most dynamic phases, symbolized by the expansion westward, technological revolution, and a desire for applied education (Pfnister, 1984). Communities were demanding flexible, practical, accessible education. The Morrill Act solidified the role of public education. The emphasis on "practical branches of knowledge" was a radical shift from the past, challenging the role of the established private liberal arts and religious colleges. The third occurrence was the introduction of the German university model, marked by the founding of Johns Hopkins University in 1876 (Patillo & Mackenzie, 1966). The German model's emphasis on scholarship and research, with a corresponding deemphasis of undergraduate education, redefined American higher education.

It was not until the latter half of the nineteenth century, however, that the "university movement" began to gain momentum and definition (Rudolph, 1962). During this period there was an increased demand for greater accessibility to public higher education, spurring the development of the land grant and state universities. And the demand at the end of the nineteenth century for elementary and secondary school teachers led to the establishment of the two-year normal schools. Later some of the normal schools were converted into four-year state colleges, and some became junior colleges (Cardozier, 1987). Thus by the beginning of the twentieth century American higher education had been transformed; the previous landscape of a relatively few single-purpose institutions had been replaced by an array of public and private two-year and four-year institutions grouped into categories on the basis of the degree offered. These categories were first introduced by Clark Kerr (Carnegie Commission on Higher Education, 1973), who grouped institutions on "the basis of their missions and educational functions" (p. 1).

Today there are over 3,600 institutions and fourteen million students in American higher education, compared to approximately 250 colleges and universities at the beginning of the Civil War (Cardozier, 1987) and an estimated sixty-two thousand students enrolled in some type of collegiate institution in 1870 (Lucas, 1994). Even during periods of fiscal woes and downturns in secondary enrollment, the overall pattern has been one of growth, both in new institutions and in student enrollment. There has been a slight decline in the number of liberal arts colleges but an offsetting increase in research and doctoral-granting institutions, community colleges, and specialized institutions.

The Carnegie Foundation for the Advancement of Teaching (1994) developed a classification scheme (revised in 1994) for American institutions of higher education, categorizing them as follows: research universities I and II; doctoral universities I and II; master's colleges and universities I and II; baccalaureate colleges I and II; associate of arts colleges; specialized institutions; and tribal colleges and universities. Student enrollment and total number of institutions for each Carnegie category are given in Table 3.1.

Although this chapter focuses primarily on institutions that have been historically underrepresented in the literature, the reader should refer to the classification of institutions by the Carnegie Foundation (1994), Rudolph (1962), and Brubacher and Rudy (1976) for a comprehensive understanding of the development and purpose of the wide array of colleges and universities.

Women's Colleges

To understand the evolution of American education for women, one must have an awareness of how societal roles for females in the United States have been perceived and articulated. During the colonial era, women were prepared for their roles in the same manner that men were prepared for theirs. They each served apprenticeships—girls served their mothers and boys served their fathers. The role for women was very simply defined—women took care of everything in the home. There was no need for formal learning.

Following the Revolutionary War, women were viewed in a different light. Given the new nation's quasi-democratic impulses, the need for an enlightened White male populace took on a new sense of urgency. Those who were to be the future electorate and representatives of the people needed to be trained to assume these responsibilities. Thus a new role emerged for women, as guardians of moral standards who provided moral training and discipline for children in the home.

Changing economic circumstances also contributed to a revision of women's defined role. With the growth of the commercial economy, the production of goods shifted away from the home, and women were no longer required to produce these goods. Therefore, women, who now had more time, logically assumed greater responsibility for the nurturing and guidance of children. If women were to now assume this expanded responsibility, they would need to be trained in a more systematic manner than the time-honored apprenticeship method. Women needed to be educated.

A major initiator of change in women's education was Emma Willard, who founded the Troy Female Seminary in 1821. She not only advocated that women should be trained for duties in the home, but also that their influence should follow the children into the schools. The teaching profession was a natural extension

TABLE 3.1. CARNEGIE CLASSIFICATION SCHEME 1994.

Enrollment in Institution of Higher Education and Number of Institutions, by Type and Control: 1994

Type of Institution	Enrollment (thousands)[a]					Number of Institutions				
	Total	Public	Private	Percent Public	Percent of Total	Total	Public	Private	Percent Public	Percent of Total
Total	15,263	12,072	3,191	79.1	100.0	3,595	1,576	2,019	43.8	100.0
Doctorate-granting institutions	3,981	3,111	869	78.2	26.1	236	151	85	64.0	6.6
Research universities I	2,030	1,652	379	81.3	13.3	88	59	29	67.0	2.5
Research universities II	641	488	153	76.2	4.2	37	26	11	70.3	1.0
Doctoral universities I	658	467	191	70.9	4.3	51	28	23	54.9	1.4
Doctoral universities II	651	505	147	77.5	4.3	60	38	22	63.3	1.7
Master's colleges and universities	3,139	2,291	848	73.0	20.6	529	275	254	52.0	14.7
Master's colleges and universities I	2,896	2,177	719	75.2	19.0	435	249	186	57.2	12.1
Master's colleges and universities II	243	114	129	46.9	1.6	94	16	68	27.7	2.6
Baccalaureate colleges	1,053	275	777	26.2	6.9	637	86	551	13.5	17.7
Baccalaureate colleges I	268	20	248	7.5	1.8	166	7	159	4.2	4.6
Baccalaureate colleges II	784	255	529	32.5	5.1	471	79	392	16.8	13.1
Associate of Arts colleges	6,527	6,234	292	95.5	42.8	1,471	963	508	65.5	40.9
Specialized institutions	548	145	404	26.4	3.6	693	72	621	10.4	19.3
Tribal colleges and universities[b]	15	15	0	100.0	0.1	29	29	0	100.0	0.8

[a]Enrollments are rounded to the nearest thousand.

[b]Figure excludes institutions with unavailable enrollment figures.

Source: Adapted from U.S. National Center for Education Statistics data. Copyright 1994, The Carnegie Foundation for the Advancement of Teaching. Reprinted with permission.

of women's nurturing responsibility and role as moral guardian. Willard wrote, "As evidence that this statement does not exaggerate the female influence in society, our sex need but be considered in the single relation of mothers. In this character, we have the charge of the whole mass of individuals, who are to compose the succeeding generation, during that period of youth, when the pliant mind takes any direction, to which it is steadily guided by a forming hand" (quoted in Woody, 1966, p. 309). To prepare women for this role, Willard insisted that their education should be on an equal par with men; however, she did not believe that women's education should extend beyond the seminary level.

Willard's curriculum consisted of instruction in moral and religious matters, literary areas, ornamentals, and domestic science. This last area was certainly not covered in the men's curriculum. Willard firmly believed that women had a responsibility for domestic pursuits. She wrote that "it is believed that housewifery might be greatly improved by being taught, not only in practice, but in theory. Why may it not be reduced to a system as well as other arts" (Woody, 1966, p. 310). Her proposal was a forerunner of what later came to be called home economics.

What Willard proposed—that women should be educated on an equal par with men and that they should pursue teaching careers—was quite radical for the early nineteenth century. Women were still expected to fulfill their domestic mission.

Building on Willard's vision of a new role for women, institutions of higher learning for women began to appear: Mount Holyoke Seminary, established in 1837; Rockford College, established in 1849; Elmira College, established in 1853; and Vassar College, established in 1865. It is estimated that by 1870, eleven thousand women were enrolled in some kind of institution of higher education. Of this number, five thousand were in normal schools (teachers' colleges), three thousand were in private seminaries and academies offering work beyond the secondary level, and three thousand were enrolled in collegiate departments of institutions offering baccalaureate degrees. Of this last figure, twenty-two hundred attended women's colleges, six hundred were enrolled in private coeducational colleges, and two hundred attended state universities (Horowitz, 1984).

Currently only a small number of women's colleges have sufficient endowments and enough support from alumnae to maintain their single-sex status. Today there are seventy-seven women's postsecondary institutions, enrolling 118,000 students (*Chronicle of Higher Education*, 1994).

Historically Black Colleges and Universities

Long before the abolition of slavery, Blacks recognized the importance and power of education. At the same time, slave owners understood the need to control slaves' access to literacy and therefore made learning to read a criminal offense for slaves. This did not keep some slaves from seizing every opportunity to acquire as much education as possible. Slaves with the highest level of literacy generally resided or worked in urban areas. Although it was more difficult for them, slaves on rural plantations also found ways to acquire learning. Some masters taught their slaves to read and write. White women did so more than White men. The greatest teaching efforts were exerted by White children. They simply ignored the law and taught their Black playmates what they knew. Slave children often had to carry White children's books to school. They would sit outside the classroom, listen, and gain literacy instruction in that manner. However slaves acquired learning, they used their skills to teach other slaves, usually in a clandestine manner (Genovese, 1972). The slaves understood that a thing denied was a thing to be desired. Although only about 5 percent of slaves emerged from bondage with any degree of literacy, as a group they exhibited a thirst for education. This burning desire to acquire formal learning was the major focus of Blacks after Emancipation (Brazzell, 1992).

At the beginning of the Civil War, fewer than thirty persons of acknowledged African descent had received baccalaureate degrees from American colleges. This is not a surprising figure given the fact that the population of free Blacks from which potential students could be drawn numbered less than five hundred thousand by 1860. Also, apart from such notable exceptions as Oberlin, Bowdoin, Franklin, and Rutland, few American colleges admitted Blacks on a continuous basis, and the only institutions of higher education specifically for Blacks, Lincoln and Wilberforce, had been created only in 1854 and 1856, respectively. And before 1860, America had not produced an overabundance of White degree holders either (Brazzell, 1991).

During the period 1865 to 1890, a major push for Black education at all levels was made. Hundreds of institutions were created all over the South. Part of this growth was facilitated by the passage of the second Morrill Act on August 30, 1890. Twelve public Black institutions of higher education were established under its auspices. The act legalized the segregation of Black and White public colleges in the South. These institutions also inculcated the legacy of industrial, mechanical, and agricultural education rather than a liberal arts curriculum. Liberal arts education in particular tended to be embraced by private Black colleges (Roebuck & Murty, 1993). Although many of these institutions called themselves colleges or universities, they were often no more than elementary and secondary schools. Their titles reflected their aspirations rather than their reality. Nonetheless, enough of these institutions had upgraded their educational content that by 1895 they had produced more than 1,150 Black college graduates.

Today there are 109 historically Black colleges and universities (HBCUs), consisting of fifty public and fifty-nine private institutions located in fourteen southern states, three northern states, three midwestern states, the District of Columbia, and the Virgin Islands. The principles on which HBCUs were founded still remain intact. Those principles are centered around the belief that Black students must be educated both to assume leadership and service roles in the Black community and to succeed in the larger community.

Until 1991 the 109 HBCUs produced approximately 70 percent of all Black college graduates. Although less than 20 percent of Black undergraduates are currently enrolled in HBCUs, they still are responsible for awarding one-third of all bachelor's degrees earned by Blacks (Roebuck & Murty, 1993). The most plausible explanation for this phenomenon seems to be that Black colleges create an esprit de corps that emphasizes leadership, responsibility, and a belief in students' capabilities, and that these values contribute to Black students' success. These emphases are less in evidence on predominantly White campuses.

Tribal Colleges

Early educational contacts between Native Americans and White Americans were framed by the latter's efforts to bring true "religion and a civil course of life" (Stein, 1992, p. 3) to the former. The first attempt to educate Indians in the English manner occurred in 1618 with the Henrico Proposal, introduced by the Virginia Company, which set up a college for Native Americans. It failed when a feud developed between the colonists and the Indians. The colonists were killed, and the college was destroyed (Stein, 1992).

The tone, however, was set, and the colonists continued their efforts to educate Native Americans. Some early colonial colleges stated their commitment to Indian education in their charters. In 1654 Harvard created an Indian college whose purpose was "the education of the English and Indian youth of this country in knowledge" (Stein, 1992, p. 3). Major fundraising campaigns were carried out for the purpose of educating Indians. These educational efforts generally ended in failure. Indian youths were removed from their homes and sent to the colonial colleges; of the twenty Indian youths sent to Harvard's school in Cambridge, only two survived to receive their bachelor's degrees. The rest died from sickness, changes in their lifestyle, and loneliness (Stein, 1992).

After the colonial period, the federal government assumed responsibility for the educational needs of Native Americans. But given the nation's preoccupation with westward expansion and the subsequent conflicts, the education needs of Native Americans were not a priority. Education, when provided, required Native

American youths to move away from their families to boarding schools where courses were conducted in English. Those who spoke in their native language were punished. Nearly all teachers were White Americans whose intent was to inculcate Native American youth with mainstream American cultural ideals (Rothschild & Hronek, 1992).

The early twentieth century and the World War II era saw an advocacy of wholesale changes in Native American education, from elementary to higher education. Among the suggested changes were to cease taking Native American children from their homes and to locate schools close to the children being served. These reform ideas culminated in the establishment of the Navajo Community College in 1969, the first tribally controlled college in the United States. Prior to its establishment, Navajos attending predominantly White colleges were dropping out at the rate of 50 percent by the end of their freshmen year. These schools were unable to meet the cultural needs Navajo students brought with them to college.

When the Navajo Community College was established, it was guided by the following principles:

1. For any community or society to grow and prosper, it must have its own means for educating its citizens.
2. Each member of that society must be provided with an opportunity to acquire a positive self-image and a clear sense of identity. This can be achieved when each individual's capacities are developed and used to the fullest possible extent.
3. Members of different cultures must develop their abilities to operate effectively, not only in their own immediate societies but also in the complexities of varied cultures that make up the larger society of men (Stein, 1992).

Currently, twenty institutions are classified as tribally controlled colleges. Though they represented only 0.07 percent of the three thousand institutions of higher education in the United States as of 1978, they held 10 percent of all Native Americans enrolled in higher education (Stein, 1992).

Hispanic-Serving Institutions

The earliest educational contact between Hispanics and White Americans was in the form of missionary work by Catholic and Protestant churches. Both groups saw themselves as agents of "Americanization," which entailed condemning "immoral" Hispanic social practices. The Catholic church sought to consolidate its control over Hispanic Catholics, and Protestant denominations sought to convert them (Yohn, 1991). While these consolidation and conversion attempts were for the most part rejected, attempts to create schools were a more welcomed activity.

While African American students were segregated from Whites by law and Native Americans were often forced to leave their homes to attend schools, Hispanic youths as a rule did not move away to schools. As was the custom (though not the law) with Native American students, however, Hispanics went to segregated schools. They were forced to speak English regardless of their native language.

Since most Hispanics lived in the border states, it is instructive to look at the historical availability of higher education in those states. For example, between 1845 and 1876, forty academies, forty-one colleges, thirty institutes, and eight educational associations were chartered in Texas. None were located in the border region, where the bulk of the Hispanic population resided. These problems have not abated; the border regions continue to have fewer campuses with narrower missions, smaller budgets, and fewer program offerings. This situation was exacerbated by the Texas Commission of Higher Education (established in 1955) and its successor, the Texas Higher Education Coordinating Board (established in 1965). Both were created to minimize program duplication and facilitate the development of a more efficient system. The Coordinating Board wields tremendous power over program development at Texas's public universities. Under the formula funding system, universities with comprehensive graduate programs are favored. The system provides more money to science and engineering courses than to others, more money to master's than bachelor's programs, and more money to doctoral than master's programs. Since the border universities lack engineering and science courses or a plethora of doctoral programs, they rank low on the formula schedule. Since 1973, three doctoral programs were added to the border region, while thirty-seven were added to the rest of the state (Hispanic Association of Colleges and Universities, 1993).

The designation Hispanic-Serving Institutions of Higher Education (HSIs) denotes accredited colleges and universities where at least 25 percent of the total student population is Hispanic (see Tables 3.2 and 3.3). In 1991, some 115 such institutions were identified. Thirty-four are located in Puerto Rico, and eighty-one are on the mainland. HSIs constitute 3 percent of all institutions of higher education in the United States, yet they enroll almost one-half (45 percent) of all Hispanics in higher education. They produce a disproportionate share of Hispanic baccalaureates who go on to earn doctorates. Of the 2,878 Hispanics who received doctorates between 1986 and 1990, 857 (30 percent) held a bachelor's degree from an HSI (Hispanic Association of Colleges and Universities, 1991).

The institutions with the greatest percentage of Hispanic students are Saint Augustine College, a two-year private institution in Chicago (99.3 percent His-

TABLE 3.2. NUMBER OF HISPANIC STUDENTS ENROLLED AT EIGHTY-ONE MAINLAND HSIs.

Hispanic Enrollment	Number of Institutions
Under 500	11
501–1,000	9
1,001–2,500	28
2,501–5,000	19
5,001–7,500	8
7,501–10,000	3
10,001 and over	3

Source: Hispanic Association of Colleges and Universities (1991). Reprinted with permission.

TABLE 3.3. PERCENTAGE OF HISPANIC STUDENTS ENROLLED AT EIGHTY-ONE MAINLAND HSIs.

Percent Hispanic	Number of Institutions
25–35	29
36–49	28
50–74	14
75–99	10

Source: Hispanic Association of Colleges and Universities (1991). Reprinted with permission.

panic); Boricua College, a four-year private institution in New York (93.4 percent Hispanic); Laredo Junior College, a two-year public college in Laredo, Texas (91.1 percent Hispanic); Texas State Technical College, a two-year public institution in Harlingen, Texas (87.7 percent Hispanic); Texas Southmost College, a two-year public institution in Brownsville, Texas (87.5 percent Hispanic); the University of Texas-Pan American, a four-year public institution (84.4 percent Hispanic); Laredo State University, a two-year upper-division university in Laredo, Texas (83.1 percent Hispanic); Hostos Community College, a two-year public college in the Bronx (81.1 percent Hispanic); the University of Texas at Brownsville, a two-year upper-division university (77.2 percent Hispanic); and El Paso Community College, a two-year public institution in El Paso, Texas (77.2 percent Hispanic).

Community Colleges

The junior college (or community college, as it is now called) is an institution unique to the United States. It was created at the turn of the twentieth century in response to a confluence of events. First, the rapidly expanding industrial sector of the economy and the shift toward mechanization in agriculture demanded a better-trained labor force. Second, the growth of public education resulted in a sharp rise in high school graduates and thus an increased demand for teachers and higher education. The higher education landscape, however, was becoming dominated by the emerging research universities. Those who controlled these institutions were less interested in undergraduate education and were eager to see the creation of another tier between high school and the university. Thus the earliest supporters and proponents of two-year institutions were leading university presidents (Tillery & Deegan, 1985).

The creation and development of community colleges was a giant step forward in opening institutions of higher education to a broader spectrum of individuals. Community colleges break through class barriers and truly provide higher education opportunities for everyone, including those with vocational interests, those seeking a terminal degree at a community college, and those seeking enrollment in two-plus-two programs with local colleges and universities.

The golden age for community colleges occurred between 1950 and 1970 (Tillery & Deegan, 1985). The number of community colleges increased from 74 in 1915 to 1,465 in 1990 (see Table 3.4), and enrollments grew from two million students to five million. During this era, there was an increased commitment to an open-door policy. The number of mature adults enrolling, particularly older women, sharply increased—as did minority enrollment. There was increased financial support from the federal government in the form of student financial aid and capital funding. State financing increased as well. Community colleges' connection to and identification with four-year colleges and universities was strengthened with the evolution of articulation agreements, interfaculty communication, and the assurance that senior institutions were willing to accept community college transfer students.

Proprietary Schools

Probably the most unusual type of postsecondary education institution is the proprietary or private career school. The purposes for which they exist and the individuals who run them are often considered to be outside the usual higher education milieu. Researchers have generally ignored this sector, and as a consequence, little data have been collected and reported on them.

Proprietary schools are one of the most recent entrants to the world of higher education. Prior to World War II, practical arts such as cosmetology, accounting, and navigation were taught by private masters. This was also true for

TABLE 3.4. NUMBER OF PUBLIC AND PRIVATE TWO-YEAR COLLEGES IN THE UNITED STATES, 1915–1990.

Year	Public	Independent	Total
1915	19	55	74
1921	70	137	207
1925	136	189	325
1930	178	258	436
1935	223	309	532
1940	258	317	575
1945	261	323	584
1950	337	311	648
1955	338	260	598
1960	390	273	663
1965	503	268	771
1970	847	244	1,091
1975	1,014	216	1,230
1980	1,049	182	1,231
1985	1,068	154	1,222
1990	1,282	183	1,465

Source: American Association of Community Colleges. *Pocket Profile of Community Colleges: Trends and Statistics, 1995–96.* Reprinted with permission.

instruction in business skills such as bookkeeping and shorthand. As a general rule, traditional colleges did not offer instruction in these areas. After World War II, technological changes and market demands dictated a more sophisticated, well-trained work force. This need required a training approach different from apprenticeships.

Growth in proprietary schools has always been tied to federal financial aid policies. After World War II, the Veterans Education Benefits program allowed thousands of returning soldiers to swell the ranks of new students. The greatest financial boost to proprietary schools came in 1972 with the passage of amendments to the Higher Education Act (Lee & Merisotis, 1990). Students in these schools now had access to federal grants and loans on a par with traditional college students.

Proprietary schools differ from traditional institutions of higher education in several major ways. First, the length of a program may last from one month to a year, and as a rule these schools do not grant degrees but rather offer certificates. Second, proprietary schools are in the business of making money. Their primary goal is to turn a profit. Third, their governance structures look nothing like those of traditional institutions. All decisions are made by the owners of the business. There are no faculty senates or venues for shared decision making. Fourth, because decision making is so narrowly concentrated and the structure of the programs is so flexible, proprietary schools can respond to market changes more rapidly than traditional institutions. The curriculum in proprietary schools is centered on developing specific job skills. There is no pretense of educating the "whole person." Most students enroll in office, technology, and personal service programs. In the technical area, programs are concentrated in auto mechanics and computer-related fields. In a particular program, all students will usually take the same sequence of courses. They receive more hands-on experience, and there is less emphasis on theory. Given the number and type of students enrolled in these schools, it is unwise to understate their role in higher education. There are currently four thousand accredited proprietary schools, enrolling about 1.8 million students. This is an increase from the 1.4 million students who attended proprietary schools in 1987. These figures account for only about two-thirds of total proprietary schools (that is, those belonging to accrediting agencies) (Lee & Merisotis, 1990). For their proponents, the value of proprietary schools is that they offer a relatively inexpensive educational option for a cadre of students who would otherwise not have access to higher education, including at community colleges.

Compared to traditional college students (see Table 3.5), proprietary school students tend to come from lower socioeconomic backgrounds and are more likely to be female, older, married, and African American. A larger proportion rely upon federal student aid programs to finance their education. They are more likely to have been away from high school for an extended period. They are more likely to have been enrolled in vocational or general curriculum programs in high school, and they are likely to have received slightly lower grades than students in college preparatory programs.

Unique Distinctions and Issues

There are lessons to be learned from institutions created to serve the needs of students who have historically been denied access to mainstream institutions or given limited opportunities for development at them. An understanding of what happens to students in these different types of institutions can be instructive for other schools and can help them educate specific subsets of students who often do not fare well in majority institutions.

One common ingredient in these alternative institutions seems to be a student-centered environment. The size of these institutions is one of their strengths. Other than community colleges, they tend to have small student bodies. Although small size is often cited as an asset, the dwindling number of liberal arts colleges demonstrates the difficulty today of competing for students, capturing sufficient resources, and maintaining a clear sense of purpose and mission. Early liberal arts colleges were created for the few. Contemporary pressures have pushed such

TABLE 3.5. PROPRIETARY SCHOOL STUDENTS COMPARED TO COMMUNITY COLLEGE STUDENTS, 1980.

	Proprietary Schools (percent)	Community Colleges (percent)
Gender		
Female	66	48
Male	34	52
Age		
Under 19	35	72
19–22	35	23
22 and over	30	5
Race		
African American	24	6
White	68	87
Other	8	7
Family income		
Under $8,000	32	19
$8,000–$15,000	34	37
$15,000–$20,000	12	19
$20,000 and over	23	26
High school grades		
A	9	9
B+ to B	41	42
B to C+	31	35
C to D	18	15
High school achievement		
High school graduate	89	98
Nongraduate, GED	6	1
No degree	5	1

Source: Lee & Merisotis (1990). Reprinted with permission.

institutions either out of existence or into a new kind of existence (for example, as comprehensive universities).

Institutions such as women's colleges, HBCUs, HSIs, and tribally controlled colleges grew out of the liberal arts tradition and still maintain the characteristics of small liberal arts colleges. For example, of the seventy-seven women's colleges in the United States, the largest is Texas Women's University, with a student population of less than 9,700. The average women's college enrollment is under 1,600.

Students attending these institutions have several advantages. First, greater opportunities are provided to participate in activities. Students serve in leadership positions in student government, cocurriculum clubs and activities, and fraternities and sororities. Second, students are enmeshed in an environment that gives positive feedback about their identity, history, and traditions—an environment that fosters pride. Part of this feedback is ingrained in these institutions' curriculum. For example, women's studies programs on all-female campuses provide an especially supportive environment for female students to learn about themselves personally and intellectually. HBCUs explore Black consciousness, culture, and history. Tribally controlled colleges emphasize tribal history and a culturally specific philosophy.

Other student-centered features of these institutions include characteristically stronger relationships between students and faculty and a greater emphasis on teaching. Proprietary schools pride themselves on the hands-on nature of the education they provide. There is much less emphasis on theory and research. The same can be said of the community college, whose whole reason for being revolves around teaching. Innovations in instruction can be said to be a major contribution of community colleges, from the use of audio tutorial teaching to instruction by telephone, television, radio, and film; computer-assisted instruction using gaming and simulation; and multistudent response systems (Cohen & Brawer, 1987). At mainstream comprehensive and research universities, by contrast, publishing is recognized and rewarded more than teaching. And graduate schools tend to be discipline-specific, with little or no emphasis on pedagogy (O'Banion, 1989).

Students in HBCUs, women's colleges, tribally controlled colleges, and HSIs are exposed to teachers who serve as role models and who can in these smaller settings instill a sense of pride and self-worth. Faculty are more apt to involve undergraduate students in their research and are instrumental in encouraging students to enter nontraditional disciplines. For example, women's colleges have been recognized for their historic strength in getting female students into careers in mathematics and science. Students at women's colleges major in economics, mathematics, the natural sciences, and the life sciences more often than women in mainstream institutions (Sharp, 1991).

Seminal research has documented the effectiveness of these institutions. Fleming's *Blacks in College* (1984); Richardson and Bender's *Fostering Minority Access and Achievement in Higher Education* (1987); Justiz, Wilson, and Bjork's *Minorities in Higher Education* (1994); and Horowitz's *Alma Mater* (1984) are but a few outstanding examples of works chronicling the success of these schools.

Financial Constraints and Opportunities

The most serious challenge for any institution in carrying out its mission is securing sufficient financial support. Liberal arts colleges have dwindled in number because too many have been unable to garner the resources to carry out their historic mission. Religious colleges found themselves competing unsuccessfully with public institutions and were subsequently outflanked in size, facilities, and total financial support.

Given their size and mission and the student populations they serve, these diverse institutional types have always faced an uphill financial struggle. The proprietary school has usually been an exception. Their lean administrative structure, their focus on profit, and access to federal student financial aid since 1972 insulates these institutions from many of the financial traumas commonly experienced by other schools (Lee & Merisotis, 1990). Until the 1970s, community colleges also enjoyed consistent and substantial financial support. That changed with taxpayer revolts and reductions in federal support.

HBCUs and HSIs, on the other hand, have always struggled from an underfinanced posture. In response to a financial crisis in the early 1940s, Black private colleges banded together and formed the United Negro College Fund (UNCF). Its first campaign was conducted in 1944. Since then, the UNCF has raised more than $690 million for twenty-seven member colleges and universities (Roebuck & Murty, 1993). The Hispanic Association of Colleges and Universities (HACU) was formed in 1986 to represent HSI interests, such as increased student financial assistance through federal and state governments (Hispanic Association of Colleges and Universities, 1991).

In 1972 the American Indian Higher Education Consortium (AIHEC) was formed to promote unity among tribally controlled colleges. The principle concern facing AIHEC in 1973 was the critical shortage of financial support. Persistent lobbying efforts resulted in the passage of the Tribally Controlled Community College Assistance Act on October 17, 1978. Title I funded all the tribal colleges, with the exception of Navajo Community College, which was separately funded under Title II (Stein, 1992).

Clearly the federal government is a major partner for these institutions and largely determines their viability. While there has been success in leveraging student financial aid, less progress has been made in securing direct institutional and research grants. As the federal government moves into a new era in which questions are being raised about the nature and level of federal support to higher education in general, the most vulnerable schools may be doubly at risk.

The future realities will require that the different institutional types become as efficient and effective as possible at managing their resources, especially federal funds. Alternative funding sources will have to be identified and vigorously pursued. The UNCF model may be an appropriate guide for the other institutional types. In the future, success may depend on the formation of coalitions among institutions that had previously competed. It is encouraging that on September 26 and 27, 1990, presidents of HSI and HBCU colleges and universities met in Washington, D.C., for the first time to seek common ground, discuss future technological challenges, address issues of minority education, and pursue increasing federal support for Hispanic and Black institutions.

Legal Remedies—Friend or Foe

Our cultural ideal of democracy and equality for all citizens is belied by the long, hard-fought efforts of excluded groups to gain access to educational opportunities. The most famous legal battles against exclusionary laws were fought by Black Americans. The landmark *Brown* v. *Board of Education* (1954 [347 U.S. 483]) decision in 1954 overturned the "separate but equal" doctrine. Yet despite this victory, segregation continued in public institutions of higher education. Not until the passage of the Civil Rights Act of 1964 did significant change occur. The act gave power to the U.S. Attorney General to file lawsuits on behalf of Black plaintiffs, and more significantly, it prohibited the release of federal funds to segregated colleges, under Title VI.

These legal rulings and the subsequent passage of the Higher Education Act of 1965, which made basic education opportunity grants and other financial aid programs available to disadvantaged students, radically altered the higher education landscape. Minority enrollment in previously predominantly White colleges and universities significantly increased. Benefits also applied to Black colleges. The increased availability of financial aid enlarged enrollments at these institutions. Funding was also secured for capital improvements on Black campuses.

In time, however, it became clear that there were unforseen consequences to these changes. The very laws that held so much promise for positive change were now being used to question the continued existence of Black colleges and universities. There were those who argued that the purposes for which HBCUs had been created were fulfilled and they were now obsolete. Opponents argued that HBCUs perpetuated a two-tiered higher education system which was duplicative from a financial, philosophical, and pedagogic standpoint.

Proponents of HBCUs countered that racial segregation still existed and that these institutions fulfilled roles, needs, and functions for Black students that were unavailable on White campuses. The reasons for the initial creation of these schools had not disappeared.

The danger for public HBCUs was that they would simply be eliminated. Their fate lay in the hands of unsympathetic and even hostile state agencies intent on engineering their demise. In *Adams* v. *Califano* (1977 [430 F. Supp. 118]), the U.S. Supreme Court ruled that states could not meet desegregation goals by closing Black colleges. Instead they had to improve Black colleges' facilities and academic offerings and ensure that these institutions could attract White as well as Black students (Roebuck & Murty, 1993).

Black public colleges are now undergoing radical changes. Desegregation plans resulted in a closer scrutiny of Black schools. The management and fiscal-planning ability of administrators were called into question, resulting in the removal of some presidents. The roles and missions of some schools changed. White students have been attracted to some campuses, altering the ethnic ratio and cultures of the institutions. White institutions, in an effort to meet affirmative action guidelines, have "raided" the faculties of HBCUs, resulting in little overall change in the number of Black faculty in the HBCU system.

The effects still unfolding from such actions have potential consequences for other institutional types. HSIs are using court rulings to press for greater access to financial and academic resources. In the push to pass Title IX, which forbade discrimination on the basis of sex by educational institutions, women's colleges asked to be exempted in order to avoid altering their admissions policies (Sharp, 1991). Although the Equal Rights Amendment did not pass, there were those who predicted that if it had, women's colleges would have been eliminated.

As nonmainstream institutions seek to rectify past discrimination, they must realize that success will likely result in unanticipated change. What had uniquely characterized them in the past may not be their defining parameters in the future.

Conclusion

The 1980s and 1990s have been confusing, challenging times for all institutions of higher education. Taxpayer revolts, protests against higher tuition, fewer funds from state legislatures, dwindling enrollments, and greater scrutiny from external entities have forced major institutional revisions. A recrafting of the higher education landscape continues.

In the midst of these changes, questions continue to arise about the continued need for the present variety of institutions. Should these schools be supported and encouraged to exist, or should the emphasis be on transforming mainstream universities to meet the needs of special populations? The obvious answer is that both should happen. Mainstream institutions have an obligation to better serve a diverse student population.

The value of nonmainstream institutions is that they successfully create milieus, techniques, and approaches that provide educational opportunities to students who would otherwise be excluded. They can set powerful examples for other institutions on how to serve unique populations. Their student-centered focus creates an environment in which all students are expected to succeed and students are given the support, encouragement, and confidence to do so. There is no reason to believe that the results achieved by HBCUs, HSIs, tribal colleges, women's colleges, community colleges, and proprietary schools cannot be replicated in other institutions. In the recrafting process, lessons must be learned from all quarters.

References

American Association of Community Colleges. (1995). *Pocket Profile of Community Colleges: Trends and Statistics, 1995–96*. Washington, DC: American Association of Community Colleges.

Brazzell, J. C. (1991). *Education as a tool of socialization: Agnes Scott Institute and Spelman Seminary, 1881–1910*. Unpublished doctoral dissertation, University of Michigan, Ann Arbor.

Brazzell, J. C. (1992). Bricks without straw: Missionary-sponsored Black higher education in the post-Emancipation era. *Journal of Higher Education, 63*(1), 26–49.

Brubacher, J. S., & Rudy, W. (1976). *Higher education in transition*. New York: Harper & Row.

Cardozier, V. R. (1987). *American higher education*. Aldershot, England: Gower.

Carnegie Commission on Higher Education. (1973). *A classification of institutions of higher education*. Berkeley: University of California Press.

Carnegie Foundation for the Advancement of Teaching. (1994). *A classification of institutions of higher education*. Princeton, NJ: Princeton University Press.

Chronicle of Higher Education. (1994, February 23).

Cohen, A. M., & Brawer, F. B. (1987). *The American community college*. San Francisco: Jossey-Bass.

Fleming, J. (1984). *Blacks in college: A comparative study of students' success in Black and White institutions*. San Francisco: Jossey-Bass.

Genovese, E. D. (1972). *Roll, Jordan, roll*. New York: Pantheon Books.

Hispanic Association of Colleges and Universities. (1991). *Annual report*. San Antonio, TX: Author.

Hispanic Association of Colleges and Universities. (1993). *Equity in financing state higher education: Impact on Hispanics*. San Antonio, TX: Author.

Horowitz, H. L. (1984). *Alma mater: Design and experience in the women's colleges from their nineteenth-century beginnings to the 1930s*. New York: Knopf.

Justiz, M. J., Wilson, R., & Bjork, L. G. (1994). *Minorities in higher education*. Phoenix, AZ: Oryx Press.

Lee, J. B., & Merisotis, J. P. (1990). *Proprietary schools: Programs, policies, and prospects* (ASHE-ERIC Higher Education Report No. 5). Washington, DC: The George Washington University, School of Education and Human Development.

Lucas, C. J. (1994). *American higher education: A history*. New York: St. Martin's Press.

O'Banion, T. (1989). *Innovation in the community college*. New York: Macmillan.

Patillo, M. M., Jr., & Mackenzie, D. M. (1966). *Church-sponsored higher education in the United States*. Washington, DC: American Council on Education.

Pfnister, A. O. (1984). The role of the liberal arts college: A historical overview of the debates. *Journal of Higher Education, 55*(2), 151–153.

Richardson, R. C., Jr., & Bender, F. W. (1987). *Fostering minority access and achievement in higher education: The role of urban community colleges and universities*. San Francisco: Jossey-Bass.

Roebuck, J., & Murty, K. S. (1993). *Historically Black colleges and universities: Their place in American higher education.* New York: Praeger.

Rothschild, M. L., & Hronek, P. C. (1992). *Doing what the day brought: An oral history of Arizona women.* Tucson: University of Arizona Press.

Rudolph, F. (1962). *The American college and university.* New York: Knopf.

Sharp, M. K. (1991). Bridging the gap: Women's colleges and the women's movement. *Initiatives Journal of NAWDAC, 53*(4), 3–6.

Stein, W. J. (1992). *Tribally controlled colleges: Making good medicine.* New York: Lang.

Tillery, D., & Deegan, W. L. (1985). The evolution of two-year colleges through four generations. In W. L. Deegan, D. Tillery, and Associates, *Renewing the American community college: Priorities and strategies for effective leadership.* San Francisco: Jossey-Bass.

Woody, T. (1966). *A history of women's education in the United States* (Rev. ed., Vols. 1–2). New York: Octagon Books.

Yohn, S. M. (1991). An education in the validity of pluralism: The meeting between Presbyterian mission teachers and Hispanic Catholics in New Mexico, 1870–1912. *History of Education Quarterly, 31*(3), 343–365.

Legal Case References

Brown v. Board of Education, 347 U.S. 483 (1954).

Adams v. Califano, 430 F. Supp. 118 (D.D.C. 1977).

CHAPTER FOUR

STUDENT DIVERSITY ON TODAY'S CAMPUSES

Elaine El-Khawas

We live in an age of complexity. The diverse elements of complexity in organized human endeavors are increasingly recognized today. Pluralism and diversity are frequently evoked to describe important values in America's communities, its workplaces, and its educational settings. College and university administrators, recognizing many aspects of difference among their students, increasingly use inclusive thinking and terminology with respect to them.

This chapter discusses some characteristics essential to understanding today's students. It emphasizes the strong degree of intersection and overlap that exists among these characteristics. An underlying theme is that a steady evolution toward increased diversity of student populations should be recognized, both as a current reality for higher education and as a continuing trend.

A theoretical perspective developed by Martin Trow (1973) helps explain this view. In a seminal essay written more than two decades ago, he described the manifold effects of the process of steadily increasing access to higher education. He argued that one of the most powerful effects of this process, best thought of as a long-term transition from elite to mass higher education, is in bringing about a greater diversity of students entering colleges and universities. As he argued, "The higher the proportion of the age grade going on to higher education, the more the democratic and egalitarian concerns for equality of opportunity come to center on the increasingly important sector of tertiary education. . . . Differences in access to higher education . . . become a sharp political issue. . . . As more students from an age cohort go to college . . . the meaning of college attendance changes . . . to being something close to an obligation. This shift . . . has enormous consequences for student motivation, and thus also for the curriculum and for the intellectual climate of these institutions" (pp. 4–5).

In this view, increasing diversity is a long-term process, its ramifications only gradually unfolding. The dimensions of diversity that are experienced today can be expected to undergo still further development. Thus, even as educators respond to greater student diversity than in the past, future generations of educators will need to respond to student populations that are even more diverse.

Trow (1973) also pointed out that greater student diversity is accompanied by a second trend, an evolving social and political consciousness in which groups that have distinctive needs and experiences increase in number and then gain a collective identity that enables them to articulate their concerns and call for appropriate responses. Through a political dynamic lasting several decades, certain groups of students have become recognized as worthy of specific attention. Colleges and universities have taken action to develop special programs appropriate for these students. The process has been a gradual one; a certain number of these students must typically be present at a given institution before they find their voice and seek group-conscious forms of assistance. Typically, too, adequate institutional response has developed slowly and unevenly, with some institutions or units within them responding more quickly than others.

One implication of this dynamic is that educators should be open to changing definitions and groupings of students. They should recognize, too, that the various dimensions of diversity reflected in current discussions represent just a few of the aspects by which students differ. A continuing challenge for educators is to use encompassing language in speaking about students. Another challenge is to acknowledge distinctive subgroupings while paying attention to broadly felt student needs. Educators must also be reflective, willing to consider ways in which changing student interests and experiences may help identify institutional practices that are outmoded or narrowly conceived.

Salient Characteristics Today

Awareness of student diversity is much different today than it was several decades ago, when college students were typically described in terms of a few background characteristics. For the 1990s, many distinctions are needed to offer even a general view of students: older and traditional age; Asian American, Hispanic, African American, and Native American; men and women; gay, lesbian, and bisexual; full-time and part-time; commuter and residential.

Thus far, demographic or personal background factors have gained the most attention. Other characteristics quite relevant to learning and academic accomplishment have not as readily entered into discussion. To spur broader thinking and to help anticipate the future, this chapter is organized according to a framework of student characteristics that includes two separate dimensions, each relevant to understanding students and their needs:

Diversity of background	*Situational differences*
Race, ethnicity	Full- or part-time
Class	Differences by degree objective
Gender	Intermittent students
Sexual orientation	Transfer students
Students with disabilities	Differences by type of institution
International students	
Older/younger students	

The first dimension, diversity of background, includes key background factors, some of which have received greater attention than others. The second dimension, situational differences, includes the necessity of studying on a part-time basis, pursuing degree studies despite geographical moves or other changes in plans or circumstances, and enrolling in some semesters and not others. Situational factors also include systematic differences arising from the degree sought and the type of institution attended. (Different institutional types are discussed by Johnetta Brazzell in Chapter Three.)

We should remember that many of these are analytical categories, constructed to meet practical objectives but nevertheless limited and necessarily narrow: an individual student's circumstances are affected by multiple, overlapping characteristics, and some characteristics are more meaningful than others for different students and at different times. (Implications of these multiple effects are discussed in Chapters Nine, Ten, and Eleven.) The task for the educator is to make use of distinctive categories as only a first step in understanding students; it is also important to develop the ability to integrate information related to several dimensions when approaching any particular situation.

Diversity of Students: Background Factors

Many background factors arising from students' family or personal circumstances affect their ability to accomplish their educational goals. Other background factors involve basic rights, including the obligation that universities and colleges protect civil rights and pursue affirmative action procedures. Some factors help the university or college to understand and facilitate different learning styles or, in other instances, to anticipate the social and personal developmental issues salient to their students.

Women. The record of progress in increasing the presence of female students on American campuses has been especially dramatic. Since the immediate postwar period, when women were severely underrepresented and faced some legal barriers to attending college, substantial change has occurred. In 1950 women represented 32 percent of total enrollment. By the mid 1960s women constituted at least 40 percent of all enrollments, and by 1978 women had achieved overall parity. Four years later, in 1982, women earned at least half of all baccalaureate degrees awarded. Today women also earn at least half of all master's degrees, although they still lag behind in the most prestigious degrees: women earn about one-third of doctoral and professional degrees (Andersen, Carter, & Malizio, 1989).

This aspect of higher education's recent history illustrates well the point Trow (1973) made about the profound ways in which an increasing numerical presence generates other effects. Along with their increased number, women students have also brought about changes in curriculum and in campus programs serving student needs. Certain fields have grown in large part due to the interests of women students, while others have contracted due to their lack of interest. Majors in education have dropped over time, for example, as fewer women students sought teaching careers. Other fields, especially business, law, and communications, have expanded, in large part due to the increasing interest of women students.

Other changes were prompted by legislation, especially federal law prohibiting discrimination against women. Because many female students are older than the traditional age for students, they have also spurred new campus programs, including child-care centers and special counseling and career placement services.

Still other changes have stemmed from the growing social and political consciousness of women, expressed by their increased attention to and understanding of subtle forms of bias and the cumulative effect of implicit, often inadvertent, behaviors. Advocates for women have contributed to higher education's general understanding of the way such behaviors, taken together, can create a negative, discouraging atmosphere—a "chilly" climate (Sandler & Hall, 1982)—that hampers the full educational achievement of female students. This understanding of subtle but powerful environmental effects also has relevance to other groups that face marginalization or other negative treatment because of their background characteristics.

Race and Ethnicity. Race and ethnicity are among the most fundamental factors in use today to monitor and understand diversity among students in higher education. Attention has been especially focused on several racial and ethnic categories—including African Americans, Asian Americans, Hispanics, and Native Americans—that fall under the legal protection of federal laws.

Colleges and universities have undertaken systematic initiatives to increase the representation of these students (El-Khawas, 1994), and federal reports show some record of progress. In 1982 American colleges, universities, and community colleges enrolled 2.1 million students from these racial and ethnic categories. This figure had increased more than 50 percent by 1993, when 3.2 million students from these backgrounds were enrolled (National Center for Education Statistics, 1994).

As Table 4.1 shows, the policy objective of achieving equal representation has not been attained. College students from African American, Hispanic, and Native American backgrounds remain underrepresented, especially in terms of degrees awarded (Carter & Wilson, 1995).

Socioeconomic Class. The socioeconomic background of students has been of long-term interest for social policy makers. Federal programs providing student financial assistance are designed to enable students to enroll for college study regardless of their family's financial circumstances. Financial circumstances may become more important for policy in the future, but with greater complexity than in the past. Today, relevant economic circumstances may involve the student's own family situation (for example, number of dependents, whether a spouse is working), not just the family circumstances in which she or he grew up. Today, too, there are a growing number of students who, although young and unmarried, are financially independent of their families (Otuya & Mitchell, 1994). College administrators and policy makers must consider this additional complexity as they try to address financial needs tied to family background. It is also important to recognize that problems related to socioeconomic circumstances may be com-

TABLE 4.1. UNDERGRADUATE ENROLLMENT OF MEMBERS OF MAJOR RACIAL AND ETHNIC GROUPS AND DEGREES EARNED, 1992.

Racial or Ethnic Group	Bachelor's Degrees Enrollment (percent)	Earned (percent)
White	74.9	82.9
African American	10.2	6.4
Hispanic	7.1	3.6
Asian American	4.9	4.1
Native American	0.9	0.5
Nonresident alien	2.1	2.5

Source: Carter & Wilson (1995). Reprinted with permission.

mingled with other characteristics, especially race and ethnicity. Among Native American students, for example, a substantial proportion are low-income.

Gay, Lesbian, and Bisexual Students. Issues of climate and the necessity of a supportive learning environment have also been salient in the growing attention to the issues facing gay, lesbian, and bisexual students. Special needs for this group, estimated to involve as many as one in six students, have been addressed at a number of colleges and universities over the last decade, although typically in limited ways (Sherrill & Hardesty, 1994). Basic rights to safety and to protection from harassment must be considered, recognizing that lesbian, gay, and bisexual students have faced both physical assaults and psychological intimidation on many campuses. Legal protections have increasingly been available, and many colleges and universities have taken steps to train police and security forces and to raise awareness about hate crimes and other acts of intolerance.

Beyond basic rights and protections, issues of whether a college climate is hostile or supportive is significant if a university or college is to be an effective learning environment for gay, lesbian, and bisexual students. Such students often feel uncomfortable on college campuses, sometimes reluctant to live in residence halls or to participate in routine college activities. Discomfort also means that gay, lesbian, and bisexual students are more likely to drop out or otherwise interrupt their studies. Feelings of depression, alienation, and fear can be present, suggesting that college administrators should not be content with preventing discriminatory treatment but should also reach out to students in ways that support them in achieving their learning goals.

Older Students. Another consequential change for higher education is greater diversity in the age of those enrolled for college study, a phenomenon affecting all degree levels. Increased numbers of older students have enrolled in higher education in response to two separate trends in the national economy: growing numbers of women entering the work force (often after some years devoted to child rearing) and the growing educational needs of American workers, whether for entry-level jobs, job retraining and advancement, or job change. By 1992, a majority of undergraduate students were over twenty-one years of age: 55 percent, or 7 million students, were over twenty-one, and 41 percent, or 5.1 million students, were over twenty-four years of age (National Center for Education Statistics, 1994).

Students above the age of twenty-four are likely to have quite distinctive needs and interests compared to younger students, because they generally are attending college after having had workplace, family, or other life experiences. Issues of dealing with older students also intersect substantially with issues concerning the needs of part-time students. In fact, the great majority (72 percent) of older students are studying part-time, although a significant segment—1.2 million students—are studying on a full-time basis (National Center for Education Statistics, 1994).

Within this older group are a sizable number of students who are thirty-five years of age or older: 1.8 million students fit this age profile, including 382,000 who are studying on a full-time basis (National Center for Education Statistics, 1994). Public community colleges are the main locus of their studies; 63 percent of students aged thirty-five or older are at public two-year institutions.

Older students may have little interest in traditional campus programs and services. They may require assistance, however, in developing a coherent academic program that builds on disparate prior experience and courses at other institutions. Curriculum planning may need to be adjusted to take into account the fact that such adults bring considerable experience of their own to the situations discussed in class. Indeed, the presence of older students has helped to sensitize many instructors to the "age-specific" focus of some undergraduate textbooks, which have traditionally been targeted to younger audiences.

Students with Disabilities. Another group that has seen recent and continuing growth is students who have physical and other disabilities that affect their learning. Since the 1970s, the percentage of freshmen who report having a disability has tripled (Henderson, 1995, p. iii). By the fall of 1994, about 9 percent of entering freshmen reported a disability. Among these students, 3 percent reported difficulties with sight or hearing, and another 3 percent reported having a learning disability (Astin, Korn, Sax, & Mahoney, 1994). Colleges and universities should anticipate further increases in these trends in the future, especially in light of the effects of recent federal legislation upholding the rights of persons with disabilities. College administrators would be well advised to work closely with high schools to stay abreast of changes they have made, as well as changes they have experienced in numbers and patterns of students with disabilities.

International Students. Students from other countries are another important constituency for American colleges and universities. In 1992–93 more than four hundred thousand international students attended U.S. institutions (Institute for International Education, 1993). Close to half were pursuing graduate degrees, 37 percent were enrolled in bachelor's degree programs, and 11 percent were enrolled in associate degree programs. About one-tenth were studying in the United States on a nondegree basis, to learn English or to obtain practical training, for example.

Although in aggregate terms international students account for only about 3 percent of all enrollments, their presence is substantial at many institutions.

International students compose more than 10 percent of enrollments at about forty U.S. institutions, mostly research universities. A few of these campuses have sizable populations of international students, ranging upward to 20 or 25 percent of enrollment or totaling more than three thousand international students (Institute for International Education, 1993). A total of 105 institutions—just 4 percent of all U.S. institutions—account for nearly half (44 percent) of all international student enrollments. Such institutions have had to develop appropriate support services to assist international students with a variety of special needs, not only in adjusting to the distinctive academic requirements of American institutions but also in adjusting to cultural factors that can be quite different from what they have experienced previously.

Diversity of Students: Situational Circumstances

While much higher education planning still presumes that the typical student is a full-time undergraduate pursuing a baccalaureate degree, many students are enrolled with other objectives. At some universities, for example, significant numbers of students are enrolled for doctoral study; these students influence the overall ethos or culture of those institutions. Other schools have had a sizable expansion in master's degree students over the past three decades. At community colleges, many students are enrolled in certificate programs of less than two years. Other differences in student circumstances—part-time study, transferring between institutions, intermittent patterns of study—have been increasing and are likely to continue to grow in the future. Another situational factor is the type of institution attended. Each of these factors will be discussed in this section, with special emphasis on their implications for college policies and practices.

Degree Status. In the fall of 1992 enrollment for all postbaccalaureate work totaled almost two million students, or 13 percent of all enrolled students. This number almost equals the number of undergraduate students enrolled at independent institutions. Most of these students (1.4 million students, or 71 percent) were studying for master's degrees (O'Brien, 1992). Doctoral students are a much smaller group, an estimated 262,000 students in 1991–92, with a similar number (280,531) enrolled for first professional degrees (mostly law or medical degrees).

Growth in master's degree enrollment has been especially significant at liberal arts colleges and four-year comprehensive universities. At independent institutions, more than 612,000 students were enrolled for graduate study in 1992, double the 1972 number. In the past many of these institutions had served baccalaureate-level students primarily, and their overall culture and the structure of their support services was shaped by the needs of baccalaureate students.

An increasing share of postbaccalaureate enrollment is accounted for by international students. In 1979 master's degrees were awarded to nineteen thousand nonresident aliens (international students with temporary visas); by 1989, this number had risen to thirty-four thousand (O'Brien, 1992). The share of doctoral degrees awarded to nonresident aliens has also risen. In 1992 thirty-two percent of all doctorates were awarded to non–U.S. citizens, up from 13 percent in 1962 (Ries & Thurgood, 1993).

The number of students enrolled for first professional degrees has also grown dramatically, more than doubling between 1972 and 1992. In another example of the intersection of several trends, this doubling is accounted for almost entirely by an increased representation of female students. In 1972 there were only 1,784 first professional degrees awarded to women, barely 5 percent of the total; twenty years later, 29,075 women were awarded first professional degrees, 39 percent of the total (National Center for Education Statistics, 1994).

At the other end of the spectrum are students who enroll for certificate programs of less than two years in length (for example, in practical nursing, police training, and health and medical technology specialties). This is also a growing population, but it is concentrated at community colleges. In 1992 a total of 182,000 certificates were awarded in such programs, including 117,000 certificates for programs lasting between one and two years (Henderson, 1995). Notably, about one in five of the recipients of these certificates is a minority student.

Part-Time Study.   There has also been rapid growth in the number of part-time students. The majority of enrollment in programs less than two years in length is part-time; similarly, the expansion of master's degree programs has taken place in evening programs, sometimes in off-campus locations or in separately administered programs addressed to specific groups (such as women returning to college after child rearing or management employees of nearby businesses). Young adult men are increasing among part-time students, as they return to school for additional coursework in their field or to pursue higher degrees in response to the changing job market.

The number of part-time students has grown steadily since World War II. Today, part-time enrollment is substantial in almost all sectors of higher education. In 1991–92 there were 5.3 million part-time undergraduates, or 42 percent of the total; there were also 1 million part-time graduate students, or 39 percent of the total (Andersen et al., 1989).

Because part-time enrollments are concentrated at community colleges, four-year institutions have been slow to adapt their procedures to the increasing presence of part-time students. In 1991–92 three million part-time students made up almost two-thirds of those enrolled at two-year institutions; however, 24 percent of students at public research universities were enrolled part-time, as were 35 percent at other public universities and colleges.

As institutions have gained experience, there has been a greater awareness that part-time students, especially those who are older than traditional students, have special needs and expectations that call for appropriate responses. Their prior experiences in the workplace and in life mean that they bring additional information to the classroom, and they often expect active participation in class dialogue. They typically have quite specific learning goals and serious constraints on their time. They may find that various institutional services—such as the registrar, financial aid office, library reference desk, and campus bookstore—are not available at convenient hours.

Transfer Students. Transfer students are another population that can be expected to have distinctive needs that require special services, both at the "sending" and the "receiving" institution. Transfer students often have very limited information and advice available, both before they transfer and after they are in their new setting. They may need more initial advising than other new students, to help them mesh their previous academic work with the requirements of their new institution, especially when terminology differs from one institution to another. Similarly, transfer students can be expected to encounter initial difficulties with a new environment that may not be addressed by orientation programs for freshmen.

The number of students who transfer from one institution to another is not monitored on a systematic basis, but some trends are known. Among students enrolled at community colleges, for example, estimates are that about one-quarter will transfer at some point, often before completing an associate degree (American Council on Education, 1991, pp. 24–25). Longitudinal studies of college students have also suggested that as many as one in four students transfers between institutions. It is likely that more transfers will occur in the future, because of several trends—increased part-time study, longer periods needed for degree completion, and increased enrollment of older students.

Intermittent Study. A related group of students may grow as well: so-called intermittent students, who enroll for one semester and then return to their studies only after some lapse of time. No clear statistics exist on the numbers of these students, although it would be consistent with several trends—higher college costs, more students combining employment with study, and so on—that the number of intermittent students will grow. Advising and adjustment problems for these students could easily be underestimated, yet they share some of the problems transfer students face. Curriculum and degree requirements may have changed during the time they were not enrolled, so academic planning and advising must consider both old and new requirements to define what remains to be completed. College and university administrators would be well advised to review their current level of services for transfer students and also explore the needs that arise among intermittent students.

Institutional Type. Another situational factor involves differences between various types of institutions. This factor has received substantial attention from researchers and planners alike (see Chapter Three). In many respects, higher education enrollments can be divided into four quite distinctive subpopulations:

- Students at community colleges. This is the largest segment, accounting for 37 percent of all enrollments.
- Undergraduates at public four-year institutions. This group accounts for 33 percent of all enrollments.
- Undergraduates at independent institutions, primarily four-year universities. This group accounts for 15 percent of all enrollments.
- Graduate students, mostly at the master's level. This group accounts for 11 percent of all enrollments.

These four subpopulations accounted for 96 percent of enrollment in 1991–92 (Otuya & Mitchell, 1994). Each is in some way distinctive compared to the others. Thus, students at community colleges are mainly part-time, more than half are over twenty-five years of age, and at least one-quarter are people of color. In contrast, undergraduates at public four-year institutions still mostly fit a traditional profile: three-quarters are less than twenty-five years of age and are studying on a full-time basis. This traditional profile also fits undergraduates at independent institutions, where 79 percent are full-time students. Graduate students at both public and independent institutions display a different overall profile, however: 65 percent are part-time, and almost all (84 percent) are at least twenty-five years old (Otuya & Mitchell, 1994).

Key Dimensions for Understanding Tomorrow's Students

Each of the characteristics that help define today's students will certainly remain important in the future. It is likely that new categories will emerge as well, possibly in response to demographic and economic changes but also because of the growing awareness that no set of categories can adequately reflect the full array of students. Further subgroupings will emerge, both in regard to student background and situational differences.

New sensitivity is already needed regarding race and ethnicity, for example. Colleges and universities should expect that steadily increasing numbers of students will be of mixed or bicultural heritage and will not identify with a single racial or ethnic group. Increasing numbers of students now check "other" on forms asking about their racial background. In 1991–92 there were half a million students for whom race information was unknown in official reports to the U.S. Department of Education (National Center for Education Statistics, 1993).

In some parts of the country, certain ethnic subgroupings have become very important. Within the Hispanic population, for example, many campuses have recognized important differences between Puerto Ricans, Cuban Americans, Mexican Americans, and students from Central and South America. Other campuses have found that Asian American students are best served when the distinctive characteristics of different subgroups are recognized: Vietnamese students, for example, have different background factors from Korean or Japanese students.

America's diversity extends far beyond the legally protected groups that currently receive direct attention. Numerous other groups can point to discriminatory treatment and bigotry or to special aspects of their history that have left them at a disadvantage. Sometimes the impact has been greatest in certain parts of the United States. In Maine, for example, Franco-Americans feel that their heritage was systematically diminished. Other cities and parts of the country have a long history of discrimination and prejudice against Irish and Italian groups, and colleges and universities in those locations have identified special needs that arise from these historical patterns. Eastern European groups, which form sizable subpopulations in parts of the United States, have developed a stronger sense of identification with their distinctive heritage in recent years in the aftermath of the collapse of communism in their homelands. Colleges and universities in geographic areas with substantial concentrations of such groups may find it important to address special aspects of their heritage.

Religious background has not received much attention in recent years, but it has certainly played a major part in America's history of discrimination. Americans of Jewish background are aware that incidents of religious prejudice can negatively affect their lives. Catholic Americans have also experienced discrimination and hateful treatment. At present, in many American communities there are increasing numbers of Muslims and Buddhists whose religious traditions are not well understood. Without careful attention, these groups may encounter difficulty in achieving acceptance and in being able to practice their customs in American settings. Another religious group of growing importance on college campuses is fundamentalist Christian denominations (Mooney, 1995). These groups also have important perspectives that set them apart from other students and that may call for special attention if their religious beliefs are to be compatible with their participation in campus life.

Emerging differences also relate to other aspects of student background. Campus offices working with students with disabilities have sensed a shift in the types of disabilities they must consider (Kroeger & Schuck, 1993; Ryan & McCarthy, 1994). There is an increasing trend toward recognizing "hidden" disabilities, conditions that are not noticeable but that nevertheless hinder student learning and call for some form of accommodation. Learning disabilities are one such category; a number of campuses have developed special programs for students so affected. Health-related disabilities, including AIDS and chemical sensitivity, are also receiving increased attention. A recent report (Henderson, 1995) indicates that students with hidden disabilities now make up more than half of all freshmen with disabilities.

Another factor that can be important, although it is not regularly discussed, is generational differences among students. They may display similar outward characteristics, but different generations of students bring very different perspectives to campus life, based on the distinctive life experiences of each cohort. Consider what is known about the students who will enroll in the early years of the twenty-first century. A significant proportion of these future students—those who will enroll directly after high school—are currently in the seventh or eighth grade. Another significant proportion—those who will enroll as adults—are in high school already or in entry-level positions in the work force.

For both groups, distinctive aspects of their life experience can shape their expectations for post–high school study. They have been heavily influenced by electronic media with strong visual imagery, fast pacing, and interactive features; many are accustomed to having access to personal computers. The effect of such experiences on their view of the world and on how information intended for them should be organized and transmitted can easily be underestimated.

This generation is also influenced by the distinctive moral conflicts of the last decade: AIDS and its threat to sexual behavior, excessive use of alcohol to relieve boredom, drug use and drug dealing, violence and its inevitable cheapening of life. College administrators should recognize that many of their entering students will have a hard time sustaining a positive outlook after the negative climates they have experienced.

Emerging Differences in Time and Place

Students of the future will also have distinctive needs arising from situational factors. Educators can expect that part-time study will grow and that further subgroups of part-time students will appear. A category that has grown recently, for example, involves students who enroll but are not seeking a degree. Currently at least 25 percent of postbaccalaureate students are enrolled on a non-degree-seeking basis. At community colleges, 19 percent of current students are enrolled on a nondegree basis. Administrators should examine whether these students need distinctive services.

Another increasing category of students will be "distance" learners (even though the exact meaning of this term will probably remain ambiguous). How will universities recognize and address the needs of students who may never set foot on campus, who may have their entire academic experience via a TV screen three hundred miles from their instructors? The number of students in such situations will grow in the future, even if appropriate support services have not been adequately identified and developed.

Ways to Explore Who Your Students Are

This section offers four maxims to underscore its general theme—the essential necessity of continually exploring and redefining the nature of any student population and its needs.

Watch Globally, Watch Locally. University administrators must be good observers, good investigative reporters, and good detectives. They should continually scan their surroundings for clues to important changes within the student populations they serve. Currently enrolled students are a special resource, if there are ways to listen to their stories and perspectives. It is useful, for example, to know what students are reading. Even better, get information on what books they've read more than once, read at various times, or talked about with close friends. Regularly watched television programs offer other insights, as does an awareness of what news events and media stories best capture the dreams and fears of students. Keeping in touch with high schools is another way to stay alert to the changing needs, interests, and expectations of soon-to-be college students. Organizing regular but brief sessions that allow high-schoolers to discuss issues of concern to them can be useful as well.

Other resources are more formal—journals, books, and conference presentations. The payoff comes from listening carefully—being alert to the trends and indicators that signal fundamental, long-term change—and seeking out and listening closely to the views of analysts and experts who have demonstrated a keen ability to characterize change.

Define and Define Again. This technique provides a hedge against complacency, a call for continuous exploration of exactly what makes students tick, what their concerns are, and how they define issues. The danger is that a certain view of students—for example, that they are increasingly materialistic because they have anxieties about the job market—can become a blinder, obscuring new meanings given by students to what otherwise appear to be the same attitudes. For example, in UCLA's annual survey of incoming freshmen, students have increasingly noted their desire to be well-off financially (Astin et al., 1994). It is important to note, however, that the period when the survey began, the mid 1960s, was a time of economic prosperity and confidence in the continuing growth of the American economy. In such a context students probably interpreted "being well-off" as extravagant, as being wealthy beyond conventional needs. In contrast, today's students, having grown to maturity during a time of greater economic uncertainty, periodic inflation, dramatic swings in the stock market, rising college costs, and rising student loan burdens, may see "being well-off" financially as just being able to make it in life.

Defining again and again may also mean rethinking what devices are effective as signals. Today's students, whatever their age, have such wide media awareness that they are more sophisticated than past generations; they have had significant exposure to sarcastic humor and are quick to poke fun at pious, high-minded statements. This means that colleges and universities must use an acceptable, believable vocabulary that fits with student perceptions. For example, reference to "heroes" may no longer be useful. Young people do continue to look to people for guidance, people who offer pivotal experiences or symbolic connections, but the word *heroes* carries too much weight (Levine, 1980). Thus alternative frames of reference—asking students whose ideas stick with them, what they regard as sources of sensible advice, or which people they find helpful—can better elicit useful information. Educators must be aware that in many aspects of communication with students, time-honored approaches may have lost their meaning.

Look to the Pioneers. Although this chapter has emphasized the continually evolving nature of student populations, the pace of change is quite gradual. Subgroups of students that receive special attention in one decade were generally present a decade earlier, although in smaller numbers, but were denied formal organizational participation. Such groups can be sought out and insights gained from their experiences. Thus, for example, the student experiences documented by Empire State College during its initial years of operation were an invaluable source of insight for other institutions expanding their services to adult learners (Palola & Bradley, 1973).

Because distance learners are likely to be a more important component of student populations in the future, it is important to listen to their views today. What can be learned from the experiences of the National Technological University, for example? Also, because two important, rapidly growing groups of students are Asian Americans and Hispanics, it would be wise to learn from the experience of colleges and universities in California, Arizona, and other locations that have already enrolled substantial numbers of them. Learning from the experience of Hispanic-serving institutions would also be valuable (see Chapter Three).

Recent changes in immigration law (Stewart, 1993, 1994) have precipitated changes in enrollment, and educators should continue to monitor the impact of such legal changes. Proposed referenda on such issues, in which California has already had some experience, need to be monitored as well.

Compare Notes and Be Open to Alternative Views. To paraphrase a saying about lawyers, the person who relies on his or her own thinking to understand the future has a fool for a teacher. The reality of student diversity is too complex for any one person to comprehend it. A pooling of experience will yield a richer, more accurate view of salient changes in student populations. Sessions at national conferences offer opportunities for such exchange, but many other, informal exchanges of insights should be sought as well.

Conclusion

Diversity and pluralism have made American life richer. To recognize and deal with the greater complexity of student characteristics may seem a difficult task, but the growing sense of diversity can be just as readily understood as an exercise in facing up to important realities. In many ways, previous generations operated with substantial perceptual blinders that made it difficult for them to understand patterns of student behavior. Educators today have an advantage: they have already become comfortable with an expanded awareness of difference and its effect on student achievement. The skills learned today in thinking about diversity will surely be put to much further use in the future.

References

American Council on Education. (1991). *Setting the national agenda: Academic achievement and transfer.* Washington, DC: Author.

Andersen, C. J., Carter, D. J., & Malizio, A. G. (1989). *1989–90 factbook on higher education.* Washington, DC: American Council on Education.

Astin, A. W., Korn, W. S., Sax, L. J., & Mahoney, K. M. (1994). *The American freshman: National norms for fall 1994.* Los Angeles: Higher Education Research Institute.

Carter, D., & Wilson, R. (1995). *Thirteenth annual status report on minorities in higher education.* Washington, DC: American Council on Education.

El-Khawas, E. (1994). *Campus trends, 1994.* Washington, DC: American Council on Education.

Henderson, C. (1995). *College freshmen with disabilities.* Washington, DC: American Council on Education.

Institute for International Education. (1993). *Open doors, 1992–93: Report on international educational exchange.* New York: Institute for International Education.

Kroeger, S., & Schuck, J. (Eds.). (1993). *Responding to disability issues in student affairs* (New Directions for Student Services No. 64). San Francisco: Jossey-Bass.

Levine, A. (1980). *When dreams and heroes died: A portrait of today's college student.* San Francisco: Jossey-Bass.

Mooney, C. J. (1995). Religious revival grips students at church colleges. *Chronicle of Higher Education, 41*(36), A39.

National Center for Education Statistics. (1993). *Fall enrollment survey, 1992–1993.* (Electronic data file). Washington, DC: Author.

National Center for Education Statistics. (1994). *Digest of educational statistics.* Washington, DC: Author.

O'Brien, E. M. (1992). Master's degree students and recipients: A profile. *Research Briefs, 3*(1), 2.

Otuya, E., & Mitchell, A. (1994). Today's college students: Varied characteristics by sector. *Research Briefs, 5*(1), 4–6.

Palola, E. G., & Bradley, A. P., Jr. (1973). *Ten out of thirty: Ten case studies of the first thirty graduates.* Saratoga Springs, NY: Empire State College.

Ries, P., & Thurgood, H. D. (1993). *Summary report 1992: Doctorate recipients from United States universities.* Washington, DC: National Academy Press.

Ryan, D., & McCarthy, M. (Eds.). (1994). *A student affairs guide to the ADA and disability issues.* Washington, DC: National Association of Student Personnel Administrators.

Sandler, B. R., & Hall, R. M. (1982). *The classroom climate: A chilly one for women?* Washington, DC: Association of American Colleges.

Sherrill, J. M., & Hardesty, C. A. (1994). *The gay, lesbian, and bisexual student's guide to colleges, universities, and graduate schools.* New York: New York University Press.

Stewart, D. (1993). *Immigration and education: The crisis and the opportunities.* New York: Lexington Books.

Stewart, D. (1994, March). Immigration laws are education laws too. *Phi Delta Kappan,* 556–558.

Trow, M. (1973). *Problems in the transition from elite to mass higher education.* San Francisco: Carnegie Commission.

PART TWO

PROFESSIONAL FOUNDATIONS AND PRINCIPLES

Part One described the historical and contemporary context of higher education at diverse institutions, demonstrating how changing societal needs for higher education have affected the philosophy of higher education and the perspective of student affairs professionals. Individuals engaged in student affairs work are guided by the common values and philosophies of the profession. They are responsible for high ethical standards and have a legal obligation to uphold a proper professional relationship with students and one another. It is impossible for any graduate program or staff development program to identify or outline what a practitioner should do in every possible scenario. Thus practitioners must be capable of making wise decisions in unpredictable situations. They must learn, practice, and model professional behavior and develop a professional perspective based on the foundational elements of the student affairs field. These basic principles serve as frames for professional practice.

The philosophy behind these principles has roots that go back to the changing nature of higher education at the turn of the century. Higher education's core commitment to individuation (that is, the development of the whole student as a unique individual) has helped the student affairs field broaden and embrace the concept of campus diversity that is so much a part of the current context. In Chapter Five, Robert Young illustrates the evolution of the key philosophies and values that ground individual student affairs practice and have become cultural norms within the profession.

As the student affairs field evolved, a recognized set of ethical standards of practice emerged. These tenets guide practitioners' behavior toward students, their expectations of other higher education professionals, and their understanding of their responsibilities to their host institution. Ethical standards guide individual behavior and ensure students are treated with appropriate respect. In Chapter Six, Harry Canon describes these standards and stresses their importance in addressing difficult dilemmas faced by student affairs professionals. Ethical practices are so indispensable to sound practice that we have included the ethical standards of both the American College Personnel Association and the National Association of Student personnel Administrators in the Resource section at the back of this book.

Increasingly, the law has prescribed how student affairs professionals and institutions must treat students. Thus it is essential for the student affairs practitioner to understand legal principles, legal thinking, and the broader culture's expectations regarding how he or she relates to others, individual practitioner rights and responsibilities, and the legal boundaries that provide a context for practice. In Chapter Seven, Peggy Barr presents key legal principles, concepts, and terms that guide professional decision making and illustrates their application in student affairs practice.

We need to understand institutional expectations, whether those of an individual office, a division, an entire college or university, or society. We must concurrently examine our individual character as it intersects with these expectations. All student affairs practitioners must examine their practices for congruence with these professional principles. Further, professionals must examine the tension points between institutional expectations due to mission or purpose and obligations for practice based on professional ethics. It is essential that we intentionally model these high standards in our care and work with each other as colleagues.

CHAPTER FIVE

GUIDING VALUES AND PHILOSOPHY

Robert B. Young

A visitor to the University of Vermont might spy a gravestone next to the chapel. Looking closer, she would see the following words: "The things in civilization we most prize are not of ourselves. They exist by grace of the doings and sufferings of the continuous human community in which we are a link. Ours is the responsibility of conserving, transmitting, rectifying, and expanding the heritage of values we have received that those that come after us may receive it more solid and secure, more widely accessible and more generously shared than we have received it" (Dewey, 1934, p. 87). The stone marks the resting place of John Dewey, whose epitaph reminds student affairs administrators and counselors to transmit solid and secure professional values to students and colleagues.

It is easy to forget the importance of values. More comfortable with practice than philosophy, members of the profession spend a great deal of time developing programs, services, and procedures and much less time musing about the values that support all those activities. Esther Lloyd-Jones said, "It would be well if we could catch a fresh view of how personnel work might more surely contribute to education the important values it seeks to serve" (Lloyd-Jones & Smith, 1954, p. 8). This chapter, written some forty years after Lloyd-Jones made her remarks, attempts to add fuel to the "fiery centrality" (Lerner, 1976) of the values of the field.

The chapter examines the historical values of student affairs and the philosophies that embrace them. After a general discussion on these values and philosophies, the early history of student affairs values is reviewed, from approximately

1900 to 1955. Next, more recent documents are examined for shifts in traditional values, the addition of new values, and information about the development of philosophies relevant to the field. The chapter concludes with commentary about the development of the profession, institutions, and individuals.

The Nature of Values

Our values define who we are. They are "the great simplicities that touch the deepest springs" (Wiggins, 1991, p. 10) of our existence. They set our course and give us something to fall back on. Some values are used consciously, like personal mission statements, but many lie beneath the surface of knowing, guiding activities such as teaching, counseling, and administration through a subconscious ideology (Rogers, 1989). For example, a resident assistant might provide counseling to a student at three in the morning because she values caring more than getting good grades, and she might not be aware of this priority until she is asked why she missed class the next day.

Usually, values reflect a real relationship between subjects and objects that gives both meaning. For example, academic freedom is one of the most important values of higher education, yet people invoke this value only when they are concerned about real people and issues: freedom for *whom* to do *what?* This linkage between subject and object can be useful; it lets researchers infer the values of a profession from real–world practices as much as from abstract philosophies.

Values form the essence of broader philosophies. They are the acorns; philosophies are the oaks. Philosophies hold values in some form that makes sense to us, whether we are Christians or Muslims, Europeans or Africans, capitalists or communists. Philosophies give us standards of truth to judge actions and ideas, ends and means, and good and bad. They help us make sense of ourselves—for a while at least; philosophy changes, not because it is ever successfully refuted but because new ideas emerge to fit a changing society (Taylor, 1952). These ideas and their concomitant values demand new philosophical forms that explain their relationships in a changing society.

The First Era of Values Development

A century ago, LeBaron Russell Briggs was appointed dean at Harvard. His appointment affirmed a historic commitment of colleges to values education while opening the door to the new field of student affairs administration. John Thelin and Elizabeth Nuss detail the heritage of higher education and the student affairs profession in Chapters One and Two; the values that guided their evolution are the subject of this chapter.

The Dawn of the Specialty

Cowley (1949) gives three reasons for the emergence of student affairs as a specialty: the secularization of higher education, the diversification of students, and the rise of the German research university. American colleges responded to the "intellectualistic impersonalism imported by American Ph.D.s trained in Germany" by expanding extracurricular activities, returning to the residential college, and appointing personnel to deal with discipline and other concerns about students (Cowley, 1949, p. 16). Cowley (unpublished handwritten manuscript, n.d.) identified three types of early student affairs administrators: the humanitarians, who wanted to help other people; the administrators, who coordinated programs; and the psychologists, who used their tests and techniques: "Despite the diversity of backgrounds . . . [each of these groups tended] to share a common set of values which [ran] counter to those of impersonalistic professors" (p. 513).

The first deans were teaching scholars and noted authors (Fley, 1979, 1980), a fact that puts "the lie to the present-day belief that the earliest deans and student personnel workers engaged in little scholarship" (Fley, 1979, p. 30). They were scholars, yet they were not hired for their research skills. For example, Lois Kimball Mathews became the first dean of women at the University of Wisconsin because her teaching put her in contact with male undergraduates, placed her in the intellectual mainstream of the academy, and gave her an educational vision instead of just a focus on details (Fley, 1979). Whatever the details of their administrative duties, the early deans primarily represented "a point of view—a point of view of the element that gives tone to the whole organization from the one [perspective] of the student, the student as an individual, the student as a complete person" (National Association of Deans and Advisers of Men, 1943, p. 33).

Two Perspectives

Since its first days, the student affairs profession has been split by two perspectives. The first perspective concerns the development of students within the overall context of higher education; the second perspective concerns the nature of specific administrative duties. Authors have differentiated the student affairs *point of view* from student affairs *work*, drawing a distinction between the profession's organic purpose and its functional realities. In a 1936 address, Hillis Miller, president of Keuka College, noted the benefits of each way of looking at the field; but he preferred the organic perspective. Miller called student affairs education itself. To him it was not a set of adjunct affairs; it was inseparable from the body and being of higher education.

An Organic Perspective. Current custom separates scientific knowledge from personal development and the classroom from student affairs. A century ago, all were connected in an organic concept of education. In 1899 William Rainey Harper, president of the University of Chicago, called for a scientific study of the physical health, character, intellectual capacity, special tastes, and social interactions of each college student (Cowley, 1949). "Scientific study" was indistinct from moral philosophy in those days; the social sciences had not yet emerged. In *School, College, and Character,* LeBaron Russell Briggs (1902) wrote that truth was truth—religious, scientific, or commercial—and the college stood for truth in any and all of its manifestations.

In 1936 W. H. Cowley (1936/1986) synthesized several historic definitions of the "student personnel point of view" into the following: a "philosophy of education which puts emphasis upon the individual" (p. 69). Like others before him, he distinguished between the student personnel point of view and student personnel work. The personnel point of view reminded everyone on campus, especially faculty, of the need to educate the whole student. Student personnel *work* consisted of essential services that were unified by an educational *point of view.*

Cowley was one of the authors of the 1937 *Student Personnel Point of View (SPPOV)* (American Council on Education, 1937/1994a), and his opinions are obvious in it. The 1937 *SPPOV* confirmed that the student was whole, that each was a unique individual, and that programs should be based on student needs.

In 1949 the *SPPOV* was revised, restating the major principles and adding several goals that reflected the national temperament. The 1949 version incorporated many ideas from *Higher Education for American Democracy,* the 1947 report of the President's Commission on Higher Education, which affirmed the need for general education for citizenship and access to higher education for diverse Americans. The commission's report said that the first goal in "education for democracy is the full, rounded, and continuing development of the person. . . . To liberate and perfect the intrinsic powers of every citizen is the central purpose of democracy, and its furtherance of individual self–realization is its greatest glory" (President's Commission on Higher Education, 1947, p. 9). These words might have been lifted directly from the writings of Cowley.

A Functional Perspective. Exploring what student affairs *does* is another way of determining what it *is.* In 1911 Gertrude Martin conducted the first national survey of deans of women. She concluded that their office was administrative but their function was social or disciplinary (Fley, 1980). By 1926 Hopkins had identified twenty areas of student affairs work (Bradshaw, 1936/1986). The 1937 *SPPOV* listed twenty-three services. And in 1938 Esther Lloyd-Jones and Margaret Smith unearthed seventy-seven different committees within the student personnel offices of 521 colleges. At that time Lloyd-Jones believed that student affairs practices were as important as the student personnel point of view. In 1952, however, she complained that author after author had described student affairs as a "collection of services." That meant that the field was being affected by the same phenomenon that affected the curriculum; it was becoming "impersonal, scientific, secular, and proliferative" (p. 219). And the larger the institution, the greater the impact of quantification, specialization, and objectification on its student affairs function.

The Dominance of the Organic Perspective

In 1954 Lloyd-Jones apologized for her 1938 attempt to describe the field through its services instead of through its philosophy. She and Smith (1954, p. 5) offered four "common beliefs" about student affairs to remedy the situation:

1. A belief in the worth of the individual; that human values are of the greatest importance; that the common good can be promoted best by helping each individual to develop to the utmost in accordance with his abilities.
2. The belief in the equal dignity of thinking and feeling and working; that these aspects are inseparable. Personnel work is interested in the *whole* person and not merely in his mind or his economic productivity or some other one of his aspects.
3. The belief that the world has a place for everybody; a place in the social world, a place in the civic world, a place in family life, and a place in the vocational world.
4. The belief that what an individual gathers from his experiences continues on in time; it is not what is imposed, but what is absorbed that persists.

Lloyd-Jones and Smith called the central mission of the profession "deeper teaching," a concept that would have comforted the first deans of men and women.

The First Major Values: Individuation and Community

Science and morality, administration and education, specific functions and an organic point of view: all reflected and affected the development of student affairs. Yet, the field was never more sure of its values than during its first fifty years.

Its services might have been new, but its point of view was as old and rock-solid as Gibraltar.

The 1949 *Student Personnel Point of View* asserted that the central concern of student affairs work was "the development of students as whole persons inter-acting in social situations" (American Council on Education, 1949/1994b, p. 122). This assertion implies the two central values of early student affairs work—indi-viduation and community. Individuation and community are also two of the cen-tral values of general education, secured through reading, writing, and reckoning. They are two of the central values of American democracy as well: free individ-uals choose to live together; they are not forced to do so—*E pluribus unum*, "from many, one." The values of the profession were in order and steady as America itself; Truman's presidential commission had verified the student personnel point of view. It would be put into practice, by *educators*.

Individuation

Sometimes referred to as human dignity (e.g., see Young & Elfrink, 1991), indi-viduation involves respect for the growing person. It represents the understand-ing that a college student's first duty is to find a unique identity—whatever a student *does* is not as important as who he or she *is*.

John Gardner (1961) has summarized the traditional conception of this value: "What we must reach for is a conception of perpetual self–discovery, perpetual reshaping to realize one's best self, to be the person one could be. This is a con-ception which far exceeds formal education in scope. It includes not only the in-tellect but the emotions, character and personality. It involves not only the surface, but deeper layers of thought and action" (p. 136). The student affairs perspective was that individuals were whole, unique, and responsible; their experience was the measure of their education and the source of student affairs programs. The stu-dent affairs dean exemplified these attributes of individuality; he or she was a model that each student should emulate.

The Whole Individual. In 1924 the first dean of men at Columbia, Herbert Hawkes, said that his college "should educate the whole [student] . . . the physi-cal, the social, the aesthetic, the religious, the intellectual aspects, each in its ap-propriate manner" (Fley, 1980, p. 42). Thirteen years later, the 1937 *Student Personnel Point of View* included the attributes of intellectual capacity, emotions, physical condition, social relationships, vocational skills, moral and religious values, eco-nomic resources, and aesthetic appreciations. Cowley created the word *holoism* (now more commonly given as *holism*) to capture this conviction that an individ-ual reacts in any situation as a totally integrated person (Lloyd-Jones, 1952).

The Unique Individual. Uniqueness is built on difference. Clothier (1931/1986) said that individual difference was a major tenet of the profession, but he did not invent this idea. Differentiation is a fact of science and a dictum of philosophy (Lloyd-Jones & Smith, 1938). Each student is a being in the process of becoming, a singularity, someone who cannot be duplicated. As famed baseball pitcher Satchel Paige said, "A person can't help being born average, but ain't nobody got to be common."

The Experiencing Individual. Knowledge is used; thus it can be measured by examining students' experiences. The 1937 *SPPOV* claimed that the interests, needs, and abilities of students are the most important factors in developing college programs. These needs, the report asserted, are not merely vocational or intellectual; they reflect both the need to *do* and the need to *be.* Thus an adequate student affairs program must be "fully as concerned with the art of living as it is with the more utilitarian aspects of education. It must concern itself with the student as he is at present, with the sort of design for living that he is working out for himself *right now*" (Lloyd-Jones & Smith, 1954, p. 8).

The Responsible Individual. The 1949 *SPPOV* declared that students are responsible participants in their development rather than passive recipients of knowledge and skills. The document linked individual development with responsibility; freedom must be disciplined for the fulfillment of human dignity. Responsible individuals form responsible communities. The first dean of men at the University of Illinois, Thomas Arkle Clark, was more blunt. He thought that there was no place in college for loafers. Character was developed by "doing things difficult enough to cut lines in a [person's] soul" (Fley, 1979, p. 32).

The Dean as Exemplary Individual. When deans first appeared on American campuses, their character was considered more important than their scholarship. Perhaps this priority grew from the religious roots of European higher education, from the time when faculty were clerics and presidents were abbots. In America, this notion of the dean's being a model of individual virtue has been embraced since Briggs was appointed at Harvard. Briggs, Mathews, Hawkes: all the early deans recognized the moral imperatives of their individual behavior; but perhaps the most glowing celebration of the dean-as-exemplary-individual is found in Stanley Coulter, the first dean of men at Purdue. To Coulter, the ideal dean was a generalist, an educator, a symbol of the finest human virtues, a personality, a role model, an inspirer, a guide, a philosopher, and a friend. It is said he lived up to his ideal (Fley, 1980).

Community

The second major value of early student affairs work was that of community, the belief that an institution of higher education must be a place where people grow by means of meaningful relationships. In the organic academy, students are involved with other people; the academic community is a reflection of the students, an extension of them, and a resource for their self-realization (Fisher & Noble, 1960).

Meaningful Relationships. A community is small. It should contain no more people than can know each other well (Redfield, 1965). In 1954 Lloyd-Jones and Smith decried the way the student affairs profession was emulating large, impersonal, specialized organizations: "The problem becomes one of how students and staff can work together to improve their community . . . to examine together how their human relationships may be improved and strengthened so as to contribute to total growth for each member" (p. 340). One of the eleven student needs listed in the 1949 *Student Personnel Point of View* is "a sense of belonging to the college" (American Council on Education, 1949/1994b, p. 128). Students must find a role in relation to others that will make them feel valued, contribute to their feelings of self-worth, and contribute to a feeling of kinship with others.

Mutual Empowerment. The 1949 *SPPOV* also reminded everyone on campus, especially faculty, of the need to empower students *mutually*. Almost all of the historical documents of the student affairs profession contain advice for faculty. The field reacted against the focus of the academy on isolated, intellectual truth, and it sought faculty cooperation in holistic individual development.

The Second Era of Values Development

Student affairs practitioners in the first half of the twentieth century had a firm conviction about the educational point of view of student affairs, guided by the values of individuation and community. Students grew holistically into unique and responsible individuals. They were helped by the campus that was similarly whole in its outlook, a community of mutually empowering colleagues. This foundation of the field seemed solid, but it would shift with changes in society and the academy.

During the second half of the century, the values of the student affairs profession were affected by three forces: the dominance of empirical science, the advancement of collective political power, and the search for professional status.

Empirical science inspired American industry—including the industry of higher education. Reputations and resources were built on the foundation of research. The empirical academy focused on the acquisition of specialized knowledge (expanding the possibilities of the *univers*–ity) while minimizing the synthesis and wholeness of knowledge (the focus of the *uni*–versity). Empirical science spawned new administrative practices that fit the rubric "scientific management." Relationships were formalized, and accountability met a scientific standard. Services were specialized and their value measured by their size and number as much as by their purpose.

Collective political power has affected student affairs at least since the 1960s. Students were legal adults; no longer could they be viewed as children, anxious to be formed by their alma mater. They were consumers, eager to judge the benefits they received from the education they bought. Legal rights required legal, logical, and linear guidelines. The roles of students and staff were put into contracts; every right and responsibility was defined.

Questions about the status of student services have hounded the field since its birth, and critics continue to view it as, at best, a half–formed profession (Stamatakos, 1981). Student services administrators were supposedly the housekeepers of the academy instead of the guardians of undergraduate education (Brown, 1972; Penney, 1969). Many student services practitioners hoped that empirical science and the political clout of students would raise the credibility and therefore the status of their field.

Preparation for Professionalism

In 1949 Cowley noted that most student affairs practitioners "drifted into personnel work because of the job demand or because someone thought they had nice personalities. The result is that most of the personnel work being done over the country is frankly disgraceful, and it will not improve until personnel people are properly trained" (p. 25). Similar comments expressed during the past fifty years have spawned a movement to develop standards for the improvement of professional preparation. Such standards have also been used to support arguments that student affairs is a distinct field of professional practice instead of a general philosophy of education.

Lloyd-Jones (1949) claimed that student affairs became a distinct profession when its preparation programs began requiring training in empirically based counseling and testing techniques. She wondered, however, whether the new "professionals" were true student affairs practitioners or just psychologists, not performing any of the other student affairs functions. Trained counselors had supplanted moral philosophers, but administrators were needed to cope with large, complex organizations: "Traditionally we think about counseling as educational, individual, personal, and facilitative. If that is true, and that is all it is, then you cut out much of what student personnel workers do" (Etheridge, 1967, p. 78).

Student affairs administrators had to become applied behavioral scientists (Zaccaria, 1968), student development specialists (Grant, 1968), and student development experts (Tripp, 1968). The application of empirical science to student living was supposed to overcome the image of some student affairs administrators as service station attendants and procedural technicians (Trueblood, 1964/1986). Tripp (1968) seemed to be using the language of the 1990s when he wrote that "in preparing professionals to be effective, . . . we must prevent being caught in the *old paradigms*" (p. 144; emphasis added). A new or alternative point of view was needed to cope with change.

Unsettled Perspectives

Two projects illustrate the continuing dialectic between the organic and functional perspectives of student affairs during the past fifty years: the Tomorrow's Higher Education project of the American College Personnel Association (Brown, 1972; Miller & Prince, 1976) and the Plan for a New Century project of the National Association of Student Personnel Administrators (1987). The Tomorrow's Higher Education project was intended to prepare a list of goals for student affairs, provide new models of practice, and test those models at various institutions. The Plan for a New Century Project undertook a fiftieth-anniversary examination of the 1937 *Student Personnel Point of View.*

Two publications resulted from the Tomorrow's Higher Education project: *Student Development in Tomorrow's Education: A Return to the Academy* (Brown, 1972), a statement of student services goals; and *The Future of Student Affairs* (Miller & Prince, 1976), which presented models of practice. The third phase of the project, application of the models, never reached maturity, but these two publications reflected the traditional bifurcation of education and student affairs functions. This chapter focuses on the Brown (1972) publication since it provides insights about the values and philosophy of the field.

Brown described "student development" as the holistic development of individual students through interactions with the college environment. It was a new, scientific way to resurrect an old value, one that had been lost in America's big, specialized institutions. Higher education took "the wrong fork in the road when it thrust personnel maintenance upon staff with specialized duties. . . [and] since then student personnel workers have been on a constant ego trip of trying to professionalize their responsibilities" (Brown, 1972, p. 37). Brown chided practitioners who claimed the "extracurricular" arena for themselves: "Extra in this instance meaning not only *outside of* or *beyond*, but to many *peripheral* and *unnecessary*" (p. 42). The term *cocurricular* sounded better, but it represented "little more than giving lip-service to an idea without program support. It is time now for student development functions to become curricular—with no prefix added" (p. 42).

In 1987 the Plan for a New Century Committee produced *A Perspective on Student Affairs* to commemorate the fiftieth anniversary of the publication of the original *Student Personnel Point of View.* The two major focuses of the new document were student diversity and the institutional context. Services for diversity were offered in support of the "preeminent academic mission" of the institution. Out-of-class environments were acknowledged to affect learning, but they were not viewed as inherently good; they could either "help or detract" (p. 11). In this document, student affairs work was not curricular; it was *co*curricular or *extra*curricular, with prefix added.

However, the New Century document reaffirmed many traditional assumptions about student affairs. Each student was viewed as unique, as a person of worth and dignity whose feelings affect his or her thinking and learning. A friendly and supportive community life would help the student learn better. Bigotry could not be tolerated, citizenship was important, and all students should assume responsibility for their lives.

Additional Viewpoints

Since the mid 1980s, authors have suggested alternative value priorities for student affairs work. Canon and Brown (1985) promoted an ethic of caring in order to humanize the rest of higher education. Sandeen (1985) argued on behalf of the values of pluralism, freedom, and altruism. Dalton and Healy (1984) deduced the following educational values from student affairs programs: self-awareness, independence, tolerance, respect, and fairness toward other individuals. Finally, Upcraft (1988) wrote that student affairs managers needed to embrace "six values that are important in managing right: honesty, fairness, integrity, predictability, courage, and confidentiality" (p. 73).

Several authors (including Barr, 1987; Brown & Krager, 1985; and Upcraft, 1988) cited the work of Kitchener (1984) in their discussions of the central values of student affairs practice. Kitchener applied the four "ethical principles" of the medical field to student affairs: respecting autonomy, doing no harm, benefiting others, and being just. Though she did not call them values, Kitchener related these ethical principles to a process for improving decision making about particular situations. Values have been related to decision making in a similar way (for example, see Rokeach, 1976).

Young and Elfrink (1991) surveyed ninety student services administrators, association leaders, and faculty about the importance and nature of seven values: aesthetics, altruism, equality, freedom, human dignity, justice, and truth. Ninety-seven percent of the respondents answered that all of these values were essential to the field. Seventy-four percent answered that the list was all-inclusive, and 26 percent responded that one or more essential values were missing from the list. As a result, "community" was added. This value incorporated cooperation, professional development, and professional commitment. It was defined as "mutual empowerment."

In Search of Community was the subtitle of the 1990 book *Campus Life,* which offered six values for the community of scholars: purposefulness, openness, justice, discipline, caring, and celebration. Even though the book was not limited to student affairs administration, it used data from the National Association of Student Personnel Administrators and the American Council on Education.

Changes in the Values System

Traditional student affairs values were based in moral philosophy. (Community was built by "responsible" individuals.) During the past fifty years, elements of both science and sociology have been added to their substance. "Science" smacks of Eurocentric, linear, left-brain logic, yet the impact of science on student development is related to the impact of collective power, not just on student affairs but on higher education in general and on the broader society. New knowledge has shredded the unity of logic, just as new groups have challenged assumptions of social superiority. Science has failed to prove that anything or anyone is superior; therefore, all things have been made—if not created—equal. Things and groups might seem superior because of their mass, not their unseen qualities—but new knowledge has exploded quantities, too. Most big things are merely aggregated specializations; chaos sits in the center of any molecule.

Two related values have become prominent in recent years, equality and justice. The concept of equality has shifted from different talents to different people. The value of justice slices through inequity to find what is fair.

Equality. Early professional conceptions of equality involved individual talent. Educating the whole student meant that character was as important as the mind. During the past fifty years, however, the value of equity has stressed the status of people in colleges and the broader culture.

Even the field of student affairs has not treated women and men equally. Deans of women had to fight for equal recognition with deans of men; they fought even harder for the rights of women students. To illustrate, Gertrude Martin, the first adviser of women at Cornell, deplored educational stereotypes. She said that the dean of women "must be able to adapt a manmade curriculum to the special needs of the woman student" (Fley, 1980, p. 39).

It was a short jump from the defense of equal rights for women to the defense of equal rights for other disadvantaged groups. The civil rights movement had a major impact on the student affairs profession (Hammond, 1981; Sandeen, 1985). Student affairs professionals have a responsibility to the "broad spectrum of persons who can profit from post–secondary education" (Council of Student Personnel Associations, 1975/1986, p. 392), presumably without bias, because "the potential for development and self-direction is possessed by everyone" (p. 393).

Justice. Justice is intertwined with equality: "The great historic struggles for social justice have centered about some demand for equal rights: the struggle against slavery, political absolutism, economic exploitation, the disfranchisement of the lower and middle classes and the disfranchisement of women, colonialism, racial oppression" (Vlastos, 1962, p. 31). The value of equal justice differs from individual responsibility because it starts with the group instead of the person.

Justice means fairness. It can be procedural, distributive, or corrective fairness. The first type relates to laws, the second to opportunities, and the last to the redress of social inequities. Procedural justice is easiest to implement, because it is based on specific procedures. Distributive justice takes more effort—for example, revising general education courses to be more representative. Corrective justice involves sacrifice by some for the benefit of others. It is much more difficult to implement and is prone to charges of reverse discrimination, but "rectification is the chief task of the fair and the just or at least of those who are institutionally constrained to be so. It is the least one can do, and far less than most of humanity can hope for" (Shklar, 1984).

Corrective justice is a form of altruism: the needs of others are treated as more important than one's own needs. While it has been convenient to separate any form of justice from caring in developmental psychology, the values are connected. As Sanford (1980) says, without some "minimum of caring and being cared for, justice will not become an important value" (p. 202).

The Profession's Philosophy

The values of individuation, community, equality, and justice are not the only values embraced by student affairs professionals during the past century, but they seem to be the primary ones mentioned in discussions about the philosophy of the field. Philosophy structures values. It puts values in context as well as in order. Philosophy provides the meanings that values suggest.

In 1952 Taylor wrote a chapter relating philosophy to general education. Three traditions were presented: rationalism, neohumanism, and pragmatism (which Taylor called instrumentalism). In her chapter in the same book, Lloyd-Jones (1952) related these traditions to student affairs. Thirty-seven years later, Knock, Rentz, and Penn (1989) confirmed the importance of these three philosophies in student affairs.

The rationalist believes that mental ability differentiates humans from other animals and that therefore the cultivation of reason is the sole aim of education and of life itself (Taylor, 1952). Faculty in rationalist colleges want student affairs administrators to identify capable students, attract them to campus, help them read better, and discipline any "who may cause ripples in the academic serenity that is so necessary to the study of universal truths and values" (Lloyd-Jones, 1952, p. 215). In the rationalist institution, student affairs administrators are subservient to faculty; student services are "extracurricular" and therefore unessential (Knock, Rentz, & Penn, 1989).

Like rationalism, neohumanism separates mind from body, reason from emotion, and thought from experience. It differs from rationalism in its refusal to state a general or specific philosophy to which all students should be committed and by which a curriculum should be constructed. Live and let live: the neohumanist believes that electives are all right and the education of the whole person might even be necessary, so long as one's passions can be ruled by reason. Lloyd-Jones (1952) noted, "How vastly extended is personnel work in institutions dominated by neohumanists beyond the scope of such work in institutions dominated by the rationalists!" (p. 218). Despite any extension of size and scope, student affairs functions remain separate and never equal with academic affairs in neohumanist institutions. Faculty cultivate intelligence in the classroom, and all of the fertile ground outside is tilled by student affairs professionals. The aggregation of these units is supposed to attain "the desired result of inner unity and harmony" (Lloyd-Jones & Smith, 1954, p. 11), but what results instead is excessive organization and specialization, not unity. Student affairs programs become "elaborate, extensive programs somewhat independent of and apart from the curriculum and the instructional programs" (Lloyd-Jones, 1952, p. 216). Neohumanism has been the philosophy that underlies the functional point of view of student affairs. It has been supported by hundreds of articles about student services management and at least one philosophical treatise, the recent *Perspective on Student Affairs* (Plan for a New Century Committee, 1987).

The instrumental philosophy, much more than that of rationalism or neohumanism, seems to represent the principles in which student services workers have protested they believe (Lloyd-Jones & Smith, 1954, p. 12). Instrumentalism—known here as pragmatism and elsewhere as radical empiricism, experimentalism, and naturalism (Childs, 1956)—puts the whole development of individuals at the center of education; techniques, services, and organization are only peripheral. This pragmatic philosophy supports the organic perspective of student affairs, and its roots and principles deserve elaboration.

Pragmatism is a term that can be used to describe anything useful, but the philosophy of pragmatism is a way of linking individuals, knowledge, and action. It is rooted in the work of William James and John Dewey, both of whom had contact with some of the pioneers of student affairs administration. To illustrate, the National Association of Deans of Women (NADW) was founded by deans who studied at Columbia University Teachers College, where John Dewey taught. Their curriculum was infused with his ideas. The first official meeting of the NADW was held at the 1916 conference of the National Education Association, a group similarly influenced by Dewey's philosophy of pragmatic, progressive education.

Progressive, pragmatic education was going to reform all of American education during the first half of the twentieth century; Cowley (1936/1986) called it the "torch" that student affairs professionals brought back to the academy, to enlighten rationalist faculty who valued only the student's mind. Even though nursery schools, elementary schools, high schools, and the President's Report on Higher Education had embraced Dewey's ideas, higher education remained firmly in the grasp of the rationalists (Taylor, 1952).

Dewey defined education as a reconstruction of experience that gives it meaning and increases a person's ability to direct subsequent experience (Brubacher, 1962). Individual experience is both the source and the end of education. James said simply that "education should be directed to what it means to be alive"—to be free, to create (Sloan, 1980, p. 257). Neither James nor Dewey conceded that loneliness and isolation were the final products of individuation. By sharing individual experiences and pooling knowledge, the world could become more democratic, more tolerant, more humane. This faith in the power of free individuals was never shaken. Nor was its moral dimension dismissed because it could not be tested in the laboratory. Dewey (like Briggs and others) saw no boundary between moral science and other science: "It is physical, biological, and historic knowledge voiced in a human context where it will illuminate and guide the activities of men" (quoted in Sloan, 1980, p. 224).

The fundamental tenets of pragmatism are as follows (Childs, 1956; Taylor, 1952):

1. The individual is an end, not a means, and is worthy of respect for what he or she is and will become.
2. Experience is the source and the test of knowledge; concepts, facts, aims, and values are validated by what people do with them.

3. Knowledge is whole: morality, thought, and action are intrinsically connected, and rationality depends on many factors, including the nonrational.
4. Knowledge is dynamic; people and the truth are always changing. We seek integration and continuity in the face of change.
5. The individual—whole, growing, making a unique life—has the potential for growth "toward cooperative ways of living, thinking, and acting . . . that . . . produce a richer and more satisfying life for the individual and his society than others reached by other methods" (Taylor, 1952, p. 37).

Lloyd-Jones was right. Pragmatism is the philosophy that has held the educational values of the field together.

The Values System Today

As Taylor said, no philosophy of education ever appears as a pure form; rather, a set of leading ideas are re-created in various forms by those who teach and those who learn (see Lloyd-Jones & Smith, 1954, pp. 22–23). Philosophers are entangled in history; they might think that they are creators of the future, but they are more surely creatures of the past. No one can step outside personal experience to describe an objective system of values, and no one can step outside time to construct a permanent one. Morrill (1981) states that "there are no enduring and general, no absolute or universal, standards for human conduct. Whatever standards exist are tied to special conditions, relative to particular times, places, and cultures" (p. 59). The essential values of individuation, community, equality, and justice represent the society in which student affairs administrators have practiced their craft. Future social priorities will alter the list as they alter our work.

Tensions Between Functional and Organic Values

Traditionally, the organic, educational, personnel point of view has reminded everyone on campus—especially faculty—of the need to empower students. The functions of student affairs were supposed to support this general educational mission. The relationship seemed straightforward, but practice has created its own philosophy of student affairs that departs from the canon of the *Student Personnel Point of View.* The canon is educational, holistic, and individualistic. The philosophy of practice starts with administration. It is specialized and institutional. Both are service philosophies, because the purpose of higher education is, ultimately, service. However, the student personnel point of view serves the individual first, while the philosophy of practice serves the institution first. The student personnel point of view requires integration; the philosophy of practice accepts segregation.

Empiricism has led to the development of an undergraduate curriculum of specialized, discipline-based courses that reflect the research interests of faculty. This is the "preeminent academic mission" that some advocates say student affairs must support (e.g., see Greenleaf, 1968; and Plan for a New Century Committee, 1987). By accepting this supportive role, student affairs practice becomes a means to maintain the current values of the academy. As a result, it becomes large and specialized and somewhat impersonal. Also, the attempts of student affairs to become a profession are based on the measures of science and training that such an academy accepts.

The advocates of specialized, large, administrative services are not troubled if they do not understand or accept an abstract educational philosophy such as pragmatism. They are too busy accomplishing specific goals. They say and with some accuracy that student services might be ancillary in the academy, but the services are given greater support and students benefit more when the services are justified on separate, administrative terms through objective, scientific means.

In 1968, however, Hoyt charged that a neohumanist position condemned many gifted students and the entire profession to mediocrity or failure. By trying too hard to be academically respectable, student affairs professionals had failed "to communicate convincingly and unambiguously" their "views on the broader meaning of educational success" (p. 271).

Hoyt might be reassured that student affairs has not abandoned all its zesty interest in improving undergraduate higher education. Many experts have used empirical techniques to study individuation, the identity development of the students they serve. At first they studied traditional adolescents, then members of ethnic groups, then women, then adults, and currently gay, lesbian, and bisexual students. These experts still want to help unique individuals emerge from whatever collective cocoons have surrounded their lives. That requires the reform of undergraduate education, a reawakening of teaching, and a reemphasis on holistic learning. Individual writers and professional associations have promoted this cause. They have been joined by many critics of the entire academic enterprise; indeed, a decadelong reform movement has railed against the accession of faculty to the German, graduate, research model of education.

Cycles of Individual and Collective Focus

Perhaps this emphasis on group values and institutional status is just a phase that student affairs is going through and not a new stage in its professional development. In 1980 Levine popularized Altbach's theory that American higher education went through cycles of individual and collective awareness. In 1919, for instance, deans of men were concerned about groups such as fraternities, but the welfare of the individual was highest on their list (Strauss, 1919). By 1968 the individualistic approach was being questioned; today the focus is cultural diversity.

Today's focus on the collective might well be replaced by individualism in a few years. However, this might be a new construction of individuation rather than a reconstruction. Some different, distant nihilism might replace democratic pragmatism. Just as the moral philosophy of the early 1900s was supplanted by scientific psychology in the 1920s, integration in the 1960s became cultural jihad in the 1990s. The emphasis on individual or community seems the same from the outside, but its inner substance might have changed.

Philosophers ponder changes in society and offer new conceptions of meaning. Already they acknowledge that the certainty of logical empiricism has broken down. Subject and object are no longer separated. New, postmodern, phenomenological, subjective, and naturalistic approaches in philosophy are being proposed (Lincoln & Guba, 1985). Some of these approaches represent only the "fallacy of the latest word" (Merton, 1984), but many of them are based on lasting precepts of pragmatism (for example, "postpositivist" concerns about the unevenness of knowledge, the importance of experience, and the role of the subject in determining objective Truth).

It might be best to leave any speculation about the future of philosophy alone for now. The specification of student affairs values might be more productive than an attempt to fit them into a single, triumphant, *historical* philosophy. It is surely easier to leave them unassembled. Some of the values are divergent, just as the values of any institution or society contain divergences (Almond & Wilson, 1988). They do not mesh readily. The symphony is more important than the scale, however (Sloan, 1980), and a fundamental obligation of student affairs has been, is, and forever will be to arrange individuation, community, equality, and justice harmoniously on our campuses. These values must make music instead of isolated sounds.

Conclusion

The remainder of this chapter examines briefly the impact of student affairs values on the profession, institutions and divisions, and individuals.

Needs of the Profession

The proponents of student affairs have filled the literature with articles about its professional status (e.g., see Crookston, 1971; Stamatakos, 1981; and Wrenn & Darley, 1949). A "profession" is an endeavor with certain conceptual, performance, and collective identity characteristics (Houle, 1980). The conceptual characteristic is the mission—in other words, the philosophy, values, and goals of the endeavor. The performance characteristics include the mastery of theory—learning how to solve problems with theory, using knowledge from the history of professional practice, and developing a spirit of continuous learning. Finally, collective identity characteristics concern the differentiation of a profession through formal training, credentialing, the creation of a subculture, the development of ethical standards, legal protection, and the maintenance of relationships with users of the professional services, other vocations, and the general public. The concept drives performance and the collective identity.

Most professions offer a mission of service as well as an array of professional services. Student affairs has that mission, and whether its service is categorized as neohumanist or pragmatic, it is still service. A distinction should be made as to whether student affairs staff serve the individual or the institution, wholeness or the intellect, the reform of education or the status quo. The easiest road to professional status is in each case the latter, but the better road might be the one less traveled. Student affairs practitioners must determine whether status is more important than using values and philosophy to create the most meaningful concept of what they do.

Institutional Needs

The student affairs profession has maintained the assumption that the student is the central concern of higher education. If so, then its values and philosophy must begin with students: "Begin with your customers" is the admonition of "quality" approaches to management. But are students the customers or the products of higher education? If students are the customers, then student affairs divisions must adopt missions to satisfy students' current interests. If students are the products of higher education, then the relationship alters, and practitioners must work to make them quality products. Either way, the field must ask whether students are served better by a mission that supports their academic growth first and then adds other elements or by one that is more synergetic than specialized, a mission that views student development holistically. If the latter mission prevails, then the field must revise its approach to practice. Rather than focusing on its uniqueness as a professional endeavor, it should focus on its mutual concerns with other educational units.

Lloyd-Jones and Smith (1954) offered several strategies for bringing "deeper teaching" into student affairs. These strategies might have been crafted by quality assurance consultants today. They wrote that the field needed to abandon its dualistic conception of teachers and personnel workers and help both work together as educators. Student affairs administrators had to downplay the importance of their services and work with faculty and students to reform the campus community. Hierarchical leadership would not work, but "chain reaction" leadership would. Centralization was bogus; small, natural communities had to be built on campus. Student affairs workers were not specialists but consultants, not experts but participants. Efficiency was less important than the quality of human relations that were being learned, and the most important people in the organization were not at the top but at the bottom.

Individual Needs

On Valentine's Day 1994 the *New York Times* asked celebrities to give one-word descriptions of themselves, one word that summed all they were. This was an important question to ask, since the word selected is a value, a "great simplicity" of who one is. If readers of this chapter were to describe themselves in one word, would it have something to do with individuation, community, equality, or justice? Would it reflect the character of the student affairs field and its practitioners? Student affairs leaders have always exemplified character, character wrought from difficulties deep enough to cut lines in a person's soul, character that reflects what it means to be free, character from *doing* and *being* one's values.

This chapter began with Dewey's epitaph. It has cited many of the writings of Esther Lloyd-Jones, one of Dewey's colleagues. A few days before his death, yet another colleague, Herbert Hawkes, the first dean of men at Columbia, said that our obligation was "to hand the torch on to the next person in the race; to keep pure and undefiled the traditions that have been handed down from the fathers, to do one's part in maintaining strong and pure the succession in which one finds himself, is an opportunity, a duty worthy of one's complete devotion" (Fley, 1980, p. 44). Hawkes's words bring us back to Dewey's epitaph. Student affairs professionals have a strong tradition of values. They believe in individuals—whole, experiencing, and responsible. They believe in community. They believe in equality and justice for all people. They accept the responsibility to conserve, transmit, rectify, and expand these values so that students and colleagues will receive them even more solid and secure than they have.

References

Almond, B., & Wilson, B. (1988). *Values: A symposium*. Atlantic Highlands, NJ: Humanities Press.

American Council on Education. (1994a). The student personnel point of view. In A. L. Rentz (Ed.), *Student affairs: A profession's heritage* (American College Personnel Association Media Publication No. 40, 2nd ed., pp. 66–77). Lanham, MD: University Press of America. (Original work published 1937)

American Council on Education. (1994b). The student personnel point of view. In A. L. Rentz (Ed.), *Student affairs: A profession's heritage* (American College Personnel Association Media Publication No. 40, 2nd ed., pp. 108–123). Lanham, MD: University Press of America. (Original work published 1949)

Barr, M. J. (1987). Individual and institutional integrity. *NASPA Journal, 24*, 2–6.

Bradshaw, F. F. (1986). The scope and aims of a personnel program. In G. L. Saddlemire & A. L. Rentz (Eds.), *Student affairs: A profession's heritage.* (Media Publication No. 40, pp. 39–46). Alexandria, VA: American College Personnel Association. (Original work published 1936)

Briggs, L. (1902). *School, college, and character.* Boston: Houghton Mifflin.

Brown, R. D. (1972). *Student development in tomorrow's education: A return to the academy* (Student Personnel Series No. 16). Washington, DC: American Personnel and Guidance Association.

Brown, R. D., & Krager, L. (1985). Ethical issues in higher education. *Journal of Higher Education, 56*, 403–418.

Brubacher, J. (Ed.). (1962). *Eclectic philosophy of education: A book of readings.* Englewood Cliffs, NJ: Prentice Hall.

Canon, H. J., & Brown, R. D. (1985). How to think about professional ethics. In H. J. Canon & R. D. Brown (Eds.), *Applied ethics in student services* (New Directions in Student Services No. 30, pp. 81–87). San Francisco: Jossey-Bass.

Carnegie Foundation for the Advancement of Teaching. (1990). *Campus life: In search of community.* Princeton, NJ: Princeton University Press.

Childs, J. (1956). *American pragmatism and education.* New York: Holt.

Clothier, R. C. (1986). College personnel principles and functions. In G. L. Saddlemire & A. L. Rentz (Eds.), *Student affairs: A profession's heritage* (Media Publication No. 40, pp. 9–20). Alexandria, VA: American College Personnel Association. (Original work published 1931)

Council of Student Personnel Associations. (1986). Student development services in postsecondary education. In G. L. Saddlemire & A. L. Rentz (Eds.), *Student affairs: A profession's heritage* (Media Publication No. 40, pp. 390–401). Alexandria, VA: American College Personnel Association. (Original work published 1975)

Cowley, W. H. (1949). Some history and a venture in prophecy. In E. G. Williamson (Ed.), *Trends in student personnel work* (pp. 12–27). Minneapolis: University of Minnesota Press.

Cowley, W. H. (1986). The nature of student personnel work. In G. L. Saddlemire & A. L. Rentz (Eds.), *Student affairs: A profession's heritage* (Media Publication No. 40, pp. 47–73). Alexandria, VA: American College Personnel Association. (Original work published 1936)

Crookston, B. B. (1971). *Professionalism and professional style in student personnel work.* Paper presented to the West Virginia Council of Student Personnel Administrators, Charleston, SC.

Dalton, J., & Healy, M. (1984). Using values education activities to confront student conduct issues. *NASPA Journal, 22*, 19–25.

Dewey, J. (1934). *A common faith.* New Haven, CT: Yale University Press.

Etheridge, R. (1967). The dilemma of professional development: Some points of view. *NASPA Journal, 4*(2), 76–80.

Fisher, M. B., & Noble, J. L. (1960). *College education as personal development.* Englewood Cliffs, NJ: Prentice Hall.

Fley, J. (1979). Student personnel pioneers: Those who developed our profession. *NASPA Journal, 17*(1), 23–39.

Fley, J. (1980). Student personnel pioneers: Those who developed our profession (Pt. 2). *NASPA Journal, 17*(3), 25–44.

Gardner, J. (1961). *Excellence.* New York: Harper & Row.

Grant, H. (1968). Higher education and student personnel work in the year 2000. *Journal of the National Association of Women Deans and Counselors, 31*(3), 140–141.

Greenleaf, E. A. (1968). How others see us. *Journal of College Student Personnel, 9*(4), 225–231.

Hammond, E. H. (1981). The new student–institutional relationship: Its impact on student affairs administration. *NASPA Journal, 19*(2), 17–21.

Houle, C. O. (1980). *Continuing learning in the professions.* San Francisco: Jossey-Bass.

Hoyt, D. (1968). The impact of student personnel work on student development. *NASPA Journal, 5*(3), 269–275.

Kitchener, K. S. (1984). Intuition, critical evaluation and ethical principles: The foundation for ethical decisions in counseling psychology. *Counseling Psychologist, 12,* 43–55.

Knock, G., Rentz, A. L., & Penn, R. (1989). Our philosophical heritage: Significant influences on professional practice and preparation. *NASPA Journal, 27*(2), 116–121.

Lerner, M. (1976). *Values in education: Notes toward a values philosophy.* Bloomington, IN: Phi Delta Kappa.

Levine, A. (1980). *When dreams and heroes died: A portrait of today's college student.* San Francisco: Jossey-Bass.

Lincoln, Y., & Guba, E. G. (1985). *Naturalistic inquiry.* Newbury Park, CA: Sage.

Lloyd-Jones, E. M. (1949). The beginnings of our profession. In E. G. Williamson (Ed.), *Trends in student personnel work* (pp. 260–264). Minneapolis: University of Minnesota Press.

Lloyd-Jones, E. M. (1952). Personnel work and general education. *Yearbook on general education* (pp. 214–229). Chicago: National Society for the Study of Education.

Lloyd-Jones, E. M., & Smith, M. R. (1938). *A student personnel program for higher education.* New York: McGraw-Hill.

Lloyd-Jones, E. M., & Smith, M. R. (1954). *Student personnel work as deeper teaching.* New York: Harper.

Merton, R. K. (1984). The fallacy of the latest word: The case of "Pietism and Science." *American Journal of Sociology, 89,* 1091–1121.

Miller, J. H. (1936, March 20). *Report of thirteenth annual meeting.* Address at annual dinner of American Council of Personnel Administrators conference. (pp. 59–64). St. Louis, MO.

Miller, T. K., & Prince, J. S. (1976). *The future of student affairs: A guide to student development for tomorrow's higher education.* San Francisco: Jossey-Bass.

Morrill, R. (1981). *Teaching values in college.* San Francisco: Jossey-Bass.

National Association of Deans and Advisers of Men. (1943, April 1–3). *Proceedings: Twenty-fifth annual conference of the National Association of Deans and Advisers of Men.* Columbus, OH.

Penney, J. F. (1969). Student personnel work: A profession stillborn. *Personnel and Guidance Journal, 47,* 958–962.

Plan for a New Century Committee. (1987). *A perspective on student affairs.* Washington, DC: National Association of Student Personnel Administrators.

President's Commission on Higher Education. (1947). *Higher education for American democracy: The report of the President's Commission on Higher Education.* New York: Harper.

Redfield, R. (1965). The folk society. In T. Lasswell (Ed.), *Life in society* (pp. 320–328). Chicago: Scott, Foresman.

Rogers, W. (1989). Values in higher education. In D. Mitchell (Ed.), *Values in teaching and professional ethics.* (pp. 1–14). Macon, GA: Mercer University Press.

Rokeach, M. (1976). *Beliefs, attitudes, and values: A theory of organizational change.* San Francisco: Jossey-Bass.

Sandeen, A. (1985). The legacy of values education in college student personnel work. In J. C. Dalton (Ed.), *Promoting values development in college students* (Monograph Series No. 4, pp. 1–16). Washington, DC: National Association of Student Personnel Administrators.

Sanford, N. (1980). *Learning after college.* Orinda, CA: Montaigne Press.

Shklar, J. (1984). Injustice, injury, and inequality: An introduction. In F. Lucash (Ed.), *Justice and equality here and now* (pp. 13–33). Ithaca, NY: Cornell University Press.

Sloan, D. (1980). *Education and values.* New York: Teachers College Press.

Stamatakos, L. (1981). Student affairs progress toward professionalism: Recommendations for action (Pt. 1 and 2). *Journal of College Student Personnel, 22,* 105–111, 197–206.

Strauss, J. A. (1919). *Secretary's report of conference of deans and advisers of men.* Handwritten manuscript, Bowling Green State University Library Archives, Bowling Green, OH.

Taylor, H. (1952). The philosophical foundations of general education. In National Society for the Study of Education, *Yearbook on general education* (pp. 20–45). Chicago: National Society for the Study of Education.

Tripp, P. (1968). Student personnel workers: Student development experts of the future. *Journal of National Association of Women Deans and Counselors, 31*(3), 142–144.

Trueblood, D. L. (1986). The college student personnel leader of the future is an educator. In G. L. Saddlemire & A. L. Rentz (Eds.), *Student affairs: A profession's heritage* (Media Publication No. 40, pp. 226–228). Alexandria, VA: American College Personnel Association. (Original work published 1964)

Upcraft, M. L. (1988). Managing right. In M. L. Upcraft & M. J. Barr (Eds.), *Managing student affairs effectively* (New Directions for Student Services No. 42, pp. 65–78). San Francisco: Jossey-Bass.

Vlastos, G. (1962). Justice and equality. In R. Brandt (Ed.), *Social justice* (pp. 31–72). Englewood Cliffs, NJ: Prentice Hall.

Wiggins, D. (1991). *Needs, values, truth: Essays in the philosophy of value* (Aristotelian Society Series, Vol. 6). Cambridge, MA: Blackwell.

Wrenn, C., & Darley, J. (1949). Appraisal of the professional status of student personnel work. In E. G. Williamson (Ed.), *Trends in student personnel work* (pp. 264–287). Minneapolis: University of Minnesota Press.

Young, R., & Elfrink, V. (1991). Essential values of student affairs. *Journal of College Student Development, 32*(1), 47–55.

Zaccaria, J. (1968). The behavioral sciences and the identity crisis of student personnel work. *Journal of the National Association of Women Deans and Counselors, 31*(3), 103–105.

CHAPTER SIX

ETHICAL STANDARDS AND PRINCIPLES

Harry J. Canon

The day-to-day realities of maintaining ethical behavior for student affairs professionals under real-life circumstances is seldom tidy, and ensuring ethically optimal outcomes is even less certain. Witness the following incident:

The division of student affairs at Preston College maintains an electronic bulletin board to post items of interest to divisional staff members. All staff members have access to the bulletin board through the division's computer network, and there is an open invitation to participate in an ongoing dialogue about divisional and professional matters. Late in the fall semester, a series of anonymous notes appears on the bulletin board, alleging sexual harassment of women staff members by a senior divisional administrator. The allegations become the focus of staff conversations, and positions are taken on their validity. The administrator, who is the target of the accusations, is clearly distraught to the point of becoming ineffective on the job.

The questions this case raises for student affairs professionals might include the following: Whose job is it to straighten out this mess, anyway? How should I react when a co-worker brings up the topic? What should I say when I see this administrator? Is this just a personal vendetta, or is there a problem in that office? and, ultimately, What is the right thing for me to do?

This range of questions leads in turn to a number of issues that emerge whenever we consider ethical conduct in student affairs settings. Key issues include (1) being able to recognize ethical dilemmas as such when they arise, (2) having a set of usable principles to guide our response to those dilemmas, (3) having a professional ethical code that addresses such matters, (4) knowing if and how to intervene, (5) determining how to respond to co-workers who may play a role in the evolution of an ethical dilemma, and finally, (6) actively fostering an environment that supports and promotes continuing inquiry into ethical matters.

This chapter addresses these key issues and suggests several conceptual models and a variety of procedures for addressing the ethical concerns that are a part of the lives of all thoughtful student affairs professionals. There is no formula or cookbook—elaborate or simple—that provides a definitive response to every ethical dilemma that a complex academic community is capable of producing. The resolution of ethical problems is an imprecise task requiring personal reflection, community concern, and, above all, tolerance for ambiguity and appreciation for the complexity of the human social condition. We need each other if the search for some approximation of ethical "truth" is to succeed. Indeed, our need for each other—community, if you will—allows us to act out for each other, or model, our best notions of what constitutes ethical conduct.

Because the case method has proved effective in generating interest in ethical matters and because it affords a process that tends to inform decision making about ethical dilemmas, a number of ethics cases are scattered throughout this chapter. You are invited—indeed, encouraged—to discuss these cases with colleagues, with the goal of heightening sensitivity to ethical issues and increasing the effectiveness of your response to them. The ultimate focus and concern of any exploration into ethical practices in student affairs has to do with the ethical and moral development of students. In her inaugural speech to the American College Personnel Association, Margaret Barr (1983) expressed her conviction that "student services professionals serve as the conscience of the campus" (p. 10). Indeed, in circumstance after circumstance, it is student affairs providers, more than any other constituent group in higher education, who attend to the human needs of students, respond to concerns about individual differences, and remind the campus community of the principles of justice and personal dignity to which it aspires. In carrying out this mission, these professionals help sustain community awareness of the inequities based on ethnicity, gender, and sexual orientation that are a part of contemporary American culture. The student affairs profession has an enviable history of willingness to be introspective, of examining the intellectual and philosophical roots of proper conduct, and, ultimately, of willingness to assert "virtuous behavior" as a desirable developmental goal for ourselves and our students.

That historical pattern serves as a mandate; it calls on us to contribute to a campus environment that reflects ethical standards of the highest quality. Only by making a commitment to this core professional value can we hope to facilitate the moral and ethical development of students. It seems obvious that the conduct of faculty and staff members has a direct bearing on the conduct students demonstrate or can be expected to aspire to. All other things being equal, the level of ethical awareness on a given campus, as reflected by the behavior of its faculty and staff, will quite likely determine the upper limits of ethical sensitivity demonstrated by its graduates. The ethical development of staff and that of students, then, can be seen as both interdependent and wholly inseparable.

Primary Approaches to Promoting Ethical Behavior

The three most common approaches to "doing ethics," or working to ensure ethical conduct in professional settings, include (1) applying broad ethical principles, (2) providing formal codes of ethics, and (3) developing an informal consensus about standards, generated and supported by a community that holds certain values in common.

The first means of promoting ethical behavior involves applying a set or sets of ethical principles—general, comprehensive, fundamental ethical statements—to problems that are perceived as having ethical implications. This tradition borrows directly from the work of scholars and philosophers of ethics; it generally yields more "shades of gray," or greater ambiguity, than a formal code of ethics. The assumption here is that ethical behavior is based on broad rules of moral conduct and that it is possible to abstract certain principles that underlie these rules. Those who favor the use of ethical principles over formal codes of ethics assert that principles are more likely to favor the spirit of the law, whereas codes lead to narrow, legalis-

---

Kimberly has been unsuccessfully referred to the campus health center and the counseling service on several occasions for treatment of a presumed eating disorder. A freshman, she is about five feet seven inches tall, appears to weigh less than one hundred pounds, and has poor abdominal muscle tone in spite of a very demanding daily schedule of running and lifting weights. The residence hall staff are deeply concerned about Kimberly's welfare and have finally decided to recommend to the director of residence life that she be given a choice between dismissal from the halls on the technical grounds of "behavior disruptive to the learning environment" or that she provide evidence of being in active treatment for her eating disorder.

tic applications. (We shall see shortly that the use of principles can shape the development of a code of ethics; therefore, the models need not be mutually exclusive.)

The second approach is to institute a formal code of ethics, usually one developed by a particular professional organization. Such codes commonly follow a quasi-legal model that offers both prescriptions and proscriptions or rules that define what is and what is not acceptable. In its most potent form a code also provides for pressing formal charges in the event of a violation. The accused is given an opportunity to respond, and a pattern of penalties may be imposed by a hearing board composed of representatives from the profession.

The community has long been assumed to play a primary role in supporting ethical inquiry and establishing the range of acceptable moral standards. Gilligan (1982), Delworth and Seeman (1984), Brown (1985), Wood (1991), Upcraft and Poole (1991), and Canon (1993) have persuasively argued for the importance of various social structures and cultures in the formation of ethical behavior. Each has addressed the role that specific social groupings (gender, professions, campuses, and so on) play in enhancing, delimiting, and otherwise defining what is ethically acceptable (or even how or if a particular individual should think about ethics). More importantly, they note the problems that arise in approaching ethical questions from the reference points of codes or principles, which neglects the social context in which behavior occurs. The social environment may be the most comprehensive force for the promotion and support of ethical behavior.

Modeling ethical behavior provides a powerful and significant means of generating ethical standards within a social environment. Behavior that reflects a consistent focus on ethical issues—particularly when modeled by visible and prestigious members of the community—has a significant impact on the larger community. Identifying those circumstances that have a moral issue at their core, having a community member take personal responsibility for assuming a stance on the matter, and affording the rest of the community an opportunity to observe and reflect on the process inevitably elevates the quality of moral sensitivity and discourse within the larger community.

These approaches can and do come into conflict with one another. An ethical principle may not take into account some behavior patterns peculiar to a particular professional subculture. A component of a given code designed to protect the interests of a professional group may risk violating the interests of the clientele it serves, straining the intent of certain ethical principles. Inevitably, the all-too-human authors of professional codes simply fail to consider the consequences of applying a particular provision under certain circumstances. Certainly no ethical code can anticipate all possible scenarios; modeling by senior professionals may help bridge any gaps. Examples of conflicts between these three approaches are provided below, as are examples of how they can complement one another.

A registered campus organization, Students for Family Values, has applied for a grant from the student fee committee to bring a nationally known speaker to campus. The content of the lecture addresses the presumed dangers of including gays, lesbians, and bisexuals in institutional antidiscrimination statements. This particular speaker is known to have been dismissed from a national professional organization because of his misrepresentations and distortions of the research literature on homosexuality. The director of student activities is concerned about using student fees for this purpose and recommends that the fee request be rejected by the committee.

Ethical Principles

In the spirit of modeling the application of ethical principles, I want to acknowledge my bias toward basing discussions and explorations of professional ethics on ethical principles, as opposed to codes of ethics or general cultural expectations.. That bias derives, in part, from my experience in seminars with graduate students, workshops at professional meetings, and a variety of campus consultations. With this bias clear, let us build on the foundation provided by Chapter Five to look at how principle-based approaches emerged in the student affairs profession, their effect on the consideration of ethical dilemmas in professional settings, how ethical principles have significantly affected the design of one association's code, and concerns expressed about the appropriateness of a commonly applied set of principles.

There are some clear advantages to the application of principles to ethical problems. Principles afford a useful degree of flexibility, permitting consistency without rigidity. The primary disadvantage of using ethical principles to solve problems is their tendency toward producing frustrating vagueness and ambiguity, when we might desire some measure of precision and certainty. Karen Kitchener (1985) identified a set of five ethical principles drawn from her careful review of the professional ethics literature which have since been widely cited in the student services literature and have provided a commonly understood set of reference points for explorations of ethical dilemmas. Those five principles are to some degree arbitrary, insofar as other ethicists might have selected from four to six or more principles. (For example, the Golden Rule consists of just one: "Do unto others as you would have them do unto you.") However, in addition to the ease with which the principles suggested by Kitchener can be understood and applied, the list has the virtue of being short and easily kept in mind (no small matter when one considers the intensity of feelings generated in almost any discussion of a presumed ethical problem). The principles she has suggested are (1) respect autonomy, (2) do no harm, (3) benefit others, (4) be just, and (5) be faithful.

Respecting autonomy means acknowledging the right of individuals to decide how they will live their own lives (so long as their actions do not interfere with the rights of others). Respecting autonomy also serves to protect student affairs professionals against our own paternalistic instincts, no matter how laudable the goal of such behavior. Students and colleagues are entitled, in significant measure, to learn from their own failures; and following exposure to whatever caveats we may choose to offer, they must remain free to chose their own course of action. Kitchener (1985) has also noted that autonomy is closely related to the right of self-determination and First Amendment rights.

By *doing no harm* we honor our obligation to avoid actions that may inflict physical or psychological injury. Despite the seemingly obvious nature of this dictum, the circumstances to which it applies are not always immediately apparent. Specifically, establishing standards or imposing stringent requirements (for the best of reasons and in our role as institutional gatekeepers) without attending to potentially adverse consequences can do significant harm. For example, requiring a student to perform volunteer service as a condition for graduation may or may not result in lifelong community involvement, but it may inflict the harm inherent in adding a barrier to graduation.

Benefiting others is our core reason for being student affairs professionals. We choose to work in this field in order to help others. Kitchener (1985) observes, however, that the intent to benefit may easily conflict with the injunction to do no harm. The potential for such conflict is present in the volunteer requirement noted in the preceding paragraph. The pitfalls of such paternalism are not always obvious, and we should be alert to them. We should, however, continue to serve as advocates for students and co-workers and sustain efforts to humanize the campus environment. Removing unreasonable barriers to tenure and promotion for our colleagues, providing opportunities for professional growth and development, and providing support that meets the needs of partners and family members are essential components of programs that benefit community members.

Being just means according equal treatment to all those who lie within our sphere of influence. Just behavior, in general, seeks to honor the Golden Rule. Each student and each colleague must be provided with his or her fair portion of the resources of the campus community. Curiously enough, ensuring equal treatment can require offering special consideration to those who do not have (or have not had) equal access to the benefits available to most citizens. Affirmative action programs, modifications of campus structures to permit access to all resources by physically challenged students and staff, and programs designed to compensate for those who have been disadvantaged by substandard educational opportunities are all provided in the spirit of according justice. Accusations of "political correctness" lose much of their impact when such programs are assessed against the ethical principle of justice. Indeed, the simple failure to confront an individual who tells an ethnic "joke" has consequences for all who witness the incident. Unaware or unsensitized members of the majority group may continue to assume that such behavior is acceptable or that it does no harm, and racial and ethnic minority group members experience one more gratuitous offense.

To be faithful may be the most demanding of ethical principles. The requirements here are to tell the truth, to be loyal, to keep promises, and to maintain respect and civility in human discourse. Civility moves us beyond merely adhering to minimum ethical standards, toward asserting virtuous behavior (more about civility later). It is usually extremely difficult to respect the personal dignity of a colleague who has just finished attacking you or has presumed to question your motives. The easiest response is to counterattack, rather than taking the time to search for and address the underlying issue. But yielding to the natural inclination to respond in kind abandons the causes of human dignity and of being faithful. Keeping a promise can be as simple as devoting the necessary time and thought to preparing a lecture or topic for class discussion. How many of us who have taught for more than a semester can claim to have kept the implicit promise of always giving our students the best we have to offer? When challenged by an aggressive investigative reporter for the student newspaper, who of us has not been tempted to respond with something less than the full truth? When supervising a staff member whose performance is less than satisfactory, who of us has not elected to postpone delivering the discomforting feedback essential to improving that performance?

On the other hand, absolute adherence to truth telling risks being self-serving and self-righteous, or worse. For example, Alcoholics Anonymous encourages its members to make amends to those they have harmed—"except when to do so would injure them or others" (Alcoholics Anonymous, 1976, p. 59). That admonition takes into account the reality that telling the full truth on all occasions can result in serious damage to the sense of self-worth of the affected individual. Similarly, to insist on keeping a promise of confidentiality when doing so places a life in danger is patently irresponsible. For example, when we take steps to prevent the suicide of a young depressed student, we are honoring the higher principle of preserving life.

Finally, faithful conduct with respect to colleagues involves the occasional "caring confrontation" that is both timely and to the point. Consistent feedback that offers a co-worker the opportunity to attend to shared values and concerns, to continue to grow in the direction of his or her aspirations, and to know that he or she is valued represents energy well invested.

> You have completed the final stages of an applicant search for an opening at your institution. The leading candidate possesses programming skills that will significantly enhance services to students. The candidate—fresh out of graduate school and short on cash—has requested moving expenses, indicating that other universities have offered such assistance. Your assistant director urges you to offer to start the candidate on salary two weeks before her arrival as compensation for the fact that your institution does not—by governing board policy—provide moving expenses.

Working with Ethical Principles

In real-life situations, Kitchener's five ethical principles regularly come into conflict with one another. For example, allowing a student group to show an X-rated film at a fundraiser honors the principle of autonomy. At the same time, however, the presumed positive value of this autonomy is in opposition to the welfare of the female members of the community, who may see the exploitative film as a direct threat to their value as persons and indeed to their very welfare and safety on campus. In a similar vein, Jewish, African American, Hispanic, and Asian American students can persuasively argue that an uncritical acceptance of the ideal of free speech is damaging, that they have the right to be free from harassment and vilification on their own campus. Thus we see again how readily the abstract principles of "autonomy" and "do no harm" can conflict with each other.

The dilemmas just noted illustrate a precept for dealing with ethical principles: if you or I elect to violate or reject an ethical principle in the course of attempting to resolve an ethical dilemma, we incur the obligation to provide a justification or rationale for that violation or rejection. In the case of the X-rated movie, we might argue that the principle of doing no harm in this case conflicts with the academy's core mission of furthering the search for truth, which requires the free expression of all ideas, even those that are wholly repugnant. On the other hand, one might argue that allowing the Ku Klux Klan to speak on campus creates a clear and dangerous potential for violence, and therefore permission for such an event must be denied; for better or worse, the principle of "do no harm" prevails over that of free expression. In each of the two examples, there is a responsibility to provide a rationale for rejecting the relevant ethical principle. Chapter Seven presents the legal foundations for making these choices.

Lest the approach offered by Kitchener be seen as unassailable or sacrosanct, it should be noted that Upcraft and Poole (1991) have taken thoughtful and serious issue with the appropriateness of the selected principles. They took particular exception to the biomedical roots of the Beauchamp-Childress (1979) model that informed Kitchener's work, suggesting that solutions from the biomedical sphere (including counseling) may be poorly suited to resolving ethical dilemmas in student affairs outside the counseling arena. Upcraft and Poole would hold that student affairs professionals make decisions that are essentially administrative in character, and the subtleties of institutional versus individual obligations are simply not addressed by Kitchener's five principles. Instead, they suggest this two-dimensional framework: the first axis represents the continuum between the management role at one end and leadership at the other, and the second axis represents the continuum between the needs of the individual and those of the community. They intend to apply this framework, by completing the intersecting cells, to the resolution of ethical problems. The relative merits and practical value of this framework and of Kitchener's five principles remain to be determined. In the meantime, Kitchener remains a consistently cited source in the professional literature, and the prospect remains of benefiting from a lively exchange about ethical issues and how they might best be resolved.

Codes of Ethics

As noted, codes of ethics tend to follow a legal model, and they are generated for the use of specific professional groups and organizations. Certain behaviors are expected of practitioners; others are prohibited. There is considerable variability from one professional group to another in the precision with which relevant behaviors are described and detailed. Indeed, and as we shall see, even organizations such as the American College Personnel Association (ACPA) and the National Association of Student Personnel Administrators (NASPA), with their markedly overlapping constituencies, can produce documents that vary substantially in detail and focus. Provisions for addressing alleged violations of professional codes of ethics can vary as well, ranging from the nonexistent to very formal, quasi-legal procedures. In their most refined form, codes specify how charges may be brought, the hearing process, and the range of penalties that can be applied.

Winston and Dagley (1985) provide a detailed review of how the codes of ethics of the major student affairs professional organizations were developed and applied. Of particular interest is their discussion of the uses served by those codes. One such use is the service these codes perform as teaching tools for new professionals and as a means of socializing new professionals to expected standards of practice. The professional values underlying these codes serve to provide general guidance—a kind of professional "feel"—wherever specific detail is lacking. They provide a concrete structure for the early stage of professional development, when specific prescriptions and proscriptions are nearly essential. Such limits are probably necessary until the apprentice practitioner can master the more complex nuances of the profession's value system. Lacking significant experience and sensitivity to the more subtle social values of the profession, the new professional can use these codes of ethics as a guide when decisions must be made quickly or in the heat of a rapidly unfolding campus crisis.

In this particular context I would underscore the utility of having proscriptions in place that head off offending behaviors before they take place. Specifically, an admonition against dual relationships, sufficiently emphasized, can help prevent the development of inappropriate feelings of affection toward clients, students, and subordinates. Suppression of such feelings has socially useful dimensions as well.

Winston and Dagley (1985) also underscore the value of codes of ethics as guides for practical decision making. Codes provide, in effect, a more or less concrete statement to support or reject a given course of action. By defining professionally responsible behavior, codes also help protect the public. At the same time, codes can serve to protect practitioners from specious or unreasonable expectations on the part of either employers or clients. Ultimately, as Winston and Dagley assert, a professional code of ethics provides official notice to the public of a commitment to self-regulation, an intent to establish benchmarks that afford reasonably objective standards for evaluation, and a sensitivity to critical issues in day-to-day practice.

Two codes, each recently revised and reaffirmed, are particularly relevant to student affairs professionals. NASPA's Standards of Professional Practice (National Association of Student Personnel Administrators, 1994) was circulated, discussed, and amended over the decade prior to adoption in its current form. ACPA's Statement of Ethical Principles and Standards (American College Personnel Association, 1993b) has undergone even more extensive revision over a fifteen-year period. The documents are radically different in format, in specificity, and in the rights and responsibilities they are designed to protect. Those differences are instructive, illuminating the range and focus of ethical concerns that lie within our profession. The codes of both associations are presented in the Resource section at the back of this book.

The NASPA Standards of Professional Practice

The NASPA standards of 1994 include eighteen defining statements that address specific subjects such as professional affairs, agreement with institutional mission and goals, management of institutional resources, employment relationships, conflict of interest, legal authority and community expectations, equal opportunity, promotion of responsible student behavior, integrity of research and information, respect for confidentiality, and similar matters that lie within the purview of senior student affairs administrators. Each statement is from one to three sentences in length and describes the intent of the membership in relatively general terms—for example: "Conflict of Interest: Members recognize their obligation to the employing institution and seek to avoid private interests, obligations, and transactions which are in conflict of interest or give the appearance of impropriety. Members clearly distinguish between statements and actions which represent their own personal views and those which represent their employing institution when important to do so" (National Association of Student Personnel Administrators, 1994, p. 15).

The preamble makes note of the fact that NASPA is "an organization of colleges, universities, agencies, and professional educators whose members are committed to providing services and education that enhance student growth and development." Further, the association "seeks to promote . . . personal integrity, belief in the dignity and worth of individuals, respect for individual differences and diversity, [and] a commitment to service," among other ethical principles (p. 15).

Consistent with its structure of institutional memberships, NASPA includes in eight of the eighteen standards specific references to members' obligations to the institutions where they are employed. For example, and not unreasonably, the standard addressing professional services asserts that "members of NASPA [must] fulfill the responsibilities of their position by supporting the educational interests, rights, and welfare of students *in accordance with the mission of the employing institution*" (emphasis added). The second standard calls on members "who accept employment with an educational institution [to] subscribe to the general mission and goals of the institution" (p. 15).

The NASPA standards may reasonably be viewed as a series of administrative principles, each tied to a moral or ethical standard of practice defined by the membership. Thus, members "honor employment relationships," "fulfill the responsibilities of their position," "ensure confidentiality," and so on. The NASPA standards can be said to fall somewhere between a very general statement of a

---

Pat is a co-worker who is actively searching for a new job. He has asked the department secretary to type correspondence related to his search, and he uses college stationery, copying facilities, and mailing privileges to send out materials associated with his numerous applications.

few selected ethical principles and the elaborate form assumed by other, more formal codes.

The ACPA Statement of Ethical Principles and Standards

In its present incarnation, the ACPA statement (American College Personnel Association, 1993b) offers guidance on addressing specific ethical violations, from holding an informal private conference to submitting formal charges; a statement of the ethical principles identified and proposed by Kitchener; enumerated groups of standards; and "Policies and Procedures for Processing Complaints of Ethical Violations" (American College Personnel Association, 1993a), a detailed accounting of the processes involved in carrying out formal adjudication of an alleged violation. Effectively, the ACPA document now meets all of the traditionally accepted criteria for a professional code of ethics.

The ACPA statement is very likely unique in that the codified statements reflect the ethics committee's decision to incorporate the principles identified by Kitchener and have the statements "informed" by the appropriate principles. The 1993 statement identifies rather specific behaviors that are subsumed under the headings of Professional Responsibility and Competence, Student Learning and Development, Responsibility to the Institution, and Responsibility to Society. Examples of the standards' prescribing and proscribing certain behaviors include their admonitions that student affairs professionals must "maintain and enhance professional effectiveness by improving skills and acquiring new knowledge"; "abstain from sexual harassment"; "submit manuscripts for consideration to only one journal at a time"; "avoid dual relationships with students that may involve incompatible roles and conflicting responsibilities"; "confront students regarding issues, attitudes and behaviors that have ethical implications"; "contribute to their institution by supporting its mission, goals and policies"; "inform appropriate officials of conditions that may be disruptive or damaging to their institution"; "demonstrate concern for the welfare of all students and work for constructive change on behalf of students"; and "demonstrate regard for social codes and moral expectations of the communities in which they live and work" (pp. 90–92). The standards conclude with a discussion of the specific steps involved in adjudicating alleged violations of the code and a description of the organizational structure within which those steps are carried out.

Compiling a code of ethics is a time- and energy-consuming task. Both the NASPA code and the ACPA code underwent a detailed and thoughtful review at many levels of their respective organizations. The testing of standards in real-life situations—with clear provision for feedback from professionals in the field—was essential if the resulting documents were to be accepted and applied. A very significant by-product of that review process is the effect that discussions and debate on ethical matters have on the membership. Those benefits include raising consciousness about and sensitivity to ethical concerns, providing support for the open discussion of ethical issues as they arise, and encouraging confrontation of those who violate the ethical standards of the professional community.

An Ethical Community

A decade ago, Brown (1985) suggested that "the common mission of the student services profession is being the moral conscience of the campus" (p. 69). He went on to point out that student affairs professionals are in a position to fill that role in light of their collective involvement with the student as a complex being (that is, the "whole student"), their virtual round-the-clock contact with students in almost every setting in which they find themselves, and their almost unique opportunity to be aware of injustices imposed on students by other students, faculty, administrators (including members of their own professional ranks), and, all too frequently, the university system itself. He held that those factors, when combined with a professional commitment to student growth and development, provide "a cohesive base for [that] common mission" (p. 69).

Brown went on to envision the possibility of building communities at a variety of levels—the campus, the state, the nation, even the world—that possess a commitment to an ethical agenda. In such communities, members would pursue the goals of ensuring peace and caring relationships, approaching careers as callings to service, moving to apply the best in theory and research findings to real-life circumstances, integrating personal development in the curricula of traditional and continuing education, and working to ensure a humane and supportive learning environment for all members of the community (pp. 72–73).

It would be unfortunate—indeed, tragic—if this seemingly utopian idea of an ethical community was cast aside as being simply too idealistic. The academic

---

Jerri is a bright but not very socially skilled and not very attractive freshman student in a coed residence hall. She has not been included in the social groups that have formed on the hall floor in the course of the semester. Lately it has become apparent that she has been spending the night in the rooms of various male residents of the floor. It is your impression that six or so of these men have been taking turns passing Jerri around.

community at large, including the student affairs profession, needs just such a model against which to assess its hopes for itself and its students. There is emerging evidence (Manning, 1994; Wilcox & Ebbs, 1992) not only that ethical communities exist on campus but also that they enjoy a measure of success in achieving their stated goals. In addition, we need look no further than the two largest organizations for student affairs professionals, NASPA and ACPA, to see how an ethical community of very modest size can effect change and enhance the moral climate for the parent body.

Professional Associations as Ethical Communities

In the late 1970s and early 1980s, a small NASPA task force proposed the set of standards for professional practice that was eventually adopted (and then revised) by the NASPA board of directors. That process involved hearings at a series of national conventions, intense discussions about the particulars, and, in its earlier stages, considerable indifference on the part of some constituents. The perseverance of members of this small task force and their sense of community was essential to achieving the organization's endorsement of a set of standards.

Concurrently and quite independently, several groups within ACPA undertook the preparation of a more formal code. Here, too, several informal and overlapping communities of ACPA members supported the labor put forth by a few of their colleagues to compose, circulate, and subsequently hold open hearings on a document that went through a number of revisions before it was adopted in 1981 (American College Personnel Association, 1981). Subsequently, a column was generated for the association's quarterly newsletter, *ACPA Developments,* which featured responses by members of the ethics committee to a series of hypothetical cases as a means of enlisting colleagues in broad ethical discourse. Workshops on professional ethics were conducted by Kitchener and others for the association's executive council, preconvention workshops on ethics became a part of the schedule of the association's annual convention, and association president Robert

> You are conducting an interview with a candidate for a staff position in the company of three of your colleagues. The candidate had mentioned in passing that she and her spouse just returned from their honeymoon in Mexico. In the course of the formal interview, one of your co-workers asks the candidate about her husband's career plans and how he would feel about moving seven hundred miles to your campus.

D. Brown selected the theme "Creating an Ethical Climate on Campus" for the 1990 ACPA convention in St. Louis. So it is—in two rather large professional organizations—that relatively small communities of persons within the organization introduced changes that enhanced the ethical sensitivity of the organization at large.

Ethical Communities on Campus

At a level closer to home, the potential power of smaller "ethical communities" is illustrated by the Jewish tradition of the minyan, which holds that a minimum of ten persons must be present before a worship service can be held. This tradition takes into account the reality that we are more likely to meet our own aspirations for virtuous behavior, to realize our individual potential, and to be more fully human and humane if we are in community with others who share our values and care for and about us. Being in community affords the nurturance, support, and challenge that Sanford (1979) posits as being the necessary and sufficient conditions for growth and change. An ethical community, then, deliberately and intentionally attends to moral concerns—day in and day out—and provides the support essential for the individual members of the community to sustain that effort. The ethical community (a secular minyan, if you will) also acts to call us into question when we fail to measure up to the ideals we hold in common. A willingness to confront a co-worker who has fallen short of the standards to which he or she would want to be held is an essential part of being a member of his or her community. Obviously, the ability to *accept* such confrontation when one has failed to measure up to the values of the community is also essential to membership in the community. Being a part of an ethical community increases the likelihood that we will recognize ethical dilemmas when they arise, that we will act on them, and that we will do so with some consistency.

Wilcox and Ebbs (1992) and Ducker and Ducker (1994) have suggested activities that would promote the enhancement of ethical sensitivity on individual campuses. Envisioning a campus division of student affairs as an ethical community has both merit and potential. By training and inclination, student affairs staff members are already receptive to the tasks and goals that are a part of membership in an ethical community.

Undertaking to adopt a personnel document for the division of student affairs that enunciates ethical standards and principles can become a significant step in the transition from student affairs as an administrative unit to student affairs as an emerging ethical community. On two campuses that undertaking has at least led to heightened awareness and increased sensitivity to ethical issues.

In the late 1970s, the personnel committee of the Division of Student Affairs at Northern Illinois University reviewed a draft version of the ACPA ethical code and subsequently adopted it as a formal part of the division's personnel policy. It is of some interest that the members of the personnel committee, at that time, determined that the section of the code that dealt with dual relationships (i.e., proscriptions against affectional relationships between staff members and persons for whom they have administrative responsibility) was impractical and deleted it from the division's personnel policies. Later, after encountering a series of messy situations resulting from dual relationships in the residence halls (the locus of the earlier judgment that the deleted portion of the code was "impractical"), action was taken to add measures explicitly prohibiting dual relationships.

More recently, the Division of Student Affairs at Colorado State University drew on standards promulgated by ACPA, NASPA, the Council for the Advancement of Standards for Student Services/Development Programs, the Association of College Unions International, and other professional organizations in preparing a draft of divisional ethical principles and standards (Colorado State University Division of Student Affairs, 1992). In that draft the preparers noted that "it is the goal for Division of Student Affairs staff members to be positive University representatives who serve as leaders and role models in the larger community" (p. 1). The draft document referenced ethical principles, enunciated ethical goals for staff members, and suggested specific steps that might be employed in resolving ethical conflicts. The positive experiences of these two divisions of student services and of those on other campuses—and their struggles—recommend the process to student services professionals on other campuses.

Putting Ethics to Work

The cynicism of the marketplace has spilled into the higher education community along with the application of entrepreneurial models and strategies that on rare occasion afford a "fit" for the increasing fiscal problems of educational establishments. It is not unusual to hear senior administrators reference the "bottom line" as the justification for a particular (usually unpalatable) decision. Similarly, "be pragmatic," "let's get real," "you wish!" or "we've got to be practical about this" are offered as justifications for less than virtuous courses of action. We continue to argue (Canon & Brown, 1985) that "being ethical in itself is a very practical pursuit. Individuals . . . (who) place a high premium on respecting autonomy, avoiding the doing of harm, benefiting others, being just, and being faithful establish a degree of credibility with others that tends to earn loyalty, trust, and respect in return" (p. 84). One need only consider the substantial number of college and university presidents who have come to grief in the last few decades— as a consequence of under-the-table bonuses to senior administrators, too-elaborate remodeling of the presidential home, or bypassing affirmative action standards in hiring a former colleague—to conclude that rejecting ethical practice in favor of "being pragmatic" can have its own hazards. Brown's ethical community, in light of these once mighty but now fallen presidents, becomes increasingly attractive.

Ethical-Legal Conflicts

Informed student affairs professionals cannot afford to be ignorant of the legal constraints on their practice nor of the legal consequences of certain professional decisions (see Chapter Seven). It is our shared good fortune that most of what is ethical is also legal, and a goodly portion of all that is legal also meets minimal ethical standards. Nonetheless, there are circumstances when the figurative—cautious—running of a traffic light is warranted. For example, the welfare of a student and his or her family may occasionally be best served by disclosing the details of a serious illness, in spite of constraints imposed by state or federal statutes or even the student's own desire to have those details remain confidential.

One needs to be particularly cautious in those circumstances in which colleagues (including the staff legal counsel) suggest that a particular course of action be followed in order to avoid a lawsuit. The first part of any decision-making process needs to draw on the experience and expertise of the student affairs professional, who very emphatically defends the ethical standards of the profession. A useful strategy for dealing with such circumstances includes advising the college or university legal counsel of the course of action you judge to be most appropriate and then seeking that professional's advice on how to best position yourself for any potential legal consequences of the decision. "Can you find grounds to defend me should this go to court?" is always a valid and useful question under such circumstances. Advice of legal counsel can never substitute for your own professional judgment, however. And ultimately, of course, a lawsuit may follow no

Fran has one of the most effective placement offices of any institution of comparable size. You have heard disturbing rumors for some time about Fran's coming back from rather leisurely lunches with staff members or other campus friends, where the drinks often added up to three or four over a period of an hour and a half. Where Fran once had several research projects under way at one time or a paper or two being reviewed for professional journals, little such activity is now observable. Late arrivals at the office and the appearance of physical fatigue are pretty obvious. A very protective staff is still doing an outstanding job in Fran's agency.

matter what course of action is chosen. So one might just as well "do the right thing" in the first place.

Using Your Ethical Community

Trusted co-workers can provide very helpful curbstone consultations when you are faced with a particularly perplexing ethical dilemma. In fact, for many of us this is where the formation of an ethical community begins. There are several direct benefits of enlisting a colleague's advice when working to resolve an ethical problem: (1) the risks of impulsive or prescriptive action are reduced, (2) the judgment of two is almost always better than one, (3) you may discover a more effective response than those you first came up with, (4) you have the sense of security that results from having garnered support, and (5) having talked it over with a colleague, you are more likely to follow through.

In addition to the benefits just listed, such consultation reinforces—at least in your immediate social-professional circle—the notion that talking about ethical matters is standard professional procedure.

Confronting the Presumed Ethical Offender

When faced with the task of confronting someone you believe to have been responsible for an ethical lapse, it may be useful to entertain the distinct possibility that we are all sinners (or at least that we all make mistakes). That touch can go a long way toward avoiding the potential for self-righteousness that lurks in most of us. With that degree of humility firmly established, the confrontation is more likely to have a favorable outcome.

The essential task is not to impose punishment (and most certainly not out of punitive motives) but rather to change behavior, to ensure that a more ethical course of action is taken on future occasions. It is much too easy to assume that you have all the facts or that you are dealing with someone who is in some way morally deficient. Your co-worker may in fact be quite unaware of the ethical implications of the situation and may be horrified to have colleagues see him or her as ethically irresponsible. It is almost always useful in such encounters to proceed on the assumption that the affected individual also wants to do the right thing. (Envision how you might feel were you approached by a co-worker with allegations of ethical impropriety.) The professional cliché about making "I" statements is worth resurrecting on such occasions. For example, "I am concerned about some statements I'm hearing from your students about the use of ridicule in class" may be heard with less defensiveness than "Your students are complaining about how you ridicule them in class." A subtle touch, perhaps, but it is one worth considering.

Blowing the Whistle

The nearly universal standard for settling ethical disputes requires that you contact the offending party prior to instituting any formal action. This is essentially the equivalent of contacting your neighbors about their barking dog before calling the police. Potential disputes are most readily solved at the lowest level of disputation. It isn't easy to do, but it may save the confronting person the embarrassment of discovering too late that the facts do not support his or her initial perception. Also, being confronted personally is the approach you and I would prefer were we thought to be guilty of an ethical lapse.

Insisting on Civility

There is an attractive elegance in the concept of focusing on civility as the minimum standard for social and intellectual discourse on campus. Indeed, if I were limited to the pursuit of a single objective in the larger domain of an ethical community, civility would very likely be my choice. Within the notion of civility lie values consistent with respect for individual worth and personal dignity. A part of that begins with our being willing to insist on (or at least assert) our personal dignity. The obvious counterpart involves approaching co-workers, students, and other members of the academic community with that same consistent pattern of civility and respect.

Conclusion

We have access to a variety of resources in the pursuit of high standards of professional conduct, including published codes, a professional literature that addresses ethical principles, and the persons with whom we carry out our day-to-day professional responsibilities. Those resources interact with one another in ways that empower us to grow as individuals and move with some consistency toward a higher level of ethical conduct in performing our duties. If civility in our exchanges with students, co-workers, and other members of the campus community represents a starting point for that growth, it is not a bad place to begin.

References

Alcoholics Anonymous. (1976). *Alcoholics Anonymous* (4th ed.). New York: Alcoholics Anonymous World Services.

American College Personnel Association. (1981). Statement of ethical and professional standards. *Journal of College Student Personnel, 22*, 184–189.

American College Personnel Association. (1993a). Policies and procedures for processing complaints of ethical violations. *Journal of College Student Development, 34*, 93–97.

American College Personnel Association. (1993b). Statement of ethical principles and standards. *Journal of College Student Development, 34*, 89–92.

Barr, M. J. (1983, March). Presidential address to the annual meeting of the American College Personnel Association, Baltimore.

Beauchamp, T. L., & Childress, J. F. (1979). *Principles of biomedical ethics.* Oxford: Oxford University Press.

Brown, R. D. (1985). Creating an ethical community. In H. J. Canon & R. D. Brown (Eds.), *Applied ethics in student services* (New Directions for Student Services No. 30, pp. 67–80). San Francisco: Jossey-Bass.

Canon, H. J. (1993). Maintaining high ethical standards. In M. J. Barr & Associates, *The handbook of student affairs administration* (pp. 327–339). San Francisco: Jossey-Bass.

Canon, H. J., & Brown, R. D. (1985). How to think about professional ethics. In H. J. Canon & R. D. Brown (Eds.), *Applied ethics in student services* (New Directions for Student Services No. 30, pp. 81–88). San Francisco: Jossey-Bass.

Colorado State University Division of Student Affairs. (1992). *Statement of ethical principles and standards.* Unpublished manuscript, Colorado State University, Fort Collins.

Delworth, U., & Seeman, D. (1984). The ethics of care: Implications of Gilligan for the student service profession. *Journal of College Student Personnel, 25*, 489–492.

Ducker, M. W., & Ducker, D. L. (1994). Educating staff on ethics and professionalism. *Journal of College Student Development, 35*, 304–305.

Gilligan, C. (1982). *In a different voice.* Cambridge, MA: Harvard University Press.

Kitchener, K. S. (1985). Ethical principles and ethical decisions in student affairs. In H. J. Canon & R. D. Brown (Eds.), *Applied ethics in student services* (New Directions for Student Services No. 30, pp. 17–30). San Francisco: Jossey-Bass.

Manning, K. (1994). Rituals and recision: Building a community in hard times. *Journal of College Student Development, 35*, 275–281.

National Association of Student Personnel Administrators. (1994). Standards of professional practice. In National Association of Student Personnel Administrators, *NASPA member handbook* (pp. 15–16). Washington, DC: Author.

Sanford, N. (1979). Freshman personality: A stage in human development. In N. Sanford & J. Axelrod (Eds.), *College and character* (pp. 107–111). Orinda, CA: Montaigne Press.

Upcraft, M. L., & Poole, T. G. (1991). Ethical issues and administrative politics. In P. L. Moore (Ed.), *Managing the political dimension of student affairs* (New Directions for Student Services No. 55, pp. 81–94). San Francisco: Jossey-Bass.

Wilcox, J. R., & Ebbs, S. L. (1992). Promoting an ethical campus culture: The values audit. *NASPA Journal, 29*, 253–260.

Winston, R. B., Jr., & Dagley, J. C. (1985). Ethical standards statements: Uses and limitations. In H. J. Canon & R. D. Brown (Eds.), *Applied ethics in student services* (New Directions for Student Services No. 30, pp. 49–66). San Francisco: Jossey-Bass.

Wood, S. A. (1991). Toward renewed collegiality: The challenge of the 1990s. *NASPA Journal, 29*, 2–9.

CHAPTER SEVEN

LEGAL FOUNDATIONS OF STUDENT AFFAIRS PRACTICE

Margaret J. Barr

The law is an important part of the professional practice of any student affairs administrator. Whether one is a new or a seasoned professional, there are legal implications to almost every decision one makes. The legal environment of higher education and student affairs has changed rapidly in recent decades; in this litigious society, the legal ramifications of student affairs practice have grown ever more intense.

The law, however, is not something to be feared. Instead, it provides a framework for guiding student affairs practice. Student affairs practitioners must be aware of both fundamental legal constraints and newly emerging areas of the law to effectively serve both their students and their institution.

This chapter is designed to provide an overview of the most salient legal issues influencing student affairs. One caveat is in order: this discussion is not intended as a substitute for competent legal advice, and each student affairs professional is strongly urged to seek appropriate legal assistance when dealing with such matters. Rather, the chapter provides an overview of those points of law that most directly influence professional practice in student affairs. Topics covered include the legal differences between public and private institutions, the sources of the law, constitutional issues, federal and state statutes, contracts, liability issues, working with legal counsel, and emerging legal issues of concern to student affairs professionals.

Private Versus Public Institutions

The differences between public and private institutions of higher education have become increasingly blurred. Financial support from the state and federal government for research or student aid has led many to believe that there are essentially no differences between such institutions. This is not the case.

A public institution's authority is derived from its statutory or constitutional entitlement. In private institutions, authority to act is derived from the institution's articles of incorporation, charter, or license. The differences between private and public institutions are most marked in regard to federal constitutional questions. The First, Fourth, Fifth, and Fourteenth Amendments to the Constitution provide the basis for the application of constitutional law to higher education. Kaplin (1985) notes that public institutions and their officers are fully subject to constitutional constraints, whereas private institutions and their officers are not. For private institutions, a clear relationship must be demonstrated between any activity alleged to be governed by constitutional mandates and the action of the state.

Most private institutions have, however, adopted guarantees similar to constitutional protections as part of their contract of enrollment with students, even though they are not bound to do so. In addition, although private institutions are technically free from federal constitutional constraints, students attending such institutions do have protection. Many individual rights are protected by statutes or by the applicable state constitution, and other rights are protected by precedent in case law (Barr, 1988).

Sources of the Law

The law has eight sources that can influence practice in student affairs in both public and private institutions; however, the degree of influence varies from one type of institution to another. The eight sources of the law are the federal Constitution; the applicable state constitution; federal, state, and local statutes; judicial decisions; the rules and regulations of administrative agencies; contracts; institutional rules and regulations; and academic tradition.

The U.S. Constitution

As Kaplin (1985) explains, "Constitutions are the fundamental source for determining the nature and extent of governmental powers. Constitutions are also the fundamental source of the individual rights guarantees that limit the power of government and protect citizens generally, including members of the academic community" (p. 10). The Constitution is the highest source of law in the country. As noted above, however, the influence of the Constitution in private institutions is limited to certain circumstances.

State Constitutions

Provisions of the applicable state constitution can influence both public and private institutions. Through the residual powers of the Constitution, all powers not specifically reserved for the federal government are ceded to the states and their citizens (Alexander & Solomon, 1972). Thus, higher education comes primarily under state control. Private institutions are also subject to some provisions of state constitutions. In some states, the constitution provides even greater protection for civil rights than the federal Constitution (*State* v. *Schmid*, 1980 [423 A.2d 615]; *Commonwealth of Pennsylvania* v. *Tate*, 1981 [432 A.2d 1382]). In both of these cases, the court found a constitutional right of access to the property of private institutions by nonaffiliated persons. Careful review of the state constitution is needed to determine the influence of specific provisions at private institutions.

Statutes

Three levels of statutes influence higher education: federal, state, and local. Federal statutes govern all citizens of the United States and must be consistent with the powers reserved for the federal government under the Constitution. Most public institutions are statutory and are subject to all provisions of the state constitution and state laws. Both public and private institutions must conform to the general laws of the state and submit to regulation by state agencies whose primary function is not education. Although private institutions are shielded from much state regulation, they are not immune from regulations derived from the general police power of the state. Private institutions also come under state control through statutes governing trusts, chartering, licensing, and coordinating bodies.

The influence of local ordinances on a given institution is determined by the legal status of the institution, the statutory entitlement of the municipality or county where the institution is located, and the facts of a particular situation. In general, both public and private institutions are subject to local ordinances regarding health and safety, such as fire codes and zoning laws. A public institution, however, as an arm of the state, has authority over local government unless such powers are restricted by state or federal constitutional provisions (Thompson, 1976).

Judicial Decisions

As Gehring (1993) explains, "The function of the judicial system is to settle controversies, decide the constitutionality of laws, and interpret them" (p. 275). The force of any judicial decision depends on the jurisdiction of the deciding court. The federal court system consists of the Supreme Court, the court of appeals, special federal courts, and district courts. In matters related to federal constitutional issues and federal statutes, only the decisions of the U.S. Supreme Court are "binding precedents throughout the country" (Kaplin, 1985, p. 13). Eleven federal districts, or circuits, constitute the court of appeals and serve as appellate courts in the federal system. In addition, the District of Columbia has a federal court of appeals. These circuit courts each have a specific geographic jurisdiction, and their decisions are only binding within that jurisdiction. Cases may be appealed as a matter of right from a district court to the appropriate circuit court. Appeals may also be heard by the U.S. Supreme Court, but the court does not agree to hear all cases. Finally, each federal district court is a one-judge trial court; its decisions are binding only in the district where judgment is rendered.

Each state court system is unique; however, most state court systems are structured like the federal courts. State district courts are usually courts of general jurisdiction and have judicial responsibilities for a geographic area within the state. Most states have separate district and appellate courts for civil and criminal matters. Generally there is one supreme court, although in some states the appellate court serves as the supreme court in criminal matters.

Although court decisions are binding only within a given court's jurisdiction (at both the state and federal levels), all decisions should be carefully reviewed. The reasoning of one court with a limited jurisdiction may be persuasive and therefore adopted by other jurisdictions.

Administrative Rules and Regulations

Kaplin (1985) indicates that the most rapidly expanding source of higher education law is the directives of state and federal agencies. Like statutes, administrative regulations at both the state and federal levels carry the force of law and must be consistent with applicable state and federal statutes and constitutional provisions. Proposed implementing regulations for federal statutes are published in the *Federal Register* with an invitation to comment. After the specified public comment period, the regulations, which have the status of law, are issued. Student affairs administrators should read the *Federal Register* and comment on proposed regulations within institutional guidelines. Recent experience with proposed regulations governing the Student Right-to-Know and Campus Security Act of 1990 illustrate that thoughtful comments can influence the final regulations.

Contracts

A contract creates a binding legal arrangement between the contracting parties, enforceable by either party if one party fails to comply with its terms. Four elements must be present in a contract: a promise or a set of promises, an offer and an acceptance, an agreement of what is to be gained or given up, and an agreement between the parties so that each has the same understanding (Gehring, 1993). In recent years, courts at all levels and jurisdictions have begun to define the relationship between a student and an institution as that of a contract. As a result, almost every oral and written statement between a student and an institutional representative has the potential to become part of a mutually binding contract (*Johnson* v. *Lincoln Christian College*, 1986 [501 N.E.2d 1380). When disputes arise, the first source of law to be checked is the elements of the contract agreed upon by the parties.

Institutional Rules and Regulations

Although institutional rules and regulations are subject to the sources of the law described above, they are also a source of the law in and of themselves. Often the question in litigation is whether an institution has followed its own rules. The key to maintaining sound institutional rules is to ensure that they are consistent with other sources of the law, that they are specific, that they are enforceable, and that they are known and consistently enforced.

Academic Tradition

Academic tradition, representing the expectations members of the academic community hold for the behavior of the institution and its members, is the most diffuse source of law influencing higher education. Academic tradition is much more informal than other sources of the law; it may be documented through speeches, correspondence, media releases, and other interpretations of how the college or university conducts its business. The use of academic tradition as a source of the law has been recognized by the courts under specific circumstances (*Krotkoff* v. *Goucher College*, 1978 [585 F.2d 675]).

Constitutional Issues

All of the sources of law described above have great potential to influence the practice of student affairs professionals, but constitutional issues are often a major part of daily practice in student affairs.

Freedom of Religion

The First Amendment to the U.S. Constitution states in part that "Congress shall make no law respecting the establishment of religion or prohibiting the free exercise thereof." The Supreme Court in *Lemon* v. *Kurtzman* (1971 [403 U.S. 602]) established a three-pronged test to determine if the government has become excessively entangled in religion: (1) Does the activity have a clearly secular purpose? (2) Does the activity have a primary effect of neither advancing nor inhibiting religion? (3) Does excessive entanglement exist between the church and the state? If so, the action may be unconstitutional.

In *Widmar* v. *Vincent* (1981 [103 Sup. Ct. 269]), the Supreme Court held that the neutral accommodation of student religious groups, in accordance with institutional policies, by public institutions is not a violation of the First Amendment. Private institutions are free to "establish" a religion or to prohibit the free exercise of religion that is not consistent with their stated policies or mission. They must, however, be consistent in applying such criteria.

Freedom of Speech

The freedom of speech clause of the First Amendment also raises a number of issues of concern to student affairs administrators. While freedom of speech is not absolute (*Schenk* v. *United States*, 1919 [249 U.S. 47]), it is an essential element in the marketplace of ideas of higher education. In *Siegel* v. *Regents of the University of California* (1970 [308 F. Supp. 832]), the Supreme Court held in part that "utterances in the context of violence, involving a definite and present danger, can lose significance as an appeal to reason and become part of an instrument of force . . . unprotected by the Constitution" (p. 838).

Most cases regarding freedom of speech have focused on outside speakers, and most courts have agreed that neither a public nor a private institution is obliged to open its doors to outside speakers. However, if a college or university allows outside speakers and "opens its lecture halls, it must do so nondiscriminately" (*Stacy* v. *Williams*, 1969 [306 F. Supp. 963], p. 971).

Tinker v. *Des Moines Independent School District* (1969 [393 U.S. 503]), although a secondary school case, established the right of students to symbolic free speech and declared that their "constitutional rights were not shed at the schoolhouse gate" (p. 736). Wright (1969) provides three principles regarding free speech which have been consistently confirmed by the courts. First, expression cannot be prohibited because of disagreement with the content expressed. Second, expression is subject to reasonable regulations of the institution regarding its time, place, and manner. Third, expression can be prohibited if it can be proved that such expression could materially and substantially disrupt the primary educational mission of the institution.

The question of commercial free speech has also been litigated. The most noted series of cases is *American Future Systems, Inc.* v. *Pennsylvania State University* (1980 [618 F.2d 252], 1982 [688 F.2d 907], 1983 [568 F. Supp. 666], 1984 [752 F.2d 854]). American Future Systems, Inc., sought to sell products in residence hall rooms through telephone solicitation and arranged demonstrations in residents' rooms. The university took the position that such solicitation violated the privacy of students and that commercial enterprises did not have absolute free speech rights in residence halls. The university prevailed under the condition that its regulations were reasonable and alternate forms of expression existed for the commercial vendor.

Hate speech has caused some institutions to introduce speech codes to regulate such behavior. This approach has been less than successful. The University of Michigan's policy prohibiting "any behavior, verbal or physical, that stigmatizes or victimizes an individual on the basis of race, ethnicity, religion, sex, sexual orientation, creed, national origin, ancestry, age, marital status, handicap, or Vietnam-era veteran status" was declared unconstitutional because it was overly broad and vague (*Doe* v. *University of Michigan*, 1989 [721 F. Supp. 852], p. 853). The prohibitions in the regulation could include speech protected by the First Amendment (Gehring, 1993). Hate speech remains a vexing problem, and it is clear that more creative ways must be found to address the issue rather than mere regulation.

Freedom of the Press

Freedom of the student press has been vigorously upheld by the courts. In *Dickey* v. *Alabama State Board of Education* (1967 [273 F. Supp. 613]) the courts declared that an institution could not exercise prior restraint by removing an editorial critical of the state governor. Furthermore, funding cannot be removed due to a disagreement or potential institutional embarrassment regarding a student newspaper's content (*Minnesota Daily* v. *University of Minnesota*, 1983 [719 F.2d 279]). Obscenity is not a reason for dismissal of a student editor or for using the campus discipline system against the editor (*Papish* v. *Board of Curators of the University of Missouri*, 1973 [93 Sup. Ct. 1197]). Removal of editorial advertisements has also not been upheld (*Lueth* v. *St. Clair County Community College*, 1990 [732 F. Supp. 1410]). Student newspapers must, however, conform to applicable statutes governing libel and slander (*Mazart* v. *State University of New York*, 1982 [441 N.Y.S. 2d 600]).

A recent Supreme Court decision (*Rosenberger* v. *Rector and Visitors of the University of Virginia*, 1995 [1155 Ct. 2510]) has implications for the funding of religious publications at state colleges and universities through student fees. The Court held that funding a Christian student newspaper does not violate the establishment clause of the First Amendment and that public universities, as centers of free expression, should not deny religious expression by refusing to fund such newspapers. Administrators at public institutions should seek legal advice on the implications of this case for specific funding approaches to the student press on their campus.

Freedom of Association

Private institutions may prevent, limit, or refuse to authorize the peaceful assembly of any group, including student organizations. Public institutions may not. Both private and public institutions must follow their own published rules; such rules should be reasonably specific, neither too vague nor too broad. In *Healy* v. *James* (1972 [92 Sup. Ct. 2338]), the Supreme Court upheld the right of a chapter of the organization Students for a Democratic Society to be recognized on a college campus. The college claimed that the organization's philosophy espoused overthrowing the U.S. government. The Court held that there was a difference between advocacy and action and declared that nonrecognition was thus unconstitutional. The *Healy* decision has been tested most recently in cases involving recognition of gay student organizations by colleges and universities (*Gay Lib* v. *University of Missouri*, 1977 [58 F.2d 848], and *Gay Student Services* v. *Texas A&M University*, 1984 [737 F.2d 1317]); the courts upheld the right of free association by students on the campus of state colleges and universities.

Freedom of Assembly

Restrictions on the use of campus facilities have been upheld by the courts as long as the regulations are fair, reasonable, and enforced in an equitable manner. As long as student organizations follow institutional rules and regulations regarding time, place, and manner of assembly, they are free to use campus facilities for meetings. Restrictions on the use of campus facilities by outside groups have been upheld by the courts, as long as the restrictions are enforced in a fair and reasonable manner

(*American Civil Liberties Union of Virginia* v. *Radford College,* 1970 [315 F. Supp. 893]). The prime educational purpose of the institution may also be protected through facility use policies (*State* v. *Jordan,* 1972 [500 P.2d 56]). Once an institution has opened its doors to outside groups, however, it must make facilities equally available to all, regardless of the content of the proposed event (*National Socialist White People's Party* v. *Ringers,* 1973 [473 F.2d 1010]). Furthermore, due process must be provided for denial of the use of facilities by outside groups (*Watson* v. *Board of Regents of the University of Colorado,* 1973 [512 P.2d 1161]). In addition, "state and local governments have trespass and unlawful entry laws that limit the use of postsecondary facilities by outsiders" (Kaplin, 1985, p. 422), and the courts have generally upheld those regulations.

Search and Seizure

The Fourth Amendment provides protection against unreasonable search and seizure. Although *Moore* v. *Student Affairs Committee of Troy State University* (1976 [284 F. Supp. 775]) permitted warrantless searches, another line of cases (*Smyth* v. *Lubbers,* 1975 [398 F. Supp. 777]; *State* v. *Moore,* 1976 [429 U.S. 1004]) has held such searches to be unlawful. In *Washington* v. *Chrisman* (1982 [455 U.S. 1]), the Supreme Court heard a residence hall search and seizure case and affirmed that the "plain view" doctrine applied to warrantless searches. *New Jersey* v. *T.L.O.* (1985 [469 U.S. 325]) also has implications for higher education. In this case the Court held that a warrantless search was permissible because the secondary school official had reasonable suspicion that contraband was present. As Weeks and Davis (1993) explain, "Because the detention of students, and the search of their persons or premises involves possible tortious invasion of privacy, false imprisonment and the integrity of evidence in criminal proceedings, this is an area of legal responsibility that should be coordinated with legal counsel" (p. V-48). Private institutions should also carefully review their various contractual relationships with students and state law in this important area. Current issues such as mandatory drug testing forecast more Fourth Amendment challenges of unreasonable search and seizure on the campuses of both public and private institutions.

Due Process

The Fourteenth Amendment provides, in part, for due process protection. The courts have held that students have a right to at least minimal due process standards in disciplinary hearings. Minimal standards include the right to a hearing, notice of the charges, an opportunity to respond to the charges, having a hearing before an impartial person or board, and having an appropriate hearing for the type of alleged offense (*Dixon* v. *Alabama State Board of Education,* 1961 [294 F.2d 150]). Gehring (1993) explains that "the process that is due depends on the nature of the right that is deprived. Thus, a minor violation in a residence hall would not demand the same amount of due process as if the student faced expulsion" (pp. 291–292). Private institutions do not need to adhere to the same due process standards as their public counterparts, but they must follow their own rules once they are established (*Harvey* v. *Palmer School of Chiropractic,* 1984 [363 N.W. 2d 443]), and they must treat students fairly (*Clayton* v. *Board of Trustees of Princeton University,* 1985 [608 F. Supp. 413]).

In general, the courts have also not interfered in academic matters. In *Ewing* v. *Board of Regents of the University of Michigan* (1985 [106 Sup. Ct. 507]), the Supreme Court declared in part that courts may not interfere in a genuine academic decision unless "it is such a departure from accepted academic norms as to indicate that the faculty member or the committee did not exercise professional judgment" (p. 507). Student affairs administrators can take immediate action to suspend a student who poses a real and genuine threat to the welfare of the community. Such summary suspensions can be made on an interim basis, but a hearing must follow, and the institution must follow its own rules in taking such a serious step (*Swanson* v. *Wesley College,* 1979 [402 A.2d 401]).

Equal Protection

The Fourteenth Amendment also provides that no person shall be denied equal protection under the law. This clause applies to private institutions when they are acting under "color of state law." Gehring (1993) indicates that "the equal protection clause means that if an institution is engaged in state action, similarly situated individuals must be treated equally. Unless a fundamental right is denied to a class of people or a 'suspect class' is created, only a rational relationship between the classes of people created by the different treatment and the legitimate interests of the state must be demonstrated" (p. 293). In combination with civil rights legislation, the Fourteenth Amendment provides powerful protection to students and others.

Civil Rights Issues

The various civil rights laws, which prohibit discrimination against certain protected classes of individuals, can influence all aspects of a student affairs operation. This section reviews applicable federal statutes; the reader is cautioned to review state civil rights laws as well.

Civil Rights Statutes

Seven broad statutes exist that prohibit discrimination for certain classes of individuals and require affirmative actions on the part of colleges and universities. The statutes include Section 1981, Section 1983, Title VI, Title VII, Title IX, Section 504, and the Americans with Disabilities Act.

The Civil Rights Act of 1966 (*U.S. Code*, Vol. 42, sec. 1981) is a broad statute regarding racial discrimination, linked to the Thirteenth Amendment and applying to both public and private acts. Under Section 1981, a showing of state action is not required for the law to apply to private institutions, but it has not been widely applied to higher education because the plaintiff must prove that there has been purposeful and intentional discrimination by the defendant (*Williams* v. *De Kalb County*, 1978 [582 F.2d 2–3]).

Unlike claims under Section 1981, claims under Section 1983 are commonly used in litigation involving institutions of higher education. Under Section 1983, a plaintiff must only prove that he or she has been deprived of federally protected rights and that the deprivation occurred under color of state law (*Weise* v. *Syracuse University*, 1982 [522 F.2d 397]).

In 1954 racial discrimination in public schools was declared unconstitutional by the Supreme Court (*Brown* v. *Board of Education of Topeka*, 1954 [347 U.S. 483]). Although *Brown* had far-reaching implications, it did not reach into the private sector. Title VI (*U.S. Code*, Vol. 42, sec. 2000d-1) was enacted to fill this gap. Title VI prohibits discrimination on the basis of race, color, or national origin in programs receiving federal financial assistance. In *Regents of the University of California* v. *Bakke* (1978 [438 U.S. 265]), a white male alleged reverse discrimination in the admissions process. The Court held that Title VI protected only certain classes. Although affirmative action and numerical quotas can be used to cure specific cases of prior racial discrimination, race cannot be the only factor in an admissions decision.

The provisions of Title VII apply only to employment. They prohibit discrimination on the basis of race, color, national origin, sex, or religion in businesses with fifteen or more employees. It has sweeping implications for the hiring, promotion, termination, and benefits of all employees in the academy. It is not possible to provide a full treatment of the subject here; see Schlie and Grossman's *Employment Discrimination Law* (1984).

Title IX (*U.S. Code*, Vol. 20, secs. 1681–1686) applies specifically to education and educational institutions. It prohibits discrimination on the basis of sex. Certain types of institutions are not subject to the provisions of Title IX, including those controlled by religious, military, or merchant marine organizations. *Grove City College* v. *Bell* (1984 [104 Sup. Ct. 1211]) established that Title IX does not cover the entire institution. Title IX also includes a prohibition against sexual harassment as part of the implementing regulations.

Section 504 of the Vocational Rehabilitation Act (*U.S. Code*, Vol. 29, secs. 791–794) prohibits discrimination on the basis of handicap for any otherwise qualified student in any program receiving federal financial assistance. The act broadly defines handicaps and the interpretation of what constitutes a handicap. The Supreme Court held in *Southeastern Community College* v. *Davis* (1979 [442 U.S. 397]) that a qualified person "is able to meet all of the program's requirements in spite of handicap(s)" (pp. 405–406), and under such conditions exclusion does not imply discrimination. Under Section 504, institutions must make reasonable accommodations for students with handicaps in housing, admissions, career counseling, and other services.

The Americans with Disabilities Act (ADA) (*U.S. Code*, Vol. 42, secs. 12101 et seq.) applies to employers, including institutions of higher education, with more than twenty-five employees. In addition to employment issues, the act and its implementing regulations focus on physical and program accommodations for people with disabilities. Any student affairs administrator with responsibility for facilities or programming open to the general public should consult with legal counsel concerning the potential influence of the ADA.

Implications for Practice

Each of these statutes has specific implications for student affairs. Racial discrimination is clearly prohibited in any form and has been condemned, when proved, in the courts.

Title IX issues include sexual harassment and gender equity in intercollegiate athletics. Two types of sexual harassment are defined in regulations issued by the Equal Employment Opportunity Commission (1980 [29 C.F.R. 1604.11]): quid pro quo and harassing behavior that creates a hostile environment. Buchanan (1993) notes that student employees may prevail in sexual harassment suits if "an institutional official knew or should have known of the harassment" (p. 499). Consensual relationships between students and faculty have also caused problems. Some institutions, including the University of Iowa, have prohibited such relationships, while others have only strongly discouraged them.

Gender equity in intercollegiate athletics is also an active agenda item. While it is not impermissible to award separate athletic scholarships for men's and women's teams on the basis of athletic ability, Title IX requires that institutions provide "reasonable opportunity for men and women to receive athletic financial assistance in proportion to the number of male and female students participating in the intercollegiate athletic program" (Weeks & Davis, 1993, p. V-84). In addition, the regulations require that men and women participating in intercollegiate athletics receive equal benefits in terms of travel, locker rooms, training opportunities, and the like. It is a complex problem with enormous financial implications for colleges and universities. In *Kelly* v. *Board of Trustees of the University of Illinois* (1993 [821 F. Supp. 237]), the Court held that the elimination of the men's swimming team, but not the women's team, did not violate Title IX when participation by men in athletics was proportionally larger than their enrollment in the university while women's participation was less than proportional. Finally, while claims under Section 504 have provided some clarity regarding what is a qualified handicap and what services must be provided to students with disabilities, ADA litigation is just now beginning to make its way into the courts.

Campus Safety and Security

Concern about the safety, security, and general health and well-being of college students has been the subject of federal legislation (which mirrors similar statutes in many states). The Drug Free Schools and Communities Act of 1989 requires institutions to develop and disseminate information to students regarding substance abuse. The Hate Crime Statistics Act of 1990 requires the U.S. attorney general to collect additional data about crimes that manifest evidence of prejudice based on race, religion, sexual orientation, or ethnicity (Buchanan, 1993).

The Student Right-to-Know and Campus Security Act of 1990 requires colleges and universities to collect data on certain defined crimes; to advise students, faculty, and staff in writing of those crimes; to have a plan for emergency notification of criminal activity; and to publish crime statistics on an annual basis. Data for the prior three years must be included in all reports, and the reports must be available to current students and applicants. Additionally, the act requires that the institution annually publish the graduation rates of all student intercollegiate athletes.

Rape and sexual assault on campus are also of great legislative interest, and a number of bills have been introduced (although not passed) regarding this important area of concern. Universities have an obligation to provide appropriate support services to victims of sexual assault and rape and should engage in prevention activities to avoid such problems.

Contracts

As indicated above, the contractual relationship between a student and an institution has been the basis of a great deal of litigation. Cases have been litigated regarding admissions in both private and public institutions (*Nuttleman* v. *Case Western Reserve University*, 1981 [560 F. Supp. 1]; *Hall* v. *University of Minnesota et al.*, 1982 [530 F. Supp. 104]). Institutions' admissions policies have been upheld by the courts in all cases where the institution included specific language in its publications reserving certain rights for the institution and clearly articulating its procedures.

Discipline cases, both academic and behavioral, have also been litigated under contract theory. The courts have been reluctant to interfere in matters involving the judgment of professionals; however, when it could be proved that institutional officials acted in an arbitrary and capricious manner, the institutions have been subject to judicial scrutiny for their actions (*McDonald* v. *Hogness,* 1979 [598 P.2d 707]).

The right of an institution to alter requirements, change fees, and make other adjustments during a student's period of enrollment has been upheld by the courts, if such changes are reasonable (*Mahavongsanan* v. *Hall,* 1976 [529 F.2d 488]). Tuition and fee refunds have also been litigated as a contractual obligation, and as long as the institution included appropriate disclaimers in its publications regarding costs, they have been upheld by the courts (*Basch* v. *George Washington University,* 1977 [370 A.2d 1364]; *Prusack* v. *State,* 1986 [498 N.Y.S. 2d 455]). Administrators would be well advised to place disclaimers in their publications, to educate their staff about the importance of oral statements, and to ensure that their regulations are fair, equitable, and reasonable.

Liability

Many factors have contributed to administrators' growing concern regarding personal and institutional liability. Litigation has increased, insurance costs have risen, and the number of contractual disputes have increased—all of these developments have contributed to concern about liability.

The question of whether a public institution—or a private institution engaging in state action—is immune from suit is difficult to answer. State law is the primary determining factor. Additional factors include whether the institution was engaged in state action, the charter provisions of the school, and other state statutes.

Tort Liability

Preventing and defending against liability claims in colleges and universities is both difficult and complex. The most common forms of liability actions fall under the doctrine of torts. As Kaplin (1985) explains, "A tort is broadly defined as a civil wrong, other than a breach of contract, for which the courts will allow a damage remedy" (p. 55). Tort actions may be brought in the event of either a direct invasion of some legal right of a person or a failure to meet a public duty or obligation toward a person.

Negligence There are three legal prerequisites for pressing a claim of negligence: (1) the defendant owed a duty of care to the claimant, (2) the defendant breached that duty, and (3) the breach of duty was the proximate cause of injury. Courts have held that, in regard to persons invited onto campus, institutions of higher education have a duty to take ordinary and reasonable care with respect to the condition of their premises (*Mead* v. *Nassau Community College,* 1985 [483 N.Y.S. 2d 953]). When a person is on the institution's property for his or her own convenience but with the sufferance of the institution, the institution owes the duty of maintaining the property in a reasonably safe condition. A trespasser is on the property without the legal permission of the owner, and under these conditions an institution may have diminished legal responsibility in claims of negligence.

Accidents are also a source of negligence claims. If an institution knows of a dangerous condition and fails to correct it, it can be held liable (*Lumbard* v. *Fireman's Fund Insurance Company,* 1974 [302 So. 2d 394]). But a person's suffering a fall or injury does not by itself establish negligence. When a person has knowingly assumed a risk, liability claims against institutions or their agents have not been upheld in the courts (*Dudley* v. *William Penn College,* 1974 [219 N.W.2d 484]).

Sexual Assault Cases of sexual assault have also been tried under claims of negligence. Such negligence claims have not been upheld when the assault was not foreseeable, there was not evidence of repeated criminal activity, and adequate security was in place (*Brown* v. *North Carolina Wesleyan College, Inc.,* 1983 [309 S.E.2d 701]). A claim of negligence was upheld, however, in *Mullins* v. *Pine Manor College* (1983 [449 N.E.2d 331]), in which the court declared that there was a special duty of care present, owing to the landlord-tenant relationship between the student and the institution.

Liability and Alcohol State law is the most important variable in determining liability with regard to alcohol. The institution may be found liable as a supervisor of student conduct, property owner, seller of alcohol, or social host. In *Bradshaw* v. *Rawlings* (1979 [612 F.2d 135]), however, an appellate court held that there was no duty on the part of a college to keep a student from getting into a car with an intoxicated person.

Unintentional injury is often associated with alcohol, and even when there was no intent to harm, both the institution and its agent may be found liable. State laws vary greatly in this area and should be clearly understood. Residence hall staff members at the University of California (*Zavala* v. *Regents of the University of California,* 1981 [125 Cal. App. 3d 648]) served alcohol to an intoxicated person who subsequently fell and was injured. Although he played a part in his own injury, the institution was held partially liable under California law.

Some institutions have established areas on campus where alcohol is sold. Special questions of liability may be involved in the operation of such premises, and the scope of state law as well as the criminal and civil penalties that attach under the law vary considerably. Roth (1986) indicates that negligence claims often arise on "failure to conduct an activity as a reasonably prudent person would do under similar circumstances" (p. 49). Potential liability connected with the sale of alcohol also extends to student organizations. Events, whether on or off campus, where alcohol is sold under the sponsorship of student organizations also involve special issues. Again, state law will prevail, including requirements for a temporary license and insurance. Social host liability statutes have also been adopted in many states.

Other Areas of Liability

There are a number of other areas of potential liability that should be of concern to student affairs administrators. These include defamation or libel, civil rights liability, and contract liability. Each is an important area of the law, and legal advice should be sought in all cases of potential liability.

Working with Legal Counsel

Throughout this chapter reference has been made to working with legal counsel and seeking legal advice. Whether the attorney is an in-house counsel, on retainer to the institution, or hired to defend a specific case, the administrator must define the relationship with the attorney and determine who is the client. In matters of policy, attorneys should provide competent legal advice; however, it is the administrator's responsibility to determine what action should be taken. Too often, administrators abrogate their decision-making responsibilities to attorneys.

Duncan (1993) provides cogent advice on working with an attorney when there is a crisis or an administrator is being sued. She cautions that the student affairs administrator should make no assumptions and should inform the attorney of all the facts, get approval prior to commenting or writing about the case, and get training for a deposition. Duncan reminds practitioners that although an out-of-court settlement may not be what an administrator wants personally, it may be in the best interest of the institution. Finally, if one is unsure about the quality of legal advice received, it is worthwhile to engage a private attorney to protect one's personal interests if they may differ from those of the institution.

Emerging Issues

As indicated earlier in this chapter, a number of points in the law and the relationship of the law to students, institutions, and administrators have not been settled. In addition, the following items may be the source of new law in the future.

AIDS and HIV

As more is learned about this deadly disease, the implications for health care, the duty to warn, and relationships with students, faculty, and staff become more profound. It is not yet clear, for example, whether AIDS is protected under Section 504.

Affirmative Action

Institutional admissions and hiring policies will be influenced by the current national review of affirmative action policies. The award of race-based scholarships as a method of increasing student diversity, for example, is currently being litigated.

Domestic Partner Benefits

Until the issue of the status of domestic partners becomes more clear legally, this will be a constant issue for administrators dealing with students and staff on campus.

Employee Expression

Where does freedom of expression end and the responsibility of the individual to the institution begin? This issue will be litigated in future years as individuals speak out on a variety of topics and issues.

Conclusion

Absent from the above discussion was a review of the Family Educational Rights and Privacy Act, immigration laws, and copyright laws. (Space does not permit a full discussion of these issues.) It is clear, however, that the law is a part of professional practice in student affairs. Staff training in the legal implications of student affairs is required for sound practice. Publications should be reviewed. Legal assistance should be sought, early and often, and the student affairs administrator should exercise sound judgment when receiving that advice. Administrators should not be afraid to challenge traditional practices if they are inappropriate. Finally, student affairs officers should exercise the best judgment possible based on the facts, including the educational mission of the institution. The law is one of many tools available to student affairs administrators to meet the goals of honesty, fairness, equity, and responsibility.

References

Alexander, K., & Solomon, E. (1972). *College and university law.* Charlottesville, VA: Michie.

Barr, M. J., & Associates (1988). *Student services and the law: A handbook for practitioners.* San Francisco: Jossey-Bass.

Buchanan, E. T. (1993). The changing role of government in higher education. In M. J. Barr & Associates, *The handbook of student affairs administration* (pp. 493–508). San Francisco: Jossey-Bass.

Duncan, M. A. (1993). Dealing with campus crises. In M. J. Barr & Associates, *The handbook of student affairs administration* (pp. 340–348). San Francisco: Jossey-Bass.

Gehring, D. D. (1993). Understanding legal constraints on practice. In M. J. Barr & Associates, *The handbook of student affairs administration* (pp. 274–299). San Francisco: Jossey-Bass.

Kaplin, W. A. (1985). *The law of higher education: A comprehensive guide to legal implications of administrative decision making* (2nd ed.). San Francisco: Jossey-Bass.

Roth, R. A. (1986). The impact of liquor liability on colleges and universities. *Journal of College and University Law, 13*(1), 45–64.

Schlie, B., & Grossman, P. (1984). *Employment discrimination law.* Washington, DC: Bureau of National Affairs.

Thompson, J. (1976). *Policymaking in American public education.* Englewood Cliffs, NJ: Prentice Hall.

Weeks, K. M., & Davis, D. (Eds.). (1993). *Legal deskbook for administrators of independent colleges and universities* (2nd ed.). Waco, TX: Baylor University Center for Constitutional Studies.

Wright, C. A. (1969). The Constitution on campus. *Vanderbilt Law Review, 22,* 1027–1088.

Legal Case References

American Civil Liberties Union of Virginia, Inc. v. Radford College, 315 F. Supp. 893 (W.D. Va. 1970).

American Future Systems, Inc. v. Pennsylvania State University, 464 F. Supp. 1252 (1979), 752 F.2d 854 (1984).

American Future Systems, Inc. v. Pennsylvania State University, 618 F.2d. 252 (3d Cir. 1980).

American Future Systems, Inc. v. Pennsylvania State University, 688 F.2d. 907 (3d Cir. 1982).

American Future Systems, Inc. v. Pennsylvania State University, 568 F. Supp. 666 (M.D. Pa. 1983).

Basch v. George Washington University, 370 A.2d 1364 (D.C. Cir. 1977).

Bradshaw v. Rawlings, 612 F.2d 135 (3d Cir. 1979); cert. den.446 U.S. 909, 100 S. Ct. 1836 (1980).

Brown v. Board of Education, 347 U.S. 483 (1954).

Brown v. North Carolina Wesleyan College, Inc., 309 S.E.2d 701 (N.C. App. 1983).

Clayton v. Trustees of Princeton University, 608 F. Supp. 413 (D. N.J. 1985).

Commonwealth of Pennsylvania v. Tate, 432 A.2d. 1382 (Pa. 1981).

Dickey v. Alabama State Board of Education, 273 F. Supp. 613 (1967).

Dixon v. Alabama Board of Education, 294 F.2d. 150 (5th Cir. 1961), cert. denied 368 U.S. 930 (1961).

Doe v. University of Michigan, 721 F. Supp. 852 (E.D. Mich. So. Div. 1989).

Dudley v. William Penn College, 219 N.W.2d. 484 (Iowa, 1974).

Ewing v. Board of Regents of the University of Michigan, 743 F.2d 913 (6th Cir. 1984); rev'd (other grounds) 106 S. Ct. 507 (1985).

Gay Lib v. University of Missouri, 58 F.2d. 848 (8th Cir. 1977).

Gay Student Services v. Texas A&M University, 737 F.2d 1317 (5th Cir. 1984).

Grove City College v. Bell, 104 S. Ct. 1211 (1984).

Hall v. University of Minnesota et al., 530 F. Supp. 104 (D. Minn. 1982).

Harvey v. Palmer School of Chiropractic, 363 N.W.2d 443 (Iowa, 1984).

Healy v. James, 92 S. Ct. 2338 (1972).

Johnson v. Lincoln Christian College, 501 N.E.2d 1380 (Ill. App. 4th Dist. 1986).

Kelly v. Board of Trustees of University of Illinois, 821 F. Supp. 237 (C.D. Ill. 1993).

Krotoff v. Goucher College, 585 F.2d. 675 (4th Cir. 1978).

Lemon v. Kurtzman, 403 U.S. 602 (1971).

Lumbard v. Fireman's Fund Insurance Company, 302 So. 2d 394 (Ct. App. La. 1974).

Lueth v. St. Clair County Community College, 732 F. Supp. 1410 (E.D. Mich. S.D. 1990).

McDonald v. Hogness, 598 P.2d 707 (Wash. 1979).

Mahavongsanan v. Hall, 529 F.2d 488 (5th Cir. 1976).

Mazart v. State University of New York, 441 N.Y.S.2d 600 (Ct. Cl. 1976).

Minnesota Daily v. University of Minnesota, 719 F.2d 279 (8th Cir. 1983).

Mead v. Nassau County Community College, 483 N.Y.S.2d 953 (Sup. Ct. 1985).

Moore v. Student Affairs Committee of Troy State University, 284 F. Supp. 775 (M.D. Ala. 1976).

Mullins v. Pine Manor College, 449 N.E.2d 331 (1983).

National Socialist White People's Party v. Ringers, 473 F.2d 1010 (4th Cir. 1973).

New Jersey v. T.L.O., 469 U.S. 325 (1985).

Nuttleman v. Case Western Reserve University, 560 F. Supp. 1 (N.D. Ohio, 1981).

Papish v. Board of Curators of the University of Missouri, 93 S. Ct. 1197 (1973).

Prusack v. State, 498 N.Y.S.2d 455 (A.D.2 Dept. 1986).

Regents of the University of California v. Bakke, 438 U.S. 265 (1978).

Rosenberger v. Rector and Visitors of the University of Virginia, No. 94–329, (1995).

Schenk v. United States, 249 U.S. 47 (1919).

Siegel v. Regents of the University of California, 308 F. Supp. 832 (N.D. Calif. 1970).

Southeastern Community College v. Davis, 442 U.S. 397 (1979).

Smyth v. Lubbers, 398 F. Supp. 777 (W.D. Mich. 1975).

Stacy v. Williams, 306 F. Supp. 963 (N.D. Miss. 1969).

State v. Jordan, 53 Hawaii 634, 500 P.2d 56 (1972).

State v. Moore, cert. denied 429 U.S. 1004 (1976).

State v. Schmid, 423 A.2d 615 (N.J. 1980).

Swanson v. Wesley College, 402 A.2d 401 (Del. Sup. Ct. Kent Co. 1979).

Tinker v. Des Moines Independent School District, 393 U.S. 503 (1969).

Washington v. Chrisman, 455 U.S. 1, 102 S. Ct. 812 (1982).

Watson v. Board of Regents of the University of Colorado, 512 P2d. 1161 (1973).

Weise v. Syracuse University, 553 F. Supp. 675 (N.D.N.Y. 1982); 522 F.2d 397 (2d Cir. 1975).

Widmar v. Vincent, 103 S. Ct. 269 (1981).

Williams v. DeKalb County, 582 F.2d (5th Cir. 1978).

Zavala v. Regents of the University of California, 125 Cal. App. 3d 648, 178 Cal. Rptr. 185 (1981).

PART THREE

THEORETICAL BASES OF THE PROFESSION

Parts One and Two set a foundational context for student affairs practice. As the contributors to those parts made clear, understanding diverse students' experience with postsecondary education requires a thorough grounding in the historical and philosophical foundations of American higher education. But student affairs professionals also need a deep understanding of how students grow, develop, and learn. Therefore, this part presents the educational, development, and organization theory essential to the work of every student affairs practitioner.

The first two editions of this book illustrated the rich and growing theoretical heritage of the student affairs profession, covering a span of thirty years. They addressed the importance of theoretical perspectives for understanding

students and for designing programs and services to facilitate their intentional development. In the first edition, written in the late 1970s, the visionaries Delworth and Hanson included chapters on student development theory as well as environmental interaction theory. They expanded that theoretical frame in the second edition, written a decade later, to include organizational theory. This edition further expands the theoretical perspective to include discussions on what theory is and how it is useful in practice, new perspectives on identity development, and theoretical explorations of how students learn. This expanded theoretical focus constitutes an important frame of reference for professional practice.

The student affairs profession proudly relies on an interdisciplinary base, drawing from such areas as anthropology, sociology, psychology, business management, and education, to name a few. All professions engage in cycles, constructing and deconstructing new and old theories so as to be responsive to changing conditions. Student affairs practitioners have been well guided by theoretical perspectives, but many professionals have perhaps been lax in learning and applying new theoretical frames and engaging in theoretically grounded research on outcomes of such applications. The contributors to Part Three have made a concerted effort to illustrate how the theoretical perspectives they present apply to diverse students and diverse settings.

In Chapter Eight, Marylu McEwen introduces the role and nature of theory applicable to students and the higher education context, including logical positivism, critical science, and social construction. Her discussion on how and why theoretical applications are useful for one's own development and in one's work with students and the higher education environment reinforces the benefits of putting theory into practice. In Chapter Nine, Nancy Evans presents an overview of theories of student development, including psychosocial development theory (emphasizing adult and career development), cognitive-structural perspectives, and typology. Her discussion is informed by individual differences that might not have been taken into account in the original development of

select theories. In Chapter Ten, Marylu McEwen expands on important aspects of identity development, emphasizing social construction of such dimensions as gender, ability, race, and class. In Chapter Eleven, Pat King presents an overview of how students learn. As a central element in student development, student learning should be a primary expertise base of student development educators. In Chapter Twelve, Carney Strange reviews the importance of understanding how environments influence learning and development, with a particular focus on understanding campus climate and culture. In Chapter Thirteen, George Kuh explores both conventional and alternative views of how organizational systems function. Organizational systems and the expectations of people in various organizational relationships have a direct influence on the student experience.

It is encouraging that student affairs professionals are engaging in healthy and critical dialogue about the role and use of theoretical perspectives in practice and research. Part Three contributes to that inquiry by presenting both the breadth and depth of theoretical perspectives that should inform student affairs practice. The challenge for theoreticians today is to reformulate and integrate theory to make it useful in practice, and the challenge for practitioners is to inform their professional actions with appropriate theory and research.

CHAPTER EIGHT

THE NATURE AND USES OF THEORY

Marylu K. McEwen

As an academic adviser to students who have not yet made a decision about their major, it is difficult for you to understand some of the differences among your advisees—why, for example, many of your first-year student advisees, regardless of their background and abilities, seem almost preoccupied with whether they can handle college-level work.

You regularly conduct diversity training with groups of student leaders. You have noticed that some students are open and excited about the training and others seem highly resistant, and you are confused by their different reactions.

As a residence hall director, you supervise resident assistants and undergraduate students in four different buildings. In two units the students seem to possess a true sense of community; in another there are difficulties with discipline, vandalism, and hate speech; in the fourth unit the students seem passive and indifferent. You just can't make sense of why this would be the case.

You observe that the administrative division and the academic affairs division in the college where you work always seem to conduct their business differently. When someone from the administrative division wants to meet with you, he or she has always involved and received permission from his or her supervisor. But when a faculty member or an assistant academic dean meets with you, it's unusual for either the department chair or the dean to know about it. On the other hand, you usually inform your supervisor but rarely ask for permission. You wonder how and why all these units within the same college function so differently.

Are the differences in the above situations just chance occurrences? Are there ways to isolate and understand them? Most likely they are not random occurrences, and they may be understood through various theories or theoretical perspectives. Theories about how college students develop can help us understand the first two examples. Theories about how people and environments interact provide clues about the differences between the four residence hall units. Organizational theory offers perspectives on how different organizations function and what kinds of outcomes might be expected in different situations.

But what is theory? How are theories created? Do theories change? If so, how? What does theory mean to student affairs professionals? How has theory evolved in student affairs? How are theories used in student affairs? Why and how do student affairs professionals turn to theory? Does a professional select one theory to understand a particular phenomenon, or does one work with many theories?

This chapter contains eight sections plus a conclusion. Each section emphasizes a different aspect of theory in professional student affairs practice. The first section discusses why student affairs professionals need theory. The second section emphasizes the importance of looking at oneself in learning, selecting, and applying theories. The third section provides a framework for understanding the purposes and development of theory. In the fourth section, the focus is on the creation and use of theories for student affairs. Discussion of contemporary challenges to theory, contexts for theory development, and the social construction of theory make up the fifth, sixth, and seventh sections. Finally, how one makes individual choices about which theories to use is the subject of the eighth section.

Why Student Affairs Professionals Need Theory

Setting a context for student affairs professionals' use of theory is an important beginning point prior to examining the nature and uses of theory in general. Why do student affairs professionals use theory? First, it is difficult for any one person to hold simultaneously in his or her understanding all the aspects of what he or she is interested in—for instance, all the characteristics of a student's identity or all the components of a particular environment. Every one of us has our own informal theories about people, environments, students, human development, and how to work with students, although these theories or perspectives may not always be a conscious or clear part of our awareness. Thus people turn to theory—both formal and informal—to make the many complex facets of experience manageable, understandable, meaningful, and consistent rather than random.

What is the role of theory within the student affairs profession? Since the primary goals of student affairs practitioners are to serve students, to be student-centered, to understand and design academic environments, and to be experts about organizations and how they function, it is of utmost importance, both professionally and ethically, for them to know and understand the individuals, groups, and institutions they work with. One way to do this is through theory. Student affairs professionals are primarily theory users, consumers, and interpreters rather than formal theorists (although they are informal theory developers).

Where do the theories, models, and perspectives used in student affairs come from? Familiar sources include the disciplines of human development, developmental psychology, organizational development, and social psychology. Researchers who have studied the development of college students and the characteristics of organizations of higher education are another source. Theories and perspectives also evolve out of our own and others' observations and experiences and from literature and stories. Student affairs professionals can acquire a comprehensive understanding of theory about student and human development, higher education, and organizations in an interdisciplinary fashion, drawing not only from the literature on psychology and education but also from work in ethnic studies, sociology, history, literature, anthropology, philosophy, business, and management, as well as from oral and written stories and from one's own observations.

The Importance of Looking at Self

Before we discuss theory in general and the use of theory in student affairs in particular, consider the importance and value of looking at yourself. Knowing and examining oneself is especially important in relation to learning, critiquing, and using theories about student and human development. It is also pertinent to understanding and using other theories, such as organizational and environmental theory. Who each of us is, including the experiences and history we carry within us, creates the filters and frameworks through which we interpret others' experiences and perspectives (including those of organizations) and the theories we use in our work.

Thus each of us must begin by examining who we are and what we believe—our identity and our perspectives or informal theories on human nature, how people change, and the nature and functioning of organizations. For example, we should look at how we see race and how we view sexual orientation, whether we behave in ageist or sexist ways, and if we have anti-Semitic attitudes. We should also examine what we think about organizations and whether we are likely to be more attuned to the structure and processes of an organization or to the individuals and groups within it. Most important, each student affairs professional must see and understand himself or herself as a person with multiple characteristics (a certain race, gender, sexual orientation, ethnicity, social class, place of origin, and so on), which are part of his or her identity.

Examples exist in the literature about how theory is closely connected to one's sense of self. Helms's 1992 book *A Race Is a Nice Thing to Have* implies that White persons' understanding of theories and literature about people of color is inextricably linked with their sense of self as White. Research has shown that encountering a disability in another person elicits feelings about the self, about one's own helplessness, needs, and dependencies (Asch & Fine, 1988), thus hampering one's ability to see beyond the disability and understand the other person as an individual. In speaking about multiculturalism, Taylor (1992) described this effect succinctly: It "is *not* a commitment to learning about *them;* instead, it is a commitment to learning about myself—and ultimately, us" (p. 1).

Student affairs professionals need to ask questions of themselves, such as Who am I, as an able-bodied, middle-class, educated White woman? or a second-generation bisexual Asian man? or an African American woman? or a person with any other combination of characteristics? Such self-reflection will help you discover and understand those frameworks you use in both the consideration and the application of theory. Thoughtful, insightful, and continuing introspection about oneself is a necessary part of a student affairs professional's journey of learning, understanding, and using theory—about organizations, environments and their interactions with students, and, especially, college students and their development.

Uses and Development of Theory

Theory can be thought of as a description of the interrelationships between concepts and constructs. These interrelationships are often represented by a particular set of hypotheses—about human development, about organizations, about how persons and environments interact—developed by an individual or a group of individuals. Some hypotheses are empirical in nature, evolving from the collection and examination of quantitative or qualitative data. Others are rational in nature, based not on formal data but rather on ideas and relationships that attempt to explain a particular phenomenon.

Theory is a framework through which interpretations and understandings are constructed. Theory is used to describe human behavior (Knefelkamp, Widick & Parker, 1978, p. xiii), to explain, to predict, and to generate new knowledge and research. Moore and Upcraft (1990) offer a fifth purpose, based on Harmon's (1978) work that theory "permits" us to "influence outcomes" (p. 3). A sixth use of theory—often not cited—is to assess practice. Presenting the uses of theory in a slightly different way, Hall (1988, p. 36 as cited in Apple, 1993) says that theory should help us to "grasp, understand, and explain—to produce a more adequate knowledge of—the historical world and its processes; and thereby to inform our practice that we may transform it" (p. 25).

Let's relate these uses of theory to student affairs. For example, different theories may help us do the following: (1) *describe* first-year college students in terms of their concerns and their behavior, (2) *explain or understand* the differences in behavior between students who live in coeducational versus single-sex residence halls, (3) *predict* how staff in an office may act when a supervisor with a collaborative style is replaced by one with an autocratic style, (4) *generate* new research and theory about first-generation college students, (5) *influence* the development of students in an honors program by designing the program in certain ways, and (6) *assess* an institution's practices for creating a positive multicultural environment.

Formal criteria exist for evaluating theories. Patterson (1980) has summarized the following eight criteria for use in considering the adequacy of a theory: it should be (1) important, not trivial; (2) precise and understandable; (3) comprehensive; (4) simple and parsimonious but still comprehensive; (5) able to be operationalized; (6) empirically valid or verifiable; (7) able to generate new research, new knowledge, and new thinking and ideas; and (8) useful to practitioners. It is quite likely that many theories that seem valid and useful do not meet all of these criteria; nevertheless, the criteria provide appropriate goals for further theory development and refinement. For example, a theory may be comprehensive but not parsimonious, or a theory may be precise, understandable, and useful but difficult to put into operation.

Theory frequently serves to simplify the complex—to connect what appears to be random and to organize what appears to be chaotic. Theory is inherently reductionist; it helps one reduce or organize many difficult-to-manage pieces or dimensions into fewer, simpler parts and an integrated, organized whole. One aspect of theory that is frequently not described or discussed is that theory—whether empirical or rational—is developed through the lenses, or perspectives, of those who create or describe it. Thus theory is not objective, as is frequently claimed, but evolves from the subjectivity of the theorist or researchers. L. L. Knefelkamp (personal communication, October 16, 1980) has suggested that all theory is autobiographical—that is, theory represents the knowledge, experience, and worldviews of the theorists who construct it. King (1994) echoes this idea in stating that "we produce ourselves as theorists and remember ourselves at the center(s) of theory building" (p. 29). For example, even if they have completed exhaustive research, scholars developing a theory about human behavior in organizations might see in their data (and thus reflect in their theory) only those dimensions that reflect their own experience in organizations. Their theory becomes, in essence, an autobiographical account of their own organizational experiences. Thus it is important to be aware of the subjectivity and relativism of any theory.

Is theory static, or does it change? In general, theories evolve. Sometimes they are changed, or new theories develop from old ones. People frequently see theory as static, existing in a given form, never changing. But if a theory meets the criteria of a good theory, then it serves to generate new research and new ideas, which in turn inform new theories. Practice also informs theory, as well as scholarly and public critiques. Theory generates new theory.

Theory development also takes place because of shifts in paradigms. Kuh, Whitt, and Shedd (1987) define a paradigm as a set of "assumptions and beliefs about fundamental laws or relationships that explain how the world works" (p. 2). A dominant paradigm represents the prevailing, overriding set of assumptions about the nature of a given subject (such as human development). Kuh, Whitt, and Shedd explain that "when paradigms shift, understandings are markedly altered" (p. 2). They elegantly describe the "silent revolution" (p. 1) that takes place when a dominant paradigm gives way to an emergent paradigm, the accompanying theoretical shifts in related disciplines, and the implications of paradigm shifts for student affairs. Conventional views or beliefs about, for example, the goal-directed nature of organizations or the highly individualistic nature of human beings are replaced within the emergent paradigm by alternate perspectives describing the relational and contextual aspects of organizations or individuals. With different or changing beliefs and assumptions now at the core of people's understanding of reality, new theories are developed. (See Chapter Fourteen for an extensive discussion of how paradigm shifts have led to new thinking and new theories about leadership.)

Theory generation and development is a constantly evolving, dynamic process. Some theories may stand the tests of time, practice, and research and continue to exist in a minimally changed state. Some theories encounter few challenges from scholars and practitioners; others face many challenges. In general, however, the evolution of a theory follows an identifiable cycle: a new theory leads to research and new forms of practice, which in turn inform the existing theory, which is then modified or changed. Sometimes a theory is changed by a theorist; other times an alternate theory is proposed by others. A couple of examples of theory evolution may be helpful.

Chickering's theory of the psychosocial development of college students (1969), described in Chapter Nine, was modified in work by Chickering and Reisser in 1993. The modifications were based both on new understandings from the original theorist (Thomas & Chickering, 1984) and on research by others. Kohlberg's (1975) theory of moral development also evolved based on his own work and that of colleagues. There were no major changes in the foundations of his theory until Gilligan (1982), formerly a student of Kohlberg (Larrabee, 1993), found that a gender-related perspective of care seemed to have been left out of Kohlberg's theory. Gilligan offered her own perspective on moral development, one related to care and responsibility as opposed to Kohlberg's rights and justice orientation. Kohlberg's and Gilligan's theories of moral development now exist side by side, one theory having provided a partial springboard for the development of the other. These two theories also represent different paradigms; Kohlberg's was the conventional paradigm, Gilligan's the emergent one.

Creation and Use of Theory in Student Affairs

Theory, some formal, some informal, has no doubt existed in student affairs from the beginning. Some of the early textbooks on student affairs provide evidence of the use of traditional psychological theories and, to some degree, theories on management, organizations, and administration.

Research specific to college students and their development can be traced to the fifties and early sixties, first to Nevitt Sanford and his colleagues at Vassar College (Canon, 1988) and then to the publication of Sanford's classic, *The American College* (1962). The 1960s were a time of much writing and research about college students, primarily by the psychologists Roy Heath, Douglas Heath, Kenneth Keniston, Stanley King, Arthur Chickering, and William Perry, in addition to Sanford. The student affairs profession embraced these theorists and their research. Robert Brown's (1972) call for student development to become central to the profession was enthusiastically answered, and student development theory became a foundation of the student affairs profession in the mid to late 1970s. Clyde Parker, Lee Knefelkamp, and Carole Widick, at the University of Minnesota, first brought the multiple theoretical and research bases of student development theory together, providing an organized schema of theories for understanding student development and practicing student affairs. Further, Knefelkamp (1982) suggests that student development theory provides a common language for both student affairs professionals and faculty in higher education. Thus the importance and centrality given to theory by the student affairs profession is primarily due to the importance of student development theory to the field, although environmental and organizational theory are also influential.

Contemporary Challenges to Theory

It can be easy to accept theory without question and use it in practice without challenge. Yet one of the important components of knowing and using theory is to evaluate it, both within practice and in relationship to new literature and new research. There are also, however, other considerations in using theory.

Sampson (1989) identified six challenges to psychological theory that can also be applied to theories used in student affairs: (1) cross-cultural investigation, which points out that a Western worldview is frequently assumed in theory and looks for perspectives that are not part of the dominant literature; (2) feminist reconceptualizations, which challenge patriarchal views and offer alternative perspectives; (3) social constructionism, which proposes that concepts and theories are "social and historical constructions, not naturally occurring objects" (p. 2); (4) systems theory, in which persons and constructs are viewed in relation to an overall whole rather than as separate individual entities; (5) critical theory, which "claims that through self-reflection it reveals the distortions and malformations of social life" (Gibson, 1986, p. 36); and (6) deconstructionism, which challenges "all notions that involve the primacy of the subject (or author)"—or theorist—in order "to undo, not to destroy" (Sampson, 1989, pp. 2, 7). These challenges, although different, are overlapping and not mutually exclusive.

What do these challenges mean for student affairs professionals' use of human development theory, organizational theory, and theories about how people interact with their environment? They suggest six ways in which student affairs professionals need to consider and examine theory. First, theory must be examined in terms of its implicit worldview and those worldviews or cross-cultural perspectives that are absent. In many theories of human behavior, for example, individualism is valued, but how one relates to others (such as seeing oneself as part of a family) is ignored or negated. Second, underlying assumptions about gender (and other individual conditions), patriarchy, dominance, and power should be identified. Theories that embrace personal independence and devalue social interdependence reflect a male orientation. Third, how a theory has been socially constructed—under what social conditions, at what point in history, by whom, and with whom—should be considered. For instance, knowing that many theories and models about college students were developed in the 1950s and 1960s—usually by male psychologists and based on research with male students at private, elitist colleges—has a significant impact on one's understanding of how student development has traditionally been conceptualized.

A fourth consideration is whether or not a theory regards the person as part of a whole or as a separate, discrete entity, seemingly without an external context and impervious to the influence of others. Excellent examples are early retention models about underrepresented student groups, in which deficits in the students were identified but the institutional systems they were recruited into were not considered. Critical theory, a fifth challenge, reminds us to engage people as active participants in theory and research rather than solely as subjects. For instance, studying the involvement of commuter students might mean not only collecting traditional data about their participation but also examining, with their participation, what it means to be involved and creating a dialogue with them about the tentative findings. The sixth challenge is to consider how a theory can be deconstructed (without destroying it). One way to deconstruct a theory of human behavior is to "peel away" the layers of the central constructs and relationships within it. For instance, to deconstruct a theory of identity development, we might first look at how the construct of identity is conceptualized, whose perspectives are reflected in such conceptualizations, what basis exists for the theory, and alternative ways to construct the theory, given that theory base.

King (1994) talks about theory as a political object. She raises a number of questions about theory: What political and personal beliefs are incorporated within a theory? How do formal, generic theories mask or hide informal, specialized ones? On the other hand, what "specialized" theories are really broad and comprehensive? King (1994) adds a question raised by Collins: "When is it important *not* to display under the sign 'theory' and for what reasons?" (p. 29). In considering environmental theories, for example, King might ask the following questions: What is implicit in a theory about what an environment should be? (That is, what is a "positive" environment?) Do formal, generic environmental theories gloss over important information about the college classroom setting or student participation in the campus community? Does a particular environmental theory presented as broad and comprehensive more accurately represent a specialized environment, such as student organizations, than some purportedly specialized theories? And drawing from Collins's (1991) question, what kinds of environments are not addressed by environmental theories, and why not? For example, theories about the culture or environment of a university president's office may not have been created, in part to keep hidden the intimate and innermost workings that may go on in such an office. Or, drawing on an example used by Collins (1991), persons who study something such as "cultures of resistance" may choose not to describe their work as "theory." Some researchers or scholars may see theory as antagonistic or contradictory to the liberation or emancipation implied in "culture of resistance" (p. 18).

Contexts for the Development of Theory

Theory is developed within different contexts or perspectives about knowledge. Earlier in this chapter, shifts in paradigms, from dominant, conventional paradigms to emergent ones, were identified as one of many reasons why new theory is developed. It is useful to examine different modes of inquiry and the kinds of knowledge they produce. One of these modes, the natural scientific method, represents a conventional paradigm concerning how knowledge is acquired. Two other modes, critical theory and interpretive science, have evolved from a newer paradigm.

In the social and human sciences, three dominant modes of inquiry are acknowledged (Coomer & Hultgren, 1989). The empirical-analytic mode of inquiry, also known as logical positivism or the natural scientific method (Copa, 1988), is the method most often used in disciplines such as psychology and the natural sciences to explain, predict, and control phenomena (including social phenomena) (Coomer & Hultgren, 1989; Copa, 1988). The second mode, interpretive science, allows scholars in the social and human sciences "to understand the assumptions and meanings of everyday life" (Copa, 1988, p. 1). The third dominant mode is critical science (Coomer & Hultgren, 1989) or critical theory, which seeks to examine and "disclose personal and social interpretations and practices that are distorted by ideology" (Copa, 1988, p. 1).

The concept of theory holds ideologically different meanings and purposes among these three modes of inquiry. In the empirical-analytic mode, theory is seen as a set of "scientific laws which describe human and social behavior. . . . Theory is objective and transcends individual involvement and experience" (Copa, 1988, p. 1). In interpretive science, theory comes out of the meanings and actions of the group studied; theory is a set of interpretations and underlying schema representing insights by the researcher into the human experiences of the participants (Copa, 1988). The purpose of critical science or critical theory, in contrast, is to discover or uncover the underlying, hidden, or unreflected aspects of social life that are distorted by ideology (Coomer & Hultgren, 1989; Copa, 1988); a basic assumption of critical theory is that theory cannot be "disinterested"—it cannot be objective (Copa, 1988, p. 1). Critical theory, then, becomes a means for enlightening or emancipating individuals so they can come to see themselves and their social situations in radically different ways (Coomer & Hultgren, 1989; Copa, 1988).

The mode of inquiry that has traditionally been used in both education and psychology is logical positivism. Borg and Gall (1989) suggest that this method "has served educational research well" (p. 18). It is important to acknowledge that the natural scientific method has provided highly significant contributions to the theory and research base of student affairs. It is this mode of inquiry that has produced most of our knowledge to date about the development of college students, how individuals and environments interact, and how organizations function.

Nevertheless, at least two contemporary trends have led to closer examination and use in education and psychology of the other two modes of inquiry. Critics of logical positivism have raised important questions about whether theory and research under that paradigm can truly be objective and value-free. According to Borg and Gall (1989), many scholars have also been rethinking many of the assumptions of logical positivism; much of this reexamination was stimulated by Thomas Kuhn's book *The Structure of Scientific Revolutions* (1962).

Critical science and critical theory provide a valuable set of tools and perspectives for the analysis and development of theory in student affairs. Many theories of human development have their roots in psychology, a discipline that has, as noted above, embraced almost unilaterally the positivist, empirical mode of inquiry. According to Comstock (1982), however, the positivist research method "reifies social processes by naturalizing social phenomena, addressing them as eternal to our understandings, and denying their socio-historical constructedness" (p. 371). Critical social science, on the other hand, evolves out of a historical-social context. Further, in critical social science it is recognized that critical knowledge is never neutral and "that social scientists are participants [rather than impartial researchers] in the socio-historical development of human action and understanding" (Comstock, 1982, p. 377). Comstock summarizes the nature of critical social science as that which "sees society as humanly constructed and, in turn, human nature as a collective self-construction" (p. 377). Social constructionism and deconstructionism, two of Sampson's challenges to psychological theory (1989), might be viewed as two outcomes of critical theory.

Theory as Social Construction

Critical science encourages self-reflection and critical analysis; thus it encourages us to unveil the hidden and underlying dimensions of a theory, including the unacknowledged aspects of constructs such as race, gender, social class, and sexual orientation. By engaging in critical science, we can come to see how concepts and theories are socially constructed. Most constructs, such as race or sexual orientation, have meaning only when they are viewed or considered within a sociohistorical context. For instance, it is not the biological meaning of race that we draw on; rather, it is how this society at this point in history conceives of race. In the United States, *race* refers to skin color, language, cultural traditions, patterns of communication, and values and beliefs. It is surrounded by the context of the civil rights movement and the shared history of specific groups of people. *Race,* therefore, is not an objective term meaning what genetically constitutes different groups of people; it is a subjective term that has been socially constructed.

Just as concepts are socially constructed, so too are theories. Theories are composed of concepts and interrelationships—concepts that are socially constructed and interrelationships formed from the social constructions of theorists. Theories are therefore extensions of social constructions, informed to a degree by the data from which they are developed. Important dimensions of the social construction of theory include who the theorist is, on whom the theory is based, for whom the theory is designed, and in what sociohistorical context the theory has been developed. Thus theories are not value-free, they are not objective, and they are not "pure" representations of human development. A significant problem with many theories is that the theorists have not put forth their concepts, assumptions, and hypotheses *as* socially constructed. In other words, theorists have not usually stated who they are in terms of socially constructed characteristics, backgrounds, values, and other factors that may influence the development and presentation of their theory. Further, in theories of human development, the basis for the theory—for example, the participants, the nature of the research, where the research was conducted—is often minimally provided, if at all. Not having adequate information about either the theorist or the basis for the theory means that the theory may be applied too broadly or that concepts and hypotheses may be readily accepted without question.

Examining the ways in which a theory is socially constructed means making the invisible social constructions visible, the hidden purposes explicit, and the camouflaged populations for whom the theory is intended known and acknowledged. This challenge also means revealing the social constructions of the concepts included in the theory. Further, it is necessary for us to examine ourselves to make known what lenses and filters we are using to understand, portray, and apply the theory.

One outcome or goal of critical science, therefore, is to reveal the social construction of theories. A second outcome may be the deconstruction or undoing of theories. We must remember that, as Sampson (1989) reminds us, to deconstruct a theory means "to undo, not to destroy" (p. 7). In studying, learning, and using theory, it may be necessary for us to undo, or unravel, some of the theory. Sampson indicates that deconstruction usually becomes "the analysis of language and symbolic practices as the key to be deciphered. Each seriously challenges the Western understanding of the person-society relationship, in particular the centrality and the sovereignty of the individual" (p. 6). The difficulty, Sampson says, is "that the tools used to deconstruct this tradition come from that very tradition" (p. 7). Sampson suggests that deconstruction involves the "task of employing the familiar and commonly known in order to deconstruct the familiar and commonly known" (p. 7). So the question is this: Can we, through our lenses created out of Western thought and understanding, undo and unveil those very structures—the language, symbolism, constructs, and theories—that are at the very heart of the Western tradition?

A third outcome of critical theory is to demonstrate that the objects of theories, including identity, learning, environments, and organizations, are themselves socially constructed. Individuals, organizations, and environments, including students and organizations of higher education, do not exist or develop in a vacuum. Individuals live in social settings, each with historical and political elements. Individuals have their unique family histories, and different cohorts of individuals have varying sociopolitical and historical experiences. The identity that one creates for oneself comes out of one's lived experience. Organizations and environments are composed of people and created by people; organizations and environments also have different heritages and various sociopolitical and historical elements. Even what I write about in this chapter is socially constructed. This chapter is constructed at a certain point in history, and it is influenced by what I know and how I see the world.

A fourth outcome of critical theory is to lay bare the dimensions of power and oppression implicit in theory, dimensions that are frequently not addressed. Fine (1992) points out that characteristics such as gender, race, and class are usually studied as differences; the power dimensions between or within genders, races, or social classes are usually not addressed. When power is not addressed, then women, people of color, and other oppressed groups appear in the research as "less than," as not meeting the "standards" or norms of the dominant group, as a special case. Fine cautions us against our vulnerability "to the possibilities of *gender essentialism* and *racial/ethnic/class erasure*" (p. 15). (Essentialism means treating a particular characteristic such as gender or race as having an inherent "biological inequality"; Frankenberg, 1993, p. 14.) Taking an activist stance toward feminist researchers, Fine (1992) offers advice that we in student affairs would do well to heed: If we "do not take critical, activist, and open stances on our own work, then we collude in reproducing social silences through the social sciences" (p. 206). In other words, Fine is suggesting that not to engage in critical inquiry is to perpetuate the errors, omissions, and overgeneralizations residing within the theories that we use in student affairs.

Collins (1991) talks about what theories should be: "Theory and intellectual creativity are not the province of a select few but instead emanate from a range of people" (p. xiii). She also points out that "oppressed groups are frequently placed in the situation of being listened to only if we frame our ideas in the language that is familiar to and comfortable for a dominant group" (p. xiii). Addressing power from the consideration of privilege, Collins encourages us to be cognizant of theory's role "in sustaining hierarchies of privilege" (p. xii).

In summary, to consider theory as social construction means taking a social constructivist view of both the central concepts of the theory and the ways in which the theory has been created. It implies that we need to engage in a "peeling away of the layers" of the theory to uncover and discover its hidden and unstated bases and intentions. How power and oppression function within a theory, its development, and its applications also should be examined. By engaging

in critical science, we in student affairs can develop deeper and clearer understandings of the theories available to us and how and why we select certain theories to aid us in practice.

Choosing Which Theories to Use

A value both explicit and implicit in student affairs is that student affairs professionals should guide and inform their professional practice with appropriate theories. As you will see in the chapters that follow, however, there are multiple
theories for the many phenomena and constructs relevant to student affairs. An
important question, often overwhelming, is How do you select which theory or
theories to guide your practice?

There are many perspectives about the selection and use of theory. One perspective offers a "purist" approach—that for a particular phenomenon, such as
understanding organizational change or students' cognitive development, one
should select and use a *single* theory. Proponents of this perspective believe a "true"
theory can stand alone—that is, it provides assumptions, defines relationships, and
describes how those relationships occur under given conditions. They also believe
that using more than one theory may violate the assumptions of individual theories and thus may invalidate the relationships and beliefs prescribed within any
theory.

A second perspective is to adopt an "eclectic" model. Eclectic use of theory
means a professional draws on the useful and relevant aspects of multiple theories and combines those aspects into a meaningful whole. Some people believe this
permits them to use the best parts of many theories, thus making the combined
usage stronger than any one theory. Opponents of such a perspective argue that
various assumptions of the individual theories may not be honored or may even
be violated. It is also possible that there is little if any consistency, for any one individual, from one usage to another, and little consistency from one individual to
another. Thus there is no common language or framework within which professionals can discuss or deal with the phenomena of common interest.

In spite of the challenges to eclectic theory, many persons do not believe that
any one theory is comprehensive enough to adequately describe any given phenomenon. And, practically speaking, there are few individuals who adopt one theory exclusive of all others in a similar family or grouping of theories. Thus, what
guidelines can a student affairs professional use in selecting theories? Several guidelines are offered below.

Select a theory or theories that you understand and that make sense to you.
For instance, if a certain theory resonates for you and seems to appropriately

describe a certain phenomenon, then you are more likely to internalize that theory, understand it more deeply, and apply it in your practice. On the other hand, if a theory isn't very clear to you or doesn't "come alive," then you may find it more difficult to apply in your practice.

Knowing yourself, as discussed earlier in this chapter, will help you decide which theories to choose and which ones to "put back on the shelf." For theories that seem to fit you and your understanding of the world, ask yourself what it is about them that fits. Is it because they describe your own experiences? If so, whose experiences do you maybe not describe?

As noted above, theories are reductionistic—they describe some relationships and concepts but not others. So, what theory or theories do you draw on for *each* phenomenon of interest? In thinking about a student, you may be interested in understanding his or her psychosocial and cognitive development as well as his or her racial identity development. How, then, do you combine a theory or theories for each of these areas with one another? Or, you may want to draw on several theories to describe a single phenomenon. In either case, think about how the theories fit together. Do the assumptions of each theory fit with one another, or do some conflict? If they conflict, how do you understand the conflict, and on what basis could you decide the incongruence is not pertinent? What parts of each theory do you draw upon? What, then, is your own modified version of this melding of certain theories? Be thoughtful, be intentional, and, as Evans says in Chapter Nine, be intelligent about using theory. Be explicit about the theories you use.

Conclusion

The theories we use in student affairs come from many different sources, and they serve multiple and varied purposes. Theories are evolving, both in their own development and in how we use them in student affairs. Yet we must remember that theories are not pure; they are not perfect; they were not created and do not exist in a vacuum. Sampson's (1989) six challenges about theory and knowing and taking into account our own personal filters and values are important complements to the selection and use of theory. Critical science offers a method by which we can examine how a theory has been socially constructed and how it may need to be deconstructed. Finally, as a student affairs professional, it is necessary that one be thoughtful, intentional, and systematic in selecting which theory or theories to draw upon. It is also important to know why one has selected a theory, to know its strengths and limitations, and to be conscious of how selecting and applying a given theory relates to who you are as a person and as a student affairs professional.

References

Apple, M. W. (1993). Constructing the "other": Rightist reconstructions of common sense. In C. McCarthy & W. Crichlow (Eds.), *Race, identity, and representation in education* (pp. 24–39). New York: Routledge & Kegan Paul.

Asch, A., & Fine, M. (1988). Introduction: Beyond pedestals. In M. Fine & A. Asch (Eds.), *Women with disabilities: Essays in psychology, culture, and politics* (pp. 1–37). Philadelphia: Temple University Press.

Borg, W. R., & Gall, M. D. (1989). *Educational research: An introduction* (5th ed.). White Plains, NY: Longman.

Brown, R. D. (1972). *Student development in tomorrow's higher education: A return to the academy* (Student Personnel Monograph No. 16). Washington, DC: American College Personnel Association.

Canon, H. J. (1988). Nevitt Sanford: Gentle prophet, Jeffersonian rebel. *Journal of Counseling and Development, 66,* 451–457.

Chickering, A. W. (1969). *Education and identity.* San Francisco: Jossey-Bass.

Chickering, A. W., & Reisser, L. (1993). *Education and identity* (2nd ed.). San Francisco: Jossey-Bass.

Collins, P. H. (1991). *Black feminist thought: Knowledge, consciousness, and the politics of empowerment.* New York: Routledge, Chapman & Hall.

Comstock, D. E. (1982). A method for critical research. In E. Bredo & W. Feinberg (Eds.), *Knowledge values in social and educational research* (pp. 370–390). Philadelphia: Temple University Press.

Coomer, D. L., & Hultgren, F. H. (1989). Considering alternatives: An invitation to dialogue and question. In F. H. Hultgren & D. L. Coomer (Eds.), *Alternative modes of inquiry in home economics research* (pp. xv–xxiii). Peoria, IL: Glencoe.

Copa, P. (1988, July). *Perspectives underlying major views of educational theory and practice.* Chart presented at the Second International Conference on Thinking and Problem Solving in Home Economics, Columbus, OH.

Fine, M. (1992). *Disruptive voices: The possibilities of feminist research.* Ann Arbor: University of Michigan Press.

Frankenberg, R. (1993). *The social construction of whiteness: White women, race matters.* Minneapolis: University of Minnesota Press.

Gibson, R. (1986). *Critical theory and education.* London: Hodder & Stoughton.

Gilligan, C. (1982). *In a different voice.* Cambridge, MA: Harvard University Press.

Hall, S. (1988). The toad in the garden: Thatcherism among the theorists. In C. Nelson & L. Grosberg (Eds.), *Marxism and the interpretation of culture* (pp. 35–73). Urbana: University of Illinois Press.

Harmon, L. W. (1978). The counselor as consumer of research. In L. Goldman (Ed.), *Research methods for counselors: Practical approaches in field settings* (pp. 29–78). New York: Wiley.

Helms, J. E. (1992). *A race is a nice thing to have: A guide to being a White person, or understanding the White persons in your life.* Topeka, KS: Content Communications.

King, K. (1994). *Theory in its feminist travels: Conversations in U.S. women's movements.* Bloomington: Indiana University Press.

Knefelkamp, L. L. (1982). Faculty and student development in the '80s: Renewing the community of scholars. In H. F. Owens, C. H. Witten, & W. R. Bailey (Eds.), *College student personnel administration: An anthology* (pp. 373–391). Springfield, IL: Thomas.

Knefelkamp, L., Widick, C., & Parker, C. A. (1978). Editors' notes: Why bother with theory? In L. Knefelkamp, C. Widick, & C. A. Parker (Eds.), *Applying new developmental findings* (New Directions for Student Services No. 4, pp. vii–xvi). San Francisco: Jossey-Bass.

Kohlberg, L. (1975). The cognitive-developmental approach to moral education. *Phi Delta Kappan, 56,* 670–677.

Kuh, G. D., Whitt, E. J., & Shedd, J. D. (1987). *Student affairs work, 2001: A paradigmatic odyssey.* Washington, DC: American College Personnel Association.

Kuhn, T. S. (1962). *The structure of scientific revolutions.* Chicago: University of Chicago Press.

Larrabee, M. J. (1993). Gender and moral development: A challenge for feminist theory. In M. J. Larrabee (Ed.), *An ethic of care: Feminist and interdisciplinary perspectives* (pp. 3–16). New York: Routledge & Kegan Paul.

Moore, L. V., & Upcraft, M. L. (1990). Theory in student affairs: Evolving perspectives. In L. V. Moore (Ed.), *Evolving theoretical perspectives on students* (New Directions for Student Services No. 51, pp. 3–23). San Francisco: Jossey-Bass.

Patterson, C. H. (1980). *Theories of counseling and psychotherapy* (3rd ed.). New York: Harper & Row.

Sampson, E. E. (1989). The deconstruction of the self. In J. Shotter & K. J. Gergen (Eds.), *Texts of identity* (pp. 1–19). Newbury Park, CA: Sage.

Sanford, N. (1962). *The American college.* New York: Wiley.

Taylor, K. (1992, March 31). Remarks at awards luncheon at the annual conference of the National Association of Student Personnel Administrators, Cincinnati, OH.

Thomas, R., & Chickering, A. W. (1984). Education and identity revisited. *Journal of College Student Personnel, 25,* 392–399.

CHAPTER NINE

THEORIES OF STUDENT DEVELOPMENT

Nancy J. Evans

Allison recently accepted a new position as an academic adviser at an urban community college. Previously she was a hall director at a small private college, and she is amazed at how different the students are in her new setting. How is Allison to make sense of the differences in age, background, concerns, interests, and approaches to life she sees in these college students?

Student development theory provides a useful guide for student affairs professionals like Allison. It describes how students grow and change throughout their college years; it provides information about how development occurs and suggests conditions that encourage development. In this chapter, three different categories of student development theory are introduced: psychosocial theory, cognitive-structural theory, and typological theory. Each perspective examines student development through a different lens.

Psychosocial theory explores the personal and interpersonal aspects of college students' lives. Cognitive-structural theory examines students' intellectual development and addresses how they interpret their experiences. Typological theory posits that individuals are innately different from one another, possessing varied sets of characteristics that influence how they process information, make decisions, and handle developmental challenges. After the basic ideas and major theories associated with each school are discussed, applications of each type of theory to student affairs practice are discussed. The chapter then closes with a critique of student development theory.

Psychosocial Perspectives

Mary is a nineteen-year-old White sophomore at the private college where Allison previously worked. She is trying to identify a career direction and discover what matters to her as a person. Mary has always looked to her parents for guidance, but now she finds it important to strike out on her own.

Shawna, also a second-year student, attends the urban community college where Allison currently works. She is a thirty-five-year-old African American single parent who enrolled in college to create a better life for herself. Her main concern is to be a good role model for her children and to make a difference in their lives and the lives of others in her community.

Although they are both sophomores, these two women face very different challenges and look at life from different perspectives. Psychosocial theorists attempt to explain such differences. The major ideas associated with their approach are based primarily on the work of Erik Erikson (1959, 1968). Erikson suggested that development occurs over a series of eight age-linked, sequential stages that arise during each individual's lifetime. Within each stage, particular issues, called developmental tasks, become preeminent and must be addressed. Basic attitudes, or orientations toward the world, arise from the successful or unsuccessful resolution of each stage. Three of the stages—Trust versus Mistrust, Autonomy versus Shame and Doubt, and Initiative versus Guilt—arise before a child begins school. Industry versus Inferiority occurs during childhood, while Identity versus Role Confusion and Intimacy versus Isolation are the stages associated with adolescence and young adulthood. (See Chapter Ten for an expanded discussion of identity development.) Generativity versus Stagnation is the stage of middle adulthood, while the last stage, Integrity versus Despair, occurs in late adulthood.

Mary and Shawna are at different stages of this schematic of psychosocial development. Mary is at an earlier stage—Identity versus Role Confusion—dealing with such developmental tasks as determining a vocational direction and identifying a personal set of beliefs and values. Shawna, at the later stage of Generativity versus Stagnation, has already worked through the issues Mary is addressing and is focused on the developmental tasks of actively nurturing her offspring and contributing in a productive way to society.

According to Erikson (1959), each new stage occurs when internal psychological and biological changes interact with external social demands to create a developmental crisis, or turning point, in a person's life. For Mary, the maturation associated with young adulthood, along with the societal expectation that college students must choose a career, has contributed to a developmental crisis:

establishing her identity. Each such crisis offers heightened opportunity as well as vulnerability for the individual (Erikson, 1968).

A successful resolution of each developmental crisis leads to the development of new skills or attitudes. A less successful resolution, however, contributes to a negative self-image and restricts the individual's ability to successfully address future crises. Regression to previous stages and recycling of developmental issues frequently occur as individuals attempt to more successfully resolve previous crises. To work through the issues associated with making a contribution to her community, for example, Shawna might have to revisit issues associated with earlier stages, such as developing a sense of accomplishment and acquiring skills and knowledge.

Erikson did not specifically address the issues facing college students. Thus this section includes a discussion of the theories of Marcia (1966), Josselson (1987), Sanford (1966), and Chickering and Reisser (1993), all of which expand upon Erikson's ideas and focus on the development of college students. A review of Super's (1957) theory, a psychosocial perspective addressing career development, follows. Three theoretical orientations to adult development are also reviewed. The section concludes with a discussion of the uses of psychosocial theory in student affairs practice.

Marcia

James Marcia (1966) expanded Erikson's work related to the Identity versus Role Confusion stage of late adolescence. In a study of eighty-six male college students, Marcia found that identity resolution was based on two factors: (1) whether or not the individual had experienced a crisis period related to vocational choice, religion, or political ideology and (2) the extent of his or her personal commitment to a particular choice. Based on their study of women, Schenkel and Marcia (1972) added sexual values and standards as a fourth area in which crisis and commitment occurs. Marcia identified four styles of identity resolution:

Identity Diffusion. A crisis may or may not have been experienced. A commitment has not been made, but the person is not particularly concerned about his or her lack of direction.

Foreclosure. No crisis has been experienced. A commitment has been made based on others', particularly parents', values.

Moratorium. The individual is in a period of crisis and is struggling to make a commitment.

Identity Achievement. A crisis period has been experienced and a commitment has been made.

The four styles of identity resolution do not constitute hierarchical stages; students do not necessarily progress through them in order, nor do they always reach Identity Achievement.

Marcia's work indicates that not all students approach the identity resolution process similarly and that students at different identity status categories need different types of interventions to progress.

Josselson

Building on the work of Schenkel and Marcia, Josselson (1987) set out to systematically examine identity development in women. Using Marcia's interview protocol to assess the styles of identity resolution of their subjects and selecting equal numbers of women from each of Marcia's styles, Josselson interviewed sixty women when they were seniors in college and followed up with thirty-four of them ten to twelve years later. She found that, for the women she interviewed, those who had reached identity-resolution by the end of college had generally reached the early adult life stage. Social, sexual, and religious values, more than occupational and political values, were the significant areas of crisis and commitment for women in young adulthood. And most important, the degree to which the women deviated from or remained connected to their parents', particularly their mother's, value system largely determined the identity they formed.

According to Josselson, crisis in relationships, more than in any other area, leads to growth and change for women. In this study, relationships with men were found to be particularly important, either to satisfy dependency needs or to provide self-validation and support. Relationships, rather than work, were found to be the most important anchor for women.

Josselson's work suggests that identity development in women is based on different factors than in men and that the issues of separation from parents and formation of meaningful relationships are particularly salient for college women.

Sanford

Nevitt Sanford's major contribution to psychosocial theory is his concept of challenge and support. Building on Erikson's notion that resolution of developmental crises is encouraged by optimal dissonance (that is, a moderate, growth-enhancing level of discomfort with one's current functioning), Sanford (1966) suggested that a balance of challenge and support must be present for development to occur. If there is too little challenge, the individual may feel safe and comfortable, but development will not take place. On the other hand, too much challenge can induce maladaptive responses. According to Sanford, the amount of challenge a person can handle is contingent on the amount of support available.

Creating an appropriate balance between challenge and support in the college environment is an important factor in facilitating student development. The necessary amounts of challenge and support will vary from student to student based on their personality, background, and previous experiences. First-generation college students, for example, who have no idea of how to navigate the university environment, will find the experience especially challenging. Programs that assist such students in learning about the college experience are a crucial support.

Chickering

Chickering's landmark study of undergraduate students in thirteen small colleges appeared in 1969. His theory expanded upon Erikson's notions of identity and intimacy and suggested that the establishment of identity is the central developmental issue during the college years. He has recently revised his theory to incorporate new research findings and to be more inclusive of various student populations (Chickering & Reisser, 1993).

Chickering proposes seven vectors of development that contribute to the formation of identity. He notes that students move through these vectors at different rates, that vectors can interact with one another, and that students often find themselves reexamining issues associated with vectors they have previously worked through. Although not rigidly sequential, Chickering's vectors do build on each other and lead to greater complexity, stability, and integration. Chickering's work incorporates emotional, social, and intellectual aspects of development.

Chickering's seven vectors, as presented in his revised theory (Chickering & Reisser, 1993), include the following:

1. *Developing Competence.* This vector focuses on the tasks of developing intellectual, physical and manual, and interpersonal competence. In addition, students develop confidence in their abilities within these arenas.

2. *Managing Emotions.* In this vector, students develop the ability to recognize and accept emotions, as well as to appropriately express and control them. Chickering's (1969) original theory focused on aggression and sexual desire. His recent work addresses a more inclusive range of feelings.

3. *Moving Through Autonomy Toward Interdependence.* At this stage, students develop increased emotional independence, self-direction, problem-solving ability, persistence, and mobility, as well as recognition and acceptance of the importance of interdependence. To underscore the greater emphasis given to interdependence in his revised theory, Chickering has renamed this vector, which was previously titled *Developing Autonomy.*

4. *Developing Mature Interpersonal Relationships.* Previously titled *Freeing Interpersonal Relationships,* this vector has been moved back in sequence to acknowledge

that experiences with relationships contribute significantly to the development of a sense of self. Its tasks include the development of acceptance and appreciation of differences as well as the capacity for healthy and lasting intimate relationships.

5. *Establishing Identity.* A positive identity includes (1) comfort with body and appearance, (2) comfort with gender and sexual orientation, (3) a sense of one's social and cultural heritage, (4) a clear conception of self and comfort with one's roles and lifestyle, (5) a secure sense of self in light of feedback from significant others, (6) self-acceptance and self-esteem, and (7) personal stability and integration. In Chickering's revised theory, this vector now acknowledges differences in identity development based on gender, ethnicity, and sexual orientation.

6. *Developing Purpose.* This vector consists of developing clear vocational goals, making meaningful commitments to specific personal interests and activities, and establishing strong interpersonal commitments.

7. *Developing Integrity.* In this vector, students progress from rigid, moralistic thinking to a more humanized, personalized value system that acknowledges and respects the beliefs of others. Values and actions become congruent.

Chickering argues that educational environments exert a powerful influence that helps students move through the seven vectors of development. Key factors in that influence include institutional objectives, institutional size, faculty-student interaction, curriculum, teaching practices, diverse student communities, and student affairs programs and services.

Researchers examining the applicability of Chickering's theory to women have found that women's development differs from men's development, particularly with regard to the importance of interpersonal relationships in fostering other aspects of development, such as autonomy (Straub, 1987; Straub & Rodgers, 1986). Female college students also score higher on measures of intimacy than do male college students (Greeley & Tinsley, 1988). Furthermore, at historically Black colleges, African American women scored higher than African American men on freeing interpersonal relationships, autonomy, and life purpose on a scale designed to measure development along Chickering's vectors (Jordan-Cox, 1987).

Several writers have questioned the applicability of Chickering's theory to students who are not from White, middle-class backgrounds. Taub and McEwen (1992), for instance, found that some aspects of psychosocial development may be delayed for African American students as they develop their racial identity. For African Americans, developing independence and autonomy seems to occur within the context of interpersonal relationships; family and extended family exert a pervasive influence. Religion, spiritual development, and social responsibility also take on particular significance for African Americans (Hughes, 1987). Research concerning the applicability of Chickering's theory to other racial and ethnic groups has yet to be conducted.

Furthermore, although Chickering and Reisser (1993) now address sexual orientation as part of identity, almost no research has been done to examine the suitability of Chickering's theory for nonheterosexual populations. In an exploratory study, Levine and Bahr (1989) found evidence that the development of sexual identity may retard other components of psychosocial development for gay, lesbian, and bisexual students. D'Augelli (1994) stressed that gay, lesbian, and bisexual youth face the added pressure of giving up a majority identity and developing a new, minority identity. "Coming out" is another developmental task not experienced by heterosexual students (Wall & Evans, 1991).

Super

Super's (1957) theory of vocational choice stresses the developmental nature of careers. Super suggests that people choose careers that reflect their self-concept and that career development is a process that continues throughout an individual's life. He identifies five stages of development. In the first stage, Growth (ages 0–14), children try out various experiences and develop an understanding of work. In the second stage, Exploration (ages 14–24), individuals investigate possible career options, become aware of their interests and abilities, and develop the skills necessary to enter a career. Stage three, Establishment (ages 25–44), consists of becoming competent in a career and advancing in it. In the fourth stage, Maintenance (ages 45–65), persons continue to enhance their skills to remain productive while making plans for retirement. The final stage, Disengagement (age 65+), involves adjusting work to one's physical capability and managing resources to remain independent. Super's theory suggests that career decision making is a process and that the role of career in a person's life is continually evolving.

Adult Development

Because so many college students are beyond the ages of eighteen to twenty-two, student affairs professionals must be aware of developmental issues facing individuals across the entire life span. In addition to Erikson, a number of theorists have explored adult development. Adult development theories can be categorized into three groups: life stage, life events, and individual timing perspectives.

Life Stage Perspectives. This approach suggests that individuals become more individuated and complex as they progress through life, with later developmental tasks building on earlier tasks in a predictable pattern. Developmental change occurs according to an internal timetable, influenced to some extent by environmental forces. Along with Erikson (1968), major theorists in this group include Levinson (1978) and Gould (1978).

The life stage perspective is based almost entirely on the experiences of heterosexual men. Research suggests that although women progress through similar developmental stages at roughly the same ages as men, they experience greater conflict in achieving their more complex goals, which involve both relationships and careers (Roberts & Newton, 1987).

Life Events Perspectives. These theories focus on the importance of the timing, duration, spacing, and ordering of life events in the course of human development. Unlike the life stage perspective, this view does not see life events as necessarily occurring in age-linked stages. Rather than stressing internal forces, life events theorists emphasize the influence of the environment on developmental change and examine the interaction of many different aspects of development over an individual's life span (Rossi, 1980). Life events theorists include Lowenthal, Thurnher, and Chiriboga (1975) and Schlossberg (1984).

Because of its focus on variability, interconnectedness, and environmental influence, the life events perspective is particularly well suited for explaining women's development across the life span. Tittle (1982), for instance, found that while men make clear distinctions between career, marriage, and parenthood, women see the three as being interrelated.

Individual Timing Perspectives. More so than life stage or life events theorists, theorists in this group stress the variability of human development and the importance of environment in growth and change. Because of an individual fanning-out process (Neugarten, 1979), they point out, people are more alike as children than they are as adults. The timing of events in a person's life is viewed as particularly important. According to these theorists, people develop "social clocks" that tell them when certain events are supposed to occur in their lives. When events are "off-time," stress results (Neugarten, 1979, p. 888). Neugarten (1979) and Vaillant (1977) are the major theorists associated with this perspective.

Using Psychosocial Theories in Practice

At this point you may be wondering what all these developmental tasks, vectors, and crises have to do with student affairs practice. Let's revisit Allison, the new academic affairs adviser at an urban community college, for some suggestions.

Certainly, psychosocial theories give Allison a better understanding of the issues that may be important to the students with whom she works. For instance, an understanding of the importance of family and community in the lives of African American students increases Allison's sensitivity as she helps Shawna plan her schedule to allow for attendance at her children's school events and involvement in church activities. Understanding psychosocial development helps student affairs professionals be more proactive in anticipating student issues and more responsive to, and understanding of, concerns that arise as they work with students.

Psychosocial theory is also helpful in program development. Whether planning orientation, educational programs for Greek chapters, or the staff development program for resident assistants, student affairs professionals can use their knowledge of the timing and content of developmental stages to guide the selection of topics for presentation. For instance, at the private college where Allison previously worked, most first-year students were probably in Chickering's early vectors. Programming in the first-year residence hall, then, might focus on academic and social skills and learning to deal with the stresses of college.

In addition, psychosocial theory can guide the formation of policy. For example, knowing that most students at the community college are adults over the age of twenty-two who are working and attending evening classes may suggest that policies concerning registration be adjusted to allow for telephone registration.

Cognitive-Structural Perspectives

Rick and Chris, twenty-two-year-old history majors who are about to graduate from the private college where Allison previously worked, are reminiscing over coffee.

Chris: Do you remember our first history course? I was so confused when Dr. Rosen kept giving us all those theories about the rise and fall of civilization. I just wanted the one right answer that I needed to know to pass the class.

Rick: And I couldn't understand why Dr. Rosen wouldn't just tell us what it was. Remember how I pressed her for it? I knew she had all the answers. That experience showed me that I had to find the answers on my own, not rely on teachers to tell me.

Chris: Yes, but I was still fairly certain that if I worked at it hard enough I could find the right answer, which was out there somewhere. Then I enrolled in that course on history of philosophy and I decided that there were no right answers and all opinions were equally worthwhile. Boy, was I mad when I got a D on my paper because I hadn't supported my ideas.

Rick: We sure have changed, haven't we? Now I really value exchanging ideas and learning from others, who bring different experiences and knowledge to the class. And I have come to realize that context is so important in evaluating information.

Cognitive-structural theories can help explain the changes in Chris's and Rick's thinking. Rooted in the work of Piaget (1952), cognitive-structural theories examine the process of intellectual development. These theories focus on how people think, reason, and make meaning out of their experiences.

The mind is thought to have structures, called schemata by Piaget (1952), positions by Perry (1968), and stages by others. These structures are sets of assumptions people use to adapt to and organize their environments. They determine *how* we think, but not *what* we think. Structures change, expand, and become more complex as a person develops. As first-year students, Rick and Chris saw learning as merely being told the right answers. As seniors, they viewed learning as a chance to gain insights from others, who bring a variety of ideas to the discussion; this change definitely suggests a more complex way of thinking.

Cognitive-structural stages are viewed as arising sequentially and always in the same order, regardless of cultural conditions. The age at which each stage occurs and the rate of speed with which the person passes through it are variable, however. Each stage derives from the previous one, incorporating aspects of it, and is qualitatively different and more complex than earlier stages (Wadsworth, 1979).

According to cognitive-structural theorists, change takes place as a result of assimilation and accommodation. Assimilation is the process of integrating new information into existing structures, rounding them out and contributing to their expansion—a quantitative change. Accommodation is the process of creating new structures to incorporate stimuli that do not fit into existing structures—a qualitative change (Wadsworth, 1979). Disequilibrium, or cognitive conflict, occurs when expectations are not confirmed by experience. When conflict is experienced, the individual first tries to assimilate the new information into the existing structure; if assimilation is not possible, then accommodation occurs in order to regain equilibrium (Wadsworth, 1979). Encountering Dr. Rosen, who would not give him "the answer," created cognitive conflict for Rick, who viewed learning as memorizing information provided by the instructor. By pressing Dr. Rosen for "the answer," Rick tried hard to use his existing structure. When this approach didn't work, accommodation was necessary, and Rick began to think of learning as a process of finding the answers for himself.

Piaget (1952) stresses the importance of heredity in cognitive development but also notes the role played by the environment, which presents experiences to which the individual must react. Social interaction with peers, parents, and other adults is especially influential in cognitive development.

The cognitive-structural perspective includes theories of intellectual and moral development as well. This section focuses on the intellectual development theories of Perry (1968) and Belenky, Clinchy, Goldberger, and Tarule (1986) and the moral development theories of Kohlberg (1969, 1976) and Gilligan (1982).

The work of Baxter Magolda (1992) and the reflective judgment approach (King & Kitchener, 1993), which are also cognitive-structural theories, are discussed in Chapter Eleven. To conclude this section, applications of cognitive-structural theories to student affairs practice are discussed.

Readers should be aware of three other important cognitive-structural theories. Kegan's (1982) self-evolution theory explores the balance between independence and dependence and the role played by relationships throughout a person's life. Rest (1986) has proposed a four-component model of moral development, which suggests that moral behavior consists of moral sensitivity, moral motivation, and moral character in addition to moral judgment. Fowler's (1981) work on faith development grew out of his study of Erikson, Piaget, and Kohlberg. Its general propositions are cognitive-structural, although Fowler acknowledges the role of affect in the development of faith.

Perry

Perry's (1968) longitudinal study, based on annual interviews with 112 Harvard and 28 Radcliffe students from 1954 to 1963, was the first systematic attempt to investigate the intellectual development of college students. From these interviews Perry developed a scheme composed of nine positions, or stages, to describe the progression of students' cognitive development. Perry divides his nine positions into three groups, which he calls the Modifying of Dualism (positions 1–3), the Realizing of Relativism (positions 4–6), and the Evolving of Commitments (positions 7–9). Others have suggested that only the first five stages in Perry's scheme represent different cognitive structures, while the final four stages reflect the development of commitment based on position 5 (King, 1978). Most reviews of Perry's scheme have identified four levels (King, 1978):

1. *Dualism* (positions 1 and 2). The student believes that right answers exist to all questions and that authorities have these answers. The world is viewed in absolute, right-wrong terms. In position 2 some uncertainty is recognized, but it is viewed as a challenge set by authorities for students to learn to find the answers on their own.
2. *Multiplicity* (positions 3 and 4). Uncertainty is now viewed as temporary in areas in which authorities have yet to find the answers. In position 4 uncertainty is seen as so extensive that all opinions are equally valid, and students begin to rely less on authorities.
3. *Relativism* (positions 5 and 6). A major shift in thinking occurs at position 5 as the student comes to view knowledge as contextual and relative and is able to make judgments based on evidence and the merits of an argument.

4. *Commitment in Relativism* (positions 7 to 9). Students test out and evaluate various commitments leading to the development of a personalized set of values, lifestyle, and identity.

Although some women were included in Perry's (1968) study, only the interviews with men were used to illustrate his scheme; in addition, the study included only White students. Beyond suggesting that development results from assimilation and accommodation in response to environmental challenges, Perry did not focus on the process of developmental change.

Belenky, Clinchy, Goldberger, and Tarule

Belenky and her colleagues (1986) undertook a study to determine if the process of intellectual development was different for women than the process reported by Perry (1968) for men. They conducted in-depth interviews with 135 women who were students or recent alumni of six diverse academic institutions, as well as with women who were users of various human services agencies. The women were, therefore, diverse in terms of age, concerns, and situations.

Belenky and her colleagues found that the Perry scheme did not fit well for the women they interviewed. Differences centered around the degree to which individuals actively engaged authorities and knowledge itself. Based on their research, they proposed five major perspectives on knowing. They indicated that further study was necessary before assuming that these perspectives could be regarded as stages. They also noted that their study did not specifically address how or why shifts in perspective occur. The five perspectives include:

1. *Silence.* These women, who tended to be from abusive families and deprived backgrounds, experienced themselves as having no independent thoughts and as being totally controlled by external authorities.
2. *Received knowledge.* Women with this perspective saw themselves as capable of learning from, and repeating, knowledge communicated to them by external authorities but as incapable of generating knowledge or thinking independently.
3. *Subjective knowledge.* Women with this perspective, viewed knowledge as personal, private, and based on intuition.
4. *Procedural knowledge.* Women with this perspective saw learning as based on identifiable procedures and rules, and they attempted to learn and use these procedures. For some the process was impersonal and logical (separate knowing); for others it was personal and subjective (connected knowing).
5. *Constructed knowledge.* These women saw knowledge as relative and contextual, viewed themselves as creators of knowledge, and used both subjective and objective methods.

Belenky and her colleagues also discussed how family life and education affect women's perspectives on knowledge. They advocated teaching that emphasizes connection rather than separation, and understanding and acceptance rather than evaluation. They suggested that collaboration and respect for students' experiences enhance intellectual development as well. Belenky and her colleagues have been criticized for failing to clearly present their research procedures and the data upon which they based their conclusions (King, 1987). In addition, since the study was not longitudinal in nature, it cannot be determined if the categories presented do indeed form hierarchical and sequential stages. Baxter Magolda's (1992) work, discussed in Chapter Eleven, clarifies gender-related differences in intellectual development.

Kohlberg

Moral development, the process by which individuals go about making decisions that affect themselves and others, follows a hierarchical, sequential progression similar to that of intellectual development. In an attempt to expand upon Piaget's (1948) study of the moral development of children, Kohlberg (1958) conducted a study of seventy-two boys between the ages of ten and sixteen. From this study he developed a six-stage model of moral development centered around concepts of justice, which was later validated on other populations in a wide variety of settings (Kohlberg, 1969). He grouped his stages into preconventional, conventional, and postconventional levels, based on the individual's relationship with the rules of society (Kohlberg, 1976). Kohlberg's stages can be summarized as follows (Kohlberg & Wasserman, 1980):

I. Preconventional Level

Stage 1. *The punishment-and-obedience orientation.* The direct consequences of actions determine right and wrong. The individual acts to avoid being punished.

Stage 2. *The instrumental-relativist orientation.* Decisions are made pragmatically, based on equal exchange. "You scratch my back and I'll scratch yours" sums up this position.

II. Conventional Level

Stage 3. *The interpersonal concordance, or "good boy, nice girl," orientation.* Good behavior is defined as that which pleases others and gains their approval. Individuals adhere to stereotyped images of "right" behavior.

Stage 4. *The "law and order" orientation.* Actions are based on upholding the system and obeying the rules of society. Showing respect for authority and maintaining the social order for its own sake are seen as important.

III. Postconventional, or Principled, Level

Stage 5. *The social contract, or legalistic, orientation.* Right action is determined by standards that have been agreed upon by society, but an awareness exists that rules can be reevaluated and changed. Individuals are bound by the social contracts into which they have entered.

Stage 6. *The universal ethical principle orientation.* Self-chosen ethical principles, including justice, equality, and respect for human dignity, guide behavior. Principles take precedence over laws.

The ability to reason logically and to see the point of view of others is necessary, but not sufficient, to achieve more advanced levels of moral reasoning (Kohlberg, 1976). Moral development, like intellectual development, occurs in response to cognitive conflict that disrupts the individual's current way of thinking. It is enhanced by opportunities to confront situations that have moral implications (Kohlberg, 1972).

Kohlberg's theory has spawned a significant amount of research, which has generally supported his major hypotheses, including its applicability in other cultures (Rest, 1986). Kohlberg's ideas have guided moral education programs in schools and universities (Kohlberg, 1972; Kohlberg & Wasserman, 1980). Kohlberg's theory has come under increasing attack, however, for being biased against women (Gilligan, 1977, 1982).

Gilligan

Gilligan (1977, 1982) asserted that Kohlberg's theory, with its focus on justice and rights, did not take into account the concern that women have with care and responsibility for others. To examine the moral development of women, Gilligan conducted interviews with twenty-nine women, ranging in age from fifteen to thirty-three and whom she described as diverse in ethnic background and social class. All of the women were considering abortions and were referred to the study by pregnancy counseling services and abortion clinics.

Based on her findings, Gilligan proposed an alternative model of moral development with three levels and two transition periods. In the first level, which Gilligan called Orientation to Individual Survival, decisions center on the self and one's own desires and needs. In the first transition, From Selfishness to Responsibility, the desire to take care of oneself remains but is in conflict with a growing sense that the right thing to do is to take care of others. In the second level, Goodness as Self-Sacrifice, acceptance by others becomes the primary criteria. This goal is achieved by caring for others and protecting them; one's own desires are relegated to a secondary position. As the woman begins to question the logic of always putting herself second, the second transition, From Goodness to Truth, begins, and the concept of responsibility is reconsidered in an effort to include taking care of oneself as well as others. In the third level, The Morality of Nonviolence, the woman "asserts a moral equality between self and other" (Gilligan, 1977, p. 504) and comes to understand that the prohibition against hurting includes not hurting herself as well as not hurting others. This principle of nonviolence becomes her main guiding force.

Gilligan's (1982) work set off much debate and led to a substantial amount of research designed to determine if there are gender differences in moral development. While most studies using the Kohlbergian model found few gender-related differences (Rest, 1986; Walker, 1984), evidence does suggest that two types of reasoning guide the moral judgments people make—one based on justice and rights and another based on care and responsibility (Gibbs, Arnold, & Burkhart, 1984). While these styles of reasoning are not gender-*specific*, they do appear to be gender-*related*; that is, while both men and women have been found to use both styles, men use justice and rights arguments more often, while women more frequently base their judgments on responsibility and care.

Using Cognitive-Structural Theories in Practice

Remember our friend Allison? Let's consider how she might use cognitive-structural theories in her work as an academic adviser. Knowing that students interpret their classroom experiences differently based on their level of intellectual development can help Allison understand the variations in feedback she receives from students about professors and classes and thus assist her in advising students about their options. A student at a lower level of development will feel more comfortable and may do better in a highly structured classroom setting. Knowledge of moral development theories can help Allison understand students' reasoning with regard to decisions they have made, perhaps involving the reporting of cheating they have observed or conflicts between academics and social life.

Understanding the process of cognitive development can also be very helpful to Allison as she designs workshops and classes. For instance, a workshop for first-year students on how to choose a major would probably enroll students at lower levels of development who need structure and a personalized atmosphere to feel comfortable. Allison would want to provide a written outline of the workshop components and specific directions for activities. She might begin with introductions and have workshop participants use name tags so she could see and use their names throughout the program.

Involving students in policy development is a way to challenge their level of thinking and create opportunities for their personal involvement in meaningful decision making, which will enhance their moral development. For example,

Allison might suggest that students be included on a committee to examine graduation requirements or to establish a policy on student cheating.

Typology Perspectives

Mike and Carla, both seniors on the student leadership council at their university, have been selected to put together a training session for new members. They are having a hard time working together. Mike prefers to take a relaxed approach; he is constantly throwing out interesting and creative suggestions, but he can't seem to get down to actually making a decision. Carla, on the other hand, would really prefer to get the program down on paper so they have time to practice the workshop several times before they give it. She would like time to think about Mike's ideas, but before she can, he moves on to something different.

Typology theories help explain problems such as Mike and Carla's difficulty working together. These theories examine individual differences in how people view and relate to the world. Unlike psychosocial and cognitive-structural theories, they are not truly "developmental" in that they do not consist of stages through which individuals progress. According to Carl Jung (1923/1971), human behavior does not vary by chance; rather, it is caused by innate differences in mental functioning. These differences appear in many aspects of life, such as how people take in and process information, how they learn, and the types of activities that interest them.

Typology theorists identify factors that create consistent ways of coping with the demands of life. When faced with similar developmental challenges or environmental situations, individuals will respond differently, depending on their type. Mike and Carla, for instance, approach the task of preparing a training session in very different ways because of their different types. These theories also give us important information about sources of support and challenge for students who are otherwise developmentally similar. Mike thrives on spontaneous activity and the freedom to "do his own thing," while Carla does better when she can plan ahead and has a structured outline.

Typology theories are nonevaluative in nature. Various types are viewed as different rather than as good or bad. Each type is seen as contributing something positive and unique to any situation. Mike and Carla both have something positive to offer to the training session. Mike is a great "idea" person, while Carla is very good at detail.

In this section, two of the best-known and most extensively used typology theories are introduced: the Myers-Briggs theory of personality type (Myers, 1980) and Holland's (1985) theory of vocational interest. Kolb's (1976) theory of learning styles, which proposes that individuals all have preferred ways of learning, is examined in Chapter Eleven. The temperament theory of Kiersey and Bates (1978) is another typology approach worthy of mention. As in the previous sections, this section concludes with an examination of the uses of typology theory in student affairs settings.

Myers-Briggs

Jung's (1923/1971) theory of psychological types is concerned with individuals' orientation to the world; how they perceive their environment (become aware of people, things, events, and ideas); how they make judgments, or reach conclusions, about the information they take in; and how they relate to their external environment.

Jung suggests that people differ between those who have a relative interest in the outer world of people and things (Extraversion, or E) and those who are more interested in the inner world of ideas and concepts (Introversion, or I). Jung also proposes two ways of perceiving: Sensing (S) and Intuition (N). Sensing involves taking in information directly through the five senses, while Intuition is an indirect method of perceiving through the use of ideas or associations by way of the unconscious (Myers, 1980). When using the Sensing process, individuals report real, observable facts or events. In contrast, an individual relying on the Intuitive mode of perception will present underlying meanings, connections, and symbolic relationships.

According to Jung, there are also two ways of judging: Thinking (T) and Feeling (F). When using the Thinking process, individuals rely on the logical analysis of causes and effects, pros and cons, and the weight of evidence in support of various positions. Individuals using a Feeling process, in contrast, base their decisions on personal, subjective values. They place human relationships ahead of other factors when making decisions (Myers, 1980).

A final preference implicitly suggested by Jung and more clearly defined by Myers is the preference for the perceptive or judgment attitude when dealing with the outside environment. People who prefer Judging (J) enjoy organization, planning, and making decisions quickly, while those who prefer Perception (P) are curious and welcome new experiences, like to keep their options open, and prefer to gather a great deal of information before making a decision (McCaulley, 1990).

Personality type theory, as proposed by Jung and further developed by Myers, suggests, then, that there are four bipolar scales, EI, SN, TF, and JP. Preferences on each scale are identified and organized into one of sixteen different types (for example, ENTP, ISFJ). Application of type theory to our understanding of the college environment is discussed in Chapter Twelve, while its contributions to our understanding of student learning is reviewed in Chapter Eleven.

Holland

Holland's (1985) theory of vocational choice examines both people's interests and the characteristics of work environments. According to Holland, vocation is an expression of personality; as such, individuals pursuing specific careers have similar personalities. They respond to situations similarly and create unique interpersonal environments. People look for environments that will allow them to pursue their interests and use their abilities and that reinforce their attitudes and values. Satisfaction and success are contingent on the interaction between one's personality and the characteristics of one's environment. Holland identifies six personality types, along with six corresponding work environments:

1. *Realistic.* This type is characterized by an interest in physical activities requiring motor skills and strength; concrete rather than abstract tasks are preferred. Individuals prefer working with things rather than with people or ideas.
2. *Investigative.* These individuals tend to be scholarly, analytic, and inquisitive. They prefer thinking to acting and they enjoy the world of ideas more than working with people or things.
3. *Social.* People exhibiting this type are friendly, helpful, cooperative, and sensitive to others. They enjoy close interpersonal contact and prefer to work with people rather than with things or ideas.
4. *Conventional.* These individuals like order and structure and work well within a system. They are conscientious, efficient, and practical. They like working with numbers, records, and data.
5. *Enterprising.* People in this category are verbally skilled, persuasive, confident, and concerned with status. They like to lead and organize others. They enjoy working with people but in a managerial rather than a helping role.
6. *Artistic.* This type is expressive, imaginative, and creative. These individuals dislike structure and prefer innovative assignments. They enjoy work that involves artistic creation.

Holland's (1985) theory has been found to be valid for both men and women and for African Americans (Herr & Cramer, 1992). Its student affairs applications are discussed in Chapter Twelve.

Using Typology Perspectives in Practice

Our friend Allison will certainly find typology theories useful in her work as an academic adviser. Understanding personality types can assist Allison in understanding and predicting students' likes and dislikes with regard to classes, the learning environment in which they will do best, and career options they might want to explore. These theories can also guide discussions about extracurricular activities students might enjoy and find rewarding.

Typology theories can also help explain interpersonal interactions and provide guidance in working through conflicts (such as the one between Mike and Carla). Individuals can learn to anticipate others' work style and use the strengths they bring to a project. Group interactions can also be analyzed using typology theory, and team-building activities can be developed to improve group functioning and cohesion.

Typology theories can be of great utility in making effective work assignments. For example, Carla would be most effective in a job requiring precision and organization, while Mike would be good at a task requiring creativity.

Typology theories can also provide guidance on the design of classes, workshops, training sessions, and other structured educational experiences. These applications are discussed further in Chapter Eleven. In addition, room assignment policies might take into consideration similarities and differences in personality type or interests suggested by various typology theories, as is discussed in Chapter Twelve.

Using Theory Intelligently

As can be seen from the examples presented, each theoretical perspective adds a piece to the puzzle of student development. It is important to remember, however, that development is a complex process for any individual. Individuals don't fit all stages perfectly or address all issues as they are "supposed" to. No theory can tell any student what to do with his or her life. Only students themselves can determine those answers.

It is tempting to label people as "ESTJs" or "Dualists" without giving much thought to what these labels really mean. "Dualist" can too easily become a pejorative adjective, suggesting that a certain student is not as good, capable, or easy to work with as students labeled "Relativist." It is important to remember that everyone is a dualist from time to time as they experience new situations and attempt to understand something they have never learned before.

It is also important to remember that the diversity of student experience is just beginning to be understood. Theories may suggest directions to explore in advising students from diverse backgrounds, and student affairs practitioners must remain open to hearing different answers than what they hear when they talk to majority students.

Theory is useful, however, in helping student affairs professionals such as Allison understand what they are hearing from students. It provides a framework for understanding students' concerns, attitudes, and thought processes. Theory helps student affairs professionals process information and respond effectively to it. Such responses may take the form of suggesting actions to students, challenging their thinking, providing support with a listening ear, creating workshops, or advocating changes in policy.

Theory can also help student affairs professionals become more proactive in their work with students. Theory suggests questions to ask, avenues to explore, and hypotheses to test. It provides shortcuts to exploring students' concerns and analyzing how they are addressing them. It also provides direction in developing appropriate programs and class offerings for particular groups of students.

Theory can also help student affairs professionals evaluate their work. First, by suggesting developmental outcomes, theory provides goals to work toward, such as helping students develop a clear sense of purpose in their lives. Then, assessing the extent to which these goals are achieved can determine the impact of students affairs programming on student development. With regard to developing purpose, for example, students' career decision-making processes could be investigated.

Conclusion

Throughout this presentation, the specific strengths and weaknesses of various theories have been noted. Taken as a whole, developmental theory has much to offer the student affairs field. With the important contributions of recent researchers, significantly more is known about student development now than was known ten years ago. Knowledge of gender similarities and differences, in particular, has substantially increased.

Much work remains to be done, however. While descriptions of developmental stages exist and the issues, attitudes, and behaviors that exist within these stages are apparent, much less is known about how to facilitate students' movement through these stages. What factors lead to cognitive conflict, for example, and how do they propel development? What can be done to ensure that change is positive? Why do some students change but not others?

More must be discovered about the forces that work against development and what can be done to intervene in a positive way. Societal forces such as economic pressures, conservative political attitudes, fear of violence, and other affectively charged concerns may influence students in ways about which very little is known. As researchers study the psychology of development, they must not lose sight of its sociology.

Researchers are starting to explore the applicability of various theories to individuals from nondominant backgrounds (see Chapter Ten for an overview). Much more needs to be done in this area. While some information exists about African American students, less is known about students from other racial backgrounds. Researchers also need to explore the impact of characteristics that are not as readily apparent as race. Very little is known about the development of students with disabilities; gay, lesbian, and bisexual students; students from non-Christian religious backgrounds; and students who are not middle-class. And as King (1994) persuasively points out, these groups need to be studied as much to determine what they have in common with dominant-culture students as to find out how they differ from them.

Assessment is also an important issue. Readers should be aware that most of the research reported in this chapter is based on interview procedures that require extensive training to interpret. More easily scored assessment techniques are needed if student affairs professionals are to accurately determine the developmental levels of their students and evaluate the developmental impact of their interventions.

More evaluation research related to student development is needed. Student affairs practitioners must know what works in terms of student development interventions and what does not work. A search of the student affairs literature turns up very few well-conceptualized and carefully evaluated programs based on student development theory.

Perhaps related to this concern, Upcraft (1994) has recently restated an often-heard complaint: student affairs practitioners don't use theory as a guide to practice. Hopefully the examples and connections provided in this chapter have demonstrated ways in which theory can be used effectively in the daily activities of student affairs professionals and have encouraged readers to become theory-based practitioners. But, obviously, reading one chapter on student development theory won't make anyone an expert. Further reading and ongoing study is needed. As Upcraft points out, it is easier to learn about theory if it is necessary for some aspect of one's position. Teaching student development theory to peer counselors, developing a program with a theory base, or heading up the staff development committee are all possible ways to gain increased familiarity with student development theory.

Another very good way to learn about student development is to talk to students in an intentional way about their experiences, concerns, beliefs, and challenges. All of the theories presented in this chapter were developed in this way. Perhaps you, too, can add to the profession's knowledge base on student development. At the very least you will become a better informed and more effective student affairs professional.

References

Baxter Magolda, M. B. (1992). *Knowing and reasoning in college: Gender-related patterns in students' intellectual development.* San Francisco: Jossey-Bass.

Belenky, M. F., Clinchy, B. M., Goldberger, N. R., & Tarule, J. M. (1986). *Women's ways of knowing: The development of self, voice, and mind.* New York: Basic Books.

Chickering, A. W. (1969). *Education and identity.* San Francisco: Jossey-Bass.

Chickering, A. W., & Reisser, L. (1993). *Education and identity* (2nd ed.). San Francisco: Jossey-Bass.

D'Augelli, A. R. (1994). Identity development and sexual orientation: Toward a model of lesbian, gay, and bisexual development. In E. J. Trickett, R. Watts, & D. Birman (Eds.), *Human diversity: Perspectives on people in context* (pp. 312–333). San Francisco: Jossey-Bass.

Erikson, E. H. (1959). Identity and the life cycle. *Psychological Issues, 1,* 1–171.

Erikson, E. H. (1968). *Identity: Youth and crisis.* New York: Norton.

Fowler, J. (1981). *Stages of faith.* New York: Harper & Row.

Gibbs, J. C., Arnold, K. D., & Burkhart, J. E. (1984). Sex differences in the expression of moral judgment. *Child Development, 55,* 1040–1043.

Gilligan, C. (1977). In a different voice: Women's conceptions of self and morality. *Harvard Educational Review, 47,* 481–517.

Gilligan, C. (1982). *In a different voice.* Cambridge, MA: Harvard University Press.

Gould, R. L. (1978). *Transformations: Growth and change in adult life.* New York: Simon & Schuster.

Greeley, A., & Tinsley, H. (1988). Autonomy and intimacy development in college students: Sex differences and predictors. *Journal of College Student Development, 29,* 512–520.

Herr, E. L., & Cramer, S. H. (1992). *Career guidance and counseling through the lifespan: Systematic approaches* (4th ed.). New York: HarperCollins.

Holland, J. L. (1985). *Making vocational choices: A theory of vocational personalities and work environments* (2nd ed.). Englewood Cliffs, NJ: Prentice Hall.

Hughes, M. S. (1987). Black students' participation in higher education. *Journal of College Student Personnel, 28,* 532–545.

Jordan-Cox, C. A. (1987). Psychosocial development of students in traditionally Black institutions. *Journal of College Student Personnel, 28,* 504–511.

Josselson, R. (1987). *Finding herself: Pathways to identity development in women.* San Francisco: Jossey-Bass.

Jung, C. G. (1971). *Psychological types.* (F. C. Hull, Ed.; H. G. Baynes, Trans.). Princeton, NJ: Princeton University Press. (Original work published 1923)

Kegan, R. (1982). *The evolving self.* Cambridge, MA: Harvard University Press.

Kiersey, D., & Bates, M. (1978). *Please understand me: Character and temperament types* (3rd ed.). Del Mar, CA: Prometheus Nemesis Books.

King, P. M. (1978). William Perry's theory of intellectual development. In L. Knefelkamp, C. Widick, & C. A. Parker (Eds.), *Applying new developmental findings* (New Directions for Student Services No. 4, pp. 35–51). San Francisco: Jossey-Bass.

King, P. M. (1987). Review of the book *Women's ways of knowing: The development of self, voice, and mind. Journal of Moral Education, 16,* 249–251.

King, P. M. (1994). Theories of college student development: Sequences and consequences. *Journal of College Student Development, 35,* 413–421.

King, P. M., & Kitchener, K. S. (1993). *Developing reflective judgment: Understanding and promoting intellectual growth and critical thinking in adolescents and adults.* San Francisco: Jossey-Bass.

Kohlberg, L. (1958). *The development of modes of moral thinking and choice in the years 10 to 16.* Unpublished doctoral dissertation, University of Chicago.

Kohlberg, L. (1969). Stage and sequence: The cognitive-developmental approach to socialization. In D. Goslin (Ed.), *Handbook of socialization theory and research* (pp. 347–480). Chicago: Rand McNally.

Kohlberg, L. (1972). A cognitive-developmental approach to moral education. *Humanist, 6,* 13–16.

Kohlberg, L. (1976). Moral stages and moralization: The cognitive-developmental approach. In T. Lickona (Ed.), *Moral development and behavior: Theory, research, and social issues* (pp. 31–53). New York: Holt, Rinehart and Winston.

Kohlberg, L., & Wasserman, E. R. (1980). The cognitive-developmental approach and the practicing counselor: An opportunity for counselors to rethink their roles. *Personnel and Guidance Journal, 58,* 559–567.

Kolb, D. (1976). *Learning styles inventory technical manual.* Boston: McBer.

Levine, H., & Bahr, J. (1989). *Relationship between sexual identity formation and student development.* Unpublished manuscript.

Levinson, D. J. (1978). *The seasons of a man's life.* New York: Ballantine.

Lowenthal, M. F., Thurnher, M., & Chiriboga, D. (1975). *Four stages of life: A comprehensive study of women and men facing transitions.* San Francisco: Jossey-Bass.

McCaulley, M. H. (1990). The Myers-Briggs Type Indicator: A measure for individuals and groups. *Measurement and Evaluation in Counseling and Development, 22,* 181–195.

Marcia, J. E. (1966). Development and validation of ego-identity status. *Journal of Personality and Social Psychology, 3,* 551–559.

Myers, I. B. (1980). *Gifts differing.* Palo Alto, CA: Consulting Psychologists Press.

Neugarten, B. L. (1979). Time, age, and the life cycle. *American Journal of Psychiatry, 136,* 887–894.

Perry, W. G., Jr. (1968). *Forms of intellectual and ethical development in the college years: A scheme.* New York: Holt, Rinehart and Winston.

Piaget, J. (1948). *The moral judgment of the child.* Glencoe, IL: Free Press.

Piaget, J. (1952). *The origins of intelligence in children.* New York: International Universities Press.

Rest, J. R. (1986). *Moral development: Advances in research and theory.* New York: Praeger.

Roberts, P., & Newton, P. M. (1987). Levinsonian studies of women's adult development. *Psychology and Aging, 2,* 154–163.

Rossi, A. S. (1980). Life-span theories and women's lives. *Signs, 6,* 4–32.

Sanford, N. (1966). *Self and society.* New York: Atherton.

Schenkel, S., & Marcia, J. E. (1972). Attitudes toward premarital intercourse in determining ego identity status in college women. *Journal of Personality, 40,* 472–482.

Schlossberg, N. K. (1984). *Counseling adults in transition.* New York: Springer.

Straub, C. (1987). Women's development of autonomy and Chickering's theory. *Journal of College Student Personnel, 28,* 198–205.

Straub, C., & Rodgers, R. F. (1986). An exploration of Chickering's theory and women's development. *Journal of College Student Personnel, 27,* 216–224.

Super, D. E. (1957). *The psychology of careers.* New York: Harper & Row.

Taub, D. J., & McEwen, M. K. (1992). The relationship of racial identity attitudes to autonomy and mature interpersonal relationships in Black and White undergraduate women. *Journal of College Student Development, 33,* 439–446.

Tittle, C. K. (1982). Career, marriage, and family: Values in adult roles and guidance. *Personnel and Guidance Journal, 61,* 154–158.

Upcraft, M. L. (1994). The dilemmas of translating theory to practice. *Journal of College Student Development, 35,* 438–443.

Vaillant, G. (1977). *Adaptation to life.* Boston: Little, Brown.

Wadsworth, B. J. (1979). *Piaget's theory of cognitive development* (2nd ed.). New York: Longman.

Walker, L. J. (1984). Sex differences in the development of moral reasoning: A critical review. *Child Development, 55,* 677–691.

Wall, V. A., & Evans, N. J. (1991). Using psychosocial development theories to understand and work with gay and lesbian persons. In N. J. Evans & V. A. Wall (Eds.), *Beyond tolerance: Gays, lesbians, and bisexuals on campus* (pp. 25–38). Alexandria, VA: American College Personnel Association.

CHAPTER TEN

NEW PERSPECTIVES ON
IDENTITY DEVELOPMENT

Marylu K. McEwen

Jonah is a senior at North City University, a large, urban university located in the Northeast. He grew up in Atlanta, Georgia, in a close-knit family that considered itself socioeconomically lower-middle-class. Jonah is African American; he lived in a historically and predominantly Black neighborhood and attended predominantly Black schools. Jonah was a hardworking, conscientious student, but he struggled as an engineering major. He was unwilling, however, to go to the Minority Engineering Center, where tutoring and other kinds of academic and personal support were offered. During his junior year Jonah started to attend meetings of the Black Student Union (BSU) and participate in its programs. As the year progressed, he became increasingly more involved with the BSU; further, almost all of Jonah's friends were involved with the BSU. Jonah's friends noticed that he dated very infrequently; when he was asked about meeting people whom he might date, Jonah usually told his friends that he had a girlfriend named Michelle back home in Atlanta. Even with all of the time Jonah was spending at the BSU, his grades improved, and his interest in engineering increased, especially when he met some members of the Society for Black Engineers. Junior year was a banner year for Jonah. During his senior year, his involvement in the BSU decreased, and eventually he withdrew from it and from his friends there. He continued, however, occasionally to mention his girlfriend Michelle. Other than his community service involvement, Jonah's only cocurricular activity during most of his senior year consisted of occasional attendance at functions of the Gay and Lesbian Student Alliance. During his senior year, Jonah acknowledged that he is gay.

◆ ◆ ◆

Amelia is a twenty-five-year-old sophomore biology major at San Antonio University (SAU). Amelia is from Agua Nueva, about fifty miles from the U.S.-Mexican border. In San Antonio she lives with her cousin, Ruth. Every weekend Amelia goes home to help care for her aging great-grandparents and to be with her family and friends. On campus, Amelia spends much of her time in class, in the laboratory, and studying. In the little free time she has during the week, she participates actively in programs sponsored by her church, works four hours for a community service project in San Antonio, and is involved in the Creative Dance Club. Each Sunday evening or Monday morning when Amelia returns to SAU from her home in Agua Nueva, she talks at length with Ruth about how unfairly the women in her hometown are treated by the men. Amelia complains that everyone at home expects her to return to Agua Nueva, marry her high school boyfriend, and have lots of children. Yet, when her boyfriend, Carlos, visits her at SAU, Amelia talks constantly with him about when they will get married, what Carlos will do for a living, and how they will live with his family for a while, have a big family themselves, and eventually get their own home in Agua Nueva. Ruth is confused; she doesn't understand why Amelia complains about Carlos and about how women are treated, yet assumes such a traditional role with Carlos when he comes to visit.

◆ ◆ ◆

Hank is a junior at Cornstock College (CC). He grew up on a family farm in southern Indiana, where as a teenager he lost an arm in an accident. Both of his parents completed college. Hank and his family consider themselves middle-class, although their average annual income, given the volatility of farm crops and farm prices, doesn't reflect their White middle-class status. Hank's family is liberal politically. From his earliest memories, Hank was taught by his parents about the dignity of all people, about community service, about supporting volunteer agencies, and about the value of other cultures. Now that Hank is at CC, however, his previous training and education doesn't seem to fare so well with him. CC has significant populations of African American students and students of Asian descent. Hank gets along fairly well with the Asian American students, but all of his efforts to include his African American roommate, Charles, and Charles's friends seem to be met with disinterest. Hank is taking an African American history course and tries to share all he is learning with Charles, but again, Charles seems like he couldn't care less. Hank just doesn't understand, and he decides that if Charles and other Black students aren't willing to do their part, then he isn't going to try anymore, either. Hank is just tired of trying to do the right thing.

Identity and Development

The illustrations above provide brief snapshots of three college students. If we as student affairs professionals or faculty members want to develop an understanding of such students, what do we want to understand, and what questions do we want to ask? In Chapter Nine, Nancy Evans described different types of student development theory and how they can be used to gain a general understanding of several aspects of development, including identity development. In this chapter, I focus on seven dimensions of identity that illuminate and add complexity to the overarching aspects of identity development described by Evans. The seven dimensions are race, sexual orientation, social class, abilities and disabilities, gender, religion, and geographic region.

This chapter has five major purposes: (1) to define the constructs of identity and development, (2) to give an overview of models and theories of identity development along the seven dimensions just identified, (3) to consider a model of multiple identities, (4) to propose a working model incorporating multiple dimensions of identity development, and (5) to suggest next steps and future directions toward a more comprehensive conceptualization and understanding of the seven dimensions of identity development in college students.

Let's return to the students portrayed above. What questions would you ask about each of them? What would those questions reveal about your identity and your understanding of who you are? How would you interpret Hank's struggle with racial issues, knowing that he holds liberal attitudes and grew up in a liberal family? What does it mean that Amelia rejects traditional notions about women when she is with her roommate but adheres to traditional roles and expectations when she is at home? Does Jonah's upbringing in the Southeast affect his development at the northern urban university he attends? Being African American seems to mean something different to Jonah than it did when he first came to college—how would you interpret that? Why does Jonah tell people he has a girlfriend in Atlanta when he knows he is gay?

What other questions would be pertinent for these three students? And for all students, what is identity? What is development? What are common beginning definitions from which we can discuss students' identity development?

Identity

One of the most frequently cited definitions of identity, especially among student services professionals, is that of Erikson (1980). Erikson and others (Chickering, 1969; Chickering & Reisser, 1993) proposed that identity development is a central part of adolescence and early adulthood; but it is also a lifelong task. Achieving an identity is the culmination of earlier developmental tasks in the life cycle, and it is a building block for later developmental tasks. To Erikson (1980), identity is "the accrued confidence that one's ability to maintain inner sameness and continuity . . . is matched by the sameness and continuity of one's meaning for others" (p. 94).

Widick, Parker, and Knefelkamp (1978) define identity as "the organized set of images, the sense of self, which express who and what we really are" (p. 2) and who we want to become. They state that an Eriksonian sense of identity means that "the person has a subjective core self-image which provides continuity and sameness" (p. 7), that the person "knows who he [or she] is and can envision those qualities which are most central to his [or her] existence" (p. 7). An Eriksonian sense of identity also involves an interpersonal dimension. "A positive sense of identity is reality-based in that others view the individual much as he [or she] views himself [or herself]. . . . One's identity is manifest behaviorally and can be confirmed and validated by others" (p. 7). These writers also underscore the psychosocial nature of identity: "[Erikson] places the developing person in a social context, emphasizing the fact that movement through life occurs in interaction with parents, family, social institutions and a particular culture, all of which are bounded by a particular historical period" (p. 1).

The word *identity* is used and interpreted in various ways. Sometimes identity refers to one's global identity, one's overall sense of self or sense of being; this sense is often used in broad, overarching theories of personality or ego development. Both Erikson's (1980) theory of identity development throughout the life cycle and Chickering's (1969) seven vectors of identity development refer to identity in this global sense. On the other hand, the word *identity* may be used in a more specific manner, to describe either the core essence of oneself or particular aspects of one's global identity. Although Chickering's theory provides a broad portrait of identity development, one of his vectors, "establishing identity," describes a particular part of an individual's identity rather than the comprehensive picture represented by the seven combined vectors. (See Chapter Nine for a description of Chickering's vectors.) This chapter examines seven specific aspects, or dimensions, of identity. It is important to understand how these dimensions are socially constructed. Each dimension represents a single—but complex—aspect of identity, and each dimension interacts with and is closely intertwined with other aspects or dimensions of the self.

Development

What, then, is development? Often the words *growth* and *change* are used synonymously with *development*. Sanford (1967), however, contrasts these three terms, suggesting that they imply different meanings. In a general sense, development is about becoming a more complex individual (with, for example, a more complex identity, more complex cognition, or more complex values). A more precise definition is that development represents the "organization of increasing complexity" (p. 47), or an increasing differentiation *and* integration of the self. Thus development involves change, and it may include growth; but more specifically, it represents a qualitative enhancement of the self in terms of the self's complexity and integration. We tend to attach many positive values to the word *development;* for example, highly developed is better than less developed, and greater development represents increased maturity.

Developmental Dimensions of Identity

The seven dimensions of identity that are the focus of this chapter can be defined and used in a variety of ways. Some of these dimensions, particularly race, gender, and sexual orientation, are frequently linked to certain "integral" characteristics or attributes, seen to exist "outside or impervious to social and historical context"; this is known as an essentialist perspective (Omi & Winant, 1994, p. 181). Social class, although not biological, may nevertheless be inherited from one's family (it can be changed, however). Abilities and disabilities are both congenital and acquired. Constructs surrounding one's geographic region and religious identity may be absorbed from family, but they also represent elements of identity about which persons may have a choice. Other dimensions of identity, not addressed in this chapter, include age, ethnicity, family history of attending college (first-generation versus second-generation students, and so on), and culture.

In considering student development, however, it is more appropriate and more useful to think about the above dimensions in terms of their social constructions. There are meaningful differences related to—but not based upon—these characteristics as they are constructed, experienced, and lived within given cultural and historical contexts.

Some of these characteristics are addressed more fully here than are others, primarily because there is more literature and research on them available. Most of the literature on the social construction of identity has focused on oppressed groups, but more recent perspectives have suggested that socially constructed dimensions must also be considered as part of identity and identity development for dominant-group persons as well. By *dominant* I mean the primary groups in the United States that *collectively* have power and whose perspectives constitute what is considered normative. Dominant is not necessarily synonymous with a numerical majority. Examples of dominant groups include White, male, heterosexual, able-bodied, and Christian. Oppressed groups include those that are not dominant: people of color; women; persons with disabilities; persons with a non-Christian religious affiliation, such as Jewish, Hindu, or Muslim; and individuals who are gay, lesbian, or bisexual.

My goal, therefore, is to present and discuss developmental theories, models, and perspectives about dominant groups as well as oppressed groups. Models of identity development do not exist for some dominant groups (for example, for heterosexual identity development).

Racial Identity Development

In the United States (and in other countries and regions, to a varying degree), racial and ethnic identity is an important dimension of an individual's overall identity, although its developmental aspects may not be apparent to every individual. The terms *race* and *ethnicity* represent different constructs with different meanings. Frequently in the literature these terms are used interchangeably; it is important, however, to differentiate between their meanings and implications.

Racial identity, according to Helms (1990f), refers to "a sense of group or collective identity based on one's perception that he or she shares a common racial heritage with a particular racial group" (p. 3). Ethnic identity, on the other hand, according to Phinney (1990) in her comprehensive review of research on the subject, is frequently defined as the "ethnic component of social identity" (p. 500); Phinney (1990, 1992) draws on Tajfel's (1981) definition of a person's social identity as "that part of an individual's self-concept which derives from his [or her] knowledge of his [or her] membership of a social group (or groups) together with the value and emotional significance attached to that membership" (p. 255). Based on these definitions, both racial identity and ethnic identity are socially constructed, and an individual's racial and ethnic heritage in one country or region therefore sets a particular context for his or her racial and ethnic identity development.

Racial identity development has been applied more frequently to persons of Asian, African, Latino, and Native American descent. It is also necessary, however, to consider the racial identity of White people and those of mixed or "blended" races. The racial identity of White persons has been denied or invisible; the racial identity of mixed-race persons has likewise been ignored. Each of us has a race, to paraphrase Helms (1992); thus, a part of each person's identity is his or her racial identity. Within this section, I focus first on White racial identity development and then on minority identity development. (The term *minority* is used here to represent people of color, or members of visible racial or ethnic groups [Cook & Helms, 1988]. I use the word cautiously and with some misgivings, as it often implies "less than" or "not equal to"; however, such is not my intent here. Further, in some parts of the United States, people of color are not a numerical minority, but rather the majority.) Ethnic identity development is not addressed here; readers are referred to works by Ruiz (1990) and Phinney (1990, 1992).

White Racial Identity Development. The racial identity of White people has historically been ignored in the United States, essentially because, as the dominant racial group, White people have not had to face or name their race and the various characteristics, attributes, and privileges associated with it. Janet Helms (1990g, 1992) has provided the most extensive theoretical and research work to date on White racial identity. She says that "in order to develop a healthy White identity, defined in part as a nonracist identity, virtually every White person in the United States must overcome one or more of these aspects [individual, institutional, and cultural] of racism. Additionally, he or she must accept his or her own Whiteness, the cultural implications of being White, and define a view of Self as a racial being that does not depend on the perceived superiority of one racial group over another" (1990g, p. 49).

Racism is central to the construction of White racial identity, both in terms of its presence in the United States and White people's role in perpetuating it. In Helms's model of White racial identity development (see Exhibit 10.1), there are two phases. In the first phase, people abandon a racist identity; in the second, they develop a nonracist identity. According to Helms, it is impossible to develop a healthy White identity without acknowledging, understanding, and working to rid oneself of deep, internalized racism. In her more recent work, she refers to "ego statuses" in her racial identity model rather than stages; these "are not assumed to be mutually exclusive or discontinuous" (Helms, 1994, p. 301).

From the brief description of Hank, who is a White male student, we can draw some hypotheses about his racial identity development. Hank's liberal attitudes, his comfort with Asian American students, his interest in taking an African American history course, and his desire to share all he is learning in African American history with Charles suggest that Hank may have racial attitudes that represent the pseudo-independent status. But when Hank becomes frustrated with Charles's not behaving and thinking the way Hank wants him to, then Hank's attitudes suggest the Reintegration status. That Hank as a White person is *not*

EXHIBIT 10.1. WHITE RACIAL IDENTITY DEVELOPMENT.

Phase 1: *Abandonment of Racism*

    Status 1: *Contact—"The Happy Racist."* This stage is marked by a White person's initial encounters with the idea or actuality of Black people or other people of color. The response to this event is characterized by naive curiosity; obliviousness to racial and cultural issues; a culture-neutral view of the world; and the automatic use of White criteria, without an awareness that other criteria are possible. There is limited interracial interaction, and the White person has positive feelings about himself or herself and about the "idea" of fair treatment of Blacks and other people of color.

        Transition: One can observe in Helms's (1990g, 1992) model that attitudes toward Blacks and other people of color range from not seeing color at all to believing that the fault for their treatment lies with the people of color themselves to trying to change them to be "more like White people" to ultimately working to eradicate racism by trying to change White people and joining people of color's efforts to help themselves. Helms (1990g) indicates that liberal Whites often have pseudo-independent attitudes—attitudes in which they try to change persons of color rather than focusing on changing themselves and other Whites.

    Status 2: *Disintegration.* This stage is characterized by conscious but conflicted awareness of the individual's Whiteness and a recognition of the moral dilemmas associated with being White. The resulting discomfort is reduced by avoiding contact with Blacks and other people of color, trying to convince others that these people are not so inferior, and/or trying to obtain validation from Whites or others that racism either does not exist or that it is not the White person's fault. The White person experiences guilt, depression, helplessness, and anxiety.

        Transition: The individual's desire to reduce his or her discomfort and to be accepted by his or her own racial group (Whites) spurs the transition to the next stage.

    Status 3: *Reintegration.* At this stage the individual acknowledges a White identity, accepts a belief in the superiority of Whites and the inferiority of others, and believes that negative race-related social conditions are the result of the inferiority of people of color and that Whites' privileges result from their having earned them. This stage is characterized by fear and anger toward Blacks and other people of color, covertly or overtly expressed, and racist behavior, either active or passive. In the United States, it is fairly easy for Whites to remain or become fixated at this stage.

        Transition: A personally jarring event, direct or vicarious, painful or insightful, spurs the individual on to the next stage. The individual begins to question his or her previous definition of Whiteness and the justifiability of racism in any form.

Phase 2: *Development of a Nonracist Identity*

    Status 4: *Pseudo-independence—"White Liberalism."* The individual begins to actively question that Blacks and other people of color are innately inferior to Whites and to acknowledge Whites' responsibility for racism. This stage is characterized by intellectual acceptance of and curiosity about Blacks and other people of color and by intellectual understanding of other cultures and the privileges of being

EXHIBIT 10.1. WHITE RACIAL IDENTITY DEVELOPMENT, cont'd.

White. Most of these feelings are submerged. Behavior involves helping Blacks and other people of color to change themselves to function more like Whites—according to White criteria. The individual looks to persons of color to explain racism.

Transition: If personal rewards are great enough to encourage continued strengthening of a positive White identity, then the individual may begin to seek positive aspects of Whiteness unrelated to racism.

Status 5: Immersion/Emersion. At this stage the individual attempts to redefine a positive White identity by replacing myths and stereotypes with accurate information about being White in the United States and the world. The individual asks questions such as "Who am I racially?" "Who do I want to be?" and "Who are you really?" He or she turns to other Whites engaged in similar journeys through biographies, autobiographies, or consciousness-raising groups. The focus is on changing White people rather than on changing Blacks and other people of color.

Transition: The transition to the next stage occurs when the individual feels secure enough in his or her White identity to use his or her knowledge about being White to eliminate racism, to change Whites, and to acquire new knowledge about being White and about Blacks and other people of color.

Status 6: Autonomy. This stage is characterized by a racially transcendent worldview. The individual has internalized a positive, nonracist White identity and seeks to acknowledge and abolish racial oppression. Autonomy represents the highest level of White racial identity; it is an ongoing process, one in which the individual is continually open to new information and new ways of thinking about race and culture.

Source: Adapted from Helms (1990g, 1992).

examining his own racism implies that his attitudes in this vignette are not at a status of Immersion/Emersion or Autonomy.

Helms's model is especially useful in that it can help White people understand what racial attitudes they hold and thus how they view and act on racial matters and racial interactions; it can also help one consider how a traditionally White institution of higher education or a predominantly White environment may perceive and handle racial issues. Helms's model also provides a blueprint for White persons to help them develop into healthy racial beings and for student affairs professionals to assist White students in developing healthy racial attitudes and behaviors. Helms (1990b, 1990c, 1990d, 1990e) also provides specific descriptions of social and group interactions between persons of different racial identity statuses and different races. In regard to groups, for instance, Helms (1990d) describes relationship dynamics and discusses dimensions such as perceptions of power, group racial norms, and racial identity coalitions.

Minority Identity Development. Racial identity development in persons of color has received increasing attention in the literature over the past twenty-five years. Both Cross (1971, 1978, 1991) and Helms (1990a) have written extensively about the racial identity development of Black persons. I have selected the Minority Identity Development (MID) model of Atkinson, Morten, and Sue (1993) for discussion here because of its broad applicability to persons of color.

Although the focus of the following discussion is on persons of a single race, it is important to acknowledge that many people who are biracial or multiracial live in the United States, and these people may not identify with a single racial group. Root's (1992) book on racially mixed people and Poston's (1990) model of biracial identity development are useful sources.

Atkinson, Morten, and Sue (1993) acknowledge that different racial and ethnic groups have different cultures; but because all the racial and ethnic groups that comprise "people of color" are subjected to various kinds and forms of discrimination and racism, they believe that these groups share a common experience in regard to their racial and ethnic identity development.

The MID model is composed of five stages (see Exhibit 10.2). Although each stage is distinct and qualitatively different, Atkinson, Morten, and Sue suggest that "the MID is more accurately conceptualized as a continuous process in which one stage blends with another and boundaries between stages are not clear" (p. 28). The developmental process evolves from an implicit acceptance of one's socially prescribed status as part of an oppressed group to a questioning of one's beliefs about oneself as a "minority." The individual then rejects the dominant society and moves toward acceptance of and immersion in one's own racial or ethnic group. In the fourth stage, the individual begins to evaluate the strengths and weaknesses of his or her own group, of other oppressed groups, and of the dominant group. In stage five, the individual makes a commitment to working toward the elimination of all oppression.

Parham (1989), in his discussion of the racial identity of Black people, suggests that from late adolescence or early adulthood on, Black people may have to repeatedly confront developmental issues connected with their racial identity. He describes this process as "recycling." Parham's concept of cycles of psychological Nigrescence adds significantly to our understanding of the racial identity development of people of color and offers an enhancement to the MID model offered by Atkinson, Morten, and Sue (1993).

Jonah's unwillingness to go to the Minority Engineering Center suggests that his attitudes still reflect the Conformity stage. It is not evident from the example what sort of experience Jonah may have had to push his thinking into the Dissonance stage. But his participation in the Black Student Union provides some indication that during his junior year he made the attitudinal transition to the

EXHIBIT 10.2. MINORITY RACIAL IDENTITY DEVELOPMENT.

Stage 1:   *Conformity Stage.* At this stage the individual exhibits an unequivocal preference for the dominant group's values and a denial of his or her own cultural heritage and upbringing. The stage is characterized by a depreciating attitude toward oneself and toward members of one's own minority group.

   Transition: Transition from this stage is often a gradual process; it may be stimulated by a significant event or experience.

Stage 2:   *Dissonance Stage.* At this stage there is a gradual breakdown of the individual's denial about his or her cultural heritage. Many conflicts are experienced—between appreciating and depreciating attitudes toward oneself and other members of the same minority group, between appreciating and depreciating attitudes toward members of the dominant group, between dominant-group views of minorities and the individual's own feelings of shared experience with other oppressed people.

   Transition: The individual begins to resolve the conflicts and confusions of the dissonance stage and begins to ask why he or she should feel shame about himself or herself and his or her cultural background and heritage.

Stage 3:   *Resistance and Immersion Stage.* The individual feels guilty about having "sold out" in the past and thereby contributed to his or her own group's oppression, feels anger bordering on rage about having been oppressed and "brainwashed" by forces in the dominant society, seeks information about his or her own cultural history and traditions. This stage is characterized by strong identification and commitment to one's own minority group. The individual totally rejects the dominant society and culture and tends to distrust and dislike all dominant-group members.

   Transition: Transition begins when the individual begins to experience discomfort and discontent with dualistic, absolutist views about his or her own minority group and about the dominant group.

Stage 4:   *Introspection Stage.* The individual experiences increasingly greater comfort with his or her own sense of identity but may experience a conflict between a feeling of responsibility and commitment to his or her minority group and a growing sense of individual autonomy. The individual reevaluates aspects of both the minority culture and the dominant culture and is increasingly concerned with other oppressed groups. He or she experiences ambivalence about embracing positive elements of the dominant culture.

   Transition: Transition begins with the resolution of the conflicts and discomforts experienced in the previous stage.

Stage 5:   *Synergistic Stage.* The individual experiences a sense of fulfillment, pride, and identification about his or her own culture. He or she has a strong sense of individual self-worth, self-confidence, and autonomy and has greater understanding and support for all oppressed people. The individual is open to constructive elements of the dominant culture and experiences selective liking and trust of dominant-group members who seek to eliminate the dominant group's repressive actions.

Source: Adapted from Atkinson, Morten, & Sue (1993, pp. 29–33).

Resistance and Immersion stage. It is not clear whether his lack of involvement in the BSU during his senior year indicates a progression to the Introspection stage or a recycling to Conformity.

Sexual Identity Development

Another important dimension of identity relates to the development and affirmation of one's sexual orientation. Most of the literature concerns the development of gay men and lesbians. There is very limited literature on bisexual persons, and virtually no attention has been given to heterosexual identity development.

Sexual orientation is commonly regarded as dichotomous—either a person is heterosexual or one is gay or lesbian. It is important, however, to begin this discussion with a more complex view of sexual orientation. Kinsey and his associates (Kinsey, Pomeroy, & Martin, 1948; Kinsey et al., 1953) proposed that sexual orientation should be considered along a continuum, ranging from exclusively heterosexual to exclusively homosexual, rather than as a dichotomy. Klein, Sepekoff, and Wolf (1990) suggested that sexual orientation is multidimensional, including variables such as sexual attraction, sexual behavior, sexual fantasies, emotional preference, social preference, self-identification, and straight or gay lifestyle.

Heterosexual Identity. Literature on heterosexuality is nearly nonexistent; in fact, in numerous books on human sexuality, the term is often not listed in the index. The reason for this lack of examination of heterosexuality is that heterosexuality is the dominant sexual orientation. Katz (1990) affirms the lack of attention to heterosexuality: "The importance of analyzing the . . . dominant sexual ideology seems obvious. . . . By not studying the heterosexual idea, . . . analysts of sex, gay and straight, have continued to privilege the 'normal' and 'natural' at the expense of the 'abnormal' and 'unnatural.' Such privileging of the norm accedes to its domination, protecting it from questions" (p. 8). McIntosh (1995), in discussing White privilege, also raises the issue of heterosexual privilege, by which persons of another dominant group hold unearned advantages, and points out an obliviousness about heterosexual privilege as well as White privilege and male privilege.

In a historical analysis of heterosexuality, Katz (1990, 1995) demonstrates that the word and its meanings are an invention of the past one hundred years. Earliest use of the word *heterosexual*, according to Katz (1990), indicated double deviance, from both gender and procreative norms, whereas *homosexual* represented only a single deviance, from the gender norm. Katz summarizes his study of the invention of heterosexuality: "Heterosexual designates a word and a concept, a norm and role, an individual and group identity, a behavior and feeling, and a peculiar sexual-political institution particular to the late nineteenth and twentieth centuries. . . . The formulation of the heterosexual idea did not create a heterosexual experience or behavior . . . but the titling and envisioning of heterosexuality did play an important role in consolidating the construction of the heterosexual's social existence" (p. 28).

Herek (1986) suggests that heterosexual masculinity is defined both positively and negatively. He indicates that "as more lesbians and gay men publicly assert their identities, . . . more people in the dominant majority must consciously label themselves as heterosexual rather than taking it for granted" (pp. 570–571). Herek reminds us that many times one's identity is both what one is not as well as what one is.

Finally, the unquestioned "natural" status of heterosexuality is illustrated effectively by Katz (1990). He quotes a character in a 1933 English novel, *Ordinary Families*, by Eileen A. Robertson: "The odd thing about me is that . . . I should be so purely 'hetero' in spite of lack of opportunity" (p. 20).

Gay and Lesbian Identity. Brown (1989) identified three elements that underlie a gay or lesbian identity: "biculturalism, with its requirements of juggling, balance, and living in and with ambiguity; marginality, with its perspective that is both outside and within the mainstream; and normative creativity, the ability to create boundaries that will work where none exist from tools that may be only partially suited to the task" (p. 452). Such outcomes of the gay and lesbian experience, albeit difficult and painful, seem to represent desirable goals for any developmental journey.

The developmental literature, however, focuses on how to "come to terms" with one's sexual orientation, particularly for gays and lesbians. Exhibit 10.3 summarizes Cass's (1979) model of homosexual identity formation. This model, widely cited in the literature (Fassinger, 1991), is one of the most frequently used models of sexual identity development among student affairs professionals. It consists of six stages, beginning with a tentative possibility that one is gay or lesbian. Unless one forecloses about one's homosexual identity, the commitment increases and deepens over the six stages as one becomes increasingly certain about and comfortable with an identity as a gay man or as a lesbian. Stages 3 and 4 are marked by increased exploration with other gays and lesbians, leading to almost exclusive participation with such others in Stage 5. Movement toward resolution of one's identity as gay or lesbian with the other components of one's identity takes place in Stage 6.

Levine and Evans (1991) provide an excellent summary of other models. Many of these models describe sequential and chronological stages or positions and evolution from periods of questioning and confusion about one's sexual identity to certainty and pride as a lesbian or a gay man.

EXHIBIT 10.3. HOMOSEXUAL IDENTITY FORMATION.

Stage 1: *Identity Confusion.* This stage is marked by a "conscious awareness that homosexuality has relevance" to the individual and his or her behavior—"either overt, as in kissing, or internal, as in thoughts, emotions, or physiological responses" (Cass, 1979, p. 222).

Stage 2: *Identity Comparison.* At the beginning of this stage, the individual admits the possibility of his or her homosexuality and "can now examine the wider implications of that tentative commitment" (Cass, 1979, p. 225). The person experiences great alienation about being and feeling different and may attempt to change, either outwardly, by "passing as straight," or inwardly, through professional help.

Stage 3: *Identity Tolerance.* This stage is characterized by an increased commitment to the possibility of being gay or lesbian, "commonly expressed in the statement 'I probably am a homosexual'" (p. 229).

Stage 4: *Identity Acceptance.* This stage is characterized by continued, increasing contacts with other homosexuals. The individual "now accepts rather than tolerates a homosexual self-image" (p. 231).

Stage 5: *Identity Pride.* At this stage, the individual employs strategies to "revalue homosexual others more positively" (p. 233).

Stage 6: *Identity Synthesis.* At this stage, the individual sees both good and bad in other homosexuals as well as in heterosexuals. He or she integrates a "homosexual identity with all other aspects of self" (p. 235).

Source: Adapted from Cass (1979).

Let's consider Jonah again. Without any mention of his sexual orientation prior to his senior year, it is difficult to make even a tentative hypothesis about the development of his sexual identity, although one might assume that he was at the earlier stages of Cass's model. His occasional participation in the Gay and Lesbian Student Alliance in his senior year may be evidence of either Identity Tolerance or Identity Acceptance. Jonah may have the added difficulty of dealing with his sexual identity development within the African American community; within this culture, religion and family both play powerful roles (Wall & Washington, 1991). The challenge for African American students of developing relationships on a traditionally White college campus may also contribute to Jonah's difficulties in dealing with his sexual orientation (Wall & Washington, 1991).

Bisexual Identity. Little has been written about bisexuality, and even less research on bisexuality has been conducted. In a personal essay about being Jewish, bisexual, and differently abled, Reichler (1991) points out the invisibility of each of these dimensions, and especially that of bisexuality, which "is not seen as an authentic way of being in almost every community" (p. 79). Zinik (1985) presents two opposing models of bisexual functioning, the "conflict" model and the "flexibility" model. In the conflict model, persons who identify as bisexual are believed

to be "experiencing identity conflict or confusion; living in an inherently temporary or transitional stage which masks the person's true underlying sexual orientation (presumably homosexual); and employing the label as a method of either
consciously denying or unconsciously defending against one's true homosexual
preference" (p. 9). In Zinik's flexibility model of bisexuality, persons who are bisexual are portrayed "somewhat as a chameleon, capable of moving easily between the heterosexual and homosexual worlds" (p. 9). Bisexual persons have both
heteroerotic and homoerotic feelings and behaviors. Bisexuality, thus, is "an integration of homosexual and heterosexual identities" (p. 9). Zinik points out that
the flexibility model, although it implies the coexistence of same sex and opposite
sex attractions and experiences, does not suggest necessarily the absence of ambivalence and confusion.

Gender Identity Development

Gender identity development can be defined as how one views oneself in relation
to one's own gender group, that is, as a woman or a man, and how these views
evolve and become more complex over time. Because of the way in which our society has constructed gender roles, the beginning point of men's gender identity
development differs from that of women's. Women's gender identity development
emerges from a societal position in which women as a group have been oppressed.
Gender identity development for White men begins from a position of dominant group status.

Let me restate that these models concern how one comes to see and understand oneself as a woman or a man in this society. This is in contrast to models
about how women or men develop their global identity. The differences between
the focus in this section and other gender-related models that seem to be similar
can be confusing. Sexism is at the heart of models concerning the development of
gender identity; this is similar (but not identical) to racism in the racial identity
models. The experience and process of becoming aware of sexism, abandoning
a sexist identity, and developing a nonsexist identity is different for women, the oppressed group, than it is for men, the dominant group. Again, these models are in
contrast to general models of identity development specific to women (for example, see Josselson, 1987, described in Chapter Nine) or to men (for example, see
Levinson et al., 1978; Moore, Parker, Thompson, & Dougherty, 1990).

Thus, hopefully with clarity for the reader, three models of gender identity
development, two for women and one for both men and women, are outlined
briefly in Exhibit 10.4. All three of these models begin with an acceptance of traditional gender roles. Also similar to all three models is that one's gender identity evolves from an external definition of what it means to be a woman or a man
to an internal, personal definition.

EXHIBIT 10.4. THREE MODELS OF GENDER IDENTITY DEVELOPMENT.

	Feminist Identity Development for Women (Downing & Roush, 1985)	Womanist Identity Development (Ossana, Helms, & Leonard, 1992)	Gender Role Journey (O'Neil, Egan, Owen, & Murry, 1993)
Stage 1	Passive acceptance	Pre-encounter	Acceptance of traditional gender roles
Stage 2	Revelation	Encounter	Ambivalence
			Anger
Stage 3	Embeddedness-emanation	Immersion/emersion	Activism
Stage 4	Synthesis	Internalization	Celebration and integration of gender roles
Stage 5	Active commitment		

In the two models for women, one by Downing and Roush (1985) and the other by Ossana, Helms, and Leonard (1992), the first four stages are similar in nature. Development proceeds from the acceptance of traditional gender roles to a questioning of societal gender constructions, usually as a result of one or more specific experiences. It then progresses to immersion in an exploration, usually with other women, of oneself as a woman, and finally to the fourth stage, which produces a positive sense of self as a woman and an integration of this part of oneself with other aspects of one's identity. In the Downing and Roush model there is a fifth stage, in which the woman takes an activist position in creating a nonsexist world. Both models for women are based on Cross's (1971, 1978, 1991) model of Black racial identity development.

There are several major differences between these two models for women. First, Downing and Roush (1985) identify their model as one of *feminist* identity development while Ossana, Helms, and Leonard identify theirs as one of *womanist* identity development. Second, according to Ossana, Helms, and Leonard (1992), "the womanist identity model characterizes 'healthy' development as personal and ideological flexibility that may or may not be accompanied by acknowledged feminist beliefs or social activism" (p. 403). Third, Ossana, Helms, and Leonard note that "Helms appropriated the term *womanist* from Black feminist writers (e.g., Brown, 1989) to emphasize that the *process* (e.g., stage-wise progression) of self-definition among women is similar regardless of race, social class, political orientation, and so forth" (p. 403).

The "gender role journey" is a portrayal of transitions in both men's and women's lives with respect to sexism and gender roles. Much of O'Neil's earlier work (O'Neil, 1981, 1990; O'Neil & Fishman, 1992; O'Neil, Helms, Gable, David,

& Wrightsman, 1986) focused exclusively on men. Although there are numerous differences among the three models, the primary difference in the O'Neil model is the Anger phase, which takes place between one's initial questioning of gender roles and one's subsequent immersion into understanding gender roles for oneself. The Anger phase involves both one's negative emotions about sexism as well as the act of expressing those emotions to individuals and groups.

Let's consider Amelia, who may be struggling with her role as a woman. On the one hand, she seems to be keenly aware of how women in her home community are treated by men. On the other hand, Amelia appears to embrace a traditional and perhaps unexamined gender role for herself with her boyfriend Carlos and in her home community. Because Amelia is a Mexican American woman, it is more appropriate to apply the womanist identity development model because in that model we can consider Amelia's gender identity development separate from feminism, often viewed by women of color as advocacy primarily for and by White women. Amelia perhaps is struggling between the Pre-encounter and Encounter stages of this model.

Other Dimensions of Identity

Ability and Disability

This discussion is about all persons, as we are all "differently abled" and "have varying levels mental and physical ability" in various circumstances; for example, "in the case of a blind and a sighted person in an unlighted room, being sightless may actually be an asset" (Atkinson & Hackett, 1995, p. 8). Remembering that each of us has abilities and disabilities, I focus here on the latter, as those are most frequently discussed in the literature.

Defining, identifying, and understanding disabilities is frequently neither an easy nor a simple process. One guide for university faculty and staff (President's Commission on Disability Issues, 1990) describes three kinds of disabilities: visible disabilities (easily recognizable physical impairments), hidden disabilities (learning disabilities, hearing impairment, psychiatric or seizure disorders), and multiple disabilities. Multiple disabilities may be caused by primary conditions such as multiple sclerosis or cerebral palsy, which, "depending on the nature and progression of the illness or injury, . . . may be accompanied by a second impairment—in mobility, vision, speech, or coordination—which may, in fact, pose greater difficulties" (p. 5). Disabilities are either congenital (blindness, absence of an arm, a seizure disorder) or acquired (paralysis resulting from an accident, AIDS, blindness, multiple sclerosis). For acquired disabilities, the age of onset is an important dimension in how the person views and is affected by the disability. Two approaches are used for defining a disability: one is "to identify specific mental or physical conditions" (Atkinson & Hackett, 1995, p. 9) that can be diagnosed; the other is to "identify the life activity affected" (p. 9).

Abilities and disabilities should be understood as socially constructed experiences that are also historically mediated (Harris & Wideman, 1988; Jones, in press; Scheer, 1994): "A disability has a social meaning and it is that indisputable fact that constitutes the major difficulty" for persons with disabilities (Harris & Wideman, 1988, p. 116). In his autobiography about dealing with the effects of a growing tumor inside his spinal column, which eventually resulted in quadriplegia, Murphy (1987) talked about how clear it became to him that illness and impairment "are psychological and social conditions as well as somatic problems" (p. 12).

Excellent illustrations of the importance of considering disability as a social construction exist in the literature. Jones (in press) demonstrates that "understanding disability as socially constructed is to celebrate the uniqueness of individual difference while directing one's attention toward social change and transformation of oppressive structures. It is to distinguish between the biological fact of disability and the handicapping social environment in which the person with disabilities exists." Wise-Mohr (1992), who has multiple sclerosis, describes a personal experience in which others did not believe she has a disability because she does not look disabled. Rousso (1984, cited in Asch & Fine, 1988) described how her mother's efforts to make her appear more "normal"—by having her try to change how she walks—made her feel like she was removing an integral part of her own identity, since she had incorporated her disability into her identity as a child.

For student affairs professionals, there are two interrelated implications of the social construction of disabilities. First, it is important to learn how an individual with a disability understands and conceptualizes that disability, rather than just relying on the socially constructed definition of it. Second, it is again important to understand oneself—specifically, in this case, in terms of how one views disability. Asch and Fine (1988), drawing on Hahn's (1983) analysis, suggest that disabilities in others "often elicit . . . powerful existential anxieties" (p. 17) about ourselves—our own helplessness, our needs, and our dependencies. Thus, if we do not know ourselves, we may act according to our own insecurities and needs rather than in the best interest of a student with a disability.

Let us consider Hank's loss of an arm in a farming accident. In terms of his identity, what is important is how Hank views this loss, whether or not he considers it disabling. While those of us who have full use of both our arms and hands may create our own understanding of what such a disability is like (that is, a social construction of the disability), Hank's perceptions and experiences with this disabling condition are the salient considerations. But it is important to attend to our personal thoughts about Hank and his disability and to determine whether those thoughts need to be altered.

Social Class

One's social class is a very important variable that relates to one's identity and that interacts with other dimensions of identity such as race and ethnicity, ability or disability, and gender. Dill (1994) points out that much of the literature about race and gender tends to omit consideration of social class, just as the class and gender literature tends to ignore race.

Langston (1995) addresses the myth of the "classless society" and discusses the effects of power in relation to social class. The myth is that one can pull oneself up by one's bootstraps, that "ambition and intelligence alone are responsible for success" (p. 101). Langston describes the chain or cycle of maintaining the classes as follows:

> The myth conceals the existence of a class society, which serves many functions. One of the main ways it keeps the working-class and poor locked into a class-based system in a position of servitude is by cruelly creating false hope. It perpetuates the false hope among the working-class and poor that they can have different opportunities in life. The hope that they can escape the fate that awaits them due to the class position that they were born into. Another way the rags-to-riches myth is perpetuated is by creating enough visible tokens so that oppressed persons believe that they, too, can get ahead. The creation of hope through tokenism keeps a hierarchical structure in place and lays the blame for not succeeding on those who don't. This keeps us from resisting and changing the class-based system. Instead, we accept it as inevitable, something we just have to live with. . . . The myth also keeps the middle class and upper class entrenched in the privileges awarded in a class-based system. It reinforces middle- and upper-class beliefs in their own superiority. (p. 101)

What about class is important to student service professionals concerned about student development? In considering this question, it is necessary to realize that class is about economic security, choices perceived and those available, and cultural background (including education, language, behavior) (Langston, 1995).

Both the examples of Jonah and Hank are useful in thinking about social class. Jonah, expecting to be a college-educated person, may anticipate a middle-class status, although his family is economically lower-middle-class. But his upbringing and experiences, regardless of his future earnings, may continue to have a strong influence on the choices he perceives and the risks he is willing to take. It is also important to consider the intersection of Jonah's race, gender, and social class. For example, not only are the options Jonah perceives likely to be connected to—and perhaps limited by—his socioeconomic class, but they are also affected by the discrimination he may face as an African American. His gender, given male privilege, might be a positive factor in relation to his social class, but as an African American man he might face greater discrimination and questions of self-esteem than a White man would.

Hank, on the other hand, comes from a rural background, and his family's earnings for the past several years reflect near-poverty status. But the fact that his family is college educated and their farm and its valuable equipment were recently inherited place Hank into a different social class than Jonah. Hank and his family probably see themselves as solidly middle-class, regardless of the fact that Hank needs to work twenty hours a week and is receiving substantial financial aid.

Religious Identity

Religious identity is an important identity dimension for those who identify with their religion or religious beliefs. I underscore *identify* because I am not speaking of simply belonging to a religious group or denomination; nor am I speaking of how religious one is or what religious beliefs one ascribes to; rather, I am referring to whether or not one views religion as an integral part of one's identity. Faith development concerns one's way of finding or making meaning (Fowler, 1981; Parks, 1986), but it is a different concept from religious identity.

Religion is an important part of U.S. society. A supreme being is referenced in the Pledge of Allegiance and on the nation's currency. Christianity is the dominant religion; its position in society is reflected in the observation of the Sunday Sabbath and major Christian holidays by government units, school systems, and businesses. Often Jewish holidays are acknowledged only in areas with large numbers of Jewish people. The holy days of other religions are often not honored in the United States.

Yet within the United States there are many different religions, beliefs, and practices. There are many different types of Christians, including Catholics, fundamentalists and evangelicals, Mennonites, Quakers, members of the Greek Orthodox church, and various groups that observe a Saturday sabbath. Among Jews there are adherents to the Orthodox, Conservative, and Reform branches of Judaism. There are also various religious organizations, many based in Christianity, that have no formal ties to a particular denomination. It is within this context of a dominant Christian society with a diversity of other religions, beliefs, and practices that many college students develop their religious identity.

Religion is an integral part of some cultures and subcultures. Religious beliefs are interwoven with their traditions and values, and religious rituals play an essential role in daily life, sometimes down to the food people eat and the clothes they wear. Especially where particular religions are marginalized (such as in the United States), religious identity may become an important part of the many complex identity issues faced by college students.

Much of the literature on religious identity comes from research on Jewish identity and the development of self-esteem in young Jewish adults. Judith Klein (1980) addresses Jewish identity as ethnic identity, which Gordon (1964) defined as a "sense of peoplehood" (pp. 23–24). This sense of peoplehood, according to Klein (1980), includes both identification with one's past and one's ancestors and a "future-oriented identification" (p. 9) with one's ethnic group. Based on her research, Klein offers a typology of three patterns of Jewish identification. Positive identifiers were able to incorporate and integrate both positive and negative aspects of being Jewish into their identity. Ambivalent identifiers ascribed both their "most valued and most despised traits to Jewishness but never resolved the conflict thus engendered" (p. 57). Negative identifiers, conversely, used denial and self-contempt to distance and disaffiliate themselves from being Jewish.

The MID model developed by Atkinson, Morten, and Sue (1993) is also applicable to religious identity development. The individual evolves from a point where he or she demonstrates a total denial of his or her religious identity and incorporates the beliefs and attitudes of the dominant culture to a stage at which he or she synthesizes both the good and bad elements of his or her religious culture and those of the dominant religious culture into his or her religious identity. So Klein's "negative identifier" (1980), someone who seems completely unaware of any religious identity and adheres to the dominant culture, might be regarded as being in the early stages of the MID model. We cannot know upon quick and simple observation or questioning, however, whether a person for whom religious identity appears to be unimportant is in the early stages of the MID model or has simply decided, after thoughtful consideration, that religious affiliation is not a relevant personal identity dimension.

The only information we have about the religious identity of our three sample students is the reference to Amelia's active participation in her church. We have no real indication of how central religion is to Amelia's identity. It may be that Amelia has simply accepted her religion from her family and that participation in her church (but not religion) is a considered part of her identity. Another possibility is that Amelia's move away from home to college may have encouraged a personal examination of religion and that a central part of Amelia's identity is who she is as a member and participant in her religion.

Geographic Region

Where one grows up, where one forms basic values, where one currently resides, and where one envisions herself or himself in the future are rarely considered in discussions of identity development. Yet if we view identity as socially constructed, is not one's region or place a salient part of such social constructions? Place may also reflect the social dimension of urban, suburban, or rural.

Garreau (1981), in identifying and describing nine regions of North America, encourages one to forget traditional notions of region, such as those that are historically, geographically, or politically defined. Rather, Garreau speaks of the sociological and psychological components of region. He indicates that "each nation [or region] has a distinct prism through which it views the world" (p. 2). According to Garreau, a region or geographic entity is limited for individuals by a "certain intuitive, subjective sense of loyalties that unify it" (p. xv). He underscores the importance of a region's feeling "right" to the individual. Although Garreau's work is not explicitly about identity, he does address it: "Your identity is shaped by your origins. Thus, to come away with a new understanding of regionalism is to come away with a better understanding of yourself" (p. xvi). He concludes by saying that one's region, locale, or place is where one has a "feeling of familiarity," where "surroundings stop feeling threatening, confusing, or strange" (p. 13).

Considering students' "home" region or place may help student affairs professionals put students' concerns, developmental struggles, and attitudes into a meaningful context that constitutes part of their overall identity. Regional identity may have implications for one's level of comfort or alienation in a given environment, one's ways of talking and interacting with others, the values one holds, and the foods one eats; it may also relate to one's connection with a sense of family.

Region or place may or may not be salient to the three students in the vignettes. Although there may be a strong geographic identity for each of the regions in which these students were raised, they may or may not connect with place as a part of their personal identity. It is possible that Jonah has a regional identity with the South, the Southeast, or Atlanta, and that he has a heightened awareness of that identity during his time in the Northeast.

Multiple Identities

Multiple oppressions and multiple identities are rarely addressed in the psychological literature, although it is not uncommon to find anthologies about multiple oppressions and multiple identities in the literature on women's studies (see, for example, Andersen & Collins, 1995, and Moraga & Anzaldúa, 1983). Reynolds and Pope (1991) focus on multiple oppressions and challenge the dichotomies or segmentation of identities seen in literature and in society—male or female; heterosexual, bisexual, lesbian or gay; Asian American, African American, White, American Indian, or Latino; lower-, middle-, or upper-class. They also point to the lack of attention to within-group differences, a complexity that goes beyond the segmentations of various identities and groups. Building on Root's biracial identity model, Reynolds and Pope (1991), in their Multidimensional Identity Model (MIM), identify two dimensions of identity development. One dimension concerns whether an individual chooses to identify with only one aspect of his or her identity or with multiple aspects. A second dimension concerns whether an individual is active or passive in taking on one or more identities.

These two dimensions result in "four possible options for identity resolution that occur within a dynamic process of self-growth and exploration" (Reynolds & Pope, 1991, p. 178). The four options are as follows:

> Identify with one aspect of self (society assigned-passive acceptance).
>
> Identify with one aspect of self (conscious identification).
>
> Identify with multiple aspects of self in a segmented fashion.
>
> Identify with combined aspects of self (identity interaction). (p. 179)

Reynolds and Pope's (1991) model describes effectively different patterns of dealing with multiple oppressions or multiple identities. What is not known is how and under what circumstances an individual's pattern may change over time. Returning to one of the premises of developmental theory, we know that development involves an interaction between what happens within a person and what takes place in his or her environment. Thus, changing environmental conditions may have an important effect on how an individual's identity develops. An example may be useful. Racial identity theory suggests that a race-related experience or series of experiences may provide a trigger for facing a new racial identity status. Similar kinds of experiences—trigger events—may challenge an individual to address an aspect of his or her identity that has been put aside or has not yet emerged. Such a situation may occur when a person is, perhaps for the first time, one of a few similar persons in a group of "others" and thus feels marginalized.

Concerning oneself with the multiple dimensions of one's identity is a highly fluid and dynamic process. Sampson (1985) suggests that identity as described by Erikson (1980), as a more or less coherent whole, may be misrepresented. Rather, Sampson encourages a somewhat more "decentralized, nonequilibrium conception of personhood that allows our multiplicity and interconnectedness a time to live" (p. 1210). The social constructions of these identity dimensions in our society challenges each of us to examine them for ourselves and determine how they are a part of our evolving and developing sense of self.

All three of our students provide nice examples of the development of multiple identity dimensions within a single individual. For Jonah, an African American gay man from Atlanta, we can hypothesize that earlier in his college years his racial identity was developing, perhaps to the exclusion of his sexual identity. His focus on his sexual orientation may have emerged after he became more secure with his identity as an African American. There is no evidence in the vignette, however, about how these two dimensions of identity development may have interacted or conflicted with each other. There is also no evidence about whether or how Jonah has struggled with his sense of himself as a man. Jonah's social class, his sense of his regional identity, and possibly his religious identity may have also interacted with the dimensions about which we have more information. A reasonable hypothesis is that some of his other identities, such as his racial, regional, and religious identity, may have challenged the development of his identity as a gay man. Finally, all of these dimensions probably play out in some way with Jonah's cognitive and psychosocial development.

Amelia's gender identity development seems integrally connected with her culture and ethnicity. Whether or how she is concerned with her ethnic or racial identity or her identity as an apparently heterosexual woman is not clear. Amelia's regional identity may be closely interwoven with her culture and ethnicity, but again we have no information about the salience of locale or place to her identity development.

Hank's racial identity development, his sense of his social class, and how he views the loss of his arm potentially interact. Although as a White man he is part of a dominant group, Hank may believe, falsely, that his socioeconomic class and his disability counterbalance his racial privilege. Hank's identification with his rural upbringing may cause the multiple dimensions of his identity to come together somewhat differently than they would if he identified with an urban or suburban background.

An Emerging Model of Multiple Dimensions of Identity Development

How might all these aspects of identity interact? Which ones intersect or overlap, and which ones exist apart from others? As I think about all the many dimensions of identity, I draw on my education in mathematics and physics in considering how they might be represented. Using Helms's (1992) idea that development can be thought of in three-dimensional terms, I would like to represent the interaction and intersection of identity development as a conical structure with varying radii and heights. As with a helix, the overall shape of this conelike structure would be one of increasing circumference and increasing complexity, becoming more extended in length with increasing age, experiences, education, and reflection. Different colors or shades might be used to represent different arenas of a person's life, such as family, work, leisure, and self.

If we were to cut horizontally through this conelike structure we would see a number of circles placed in relation to one another. Each cut or circle would represent a certain point in time. Each circle might give us a comprehensive picture of an individual's development at that particular point in time. It would not, however, provide any sense of that individual's developmental patterns.

Let us consider, however, looking at a vertical cross-section of this conelike shape. In such a cross-section we might see only one dimension of identity, or only a couple, but we would have the opportunity to gain a sense of how the individual's identity in that dimension or those dimensions evolved over his or her lifetime.

We could also consider other kinds of cross-sections of this conelike representation. What if we created a diagonal cross-section across multiple areas of development? This might portray intersections or interactions between dimensions or between multiple identities and other kinds of development, such as psychosocial, cognitive, or career development.

Conclusion

Let's return to some of the questions raised near the beginning of this chapter. Many other questions are also important to consider. For instance, which identity dimensions are salient for any given individual? Which are "on hold," or not yet addressed? Which have yet to appear? How do we know? In what situations or life statuses are certain dimensions salient, and when are they not? When and how do they emerge, and when do they fade or seemingly disappear? What about other dimensions of identity — do they play a role? If so, what is it, and how is it constructed? How do an individual's identity dimensions interact with one another? How do they interact with other kinds of development (such as psychosocial and cognitive)? How do they interact with that individual's learning process and career development? How does personality affect the development of identity dimensions? What is the role of environment in identity development, especially in relation to the seven dimensions of identity discussed in this chapter? How are the dimensions of an individual's identity socially constructed? How do our own lenses, experiences, and identities filter what we see and how we understand identity development?

How do the various identity dimensions interact together and with one's overall development and sense of self? How do student affairs professionals address the holistic development of the student and yet also consider these specific dimensions of development? How do we help students to have a whole and complete experience in terms of their development? How can we learn to use theories complexly to think about and understand the whole student?

There may not be complete answers to these questions, but it is imperative for us to struggle with them. It is hard work to understand students and to apply theory to their development. We need to struggle regularly and consistently with these questions through continued reading, discussion with colleagues, and reflection. Reflection is the component most central to critical science inquiry.

And the questions continue. How does Helms's (1994) shift from "stages" in identity development to "ego statuses" help us conceptualize and understand the complexities of human development? What does "developmental recycling" mean, and how do individuals portray it in their own development? What do we believe about human development, and what is our role in supporting, facilitating, and/or promoting it?

What is the role of theory? How should we use theory? Should we use theory to predict? We should probably use it to predict only with the greatest of cautions, given that both theory and identity are socially constructed. Should we use theory to understand? Yes, theory can help us to understand, not in an absolute sense but with greater complexity and with more integrated meanings. Should theory be used to generate research and new theory? Yes, along with critical science, critical theory, and deconstruction. What are some of the critical points in various developmental processes, and how do our programming and interventions with students facilitate (or hinder) their development at those critical points?

In conclusion, an objective of this chapter has been to demonstrate that identity and its development in college students are very complex. Identity in its most comprehensive sense encompasses not only the traditional Eriksonian notions of identity but also identity dimensions viewed through important social constructions such as race, gender, sexual orientation, social class, and ability and disability.

Individuals, including students, who live in the United States must contend with the dominant society and its constructions of race, gender, sexual orientation, and other dimensions of difference. People can never be free from the external pressures of these social constructions to develop themselves without incorporating these dimensions. Thus we as student affairs professionals must examine how an individual looks at and incorporates these dimensions of identity within the individual's sense of self. Such considerations must include racial, sexual, and gender identity development, as well as aspects of ability and disability, social class, religion, and geographic region.

The developmental models of racial, sexual, and gender identity described in this chapter suggest that as an individual develops in each of these areas, the individual's perspectives evolve from an acceptance of and adherence to the views of the relevant dominant group to an increasing acceptance and appreciation of oneself as different from the dominant-group perspectives. One who is part of an oppressed group develops understanding, affirmation, and pride in being part of one's own cultural group, such as being Black, gay, or female. An individual who is part of a dominant group also develops an identity as part of that group; but rather than an unexamined acceptance of and adherence to such group membership, the individual has carefully examined the privileges garnered from membership in that group, the group's oppression of others, and the positive values of being a member of that group.

Other dimensions, including ability and disability, social class, religion, and geographic region, although they may not be developmental in nature, may also be important components of identity. In the simplest description, an individual either incorporates the society's dominant views of these dimensions or develops a more self-defined identity.

Not only may each of the seven dimensions described in this chapter be an important component of an individual's identity, but how these dimensions intersect and how they collectively fit into an individual's identity may be even more important. Theory and research are beginning to address how these various dimensions may interact with one another and whether or not and when they are salient to an individual (for example, see Reynolds & Pope, 1991, and Jones, 1995). Along with the privilege of working with college students go our responsibilities as student affairs professionals to understand the complexities of college students' identities and how these identities are differentially meaningful to students and in what contexts.

References

Andersen, M. L., & Collins, P. H. (Eds.). (1995). *Race, class, and gender: An anthology* (2nd ed.). Belmont, CA: Wadsworth.

Asch, A., & Fine, M. (1988). Introduction: Beyond pedestals. In M. Fine & A. Asch (Eds.), *Women with disabilities: Essays in psychology, culture, and politics* (pp. 1–37). Philadelphia: Temple University Press.

Atkinson, D. R., & Hackett, G. (1995). *Counseling diverse populations.* Dubuque, IA: Brown & Benchmark.

Atkinson, D. R., Morten, G., & Sue, D. W. (1993). *Counseling American minorities: A cross-cultural perspective* (4th ed.). Dubuque, IA: Brown & Benchmark.

Brown, L. S. (1989). New voices, new visions: Toward a lesbian/gay paradigm for psychology. *Psychology of Women Quarterly, 13,* 445–458.

Cass, V. C. (1979). Homosexual identity formation: A theoretical model. *Journal of Homosexuality, 4,* 219–235.

Chickering, A. W. (1969). *Education and identity.* San Francisco: Jossey-Bass.

Chickering, A. W., & Reisser, L. (1993). *Education and identity* (2nd ed.). San Francisco: Jossey-Bass.

Cook, D. A., & Helms, J. E. (1988). Visible racial/ethnic group supervisees' satisfaction with cross-cultural supervision as predicted by relationship characteristics. *Journal of Counseling Psychology, 35,* 268–274.

Cross, W. E., Jr. (1971). The Negro-to-Black conversion experience: Toward a psychology of Black liberation. *Black World, 20*(9), 13–27.

Cross, W. E., Jr. (1978). The Thomas and Cross models of psychological Nigrescence: A review. *Journal of Black Psychology, 5,* 13–31.

Cross, W. E., Jr. (1991). *Shades of Black: Diversity in African-American identity.* Philadelphia: Temple University Press.

Dill, B. T. (1994). Race, class, and gender: Prospects for an all-inclusive sisterhood. In L. Stone (Ed.), *The education feminism reader* (pp. 42–56). New York: Routledge.

Downing, N. E., & Roush, K. L. (1985). From passive acceptance to active commitment: A model of feminist identity development for women. *Counseling Psychologist, 13,* 695–709.

Erikson, E. H. (1980). *Identity and the life cycle.* New York: Norton. (Original work published 1959).

Fassinger, R. E. (1991). The hidden minority: Issues and challenges in working with lesbian women and gay men. *Counseling Psychologist, 19,* 157–176.

Fowler, J. (1981). *Stages of faith: The psychology of human development and the quest for meaning.* New York: Harper & Row.

Garreau, J. (1981). *The nine nations of North America.* Boston: Houghton Mifflin.

Gordon, M. M. (1964). *Assimilation in American life: The role of race, religion, and national origins.* New York: Oxford University Press.

Hahn, H. (1983). Paternalism and public policy. *Society, 20*(2), 36–46.

Harris, A., & Wideman, D. (1988). The construction of gender and disability in early attachment. In M. Fine & A. Asch (Eds.), *Women with disabilities: Essays in psychology, culture, and politics* (pp. 115–138). Philadelphia: Temple University Press.

Helms, J. E. (1990a). An overview of Black racial identity theory. In J. E. Helms (Ed.), *Black and White racial identity: Theory, research, and practice* (pp. 9–32). New York: Greenwood Press.

Helms, J. E. (1990b). Applying the interaction model to social dyads. In J. E. Helms (Ed.), *Black and White racial identity: Theory, research, and practice* (pp. 177–185). New York: Greenwood Press.

Helms, J. E. (1990c). Counseling attitudinal and behavioral predispositions: The Black/White interaction model. In J. E. Helms (Ed.), *Black and White racial identity: Theory, research, and practice* (pp. 135–143). New York: Greenwood Press.

Helms, J. E. (1990d). Generalizing racial identity interaction theory to groups. In J. E. Helms (Ed.), *Black and White racial identity: Theory, research, and practice* (pp. 187–204). New York: Greenwood Press.

Helms, J. E. (1990e). Interventions for promoting better racial identity development. In J. E. Helms (Ed.), *Black and White racial identity: Theory, research, and practice* (pp. 205–219). New York: Greenwood Press.

Helms, J. E. (1990f). Introduction: Review of racial identity terminology. In J. E. Helms (Ed.), *Black and White racial identity: Theory, research, and practice* (pp. 3–8). New York: Greenwood Press.

Helms, J. E. (1990g). Toward a model of White racial identity development. In J. E. Helms (Ed.), *Black and White racial identity: Theory, research, and practice* (pp. 49–66). New York: Greenwood Press.

Helms, J. E. (1992). *A race is a nice thing to have: A guide to being a White person, or understanding the White persons in your life.* Topeka, KS: Content Communications.

Helms, J. E. (1994). The conceptualization of racial identity and other "racial" constructs. In E. J. Trickett, R. J. Watts, & D. Birman (Eds.), *Human diversity: Perspectives on people in context* (pp. 285–311). San Francisco: Jossey-Bass.

Herek, G. M. (1986). On heterosexual masculinity: Some psychical consequences of the social construction of gender and sexuality. *American Behavioral Scientist, 29,* 563–577.

Jones, S. R. (1995). *Voices of identity and difference: A qualitative exploration of the multiple dimensions of identity development.* Unpublished doctoral dissertation, University of Maryland, College Park.

Jones, S. R. (in press). Toward inclusive theory: Disability as social construction. *NASPA Journal.*

Josselson, R. (1987). *Finding herself: Pathways to identity development in women.* San Francisco: Jossey-Bass.

Katz, J. N. (1990). The invention of heterosexuality. *Socialist Review, 20* (1), 7–34.

Katz, J. N. (1995). *The invention of heterosexuality.* New York: Dutton.

Kinsey, A. C., Pomeroy, W. B., & Martin, C. E. (1948). *Sexual behavior in the human male.* Philadelphia: Saunders.

Kinsey, A. C., et al. (1953). *Sexual behavior in the human female.* Philadelphia: Saunders.

Klein, F., Sepekoff, B., & Wolf, T. J. (1990). Sexual orientation: A multi-variable dynamic process. In T. Geller (Ed.), *Bisexuality: A reader and sourcebook* (pp. 64–81). Ojai, CA: Times Change Press.

Klein, J. W. (1980). *Jewish identity and self-esteem: Healing wounds through ethnotherapy.* New York: Institute on Pluralism and Group Identity, American Jewish Committee.

Langston, D. (1995). Tired of playing monopoly? In M. L. Andersen & P. H. Collins (Eds.), *Race, class, and gender: An anthology* (pp. 100–110). Belmont, CA: Wadsworth.

Levine, H., & Evans, N. J. (1991). The development of gay, lesbian, and bisexual identities. In N. J. Evans & V. A. Wall (Eds.), *Beyond tolerance: Gays, lesbians, and bisexuals on campus* (pp. 1–24). Alexandria, VA: American College Personnel Association.

Levinson, D. J., Darrow, C. H., Klein, E. B., Levinson, M. H., & McKee, B. (1978). *The seasons of a man's life.* New York: Knopf.

McIntosh, P. (1995). White privilege and male privilege: A personal account of coming to see correspondences through work in women's studies. In M. L. Andersen & P. H. Collins (Eds.), *Race, class, and gender: An anthology* (2nd ed., pp. 76–87). Belmont, CA: Wadsworth.

Moore, D., Parker, S., Thompson, T., & Dougherty, P. (1990). The journey continues. In D. Moore & F. Leafgren (Eds.), *Problem solving strategies and interventions for men in conflict* (pp. 277–283). Alexandria, VA: American Association for Counseling and Development.

Moraga, C., & Anzaldúa, G. (1983). *This bridge called my back: Writings by radical women of color.* New York: Kitchen Table.

Murphy, R. F. (1987). *The body silent.* New York: Holt.

Omi, M., & Winant, H. (1994). *Racial formation in the United States from the 1960s to the 1990s* (2nd ed.). New York: Routledge.

O'Neil, J. M. (1981). Patterns of gender role conflict and strain: Sexism and fear of femininity in men's lives. *Personnel and Guidance Journal, 60,* 203–210.

O'Neil, J. M. (1990). Assessing men's gender role conflict. In D. Moore & F. Leafgren (Eds.), *Problem solving strategies and interventions for men in conflict* (pp. 23–38). Alexandria, VA: American Association for Counseling and Development.

O'Neil, J. M., Egan, J., Owen, S. V., & Murry, V. M. (1993). The Gender Role Journey Measure: Scale development and psychometric evaluation. *Sex Roles, 28,* 167–185.

O'Neil, J. M., & Fishman, D. M. (1992). Adult men's career transitions and gender-role themes. In H. D. Lea & Z. B. Leibowitz (Eds.), *Adult career development: Concepts, issues, and practices* (pp. 161–191). Alexandria, VA: National Career Development Association.

O'Neil, J. M., Helms, B. J., Gable, R. K., David, L., & Wrightsman, L. S. (1986). Gender-role conflict scale: College men's fear of femininity. *Sex Roles, 14,* 335–350.

Ossana, S. M., Helms, J. E., & Leonard, M. M. (1992). Do "womanist" identity attitudes influence college women's self-esteem and perceptions of environmental bias? *Journal of Counseling and Development, 70,* 402–408.

Parham, T. A. (1989). Cycles of psychological Nigrescence. *Counseling Psychologist, 17,* 187–226.

Parks, S. (1986). *The critical years: The young adult search for a faith to live by.* New York: Harper & Row.

Phinney, J. S. (1990). Ethnic identity in adolescents and adults: Review of research. *Psychological Bulletin, 108,* 499–514.

Phinney, J. S. (1992). The Multigroup Ethnic Identity Measure: A new scale for use with diverse groups. *Journal of Adolescent Research, 7,* 156–176.

Poston, W. S. C. (1990). The biracial identity development model: A needed addition. *Journal of Counseling and Development, 69,* 152–155.

President's Commission on Disability Issues. (1990). *Reasonable accommodations: Teaching college students with disabilities.* College Park: University of Maryland.

Reichler, R. (1991). A question of invisibility. In L. Hutchins & L. Kaahumanu (Eds.), *Bi by any other name: Bisexual people speak out* (pp. 78–79). Boston: Alyson Publications.

Reynolds, A. L., & Pope, R. L. (1991). The complexities of diversity: Exploring multiple oppressions. *Journal of Counseling and Development, 70,* 174–180.

Root, M. P. P. (Ed.). (1992). *Racially mixed people in America.* Newbury Park, CA: Sage.

Rousso, H. (1984, December). Fostering healthy self-esteem (Pt. 1). *Exceptional Parent,* 9–14.

Ruiz, A. S. (1990). Ethnic identity: Crisis and resolution. *Journal of Multicultural Counseling and Development, 18,* 29–40.

Sampson, E. E. (1985). The decentralization of identity: Toward a revised concept of personal and social order. *American Psychologist, 40,* 1203–1211.

Sanford, N. (1967). *Where colleges fail: A study of the student as a person.* San Francisco: Jossey-Bass.

Scheer, J. (1994). Culture and disability: An anthropological point of view. In E. J. Trickett, R. J. Watts, & D. Birman (Eds.), *Human diversity: Perspectives on people in context* (pp. 244–260). San Francisco: Jossey-Bass.

Tajfel, H. (1981). *Human groups and social categories: Studies in social psychology.* Cambridge: Cambridge University Press.

Wall, V. A., & Washington, J. (1991). Understanding gay and lesbian students of color. In N. J. Evans & V. A. Wall (Eds.), *Beyond tolerance: Gays, lesbians, and bisexuals on campus* (pp. 67–78). Alexandria, VA: American College Personnel Association.

Widick, C., Parker, C. A., & Knefelkamp, L. (1978). Erik Erikson and psychosocial development. In L. Knefelkamp, C. Widick, & C. A. Parker (Eds.), *Applying new developmental findings* (New Directions for Student Services No. 4, pp. 1–17). San Francisco: Jossey-Bass.

Wise-Mohr, C. (1992, March 1). MS, the world and me: Who says I'm disabled? *Washington Post,* p. C5.

Zinik, G. (1985). Identity conflict or adaptive flexibility? Bisexuality reconsidered. In F. Klein & T. J. Wolf (Eds.), *Bisexualities: Theory and research* (pp. 7–19). New York: Haworth.

CHAPTER ELEVEN

STUDENT COGNITION AND LEARNING

Patricia M. King

The central mission of higher education is to enhance learning. All those who have a responsibility for contributing to this process should be able to articulate how they do so. This is the most important reason student affairs practitioners should be knowledgeable about student learning. While learning is sometimes seen as the sole responsibility of faculty, it is a premise of this chapter that both faculty and student affairs practitioners have a mutual responsibility—and complementary opportunities—to enhance student learning. Also, student affairs practitioners often serve as a resource to faculty and campus administrators on student issues; understanding student learning will help practitioners better assist others respond more effectively when dealing with student problems related to learning. Further, as we near the end of the twentieth century, issues of learning have taken on a special significance and urgency. The knowledge explosion continues unabated, and electronic media provide virtual mountains of information that must be understood and interpreted in order to be useful. Global issues, from pollution to terrorism, demand informed, creative responses. As Davis (1993) has noted, "People need to learn, as never before, how to deal with each other as human beings, across, within, and in spite of their differences" (p. 17). These are pressing reasons to attend to student learning.

The focus of this chapter is how students learn. It is intended to help educators choose and design educational strategies that are appropriate for their educational purposes, acknowledging the diverse educational needs of college students. It begins with a brief discussion of three related questions: What is learning? What should college students learn? and How do students learn?

What Is Learning?

Learning is sometimes regarded as synonymous with education ("to be a learned person") and knowledge ("book learning"). Learning is also associated with acquired wisdom, which involves showing good judgment; being able to discern what is true, right, or lasting; and being prudent and informed. Learning thus defined— as an *outcome*—includes the knowledge, skills, and attitudes that serve as a foundation for wisdom. Learning defined as a *process*, on the other hand, focuses on the kinds of strategies people use to solve new problems, how they respond to feedback and new information, how they gather and interpret data, how they determine its relevance, and how strong the evidence needs to be before they are satisfied that they can make a decision or solve a problem. *Learning* is both a noun and a verb, representing both an outcome and a process of education. How college students define learning has been found to be closely related to how they approach it (van Rossum & Schenk, 1984).

The field of learning (especially what used to be called learning theory, now known as cognition or cognitive science) has undergone a dramatic transformation in the past twenty-five years. Brown (1994) refers to the "cognitive revolution" (p. 6) during this period, which has changed many beliefs about learning and learners. She notes that "learners came to be viewed as *active constructors*, rather than passive recipients of knowledge" (p. 6). It is now widely accepted that learning involves metacognitive functions and the construction of knowledge by the learner.

The question "What is learning?" is one that many people who work on college campuses should be able and willing to discuss with students, parents, and other constituent groups. Educators should be able to both explain and model meaningful learning. Students should be encouraged to identify their own definition of learning and examine how their approach to learning and their prior learning experiences affect their learning goals and strategies. These would be excellent topics of discussion for an orientation program or as part of a senior outcomes assessment. Discussion of such issues provides an excellent point of contact between student affairs staff and faculty members.

What Should College Students Learn?

Institutional expectations for student learning influence the kind of learning that takes place. Educators should be able to identify what they intend students to learn from their educational programs and the attributes they hope their graduates will have. Student learning goals are typically described in terms of the knowledge, skills, and attitudes students are expected to demonstrate by the time they graduate. While these three sets of attributes are separated for clarity as goals, they are interrelated in the developing person. For example, gaining global awareness requires students to be knowledgeable about such topics as world history; current events; and cultural, economic, and social influences. They also need to be able to discern others' values and understand the sources and implications of their own value systems. Students should be aware of the interdependence of knowledge, skills, and attitudes so they can more intentionally target their educational efforts and more effectively respond to the problems they confront.

Students' attitudes and values play an important role in what and how they learn. Do students have the disposition to apply critical thinking skills to "everyday" problems? Do they seek out different perspectives on controversial problems? Do they demonstrate a fundamental respect for other persons in their daily interactions? Do they strive to act ethically in support of the common good? Students should be aware that what and how they learn will influence the kind of people they become. They should actively consider the questions, "What kind of person (citizen, parent, worker) do I want to be?" "What do I need to learn (about myself, about others, about the world around me) to become this kind of person?" and "What do I want to learn while I am a student here?" Faculty and staff should be available and ready to help students develop answers to these questions of personal and professional identity and to support them in recognizing this as a difficult and important part of the process of becoming educated and gaining wisdom.

Proposing a list of the knowledge, skills, and attitudes that students should learn by the time they graduate from college is beyond the scope of this chapter. However, several excellent resources are available for this purpose (Alverno College, 1992; Association of American Colleges, 1985, 1991; Bok, 1986; Bowen, 1980; Hirsch, 1987; Rosovsky, 1990).

How Do Students Learn?

We now turn to the major topic of this chapter—how students learn. A dizzying array of approaches to student learning exists in the professional literature. A common theme of these approaches is that the key to understanding student learning is understanding student differences. This section opens with a description of three major factors that affect student learning, starting with cognitive factors (how individuals recognize, process, and evaluate information). Here, student learning is examined from two major perspectives, learning styles and strategies (a broad category that includes many diverse approaches to understanding *how* students reason) and learning and epistemology (which looks at the assumptions underlying students' learning strategies, with greater emphasis on *why* students reason as they do). Next, two other sets of factors that affect learning are briefly addressed: motivational factors (what encourages and sustains students' interest in learning and performing well in educational settings) and social factors (the dynamics of the social context in which learning occurs, situations that require interpersonal as well as cognitive skills). While these three sets of factors are treated separately here for clarity, they overlap and interact in any given educational context. This section describes a variety of approaches students use in situations where they are asked to think about and solve unfamiliar problems.

Cognitive Factors That Affect Learning

Learning Styles and Strategies

The term *learning style* has become quite familiar to educators seeking to respond helpfully to individual differences among the students with whom they work. Several researchers have suggested that understanding learning styles requires an understanding of learning strategies. A learning strategy is "a sequence of procedures for accomplishing learning" (Schmeck, 1988, p. 5). A strategy must be intentionally invoked; it requires a conscious decision to follow a specified plan of action. For example, Brown and Campione (1990) asked a group of high school students about their preferred study strategies. Three of their responses were as follows: "I stare real hard at the page, blink my eyes and then open them—and cross my fingers that it will be right here [pointing at his head]." A somewhat better informed peer replied, "It's easy; if she [the teacher] says study, I read it twice. If she says read, it's just once through." A third answered, "I just read the first line in each paragraph—it's usually all there" (p. 111).

More effective learners draw from a broad repertoire of strategies, such as clarifying the author's purpose, outlining the chapter to identify the main points and supporting evidence, making evaluative judgments about the strength of the arguments presented, making predictions, identifying implications, or exchanging sample test questions with friends. Failure to solve a problem may reflect not only a poor choice of strategy but also a wide variety of other factors, such as a lack of necessary skills to implement the strategy, a misunderstanding of the purposes of the activity, or an unwillingness to take the time to use the preferred strategy.

By contrast, a learning style is "a predisposition to adopt a particular learning strategy" (Das, 1988, p. 101) or the habitual use of similar strategies (Kirby, 1988) across situations or contexts. For example, a student might typically study a text by reviewing the chapter outline, main headings, and summaries, comparing these to his or her class notes, looking up unfamiliar words or concepts, and periodically reviewing memorized information. Establishing this as a student's style requires multiple observations of that student in similar circumstances, not just one observation of a single event (Schmeck, 1988).

The next section of this chapter summarizes several models that describe different learning styles and strategies. Following these summaries is a discussion that attempts to integrate the major features of the various models, noting their implications for working with college students.

Surface and Deep Approaches

Marton and Säljö (1976a, 1976b) investigated two distinct strategies students use when reading academic texts. Students who use a surface approach focus on verbatim recall of facts or ideas as if they were self-standing and self-explanatory. They "may well fail to distinguish between essential points and incidental facts or between principles and examples. They are unlikely to relate evidence and conclusions or examine the argument in a critical way" (Entwistle, 1988, p. 25). As a result, they risk missing the main point of the reading.

By contrast, students who use a deep approach to learning intentionally try to establish connections between new information or ideas in the text and their prior learning. They have a personally meaningful purpose for learning, and their role as learner includes evaluating and reconstructing knowledge. (This assumption is discussed further below, in the section on learning and epistemology). These students use "an active process of learning in which the student challenges the ideas, evidence, and arguments presented by the author, tries to see interrelationships among the ideas presented, and seeks links with personal experience and the outside world" (Entwistle, 1988, p. 24).

A similar pair of contrasting learning styles are Schmeck's (1981) "shallow-reiterative" and "deep-elaborative" information processing approaches. In the first style, students "prefer to assimilate information as given rather than rewording, restating, or rethinking it" (p. 385). Students who used the deep approach "classify, contrast, analyze, and synthesize information from different sources" (p. 385). The success of the deep approach was documented by Miller, Alway, and McKinley (1987), who found that students who used the deep approach had higher GPAs.

These learning styles reflect not only differences in approaches to learning but also differences in students' conceptions of learning itself. Van Rossum and Schenk (1984) asked students to indicate which of five different conceptions of learning they endorsed; they then compared the responses to the students' approach to learning (surface or deep). They found that virtually all those who used a surface approach defined learning according to one of the two simplest categories—an increase in knowledge or memorization. By contrast, virtually all those who used a deep approach to learning defined it using the two most cognitively complex definitions—learning as the abstraction of meaning or as an interpretive process aimed at understanding the world. Surface and deep learners were equally split on the midlevel definition of learning—learning as the acquisition and utilization of facts.

The deep approach to learning is clearly more consistent with the aim of colleges to teach students to think more critically. Educators should encourage students to read and listen actively, to use a more complex frame of reference than the immediate text or speaker, and to try to make a personal connection to the ideas presented.

Modes of Consciousness: Left Brain–Right Brain

A considerable amount of research over the last 150 years on brain functioning has greatly expanded our understanding of processes related to thinking and reasoning. Research on the hemispheric structure of the brain was originally based on patients with injuries to one side of the brain. Such research has since evolved into a major theoretical school, addressing "the psychological and physiological mechanisms of the two major modes of consciousness" (Ornstein, 1972, p. 51). Dual modes of thinking have been observed in many cultures around the world. Each hemisphere of the brain is associated with different capabilities: the left emphasizes analytic and sequential approaches, and the right emphasizes more holistic and relational styles. Ornstein describes the two modes of consciousness as follows. The left hemisphere "is predominantly involved with analytic, logical thinking, especially in verbal and mathematical functions. Its mode of operation is primarily linear. This hemisphere seems to process information sequentially" (p. 51). Logic, language, and mathematics are considered left-brain activities. The right hemisphere, by contrast, "is primarily responsible for our orientation in space, artistic endeavor, crafts, body image, recognition of faces. It processes information more diffusely than does the left hemisphere, and its responsibilities demand a ready integration of many inputs at once" (p. 52).

Both types of functions are available to most individuals, though some people do show hemisphere-dominant characteristics. It is an oversimplification to suggest that the left hemisphere controls rational and logical thinking and the right controls intuition and creativity. Educators should encourage students to learn with both sides of their brain, since some problems (or parts of problems) call for strategies associated with one side more than the other.

Global and Analytic Strategies

In his studies of the reading strategies used by poor readers, Kirby (1988) observed individuals who focused their attention at too broad a level, did not retain most details, and missed even main points. Kirby refers to this type of surface strategy as highly *global* ("seeing the forest"). He also observed a second group of poor readers who erred in the opposite direction: *analytic* readers, by contrast, focused on the specific details of the text ("seeing the trees"), using rote memory to remember the exact words and phrases. In the process, they also missed the main points, could not explain how the main points were related in the text, and did not engage in interpretive analyses of the arguments presented.

Since Kirby's descriptions were developed by examining students who used ineffective approaches to learning through reading, his work brings a different vantage point to this cluster of models. He suggested that a better strategy is to combine elements of each approach, what he called a *synthetic* style. Using this style, the reader attends to details but retains them only if doing so is consistent with his or her purpose. Schmeck (1981) also noted that the most competent students use versatile learning strategies, "alternately employing analogy to get an overall model and then testing its applicability by examining details. The versatile learning style leads to a very high level of understanding" (p. 236).

Reading is an essential skill for achieving success in many academic contexts. For practitioners working with academically at-risk students, identifying whether and how a student's reading strategy is ineffective can suggest ways to improve the process and thus enhance the likelihood of the student's success.

Field Dependence or Independence

Witkin's (1976) work on cognitive style has received a great deal of attention in educational circles. Witkin focused on the dimension of field dependence or independence, measuring the degree to which individuals are heavily influenced by (dependent upon) or relatively uninfluenced by (independent of) their surrounding context. Whereas a field-dependent person tends to see a situation globally (seeing the whole instead of its parts), the field-independent person tends to see a situation more analytically (separating the parts from the whole).

Witkin's model has an extensive (but dated) research base (Witkin & Goodenough, 1981; Witkin, Moore, Goodenough, & Cox, 1977). In his major review in the mid 1970s, Witkin (1976) reported that field-dependent students tended to be involved in majors and careers that have a strong interpersonal dimension, such as teaching, counseling, and sales. Field-independent students tended to be involved in majors and careers that focus on analytic skills, such as mathematics, engineering, and science. Whether these findings apply to today's students is open to speculation and further research.

Psychological Type and Learning Styles

The Myers-Briggs Type Indicator (MBTI) (Myers, 1980) has been used extensively to document differences based on the ways individuals tend to take in information (the perception function) and make judgments (the judgment function). Since the Myers-Briggs model is described elsewhere in this volume (Chapter Nine), only a brief overview is given here. The perceiving and judging functions are broken down into four polar dimensions, Introversion-Extraversion (I-E), Sensing-Intuition (S-N), Thinking-Feeling (T-F), and Perceiving-Judging (P-J), which when combined yield sixteen different types (ENFP, INTJ, and so on).

The MBTI has enjoyed immense popularity, yet literature reviews report mixed results in terms of validating the model's theoretical claims (e.g., see Murray, 1990, and Pittenger, 1993). Nevertheless, the model has been widely applied in both business and higher education settings (Provost & Anchors, 1987). Jensen (1987) summarized the preferred learning styles by type; these are reprinted here as Exhibit 11.1.

Kolb's Experiential Learning Theory

Kolb (1984) defines learning as "the process whereby knowledge is created through the transformation of experience" (p. 38). Kolb described four adaptive modes of learning, based on how individuals perceive information (through concrete experience or abstract conceptualization) and how they process it (through reflective observation or active experimentation). From these two dimensions, Kolb identified four distinct types of learners (divergers, assimilators, convergers, and accommodators), each characterized by specific competencies.

Divergers take in information through concrete experience and transform it through reflective observation. This style "is associated with *valuing skills:* being sensitive to people's feelings and to values, listening with an open mind, gathering information, and imagining implications of ambiguous situations" (pp. 93–94).

Assimilators take in information through abstract conceptualization and transform it through reflective observation. This style "is related to *thinking competencies:* organizing information, building conceptual models, testing theories and ideas, designing experiments, and analyzing quantitative data" (p. 94).

EXHIBIT 11.1. TYPE AND LEARNING STYLES.

Extraversion (E)

E's learn best in situations filled with movement, action, and talk. They prefer to learn theories or facts that connect with their experience, and they usually come to a more thorough understanding of these theories or facts during group discussions or when working on cooperative projects. E's tend to leap into assignments with little forethought, relying on trial and error rather than anticipation to solve problems.

Introversion (I)

Since I's may be more quiet and less active in the classroom, teachers may feel the need to press them into taking part in group discussions. Such pressure, however, will often only increase their withdrawal. Teachers need to respect their need to think in relative solitude, for that is how they think best. I's are more willing to share their ideas when given advance notice. This allows them time to think about how they will become active in the classroom.

Sensory Perception (S)

S's learn best when they move from the concrete to the abstract in a step-by-step progression. Thus they are most at home with programmed, modular, or computer-assisted learning. They value knowledge that is practical, and they want to be precise and accurate in their own work. They tend to excel at memorizing facts.

Intuitive Perception (N)

N's tend to leap to a conceptual understanding of material and may daydream or act out during drill work or predominantly factual lectures. They value quick flashes of insight but are often careless about details. They tend to excel at imaginative tasks and theoretical topics.

Thinking Judgment (T)

T's are most motivated when provided with a logical rationale for each project and when teachers acknowledge and respect their competence. They prefer topics that help them understand systems or cause-and-effect relationships. Their thought is syllogistic and analytical.

Feeling Judgment (F)

F's are most motivated when they are given personal encouragement and shown the human angle of a topic. F's think in order to clarify their values and establish networks of values. Even when their expressions seem syllogistic, they usually evolve from some personally held belief or value.

Judgment (J)

J's tend to gauge their learning by the completion of tasks: reading *x* amount of books, writing *x* amount of papers, or making *x* amount of reports. They thus prefer more structured learning environments that establish goals for them to meet.

Perception (P)

P's tend to view learning as a freewheeling, flexible quest. They care less about deadlines and completing tasks. They prefer open and spontaneous learning environments and feel imprisoned in highly structured classrooms.

Convergers take in information through abstract conceptualization and transform it through active experimentation. This style "is associated with *decision skills:* creating new ways of thinking and doing, experimenting with new ideas, choosing the best solution to problems, setting goals, and making decisions" (pp. 94–95).

Accommodators take in information through concrete experience and transform it through active experimentation. This style "encompasses a set of competencies that can best be termed *acting skills:* committing oneself to objectives, seeking and exploiting opportunities, influencing and leading others, being personally involved, and dealing with people" (p. 93).

In contrast to other learning models described above, Kolb (1984) not only describes the characteristics of the various learning styles but also discusses the need for development within dimensions, reflected by increasing competence in each dimension (for example, refined perceptual complexity in the reflective observation dimension). He suggests that development "is marked by increasing complexity and relativism in dealing with the world and one's experience and by higher-level integrations of the dialectic conflicts among the four primary learning modes" (p. 140). (For a related model of learning style, see Gregorc, 1982.)

Multiple Intelligences

Gardner's (1987, 1993) theory of multiple intelligences describes seven distinctive ways people process information. It helps explain what people can and cannot do well and how they become different kinds of problem solvers and problem finders. He defines intelligence as "an ability to solve a problem or to fashion a product which is valued in one or more cultural settings" (Gardner, 1987, p. 25). His theory includes seven domains of intelligence (see Exhibit 11.2), which are assumed to be largely independent. For example, a person who can readily remember names and faces often cannot as readily remember math formulas or words in a poem; linguistic ability does not predict spatial ability. Further, each intelligence is assumed to have its own developmental trajectory, so development across intelligences is assumed to proceed at different paces.

Different roles or occupations are associated with each type of intelligence, as well as with combinations of the different types. For example, spatial intelligence is required for navigators and sculptors, and interpersonal intelligence is required for counselors and salespeople. Surgeons require not only spatial but bodily-kinesthetic intelligence to manipulate their scalpels with accuracy and dexterity.

Although Gardner's theory is based in biology, it focuses on cultural roles and assumes that intelligence is content-based. Different learning situations are better

EXHIBIT 11.2. GARDNER'S MULTIPLE INTELLIGENCES.

Intelligence	Associated Abilities
Linguistic	Sensitivity to the sounds, rhythms, and meanings of words; sensitivity to the different functions of language
Logical-Mathematical	Sensitivity to and capacity to discern logical or numerical patterns; ability to handle long chains of reasoning
Musical	Abilities to produce and appreciate rhythm, pitch, and timbre; appreciation of the forms of musical expressiveness
Spatial	Capacities to perceive the visual-spatial world accurately and to perform transformations on one's initial perceptions
Bodily-Kinesthetic	Abilities to control one's body movements and to handle objects skillfully
Interpersonal	Capacities to discern and respond appropriately to the moods, temperaments, motivations, and desires of other people
Intrapersonal	Access to one's own feelings and the ability to discriminate among them and draw upon them to guide behavior; knowledge of one's own strengths, weaknesses, desires, and intelligences

Source: Gardner & Hatch (1989, p. 6). Copyright 1989 by American Educational Research Association. Reprinted with permission.

suited to different types of intelligences. Gardner (1993) criticizes standardized testing and schooling approaches for focusing too heavily on linguistic and logical-mathematical intelligence, to the detriment of students whose strengths lie in other domains. He argues that the purpose of education should be to develop diverse intelligences, to help individuals become intelligent in more than one domain.

Educators can use Gardner's concept of the seven intelligences to clarify both the content of what they teach (for example, interpersonal or linguistic skills) and the means for students to respond to it (for example, through language, music, or space). Such an approach gives educators a new tool for analyzing and selecting appropriate responses to students who possess intelligences that have not traditionally been stressed in academic environments. For example, it offers more support for the idea that some people prefer to learn using their sight (visual learners), others learn better using their ears (auditory learners), and still others learn better using their tactile or kinesthetic senses.

Research on Scientific Reasoning

Other lines of research on learning have used scientific reasoning as the basis for information about students' information processing (for example, see Baron, 1988; Kuhn, 1989). These studies have focused on such specific skills as hypothesis generation, experimentation, data interpretation, and hypothesis revision. They found that the strategies of "better" and "poorer" learners differed in *evidence generation* (better learners tested experimental predictions and used effective experimental designs; poorer learners used unsystematic approaches), *evidence interpretation* (better learners tested newly discovered concepts in different markets; poorer learners generalized findings without testing them), and *data management* (better learners systematically recorded relevant data more often than did poorer learners).

Schauble and Glaser (1990) offer an alternative explanation for poor learners' use of ineffective problem-solving strategies. They suggested that their choice of strategies may reflect a different understanding (or a misunderstanding) of the goal of the activity. They asked students, "What are you going to learn from this experiment?" or "What are you trying to accomplish here?" and found that "differences in students' plans reflected fundamentally different understandings of the experimentation task they were engaged in" (p. 24). Thus educators should encourage students to be clear about the purpose of their assignments, class activities, and readings, so they have a better idea of the task at hand and can focus their attention and efforts accordingly.

What about students who are overconfident in their beliefs and tend to ignore evidence against their initially favored views? Baron (1988, 1990) has argued that educators should encourage students to use "actively open-minded" thinking and its associated learning strategies. That is, students should be taught "to consider alternative possibilities, neglected goals, and counterevidence" (1990, p. 28).

Integrating Models of Learning Styles and Strategies

Several of these models of learning styles and strategies include similar sets of elements. Several researchers use contrasting pairs of strategies to describe observed differences. Different combinations of strategies are characterized by a preferred strategy for approaching a problem or situation—for example, a "big picture" approach (seeing the forest) versus a detailed approach (seeing the trees). Some readers may think the prevalent use of dichotomies in strategies conveys an unduly bifurcated view of the world. However, this degree of consistency between theories has led Schmeck (1988) to speculate that these dichotomies are collectively describing an underlying construct, which he refers to as *global-holistic* and *focused-detailed* approaches. For example, compare the preferred learning "styles" or reasoning strategies of Ornstein's left-brain thinkers, Kirby's analytic thinkers, Witkin's field independents, Kolb's assimilators, those who prefer Myers-Briggs's sensing and thinking approaches, and those with what Gardner would call high logical-mathematical intelligence. Students who prefer these approaches might need more encouragement and practice in seeing the big picture and the main points, undertaking independent projects, seeing implications, considering "What if?" questions, and solving problems that require understanding of conceptual distinctions or theories.

By contrast, consider Ornstein's right-brain thinkers, Kirby's global thinkers, Witkin's field dependents, Kolb's divergers, those who prefer Myers-Briggs's intuitive and feeling approaches, and those with what Gardner would call high interpersonal intelligence. Students who prefer these approaches might need more encouragement and practice keeping track of relevant details, being accurate and precise, developing logical arguments, solving deductive problems that require step-by-step procedures, and thinking analytically and deductively.

Most learning style models present such contrasting approaches as two equally effective means of addressing and resolving problems. (In fact, only two of the models summarized above designated educationally preferable strategies—the deep versus the surface approach to learning and the scientific reasoning studies, which are developmentally based). This stance has the advantages of affirming individuals "where they are" and showing respect for individual differences. This focus on appreciating differences and making nonevaluative judgments is appealing to faculty and staff alike, in part because giving feedback to students about their approach is correspondingly descriptive rather than judgmental, which helps create a more inviting and affirming type of contact with students.

The nonjudgmental approach creates difficulties, however, when the student faces problems for which his or her preferred approach is not effective. At such times the student needs to strengthen skills associated with his or her "auxiliary" (nonpreferred) approach; the role of the educator then changes to someone who can help the student overcome whatever obstacles impede his or her success, including acknowledging the weaknesses of the preferred approach.

While this group of learning models uses contrasting styles to point out differences, it is important for educators to note that these styles are frequently the extreme endpoints of a continuum with many variations—that is, many students—falling between them. In other words, most people do not rely exclusively on the skills associated with one approach to learning or one end of a given continuum of learning styles. This is an encouraging observation, as the most advanced or adaptive styles and the most effective learning strategies often require integration of elements from both extremes. Educators should be cautioned against the temptation to label a student as though he or she possesses only one set of talents, skills, or sensitivities— as a "visual learner," a "feeling type," or a "right-brained thinker," for example— instead of acknowledging the student's attributes as points on a continuum.

Taking these different learning strategies into account, educators can help students effectively adapt their methods of learning to the specific tasks and contexts at hand. As Weinstein and Meyer (1991) note, "to be successful in selecting and using a strategy, students must understand under what circumstances a given strategy is or is not appropriate" (p. 17). As these models show, research on the development of sound reasoning strategies and the appeal of faulty strategies have yielded important insights into our understanding of how students learn.

Learning and Epistemology

As Kolb (1984) states, "to understand knowledge, we must understand the psychology of the learning process, and to understand learning, we must understand epistemology—the origins, nature, methods, and limits of knowledge" (p. 37). The models summarized in this section describe students' epistemological assumptions as a way to understand how they define, approach, and interpret learning. In contrast to the work discussed above on learning strategies, these models focus on a more fundamental level of thinking—the underlying assumptions that appear to guide the process of knowing. From this perspective, strategies for learning reflect more than preferred study techniques or procedures for gathering information; they reflect the individual's way of constructing meaningful interpretations of their experiences. Constructing one's own knowledge instead of relying on knowledge received from another source reflects a major distinction between deep and surface approaches to learning.

Several scholars have studied developmental changes in students' assumptions about knowledge, with varying degrees of specificity about how these are related to learning (Basseches, 1984; Baxter Magolda, 1992; Belenky, Clinchy, Goldberger, & Tarule, 1986; Broughton, 1978; King & Kitchener, 1994; Kramer, 1989; Perry, 1970; Sinnott, 1989). Two that have strong research bases and a clear connection to college students' learning are discussed next.

The Reflective Judgment Model

The reflective judgment model (King & Kitchener, 1994; Kitchener & King, 1981, 1990) describes a developmental progression in people's assumptions about knowledge (what can be known, how knowledge is gained, certainty of knowledge claims) and how these assumptions are related to how people justify their beliefs. This progression may be observed in the ways people use evidence in making decisions about problems that cannot be defined and resolved with completeness and certainty (for example, for current events where evidence is incomplete or contradictory or historical events where evidence has been lost over time). Using evidence intentionally and honestly reflects the difference "between developing and justifying a position and merely asserting one" (Association of American Colleges, 1991, p. 14). Research on the reflective judgment model has shown that people's assumptions about knowledge correspond closely to the ways they evaluate knowledge claims (including their own beliefs). For example, those who believe judgments can only be made with a measure of certainty (and not absolutely) tend to be skeptical when faced with dogmatic assertions made by others.

The progression of thinking described by the reflective judgment model is summarized in Exhibit 11.3. In this model it is not assumed that individuals are "in" one stage at a time; rather, they work within a "developmental range" of stages (Lamborn & Fischer, 1988, p. 1), and their performance varies depending on such factors as support and feedback (Kitchener, Lynch, Fischer, & Wood, 1993).

Teaching for reflective thinking requires that educators create and sustain learning environments conducive to the thoughtful consideration of controversial topics, that they help students learn to evaluate others' evidence-based interpretations, and that they provide supportive opportunities for students to practice making and explaining their own judgments about important and complicated problems. (For examples of specific strategies for promoting reflective thinking, see Kitchener & King, 1990; King, 1992; King & Kitchener, 1994; and Kroll, 1992.)

The Epistemological Reflection Model

Baxter Magolda (1992) described four "qualitatively different ways of knowing, each characterized by a core set of epistemic assumptions" (p. 29). These four approaches (absolute, transitional, independent, and contextual) are associated with different expectations of the learner and his or her peers and instructors about how learning should be evaluated and how educational decisions should be made. In addition to the structural differences between the ways of knowing, Baxter Magolda also describes gender-related patterns within each of the first three ways of knowing, patterns that were more often used by either men or women (but not exclusively by either gender).

Baxter Magolda (1992, 1994) has examined a variety of educational issues in light of these four ways of knowing. She suggests that three principles be used to support student learning—"validating the student as a knower, situating learning in the students' own experience, and defining learning as jointly constructing meaning" (1992, p. 270)—and she has called for transforming (not just redesigning)

EXHIBIT 11.3. SUMMARY OF REFLECTIVE JUDGMENT STAGES.

Prereflective Thinking

Stage 1   *View of Knowledge:* Knowledge is assumed to exist absolutely and concretely; it is not understood as an abstraction. It can be obtained with certainty through direct observation.

Concept of Justification: Beliefs need no justification since there is assumed to be an absolute correspondence between what is believed and what is true. Alternative beliefs are not recognized.

"I know what I have seen."

Stage 2   *View of Knowledge:* Knowledge is assumed to be absolutely certain, or certain but not immediately available. Knowledge can be obtained directly through the senses (such as direct observation) or via authority figures.

Concept of Justification: Beliefs are unexamined and unjustified, or justified by their correspondence with the beliefs of an authority figure (such as a teacher or parent). Most issues are assumed to have a right answer, so there is little or no conflict in making decisions about disputed issues.

"If it is on the news, it has to be true."

Stage 3   *View of Knowledge:* Knowledge is assumed to be absolutely certain or temporarily uncertain. In areas of temporary uncertainty, only personal beliefs can be known until absolute knowledge is obtained. In areas of absolute certainty, knowledge is obtained from authorities.

Concept of Justification: In areas in which certain answers exist, beliefs are justified by reference to authorities' views. In areas in which answers do not exist, beliefs are defended as personal opinion, since the link between evidence and beliefs is unclear.

*"When there is evidence that people can give to convince everybody one
way or another, then it will be knowledge; until then, it's just a guess."*

Quasi-Reflective Thinking

Stage 4   *View of Knowledge:* Knowledge is uncertain, and knowledge claims are idiosyncratic to the individual, since situational variables (such as incorrect reporting of data, data lost over time, or disparities in access to information) dictate that knowing always involves an element of ambiguity.

Concept of Justification: Beliefs are justified by giving reasons and using evidence, but the arguments and choice of evidence are idiosyncratic (for example, choosing evidence that fits an established belief).

*"I'd be more inclined to believe in evolution if they had proof.
It's just like the pyramids: I don't think we'll ever know.
Who are you going to ask? No one was there."*

Stage 5   *View of Knowledge:* Knowledge is contextual and subjective since it is filtered through a person's perceptions and criteria for judgment. Only interpretations of evidence, events, or issues may be known.

Concept of Justification: Beliefs are justified within a particular context, using the rules of inquiry for that context and by context-specific interpretations of evidence. Specific beliefs are assumed to be context-specific or are balanced against other interpretations, which complicates (and sometimes delays) conclusions.

*"People think differently, and so they attack the problem differently.
Other theories could be as true as my own, but based on different evidence."*

EXHIBIT 11.3. SUMMARY OF REFLECTIVE JUDGMENT STAGES, cont'd.

Reflective Thinking

Stage 6   *View of Knowledge:* Knowledge is constructed into individual conclusions about ill-structured problems based on information from a variety of sources. Interpretations that are based on evaluations of evidence across contexts and on the evaluated opinions of reputable others can be
known.

Concept of Justification: Beliefs are justified by comparing evidence and opinion on different sides
of an issue or across contexts and by constructing solutions that are evaluated by criteria such as
the weight of the evidence, the utility of the solution, or the pragmatic need for action.

> *"It's very difficult in this life to be sure. There are degrees of sureness. You come
> to a point at which you are sure enough to take a personal stance on an issue."*

Stage 7   *View of Knowledge:* Knowledge is the outcome of a process of reasonable inquiry, in which solutions to ill-structured problems are constructed. The adequacy of those solutions is evaluated
in terms of what is more reasonable or probable based on the current evidence, and it is reevaluated when relevant new evidence, perspectives, or tools of inquiry become available.

Concept of Justification: Beliefs are justified probabilistically, based on a variety of interpretative
considerations such as the weight of the evidence, the explanatory value of the interpretations,
the risk of erroneous conclusions, consequences of alternative judgments, and the interrelationships of these factors. Conclusions are defended as representing the most complete, plausible, or compelling understanding of an issue, based on the available evidence.

> *"One can judge arguments by how well thought out the positions are, what
> kinds of reasoning and evidence are used to support it, and how consistent
> the way one argues on this topic is as compared with other topics."*

Source: King & Kitchener (1994, pp. 14–16). Reprinted with permission.

educational practices to enhance intellectual development. She has emphasized
that relational modes of knowing are essential to intellectual development and are
often learned in cocurricular settings. Examples of ways educators can assist students to learn from their out-of-class experiences are summarized in Exhibit 11.4
for each way of knowing.

Implications

How can educators try to improve college students' learning experiences? Svinicki
(1991) suggests six principles from cognitive learning for this purpose:

1. Students need to recognize the important information and concepts in what
   they are learning.
2. Learners act on information to make it more meaningful.
3. Learners store information in a way that reflects their prior understanding.
4. Learners continually check, refine, and revise their understanding.
5. Transfer of learning to new contexts is not automatic.
6. Learners should be aware of their learning strategies and monitor their use.

EXHIBIT 11.4. STUDENTS' ADVICE FOR COCURRICULAR EDUCATION.

	Absolute Knowing	Transitional Knowing	Independent Knowing	Contextual Knowing
Peer relationships	Create opportunities for positive peer interaction.	Encourage development of support network of friends. Help students respond to peer influence. Help maximize learning about diversity.	Support peer interaction that fosters appreciation of diversity. Encourage efforts to balance personal needs with those of close friends. Teach students how to create new support networks.	Reinforce peers as legitimate source of knowledge.
Student organizations	Create opportunities for positive peer interaction. Create opportunities for student responsibility.	Promote leadership development. Offer opportunities for practical experience. Use as a source of friendship and for dealing with diversity.	Validate voice through leadership opportunities.	Provide freedom to exercise choice.
Living arrangements	Create opportunities for positive peer interaction. Create opportunities for student responsibility.	Organize around themes of responsibility and community.		
Internships/ employment		Build human relations skills. Offer practical experience.	Help students process insights gained. Reinforce self-confidence gained.	Reinforce expanding horizons.
Educational advising	Create opportunities for student responsibility, combined with support from authority.	Provide direct experience and stress-management assistance.		
General campus environment	Create opportunities for student responsibility.	Provide opportunity for self-discipline.		Create possibilities for freedom and development of voice.
International and/or cultural exchange		Provide direct encounters with diversity.	Create opportunity for students to reevaluate their beliefs.	

Source: Baxter Magolda (1992, pp. 298–299). Reprinted with permission.

Student affairs staff who are aware of these phenomena can help students understand and evaluate their preferred learning strategies and the experiences on which their preferences might be based. Educators can also discuss how different learning contexts call for different strategies (for example, strategies for gathering background information for a concert differ from strategies for identifying solutions to an interpersonal conflict) and encourage students to vary their strategies according to the specific characteristics of the problem at hand. (For a discussion of the importance of fostering personal development concurrently with learning, see King & Baxter Magolda, in press.)

Motivational Factors That Affect Learning

Why do some students eagerly engage in the learning process? What encourages them to perform well in educational settings? What helps them sustain their interest when they are not performing as well as they or their teachers hope? The study of how these and other dispositional features affect learning is the topic of interest for many researchers in the field of motivation. According to McMillan and Forsyth (1991), students' motivation is heavily influenced by what they perceive as important and what they believe they can accomplish. For example, students are motivated by activities that help them achieve a goal, gain social approval, or attend to developmental tasks. Students' motivation is not only affected by such "needs" but also by their expectations for success. These expectations are based on such factors as prior learning experiences (positive and negative), how feedback is given and received, and whether they feel they have earned their successes. McMillan and Forsyth conclude that "students are more likely to be motivated if their needs are being met, if they see value in what they are learning, and if they believe that they are able to succeed with reasonable effort" (p. 50). Taking advantage of opportunities to practice new strategies for learning will require extra effort on the student's part—and extra motivation to exert it.

Social Factors That Affect Learning

Learning often occurs in social contexts, such as classrooms, computer labs, residence halls, and snack bars. Understanding social contexts is important for understanding learning because they affect the roles played by individuals within them. For example, students typically take less responsibility for how they learn in classroom contexts than in study groups, and they are more likely to help one another learn in computer labs than in lecture halls. The social context includes "the entire spectrum of roles, responsibilities, expectations, and interactions between students and teachers, and among students" (Tiberius & Billson, 1991, p. 68). Attending to the social context of education is important, because being socially effective requires interpersonal as well as cognitive skills. The social context can either strongly encourage students to take an intellectual or interpersonal risk in the service of learning, or it can discourage them from persevering in a difficult subject.

Student affairs staff members can play a pivotal role in helping students understand the social contexts of their formal learning environments, especially since they are often privy to students' early reactions to course-related activities. For example, they should encourage students to think about the types of questions they volunteer to answer in class, whether they initiate a study group and with whom, and what level of responsibility they take for preparing for class. They should also help students understand the social contexts of their out-of-class learning environments (for example, judicial affairs, residence hall councils, special interest student groups) and deliberately create interactions for students that are sensitive to the power of these contexts. For example, staff should encourage students to identify the meaning of their service at a local soup kitchen, the role of ritual in their Greek letter organization, or interests that may be shared by residents of their floor that can then serve as the basis for a floor event.

What features of the social context are particularly important for fostering student learning? Tiberius and Billson (1991) identified the following: mutual respect, shared responsibility for learning and mutual commitment to goals, effective communication and feedback, cooperation and a willingness to negotiate conflicts, and a sense of security in learning environments. They describe a social context that discourages learning by noting, "The social context will be toxic if discriminatory comments are allowed to float unchallenged in the classroom. Students who feel excluded or slighted are likely to withdraw; both the victims and other students suffer from the loss of ideas" (p. 90).

In light of the access student affairs staff members have to information about students' academic activities (from students' study habits to students' reactions to their course assignments), they are in an excellent position to help students make connections between in-class and out-of-class learning. Further, they are in a position to offer many opportunities for students to practice their skills and apply them in diverse campus and off-campus settings. To be successful in making these kinds of connections with students may require the use of a common vocabulary across the campus, so the many individuals with whom students are learning can talk about goals, skills, strategies, and educational assumptions.

Practices That Encourage Student Learning

Learning takes place in many settings, both formal and informal, and it takes place both intentionally and serendipitously. How educators choose to encourage learning varies as they respond to many different factors, including cognitive, motivational, and social context factors. Educators select strategies based on their assumptions about students and the process of learning as well as on their own preferred styles of teaching (Davis, 1993). Students' selection of learning strategies also depends on their assumptions about the teacher and about the process of learning, as well as on their awareness of themselves as learners (awareness of their strengths, weaknesses, and preferences). Many excellent resources are now available that identify educational practices that enhance learning (Baxter Magolda, 1992; Brown, 1994; Brown & Campione, 1990; Chickering & Gamson, 1987; Chickering & Reisser, 1993; Claxton & Murrell, 1987; Davis, 1993; Davis & Murrell, 1993; Johnson, Johnson, & Smith, 1991; Menges & Svinicki, 1991; Vasquez & Wainstein, 1990).

Davis (1993) identified five instructional strategies used by educators; each reflects a different educational purpose and set of assumptions about learning and teaching. They are as follows:

> Training and coaching: "developing basic and advanced skills by using clear objectives, breaking instruction into steps, and reinforcing progress" (p. 13)
>
> Lecturing and explaining: "presenting information in ways that it can be attended to, easily processed, and remembered" (p. 13)
>
> Inquiry and discovery: "teaching thinking skills, problem-solving, and creativity through inquiry and discovery" (p. 13)
>
> Groups and teams: "sharing information, working cooperatively on projects, and exploring attitudes, opinions, and beliefs through group processes" (pp. 13–14)
>
> Experience and reflection: "enabling students to reflect on learning that takes place in work settings, internships, travel, or outdoor activities" (pp. 14).

In order to meet the needs of diverse learners, educators must employ a diverse range of teaching strategies. All of Davis's strategies have been used successfully in both academic and student affairs contexts. As educators select strategies, they will have to consider their educational purpose, which strategy is best suited to that purpose, and decide whether to select a strategy that complements or challenges students' preferred approach to learning.

When a student is encouraged to learn about his or her "learning style," it erroneously implies that the student has just one style. This in turn suggests rigidity rather than flexibility or development as the educational goal. The same concerns apply to a student's "leadership style," which suggests inflexibility or resistance to different styles and an inability to adapt to different needs. Instead students should be encouraged to learn about and evaluate their own preferences for learning, since approaches, styles, and strategies are typically defined in terms of both strengths and weaknesses. They should also be encouraged to develop new strategies for learning that are appropriate to the situation at hand and to practice thinking through their own selection of strategies.

Should educators select their strategies based on culture and race? There appears to be a widespread assumption that learning styles differ for students of different ethnic minority groups. This conclusion may be premature, however: "Although the current research base does not demonstrate definitive links between learning style and race, culture, or gender, consistent cultural and educational findings across such disciplines as psychology, sociology, anthropology and linguistics suggest some correlations" (Anderson & Adams, 1992, p. 20). Most studies of cultural differences in learning styles and strategies have been conducted using school-age children; comparable research using college students has been rather limited. The assertion that significant cultural differences in learning styles can be observed—for example, that African American students and women are field-dependent learners and White males are field-independent learners—is at this point a sweeping generalization unsubstantiated by the research (Frisby, 1993). As Tharp (1989) noted, "Within all cultures, there are variations of considerable magnitude. . . . For example, within any cultural group, motivation, social organization, and ways of speaking and thinking vary with education, income, and class status. Broad educational prescriptions for 'Hawaiians' or 'Blacks' or 'Native Americans' are often, and rightly, resented by culture members who are not well described by these generalizations" (p. 357). Students of all cultural and racial backgrounds should be encouraged to develop learning strategies that are flexible and suited for the specific demands and constraints of the problem at hand. In this regard ethnic minority college students may have an advantage. Persons of color in the United States often live in a bicultural world. They move between two cultures, the dominant culture and their own, adapting their learning style, language, and dress to the two cultures as needed. Presumably, college students of color also live bicultural lives, especially those at predominantly white institutions. Having learned to adapt their strategies to meet cultural demands, they may be more able to adapt to situational demands of different learning environments, such as adopting strategies needed to succeed in analytical, field-independent classrooms (Shuford, 1995). Whether a bicultural background contributes to the paucity of learning style differences among minorities documented in the literature is a topic worthy of additional research.

Conclusion

Kegan (1994) used the metaphor of crossing bridges to describe the process of learning and development. He noted that "a bridge must be well anchored on both sides, with as much respect for where it begins as for where it ends" (p. 62). This observation reflects the importance of respectful, collaborative relationships between teachers and students. Educators must both respect students as unique human beings—whatever their preferred learning strategies or epistemic assumptions—while encouraging them to develop their full capacities. It is the role of educators to help create developmental bridges and to invite students to cross new bridges (King & Baxter Magolda, in press), thus enhancing student learning.

References

Alverno College. (1992). *Liberal learning at Alverno College.* Milwaukee, WI: Author.

Anderson, J., & Adams, M. (1992). Acknowledging the learning styles of diverse student populations: Implications for instructional design. In L.L.B. Borders and N.V.N. Chism (Eds.), *Teaching for diversity* (New Directions for Teaching and Learning No. 49, pp. 19–33). San Francisco: Jossey-Bass.

Association of American Colleges. (1985). *Integrity in the college curriculum: A report to the academic community.* Washington, DC: Author.

Association of American Colleges. (1991). *The challenge of connecting learning.* Washington, DC: Association of American Colleges.

Baron, J. (1988). *Thinking and deciding.* New York: Cambridge University Press.

Baron, J. (1990). Harmful heuristics and the improvement of thinking. In D. Kuhn (Ed.), *Developmental perspectives on teaching and learning thinking skills* (Contributions to Human Development, Vol. 21, pp. 28–47). Basel, Switzerland: Karger.

Basseches, M. (1984). *Dialectical thinking and adult development.* Norwood, NJ: Ablex.

Baxter Magolda, M. B. (1992). *Knowing and reasoning in college: Gender-related patterns in students' intellectual development.* San Francisco: Jossey-Bass.

Baxter Magolda, M. B. (1994). Post-college experience and epistemology. *Review of Higher Education, 18*(1), 25–44.

Belenky, M. F., Clinchy, B. M., Goldberger, N. R., & Tarule, J. M. (1986). *Women's ways of knowing: The development of self, voice, and mind.* New York: Basic Books.

Bok, D. C. (1986). *Higher learning.* Cambridge, MA: Harvard University Press.

Bowen, H. (1980). *Investment in learning.* San Francisco: Jossey-Bass.

Broughton, J. (1978). Development of concepts of self, mind, reality, and knowledge. In W. Damon (Ed.), *Social cognition* (New Directions for Child Development No. 1, pp. 75–100). San Francisco: Jossey-Bass.

Brown, A. L. (1994). 1994 AERA presidential address: The advancement of learning. *Educational Researcher, 23*(8) 4–12.

Brown, A. L., & Campione, J. C. (1990). Communities of learning and thinking, or a context by any other name. In D. Kuhn (Ed.), *Developmental perspectives on teaching and learning thinking skills* (Contributions to Human Development, Vol. 21, pp. 108–125). Basel, Switzerland: Karger.

Chickering, A. W., & Gamson, Z. (1987). *Seven principles for good practice in undergraduate education.* Winona, MN: Winona State University, Seven Principles Resource Center.

Chickering, A. W., & Reisser, L. (1993). *Education and identity* (2nd ed.). San Francisco: Jossey-Bass.

Claxton, C. S., & Murrell, P. H. (1987). *Learning styles: Implications for improving education practices* (ASHE-ERIC Higher Education Report No. 4). Washington, DC: Association for the Study of Higher Education.

Das, J. P. (1988). Simultaneous-successive processing and planning: Implications for student learning. In R. R. Schmeck (Ed.), *Learning strategies and learning styles* (pp. 101–129). New York: Plenum Press.

Davis, J. R. (1993). *Better teaching, more learning: Strategies for success in postsecondary settings.* Phoenix, AZ: Oryx Press.

Davis, T. M., & Murrell, P. H. (1993). *Turning teaching into learning: The role of student responsibility in the collegiate experience* (ASHE-ERIC Higher Education Report No. 8). Washington, DC: George Washington University, School of Education and Human Development.

Entwistle, N. (1988). Motivational factors in students' approaches to learning. In R. R. Schmeck (Ed.), *Learning strategies and learning styles* (pp. 21–51). New York: Plenum Press.

Frisby, C. L. (1993). One giant step backward: Myths of Black cultural learning styles. *School Psychology Review, 22,* 535–557.

Gardner, H. (1987). The theory of multiple intelligences. *Annals of Dyslexia, 37,* 19–35.

Gardner, H. (1993). *Multiple intelligences: The theory in practice.* New York: Basic Books.

Gardner, H., & Hatch, T. (1989). Multiple intelligences go to school: Educational implications of the theory of multiple intelligences. *Educational Researcher, 18,* 4–10.

Gregorc, A. R. (1982). *An adult's guide to style.* Maynard, MA: Gabriel Systems.

Hirsch, E. D., Jr. (1987). *Cultural literacy: What every American needs to know.* Boston: Houghton Mifflin.

Jensen, G. H. (1987). Learning styles. In J. Provost & S. Anchors (Eds.), *Applications of the Myers-Briggs Type Indicator in higher education* (pp. 181–206). Palo Alto, CA: Consulting Psychologists Press.

Johnson, D. W., Johnson, R. T., & Smith, K. A. (1991). *Cooperative learning: Increasing college faculty instructional productivity* (ASHE-ERIC Higher Education Report No. 4). Washington, DC: George Washington University, School of Education and Human Development.

Kegan, R. (1994). *In over our heads: The mental demands of modern life.* Cambridge, MA: Harvard University Press.

King, P. M. (Ed.). (1992). [Special issue on reflective judgment.] *Liberal Education, 78*(1).

King, P. M., & Baxter Magolda, M. B. (in press). A developmental perspective on learning. *Journal of College Student Development.*

King, P. M., & Kitchener, K. S. (1994). *Developing reflective judgment: Understanding and promoting intellectual growth and critical thinking in adolescents and adults.* San Francisco: Jossey-Bass.

Kirby, J. R. (1988). Style, strategy and skill in reading. In R. R. Schmeck (Ed.) *Learning strategies and learning styles* (pp. 229–274). New York: Plenum Press.

Kitchener, K. S., & King, P. M. (1981). Reflective judgment: Concepts of justification and their relationship to age and education. *Journal of Applied Developmental Psychology, 2*(2), 89–116.

Kitchener, K. S., & King, P. M. (1990). The reflective judgment model: Transforming assumptions about knowing. In J. Mesirow & Associates (Eds.), *Fostering critical reflection in adulthood: A guide to transformative and emancipatory learning* (pp. 159–176). San Francisco: Jossey-Bass.

Kitchener, K. S., Lynch, C. L., Fischer, K. W., & Wood, P. K. (1993). Developmental range of reflective judgment: The effect of contextual support and practice on developmental stage. *Developmental Psychology, 29,* 893–906.

Kolb, D. A. (1984). *Experiential learning: Experience as the source of learning and development.* Englewood Cliffs, NJ: Prentice Hall.

Kramer, D. A. (1989). The development of an awareness of contradiction across the life span and the question of postformal operations. In M. L Commons, J. D. Sinnott, F. A. Richards, & C. Armon (Eds.), *Adult development. Vol. 1: Comparisons and applications of developmental models* (pp. 133–159). New York: Praeger.

Kroll, B. (1992). *Teaching hearts and minds: College students reflect on the Vietnam War in literature.* Carbondale: Southern Illinois University Press.

Kuhn, D. (1989). Children and adults as intuitive scientists. *Psychological Review, 96,* 674–689.

Lamborn, S. D., & Fischer, K. W. (1988). Optimal and functional levels in cognitive development: The individual's developmental range. *Newsletter of the International Society for the Study of Behavioral Development, 14*(2), 1–4.

Lawrence, G. (1984). A synthesis of learning style research involving the MBTI. *Journal of Psychological Type, 8,* 2–15.

McCaulley, M., & Natter, F. L. (1984). *Psychological (Myers-Briggs) type differences in education.* Gainesville, FL: Center for Applications of Psychological Type.

McMillan, J. H., & Forsyth, D. R. (1991). What theories of motivation say about why learners learn. In R. J. Menges & M. D. Svinicki (Eds.), *College teaching: From theory to practice* (New Directions for Teaching and Learning No. 45, pp. 39–52). San Francisco: Jossey-Bass.

Marton, F., & Säljö, R. (1976a). On qualitative difference in learning: I. Outcome and process. *British Journal of Educational Psychology, 46,* 4–11.

Marton, F., & Säljö, R. (1976b). On qualitative difference in learning: II. Outcome as a function of the learner's conception of the task. *British Journal of Educational Psychology, 46,* 115–127.

Menges, R. J., & Svinicki, M. D. (Eds.). (1991). *College teaching: From theory to practice* (New Directions for Teaching and Learning No. 45). San Francisco: Jossey-Bass.

Miller, C. D., Alway, M., & McKinley, D. (1987). Effects of learning styles and strategies on academic success. *Journal of College Student Personnel, 28,* 399–404.

Murray, J. B. (1990). Review of research on the Myers-Briggs Type Indicator. *Perceptual and Motor Skills, 70,* 1187–1202.

Myers, I. B. (1980). *Gifts differing.* Palo Alto, CA: Consulting Psychologists Press.

Ornstein, R. E. (1972). *The psychology of consciousness.* San Francisco: Freeman.

Perry, W. G., Jr. (1970). *Forms of intellectual and ethical development in the college years: A scheme.* New York: Holt, Rinehart and Winston.

Pittenger, D. J. (1993). The utility of the Myers-Briggs Type Indicator. *Review of Educational Research, 63,* 467–488.

Provost, J. A., & Anchors, C. (1987). *Applications of the Myers-Briggs Type Indicator in higher education.* Palo Alto, CA: Consulting Psychologists Press.

Rosovsky, H. (1990). *The university: An owner's manual.* New York: Norton.

Schauble, L., & Glaser, R. (1990). Scientific thinking in children and adults. In D. Kuhn (Ed.), *Developmental perspectives on teaching and learning thinking skills* (Contributions to Human Development, Vol. 21, pp. 9–27). Basel, Switzerland: Karger.

Schmeck, R. R. (1981, February). Improving learning by improving thinking. *Educational Leadership,* 384–385.

Schmeck, R. R. (1988). An introduction to strategies and styles of learning. In R. R. Schmeck (Ed.), *Learning strategies and learning styles* (pp. 3–19). New York: Plenum Press.

Shuford, B. (1995). *Learning styles of African American college students.* Unpublished manuscript, Bowling Green State University, Bowling Green, OH.

Sinnott, J. D. (1989). Life-span relativistic post-formal thought: Methodology and data from everyday problem-solving studies. In M. L Commons, J. D. Sinnott, F. A. Richards, & C. Armon (Eds.), *Adult development: Vol. 1. Comparisons and applications of developmental models* (pp. 239–278). New York: Praeger.

Svinicki, M. D. (1991). Practical implications of cognitive theories. In R. J. Menges & M. D. Svinicki (Eds.), *College teaching: From theory to practice* (New Directions for Teaching and Learning No. 45, pp. 27–37). San Francisco: Jossey-Bass.

Tharp, R. G. (1989). Psychocultural variables and constants. *American Psychologist, 44,* 349–359.

Tiberius, R. G., & Billson, J. M. (1991). The social context of teaching and learning. In R. J. Menges & M. D. Svinicki, (Eds.), *College teaching: From theory to practice* (New Directions for Teaching and Learning No. 45, pp. 67–86). San Francisco: Jossey-Bass.

van Rossum, E. J., & Schenk, S. M. (1984). The relationship between learning conception, study strategy and learning outcome. *British Journal of Educational Psychology, 54,* 73–83.

Vasquez, J. A., & Wainstein, N. (1990). Instructional responsibilities of college faculty to minority students. *Journal of Negro Education, 59,* 599–610.

Weinstein, C. E., & Meyer, D. K. (1991). Cognitive learning strategies and college teaching. In R. F. Menges & M. D. Svinicki (Eds.), *College teaching: From theory to practice* (New Directions for Teaching and Learning No. 45, pp. 15–26). San Francisco: Jossey-Bass.

Witkin, H. A. (1976). Cognitive style in academic performance and in teacher-student relations. In S. Messick & Associates (Eds.), *Individuality in learning* (pp. 38–72). San Francisco: Jossey-Bass.

Witkin, H. A., & Goodenough, D. R. (1981). *Cognitive styles: Essence and origins* (Psychological Issues Monograph 51). New York: International Universities Press.

Witkin, H. A., Moore, C. A., Goodenough, D. R., & Cox, P. W. (1977). Field-dependent and field-independent cognitive styles and their educational implications. *Review of Educational Research, 47,* 1–64.

CHAPTER TWELVE

DYNAMICS OF
CAMPUS ENVIRONMENTS

C. Carney Strange

Much has changed in American higher education since James Garfield said, "The ideal college is Mark Hopkins at one end of a log and a student at the other." Hopkins, a renowned educator who taught philosophy and rhetoric for fifty-seven years at Williams College and served as its president from 1836 to 1872, was the consummate "gentleman scholar" of his day. Since his time, the "log" has grown into an enormous academic enterprise of stone, brick, concrete, and steel—a gallery of architectural designs, functions, and purposes. The gentleman scholar has evolved into a complex web of new faculty roles and responsibilities. And, at the other end of the log, the awestruck student has been replaced by a chorus of learners voicing an increasingly rich score of liberal, technical, and vocational educational interests and goals. Higher education in America has indeed changed, giving rise to a maze of state, private, and community-based institutions that is as difficult to comprehend for the faculty and administrators who work within these institutions as it is for the students who must choose between them.

An essential challenge facing postsecondary educators today is the creation and maintenance of a campus environment that attracts a variety of students and satisfies and sustains them in their efforts to achieve their educational goals. Student affairs practitioners play a major part in achieving this goal. As campus enrollment managers and orientation directors, they recruit and acclimate new students to the college environment. As residence hall directors, they assist students in meeting the challenges of communal living and learning. As directors of adult and commuter education programs, they enhance students' sense of belonging and their belief that they matter to their institution (Schlossberg, Lassalle, & Golec, 1988). As student activity and organization advisers, they engage students in the opportunities of campus involvement and leadership. As personal counselors, they aid students in understanding the adjustments required of life transitions. And as academic, career, and vocational advisers, they assist students in choosing a personally fulfilling academic and occupational goal. What is needed to guide these functions and practices is a comprehensive model of the college environment that describes various features and assists campus participants in understanding how such features can encourage student development (Strange, 1983; Strange & King, 1990).

Concepts Related to Campus Environments

Although a comprehensive model of campus environments does not yet exist, a number of conceptual reviews have highlighted various models that are useful for understanding the interaction between students and their campus (e.g., see Baird, 1988; Huebner & Lawson, 1990; Moos, 1979; Pascarella, 1985; and Strange, 1991, 1993, 1994). This chapter presents an overview of a selection of these models, organized within a framework of four dimensions of campus environments that have received substantial attention in the literature: the design and quality of campus physical features; the collective characteristics of campus human aggregates, or groups; the dynamics of campus organizational structures; and the meaning campus members construct around these dimensions and attach to them.

A thirty-minute tour of most any campus can reveal much about its essential institutional characteristics and dynamics. From the size, layout, and design of its buildings, facilities, and spaces; from the appearance and style of its students, faculty, and staff; from the structure and organization of its administrative systems; and from the nature of its traditions, customs, and symbols emerge immediate and powerful impressions of whether or not "this is a good place to be." All of these features blend to create campus environments that influence, in varied and complex ways, the behavior of those who interact with them.

Physical Environments

All campuses contain physical features, both natural and synthetic, that influence the attitudes and behaviors of campus participants. Natural features include geographic location, terrain, climate, and weather; synthetic features include architectural design, space, and amenities. Both sets of features contribute to various conditions of light, density, noise, temperature, air quality, and aesthetics to create a powerful influence on individuals' attraction to and satisfaction with the physical setting.

The physical features of a campus are often among the most important factors in creating a prospective college student's critical first impression of an institution (Sturner, 1973; Thelin & Yankovich, 1987). The basic layout of the campus; open spaces and shaded lawns (Griffith, 1994); the accessibility and cleanliness of commuter parking lots; interior color schemes; the shape and design of residence halls, classroom buildings, libraries, and galleries; an impressive fitness center; and even the weather on the day of a campus visit all shape applicants' initial attitudes in subtle ways (Stern, 1986). In a firsthand study of campus life at twenty-nine different colleges, Boyer (1987) concluded that "it was the buildings, the trees, the walkways, the well-kept lawns—that overwhelmingly won out. The appearance of the campus is, by far, the most influential characteristic during campus visits, and we gained the distinct impression that when it comes to recruiting students, the director of buildings and grounds may be more important than the academic dean" (p. 17). Admissions offices have recently begun to understand and exploit the power of these images, using videotapes and virtual tours on the Internet to provide potential students with a quick, economical, manicured survey of campus life in the privacy of their home.

Concepts of campus physical environments draw from a variety of fields, such as art and architecture (e.g., Dober, 1992; Gaines, 1991; Sommer, 1969), ecological psychology (e.g., Barker, 1968), and cultural anthropology (e.g., Moffatt, 1989). All of these disciplines contribute to an understanding of the college campus as a "place apart" (Stern, 1986) whose physical features interact with and influence a range of behaviors, attitudes, and outcomes relative to its educational mission. Physical features also set broad limits on the phenomena that can occur, making some behaviors more or less likely than others—a concept labeled "intersystems congruence" (Michelson, 1970, p. 25). Accordingly, various aspects of the physical environment interact with other features of the setting (such as its social systems) to affect the probability of various phenomena occurring. For example, a large theater-style classroom with immovable seating may set limits on the extent to which group discussions can occur, regardless of the types of students involved or the best efforts of the instructor. On the other hand, some phenomena are encouraged because of physical limitations, as is evident on many campuses where bare paths are quickly worn through green lawns to find the shortest distance between two points. Although the physical environment may not directly cause specific behaviors or attitudes, its limitations present challenges that must be negotiated by campus inhabitants.

For some students, the features of an institution's on-campus residence halls shape their first impressions of campus life. The number of floors, the location of stairwells and elevators, the design of inner spaces, and the use of amenities all play an important role in the quality of residents' campus experience (Heilweil, 1973). For many others, pathways from commuter parking lots and garages to classroom buildings do the same. Distances to communal facilities, the location of maintenance and disposal equipment, and the marking and lighting of walkways can all create quick impressions of comfort or risk. Further, opportunities for the development and expression of personal identity often lie in the flexibility students enjoy in shaping and arranging the spaces they use. Where students are encouraged to assume greater responsibility for individualizing the design of their own spaces (whether residence hall rooms, classrooms, or other organizational facilities), a sense of territoriality (Schroeder, 1979), personal space (Anchors, Schroeder, & Jackson, 1978), and community (Ender, Kane, Mable, & Strohm, 1980) prevails.

All aspects of the campus physical environment are important to the quality of students' campus experiences and can serve as prohibitive or positive forces for development in students' lives (Strange, 1983). As Dober (1992) explains, "Each campus deserves to be a special place and to have a distinctive image that communicates, at the least, the institution's purpose, presence, domain, and values" (p. 280). To the extent that various campus physical features contribute to students' sense of safety and security, their sense of belonging and familiarity with an institution, their ease of access and movement through its spaces, and their experience of membership in an educational community is the ultimate test of their design and purpose.

Human Aggregates

The human aggregates (that is, groups) present in campus environments are addressed using many of the same models and theories used to understand interpersonal styles and differences among students (see Chapters Nine and Eleven). Recognizing that individuals differ in characteristic ways as they approach a variety of tasks and problems, these models examine such differences from a human aggregate focus, asserting that an environment's characteristics are transmitted collectively through its inhabitants. A key assumption of this perspective is that the dominant features of any particular environment are a reflection of the dominant characteristics of the people within it (Astin, 1962, 1968; Astin & Holland, 1961). Therefore, in order to understand the likely impact of an environment, knowledge of its inhabitants' collective characteristics is essential.

Subcultures, Typologies, and Styles. Various models have identified patterned differences among students—subcultures, types, and styles—thought to be important for understanding how students function collectively. Clark and Trow (1966) were among the first to explore the implications of campus subcultures with their identification of four such types—academic, nonconformist, collegiate, and vocational. Since then, the work of Holland (1973) on vocational interests, the psychological styles of Myers (1980), and the learning orientations of Kolb (1983) have received the attention of researchers and educators seeking to understand the dynamics of human aggregates on campus. A more recent model with similar assumptions is found in Astin (1993).

Employing "taxonomic or typological language that implicitly sorts students into a variety of discrete categories or boxes" (p. 36), Astin constructed an empirically derived typology of college students from self-reported student responses to the Cooperative Institutional Research Program's (CIRP) national freshman survey. According to Astin, seven verifiable student types emerged from their responses: Scholars, Social Activists, Artists, Hedonists, Leaders, Status Strivers, and Uncommitted Students. Each type is characterized by select values, background characteristics, institutional preference, and academic major preference. For example, Scholars are "characterized by a high degree of academic and intellectual self-esteem, high expectations for academic success in college, and aspirations for high-level academic degrees" (p. 38). "Overrepresented in the private four-year colleges, public universities, and especially in the private universities," Scholars are younger, come from well-educated families, rank in the top quarter of their high school classes, have A averages, and are "disproportionately concentrated in mathematics, science, and engineering and show strong inclinations for careers in engineering, science, military service, and computer programming. . . . Scholars show a significant disinclination toward careers in business and social work" (p. 41–42). In contrast, Status Strivers are "committed to being successful in [their] own business, having administrative responsibility for the work of others, being very well-off financially, obtaining recognition from colleagues for contributions in [their] special field, and becoming an authority in [their] field" (p. 40). Students of this type include "a relatively large percentage of African-American and Chicano students and tend to have parents who are somewhat less-well educated. . . . Their academic performance in high school was poorer than that of all other types except the Hedonists. The strongly materialistic values of the Status Striver are reflected in their inclination toward college majors and careers in accounting and business" and "toward partying, watching television, and joining fraternities or sororities." They are "underrepresented in careers such as the clergy, college teaching, and writing" (p. 44).

In addition to these seven types, Astin (1993) also identified a group labeled No Type students, which constituted about 40 percent of the students in his sample. These students exhibited a very distinctive pattern; they came "from families with less education and lower incomes than any of the types" (p. 44), were less involved in leadership and extracurricular activities, and had lower degree aspirations and poorer high school academic records. They also were "heavily concentrated in community colleges and underrepresented in public universities and all types of private institutions" (p. 44). Other patterns observed suggest that No Type students "show a lower degree of involvement in their undergraduate experience than any other student type, including the Uncommitted student" (p. 44).

Astin's types are helpful in describing and understanding the characteristics and attributes of various student aggregates on campus. A student body dominated by Scholars, for example, would likely create an institutional milieu supportive of an academic or intellectual nature. In contrast, Social Activists and Artists would create a greater emphasis on social action and involvement. Whole institutional cultures and images have emerged from the distinctions attributed to these types. Where would an Oberlin College be without the presence of Social Activists and Artists? Could Princeton survive without its Scholars? Faculty and administrators at many large state universities recognize the impact of Hedonists and of Status Strivers, with their rich traditions of involvement in residence hall life, campus activities, Greek letter organizations, and intercollegiate athletics. Likewise, a Howard University or a Spelman would be radically different without its Leaders.

Human aggregate models reduce environmental differences to the collective effects of individual members' personalities and styles. An environment dominated by a particular type (that is, containing a majority of one type) is presumed to exhibit the characteristics of that type. Holland (1973) would say that an environment dominated by Social types (for example, a classroom of social work students or a student volunteer service organization) would foster its inhabitants' social competencies, stimulating them to engage in social activities and to see themselves as liking to help others. Similarly, an environment dominated by Judging and Sensing types (Myers, 1980) (such as a campus registrar or bursar's office) would place an emphasis on organization, systematic processes, and predictability. A classroom composed primarily of Accommodators (Kolb, 1983) would place an emphasis on active and concrete forms of learning. Thus assessments of the collective characteristics of an environment's inhabitants, whether demographic (by gender, age, or racial-ethnic composition, for example) or psychological (by personality types or learning styles), provides a descriptive measure of the environment's dominant features.

Person-Environment Interactions. Much of the value of these human aggregate models lies in their illumination of the dynamics of the interactions between people and their environment. The design, strength, or character of any human environment is a function of its degree of differentiation and its consistency (Holland, 1973). A highly differentiated, or focused, environment is dominated by one single type or characteristic (all women, all African Americans, all individuals of high socioeconomic status, all urban residents, all southerners, and so on); a highly undifferentiated environment is more diffuse and characterized by the presence of several different types. Undifferentiated environments are readily distinguished by their inhabitants and by outside observers, precisely because they encourage certain behaviors, values, attitudes, and expectations and discourage those that are dissimilar. Undifferentiated environments "stimulate a broad range of behavior and provide ambiguous guidance" (Holland, 1973, p. 34), are more flexible and open to a variety of inputs and influences, and are consequently more difficult to understand and describe because of their lack of a clear focus.

The degree of consistency, or similarity of type, of a human environment also affects its dynamics. In Holland's hexagonal model, interest types that are adjacent (for example, Social and Enterprising) are presumed to share greater similarity than those that are opposite (such as Artistic and Conventional). Similarly, Astin's Leader and Social Activist (1993), Myers's (1980) ENTP (Extraverted, Intuitive, Thinking, and Perceiving) and ENFP (Extraverted, Intuitive, Feeling, Judging) types, and Kolb's (1983) Assimilator and Converger might be thought of as consistent in that each pair shares significant similarities. Highly consistent environments contain individuals of similar types and "provide similar rewards and demands"; inconsistent environments "provide divergent rewards and demands" (Holland, 1973, p. 34).

Person-environment congruence, or the degree of "fit" between people and their environment, is another concept implicit in human aggregate models. A person is said to be congruent with a given environment if his or her type is the same or nearly the same as the dominant type within that environment. Understanding the degree of congruence between an individual and his or her environment is critical for understanding the extent to which he or she is likely to be attracted to, satisfied, and stable within that environment. Individuals who share much in common with an environment are predicted to be most attracted to that environment. Once inside, they are likely to be encouraged for exactly those behaviors, values, attitudes, and expectations that attracted them to that particular environment in the first place, thus reinforcing the similarities between them. Congruent person-to-environment matches allow individuals to exercise their strengths, "but of equal importance, [they also allow them] to avoid the activities [they] dislike, the demands for competencies [they] lack, the tasks and self-images [they] do not value, and the situations in which [their] personality traits are not encouraged" (p. 38). Consequently, the likelihood of any given person's remaining in a congruent environment is quite high.

People are presumed to prefer and to be satisfied in a state of congruence, and according to Holland (1973), "the interaction of a differentiated person and a differentiated environment will be most predictable and intense because a well-defined (predictable, and therefore understandable) person is interacting with a well-defined environment that has a focused influence" (p. 39). Thus degrees of congruence, differentiation, and consistency are important for understanding how an individual will function within any human environment and whether they are likely to adapt to it, leave it, or try to change it. Such an analysis lies at the heart of many campus retention issues; it also underscores current critiques of the "chilly climate" for women and students of color on campus (Hall & Sandler, 1982, 1984), which assert that these groups have been historically disadvantaged by a White- and male-dominated culture.

Organized Environments

Most any educational environment, whether a classroom, academic department, student group, residence hall, or entire campus, exhibits characteristics of an organized system, regardless of the actual degree of formal organization present (Blau, 1973). In each of these settings, certain goals or outcomes (explicit or implicit) shape decisions about the use of various resources and strategies for maintaining or changing those settings. To facilitate such decisions, it is common practice to "get organized" by establishing plans, rules, and guidelines for group functioning; by allocating resources; and by identifying those who will share authority and responsibility for making various substantive and procedural decisions (Etzioni, 1964). Thus faculty develop syllabi to outline course goals and assignments; departments define procedural guidelines and degree requirements; student groups plan for and implement programs; residence life staff create structures for encouraging student participation and leadership; and campus administrators establish rules for effective and efficient use of limited resources.

Organizational Structures. Hage and Aiken's (1970) model of complex organizations is useful for understanding these various structural-organizational aspects of campus environments. They posited that organized environments can generally be characterized along a continuum from dynamic to static. Dynamic environments are flexible in design and respond more readily to change; static environments resist change. The extent to which organized environments are likely to exhibit dynamic or static characteristics can be understood with reference to their complexity, centralization, formalization, stratification, production, and efficiency.

Organizational complexity refers to the number of occupational subunits and specialties present within a particular setting, as well as to the extent and intensity of knowledge and expertise that they require (Hage & Aiken, 1970). Colleges and universities are typically characterized by a high degree of complexity, with a variety of highly credentialed professionals conducting the business of postsecondary education. Many different departmental subunits require a variety of specialties dedicated to meeting the needs of campus constituents. Departments of natural sciences require advanced training and preparation of appropriate personnel in order to meet the goals of teaching chemistry and biology courses. Career planning and placement offices require the services of professionally prepared counselors who can effectively assist students in sorting through the maze of their occupational interests, skills, and choices. In the context of various campus subenvironments, such as classes or student organizations, complexity might be reflected in the number of discussion groups in the case of a classroom or the number of specialized task groups in the case of student organizations or residence hall governments. Complexity is also evident in "the degree to which members of an organization attempt to gain greater knowledge about their respective work activities and the overall activities of their organization" (p. 18). Colleges and universities are, by nature, professional organizations that generally place a concerted emphasis on staff development and continuing education.

Degree of centralization describes the way in which power, or "the capacity of one social position to determine the actions of other social positions" (Hage & Aiken, 1970, p. 19), is distributed in an organization. "Every organization needs to make decisions about the allocation of its funds, the promotion of its personnel, and the initiation of new programs. Responsibilities for these decisions must be allocated to some jobs; this helps ensure coordination of many different occupations" (p. 19). Thus academic administrators must decide what courses will be offered and when they will be scheduled; faculty determine the number, type, and due dates of assignments for individual classes; and staff implement plans for the expenditure and accounting of various budgets. Where few individuals share such power for decision making, organizations are said to be highly centralized; organizations where many or all share decision-making power equally are said to be decentralized. In a classroom, for example, a high degree of centralization might be evident when the instructor makes all the decisions about the course syllabus, assigned readings, and papers and relies principally on lectures for presenting course material. In contrast, a seminar format, where the students and instructor work collaboratively to create the syllabus around student interests and learning styles, grading practices are negotiated, and an open discussion format is preferred, might be described as a decentralized learning environment.

A third feature bearing on the quality of organizational dynamics is the degree of formalization. Formalization refers to the importance of rules and regulations (whether formal, written rules or customary, understood rules) in a given setting (Hage & Aiken, 1970). Three aspects influence formalization: the number of rules, their specificity, and their degree of enforcement. Highly formalized units enforce many explicit rules, which are thought to provide guidelines for efficient functioning and to lend a degree of predictability to organizational efforts. Degrees of formalization in various campus environments might be reflected in the nature of student codes, administrative manuals and job descriptions, college catalogs, course syllabi, organizational constitutions and bylaws, and customary understandings of "how things are done." A high degree of formalization is associated generally with organizational rigidity and inflexibility.

Organizational stratification has to do with the differential distribution of rewards in a system (Hage & Aiken, 1970). Highly stratified systems have many different levels of status, distinguished by differential rewards (such as income, esteem, and prestige). Those at higher status levels in the organization receive higher recognition and rewards. Stratification also reflects the degree of mobility members have between lower and higher status levels; highly stratified systems tend to preserve status distinctions and restrict members' mobility. The relevance of this concept can be seen in the various campus systems that affect students' experiences. For example, high stratification might be apparent in classrooms where the distance between the students and the instructor is maintained by formal titles and formal academic authority, in student organizations where rewards (such as access to office space and equipment, titles, and campus recognition) are differentially distributed to group leaders, and in residence halls where the head resident and resident assistants are distinguished significantly from others by higher status and appreciably better living arrangements. Other relevant distinctions might include class levels (for example, seniors have greater claim on campus facilities than first-year students), majors (students in the "hard sciences" may be perceived by peers to possess greater intellectual acuity than other students), or status (sports teams may have access to preferential course schedules and special campus living arrangements). While power and rules exert a conforming influence, stratification tends to be more divisive, since reward structures are cast into a competitive framework, and those who share disproportionately in the rewards are vested in maintaining the status quo.

Degree of production refers to the relative emphasis on quantity or quality of an organization's products or services (Hage & Aiken, 1970). All organizations need to "produce" in order to justify their existence, maintain current resources or attract additional ones, and create a sense of accomplishment among organizational members who contribute to its goals. When quantity of production is high, or at least sufficient, a well-functioning system is assumed. A drop in quantity of production often signals a need for reexamination and evaluation. As organized systems, colleges are often driven by production mandates. For example, students might request that certain classes be held more frequently, or trustees might inquire about the number of graduates placed from various programs as an indicator of mission fulfillment. Credit hours completed, retention rates, proportion of minorities, advisee contacts, number of research grants received, and articles published, to name a few, are all familiar indicators of production in an academic environment. Annual reports teem with such data, often under the presumption that appropriate increases are indicative of improvement and success; measures like these are frequently invoked for purposes of resource reallocation to units perceived to have a greater need (that is, those already most productive). Increased production often involves a trade-off with quality, however. Student credit hours can be stimulated easily by employing economies of scale, increasing both enrollments and class sizes, raising the ratio of students to faculty, and using resources (such as faculty salaries) more efficiently. Questions about the quality of student experiences must figure in any formula of institutional success, however. How do greater numbers of students in the classroom affect the quality of intellectual exchange, which is known to contribute to the development of critical reasoning? Are there fewer opportunities to communicate in the form of written papers and essays, and is there sufficient time for the instructor to give quality feedback to all students? Answers to such questions have implications not only for the productivity of various institutional environments but also for their ability to meet educational goals.

Another aspect affecting the overall dynamics of an organized system is its degree of efficiency, or its emphasis on reducing the cost of production (Hage & Aiken, 1970). Maximum efficiency, like high productivity, is often assumed to reflect a smooth, well-functioning system. Like other complex organizations, colleges and universities pursue efficient use of resources by means of a variety of institutional strategies. For example, restricting access to copying machines, raising minimum enrollment levels on courses before they're allowed "to make," and assigning lower-salaried graduate teaching assistants to large introductory courses all have the effect of lowering the cost of production. Ensuring full occupancy rates in residence halls, usually by overbooking them, and keeping classrooms full also reduce the cost of physical plant investments. While cost reduction is a necessary goal in any organized system, it is particularly difficult to measure and evaluate in the context of an academic setting. What is an efficient number of resources to produce a graduate of a program, a student leader, a publication in a professional journal, or a grade of B in a particular course? What is the cost of a new idea? Without a clear and succinct definition of an organization's goals, how can the accomplishment of such goals be demonstrated? Answers to these questions are inherently value-laden—and invariably contested—serving to complicate any discussion about efficiency in higher education. Perhaps too often, though, the most important outcomes of the college experience (for example, development of personal autonomy and tolerance for ambiguity) are reduced to manageable metrics that may not capture the essence of such goals.

Organizational Dynamics. The import of these organizational characteristics lies in their illumination of the nature of dynamic systems, which are most often associated with successful educational experiences. Dynamic environments combine a higher degree of complexity with lower centralization, formalization, stratification, and efficiency, and they place a relatively high emphasis on the quality of products or services (Hage & Aiken, 1970). In a classroom, higher complexity might be reflected in the utilization of multiple perspectives and in the nature of the assignments and learning tasks. Degrees of centralization and formalization are lowered by engaging students actively in the planning and implementation of course goals, employing a variety of creative options (such as cooperative projects, independent assignments, and multiple-format exams). This, of course, demands a more labor-intensive process for instructors and students alike, therefore lowering the degree of efficiency. But dynamic educational environments, like self-organizing systems evolving toward nonequilibrium (Caple, 1987), encourage substantive involvement, responsibility, and creativity on the part of members— the effective essences of developmentally powerful systems (Astin, 1985; Strange, 1981, 1983).

Static environments, characterized by lower complexity; higher centralization, formalization, stratification, and efficiency; and a greater emphasis on the quantity of products or services, tend to discourage change and innovation. For example, a course syllabus prepared without student input requires little investment from students and may not reflect their learning interests and goals; rigidly formatted class assignments are less likely to be responsive to individual learning styles and needs; insistence on formal titles and status structures may diminish the kind of personal atmosphere that supports the risk taking needed to explore new ideas; and an overemphasis on efficiency ("We just don't have time to explore that") and quantity of readings or assignments tends to invoke a "just get it done" attitude among students as the term unfolds. A key point in this analysis is that developmental environments, whatever the setting, exhibit characteristics of dynamic organizations, in which individual differences are appreciated, participation is expected, interactions are personal, and risk taking is encouraged (Strange, 1983).

Organizational dynamics can also affect the morale of participants, depending upon their individual differences. A static classroom, for example, where the professor makes all the decisions about course timing and content (high centralization), assignments are specific and inflexible (high formalization), and questions are discouraged for fear of wasting time (high efficiency) might prove comforting to students at one level of development (such as Dualism), but it may be very boring and discouraging to students at other levels (such as Relativism) (Perry, 1970). Varying personalities may respond differently to the same environment as well. Sensing and Judging types (Myers, 1980) or Conventional and Realistic types (Holland, 1973), for example, might enjoy the routine and standardization of a predictable, static class arrangement, but such an environment may ultimately frustrate Intuitive Perceivers and Artistic or Social types. Likewise, student organizations structured around a hierarchical model of charter-based roles and powers may be less attractive to students socialized in an ethic of care and "connectedness" (Forrest, Hotelling, & Kuk, 1986; Gilligan, 1982), who may prefer a more heterarchic, less legalistic arrangement. The overall degree of structure reflected in how various student groups' and organizations' goals are set, their rules implemented and enforced, their policies decided, and their resources expended may or may not be compatible with the characteristics of their participating students. For example, students who know little of the fundamentals of organizational leadership and participation (or who are simply inexperienced) may not be immediately ready to assume the responsibilities of membership in a self-directed group. In such cases, a more highly structured organizational environment may be appropriate. On the other hand, a more advanced student group, whose talents and styles have been tested in a variety of settings, may become disinterested and "turned off" by a highly structured system that allows for little student input and involvement. Thus a general understanding of students' developmental characteristics (see Chapter Nine) is a critical source of information for constructing appropriate organizational environments.

Constructed Environments

Models of constructed environments recognize that a consensus of individuals who perceive and characterize their environment similarly creates a measure of environmental "press" or a certain environmental climate. These perceptions, in turn, exert a directional influence on behavior (Moos, 1986). In contrast to the models discussed previously, these theories focus on the subjective views of participant-observers, assuming that environments are understood best through their collective perceptions. They also suggest that such information is critical for understanding how people are likely to react to environments. Thus whether people are attracted to a particular environment or remain satisfied and stable within it is a function of how they perceive, construct, and evaluate the environment. In effect, their perception of the environment is its reality.

Environmental Press. Pace and Stern (1958), in their development of an interactive model of needs "press," drawing on earlier work by Murray (1938), were among the first to apply a perceptual approach to the study of college campuses. *Press,* inferred from concordant self-reports of perceived activities in an environment, refers to "the characteristic demands or features of the environment" (Walsh, 1973, p. 114). For example, if 80 percent of a representative sample of students on a particular campus report that students frequently spend time studying in the library, a significant "press toward academic achievement" might be inferred. Pace and Stern (1958) developed the College Characteristics Index (CCI), a self-administered questionnaire of three hundred items, later reduced by Saunders (1969) to a factorial structure of eleven potential environmental presses: aspiration level, intellectual climate, student dignity, academic climate, academic achievement, self-expression, group life, academic organization, social form, play-work, and vocational climate. Accordingly, a public two-year community college might lend itself to greater presses toward work and vocational climate, while a small, selective institution might exhibit a greater press toward aspiration level, intellectual climate, and academic achievement.

Social Climate. Sharing a similar set of assumptions about group construction of environments, Moos (1986, 1979) authored a model of social climate, which describes the nature and effects of various "environmental personalities." Social climate is composed of three domains or sets of dimensions: (1) relationship dimensions, reflecting "the extent to which people are involved in the setting, the extent to which they support and help one another, and the extent to which they express themselves freely and openly" (Moos, 1979, p. 14); (2) personal growth and development dimensions, which define the "basic goals of the setting, that is, the areas in which personal development and self-enhancement tend to occur," the nature of which "varies among settings according to their underlying purposes" (p. 16); and (3) system maintenance and system change dimensions, reflecting "the extent to which the environment is orderly and clear in its expectations, maintains control, and responds to change" (p. 16). These three domains guide the assessment and understanding of the key aspects of any social environment and manifest themselves in specific ways, depending upon the context of the environment being examined. For example, in classrooms, relationship dimensions include the degree of student involvement, affiliation among students, and teacher support; personal growth and development dimensions assess task orientation and competition; and system maintenance and system change dimensions include order and organization, rule clarity, teacher control, and innovation (Moos & Trickett, 1974). In residence halls, relationship dimensions include students' involvement and the emotional support they offer one another; personal growth dimensions are reflected in the degree of student independence, the traditional social orientation, and the level of emphasis on competition, academic achievement, and intellectuality; and system maintenance dimensions are expressed in the degree of order, student influence, and innovation present (Moos, 1979).

To complete his picture of the various interactive social climates that affect students' lives, Moos (1981) also described the social climate dimensions of social or task-focused group environments, helpful for understanding students' experiences as participants in various campus groups and organizations; work environments (Moos & Insel, 1974), important for examining the experiences of students who hold jobs (either on or off campus); and family environments (Moos, 1974), essential for understanding the basic set of relationships that students, traditional and nontraditional alike, bring with them to college and that form a foundation for their experiences there. Each of these social climate dimensions may vary along a continuum, from high to low, depending upon the characteristics of the setting and creating a special focus or orientation for it. For example, with the University Residence Environment Scale, Moos (1979; Moos & Gerst, 1974) identified six characteristic environments or "personalities" he attributed to various living groups: relationship-oriented environments; traditionally socially oriented environments; supportive, achievement-oriented environments; competition-oriented environments; independence-oriented environments; and intellectually oriented environments. Likewise, varying emphases on certain dimensions in classrooms, task groups, work settings, and family environments may create a cumulative tendency toward one orientation or another: one work environment might be very competitive and another one very supportive; one family environment may express a strong achievement orientation while another might emphasize independence.

These various environmental orientations or "personalities" have been found to be related, as well, to differing human aggregate and physical configurations, at least in the context of living environments. For example, Moos (1979) found that all-male residence halls tend to be more competition-oriented, all-female units tend to be more traditionally socially oriented, and coed units tend to be independence-oriented and intellectually oriented. Further, supportive, achievement-oriented and relationship-oriented residence halls tend to be almost exclusively female or coed, and units composed of a greater proportion of single rooms are more oriented toward competition and less toward supportive achievement, independence, intellectuality, and relationships.

Campus Culture. Another set of ideas emerging from this focus on constructed environments comes from a growing literature that applies concepts of campus and organizational culture to understanding college environments (Chaffee & Tierney, 1988; Horowitz, 1987; Kuh, 1993; Kuh & Whitt, 1988; Moffatt, 1989). "Culture," with roots in anthropology, sociology, and social psychology, is inherently a perceptual construct in that it reflects the assumptions, beliefs, and values environmental inhabitants construct and use to interpret or understand the meaning of events and actions. Schein (1985) referred to culture as "a pattern of basic assumptions—invented, discovered, or developed by a given group as it learns to cope with its problems of external adaptation [that is, what a group must do to maintain survival in a changing environment] and internal integration [what the group must do to maintain internal relationships and functioning]—that has worked well enough to be considered valid and, therefore, to be taught to new members as the correct way to perceive, think, and feel in relation to those problems" (p. 9). Problems of external adaptation include establishing a core mission, specific goals derived from that mission, a means to attain the goals, criteria for measuring success, and strategies for remediation when goals are not being met. Internal integration includes establishing and maintaining a common language and set of concepts, determining criteria for membership, deciding how power is used, delimiting relationships, discerning the nature of rewards and punishments, and defining an ideology that helps the group face inexplicable events (Schein, 1985). Kuh and Hall (1993) defined campus culture as the "confluence of institutional history, campus traditions, and the values and assumptions that shape the character of a given college or university" (pp. 1–2). Culture, then, is essentially "a social construction" (Chaffee & Tierney, 1988, p. 10), reflected in traditions, stories, ceremonies, histories, myths, heroines and heroes, interactions among members, policies and practices, symbols, and missions and philosophies.

There are essentially four levels of campus culture—artifacts, perspectives, values, and assumptions (Dyer, 1986; Kuh & Hall, 1993; Lundberg, 1985; Schein, 1985). Cultural artifacts include those tangible aspects (physical, verbal, and behavioral), "the meaning and functions of which may be known by members" (Kuh & Hall, 1993, p. 4). Virtually all campuses have some distinctive physical artifacts—usually buildings, landscape features, or various other physical attributes—that mark points of interest on a typical admissions or orientation tour. A "founders' hall," a majestic library, a multicultural center, or a technologically advanced classroom building can all serve to convey some of the core values that shape an institution's culture and the historical roots from which it came. Verbal artifacts incorporate language, stories, and myths, including "terms of endearment" (Kuh et al., 1991, p. 84) associated with specific institutions, as well as slang terms typical of traditional college-age subcultures (Hancock, 1990). Stories about significant campus leaders, personalities, and even mythical figures convey key moments of institutional history and construct personal models of emulation consistent with institutional values. Behavioral artifacts might include a host of celebratory activities and events that connect members to the institution (such as orientation and convocation), acknowledge their participation in institutional subcultures and groups (Gospel choir), or send them on their way following completion of their institutional experience (commencement). Various campus rituals, another form of behavioral artifact, also serve to connect the past to the present (Masland, 1985), as happens regularly, for example, when anniversary classes are remembered at homecoming or during alumni week.

Perspectives, or "socially shared rules and norms" (Kuh & Hall, 1993, p. 6), constitute a second level of institutional culture. As "social conventions manifested through behavior," perspectives define the "way things are done" and "determine what is 'acceptable behavior' for students, faculty, staff and others in various institutional settings. They are relatively easy to determine and the members of various groups who adhere to perspectives are usually aware of them" (p. 6). Thus students become quickly aware of appropriate campus customs, attire, and ideologies and are able to recognize certain perspectives as "typical" of those who reflect and construct institutional culture.

Values, a third level of institutional culture, are more abstract than perspectives. They reflect the "espoused as well as the enacted ideals of an institution or group . . . and serve as the basis on which members of a culture or subculture judge situations, acts, objects and people" (Kuh & Hall, 1993, p. 6). College catalogs, convocation speeches, campus philosophy and mission statements, and significant planning documents are important sources for understanding institutional values in their espoused form.

Finally, the fourth and deepest level of institutional culture includes assumptions, or "tacit beliefs that members use to define their role, their relationship to others, and the nature of the organization in which they live" (Kuh & Hall, 1993, p. 7). Schein (1992) suggested that all the various other artifacts of organizational culture reflect these fundamental assumptions and define and shape the core elements of institutional culture. Campus culture is a critical lens through which institutional members view and evaluate their experiences, and these socially constructed aspects of campus environments offer important clues for understanding how students interact with their various features.

Creating Effective Educational Environments

These models of campus environments suggest that colleges can positively influence students through physical features that are enabling, human aggregate characteristics that are reinforcing, and organizational structures that are dynamic. The effects of such features, characteristics, and structures are mediated through meanings attached to them by participant members, however. A distillation of the literature supports several key institutional concerns educators need to address if their commitment to student learning is to be realized: human-scale design, student-institution congruence, participant involvement, sense of community, and campus culture. Careful reflection on these concerns can yield important information for the design of vital educational environments.

Human-Scale Design

The concept of human-scale design involves both the physical and organizational properties of campus environments, as well as the behaviors and feelings these features engender. Human-scale environments accommodate small numbers of people and cultivate a sense of efficacy and confidence among participants (Hall, 1966; Kuh et al., 1991). In doing so they offer key ingredients for a meaningful educational experience. The most significant challenges to human-scale qualities in higher education today are institutional and organizational size. Emphasis on economies of scale has resulted in many large, "overmanned" institutions (Wicker, 1973) where too many people compete for too few opportunities for meaningful achievement, a condition Barker and Gump (1964) labeled "redundancy." Chickering and Reisser (1993), reflecting on the consequences of this condition, concluded that "as the number of persons outstrips the opportunities for significant participation and satisfaction, the developmental potential of available settings is attenuated for all" (p. 269). Generally speaking, large settings often mitigate against an "economy of learning" (Strange & Hannah, 1994), jeopardizing conditions known to contribute to a successful educational experience (for example, a sense of community, opportunities for involvement and creativity).

Human scale (or the lack of it) is also reflected in the design and layout of the physical spaces on campus. Sommer (1974) warned against "hard architecture . . . designed to be strong and resistant to human imprint" (p. 2). Straight-backed chairs, immovable desks, unbreakable lamps, uniform colors, Spartan amenities, unimaginative maintenance-free spaces, unusable wall surfaces, and permanently sealed windows are all examples of such designs, found today on most any college campus. Sommer, recognizing the intent of hard architecture to economize by employing durable and cost-effective features, nevertheless concluded that the "major defects of hard architecture are that it is costly, dehumanizing, and it isn't effective. Besides that, it doesn't look very nice" (p. 11). An antidote, he suggested, lies in greater use of "soft architecture," a prime ingredient of which is personalization, or "the ability to put one's individual imprint on one's surroundings" (p. 19). The flexibility and personalization offered by campus territoriality programs is one example of such a remedy that has met with success at a number of institutions (Schroeder, 1979, 1981). Maintenance of physical spaces (Kuh et al., 1991), which offer opportunities for privacy as well as social interaction, is also important.

Whether large or small, institutions guided by human-scale design place an emphasis on achieving their mission in settings and spaces that are manageable, personable, and flexible and reflect the needs of those who participate in them.

Congruence

Congruence between people and their environment are also important for effective educational experiences. Assuming that successful attraction, matriculation, and retention of students are desirable goals for all campuses, those responsible for recruitment and admissions need to pay special attention to the degree of institutional "fit" for any potential student. Careful and accurate representation of the institution's and its various departments' dominant features (often accomplished through catalogs, brochures, and other publications) is critical in encouraging an informed decision on the part of students that maximizes congruence. Orientation programs offer perhaps the best opportunity for discussing and understanding this kind of campus information.

Understanding the potentially negative consequences of incongruence is particularly important for understanding the experiences of minority students and others who may not share the characteristics of the dominant campus population (including international students, adult learners, and students with disabilities). The inevitable stress and "associated symptoms" (Moos, 1986, p. 413) resulting from incongruence between a student and the educational environment often place additional burdens on such students, and higher attrition rates and greater adjustment problems are to be expected. A centralized administrative model, in which a single umbrella office provides comprehensive services in an intensive, focused manner (such as an office of multicultural affairs or adult learner services) might be the most effective in initially acclimating these students to campus. Although it is yet to be established empirically, such an arrangement likely provides students with a more highly visible and homogeneous educational experience, by which conditions of cultural consistency and congruence can be maximized. For purposes of identity recognition and support, this arrangement is more likely to result in the highest level of initial satisfaction and stability, while offering a highly differentiated source of congruence at a critical point of transition in these students' lives.

From the human aggregate literature it appears that highly focused human environments exert a strong influence on members, who follow the direction already established by the dominant characteristics of the group. Such homogeneous groupings offer a powerful educational tool for establishing a sense of satisfaction, fit, and stability with the institution and for reinforcing behaviors related to its educational mission (such as involvement and leadership in the campus community).

Involvement

According to Astin (1985), "The effectiveness of any educational policy or practice is directly related to the capacity of that policy or practice to increase student involvement" (p. 136). In light of the discussion on organizational size and style, it is implicit that a truly involving environment is of human scale and exhibits a dynamic organizational style.

How people function and evaluate their experiences in an organizational setting is also related to their degree of involvement, which, again, is often a function of organizational size. Moos (1986) warned that as group size increases, "morale and attitudes become less positive, and absenteeism is more frequent" (p. 410). Banning (1989) also observed that "the ratio of persons per setting is critical to what happens to the people within the setting. In the 'undermanned setting,' people more frequently serve in responsible positions, engage in actions that are challenging, perform activities that are important to the setting, engage in a wide range of activities, see themselves as important and responsible for the setting, and work hard to maintain the function of the setting" (p. 59). The challenge to educational institutions is to create and support smaller campus subenvironments (or "undermanned" settings), such as cluster colleges, residence hall units, student organizations, and class sections, that more fully engage students in meaningful ways and in which students can experience a sense of functional importance and identity.

Community

From earlier prescriptions of an "intentional democratic community" (Crookston, 1974, p. 55) as a model for campus residence halls to more recent recommendations for creating higher education communities that are purposeful, open, just, disciplined, caring, and celebrative (Carnegie Foundation for the Advancement of Teaching, 1990), community building has remained a persistent theme in discussions of educational policy, design, and practice (Palmer, 1987; Spitzberg & Thorndike, 1992; Tierney, 1993). Palmer (1987) urged that "community must become a central concept in ways we teach and learn" (p. 25), as it incorporates all the essential features associated with effective learning environments—a compelling and unifying purpose, traditions and symbols of membership and participation, and mutual support among institutional members. A commitment to community in higher education, Boyer (1987) concluded, "helps students to go beyond their own private interests, learn about the world around them, develop a sense of civic and social responsibility, and discover how they, as individuals, can contribute to the larger society of which they are a part" (pp. 67–68).

The creation and maintenance of community on campus is particularly challenging to educators, especially at institutions that are redundant or fragmented by various subgroups. The challenge of establishing a balance between "community of the parts and community of the whole" (Spitzberg & Thorndike, 1992, p. 154) is paradoxical, however: that which contributes to strong subcommunities usually detracts from the community of the whole, and that which sustains the whole community often fails to meet the needs of various subcommunities. The solution is also elusive, but ever more urgent: "healthy subcommunities are not enough, . . . in today's complex and diverse world, more than ever, students, and everyone else working on our campuses, must connect with the institution" (p. 151). Perhaps especially for large institutions, structural accommodation of subcommunities and intermediate networks may be a necessary step for reducing institutional scale and connecting members to the whole campus. A compelling organizational vision detailing what the institution seeks to accomplish is a vital ingredient for effective colleges (Boyer, 1987; Kuh et al., 1991); the framework of community is perhaps the best mode for encouraging institutional members to share in that vision.

Campus Culture and Purpose

In a study of institutions perceived to be highly successful in encouraging student involvement and learning, Kuh and his colleagues (1991) underscored the importance and complementarity of educational practices, campus culture, and institutional mission. Policies, practices, and environmental features unsupported by the institution's educational purposes or incompatible with its organizational culture do little to encourage learning. Synergy of purpose, value, and action is a key ingredient of educationally powerful environments. For example, educational models and practices that rely on formal, stratified organizational arrangements will likely fail at an institution whose culture and tradition is egalitarian and participative. Likewise, a more hierarchical institutional culture might thrive on such arrangements, since they support a more competitive, individualized campus style and ethos. The point of this analysis is that what works well at one institution may conflict with the organizational culture of another. The human aggregate characteristics, physical features, and organizational structures that sustain satisfaction, stability, and involvement among students often differ significantly from one campus to the next, affirming the centrality of institutional purpose and culture in the design of effective educational environments.

Conclusion

Campus educators and policy makers would do well to review how their practices and policies reflect the principles highlighted in the literature on campus environments. The potency of any educational environment, whether a classroom, a residence hall, a student organization, or an entire campus, is a function of its design (planned or not), what it encourages and expects students to do, and what ends it serves. Effective educational environments present human-scale communities that offer opportunities for congruence, encourage involvement, and fulfill educational purposes consistent with the institution's organizational culture.

References

Anchors, S., Schroeder, C., & Jackson, S. (1978). *Making yourself at home: A practical guide to restructuring and personalizing your residence hall environment.* Washington, DC: ACPA Media Publications.

Astin, A. W. (1962). An empirical characterization of higher educational institutions. *Journal of Educational Psychology, 53,* 224–235.

Astin, A. W. (1968). *The college environment.* Washington, DC: American Council on Education.

Astin, A. W. (1985). *Achieving educational excellence: A critical assessment of priorities and practices in higher education.* San Francisco: Jossey-Bass.

Astin, A. W. (1993). An empirical typology of college students. *Journal of College Student Development, 34,* 36–46.

Astin, A. W., & Holland, J. L. (1961). The environmental assessment technique: A way to measure college environments. *Journal of Educational Psychology, 52,* 308–316.

Baird, L. L. (1988). The college environment revisited: A review of research and theory. In J. C. Smart (Ed.), *Higher education: Vol. 4. Handbook of theory and research* (pp. 1–52). New York: Agathon Press.

Banning, J. H. (1989). Impact of college environments on freshman students. In M. L. Upcraft, J. N. Gardner, & Associates. *The freshman year experience* (pp. 53–62). San Francisco: Jossey-Bass.

Barker, R. G. (1968). *Ecological psychology: Concepts and methods for studying the environment of human behavior.* Stanford, CA: Stanford University Press.

Barker, R. G., & Gump, P. V. (1964). *Big school, small school.* Stanford, CA: Stanford University Press.

Blau, P. M. (1973). *The organization of academic work.* New York: Wiley.

Boyer, E. L. (1987). *College: The undergraduate experience in America.* New York: Harper & Row.

Caple, R. B. (1987). The change process in developmental theory: A self-organization paradigm (pt. 1). *Journal of College Student Personnel, 28,* 4–11.

Carnegie Foundation for the Advancement of Teaching. (1990). *Campus life: In search of community.* Princeton, NJ: Author.

Chaffee, E. E., & Tierney, W. G. (1988). *Collegiate culture and leadership strategies.* New York: American Council on Education/Macmillan.

Chickering, A. W., & Reisser, L. (1993). *Education and identity* (2nd ed.). San Francisco: Jossey-Bass.

Clark, B. R., & Trow, M. (1966). The organizational context. In T. M. Newcomb & E. K. Wilson (Eds.), *College peer groups: Problems and prospects for research* (pp. 17–70). Chicago: Aldine.

Crookston, B. B. (1974). A design for an intentional democratic community. In D. A. De Coster & P. Mable (Eds.), *Student development and education in college residence halls* (pp. 55–67). Washington, DC: American College Personnel Association.

Dober, R. P. (1992). *Campus design.* New York: Wiley.

Dyer, W. G., Jr. (1986). The cycle of cultural evolution in organizations. In R. H. Kilman, M. J. Saxton, R. Serpa, & Associates (Eds.), *Gaining control of the corporate culture* (pp. 200–229). San Francisco: Jossey-Bass.

Ender, K., Kane, N., Mable, P., & Strohm, M. (1980). *Creating community in residence halls.* Washington, DC: ACPA Media Publications.

Etzioni, A. (1964). *Modern organizations.* Englewood Cliffs, NJ: Prentice Hall.

Forrest, L., Hotelling, K., & Kuk, L. (1986). *The elimination of sexism in the university environment* (ERIC Document Reproduction Service No. ED 267348). Paper presented at the second annual Student Development Through Campus Ecology symposium, Pingree Park, CO.

Gaines, T. A. (1991). *The campus as a work of art.* New York: Praeger.

Gilligan, C. (1982). *In a different voice: Psychological theory and women's development.* Cambridge, MA: Harvard University Press.

Griffith, J. C. (1994). Open space preservation: An imperative for quality campus environments. *Journal of Higher Education, 65,* 645–669.

Hage, J., & Aiken, M. (1970). *Social change in complex organizations.* New York: Random House.

Hall, E. T. (1966). *The hidden dimension.* Garden City, NY: Doubleday.

Hall, R. M., & Sandler, B. R. (1982). *The classroom climate: A chilly one for women?* Washington, DC: Project on the Status and Education of Women, Association of American Colleges.

Hall, R. M., & Sandler, B. R. (1984). *Out of the classroom: A chilly campus climate for women?* Washington, DC: Project on the Status and Education of Women, Association of American Colleges.

Hancock, E. (1990). Zoos, tunes, and gweeps: A dictionary of campus slang. *Journal of Higher Education, 61,* 98–106.

Heilweil, M. (1973). The influence of dormitory architecture on resident behavior. *Environment and Behavior, 5,* 377–412.

Holland, J. L. (1973). *Making vocational choices: A theory of careers.* Englewood Cliffs, NJ: Prentice Hall.

Horowitz, H. L. (1987). *Campus life: Undergraduate cultures from the end of the eighteenth century to the present.* New York: Knopf.

Huebner, L. A., & Lawson, J. M. (1990). Understanding and assessing college environments. In D. Creamer & Associates, *College student development: Theory and practice for the 1990s* (American College Personnel Association Media Publication No. 49, pp. 127–151). Alexandria, VA: American College Personnel Association.

Kolb, D. (1983). *Experiential learning: Experience as the source of learning and development.* Englewood Cliffs, NJ: Prentice Hall.

Kuh, G. D. (Ed.). (1993). *Cultural perspectives in student affairs work.* Lanham, MD: American College Personnel Association.

Kuh, G. D., & Hall, J. E. (1993). Using cultural perspectives in student affairs. In G. D. Kuh (Ed.), *Cultural perspectives in student affairs work* (pp. 1–20). Lanham, MD: American College Personnel Association.

Kuh, G. D., Schuh, J. H., Whitt, E. J., Andreas, R. E., Lyons, J. W., Strange, C. C., Krehbiel, L. E., & MacKay, K. A. (1991). *Involving colleges: Encouraging student learning and personal development through out-of-class experiences.* San Francisco: Jossey-Bass.

Kuh, G. D., & Whitt, E. J. (1988). *The invisible tapestry: Cultures in American colleges and universities* (ASHE-ERIC Higher Education Report Series No. 1). Washington, DC: Association for the Study of Higher Education.

Lundberg, C. C. (1985). On the feasibility of cultural intervention in organizations. In P. J. Frost, L. F. Moore, M. R. Louis, C. C. Lundberg, & J. Martin (Eds.), *Organizational culture* (pp. 169–186). Beverly Hills, CA: Sage.

Masland, A. T. (1985). Organizational culture in the study of higher education. *Review of Higher Education, 8,* 157–168.

Michelson, W. (1970). *Man and his urban environment: A sociological approach.* Reading, MA: Addison-Wesley.

Moffatt, M. (1989). *Coming of age in New Jersey: College and American culture.* New Brunswick, NJ: Rutgers University Press.

Moos, R. H. (1974). *Family environment scale—Form R.* Palo Alto, CA: Consulting Psychologists Press.

Moos, R. H. (1979). *Evaluating educational environments.* San Francisco: Jossey-Bass.

Moos, R. H. (1981). *Group environment scale manual.* Palo Alto, CA: Consulting Psychologists Press.

Moos, R. H. (1986). *The human context: Environmental determinants of behavior.* Malabar, FL: Krieger.

Moos, R. H., & Gerst, M. (1974). *The university residence environment scale manual.* Palo Alto, CA: Consulting Psychologists Press.

Moos, R. H., & Insel, P. (1974). *Work environment scale technical report.* Palo Alto, CA: Stanford University, Department of Psychiatry, Social Ecology Laboratory.

Moos, R. H., & Trickett, E. J. (1974). *Classroom environment scale manual.* Palo Alto, CA: Consulting Psychologists Press.

Murray, H. (1938). *Explorations in Personality.* New York: Oxford University Press.

Myers, I. B. (1980). *Gifts differing.* Palo Alto, CA: Consulting Psychologists Press.

Pace, C. R., & Stern, G. G. (1958). An approach to the measurement of psychological characteristics of college environments. *Journal of Educational Psychology, 49,* 269–277.

Palmer, P. (1987, September-October). Community, conflict, and ways of knowing. *Change,* 20–25.

Pascarella, E. T. (1985). College environmental influences on learning and cognitive development: A critical review and synthesis. In J. C. Smart (Ed.), *Higher education: Vol. 1. Handbook of theory and research* (pp. 1–61). New York: Agathon Press.

Perry, W. G. (1970). *Forms of intellectual and ethical development in the college years: A scheme.* New York: Holt, Rinehart and Winston.

Saunders, D. R. (1969). A factor analytic study of the AI and CCI. *Multivariate Behavioral Research, 4,* 329–346.

Schein, E. H. (1985). *Organizational culture and leadership.* San Francisco: Jossey-Bass.

Schein, E. H. (1992). *Organizational culture and leadership* (2nd ed.). San Francisco: Jossey-Bass.

Schlossberg, N. K., Lassalle, A., & Golec, R. (1988). *The mattering scale for adults in higher education* (6th ed.). College Park, MD: University of Maryland.

Schroeder, C. C. (1979). Territoriality: Conceptual and methodological issues for residence educators. *Journal of College and University Housing, 8,* 9–15.

Schroeder, C. C. (1981). Student development through environmental management. In G. S. Blimling & J. H. Schuh (Eds.), *Increasing the educational role of residence halls* (New Directions for Student Services No. 13, pp. 35–50). San Francisco: Jossey-Bass.

Sommer, R. (1969). *Personal space.* Englewood Cliffs, NJ: Prentice Hall.

Sommer, R. (1974). *Tight spaces: Hard architecture and how to humanize it.* Englewood Cliffs, NJ: Prentice Hall.

Spitzberg, I. J., Jr., & Thorndike, V. V. (1992). *Creating community on college campuses.* Albany: State University of New York Press.

Stern, R. A. (1986). *Pride of place: Building the American dream.* Boston: Houghton Mifflin.

Strange, C. C. (1981). Organizational barriers to student development. *National Association of Student Personnel Administrators Journal, 19*(1), 12–20.

Strange, C. C. (1983). Human development theory and administrative practice in student affairs: Ships passing in the daylight? *National Association of Student Personnel Administrators Journal, 21,* 2–8.

Strange, C. C. (1991). Managing college environments: Theory and practice. In T. K. Miller, R. B. Winston, Jr., & Associates (Eds.), *Administration and leadership in student affairs: Actualizing student development in student affairs* (2nd ed., pp. 159–199). Muncie, IN: Accelerated Development.

Strange, C. C. (1993). Developmental impacts of campus living environments. In R. B. Winston, Jr., S. Anchors, & Associates, *Student housing and residential life: A handbook for professionals committed to student development goals* (pp. 134–166). San Francisco: Jossey-Bass.

Strange, C. (1994). Student development: The evolution and status of an essential idea. *Journal of College Student Development, 35,* 399–412.

Strange, C. C., & Hannah, D. (1994, March). *The learning university: A model for the twenty-first century.* Paper presented at the meeting of the American College Personnel Association, Indianapolis, IN.

Strange, C. C., & King, P. (1990). The professional practice of student development. In D. Creamer & Associates (Eds.), *College student development: Theory and practice for the 1990s* (ACPA Media Publication No. 49, pp. 9–24). Alexandria, VA: American College Personnel Association.

Sturner, W. F. (1973). The college environment. In D. W. Vermilye (Ed.), *The future in the making* (pp. 71–86). San Francisco: Jossey-Bass.

Thelin, J. R., & Yankovich, J. (1987). Bricks and mortar: Architecture and the study of higher education. In J. C. Smart (Ed.), *Higher education: Vol. 3. Handbook of theory and research* (pp. 57–83). New York: Agathon Press.

Tierney, W. G. (1993). *Building communities of difference: Higher education in the twenty-first century.* Westport, CT: Bergin & Garvey.

Walsh, W. B. (1973). *Theories of person-environment interaction: Implications for the college student.* Iowa City, IA: American College Testing Program.

Wicker, A. W. (1973). Undermanning theory and research: Implications for the study of psychological and behavioral effects of excess populations. *Representative Research in Social Psychology, 4,* 185–206.

CHAPTER THIRTEEN

ORGANIZATIONAL THEORY

George D. Kuh

The accelerating pace of change in higher education is forcing institutions to become more agile and responsive (Belasco & Stayer, 1993; "Higher Education Must Change," 1992; "To Dance with Change," 1994; "An Uncertain Terrain," 1993; Wingspread Group on Higher Education, 1993). Virtually every institution is reexamining its core functions—including student affairs—to determine whether they are necessary and, if so, organized in an efficient and effective manner (El-Khawas, 1994). More than ever, student affairs professionals must understand how people, organizational structures, and governance processes influence one another. To describe and understand these phenomena, theories about organizational behavior have been developed.

The term *organizational behavior* represents a personification, an attempt to give human characteristics to inanimate entities such as colleges and universities (Weick, 1979). A student affairs office does not perform; it is the people in the office that are responsible for what is accomplishes. In this chapter, "organizational behavior" refers to the interactions among organizational actors; organizational events are the outcomes of their attitudes, beliefs, and actions. Identifying the actors, the actors' roles, and the relationships between the actors and organizational actions is difficult, as institutions of higher education are increasingly vulnerable to such external influences as changing economic conditions and the agendas of legislators, corporate and philanthropic foundations, accrediting bodies, and state education commissions. These influences, coupled with an increase in the number of students, faculty, and administrators from historically underrepresented groups, add another measure of complexity to an environment already characterized by competing values and preferences among faculty, professional staff, administrators, and students (Birnbaum, 1988; Cohen & March, 1974).

Organizational theory is an eclectic field, drawing from sociology, social psychology, anthropology, philosophy (Morgan, 1986; Pfeffer, 1982), cybernetics (Birnbaum, 1988), and the study of chaos and complexity (Peters, 1987; Waldrop, 1992; Wheatley, 1992) to explain such processes such as resource allocation, policy making, personnel management, leadership, restructuring, and reengineering. Just as different student development theories account for some aspects of growth and behavior but not others, so it is with organizational theories. In this sense, an organizational theory is a window through which to view the behavior of individuals and groups (students, faculty members, student affairs professionals) in the context of a complex organization interacting with and being shaped by external exigencies and special interest groups. What one sees depends on which window one looks through (Birnbaum, 1988; Bolman & Deal, 1991). That is, by looking at behavior through one window, certain events, actions, and relationships appear coordinated and purposeful; viewed through another window, however, the same interactions may look chaotic or dysfunctional.

In a practitioner's mind, concepts from various organizational views are mixed with experience, becoming theories-in-use (Argyris & Schön, 1978)—highly personal, individualized patterns of understanding. Being familiar with multiple theoretical windows increases the possibility that one's theories-in-use will generate more accurate interpretations of events and actions than are possible using any single view (Kuh, 1984). In this chapter, three conventional and three postconventional views of organizational behavior are discussed, including their implications for student affairs professionals. (Exhibit 13.1 summarizes the differences between the conventional and postconventional views.)

Conventional Views of Organizations

Conventional views of organizational behavior developed during an era (1900 to 1960) when the closed-system approach to understanding organizations was dominant. That is, complex organizations, including institutions of higher education, were generally portrayed as impermeable to external influences. In addition, all variables (including people) with the potential to affect institutional performance could be manipulated by a competent administrator (Katz & Rosenzweig, 1974). A closed-systems approach to alcohol abuse in residence halls would focus exclusively on a student's behavior (and, perhaps, differences in hall

EXHIBIT 13.1. CONVENTIONAL AND POSTCONVENTIONAL VIEWS OF ORGANIZATIONS.

Conventional Views	PostConventional Views
Hierarchical structures are normal, necessary, functional, and desirable.	Heterarchical or cross functional interactions are uninhibited by structures and facilitate organizational learning and effective management; organizational processes and structures evolve over time.
Communication channels are clearly delineated and consistently used.	Information is available from many sources inside and beyond the institution and flows in many directions.
Expertise, control, and authority are commensurate with position and exercised by superordinates.	Any person at any level has the potential to influence organizational behavior in an effective, positive, creative manner.
Goals and means to attain goals are clear, are shared, give direction to behavior, and are tied directly to outcomes.	Relationships among events, individual behavior, technologies, and outcomes are unpredictable, frequently ambiguous, and constantly changing.
Intentions are directly linked to actions.	Intentions and actions, by units or individuals, are loosely coupled and can be understood only in retrospect.
Reliability and predictability of organizational processes are hampered only by factors such as knowledge and technology.	Qualities of indeterminacy, morphogenesis, action learning, and self-organizing compromise expectations for reliability and predictability but are necessary for organizational adaptation and change.

Source: Adapted from Kuh, Whitt & Shedd (1987).

environments) but would ignore societal drinking habits, drinking customs common to ethnic groups, family histories of alcohol use, and so on (Kuh, 1994).

Conventional approaches emphasize three properties: (1) hierarchical structures and controls; (2) clear communication channels; and (3) stability, reliability, and predictability (Clark, 1985; Kuh, Whitt & Shedd, 1987, Table 1). Three views of organizations emphasize these characteristics, to varying degrees: rational-bureaucratic, collegial, and political. The collegial and political views were developed specifically to understand behavior in colleges and universities.

Rational-Bureaucratic View

The objective of the rational-bureaucratic organization is to routinize tasks, functions, and processes, much like an assembly line routinizes production (Weber, 1947). The guiding premise is that routinization leads to improved organizational effectiveness and efficiency. No wonder "an efficient, well-oiled, smooth-running machine" was once a popular metaphor for organizations!

Viewed through the rational-bureaucratic window, institutions of higher education have seven characteristics:

1. Hierarchical authority or a clear chain of command. Every individual is responsible to someone in a higher office (for example, the senior student affairs officer, or SSAO, has more authority and responsibility than associate deans or entry-level staff).
2. Limits on authority. Specific people are responsible for specific, clearly defined areas of organizational performance.
3. Division of labor. Efficiency is maximized and duplication of effort is minimized by assigning responsibility for specific functions to certain persons and groups.
4. Technical competence. Workers have the requisite training.
5. Standard operating procedures. The tasks that must be performed to attain the organization's objectives are carefully prescribed.
6. Rules for work. Requirements and competence levels for various positions are specified.
7. Differential rewards. Salary and perquisites are tied directly to seniority and position in the hierarchy (Hage, 1980; Morgan, 1986).

To impose order, exert control, and produce desired outcomes, the rational-bureaucratic manager must

- Clarify values
- Set goals
- Determine the tasks needed to attain the goals
- Standardize tasks so anyone can perform them
- Designate responsibility for various functions to specific groups and individuals
- Delineate standard operating procedures in policy and procedure manuals
- Establish contingency plans, including who is to take what actions when (Allison, 1971; Chaffee, 1983; Pfeffer, 1982).

Policy decisions are centralized; that is, a handful of senior staff make decisions to ensure high-quality performance and progress toward organizational goals. The organizational structure indicates who is responsible for sharing what kind of information with whom. Certain people evaluate information for accuracy and disseminate it as necessary to appropriate individuals and groups. For example, resident assistants (RAs) convey information about residence hall policies and practices to students and report problems to supervisors. The director of residence life reports the most important information from RAs to the SSAO on a need-to-know basis. In turn, the SSAO informs the campus senior executive officer about events in the residence halls and usually represents student life to external audiences, such as parents and community leaders. Effectiveness depends on accurate information and appropriate "technology" (that is, the means by which the organization does its work). Inadequate information or flawed technology creates problems. For example, tardy financial aid awards may be explained by obsolete or poorly designed software that does not accommodate recent changes in federal aid guidelines. Flawed technology could also include cumbersome communication networks, such as decision-making processes that exclude legitimate stakeholders, or human error, such as failure to consult with student government officers with regard to tuition and technology-related fee increases.

Rational-bureaucratic principles coupled with scientific management concepts (Fayol, 1949; Gulick & Urwick, 1937; Taylor, 1911) are the foundation of such management techniques as management by objectives (MBO), planned programming and budgeting systems (PPBS), and other hyperrational planning and control mechanisms (Clark, 1985). The human relations management approach (Argyris, 1964; Likert, 1967; Mayo, 1945; McGregor, 1960) was developed subsequently to emphasize the importance of such factors as motivation and morale to organizational performance.

As with all organizational views, the rational-bureaucratic window has some limitations, particularly when applied to an institution of higher education. For example, people can assimilate only so much information at any one time (see Exhibit 13.2). Because of this "bounded rationality" (Simon, 1957), no one can be aware of everything that takes place in a complex organization. People must "satisfice"—that is, they must act on incomplete knowledge (Simon, 1957; Weick, 1979). Specialization, standardization, routinization, and repetition inhibit organizational flexibility (Hage & Aiken, 1970; Strange, 1983) and blunt change efforts (Morgan, 1986), and they discourage individual initiative, innovation, and risk taking (Peters & Waterman, 1982; Vaill, 1984). In addition, faculty and professional staff expect autonomy, not close supervision. Standardization is difficult when activities are not similar across jobs. Although some functions are more effective when routinized (for example, registration and financial aid), others may not be (such as career planning and student activities). For these reasons, a hybrid organizational form—the professional bureaucracy—evolved in institutions of higher education and other organizations with large numbers of highly educated personnel to take advantage of the unusual amount of expertise they possess (Mintzberg, 1979).

EXHIBIT 13.2. ADVANTAGES AND LIMITATIONS OF CONVENTIONAL VIEWS OF ORGANIZATIONS.

View	Advantages	Limitations
Rational-bureaucratic	Appeals to reason and logic. Clearly defined roles, functions, responsibilities, scope of authority, and relationships. Performance is standardized. Prospective approach. Emphasizes productivity.	Incompatible with certain values of the academy (such as autonomy, multiple areas of expertise, decisions by peers). Expectations for goal consensus and control are often not met. Oversimplifies complex problems. Constrained by information-processing limits. Resistant to change. Measures of productivity not well suited to purposes of higher education.
Collegial	Consistent with traditions of the academy. Responsive to persuasive argument of colleagues. Based on democratic principles. Ensures representation.	Inefficient (labor-intensive and time-consuming). Insensitive to power differentials, resource availability, and policy implementation issues.
Political	Acknowledges importance of power and conflict resolution. Emphasizes policy making as a process for issue management. Encourages collaboration among disparate stakeholder groups.	Incongruent with certain values of the academy (such as openness, fairness, self-governance). Reinforces the status quo. Exchanges achievement and merit for influence in decision making.

These limitations do not mean that expert judgment and logical analysis are lacking in merit or that reason never prevails. In fact, most actions in a college or university are rational—to someone. The fatal flaw of the rational-bureaucratic view is the assumption that managers can and should anticipate, account for, and attempt to control all the possible contingencies that may bear on a decision (see Exhibit 13.2), an expectation that cannot be met by any individual or organization. Equally important, such traditions as academic freedom and collegial governance are incompatible with certain rational-bureaucratic principles, as explained below.

Collegial View

The collegial view is based on two enduring values of the academy: professional autonomy and a normative compliance system (Austin & Gamson, 1983). Faculty and staff are highly trained in their respective fields, and therefore they are uniquely capable of determining the conditions under which they perform best. Compliance is normative in that faculty and professional staff are motivated more by the belief that their work is significant than by fear of sanctions from superiors (Etzioni, 1961). As a result of its allegiance to these two values, the collegial view of organizations is almost universally endorsed by faculty and student affairs professionals as the preferred way to organize and govern an institution of higher education.

Collegial processes foster commitment, satisfaction, and productivity by allowing people to shape their destiny through participating in governance structures. These governance structures (for example, personnel committees, the faculty senate) determine priorities, work conditions, and standards of quality; they also have responsibility for selecting new colleagues and evaluating peer performance (Baldridge, Curtis, Ecker, & Riley, 1977; Birnbaum, 1988; Chaffee, 1983; Kanter, 1983). The structures are reproduced at various levels (for example, the entire institution, academic departments, student organizations, and residences).

For collegial processes to be effective, people must be open to new ideas. They must share and clarify their positions through discussion, and they must change their position when presented with compelling reasons to do so. While some roles and processes are delineated, such as the role of the president pro tempore of the faculty senate and the use of *Robert's Rules of Order*, specific procedures are not prescribed for universal use but emerge through reasoned discourse among peers at each individual campus.

However, the collegial view tends to oversimplify life in institutions of higher education. In addition, collegial decision making and policy formulation are time-consuming. The increasing influence of external agencies and factors, such as the economy, sunshine laws, threats of litigation, and parental wishes, have eroded the integrity of collegial processes. For these reasons and others, faculty members are less willing to spend time and resources on institutional governance (Austin & Gamson, 1983). Taken together, these factors have reduced the utility of the collegial view for making certain types of decisions, such as resource allocations and decisions concerning physical plant expansion. Finally, the collegial view does not explicitly address conflict resolution or the role of power in decision making, two realities of life in colleges and universities that are featured in the political view of organizations.

Political View

When powerful stakeholders compete for limited resources or differ on important issues, conflict is inevitable. Policy alternatives may be proposed to address differences in views or to respond to the interests of various groups. People with similar interests often form coalitions to advocate a particular alternative. Lobbying and debating take place both in public forums and in private. Sometimes these negotiations result in new or changed policies (Baldridge, Curtis, Ecker, & Riley, 1977). Some form of ratification, such as voting or formal acknowledgment by institutional leaders, usually determines the preferred policy option (Baldridge, 1971).

Although the political view implies that many faculty and staff will be involved in decision and policy making, this is not necessarily the case. In part this is because few issues are of sufficient importance to stimulate active involvement by large numbers of stakeholders (March & Olsen, 1976). Unless an issue is of high salience to members of one or more groups, people are not likely to invest limited energy and time in the deliberations.

The political view acknowledges the uneven distribution of power within an institution of higher education, which challenges the "myth of organizational rationality" (Morgan, 1986, p. 195), including expectations for rational decision making and goal-directed, functionally interdependent units. For example, sometimes a decision is made without the knowledge of those individuals who will be affected by it, leading to feelings of alienation and problems in implementing decisions or policies (see Exhibit 13.2). And when implemented, a policy or practice may look very different from what was adopted (Lipsky, 1980). Also, the debates and lobbying associated with decisions may exacerbate, rather than ameliorate, differences between groups, thus creating more tension.

Faculty and student affairs staff who expect their institution to be a community of equals may reject or feel threatened by the political view. Conflict and competition are perceived as antithetical to the traditions of collegial decision making and governance. Some people associate institutional politics with Machiavellian behavior and ruthless self-interest, considering conflict to be a dysfunctional condition triggered by lamentable circumstances such as personality problems, rivalry, and role dissonance. Conflict associated with self-interest cannot be avoided, however. For example, when faculty and students learn that funds have been allocated for additional scholarships for students with certain talents, such as athletes and musicians, but no financial need, one or more groups will likely challenge the wisdom of such decisions. Staff may disagree on how to allocate funds for professional development or programming, who remains on duty during spring break, which student groups get offices in the union, or the institution's policies on student activism or hate speech. As resources become more scarce and the number of special interest groups increases ("An Uncertain Terrain," 1993), colleges and universities will experience more, not less, competition. The political view is particularly useful for identifying those who are most likely to be influential in the process and for maximizing the potential benefits of conflict management and collaborative policy making.

Implications of Conventional Views

In conventional views of organizations, goals are presumed to be clear and uniformly validated; people either decide together (as in the collegial and political views) or are told by a superior (as in the rational-bureaucratic view) how to attain the organization's goals. Logic and reason are instrumental in problem solving, planning, and policy making. Control and responsibility are exercised from the top down. Confusion, poor performance, and differences of opinion are addressed by following the rules of engagement specific to the preferred view. In the collegial approach, for example, disagreements are ameliorated via the appropriate governance committee; in the rational-bureaucratic approach, managers use the chain of command to fix the "part" of the organizational machine that is not functioning properly. Occasionally the preferences of some persons or coalitions may supersede the goals of others, creating conflict and, perhaps, confusion (the political view) (see Exhibit 13.1). Change is brought about intentionally in response to threats and opportunities in the external environment (Di Maggio & Powell, 1983; Lawrence & Lorsch, 1967; Thompson, 1967; Pfeffer & Salancik, 1978; Zucker, 1987). Success is measured by accuracy of predictions, comprehensiveness of plans, and the degree to which predetermined objectives are attained. That is, if staff serve students well and the student affairs division runs smoothly and meets the expectations of the president and governing board, student affairs is considered effective.

For more than half a century, conventional views shaped expectations of how people should behave in institutions of higher education. They were developed assuming that colleges and universities were closed systems, independent of external forces for the most part. But circumstances have changed. As Heydinger (1994) asserts, "Twenty-first century higher education must become mission-driven, customer-sensitive, enterprise-organized, and results-oriented. . . . We need a new organizational paradigm: one that will focus us on those we serve; allocate resources based on demonstrable success; provide flexibility that will permit timely responses to changing student and research needs; eliminate unnecessary layers of oversight by placing more responsibility with those we serve" (p. 1).

As mentioned earlier, institutions of higher education are increasingly vulnerable to forces in their turbulent, unpredictable external environment. In addition, people from more diverse backgrounds are working and studying in postsecondary institutions (Katz, 1989). Therefore, student affairs staff need different windows to look through in order to make sense of the complicated and rapidly changing institutions in which they work.

Postconventional Views of Organizations

Postconventional views hold that colleges and universities are complex open systems, influenced by external events and changing conditions. Instead of being orderly, linear, and goal-directed, the postconventional organization encourages sharing information simultaneously in various directions and interactions within, across, and beyond organizational boundaries to respond to developing circumstances (see Exhibit 13.1). Moreover, colleges have the capacity to evolve into qualitatively different forms as they adapt to changes in their external environment and internal conditions. Indeed, they must change and adapt to survive (Heydinger, 1994; Hollyman & Howie, 1994; "To Dance with Change," 1994)! This perspective on organizations shares many of the qualities characteristic of shifting paradigms in other fields, such as history, law, economics, psychology, and physics (Capra, 1983; Gleick, 1987; Kuhn, 1970; Lincoln, 1985; Schwartz & Ogilvy, 1979; Waldrop, 1992; Wheatley, 1992).

To stimulate creative thinking about how organizations function under conditions of instability and uncertainty, imaginative metaphors for organizations have been invoked by various authors (Morgan, 1986), including "flying seesaws" (Hedberg, Nystrom, & Starbuck, 1976), "garbage cans" (Cohen, March, & Olsen, 1972), "psychic prisons" (Morgan, 1986), and "rain-forest tribes" (Schroeder, Nicholls, & Kuh, 1983). In this section, three postconventional views are described: organized anarchy, culture, and the learning organization. Although we have less experience looking through the newer, postconventional windows, they more accurately describe many of the rapidly changing external and internal conditions student affairs professionals must contend with.

Organized Anarchy

The "organized anarchy" view (Cohen & March, 1974) is the most familiar of the postconventional windows. It was developed specifically to describe six characteristics peculiar to colleges and universities: ambiguous, conflicting goals; unclear technologies; loose coupling; fluid participation; a professional work force; and clients who participate in institutional governance (Baldridge et al., 1977; Birnbaum, 1988; Cohen & March, 1974; Weick, 1976, 1979).

Colleges and universities have multiple goals that occasionally conflict (Gross

& Grambusch, 1968). For example, many faculty at research universities complain about getting mixed messages regarding the relative value of teaching and research. Administrators receive many more legitimate requests for funding than they can accommodate (for salary increases, new equipment, and student aid, to name a few). A student activities director wants to create additional leadership opportunities for students of color; a career counselor is charged with increasing the number of employers recruiting on campus; the director of commuter affairs wants to increase security in the parking lots—all of these goals are worthwhile, but some of them cannot be realized because of limited resources (Hull, Hunter, & Kuh, 1983).

Unclear technology (Cohen & March, 1974) refers to an inability to consistently describe and replicate important processes, such as the use of relationship therapy in the campus mental health center or in theory-based residence hall programs. In almost every field, professionals rely on tacit information, their experience, and enlightened judgment when working with clients (Schön, 1987). For example, an estimated 80 percent of the vision problems encountered by optometrists do not fit the correction categories taught in professional school (Schön, 1983). When many different individuals exercise professional judgment in an organization, numerous approaches to performing tasks typically develop. The complexity of tasks such as student development programming and the absence of reliable, comparative data about the efficacy of various approaches contribute to unclear technology in student affairs (Hull, Hunter, & Kuh, 1983; Kuh, Whitt, & Shedd, 1987).

Coupling refers to the strength of the relationships between or among elements in an organization (Clark, Astuto, & Kuh, 1986; Weick, 1976). For example, residence life may be affected by the performance of admissions and financial aid staff—rooms might be left vacant if enough students do not apply or if financial aid awards are not made promptly. Conventional views expect such organizational units as the admissions office, residence halls, and student activities offices to be tightly coupled (Kuh, 1983), meaning that communication is direct and immediate and responses are immediate and predictable. For various reasons, however, tight coupling is the exception, not the rule, in most educational institutions (Clark, Astuto, & Kuh, 1986; Hull, Hunter, & Kuh, 1983; Weick, 1985) (see Exhibit 13.3).

In part this is due to the complexity and range of specialized functions performed in institutions of higher education (admissions, student development programming, legal services, career planning, psychological and health services, financial aid, food services, recreation, entertainment, and so on). Although the SSAO is responsible for all division employees, relatively few are in daily or weekly contact with him or her. Further, information (or a lack thereof) about what takes

EXHIBIT 13.3. ADVANTAGES AND LIMITATIONS OF POSTCONVENTIONAL VIEWS OF ORGANIZATIONS.

View	Advantages	Limitations
Organized anarchy	More descriptive of life in institutions of higher education. Images are intuitively appealing and evocative. Compatible with academy values (such as autonomy, minimal supervision). Acknowledges retrospective understanding rather than prescriptive models.	Information not always available to those who need it. Legitimizes and encourages divided loyalties. Hinders coordinated response to issues and crises. Does not suggest implications for staff and leader behavior. Challenges basic assumptions about effective organizing.
Culture	Acknowledges context as an important variable in understanding behavior. Explains unusual and routine behavior. Accommodates different behaviors (subcultures) within the institution or student affairs units. Acknowledges validity of subjective views. Emphasizes the importance of mutual shaping.	Lacks conceptual specificity. Insights gleaned from one experience or institution not transferable to others. Organizational properties cannot be manipulated or controlled. Requires different expectations for leader behavior.
Learning organization	Compatible with cybernetic, action learning principles (such as mutual shaping, evolutionary change). Acknowledges the importance of all members of the organization. Deemphasizes formal structures and procedures, thereby encouraging innovation, creativity, and organizational change. Encourages continuous personal and professional development of staff through role expansion, involvement in problem solving, and changing of norms.	Based on unfamiliar concepts. Contradicts conventional wisdom about organizations. Emphasizes complexity, paradox, and continuous change over simplicity and the search for correct solutions. Requires policies and practices that many institutions are not prepared to adopt.

place in the career planning office rarely affects what recreational sports, student activities, or judicial affairs staff do, particularly in larger institutions. Information does not always get to those individuals who are in the best position to act. If the counseling center's staff are not aware of a student's conflict with a roommate, the student may perceive the institution or its student affairs unit as inefficient, poorly managed, or—worse—uncaring and unresponsive. At the same time, loose coupling can be advantageous. In loosely coupled organizations, staff operate with minimal supervision and interference and assume greater responsibility for their work (Weick, 1976, 1979, 1985). For example, poor attendance at the student union's film series does not, fortunately, affect the financial aid or health services offices. Because mistakes in one area are isolated from other parts of the system, staff may be more likely to seek their own solutions to problems or to respond to opportunities independently; greater risk taking and innovation are encouraged.

Fluid participation, common in institutions of higher education, describes situations in which people who might ordinarily participate in decision making are absent when decisions are made (which may affect the quality of the decision) or in which people may not be available to implement a decision they made (which may affect the quality of the implementation) (Cohen & March, 1974). Because the student activities director is attending a professional meeting, a decision about raising the activity fee may be delayed another year. Or those present may decide to raise the fee without the input of the student activities office, which could have a deleterious effect on future relations between students and administrators. Fluid participation is also illustrated by the high turnover of both students and staff. At most institutions the students are around only eight months a year, and more than a quarter are new to the institution each year. Some institutions expect entry-level student affairs staff to leave after two or three years for financial reasons (Kuh & McAleenan, 1986). As a consequence, considerable effort is required to teach newcomers how to advise student government or what to expect during orientation activities.

Anarchistic qualities of colleges and universities are exacerbated by the presence of highly autonomous professionals who expect to determine the character of their work environment, such as program development and availability to students. Many faculty members, particularly those at prestigious institutions, have a stronger allegiance to their discipline and national network of peers than to their employing institution (Clark, 1985). Obligations to professional associations sometimes conflict with institutional expectations, creating tensions (Baldridge et al., 1977).

Until recently, colleges and universities were the only large, complex organizations that actively encouraged their primary client group (students) to participate in institutional governance (Baldridge et al., 1977). Although student involvement has numerous benefits (for example, it allows students to practice enlightened citizenship), decisions require more time, as student representatives must be oriented to governance structures and processes once or twice a year, and meetings must be scheduled when students are available. In the past few decades, the number of stakeholders expecting to participate in institutional decisions has expanded to include alumni, corporate and philanthropic sponsors, local and federal government officials, and parents (Birnbaum, 1988). As the number of stakeholders seeking a voice increases, decision-making processes become more complicated and time-consuming.

The organized anarchy view is unsettling to those who expect their institution to act rationally in predictable ways. The playful terms used to describe decision making seem incongruent with serious social science and firm, visionary institutional leadership. Nevertheless, the organized anarchy perspective is descriptively rich and intuitively appealing because it accurately portrays the special qualities of life in colleges and universities that are overlooked by conventional views (Kuh, 1983). For example, perhaps new procedures must be developed to allocate student activity fees because the people involved did not participate in the process the previous year or do not remember the decision-making rules (unclear technology). Or the assistant dean who conceptualized the recent reorganization of student government is pursuing a doctorate at another institution (fluid participation), and someone unfamiliar with the new structure becomes the student government advisor. Such experiences are not necessarily random or without meaning, as is suggested by the term *anarchy*. Certain patterns and themes emerge out of annual events and daily interactions; some are even predictable. For example, students arrive in early September, the spring term class schedule must be prepared the preceding fall, and the annual spring fling weekend irritates the faculty, tests the patience of student affairs staff, and brings great pleasure to students and local merchants. Therefore, student affairs staff should not forget the first word of the phrase "organized anarchy."

A Cultural Phenomenon

Another way to view college or university life is to think of it as a cultural phenomenon. An institution's culture represents a complex, elusive web of assumptions, beliefs, and values (Kuh & Whitt, 1988; Schein, 1985; Smircich, 1983; Tierney, 1988) that encourage, support, and reward certain behaviors over others. It imposes order and brings coherence to daily life by determining what people consider important and what they will and will not do (Louis, 1983). And because people have their own constructions of institutional life, multiple interpretations are legitimate. That is, the interpretations of events depend on the context in which the events occur and the meaning given to the events by the actors, or "culture-bearers" (Allaire & Firsirotu, 1984). This explains in part why members of historically underrepresented groups may feel alienated by the way their institution does things (Katz, 1989), why debates occur annually about the best way to conduct performance reviews, and why student affairs staff rarely modify their behavior following the arrival of a new dean or president.

Culture is not a static entity, however; it is continually evolving. An institution's culture is shaped in part by its external environment—economic and social conditions, the background and values of the people who live near the college, and so on. Also, while the institution's culture may influence how an individual thinks and behaves, new faculty, staff, and students from historically underrepresented groups bring with them different attitudes and perspectives that have a shaping influence on the institution's culture (Van Maanen, 1984). New staff members committed to using student development theory can influence certain features of the culture, such as the language used to communicate ideas. All these influences and more must be taken into account when trying to understand and appreciate an institution's culture.

Levels of Culture. As mentioned by Carney Strange in Chapter Twelve, cultural properties can be divided into four levels (Schein, 1985): artifacts, perspectives, strategic values, and assumptions (Kuh & Hall, 1993; Lundberg, 1990). Artifacts, the most visible level, include such physical, verbal, and behavioral properties as language, stories and sagas (Clark, 1972/1984), images, daily and periodic rituals, ceremonies, signs, and symbols (Kuh & Hall, 1993; Morgan, 1986; Van Maanen, 1984)—"the physical layout, the dress code, the manner in which people address each other, the smell and feel of the place . . ." (Schein, 1990, p. 111). Perspectives are patterns of behavior that have become widely shared; they define the way things should be and how things are done. An organization's strategic values are reflected in the sense of "what should be" compared with "what is." Many values are conscious, explicitly articulated, and guide group members in dealing with new or key situations. Espoused values are reflected in what people say but not necessarily in what they do (Argyris & Schön, 1978). Taken together, assumptions constitute a worldview (Lundberg, 1990) and define the nature of relations between people in their environment—how we treat each other, what constitutes "truth," and the relative importance of various tasks and activities. Assumptions essentially define the organization's "reality" (Morgan, 1986), determining how its members perceive, think about, and feel about things (Schein, 1985).

Subcultures. Most colleges and universities have several clearly differentiated subgroups among their students, faculty, and administrators; these groups tend to differ from one another in their values and beliefs (Clark, 1989; Clark & Trow, 1966; Martin, 1992; Sergiovanni, 1984). For example, student affairs staff often perceive events and activities differently from some of their faculty colleagues. This is due, in part, to their being socialized in different "cultures of orientation" (Van Maanen, 1984, p. 215). Subcultures are positive forces when they engender a sense of identity, cohesiveness, and loyalty to the institution or when they make success possible for persons in an alienating environment, such as African American students at a predominantly White campus. But when a subculture's values and norms deviate significantly from the institution's expectations of appropriate behavior, such as when a fraternity tolerates hazardous use of alcohol by its members (Kuh & Arnold, 1993), the group can have a deleterious influence. On the other hand, the presence of such groups can stimulate productive disagreements about institutional goals and values. Such disagreements are inevitable, in fact, and they can provoke appropriate institutional change if the institution is forced to examine culturally embedded practices that inhibit certain individuals and groups from realizing their learning and personal development goals.

The culture window is best used as an interpretive lens for understanding and appreciating the nuances of a particular group's behavior (Kuh, 1993). For example, culture may explain why the goals of student affairs professionals are sometimes perceived as being inconsistent with the expectations of faculty and students, or why newcomers perceive certain aspects of institutional life differently from people who have been there some time. By examining values and beliefs, events can be understood that otherwise might seem mysterious, out of place, debilitating, or irrational. Looking through the culture window also provides a constant reminder that while institutions may be similar in many ways, they also differ in ways that affect how their members interpret and respond to what seem to be the same phenomena. Student affairs staff also resonate to the culture view's emphasis on holism, history, tradition, evolving circumstances, and individual differences.

However, the culture window does not reveal everything that one needs to know about what takes place in a college or university. Culture concepts lack semantic precision, which limits their analytical power. Because meaning is context-bound, insights from one setting are not necessarily applicable to other settings; thus those who hope to develop a set of generalizable guiding principles will not be satisfied with the contextual restrictions imposed by a cultural perspective (Kuh, 1993) (see Exhibit 13.3). Some observers suggest that culture is not controllable and is therefore difficult—if not impossible—to change, at least in the short term (Kuh & Whitt, 1988). Others see culture as just another set of organizational properties that must adapt to changing external forces and internal circumstances (Bolman & Deal, 1991). These conflicting interpretations point to a potential limitation of the value of the cultural view for administrators coping with a rapidly changing external environment. As Pritchett and Pound (1993) put it, "We've entered an era where the organization must adopt a 'do what works' mentality. . . . In times past it was acceptable to settle for gradually evolving culture change. . . . [Today,] if the culture doesn't adapt—rapidly—everybody loses" (p. 8). Those who do use a cultural view are encouraged to experiment with ways of intentionally changing dysfunctional elements of their institutional culture.

Learning Organizations

The learning organization view is the newest of the three postconventional windows, and it is thus the least well understood. This view draws on three metaphors—the hologram, the brain, and the thermostat—that provide insight into how colleges and universities cope with the turbulent environmental forces that demand continuously changing institutional functions, processes, and structures.

A hologram is a photographic record of a dynamic process of interaction, integration, and differentiation. If a hologram breaks, any of its parts can be used to re-create the entire image (Morgan & Ramirez, 1983); that is, everything is encoded into everything else (Morgan, 1986). The institution-as-hologram metaphor suggests that each student affairs staff member reflects the character of the entire division of student affairs and indeed the greater institution's mission and values.

The brain combines features found nowhere else in nature: it acquires, stores, organizes, retrieves, and manipulates disparate pieces of information in a resilient, flexible, inventive, and integrative way; moreover, it has an elastic capacity to improve these functions (Morgan, 1986). Given the complex, rapidly changing circumstances institutions of higher education must contend with, it is highly desirable for a college or university to develop brainlike qualities.

A thermostat engages a furnace or air conditioner to respond to temperature changes (Birnbaum, 1988; Morgan, 1986). Similarly, a learning organization senses, monitors, and scans its internal and external environments and measures what they require against the organization's capacity to respond. When significant gaps exist between environmental demands and institutional processes and structures, the institution must adapt in order to survive. As the scope and magnitude of changes reach a certain point, a qualitatively different organizational form may emerge. This morphogenetic change process is called self-organizing (Bertalanffy, 1968; Caple, 1985; Prigogine & Stengers, 1984); it requires four conditions: redundancy, requisite variety, minimum critical specification, and action learning (Morgan, 1986).

Redundancy means that staff members can perform a range of functions and can do the jobs of others; thus, generalists are valued over specialists. By sharing information, people learn how their work affects others, fostering teamwork and improved productivity (Wheatley, 1992). Both self-knowledge and organizational knowledge increase as staff learn more about student affairs and how their work influences others and the institution as a whole (Senge, 1990). Total Quality Management approaches emphasize this approach (Seymour, 1992).

Requisite variety means that the "internal diversity of any self-regulating system must match the variety and complexity of its environment" (Morgan, 1986, p. 100). For example, as increasing numbers of students of color matriculate, student affairs divisions must reflect the values of a more diverse student body by hiring more people of color. In this way the values and attitudes of the student affairs staff may become more compatible with important characteristics of the external and internal environments. The personal values of staff must also be in harmony with institutional values. This does not imply unyielding, dogmatic adherence to institutional norms or policies, but rather respect for collective purposes and goals.

Minimal critical specification refers to having the fewest number of people needed to perform essential functions and adapt to changing circumstances—whatever it takes to get the job done. Thus, to increase organizational flexibility, staff and students should not be unduly constrained by rules, customs, and time-honored customs. Like restructuring in the for-profit sector, minimum critical specification implies that fewer full-time professionals may be needed for any given function in the future.

The most common response to problems is single-loop learning—that is, error detection and correction (Argyris & Schön, 1978). When problems arise, the usual response is to provide whatever is required to return the system to normal functioning. Action learning, on the other hand, is a form of purposeful reflection (Morgan, 1986; Senge, 1990) similar to double-loop learning. Double-loop learning is "learning to learn, an acquired ability to question normative behavior and guiding principles. Action learners take risks . . . and are skeptical about what their experiences teach them. They never assume they have discovered the 'best' way or 'correct' answer." (Kuh, Whitt, & Shedd, 1987, p. 67). In a rapidly changing environment, taking risks is one way of trying to take a measure of control (Peters, 1995); thus cautious, routine behavior may be counterproductive, because it prevents one from being creative and responsive and taking initiative.

For a student affairs unit to become a learning organization, its practitioners must cultivate five skills, or "disciplines" (Senge, 1990):

1. Systems thinking—the ability to see that individual events and actions are interrelated and are part of a bigger pattern that is often difficult to discern
2. Personal mastery—a commitment to lifelong learning, whereby one continually clarifies and deepens one's personal vision, focuses one's energies, and develops patience

3. Mental models—an ability to discover and modify the assumptions, general-izations, and visual images that shape the way faculty, staff, students, and others perceive the world and affect how they behave

4. Shared vision—an ability to unite people around a common sense of purpose and commitment

5. Team learning—an ability to contribute to collaborative problem solving with coworkers and students, producing accelerated results

Holograms, cybernetics, minimum critical specifications, and double-loop learning may seem irrelevant or nonsensical to student affairs staff expecting (or hoping for) stability, order, and control (see Exhibit 13.3). These ideas are essen-tial, however, for understanding and experimenting with ways to respond to chang-ing circumstances. Indeed, "sensing direction through variety, action, and involvement of many persons throughout the student affairs division is quite com-patible, humane, and even sensible in the ambiguous, loosely coupled context of colleges and universities" (Kuh, Whitt, & Shedd, 1987, p. 67).

Implications of Postconventional Views of Organizations

Postconventional views of organizations share four qualities. First, they assume that colleges and universities are open systems shaped by rapidly changing and unpredictable external forces and internal circumstances. Change occurs mor-phogenetically, via a natural, seemingly spontaneous formation and differentia-tion of structures sparked by interactions between the external environment and intentional (or unintentional) acts by the institution's leadership and management (Schwartz & Ogilvy, 1979). Second, because each institution is unique, policies and practices that work in one setting may not work in another (see Exhibit 13.3). Moreover, there are no single right answers in most situations. Third, people con-struct reality for themselves. This runs counter to conventional views' assumption of a single shared reality. As with a hologram, multiple constructions of reality re-flect the whole of the institution, but from different perspectives. Through mu-tually shaping interactions, faculty, staff, and students develop a "collective unconscious" or culture that bonds people; this culture is continually evolving, but it cannot be directly or intentionally manipulated by any person or group.

Finally, postconventional views suggest that all members of an organization have expertise, power, and responsibility. Contrary to conventional views, in which those near the top of the hierarchy are seen as having more expertise, postcon-ventional views suggest that those persons closest to the effective point of action should be directly involved in resolving issues and developing policy (Kuh, 1985). Many entry-level staff members, for example, are competent—perhaps uniquely qualified—to help students deal with problems and to revise institutional policies. The biggest challenge, then, "is to reach out to all our people and then have them own these changes" (Bostdorff, quoted in Hollyman & Howie, 1994, p. 3). This means that student affairs professionals must exploit their autonomy, share their expertise, and collaborate with students and faculty (Kuh, in press).

To assist their institution in discovering novel and increasingly progressive solutions to complex problems, student affairs staff must practice action learning (Argyris & Schön, 1978), by testing their assumptions; reflect on and question how the division of student affairs is operating; and—if appropriate—work toward changing the institution's norms, policies, and processes (Garvin, 1993). Though institutions have hierarchical structures, the relationships between subsystems, such as the student activities office or a particular student organization, and higher-order systems, such as the division of student affairs or the institution, must be allowed to evolve into new forms through experience (Morgan, 1986; Senge, 1990). Reflection, flexibility, and adaptability are indispensable.

The learning organization view discourages people from concentrating on isolated problems (such as low voter turnout for student government elections or poor class attendance in lower-division courses) and emphasizes understanding big-picture issues (such as inadequate levels of student engagement in the institution's social and academic subsystems) (Garvin, 1993; Senge, 1990). For example, to learn why students cannot make tuition payments requires knowledge about their background and cultural orientation to incurring debt, the local cost of living, the current availability of loans, and so on. Thus student affairs staff need to look beneath the surface and discover the motivations and desires grounded in people's mental models or "tacit assumptions (unquestioned beliefs behind all decisions and actions) and hidden cultures (shared but unwritten rules for each member's behavior)" (Kilmann, 1985, p. 8).

Over time, faculty and student affairs professionals have developed different mental models guiding their interactions with students and one another. Most people are unaware of how their mental models influence their behavior. Therefore, discovering these models and the assumptions and values they represent is necessary if student affairs and faculty are to collaborate successfully to enhance student learning (American College Personnel Association, 1994; Kuh, in press). Through this process, student affairs staff may learn that certain of their assumptions (and thus their actions) are counterproductive. By being "unreasonable" and asking questions like "What are we doing?" and "Why are we doing it this way?" staff can determine whether routine practices are responsive to the changing needs and interests of students and changing institutional conditions. As student affairs staff, faculty, and students learn more about their institution and themselves, knowledge and understanding about the institution as a whole will increase. This is not simply desirable; it is necessary, given the economic realities facing higher education today.

Conclusion

No single view of organizations can account for everything that takes place in an institution of higher education or its division of student affairs. The six organizational windows described in this chapter are grounded in different assumptions about power, control, causality, and change. Although the different views produce conflicting descriptions and interpretations, taken together they can help student affairs staff understand why restructuring is a fait accompli as institutions respond to external conditions and internal pressures (El-Khawas, 1994). For this reason, each window is useful, depending on the events and behaviors one wishes to understand. Conventional views, for example, adequately describe some of the more predictable institutional functions (such as registration, record keeping, and payroll). At the same time, however, they often impose unnecessary and undesirable psychological limits on the actions of leaders and followers alike, obfuscating action learning and evolutionary change processes. Whereas stability, reliability, predictability, and control are valued in conventional views, ambiguity, surprise, and change are featured in postconventional views.

Indeed, working in student affairs today is like going white-water rafting. To negotiate the rapids, one must use a variety of psychological and behavioral skills to change course. One also must take into account as many variables as possible: the current, eddies, rocks, the laws of physics, other rafts and paddlers, and so forth. Moment by moment, student affairs professionals must decide when to let the river have its way and when to use their professional knowledge, judgment, and skill to change its direction. To survive in the white water of the 1990s, student affairs staff must learn to think and behave differently. Relying on authority, control, and predictability are anachronisms; ambiguity and risk taking must be encouraged and embraced, not merely tolerated. Collaboration—with faculty, students, and others—is essential (American College Personnel Association, 1994; Johnstone, 1993; Kuh, in press; National Association of Student Personnel Administrators, 1995). The key challenge is to become masters of change (Kanter, 1983), dedicated to radically redesigning student affairs work and institutions of higher education on a continuing basis. Such masters of change are institutional treasures. Support them. Better yet, become one of them. Your life will be more interesting, and your institution will be more productive!

References

Allaire, Y., & Firsirotu, M. E. (1984). Theories of organizational culture. *Organization Studies, 5,* 193–226.

Allison, G. T. (1971). *Essence of decision: Explaining the Cuban missile crisis.* Boston: Little, Brown.

American College Personnel Association. (1994). *Student learning imperative: Implications for student affairs.* Alexandria, VA: American College Personnel Association.

Argyris, C. (1964). *Integrating the individual and the organization.* New York: Wiley.

Argyris, C., & Schön, D. A. (1978). *Organizational learning: A theory of action perspective.* Reading, MA: Addison-Wesley.

Austin, A. E., & Gamson, Z. F. (1983). *Academic workplace: New demands, heightened tensions* (ASHE-ERIC Higher Education Research Report No. 10). Washington, DC: Association for the Study of Higher Education.

Baldridge, J. V. (1971). *Power and conflict in the university: Research in the sociology of complex organizations.* New York: Wiley.

Baldridge, J. V., Curtis, D. V., Ecker, G. P., & Riley, G. L. (1977). *Alternative models of governance in higher education.* In J. V. Baldridge & T. E. Deal (Eds.), *Governing academic organizations* (pp. 2–25). Berkeley, CA: McCutchan.

Belasco, J. A., & Stayer, R. C. (1993). *The flight of the buffalo.* New York: Warner Books.

Bertalanffy, L. von. (1968). *General system theory* (2nd ed.). New York: Braziller.

Birnbaum, R. (1988). *How colleges work: The cybernetics of academic organization and leadership.* San Francisco: Jossey-Bass.

Bolman, L. G., & Deal, T. E. (1991). *Reframing organizations: Artistry, choice, and leadership.* San Francisco: Jossey-Bass.

Caple, R. B. (1985). Counseling and the self-organization paradigm. *Journal of Counseling and Development, 64,* 173–178.

Capra, F. (1983). *The turning point: Science, society, and the rising culture.* New York: Basic Books.

Chaffee, E. E. (1983). *Rational decision-making in higher education.* Boulder, CO: National Center for Higher Education Management Systems.

Clark, B. R. (1984). The organizational saga in higher education. In R. Birnbaum (Ed.), *ASHE reader in organization and governance in higher education* (pp. 36–41). Washington, DC: Association for the Study of Higher Education. (Reprinted from *Administrative Science Quarterly, 17,* 178–184, 1972.)

Clark, B. R. (1989). The academic life: Small worlds, different worlds. *Educational Researcher, 18*(5), 4–8.

Clark, B. R., & Trow, M. (1966). The organizational context. In T. Newcomb and E. Wilson (Eds.), *College peer groups: Problems and prospects for research* (pp. 17–70). Chicago: Aldine.

Clark, D. L. (1985). Emerging paradigms in organizational theory and research. In Y. S. Lincoln (Ed.), *Organizational theory and inquiry: The paradigm revolution* (pp. 43–78). Newbury Park, CA: Sage.

Clark, D. L., Astuto, T. A., & Kuh, G. D. (1986). Strength of coupling in the organization and operation of colleges and universities. In G. Johnston and C. Yeakey (Eds.), *Research and thought in educational administration* (pp. 69–87). Lanham, MD: University Press of America.

Cohen, M. D., & March, J. G. (1974). *Leadership and ambiguity: The American college president.* New York: McGraw-Hill.

Cohen, M. D., March, J. G., & Olsen, J. P. (1972). A garbage can model of organizational choice. *Administrative Science Quarterly, 17*(1), 1–25.

Di Maggio, P. J., & Powell, W. W. (1983). *Power and the structure of society.* New York: Norton.

El-Khawas, E. (1994). Restructuring initiatives in public higher education: Institutional response to financial constraints. *ACE Research Briefs, 5*(8), 1–7.

Etzioni, A. (1961). *A comparative analysis of complex organizations: On power, involvement, and their correlates* (2nd ed.). New York: Free Press.

Fayol, H. (1949). *General and industrial management.* London: Pitman.

Garvin, D. A. (1993, July-August). Building a learning organization. *Harvard Business Review,* pp. 78–91.

Gleick, J. (1987). *Chaos: Making a new science.* New York: Viking.

Gross, E., & Grambusch, P. (1968). *University goals and academic power.* Washington, DC: American Council on Education.

Gulick, L., & Urwick, L. (1937). *Papers on the science of administration.* New York: Columbia University Institute of Public Administration.

Hage, J. (1980). *Theories of organization: Form, process, and transformation.* New York: Wiley.

Hage, J., & Aiken, M. (1970). *Social change in complex organizations.* New York: Random House.

Hedberg, B., Nystrom, P., & Starbuck, W. (1976). Camping on seesaws: Prescriptions for self-designing organization. *Administrative Science Quarterly, 21,* 41–65.

Heydinger, R. B. (1994). A reinvented model for higher education. *On the Horizon, 3*(1), 1–5.

Higher education must change. (1992). *AGB Reports, 34*(3), 6–9.

Hollyman, B. P., & Howie, R. L., Jr. (1994, December 19). Mastering change: Information technology integration in successful enterprises. *Business Week* (Special Advertising Section), pp. 1–12.

Hull, D. F., Jr., Hunter, D. E., & Kuh, G. D. (1983). Alternative perspectives on student affairs organizations. In G. D. Kuh (Ed.), *Understanding student affairs organizations* (New Directions for Student Services No. 23, pp. 27–38). San Francisco: Jossey-Bass.

Johnstone, D. B. (1993). *Learning productivity: A new imperative for higher education* (Studies in Public Higher Education No. 3). Albany: Office of the Chancellor, State University of New York.

Kanter, R. M. (1983). *The change masters.* New York: Simon & Schuster.

Katz, F. E., & Rosenzweig, J. E. (1974). *Organization and management: A systems approach.* New York: McGraw-Hill.

Katz, J. (1989). The challenge of diversity. In C. Woolbright (Ed.), *Valuing diversity on campus: A multicultural approach* (pp. 1–21). Bloomington, IN: Association of College Unions—International.

Kilmann, R. H. (1985). *Beyond the quick fix: Managing five tracks to organizational success.* San Francisco: Jossey-Bass.

Kuh, G. D. (1983). Guiding assumptions about student affairs organizations. In G. D. Kuh (Ed.), *Understanding student affairs organizations* (New Directions for Student Services No. 23, pp. 15–26). San Francisco: Jossey-Bass.

Kuh, G. D. (1984). A framework for understanding student affairs work. *Journal of College Student Personnel, 25,* 25–31.

Kuh, G. D. (1985). What is extraordinary about ordinary student affairs organizations. *NASPA Journal, 23*(2), 31–43.

Kuh, G. D. (1993). Appraising the character of a college. *Journal of Counseling and Development, 71,* 661–668.

Kuh, G. D. (1994). The influence of college environments on student drinking. In G. Gonzalez and V. Clement (Eds.), *Research and intervention: Preventing substance abuse in higher education* (pp. 45–71). Washington, DC: Office of Educational Research and Improvement, U.S. Department of Education.

Kuh, G. D. (in press). Guiding principles for designing seamless learning environments for undergraduates. *Journal of College Student Development.*

Kuh, G. D., & Arnold, J. A. (1993). Liquid bonding: A cultural analysis of the role of alcohol in fraternity pledgeship. *Journal of College Student Development, 34,* 327–334.

Kuh, G. D., & Hall, J. (1993). Using cultural perspectives in student affairs. In G. D. Kuh (Ed.), *Using cultural perspectives in student affairs work* (pp. 1–20). Alexandria, VA: American College Personnel Association.

Kuh, G. D., & McAleenan, A. C. (Eds.). (1986). *Private dreams, shared visions: Student affairs work in small colleges.* Columbus, OH: National Association of Student Personnel Administrators.

Kuh, G. D., & Whitt, E. J. (1988). *The invisible tapestry: Culture in American colleges and universities* (ASHE-ERIC Higher Education Report No. 1). Washington, DC: Association for the Study of Higher Education.

Kuh, G. D., Whitt, E. J., & Shedd, J. D. (1987). *Student affairs, 2001: A paradigmatic odyssey* (ACPA Media Publication No. 42). Alexandria, VA: American College Personnel Association.

Kuhn, T. S. (1970). *The structure of scientific revolutions* (2nd ed.). Chicago: University of Chicago Press.

Lawrence, P., & Lorsch, J. (1967). *Organization and environment.* Cambridge, MA: Harvard University Press.

Likert, R. (1967). *The human organization.* New York: McGraw-Hill.

Lincoln, Y. S. (1985). [Introduction]. In Y. S. Lincoln (Ed.), *Organizational theory and inquiry: The paradigm revolution* (pp. 29–40). Newbury Park, CA: Sage.

Lipsky, M. (1980). *Street-level bureaucracy: Dilemmas of the individual in public services.* New York: Russell Sage Foundation.

Louis, M. R. (1983). Organizations as culture-bearing milieux. In L. Pondy, P. Frost, G. Morgan, & T. Dandridge (Eds.), *Organizational symbolism* (pp. 39–54). Greenwich, CT: JAI.

Lundberg, C. C. (1990). Surfacing organizational culture. *Journal of Managerial Psychology, 5*(4), 19–26.

McGregor, D. (1960). *The human side of enterprise.* New York: McGraw-Hill.

March, J. G., & Olsen, J. P. (1976). *Ambiguity and choice in organizations.* Bergen, Norway: Universitetsførlaget.

Martin, J. (1992). *Cultures in organizations: Three perspectives.* New York: Oxford University Press.

Mayo, E. (1945). *The social problems of an industrial civilization.* Boston: Harvard University Graduate School of Business.

Mintzberg, H. (1979). *The structuring of organizations.* Englewood Cliffs, NJ: Prentice Hall.

Morgan, G. (1986). *Images of organization.* Newbury Park, CA: Sage.

Morgan, G., & Ramirez, R. (1983). Action learning: A holographic metaphor for guiding social change. *Human Relations, 37,* 1–28.

National Association of Student Personnel Administrators. (1995). *Reasonable expectations.* Washington, DC: Author.

Peters, T. J. (1987). *Thriving on chaos: Handbook for a management revolution.* New York: Harper & Row.

Peters, T. J. (1995). *Pursuit of wow.* New York: Random House.

Peters, T. J., & Waterman, R. H., Jr. (1982). *In search of excellence: Lessons from America's best run companies.* New York: Harper & Row.

Pfeffer, J. (1982). *Organizations and organizational theory.* Boston: Pitman.

Pfeffer, J., & Salancik, G. (1978). *The external control of organizations: A resource dependence perspective.* New York: Harper & Row.

Prigogine, I., & Stengers, I. (1984). *Order out of chaos.* New York: Bantam Books.

Pritchett, P., & Pound, R. (1993). *High-velocity culture change: A handbook for managers.* Dallas, TX: Pritchett.

Schein, E. H. (1985). *Organizational culture and leadership.* San Francisco: Jossey-Bass.

Schein, E. H. (1990). Organizational culture. *American Psychologist, 45*(2), 109–119.

Schön, D. A. (1983). *The reflective practitioner: How professionals think in action.* New York: Basic Books.

Schön, D. A. (1987). *Educating the reflective practitioner: Toward a new design for teaching and learning in the professions.* San Francisco: Jossey-Bass.

Schroeder, C. C., Nicholls, G. E., & Kuh, G. D. (1983). Exploring the rain forest: Testing assumptions and taking risks. In G. D. Kuh (Ed.), *Understanding student affairs organizations* (New Directions for Student Services No. 23, pp. 51–65). San Francisco: Jossey-Bass.

Schwartz, P., & Ogilvy, J. (1979). *The emergent paradigm: Changing patterns of thought and belief* (SRI International Analytical Report No. 7). Menlo Park, CA: Values and Lifestyles Program.

Senge, P. M. (1990). *The fifth discipline: The art and practice of the learning organization.* New York: Doubleday/Currency.

Sergiovanni, T. J. (1984). Cultural and competing perspectives in administrative theory and practice. In T. J. Sergiovanni and J. Corbally (Eds.), *Leadership and organizational culture: New perspectives on administrative theory and practice* (pp. 1–11). Urbana: University of Illinois Press.

Seymour, D. T. (1992). *On Q: Causing quality in higher education.* New York: Macmillan.

Simon, H. A. (1957). *Administrative behavior.* New York: Free Press.

Smircich, L. (1983). Concepts of culture and organizational analysis. *Administrative Science Quarterly, 28,* 339–358.

Strange, C. C. (1983). Traditional perspectives on student affairs organizations. In G. D. Kuh (Ed.), *Understanding student affairs organizations* (New Directions for Student Services No. 23, pp. 5–13). San Francisco: Jossey-Bass.

Taylor, F. W. (1911). *The principles of scientific management.* New York: Harper.

Thompson, J. D. (1967). *Organizations in action.* New York: McGraw-Hill.

Tierney, W. G. (1988). Organizational culture in higher education: Defining the essentials. *Journal of Higher Education, 59,* 2–21.

To dance with change. (1994). *Policy Perspectives, 5*(3), A1–12.

An uncertain terrain. (1993). *Policy Perspectives, 5*(2), A1–11.

Vaill, P. B. (1984). The purposing of high-performing systems. In T. J. Sergiovanni and J. Corbally (Eds.), *Leadership and organizational culture: New perspectives on administrative theory and practice* (pp. 85–104). Urbana: University of Illinois Press.

Van Maanen, J. (1984). Doing old things in new ways: The chains of socialization. In J. Bess (Ed.), *College and university organization: Insights from the behavioral sciences* (pp. 211–247). New York: New York University Press.

Waldrop, M. M. (1992). *Complexity: The emerging science at the edge of order and chaos.* New York: Simon & Schuster.

Weber, M. (1947). *The theory of social and economic organization.* London: Oxford University Press.

Weick, K. E. (1976). Educational organizations as loosely coupled systems. *Administrative Science Quarterly, 21,* 1–19.

Weick, K. E. (1979). *The social psychology of organizing* (2nd ed.). Reading, MA: Addison-Wesley.

Weick, K. E. (1985). Sources of order in underorganized systems: Themes in recent organizational theory. In Y. S. Lincoln (Ed.), *Organizational theory and inquiry: The paradigm revolution* (pp. 106–136). Newbury Park, CA: Sage.

Wheatley, M. J. (1992). *Leadership and the new science: Learning about organization from an orderly universe.* San Francisco: Berrett-Koehler.

Wingspread Group on Higher Education. (1993). *An American imperative: Higher expectations for higher education.* Racine, WI: Johnson Foundation.

Zucker, L. G. (1987). Institutional theories of organization. *Annual Review of Sociology, 13,* 443–464.

PART FOUR

ESSENTIAL COMPETENCIES AND TECHNIQUES

Student affairs professionals need the proper knowledge base, attitudes, and skills to perform their professional roles effectively. Developing professional, competence is a constant, experiential process of knowing, being, and doing. Competence supports effective implementation, grounding each professional action in the appropriate philosophies and values—the research, theory, and good judgment that form the basis of student affairs practice. Staying competent is an ongoing process. The student affairs professional must remain knowledgeable, pursue essential new skills, and link up with other resources to benefit both the institution and its students. Formal graduate preparation in any field is often focused on expanding knowledge, with limited time devoted to how to apply that knowledge. Thus new pro-

fessionals must seek mentors and practical learning experiences, and they must solicit feedback from trusted colleagues as they add to their competencies.

Competencies are an embedded component of professional roles. The first two editions of *Student Services* included a section on the primary roles and models of practice of student affairs professionals. That section connected the theoretical bases of the field to the roles student affairs staff play on campus: administrators, counselors, student development educators, and ecology managers. In this edition we decided to expand other sections; therefore, we had to make the difficult decision to remove the former, very valuable section on roles and models for practice. We encourage the reader to read that section in the second edition. It would be unfortunate for

generations of new student affairs professionals to miss the frame provided by
these models to link the historical, philosophical, and theoretical context of the
profession to their daily practice.

An overview of these key roles provides the context for practice. As Delworth and Hanson note in the second
edition, student affairs professionals were
in the past regarded as surrogate parents
and disciplinarians, administrators, and
counselors. Legal and societal changes
have diminished the surrogate parent
role. Professional developments outlined
in the previous chapters have signaled
the emergence of the student development educator and ecology manager
roles. As student development educators,
student affairs staff apply theoretical
frames to help students achieve a positive educational experience and to learn
about themselves and others. As ecology
managers, student affairs staff seek to
shape the educational environment to
enhance student experiences and build
and nurture the educational community.
Each student affairs professional's role
likely includes some combination of
these four roles and models. Practitioners
need to assess their personal and professional interests to determine which combination of roles matches their interests,
personal philosophy, skills, career goals,
and convictions concerning how they
can best impact the student experience.

Each student affairs role requires a
specialized set of competencies, and
many competencies are shared among
several roles. While there are dozens of
specialized competencies that could be

addressed for each role, the seven chapters in Part Four identify and describe a
dozen key competencies used by many
student affairs professionals for all roles.

The part begins with Judy Rogers's
exploration in Chapter Fourteen of why
leadership is so essential for administrative roles, particularly in effecting campus change. In Chapter Fifteen, Larry
Roper presents teaching and training,
the key competencies required for student development educators. In Chapter
Sixteen, Roger Winston presents an
overview of counseling, with an emphasis on career counseling and academic
advising. In Chapter Seventeen, Clyde
Crego presents the basics of consultation and mediation, important competencies for the counselor, administrator,
and ecology manager roles. In Chapter
Eighteen, Donna Talbot explores multiculturalism and diversity, important
competencies in all roles. In Chapter
Nineteen, Michael Cuyjet presents program development and group advising
competencies, crucial for the student development educator and administrator
roles. In Chapter Twenty, Dary Erwin addresses the competencies of assessment,
evaluation, and research, which utilize
different but related knowledge bases
and are essential for all four primary student affairs roles.

Many of these competency domains
have become very specialized areas requiring extensive education and experience. Each chapter might be explored to
determine if advanced education in that
area would benefit your individual practice. For example, no professional should

claim to be a counselor without proper preparation. Those interested in counseling might study Chapter Sixteen to determine its place in student affairs practice and to make decisions concerning their need for further training in order to help students in a caring, responsive manner.

The competencies presented in this part are applicable to many functional areas beyond student affairs as well. Staff in such areas as commuter affairs, residence life, or student activities will see direct applications of the information presented in these chapters to their work. Also, other competencies could have been addressed, and we encourage readers to explore such needed competencies as community building, technological applications, futures forecasting, facilities management, and developmental supervision. Student affairs professionals must continually scan the developing needs of the profession and the changing needs of students and institutions to stay helpful and timely.

We encourage each student affairs professional to approach his or her professional development as if recertification were required on a regular basis. If that were the case, what new competencies, skills, awareness, and knowledge bases would you need to develop? This part provides basic information and referrals for additional information on many important competencies.

CHAPTER FOURTEEN

LEADERSHIP

Judy Lawrence Rogers

In the twenty-first century, change will be constant and rapid, and coping with ambiguity will be a fact of life (Kennedy, 1993; Mossberg, 1994). Already, profound transformations are occurring in every sector of U.S. society, as we reengineer the corporation (Hammer & Champy, 1993), reinvent government (Osborne & Gaebler, 1992), and reform our educational system (Schlechty, 1990) to respond to the turbulent environment in which we find ourselves. During this time of transformation and upheaval, the call for leadership, especially "visionary" leadership, has grown loud and persistent (Bennis & Nanus, 1985). We seek individuals to lead us through the chaos, to help us make meaning of the ambiguity we face. In the new millennium, student affairs professionals will be expected to exercise leadership to successfully initiate and implement change processes in institutions of higher education, and they will be expected to create and implement campus programs to empower students to develop such leadership as well.

A discussion of the competencies needed for twenty-first-century leadership might best begin with a definition of the term. Defining leadership has proved to be a difficult task, however. As Warren Bennis (1959) observed, "Always, it seems, the concept of leadership eludes us or turns up in another form to taunt us again with its slipperiness and complexity. So we have invented an endless proliferation of terms to deal with it . . . and still the concept is not sufficiently defined" (p. 259). James MacGregor Burns (1978) agreed: "Leadership is one of the most observed and least understood phenomena on earth" (p. 2). Without a commonly accepted definition of leadership, it is even more difficult to discuss the competencies, behaviors, and beliefs needed to develop it. Different perspectives of leadership call for a different set of skills and attitudes. This chapter presents an overview of the dominant theories of leadership that have shaped our understanding of the concept in the twentieth century. Then, given this theoretical foundation, it explores the competencies, behaviors, and beliefs that these theories suggest one needs in order to successfully practice leadership. In order to put the "messiness" of the leadership literature in perspective, the chapter begins with a brief discussion of how theories are created and how they gain credibility.

In his celebrated study entitled *The Structure of Scientific Revolutions,* Thomas Kuhn (1970) describes the rise and fall of dominant paradigms in scientific thought. He defines a paradigm as a set of assumptions that guides our thinking and behavior, shaping our view of the world and how it operates. "To be accepted as a paradigm, a theory must seem better than its competitors [at describing reality], but it need not, and in fact never does, explain all the facts with which it can be confronted" (pp. 17–18). A widely accepted paradigm becomes a foundation for research and practice. For example, in student affairs we believe we can intentionally prompt students' psychosocial and cognitive development. A perusal of college student affairs journals demonstrates how the research assumes that students' development can be intentionally influenced; numerous articles describe various ways to promote such development. The value of a paradigm is that it allows researchers to operate from an accepted conceptual foundation, a common baseline, rather than having to continually explain and argue for the assumptions that guide their research. Thus a paradigm shapes what we "see," and consequently it shapes what we study and how we study it.

But as Kuhn explains, no paradigm can explain all the facts that confront it. While a paradigmatic lens allows us to see certain things about the world, it can blind us to other aspects. Anomalies arise in the research which cannot be explained by the prevailing paradigm, prompting us to question the paradigm's basic assumptions. Research begins to either address the anomalies within the parameters of the existing paradigm (if it can) or to present a new paradigm altogether, one that can better explain and respond to the anomalies. Thus a new paradigm is born, which after a period of debate and validation becomes a new set of common assumptions that guides our thinking and behavior. It is by this process of establishing new paradigms, researching their parameters, applying them to practice, dealing with their anomalies, and debating their value for explaining reality that we create new knowledge. Kuhn says this process forms the structure of scientific revolutions.

The idea that paradigms come and go attests to the fact that our understanding of nature is only partial at best; at any given time, depending on the lens we use, there are aspects of the world that we see and aspects we do not see. In order for us to compensate for the blind spots inherent in our strongly held assumptions and paradigms, it has been suggested that we use multiple perspectives to more fully understand the world around us and to better guide our practice as professionals (Morgan, 1986). In Chapter Thirteen, George Kuh takes a multiperspective approach to organizational theory, presenting both conventional and emergent views. Each theory explains some aspects of organizational functioning, but we must view organizations through all of these lenses together in order to come closer to understanding the realities of organizational life. This chapter takes the same approach. Since the industrial revolution, when it first became a popular subject of study, there have been several prevailing paradigms about the nature of leadership. Each has contributed to our understanding of the concept, but none can stand alone as a definitive set of assumptions about what leadership is. Therefore this chapter provides several lenses for examining the concept of leadership; you can then draw conclusions about the behavior of both leaders and followers based on the assumptions you choose to operate from. It is hoped that the ideas in this chapter will prompt you to examine your own "theories in use" about leadership. The perspectives offered here, based on emerging conceptions of leadership for the twenty-first century, can help you uncover your assumptions about leadership, examine them, and decide which to keep or modify and which to discard. Let us begin the journey by examining conventional definitions of leadership.

Conventional Views of Leadership

One of the most comprehensive reviews of the literature on leadership was conducted by Stogdill (1974), who found that "there are almost as many definitions of leadership as there are persons who have attempted to define the concept" (p. 259). A few representative definitions illustrate how leadership has been conceptualized in the twentieth century:

> Leadership is "the ability to impress the will of the leader on those led and induce obedience, respect, loyalty, and cooperation" (Moore, 1927, p. 124).

> "Leadership can be conceptualized as an interaction between a person and the members of a group. . . . One person, the leader, influences, while the other person responds" (Gordon, 1955, p. 10).

> Leadership is "the process of influencing human behavior so as to accomplish the goals prescribed by the organizationally appointed leader" (Prince & Associates, 1985, p. 7).

> "Managers do things right. Leaders do the right thing" (Bennis & Nanus, 1985, p. 21).

If we examine these definitions for their underlying assumptions, we can identify several themes that have characterized conventional notions of leadership
throughout most of the twentieth century. The first theme is that leadership is the
property of an individual. One person—a leader—provides leadership. A leader
interacts with followers primarily to get them to do what he or she wants them
to do. A leader may influence either through persuasion or power, but the point
is to get the followers to accomplish the goals the leader sets (Rost, 1991).

The second theme is that leadership pertains primarily to formal groups or
organizations. Leaders are those who hold authority within organizations and have
a complement of subordinates reporting to them. The role of the leader is to monitor, control, and direct subordinates to ensure maximum effectiveness in completing organizational tasks. Subordinates—persons who hold positions lower in
the organizational hierarchy—are not usually considered leaders. Leadership is
reserved for those who have been given a certain rank within the organization.

A third theme or assumption about leadership stems directly from the previous one; throughout the twentieth century, the concepts of leadership and management have been integrally intertwined. The words *leadership* and *management* are
often used interchangeably (Rost, 1991; Yukl, 1994). When a distinction *is* drawn,
as in the above quote from Bennis and Nanus, leadership is simply considered to
be *good* management: "Hence there is no such thing as bad leadership because
when leadership is bad, it is characterized as management" (Rost, 1994, p. 3). The
confusion of leadership with management points to a deeply embedded assumption in the conventional perspective on leadership, an assumption that has shaped
studies of what constitutes a good leader.

These assumptions about leadership have shaped the dominant image of
effective leadership in U.S. society. An effective leader is a hero, a masterful planner who sits atop a pyramid of power, controlling the people and processes of
an organization. A leader is decisive, tough-minded, unemotional, analytical, and
skilled at wielding power. A leader is an expert who creates a vision for his or her
organization and through a process of exchange with followers motivates them to
buy into it. Leadership is the domain of individuals—powerful, all-knowing individuals. This view of leadership, which resonates with the values of the rational-
bureaucratic model of organizations (see Chapter Thirteen), has been labeled the
industrial paradigm of leadership (Rost, 1991).

Think for a moment about your own perspective on leadership. How many
of the concepts embodied in the industrial paradigm of leadership are embraced
by your image of a leader? How do those concepts influence your ideas about who
can play a leadership role in the groups or organizations you participate in? How
do they shape your assessment of your own ability to be a leader? How do they
shape your behavior when you are placed into a position of leadership? How do

they shape the way you design leadership development programs for the students you work with? It is important that you recognize the assumptions that guide your thinking and behavior related to leadership. The industrial paradigm of leadership presents *one* way to conceptualize leadership; although it has been the dominant perspective for most of the twentieth century in the United States, it is not the only perspective. Let us now examine some other perspectives.

Alternative Views of Leadership

A number of scholars broke with mainstream thinking about leadership in the latter part of the twentieth century. The work of three of these authors—Robert Greenleaf (1970), James MacGregor Burns (1978) and William Foster (1986)—is highlighted here. Each represents a shift away from the assumptions of the industrial paradigm of leadership and provides us with additional insights about the nature and definition of leadership.

Servant Leadership

In his 1970 book *The Servant as Leader,* Robert Greenleaf made a radical departure from the industrial paradigm's conception of leaders as all-knowing, all-powerful heroes. He proposed instead that "the great leader is seen as servant first" (p. 2). Greenleaf based this conclusion on changes he saw emerging in U.S. society. The concepts of power and authority were being critically examined, and cooperation and support were emerging as more productive ways for people to relate to one another.

Greenleaf stressed that a servant leader is not only *seen* as a servant, he or she *is* first and foremost a servant. The servant leader takes care to ensure that other people's greatest needs are met and that they therefore "become healthier, wiser, freer, more autonomous, more likely themselves to become servants" (p. 7). The qualities, abilities, and beliefs of servant leaders include listening before acting (in order to better understand a situation), exhibiting empathy for and acceptance of those who follow their lead, developing their intuition and an ability to "foresee the unforeseeable" (p. 14), leading by persuasion, forging change by "convincement rather than coercion" (p. 21), being able to conceptualize reforms and make others see the same possibilities, and empowering those they serve by creating opportunities and alternatives for them. The servant leader recognizes that the first step to changing the world is to change oneself. A well-known example of servant leadership is Mother Theresa. Through her work serving and advocating for the poor, leadership has accrued to her.

Transformational Leadership

In 1978, James MacGregor Burns further extended the debate about what leadership comprises by describing two forms of leadership, transactional and transformational. According to Burns, transactional leadership results in organizational bartering, exchanging wants and needs between leaders and followers. People follow a transactional leader because he or she will help them achieve their goals; it is obvious to followers that it is in their own best interest to do so (Kellerman, 1984). The transactional image of leadership closely parallels the industrial paradigm.

Transformational leadership, on the other hand, goes beyond the notion of exchange. Burns asserted that transformational leadership demonstrates two essential qualities—it is relational, and it is about producing real change. Burns explains that "transformational leadership occurs when one or more persons engage with others in such a way that leaders and followers raise one another to higher levels of motivation and morality" (p. 20). Thus transformational leadership inspires a commingling of needs, aspirations, and goals in a common enterprise. The purpose of this engagement between leaders and followers is to bring about change. In fact, in Burns's view, the ultimate test of practical leadership is the realization of intended, necessary change. Transformational leadership has a moral dimension as well, because those engaged in it "can be lifted *into* their better selves" (p. 462). Burns cites Gandhi as an example of a transformational leader.

Burns's seminal work enlightened us to the fact that leadership is really about transformation. Transforming leadership forges a relationship between leaders and followers in which both are elevated to more principled levels of judgment. It is about leaders and followers engaging one another in a change process. It is about power "to" rather than power "over." And, in the manner described by Kuhn (1970), Burns's and Greenleaf's ideas began to transform our notions of leadership over the past two decades.

Critical Leadership

William Foster (1986) and other critical theorists (such as Smyth, 1989) homed in on the idea of transformational leadership by examining the content of the change leadership can bring about. They believed leadership should focus on restructuring society: "Leadership is and must be socially critical, it does not reside in an individual but in the relationship between individuals, and it is oriented towards social vision and change, not simply, or only, organizational goals" (Foster, 1986, p. 46). Transformational leaders and their followers can pursue a vision of greatness together, but the critical question is, "Whose vision is it?" According to the critical perspective, for transformational leadership to actually transform, it must prompt those engaged in the process to question the assumptions their vision is based upon. Thus, critical transformational leadership requires reflection and analysis. It causes us to ask on whose behalf we use our power. It makes a place for all voices and arguments, regardless of race, class, or gender (Quantz, Rogers, & Dantley, 1991). Since the critical model of leadership is about changing the human condition, leadership can spring from anywhere; it is not confined to an organizational hierarchy. In this view, leadership is a courageous political act aimed at empowering followers to become leaders themselves. And, finally, Foster (1989) offers that critical transformational leadership is not "a special or unique occurrence, one that is found only in certain grand moments of human history. Rather, it happens in everyday events, when commonplace leaders exert some effect on their situations" (p. 52). A good example of critical transformational leadership is the work of the Brazilian educator Paulo Freire, who through his teaching methods empowered the peasants in his country (Freire, 1970).

Implications of Alternative Views of Leadership

There are several common themes that emerge in analyzing these three alternative perspectives on leadership. First, leadership is a relationship; it is not the "property" of any individual. Leadership tasks are accomplished with both leaders and followers—followers are an essential part of the equation. The role of the leader is to serve followers and empower them to become leaders themselves. Second, leadership is about change. For both leaders and followers, change begins within and then emanates outward into the community. Leadership requires critical reflection and analysis in order to determine if the vision of change being pursued is inclusive or if it excludes or diminishes some members of the community. Third, leadership can be done by anyone, not just by people who are designated leaders.

Again, reflect on your current image of leaders and leadership. Do you see leaders as servants, change agents, and people who facilitate others' empowerment? Have you considered that leadership can come from anyone, whether or not they are a designated leader? Have you considered leadership as a relationship between leaders and followers rather than as something a leader practices independently? Have these perspectives shaped the way you practice leadership with colleagues and students? These alternative perspectives on leadership have gained credence because they capture some aspects of our experience with leadership better than the conventional view. These perspectives involve aspects of leadership that are not addressed by the industrial paradigm, and thus they have prompted a search for a new paradigm of leadership for the twenty-first century.

The Postindustrial Paradigm of Leadership

In his book *Leadership for the Twenty-First Century,* Joseph Rost (1991) offered a new definition of leadership for the next millennium. He boldly proclaimed it to be the postindustrial paradigm of leadership. But as Kuhn (1970) has made clear, one does not pronounce a new paradigm without substantial evidence of its need. And so it is with Rost. He argued convincingly that the industrial paradigm is not adequate to explain the realities of leadership in the 1990s or to define the type of leadership we need in the twenty-first century. What are the realities that have prompted us to establish a new leadership paradigm?

U.S. culture is in the midst of a major shift in the way we make sense of our world. The globalization of the economy, rapid and continual change resulting from new technologies, the information explosion, and the increasing diversity of our population have created a reality that is messy and ambiguous rather than orderly and predictable (Rogers & Ballard, 1995). As a result we are moving away from a mechanistic worldview, in which objectivity, control, and linear causality reign supreme, to a worldview marked by a more contextual, complex, and relational paradigm (Kuh, Whitt, & Shedd, 1987). In Chapter Thirteen, George Kuh concludes that conventional organizational models are not useful for understanding events and actions in uncertain, turbulent times. In a similar vein, Rost (1994) debunks the industrial paradigm of leadership because of its grounding in a mechanistic worldview. He says that "the industrial paradigm of leadership is industrial because . . . it has a structural-functionalist [that is, bureaucratic] view of organizations; it has a personalistic focus since only great leaders do leadership; it is dominated by a goal achievement sense of purpose; it promotes an individualistic and even a self-interested outlook on life; it accepts a male model of behavior and power (which has been labeled leadership style); it articulates utilitarian and materialistic ethical perspectives; it has been enveloped in a rational, technocratic, linear, quantitative and positivistic epistemology; and it asserts a managerial perspective as to what makes organizations tick" (p. 4). It is in the context of our increasingly complex and ambiguous world that Rost, expanding on the work of Burns, Greenleaf, and Foster, offers a postindustrial paradigm of leadership for our consideration.

Rost's definition of leadership is this: "Leadership is an influence relationship among leaders and their collaborators who intend real changes that reflect their mutual purposes" (1994, p. 7). There are four essential elements in this definition of leadership, and Rost states that each of these elements must be present in order to call a relationship leadership.

First, the relationship must be based on influence rather than positional authority. Noncoercive persuasion is used to influence people in Rost's leadership relationship; the influence is multidirectional, coming from all members rather than only from the top down. People are free to agree or disagree and to stay in or leave the relationship. Second, it is leaders and collaborators who do leadership. Collaborators are active, not passive. Leaders are simply those who at particular moments commit more of their resources (such as expertise, passion, and political savvy) to influence the process. Third, collaborators and their leaders must intend real change. Rost explains, "*Intend* means that the leaders and their collaborators do not have to produce changes to do leadership, only intend them and then act on that intention. Real means that the changes are substantive or transforming" (p. 7). Fourth, the changes leaders and collaborators pursue together must reflect a mutual purpose. The changes must comprise what both leaders and collaborators want; leadership is a shared enterprise.

There are several important implications embedded in this definition of leadership. Collaborators choose the leaders they want to affiliate themselves with, and they may or may not be people who hold authority over them. Leaders and collaborators often change places in the ebb and flow of the leadership process. In any organization there may be a number of leadership relationships, and the leaders in one relationship may be collaborators in another. Leadership is "episodic." One is not a leader all of the time; rather, one is a leader when one chooses to exert the greatest influence on the change process. Rost (1994) concludes that "leadership is people bonding together to institute a change in a group, organization or society. Leadership is a group of activists who want to implement a reformist agenda. Leadership is a band of leaders and collaborators who envision a better future and go after it" (p. 6).

One other major purpose of Rost's work is to clearly distinguish leadership from management. In the industrial paradigm, leadership is defined as good management. In the postindustrial paradigm, the two are defined as distinct activities. One is not better than another; they are simply different processes. A key element separating the two in Rost's view is that management is based on positional authority, while leadership is based on noncoercive influence or persuasion.

Numerous other scholars have contributed to the understanding of postindustrial leadership. For example, Bensimon and Neumann (1993) discuss leadership in its collective form as "occurring among and through a group of people who think and act together" (p. 2). Drath and Palus (1994) describe leadership as meaning making in a community of practice—a process in which everyone in the group is engaged. Wheatley (1993) reinforces the relational nature of postindustrial leadership in her intriguing comparison of leadership and the principles of chaos theory and quantum mechanics. The postindustrial view of leadership is gaining credence as the paradigm that will better assist us in maneuvering through the white water of the twenty-first century.

Implications and Application of the Postindustrial Paradigm

The fact that we have only recently recognized a postindustrial paradigm of leadership does not mean that this kind of leadership has never existed before. In fact it has been all around us. But because of our industrial paradigm lens, we didn't see these actions and behaviors as leadership. For example, some student groups likely demonstrate postindustrial leadership. Consider the example of the peer education drama troupes that are becoming prevalent on many college campuses across the country. The students in these troupes come together because of their mutual dedication to educating their peers about important social issues. Their goal is to change society, to free it from drug abuse, sexual assault, racism, homophobia, sexual harassment, and so on through education in the form of skits and role plays. While these groups typically have a designated leader (sometimes a student affairs professional who serves as coordinator), leadership does not rest solely with this person. Leadership roves among the members of the troupe, depending on the task to be performed, the issue to be addressed, and the expertise of the members. For example, the most skilled writer in the troupe takes a leadership role when new scripts must be conceptualized and written. The most experienced actors or actresses take the leadership position when skits are rehearsed and new members trained. The most visionary or articulate member of the group may have the most influence on defining the troupe's values, setting its policies, and deciding on new projects. Members who can engender the greatest enthusiasm for the troupe's work and explain its impact on student development to external constituents may become leaders in obtaining funds. What is important to understand is that while the designated "leader"—the coordinator—may take a leadership role at times, he or she is not the real leader all the time. In fact, in an empowered group the coordinator may play a primarily collaborative role, with short periods of being a leader. The student members are also collaborators as well as leaders, depending on the context and the task. The influence such leaders and collaborators exert is in the form of noncoercive persuasion; it comes from all directions, not just from the coordinator (from the top down). The leaders and collaborators are engaged in a give-and-take relationship because they desire to bring about real change. The changes they intend reflect their mutual purposes.

Examples of postindustrial leadership can also be found among other constituents of a university community, including student affairs staff, academic administrators, support staff, and faculty. For instance, Total Quality Management is being implemented on many campuses today (Marchese, 1993). In order to understand and implement this new management philosophy, cross-functional task forces and committees are created. When these committees are truly empowered to make decisions, establish new policy, and transform the institution, postindustrial leadership is likely taking place. If so, then the support-staff members of these task forces will at times be leaders, as might be faculty, student affairs staff, and students. When conditions are created that allow organization members to break free of the roles and rules of the rational-bureaucratic model, then leadership comes from anywhere and everywhere. A staff group in student affairs (such as residence life, student activities, or admissions) might just also adopt principles of postindustrial leadership and operate primarily in this way. It simply requires individuals who have the commitment and the competencies necessary to create the conditions in which postindustrial leadership relationships can form; together, such a community of believers can pursue a transformational cause.

The Central Role of Ethics in Postindustrial Leadership

James MacGregor Burns (1978) and the critical theorists challenged us to consider the content of the change transformational leaders seek to make. In their eyes, change should have a moral purpose. Rost (1993a) continued this emphasis on the moral dimension of leadership in his exposition of postindustrial leadership. He argued that there are two general ethical issues to be considered if we operate from the premise that leadership is a relationship. The first is about the *process* of the leadership relationship. The question to ask about process, Rost asserts, is this: "Is the way that leadership is being done in the organization at this moment in time ethical?" (p. 7). For Rost, ethical leadership revolves around whether the influence processes used are noncoercive and whether the group is pursuing mutual goals. Are the participants in the relationship free to disagree and to leave the relationship if they do not like the direction it is taking?

The second issue has to do with the *content* of leadership, the actual changes that leaders and collaborators wish to accomplish. The question to ask about content, Rost says, is this: "Are the proposed changes (decisions, policies, positions) that the leaders and collaborators intend for the organization morally acceptable or, in a word, ethical?" (p. 7). It is this issue—whether the proposed changes are ethical—that receives the most attention from scholars as well as from people involved in a leadership relationship.

How are we to evaluate whether the process of change and the change itself are ethical? First, it seems important that the ongoing reflection and process evaluation advocated by the postindustrial paradigm always include a consideration of ethics. Continually assessing whether noncoercive influence is being used to forge mutual purposes and ascertaining if all voices have been included in deciding which purposes to pursue promotes the integrity of the process. These ethical discussions are an integral part of postindustrial leadership, and they can be raised by both leaders and collaborators.

Evaluating whether the change itself is ethical presents more of a dilemma. In fact, Rost (1993a) seems rather pessimistic about whether we can do this with any consistency: "In the end, it is virtually impossible to determine what the moral high ground is regarding many complex, controversial, and difficult ethical dilemmas with which the leadership dynamic in many organizations can often present us " (p. 9). Nevertheless, it is imperative for us as student affairs professionals to consider the ethical dimensions of the decisions we make. The ethical codes developed by our professional associations and the ethical principles outlined by Harry Canon in Chapter Six can serve to inform and guide us. However difficult it may be to sort out the complexities of the choices we make as members of leadership relationships, it is our obligation as professionals to use appropriate ethical frameworks to analyze the process and content of the changes we advocate.

Competencies, Behaviors, and Beliefs

The next question for consideration is this: what are the competencies, behaviors, and beliefs that will enhance one's ability to successfully participate in leadership relationships in the twenty-first century? In the twentieth century's "Lone Ranger" approach to leadership, training emphasized skills, personality characteristics, and behaviors necessary to be a good leader (Rost, 1993b). The industrial view of leadership led us to focus our leadership development efforts almost exclusively on teaching *individuals* to be leaders (Drath & Palus, 1994). The "one best way" mentality of the industrial paradigm prompted us to search for the right formula for making an effective leader. A quick review of the literature, including student affairs publications, demonstrates how deeply our leadership development programs are invested in the belief that developing individuals is the primary objective of leadership training.

In the postindustrial view of leadership, the focus of training shifts from developing a leader to enhancing everyone's ability to participate in the process of leadership (Drath & Palus, 1994; Rost, 1993b). Since both leaders and collaborators do leadership, the emphasis is on training all persons who take part in the relationship.

The following list of competencies is suggested as a foundation for student affairs professionals seeking to successfully engage in postindustrial leadership. This is not meant to be a recipe for how to engage in leadership, since it is clear that each leadership relationship is unique and takes on the characteristics of those leaders and collaborators who have chosen to participate in a particular change effort. But the following competencies will surely enhance the effectiveness of any leadership relationship.

Understanding, Valuing, and Nurturing the Group Process

Postindustrial leadership is a process by which leaders and collaborators come together around mutual purposes and influence each other in their intention to bring about real change. In the postindustrial paradigm the focus is on the process as well as on the task. How do leaders and collaborators come together and forge mutual purposes? What are the modes of influence they can use to bring about change? How can leaders and collaborators bring more people into the process so that their mutual purposes can be advanced? Clearly, one must develop group process skills to engage in postindustrial leadership. These skills include understanding groups and how they develop; reading the group, analyzing and interpreting its actions; understanding the roles group members play; knowing how to influence the group's process; and providing feedback to group members.

Bensimon and Neumann (1993) published an intriguing study examining the processes used by successful leadership teams in colleges and universities. Rather than serving as a rubber stamp for the president and his or her ideas, the successful leadership groups were "thinking" teams. They engaged and fully included the multiple perspectives each team member brought to the process. They examined issues from many angles, valuing criticism as well as support of suggested courses of action. Bensimon and Neumann identified eight specific roles group members played in the successful teams they studied: definer, analyst, interpreter, critic, synthesizer, disparity monitor ("How will our decisions sit with our constituents?"), task monitor, and emotional monitor (p. 59). In real or functional teams (as opposed to "illusory" teams, teams in name only), all of these roles were evident. The team builder recognized the value of each role and worked to ensure that every perspective was included in the decision-making work of the team. Bensimon and Neumann's study provides one frame for making sense of the process by which leaders and collaborators bring about real change. As we move into the twenty-first century, with its emphasis on teams and teamwork, there will undoubtedly be others. Postindustrial leaders and collaborators recognize the value of process and make time for group members to reflect on and make sense of it.

Collaborating and Engaging in Creative Conflict

In the postindustrial view, members of a leadership relationship collaborate rather than compete with one another. Competitive individualism is a dominant value of U.S. culture (Bellah, Madsen, Sullivan, Swidler, & Tipton, 1985; Kohn, 1986). We focus much attention in our educational system on how to compete and not nearly as much on how to collaborate. But in the face of increasing diversity we must learn to collaborate and to find common ground in order to advance as a society (Lappé & Du Bois, 1994). We must also work through and learn from the inevitable conflict that will result from engaging so many diverse perspectives as we forge mutual purposes.

Lappé and Du Bois (1994) have identified ten essential skills for successful community collaboration. Labeled the "democratic arts," they include active listening, creative conflict, mediation, negotiation, political imagination (visioning the future according to one's values), public dialogue (public talk about community issues), public judgment (public decision making that allows community members to make choices they are willing to implement), celebration and appreciation, evaluation and reflection, and mentoring. Lappé and Du Bois present inspirational stories of communities from all over the United States that have been successful in using these arts to find common ground and achieve shared goals. These arts are clearly wonderful tools for residence halls choosing their community standards and for any student group or university committee that desires to engage in collaborative decision making. They are important competencies for student affairs leaders and collaborators to acquire, practice, and teach.

Creating Environments Based on Trust and Empowerment

Trust is essential if all members of a leadership relationship are to participate in the process. Trust is necessary to encourage members to take the risks necessary to bring about real change. Trust develops when leaders model and encourage openness, vulnerability, and self-disclosure (Bensimon & Neumann, 1993). Empowerment means that collaborators, not just leaders, have a voice in decision making, in influencing the agenda of the group, and in building mutual purposes. Thus postindustrial leaders must let go of control and instead create opportunities and alternatives so that collaborators can choose autonomy (Greenleaf, 1970). Bensimon and Neumann (1993) refer to these skills as the relational work of the team builder. The team builder is committed to including others in the process and to sharing power in ways that generate more power for all.

Encouraging Diverse Voices

Postindustrial leaders and collaborators recognize that all concerned voices must be heard for the leadership process to have integrity and for the intended change to be reflective of the relevant larger context. In Bensimon and Neumann's study

(1993), successful team builders brought the voices of those on the margin (often women and people of color) to the center so that their perspective would be considered. Lappé and Du Bois (1994) found that in successful communities, members were able to take the role of the "other": "putting oneself in another's shoes, seeing the world—even if for just a fleeting moment—from their vantage point" (p. 240). The service learning movement on college campuses would seem to provide just such an opportunity to stand in the other's shoes. For example, the experience of entering others' neighborhoods, of engaging with them in some community project, pushes student and staff participants to consider an action, situation, or assumption from their perspective. This is just one example of how student affairs practitioners and students can engage in activities that teach taking the role of the other.

Knowing Yourself and Changing Yourself First

Robert Greenleaf (1970) eloquently taught that change begins with us: "If a flaw in the world is to be remedied, to the servant, the process of change starts in here, in the servant, not out there" (p. 33). Gandhi helped free his country from the British by spinning his own cloth and collecting his own salt from the sea rather than continuing to support British monopolies that kept his country in servitude. His example prompted a revolution. Rosa Parks decided she would no longer be discriminated against and humiliated by segregation and so refused to move to the back of a bus. Her act of individual courage set an example that mobilized the civil rights movement. Candy Lightner, out of her grief and a fierce determination that the death of her child would have a greater purpose, founded Mothers Against Drunk Driving, the grassroots movement that changed U.S. social consciousness about drinking and driving. Her commitment to this cause has saved innumerable lives. The point here is that postindustrial leaders and collaborators must identify what they believe in deeply and demonstrate by example and personal courage their commitment to change. Their example will influence others and initiate the process of building a community of believers.

Knowing oneself is enhanced through continual critical reflection and evaluation. Reflection consists of deep thought about the meaning of one's actions and experiences. What did I just do? Why did I do it? What did I learn from this? What would I do differently to become more effective in the future (Lappé & Du Bois, 1994)? Parker Palmer (1990) feels that this kind of deep reflection is the foundation of exceptional leadership: "Great leadership comes from people who have made that downward journey, . . . who have touched the deep place where we are in community with each other and who can help take other people to that place" (p. 7). This kind of critical evaluation also pushes us to be consistent, to behave in a manner in line with the values and beliefs we espouse. Service learning programs that make reflection and evaluation an integral part of the volunteers' experiences teach participants these crucial skills for postindustrial leadership.

Creating and Articulating a Shared Vision

Much has been written in the last decade about creating shared visions (for example, see Block, 1987). If the process of creating a shared vision (or, in Rost's terms, forging mutual purposes) is an inclusive one, then members of the leadership relationship come to share congruent images of what the group is trying to accomplish. The vision becomes an internal control for members' behavior and guides their decision making. The vision is invoked continually as the process of change unfolds, fueling the members' commitment to change. Drath and Palus (1994) refer to this aspect of leadership as "meaning making in a community of practice" (p. 4). Bensimon and Neumann (1993) similarly describe it as the shared construction of meaning. They eloquently elaborate: "Leadership requires skill in the creation of meaning that is authentic to oneself and to one's community. It also requires the uncovering of meaning that is already embedded in others' minds, helping them to see what they already know, believe, and value, and encouraging them to make new meaning. In this way, leadership generates leadership" (p. xv). The ability to engage persons in creating a shared vision, to help them make meaning of their involvement in the community and its purposes, and to articulate those purposes as a means to prompt change is at the heart of postindustrial leadership.

Understanding and Using Political Processes

Politics is often a dirty word, especially among those in the helping professions. Yet humans are political animals, and an understanding of the political process is essential in order to enact change. Morgan (1986) describes politics as comprising three elements: interests, conflict, and power. All individuals have interests they seek to fulfill. When these interests collide with the interests of others, conflict often results. Power is used to resolve the conflict. There are many sources of power one can use to resolve a conflict—for example, knowledge, authority, persuasion, or force (Morgan, 1986). In postindustrial leadership, noncoercive persuasion is used to build support for the change that members intend and to create coalitions with outside groups who also believe in the proposed change. Understanding the political process and becoming skilled at identifying the interests of others, forming coalitions, and using noncoercive means of persuasion are key if leaders and collaborators in student affairs organizations are to achieve the real changes they intend. Student government, residence hall governments, and university senates are obvious places where students and student affairs staff engage these political skills, but they can also be experienced in every group that seeks to pursue a particular agenda.

Developing a Multiperspective View

Finally, leaders and collaborators must be able to take a step back and see the bigger picture, the context within which they wish to initiate change. For student affairs professionals this means understanding higher education organizations and how they function, as well as understanding the societal milieu in which they exist. The use of multiple perspectives to make sense of how organizations operate provides a much richer analysis than the use of only one view. Using the different "logics" that emanate from different organizational models (see Chapter Thirteen) provides leaders and collaborators with a variety of strategies to employ in making the changes they intend. Also, recognizing that the internal and external environments in which student affairs professionals operate are becoming more uncertain and turbulent helps us frame the processes of change in multiperspective terms, instead of relying on the language and images of the linear, rational perspective that is rapidly losing credibility as we shift to a postindustrial society. Using multiple frames to interpret the experiences of the leadership group and to more fully understand the context in which change is to be initiated will enhance the work of student affairs professionals as postindustrial leaders and collaborators.

Putting Competencies into Practice

Let us return briefly to the peer education drama troupe used earlier in the chapter as an example of postindustrial leadership. By examining the activities of such a group we can see how the competencies outlined above are likely to play out in practice. Trust and empowerment create the conditions necessary for leadership to rotate among group members. The coordinator (the designated leader) lets go of the bureaucratic imperative that her role is to control the group. By doing this, she encourages the group's members to express their autonomy. Going hand in hand with this release is the recognition that each member brings important talents and perspectives to the work of the troupe. These perspectives are valued and actively sought. The troupe collaborates in conceptualizing the skits and in performing them. The troupe's shared vision about fostering a more socially conscious and responsible student body serves as the foundation for what they do and how they do it. It serves to help the students make meaning of their experiences.

The values of the troupe's particular campus likely influence the language and images it uses in its skits. Understanding this context is an example of being politically savvy. Also, the group is likely to have greater success with funding if its goals reflect campus values. Finally, for the troupe to maintain its cohesiveness and its focus, critical reflection and analysis of its leadership and development processes must occur regularly.

Teaching Postindustrial Competencies

How should postindustrial leadership training be conceptualized and implemented? Two central values have emerged. First, as noted earlier, leadership development is not focused on teaching individuals to be leaders; instead it is focused on teaching people to engage in leadership. Therefore, postindustrial leadership training programs are not reserved for "designated" or "positional" leaders (for example, the elected officers of student groups or the directors of students affairs units); they are for anyone who wants to learn more about how leaders and collaborators engage one another in a change process. Expanding the notion of who is included in leadership development programs is a crucial first step in training for postindustrial leadership.

Second, the methods used to teach leadership must reflect the principles of postindustrial leadership. For instance, a lecture format sends a mixed message—it still represents an "expert" dispensing wisdom about the best way to do things. More congruent methods include teachers' and learners' mutually constructing their conceptualization of postindustrial leadership and fleshing out their understanding with examples from their own experiences. Such collaborative methods of learning can be instituted in every arena where leadership education occurs. For example, a study by Rogers (1992) found that faculty in student affairs preparation programs recognized that an essential part of teaching students about shared leadership is to create collaborative environments in the classroom and in graduate programs. Student input was sought, and students were encouraged to take responsibility for their learning community.

The idea of modeling the principles of postindustrial leadership is a powerful teaching tool. This can occur in every area of student affairs. Professional development programs, student leadership retreats, and staff training sessions can not only be used to explain postindustrial leadership competencies but also to demonstrate them, in the very way the programs are structured and the participants included in the process. Even more ideal, the entire student affairs function could become a living laboratory for students and staff alike to engage in the processes of postindustrial leadership and acquire the skills necessary to engage in it. This would entail putting the principles and competencies of postindustrial leadership into practice in the day-to-day functions of student affairs offices.

Conclusion

The fact that "there are almost as many definitions of leadership as there are persons who have attempted to define it" (Stogdill, 1974, p. 259) is even more reason for student affairs professionals to engage in rigorous intellectual analysis and personal self-assessment concerning what it means to be a leader. The purpose of this chapter has been to introduce you to the debate about what leadership comprises and to challenge you to examine your currently held assumptions about leadership. Your assumptions shape how you think about and practice leadership and also how you approach leadership development activities with the students you work with. It is important that you recognize which paradigms of leadership have the greatest influence on you. It is also important to critically examine your assumptions throughout your professional career so that they remain relevant in a rapidly changing world.

The postindustrial perspective presents an intriguing new definition of leadership, one that many scholars and practitioners are convinced is better for responding to the dynamic conditions that confront us. There are those who wholeheartedly embrace postindustrial principles and attempt to put them into practice. There are others who continue to value and operate from the industrial paradigm. This duality will remain for some time to come. Old paradigms die hard. People's assumptions are constructed of deeply held beliefs that not only shape their view of the world and direct their behavior but also are integral to their self-concept. Such beliefs are not abandoned lightly. Undoubtedly student affairs professionals will find themselves in work environments in which some supervisors and colleagues operate from a conventional perspective and others hold postindustrial views. Their particular perspectives will shape their expectations of staff. Contradictory expectations may create conflict. These are the consequences, for better or worse, of living in a time when our culture is undergoing a transition from one paradigm to another. Understanding the assumptions and language of both the postindustrial and industrial perspectives on leadership will help you make better sense of a world in transition. Also, being clear about your own theoretical framework and understanding the frameworks of the people you work with will increase your ability to understand others, lead with them, and thus bring about real and positive change.

References

Bellah, R. N., Madsen, R., Sullivan, W. M., Swidler, A., & Tipton, S. M. (1985). *Habits of the heart*. New York: Harper & Row.

Bennis, W. G. (1959). Leadership theory and administrative behavior: The problem of authority. *Administrative Science Quarterly, 4*, 259–260.

Bennis, W. G., & Nanus, B. (1985). *Leaders: The strategies for taking charge*. New York: Harper & Row.

Bensimon, E. M., & Neumann, A. (1993). *Redesigning collegiate leadership*. Baltimore: Johns Hopkins University Press.

Block, P. (1987). *The empowered manager: Positive political skills at work*. San Francisco: Jossey-Bass.

Burns, J. M. (1978). *Leadership*. New York: Harper & Row.

Drath, W. H., & Palus, C. J. (1994). *Making common sense: Leadership as meaning making in a community of practice*. Greensboro, NC: Center for Creative Leadership.

Foster, W. (1986). *Paradigms and promises*. Buffalo, NY: Prometheus Books.

Foster, W. (1989). Toward a critical practice of leadership. In J. Smyth (Ed.), *Critical perspectives on educational leadership* (pp. 39–62). London: Falmer.

Freire, P. (1970). *Pedagogy of the oppressed*. New York: Continuum.

Gordon, T. (1955). *Group-centered leadership*. Boston: Houghton Mifflin.

Greenleaf, R. K. (1970). *The servant as leader*. Newton Center, MA: Robert K. Greenleaf Center.

Hammer, M., & Champy, J. (1993). *Reengineering the corporation*. New York: HarperCollins.

Kellerman, B. (1984). Leadership as a political act. In B. Kellerman (Ed.), *Leadership: Multidisciplinary perspectives* (pp. 63–89). Englewood Cliffs, NJ: Prentice Hall.

Kennedy, P. (1993). *Preparing for the twenty-first century*. New York: Random House.

Kohn, A. (1986). *No contest: The case against competition*. Boston: Houghton Mifflin.

Kuh, G. D., Whitt, E. J., & Shedd, J. D. (1987). *Student affairs work, 2001: A paradigmatic odyssey*. Alexandria, VA: American College Personnel Association.

Kuhn, T. S. (1970). *The structure of scientific revolutions* (2nd ed.). Chicago: University of Chicago Press.

Lappé, F. M., & Du Bois, P. M. (1994). *The quickening of America: Rebuilding our nation, remaking our lives*. San Francisco: Jossey-Bass.

Marchese, T. (1993). TQM: A time for ideas. *Change, 25*(3), 10–14.

Moore, B. V. (1927). The May conference on leadership. *Personnel Journal, 6*, 124–128.

Morgan, G. (1986). *Images of organization*. Newbury Park, CA: Sage.

Mossberg, B. (1994). *CHAOS: A primer to round world thinking*. Washington, DC: American Council on Education.

Osborne, D., & Gaebler, T. (1992). *Reinventing government: How the entrepreneurial spirit is transforming the public sector*. Reading, MA: Addison-Wesley.

Palmer, P. J. (1990). *Leading from within: Reflections on spirituality and leadership*. Indianapolis: Indiana Office for Campus Ministries.

Prince, H. T., & Associates (Eds.). (1985). *Leadership in organizations* (3rd ed.). West Point, NY: United States Military Academy.

Quantz, R. A., Rogers, J. L., & Dantley, M. (1991). Rethinking transformative leadership: Toward the democratic reform of schools. *Journal of Education, 173*(3), 96–118.

Rogers, J. L. (1992). Graduate student views of leadership education in college student personnel preparation programs. *NASPA Journal, 29*(3), 169–180.

Rogers, J. L., & Ballard, S. C. (1995). Aspirational management: Building effective organizations through shared values. *NASPA Journal, 32*(3), 162–178.

Rost, J. C. (1991). *Leadership for the twenty-first century.* New York: Praeger.

Rost, J. C. (1993a). *Leadership: A discussion about ethics.* Unpublished manuscript, University of San Diego.

Rost, J. C. (1993b). Leadership development for the new millennium. *Journal of Leadership Studies, 1*(1), 91–110.

Rost, J. C. (1994). *Moving from individual to relationship: A postindustrial paradigm of leadership.* Paper presented at the meeting of the American Educational Research Association, New Orleans.

Schlechty, P. C. (1990). *Schools for the 21st century: Leadership imperatives for educational reform.* San Francisco: Jossey-Bass.

Smyth, J. (1989). *Critical perspectives on educational leadership.* London: Falmer.

Stogdill, R. M. (1974). *Handbook of leadership: A survey of the literature.* New York: Free Press.

Wheatley, M. J. (1993). *Leadership and the new science: Learning about organization from an orderly universe.* San Francisco: Berett-Koehler.

Yukl, G. (1994). *Leadership in organizations* (3rd ed.). Englewood Cliffs, NJ: Prentice Hall.

CHAPTER FIFTEEN

TEACHING AND TRAINING

Larry D. Roper

Our primary responsibilities as student affairs professionals are to facilitate student development and to support the educational mission of our institution. No other activities can immerse us so intimately in the life and success of our institution as our involvement as educators and student development professionals. By virtue of our role we have many opportunities to create and respond to learning situations: as employers we provide orientation, training, and education for professional and student employees; on some campuses we are accorded faculty status and assume classroom teaching roles; and as supervisors of functional areas we offer workshops and organize other developmental experiences. We also provide educational activities for faculty and other peers at our own institutions and on other campuses. We educate directly and formally through our roles as teachers and trainers; in addition, we informally teach colleagues, employees, and students. The degree to which we are effective in these educational roles determines how well we are linked to the primary mission of our institution. The purpose of this chapter is to provide information on the essential skills we must possess if we are to be effective student development educators, actively engaged in teaching and training.

Teaching and training roles vary widely from campus to campus, but certain criteria for effectiveness are common. These criteria are based on current thinking about the essential considerations for maximizing learning. Other chapters in this book provide grounding for important subject matter to be taught and address how students learn. This chapter provides thoughts on the importance of assuming teaching roles and details essential teaching skills. Specifically, this chapter identifies the essential competencies and related knowledge necessary for effective teachers and trainers.

This chapter is aimed at all student affairs professionals, given the fact that our primary responsibility is to serve as educators. The research cited here is especially helpful for developing a rationale for student affairs professionals' teaching and training roles and for identifying specific strategies to achieve desired outcomes. The emphasis in this chapter is on information related to active, cooperative, and collaborative learning; facilitating groups; leading discussions; team building; teaching multicultural populations; and training other trainers. These topics are highlighted because they represent the core activities in the daily lives of student affairs professionals.

The Challenge of Teaching

The state of college teaching in the United States has been the focus of much discussion and activity in recent years. Concerns have been raised about the effectiveness of teaching and the appropriateness of dominant pedagogical approaches for contemporary college students. Critics have suggested that college teachers are afflicted with such maladies as "narration sickness" (Freire, 1970, p. 57) and the tendency to enact "rituals of control" in the classroom (Hooks, 1994). Further, the growing presence and assertiveness of a diverse population of adult learners has raised new challenges to traditional teaching styles (Barnes, Christensen, & Hansen, 1994; Christensen, Garvin, & Sweet, 1991; Meyers & Jones, 1993).

Traditional instruction consists of teachers lecturing and students listening. This "teaching as telling" approach (Christensen et al., 1991, p. 3) is described as teacher-centered (Bruffee, 1993). In this model of teaching, there is little student-to-student interaction, and teacher-student interaction is often brief and impersonal. In the traditional classroom, students learn as isolated, independent individuals (Hooks, 1994). Much current research suggests that this approach to teaching does not maximize learning (for example, see Barnes et al., 1994; Bruffee, 1993; Johnson & Johnson, 1991; Meyers & Jones, 1993). The message is crystal clear—the dominant method of college teaching must change. Teaching must be revolutionized; educators must be "reacculturated"—they must undergo a culture change (Bruffee, 1993, p. 19).

It is well understood that good teaching does not necessarily consist of lecturing. So, what is good teaching? Passmore (1970) describes teaching as an activity aimed at *achieving* learning, a process that includes respecting the intellectual integrity of the student and the student's capacity for independent judgment. Menges (1981) further asserts that teaching is "the intentional arrangement of situations in which appropriate learning will occur" (p. 556). Good teachers possess such qualities as "enthusiasm; knowledge of the subject area; organization; clarity; concern and caring for students; use of higher cognitive level skills in discussions and examinations; use of visual aids; encouragement of student learning and student discussion; provision of feedback; and avoidance of harsh criticism" (Goodwin & Stevens, 1993, p. 166).

The dimensions of good teaching, as described in *Seven Principles for Good Practice in Undergraduate Education* (Chickering & Gamson, 1991), include the following: encouraging student-faculty interaction, encouraging cooperation among students, encouraging active learning, providing prompt feedback, emphasizing time on task, communicating high expectations, and respecting diverse talents and ways of knowing. Teaching is a transformational activity in which the teacher is a guide, coach, and facilitator of student learning (McLaughlin & Talbert, 1993). But teaching is much more than an activity. Teaching is a relationship with learners (Passmore, 1970) and a process of engagement, or a "performative act" (Hooks, 1994, p. 11). Teaching is also a role—one can still be called a teacher even if the student doesn't learn (Bennett, 1995). Bruffee (1993) suggests that teachers' most important responsibilities are to build "knowledge communities" and to represent these communities in such a way as to "reacculturate" potential members (p. 3).

If student affairs professionals are to be representatives of a knowledge community, we must have a clear understanding of and direction for our role as educators. We must challenge ourselves to develop our own curriculum and methodologies appropriate to our subject matter and a commitment to promoting learning as the primary activity of our institution, our profession, and our students. One example of such an approach is seen in the work of the student affairs division at Longwood College in Virginia. The student affairs staff at Longwood identified fourteen specific learning goals (desired outcomes) for students; they then provided descriptions of available learning opportunities on campus for each goal and offered "learning maps" to assist students in selecting the most appropriate experiences to develop particular knowledge, skills, and attitudes. In short, the staff made explicit what had previously been a "hidden curriculum" (P. Mable, personal communication, June 14, 1995). At the same time, student affairs professionals must go beyond merely defining teaching as a major role of our position. Teaching is much more than a role—it is an activity, it involves relationships, and it is a process. Student affairs professionals should possess a clear vision that lets us know whether we are good teachers. Important questions to ask ourselves include the following: How do I define good teaching? What kind of teacher am

I? What is my relationship with my learners? How do I engage them? How do I go beyond my *role* as a teacher to act on my *responsibilities* as one?

As educators, we have a responsibility to prepare students to lead socially and professionally meaningful lives in a changing and challenging world. Students must be prepared not only to solve their own problems but also to confront and respond appropriately and creatively to social and institutional dilemmas. Our challenge as teachers is to effectively define our roles, frame our teaching sphere (our sphere of educational influence), organize our curriculum (the topics we address), identify our potential learning audiences, and choose appropriate teaching methods. As Mines, King, Hood, and Wood (1990) suggest, student affairs practitioners have abundant opportunities to create learning environments in which we can effectively link our work to the major goals of our institution. As we create teaching situations, we can use them to impart whatever knowledge and skills we believe are important for learners to acquire. We have an obligation to identify those skills and knowledge and to create learning situations that foster their development.

Typically the goals associated with teaching are related to enhancing students' knowledge, awareness, or skills. Among the goals generally ascribed to college teaching are enhancing students' problem solving, critical analysis, and higher-order thinking (McLaughlin & Talbert, 1993); fostering their identity resolution (Widick & Simpson, 1978); challenging them to think critically and reflect on the assumptions underlying their ideas and actions; helping them understand different forms of knowledge, our current social condition, the meaning of past events, and possibilities for the future; helping them place themselves in the world (Shor, 1992); and helping them (and ourselves) uncover their own and others' reality and re-create knowledge (Freire, 1970). These goals are consistent with the developmental goals we draw upon for our work (see Chapters Ten and Eleven). Student affairs professionals should conclude that good student affairs work is synonymous with good teaching—if we achieve the goals identified for effective teaching, we have honored the core values of our profession.

Our roles as employers, supervisors, and administrators responsible for and working within specific functional areas provide us with numerous teaching opportunities. The obligations of our various roles dictate that we are responsible for the orientation, growth, and development of students and staff. Our responsibilities include teaching others the knowledge, skills, and awareness needed to function inside and outside our institution. In some instances we refer to our efforts to help others learn as teaching. At other times we describe our initiatives to provide individuals and groups with specific information as training. Clearly there are times when we might use the terms interchangeably. What we call our efforts may not be as important as our understanding of the processes involved.

Training as a Professional Function

Budget constraints and fiscal cutbacks have placed student affairs professionals in positions where they have to assume greater responsibility for staff training. Financial constraints challenge us to become more active in creating structures to provide staff members with the information they need to perform well in their roles (Delworth & Yarris, 1982). At the same time, there has been a growing trend toward using paraprofessionals in helping and advising roles. Employing students in roles such as AIDS educators, peer counselors, resident advisers, and conflict mediators dictates that we provide them with adequate and appropriate training to fulfill those roles (Carns, Carns, & Wright, 1993). Additionally, when new staff members come to our institution, we must have a process for helping them become familiar with its people, culture, and structures. Training serves this purpose as well (Merriam & Caffarella, 1991). Training comes in the form of pre-service and in-service activities, credit courses, collaborative programs with other campuses, teleconferences, consultants, and off-campus workshops and conferences. Offering appropriate training programs influences our ability to be successful in our roles and increases the effectiveness of our staff and institutions (Creamer & Shelton, 1988).

Training can be conducted on either an individual or a group basis. Training allows organizational members to respond effectively to changing political, technological, and social influences (Gallessich, 1982). Student affairs training serves many functions: it is a form of continuous professional development (Creamer & Shelton, 1988), it provides a means of teaching needed skills and reducing stress (Winston & Buckner, 1984; Woodard & Komives, 1990), it is used to educate staff to teach others (Fulton, 1982), it provides a way for us to prepare staff to perform specific tasks (Delworth & Yarris, 1982), and it is used to teach evaluation techniques.

The goal of training is to enhance individuals' knowledge, skills, and attitudes. In general, training serves organizations by preparing those who have been charged with managing organizational processes to respond to particular situations, manage change, and support organizational effectiveness (Stewart, 1991). Sometimes training is approached as a means of improving performance or compensating for performance deficiencies (Gallessich, 1982). In other situations training is used as a means of preparing people for new roles within an organization. Margolis and Bell (1989) describe four types of training:

1. *Administrative training* provides information on policies, procedures, and rules. This type of training usually covers such things as organizational paperwork, requisition procedures, and other information needed to get work done.

2. *Professional-technical training* emphasizes skills needed to complete one's job responsibilities. In student affairs this might include such things as counseling skills, teaching skills, and confrontation skills. This type of training is directed at enhancing the skills of analysis and judgment.
3. *Mechanical-technical training* focuses on such things as how to operate and maintain office equipment, how to access electronic mail, how to use computers and voice mail, and how to transfer telephone calls.
4. *Interpersonal training* teaches staff how to work with others and resolve work-related issues. Training in this area may focus on such skills as interviewing, conflict resolution, and communication skills.

Student affairs professionals will find themselves involved in each of these four types of training. Housing professionals will teach resident assistants to complete incident reports and room inventories; peer advisers will need to be taught basic helping skills; new employees will need to be guided through how to complete travel vouchers and operate a copy machine; and frontline staff will be taught how to handle upset and demanding students. This training is necessary in order to ensure that staff can meet the basic demands of their jobs. Because of the irregularity with which people join and leave our organizations, training may occur either in planned or impromptu situations. No matter the conditions under which training is provided, the goal is to help people master knowledge, skills, and awareness (Nilson, 1990).

Simply stated, effective training is achieved when the learners master the information conveyed and are able to translate it into appropriate behavior (Warshauer, 1988). There are certain required steps we must follow, however, if we are to make formal training programs effective. Among those steps are the following: properly identifying the needed skills and knowledge; stating the needed affective, cognitive, and skill requirements in behavioral terms; assessing trainees' knowledge and skill levels; developing a format and sequence for training (moving from simple to complex skills); determining training techniques; planning for ongoing supervision and monitoring; evaluating the procedures; developing a process to train cotrainers, if needed; implementing and evaluating the training program; and redesigning the program based on feedback (Delworth & Yarris, 1982).

In both teaching and training, the leader of the learning activity is responsible for planning, implementing, and evaluating the learning experience. Teaching and training are most effective when the teacher-trainer forges a partnership with the learners and involves them in diagnosing their learning needs, formulating their learning goals, designing their learning activities, and evaluating their learning outcomes. Such partnerships make the learning program more learner-centered and potentially more effective than programs in which the learner is not actively involved (Merriam & Caffarella, 1991). Teaching and training techniques should be respectful of learners and acknowledge their diversity. (In Chapter Eleven, Patricia King describes diversity in learning styles and issues affecting learning readiness.) Our challenge is to create mechanisms to facilitate the professional effectiveness of individuals; provide them with the knowledge, skills, and awareness necessary to function in their role; and achieve some level of uniformity in carrying out our institution's policies and procedures. This should be done in a way that contributes positively to the achievement of our institution's missions.

Essential Knowledge and Skills

The essential skills and knowledge necessary to be effective in our roles as teachers and trainers include the following: knowledge of active, cooperative, and collaborative learning and the ability to promote it; an understanding of group dynamics and the ability to facilitate groups; an understanding of discussions and the ability to lead them and to promote reflection; knowledge of the use of teams in organizations and the ability to promote team building; an understanding of multicultural populations and the ability to teach diverse learners; and the ability to train other trainers. Effective student affairs professionals are able to translate these skills and knowledge into professional behavior in their roles as teachers and trainers.

Active, Cooperative, and Collaborative Learning

Research leaves no doubt that actively involving learners increases their learning, enhances their relationships with their peers and with the teacher, and leads to greater learner satisfaction with the learning experience. The approaches used to achieve maximum learning outcomes include such methods as active learning, cooperative learning, collaborative learning, and the case study method (Barnes et al., 1994; Bruffee, 1993; Erickson & Strommer, 1991; Garibaldi, 1992; Johnson, Johnson, & Smith, 1991; Tiberius & Billson, 1991). These approaches are all learner-centered, and they all focus on creating a participatory learning environment. Effective educators possess knowledge of each of these approaches and can readily determine appropriate situations in which to utilize them.

Active learning techniques display the following basic characteristics: student tasks involve more than sitting and listening; emphasis is placed on skill development rather than on transmitting information; learners are involved in higher-order cognitive activities such as analysis, synthesis, and evaluation; involvement includes experiential activities; and emphasis is placed on exploring learners' attitudes and values (Bonwell & Eison, 1991). The use of active learning strategies is viewed as one of the major commitments educators can make to acknowledging the diversity of learners on our campuses. Because women and culturally diverse students bring unique ideas and needs to campus, traditional teaching styles are not viewed as being responsive to them (Meyers & Jones, 1993). Active learning techniques are promoted for cognitive, philosophic, and pragmatic reasons. Students retain less information when they learn passively. Critical thinking and artistic sensibilities cannot be cultivated through lectures, and students are generally dissatisfied with passive learning (Christensen et al., 1991).

Active learning strategies include role plays, simulations, computer-based instruction, debates, peer teaching, in-class writing, and cooperative learning (Bonwell & Eison, 1991). Student affairs professionals must make use of the resources available to them to create active learning situations when they teach or train.

Cooperative learning involves the use of small groups to maximize learning by fostering positive interdependence, requiring face-to-face interaction, exacting individual accountability, and offering opportunities for group processing (Johnson et al., 1991). Cooperative learning also offers team rewards and equal opportunities for success (Slavin, 1990). The teacher is responsible for specifying learning objectives, placing students in groups, explaining goals and tasks, monitoring groups and intervening as necessary, evaluating student achievement, and helping learners process their involvement and contributions (Johnson et al., 1991). Cooperative learning activities are based on two goals: increasing learning outcomes and developing social skills such as conflict management, decision making, and problem solving (Bonwell & Eison, 1991). There are three types of group structures used in cooperative learning: formal groups, informal groups, and base groups. When formal groups are used, members are assigned to a group, taught specific concepts, assigned a task to complete cooperatively, monitored by the teacher, taught collaboration skills by the teacher, evaluated, and given an opportunity to process their learning. Informal groups meet for three to five minutes during a learning session to share learning on a particular activity. Base groups meet every time the class meets, providing long-term peer relationships. Student affairs professionals can employ cooperative learning strategies in academic courses or staff training situations. Peer advisers, orientation leaders, and resident assistants are good examples of individuals that may be placed into formal groups.

Collaborative learning involves a partnership between the teacher and his or her students. In this model, the students and teacher jointly construct knowledge on a particular subject or issue. Generally the goal of collaborative learning is to encourage critical thinking, improve problem solving capabilities, and broaden learners' perspectives (Bruffee, 1993). Learners are assigned specific learning tasks to complete in a specified time frame. Because there is no "right" answer, creative thought is encouraged. A typical activity might be to read this passage from the Declaration of Independence: "We hold these truths to be self-evident, that all men are created equal, that they are endowed by their Creator with certain unalienable rights, that among these are life, liberty and the pursuit of happiness." Students would then be asked to reach a consensus on the meaning of the words *truths, self-evident, unalienable rights, life, liberty,* and *happiness* (Bruffee, 1993, p. 37). The goal of exercises such as this is to expose learners to different meanings that people may perceive in the same document. It also provides a setting for learners to express themselves and to learn to value others' opinions. In collaborative learning situations, the teacher provides instructions, organizes groups (including assigning roles), provides stimulus questions, facilitates processing of group work, and brings closure to the discussion (Bruffee, 1993). Student affairs professionals might employ collaborative learning techniques by giving a copy of their institution's mission statement to a group of new employees. The trainer may want to identify key words in that statement and ask the group to reach a consensus on what those words mean. In subsequent sessions the trainer might help the learners grapple with the challenges inherent in attempting to translate a confusing document into appropriate professional practice.

Facilitating Groups

There are clear differences between teaching and facilitating learning. Teaching sometimes takes the form of giving people information, whereas facilitating involves acknowledging the different ways people learn and creating environments to nurture and support their learning (Warshauer, 1988). Teachers and trainers may be categorized as facilitators of learning groups—groups whose purpose is to ensure that members learn certain knowledge, skills, information, or procedures (Johnson & Johnson, 1982). The primary role of facilitators is to create an environment that allows group members to learn easily (Stewart, 1991). Facilitators need the following knowledge: an understanding of the potential that group experiences have for enhancing individual growth, an understanding of the variables that can influence group functioning, clarity about the group's goals, and strategies for advancing the group through the learning process (Johnson & Johnson, 1982). Facilitators must possess intervention skills to solve problems that arise in groups and an ability to turn those situations into learning experiences (Warshauer, 1988). Effective facilitators are good communicators. They are able to show that they value individual group members, and they are willing to share power and leadership. They are flexible and open to new ideas, and they are honest (Stewart, 1991). Whether one is teaching or training, good facilitation skills are essential.

Leading Discussions

Discussions are the core activity in active learning situations. Discussions help learners resolve contradictions; they are the primary means by which learners personalize their relationships with their peers, share their reflections, and crystalize their thinking on a issue (Johnson et al., 1991). Thus specific skills are needed in this area if teachers and trainers are to be effective. Our ability to lead discussions is a key indicator of our ability to effectively grasp active learning concepts. The act of fostering discussion graphically illustrates a fundamental shift in our teaching approach. In discussions, the balance of power shifts toward a more democratic paradigm than a traditional learning environment. We move away from focusing solely on content, considering the learning process and classroom climate as well. We shift from the traditional stance of making declarative explanations to using questioning, listening, and responding (Christensen et al., 1991). Discussion leaders must be sensitive to the fact that learners may feel threatened. They must effectively design activities that provide a safe climate for students to share their thoughts, feelings, and observations. Discussion leaders must also be skilled at using questions to inspire involvement and motivate learning (Bonwell & Eison, 1991).

Team Building

Colleges and universities, like many other organizations, have increasingly come to rely on cross-functional and interdepartmental groups to accomplish various tasks. Because of decreases in the size of the work force and increases in educational initiatives on our campuses, we have had to respond with creative arrangements to further our institutions' missions. Our use of task forces, strategic planning committees, search committees, Total Quality Management techniques, and self-directed work groups has created situations where members of our organizations are brought together to work with people they may not be familiar with. Campus leaders have an obligation to make sure these groups are equipped to function effectively (Lubin & Eddy, 1987). We often call these groups "teams" (quality teams, diversity teams, programming teams), but we don't often acknowledge them as such by providing them with proper training. Teams that receive training are better able to respond to change and are more likely to achieve their stated objectives (Stewart, 1991). Providing members with shared learning experiences is one way to build effective teams.

As teachers and trainers, we need knowledge of group- and team-building strategies. We should help group members get to know one another, clarify their goals, establish communication, define and solve problems, and make decisions. The goal of the teacher or trainer is to improve the group's effectiveness so that it can achieve the desired results (Dyer, 1995). Leaders of groups require the knowledge and skills to guide them through the team-development process. Most importantly, teachers and trainers should possess knowledge about team building and utilize the proper resources to facilitate it. Among the techniques to know and use are ice breakers, trust-building activities, consensus-building activities, experience-based activities (such as rope courses and adventure training), communication enhancement activities, and conflict resolution strategies.

Teaching Multicultural Populations

One of the major challenges facing higher education today is to create positive learning environments that support diversity. Teachers are challenged to find appropriate and effective means of teaching the ethnically, racially, and culturally diverse students on our campuses. As teachers and trainers, our challenge is to be cognizant of the presence of racism, sexism, classism, and other negative attitudes and behaviors directed at certain groups. Our educational efforts must be truly multicultural in that they should provide information, explore attitudes, and influence behaviors (Roper & Sedlacek, 1988). The methods employed should draw upon the strengths of diversity rather than focusing on the negative issues that grow out of having a diverse learning community.

There are dimensions of cooperative and collaborative learning that build positive intergroup relations—namely, aspects of contact theory (Allport, 1954). Contact theory suggests that positive relationships are more likely to develop between people of different racial and ethnic backgrounds if they possess equal status, their interaction is institutionally sanctioned and supported, and they work toward a common goal. Contact theory is the basis of cooperative learning techniques (Slavin, 1990). As we design teaching and training activities, it is necessary to be aware of the role these activities can play in advancing the relationship-building component of our institution's mission statement. There are specific strategies we can use to facilitate more positive relationships between members of different groups (Roper, 1988); these include creating equal-status environments, using activities that require cooperation, and illustrating to learners that there is institutional support for group interaction. The group investigation method, which requires group inquiry, data gathering, group discussion, interpretation of information, and synthesis of information into a group product, is an effective approach to building positive intergroup relationships.

Training Other Trainers

Organizations have increasingly come to rely upon members of their own work force to act as trainers for other employees. In many organizations, after certain employees have gone through particular learning experiences, they are called upon to train other potential trainers (Fulton, 1982). Through the use of train-the-trainer workshops, staff members are able to pass their knowledge and skills directly to their peers (Leinfuss, 1993). In some organizations the use of peers to train others serves to increase commitment, such as in the area of diversity training (Cox, 1994). In student affairs we have numerous situations where we are called upon to train other trainers. Our challenge is to understand the difference between how to teach learners purely for their own sake and how to teach learners so that they might in turn teach others. In train-the-trainer workshops, leaders may need to employ more demonstration and simulation activities so that learners can have the opportunity to apply the teaching and training activities they will use when they train others. Trainers need to be aware of learners' feelings, provide them with appropriate and sensitive feedback, and support them as they offer training to others. Train-the-trainer workshops are typically used for training orientation leaders, resident advisers, sexuality educators, peer helpers, teaching assistants, and student coaches, to name a few.

Gallessich (1982) asserts that training is most effective when it meets the following conditions.

1. The trainer involves the intended audience in the collaborative planning of training exercises whenever possible.
2. The training has relevance and responds to an identified need.
3. The training program is unique. It is not prepackaged; it is designed for the specific group it is intended for.
4. The program has flexibility and the capacity to adapt to changing or unpredictable circumstances.
5. The trainer employs alternative methods that acknowledge learners' diversity.
6. The program has clarity. The goals and training activities are easy to understand (especially the instructions).
7. Whenever possible, participation is voluntary. Learners have the freedom to opt out of certain activities.
8. There is a thoughtful sequence of learning tasks, moving from simple to complex.
9. The program's pace fits the learners and the material to be learned. The trainer is sensitive to boredom, overload, fatigue, and other signs that learners are not engaged.
10. The trainer pays attention to learners' comfort, including both their physical and their emotional comfort. The trainer attends to the learning environment.
11. There are supportive group norms; the learners have shared expectations and desired outcomes.
12. There is a high level of learner readiness. Learners are well prepared for the experience.

13. There is a high level of learner activity. The training program involves learners in active roles.
14. There is a feedback loop that allows the trainer to check for learning and the effectiveness of his or her methods.
15. There is leader support. The trainer feels supported in his or her work. This support may come from a cotrainer.

Conclusion

Teachers and trainers build relationships with learners while providing them with the knowledge, skills, and awareness necessary to function in their social and professional roles. Our roles and responsibilities as teachers and trainers can no longer be carried out according to a script. We must construct each learning experience as a unique situation, directly in response to the group or individual it is intended for—taking their needs, challenges, life situations, and personal characteristics into account. We must consciously develop the competencies we need in order to be good teachers and trainers. Content is important, but it loses meaning if it is not presented in a way learners can understand and translate into the desired behavior.

The information in this chapter has been aimed at helping student affairs educators find grounding for our roles as teachers and trainers. It was not meant to be a how-to piece as much as to provide exposure to important concepts in teaching and training. Specifically, regardless of whether we are in teaching or training roles, we must utilize techniques that are respectful of the diversity and capabilities of learners. Traditional lecture and presentation formats are no longer appropriate. A wide range of strategies should be utilized to reach and engage learners. As we work with groups of learners, we act as representatives of our knowledge community. Our knowledge community is rooted in a tradition of attending to the needs of individuals, respecting individual dignity, promoting high-level understanding and critical thinking, celebrating diversity while recognizing commonalities, and encouraging openness to new ideas and perspectives. As teachers and trainers we are challenged to honor that tradition. Finally, as we teach and train we should not lose sight of the fact that we are working to achieve the grand aims of our institution's mission. We are attempting to move individuals to the highest level of human functioning they can achieve.

References

Allport, G. W. (1954). *The nature of prejudice.* Garden City, NY: Doubleday/Anchor.

Barnes, L. B., Christensen, C. R., & Hansen, A. J. (1994). *Teaching and the case method: Text, cases, and readings* (3rd ed.). Boston: Harvard Business School Press.

Bennett, C. I. (1995). *Comprehensive multicultural education: Theory and practice* (3rd ed.). Boston: Allyn & Bacon.

Bonwell, C. C., & Eison, J. A. (1991). *Active learning: Creating excitement in the classroom* (ASHE-ERIC Higher Education Report No. 4). Washington, DC: School of Education and Human Development, George Washington University.

Bruffee, K. A. (1993). *Collaborative learning: Higher education, interdependence, and the authority of knowledge.* Baltimore: Johns Hopkins University Press.

Carns, A. W., Carns, M. R., & Wright, J. (1993). Students as paraprofessionals in four-year colleges and universities: Current practice compared to prior practice. *Journal of College Student Development, 34,* 358–363.

Chickering, A. W., & Gamson, Z. F. (1991). Seven principles for good practice in undergraduate education. In A. W. Chickering & Z. F. Gamson (Eds.), *Applying the seven principles of good practice in undergraduate education* (New Directions for Teaching and Learning No. 47, pp. 63–69). San Francisco: Jossey-Bass.

Christensen, C. R., Garvin, D. A., & Sweet, A. (1991). *Education for judgment: The artistry of discussion leadership.* Boston: Harvard Business School Press.

Cox, T., Jr. (1994). *Cultural diversity in organizations: Theory, research, and practice.* San Francisco: Berrett-Koehler.

Creamer, D., & Shelton, M. (1988). Staff development: A literature review of graduate preparation and in-service education of students. *Journal of College Student Development, 29,* 407–414.

Delworth, U., & Yarris, E. (1982). Concepts and processes for the new training role. In U. Delworth (Ed.), *Training competent staff* (pp. 1–15). San Francisco: Jossey-Bass.

Dyer, W. G. (1995). *Teambuilding: Current issues and new alternatives* (3rd ed.). Reading, MA: Addison-Wesley.

Erickson, B. L., & Strommer, D. W. (1991). *Teaching college freshmen.* San Francisco: Jossey-Bass.

Freire, P. (1970). *Pedagogy of the oppressed* (M. B. Ramos, Trans.). New York: Continuum.

Fulton, D. R. (1982). Teaching staff to be trainers. In U. Delworth (Ed.), *Training competent staff* (pp. 75–81). San Francisco: Jossey-Bass.

Gallessich, J. (1982). *The profession and practice of consultation: A handbook for consultants, trainers of consultants, and consumers of consultation services.* San Francisco: Jossey-Bass.

Garibaldi, A. (1992). Preparing teachers for culturally diverse classrooms. In M. E. Dilworth (Ed.), *Diversity in teacher education: New expectations* (pp. 23–39). San Francisco: Jossey- Bass.

Goodwin, L. D., & Stevens, E. A. (1993). The influence of gender on university faculty members' perceptions of "good" teaching. *Journal of Higher Education, 64,* 166–185.

Hooks, B. (1994). *Teaching to transgress: Education as the practice of freedom.* New York: Routledge.

Johnson, D. W., & Johnson, F. P. (1982). *Joining together: Group theory and group skills* (2nd ed.). Englewood Cliffs, NJ: Prentice Hall.

Johnson, D. W., & Johnson, R. T. (1991). *Learning together and alone: Cooperative, competitive, and individualistic learning* (3rd ed.). Boston: Allyn & Bacon.

Johnson, D. W., Johnson, R. T., & Smith, K. A. (1991). *Cooperative learning: Increasing college faculty instructional productivity* (ASHE-ERIC Higher Education Report No. 4). Washington, DC: School of Education and Human Development, George Washington University.

Leinfuss, E. (1993). Training in the age of downsizing [CD-ROM]. *Computerworld, 27.* Abstract from: Expanded Academic Index: AN: 13400856.

Lubin, B., & Eddy, W. B. (1987). The development of small group training and small group trainers. In W. B. Reddy & C. C. Henderson, Jr. (Eds.), *Training theory and practice* (pp. 3–15). Alexandria, VA: NTL Institute.

McLaughlin, M. W., & Talbert, J. E. (1993). New visions of teaching [Introduction]. In D. K. Cohen, M. W. McLaughlin, & J. E. Talbert (Eds.), *Teaching for understanding: Challenge for policy and practice* (pp. 1–10). San Francisco: Jossey-Bass.

Margolis, F. H., & Bell, C. R. (1989). *Understanding training: Perspectives and practices.* San Diego, CA: University Associates.

Menges, R. J. (1981). Instructional methods. In A. W. Chickering & Associates, *The modern American college: Responding to the new realities of diverse students and a changing society* (pp. 556–581). San Francisco: Jossey-Bass.

Merriam, S. B., & Caffarella, R. S. (1991). *Learning in adulthood: A comprehensive guide.* San Francisco: Jossey-Bass.

Meyers, C., & Jones, T. B. (1993). *Promoting active learning: Strategies for the college classroom.* San Francisco: Jossey-Bass.

Mines, R. A., King, P. M., Hood, A. B., & Wood, P. K. (1990). Stages of intellectual development and associated critical thinking skills in college students. *Journal of College Student Development, 31,* 538–547.

Nilson, C. (1990). *Training for non-trainers: A do-it-yourself guide for managers.* New York: AMACOM.

Passmore, J. (1970). *The philosophy of teaching.* Cambridge, MA: Harvard University Press.

Roper, L. D. (1988). *Relationship among levels of social distance, dogmatism, affective reactions, and interracial behaviors in a course on racism.* Unpublished doctoral dissertation, University of Maryland, College Park.

Roper, L. D., & Sedlacek, W. E. (1988). Student affairs professionals in academic roles: A course on racism. *NASPA Journal, 26,* 27–32.

Shor, I. (1992). *Empowering education: Critical teaching for social change.* Chicago: University of Chicago Press.

Slavin, R. E. (1990). *Cooperative learning: Theory, research, and practice.* Boston: Allyn & Bacon.

Stewart, J. (1991). *Managing change through training and development.* San Diego, CA: Pfeiffer.

Tiberius, R. G., & Billson, J. M. (1991). The social context of teaching and learning. In R. J. Menges & M. D. Svinicki (Eds.), *College teaching: From theory to practice* (pp. 67–86). San Francisco: Jossey-Bass.

Warshauer, S. (1988). *Inside training and development: Creating effective programs.* San Diego, CA: University Associates.

Widick, C., & Simpson, D. (1978). Developmental concepts in college instruction. In C. A. Parker (Ed.), *Encouraging development in college students* (pp. 27–59). Minneapolis: University of Minnesota Press.

Winston, R. B., Jr., & Buckner, J. D. (1984). The effects of peer helper training and timing of training on reported stress in resident assistants. *Journal of College Student Personnel, 25,* 430–436.

Woodard, D. B., Jr., & Komives, S. R. (1990). Ensuring staff competence. In M. J. Barr, M. L. Upcraft, & Associates, *New futures for student affairs: Building a vision for professional leadership and practice* (pp. 217–238). San Francisco: Jossey-Bass.

CHAPTER SIXTEEN

COUNSELING AND ADVISING

Roger B. Winston, Jr.

As E. G. Williamson (1939) observed over fifty years ago, all students have problems that their college or university can and should help them address. Another pioneer of the student affairs field, C. Gilbert Wrenn (1951), argued that "the only justification for student personnel services is that they can be shown to meet the needs of students. . . . These include both the basic psychological needs of all young people and the specific needs that are the direct results of the college experience" (pp. 26–27).

There is probably no student affairs division in the country that has sufficient counseling and academic advising staff to address the plethora of student needs, wants, and legitimate expectations for assistance. If a student affairs division is to satisfy Wrenn's raison d'être for the profession, then all or most of its staff must possess well-developed helping skills and utilize them in their daily interactions with students. This chapter is based on this premise. It addresses counseling and advising competencies from the perspective of the student affairs professional, who may work in a wide variety of settings, such as student activities, housing, financial aid, international student services, and admissions. This chapter is addressed to student affairs professionals and academic advisers who do not view themselves, either by reason of academic preparation or the responsibilities of their position, as professional counselors but who work with students with needs that can be adequately addressed only by the adroit use of counseling skills and knowledge. I call these professionals "allied professional counselors," adopting the terminology of Delworth and Aulepp (1976). Professionals who work in counseling centers and career planning offices are expected to have more advanced counseling skills, experience, and knowledge and can properly be called professional counselors. Likewise, professional advisers are expected to be more skilled and experienced than student affairs staff or faculty members who provide academic advising in addition to other, not directly related responsibilities. Particular attention is focused on helping students select an academic major and make career decisions, because these are the most common concerns of all types of undergraduates.

As student affairs professionals' careers advance, they tend to spend less time in direct contact with students and more time interacting with staff members. Helping skills are still needed, however, in this capacity; only the clientele has changed, from students to staff. Several well-known leadership theorists—for example, Hersey and Blanchard (1993); Blake, Mouton, and Williams (1981); and Block (1987)—emphasize the essential skills of communicating care and concern, creating a supportive atmosphere, and sharing decision making as the foundations of effective organizational leadership. A working knowledge of counseling skills and interventions greatly increases a work supervisor's capability to create positive relationships and environments.

This chapter addresses the helping skills all student affairs professionals should possess. It presents the essential components of helping and various models for understanding the helping process and determining appropriate interventions (including making effective referrals). Counseling approaches for dealing with career concerns are given particular attention. Developmental academic advising is defined, and the roles and skills needed to put the concept into practice are outlined. Some of the factors that affect the nature of helping relationships in counseling and advising, such as gender and ethnicity, are briefly identified. Finally, ethical issues particularly pertinent to counseling and academic advising are examined.

Components of the Helping Relationship

Carl Rogers (1957, 1961) initiated the great debate—which has continued for over thirty years—about the necessary and sufficient conditions for helping individuals change their behavior and attitudes. He argued that it is the character and attitudes of the helper that are most crucial to facilitation of constructive change, much more so than his or her knowledge and expertise. He asserted that "if I can provide a certain type of relationship, the other person will discover within himself the capacity to use that relationship for growth and change, and personal development will occur" (Rogers, 1961, p. 33). He identified three personal characteristics or necessary conditions that he considered to be of supreme importance: genuineness, or congruence; unconditional positive regard, or acceptance; and accurate empathic understanding.

Genuineness is the extent or degree to which the helper is nondefensive and authentic in interacting with the helpee. Genuine helpers do not play roles, do not attempt to change or conceal their values from the helpee, and are "real." To be an effective helper, one must truly want to help. Acting solely on a perceived responsibility to "help students" because of one's position cannot be concealed for long, and it will ultimately be recognized by helpees as fraudulent.

Unconditional positive regard, or nonpossessive warmth, refers to the extent that helpers communicate an attitude of nonevaluative caring and respect for the helpee as a person. Rogers (1967) asserted that because helpers often encounter persons who hold contrary values systems, they should be aware of their own values and beliefs and not try to conceal them. To pretend acceptance interferes with the helping relationship and destroys genuineness, and it can seldom be concealed from the helpee for extended periods of time. Helpers must be careful, however, not to attempt to impose their values upon the helpee or communicate disrespect toward or disapproval of the helpee's values.

Empathy refers to the degree to which helpers can successfully communicate their awareness and understanding of another person's frame of reference and feelings in language attuned to that individual. Empathy involves two processes. First, helpers must understand the inner world (values, attitudes, and feelings) of the other person. Then they must communicate that understanding by using the other person's frame of reference in their dialogue. Branner and Shostrom (1982) maintain that in responding empathetically, a helper tries to "think with, rather than for or about the client. [Empathy] is . . . the capacity to respond to another's feelings and experiences as if they were your own" (p. 160).

Other theorists (Carkhuff, 1969; Egan, 1990; Gazda et al., 1995; Ivey & Authier, 1978) have also described necessary conditions for creating a helping interaction. They depart somewhat from Rogers by maintaining that there are specific, identifiable skills that effective helpers intentionally utilize. These skills can be taught and explained from a basically behavioral frame of reference. Unlike Rogers, who emphasized the primacy of being a certain kind of person rather than of employing certain techniques, these theorists argue that successful helpers need to learn certain skills and to behave in specific ways designed to assist others. These additional skills and techniques include concreteness, self-disclosure, immediacy, and confrontation.

Concreteness refers to the helper's assisting the helpee in identifying the specific feelings associated with the experiences being described. The helper's task is to assist helpees to convert vague statements about themselves and their concerns into concrete expressions. This can prove revelatory for helpees, who are often unaware of the intensity or even the presence of some emotions associated with an event until called upon to verbalize them.

Self-disclosure involves judicious revelation of the helper's past or present situation as a means of communicating the helper's understanding of the helpees' concerns and offering reassurance about the helpee's ability to deal with his or her problems. There is often a danger, however, that through self-disclosure the helper may begin to focus on his or her needs rather than those of the helpee. As Gazda and his colleagues (1995) have noted, "When helper self-disclosure is premature or irrelevant to the helpee's problem, it tends to confuse the helpee or put the focus on the helper. The helper steals the spotlight" (p. 16). Self-disclosure, if used appropriately and timed sagaciously, can allow the helper to model attitudes and behaviors that helpees may find useful in changing their attitudes and behaviors.

Immediacy is a form of self-disclosure that deals with what is going on between the helper and the helpee at the present moment. Its principal value is to facilitate helpees' becoming more aware of their behaviors in the relationship and to help them bring out into the open unverbalized thoughts and feelings associated with the helper. This is a powerful tool, but only after a trusting relationship has been developed. If inappropriately timed, immediacy may frighten helpees and lead to premature termination of the relationship.

Finally, confrontation is viewed as an action tool that invites helpees to examine their behaviors and attitudes more carefully and to become aware of discrepancies between their feelings or words and their behavior. Confrontation assists helpees in coming to grips with the reality of their situation. To be effective, confrontation must be preceded by the establishment of a caring and trusting relationship. Corey (1991) asserts that confrontation is an invitation for helpees to look at the "discrepancies between [their] attitudes, thoughts, or behaviors. Confrontation that is done in a tentative (yet direct and honest) manner can be an extension of caring and respect for clients. It can encourage them to examine certain incongruities and to become aware of . . . ways that they might be blocking their personal strengths" (p. 90). It must be emphasized that confrontation can only be effective after helpers and helpees have established firm relationships committed to solving problems. If used prematurely, it can often be perceived by helpees as either an attack or a personal rejection, and it will usually lead to termination of the relationship without resolution of the problems.

A Model of the Helping Process

Carkhuff (1969) proposed a four-phase model of the helping process that, although somewhat oversimplified, has proven effective as the basis for the initial

FIGURE 16.1 CARKHUFF'S BASIC MODEL OF THE HELPING PROCESS.

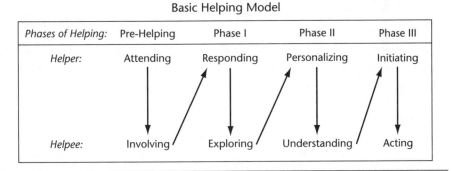

Basic Helping Model

Phases of Helping:	Pre-Helping	Phase I	Phase II	Phase III
Helper:	Attending	Responding	Personalizing	Initiating
Helpee:	Involving	Exploring	Understanding	Acting

Source: Anthony & Vitalo (1982, p. 70).

training of professional, paraprofessional, and allied professional counselors. (See Figure 16.1.)

In the initial phase, pre-helping, the helper attends to the helpee as she or he begins to talk about her or his concerns. The helper assumes a physical posture that reflects concentration on and concern for what the helpee is saying and feeling. The helper observes "the context, appearance, and behavior of the helpee for cues to the helpee's physical, emotional, and intellectual state" and listens for content, feeling, and meaning—the reason behind the helpee's feelings (Anthony & Vitalo, 1982, p. 70). This has the effect of involving helper and helpee in a mutual effort to deal with the helpee's concerns or problems, and it clearly communicates the helper's interest and desire to be of assistance.

Phase I calls for the helper to use responding skills to communicate to the helpee that he or she understands the content, feeling, and meaning of the helpee's message. The Carkhuff training model involves using the now-familiar "You feel _____ because _____" type of statement. This assists helpees in exploring themselves and their problems more fully. Often helpees develop important insights into themselves when they hear a concerned person orally expressing what they have been feeling but were either unaware of or unwilling to acknowledge. Responding can also help a troubled person discover feelings he or she has been attempting to suppress or deny.

Phase II is called personalizing. The helper attempts to hold the helpee directly accountable for her or his current state. Anthony and Vitalo (1982) explain that "personalizing the problem means developing the response deficit or vulnerability that the helpee experiences by making the helpee directly accountable for the problem he or she is having" (p. 72). Typical statements include "You

feel _____ because you _____" or "You feel _____ because you cannot
_____." For example, "You feel disappointed in yourself because you didn't
take preparing for the test seriously enough." This may be expanded to responses
such as, "You feel _____ because you cannot _____ and you want to _____."
For example, "You feel confused because you asked Mary for a date after she
seemed so friendly, and then she not only refused but put you down as well,
and you want to know why you misread her interest in you so badly." The
latter kind of response can be the transition from the helpee's understanding
his or her problem to an action phase in which the helpee begins to establish
goals and make plans for accomplishing them. As Anthony and Vitalo (1982) comment, "The ultimate test of the helper's personalizing skills is the level of self-
understanding the helpee achieves concerning what he or she wants to achieve
in the world" (p. 73).

Initiating, Phase III in the model, involves assisting the helpee to specify goals,
make plans for accomplishing them, and move toward action. The helper must
remain focused on the helpee's goals, not his or her own goals. The helper must
be aware that if the helpee's goals are to be accomplished, the helpee must "own"
them and approach accomplishing them in ways that fit his or her typical life pattern. The helper plays somewhat of a teacher's role; the helper must assist the
helpee to act in ways he or she feels most comfortable with, even if they are not
necessarily the most efficient methods available.

Most effective helpers possess the basic skills identified in this model, whether
or not they subscribe to it. Some people are somewhat offended by the use of for-
mulaic techniques such as "You feel _____ because _____" statements. One can
appreciate the importance and therapeutic benefits of establishing a relationship between the helper and the helpee, as Rogers advocates, without accepting
all the phenomenological baggage Rogers attaches to the process. Substantial
research documents the effectiveness of these types of models for teaching basic
helping skills (Carkhuff, 1969; Kasdorf & Gustafson, 1978; Lambert, 1982). I contend that basic helping skills are learned (through extensive practice accompanied
by critical feedback) and that student affairs practitioners need to master them
as part of their repertoire of essential student development and administrative-
management skills.

Application of Helping Skills

One of the essential tasks the allied professional counselor must accomplish when
dealing with issues or concerns that students have been unable to satisfactorily resolve is to determine the nature of the problems and whether the counselor can

(or should) offer assistance or whether different expertise is required. In other words, the counselor needs to make an assessment of the person, her or his situation or context, and the counselor's ability to deal with it.

Central to the process of making an assessment is how students' problems and concerns are conceptualized. As can be seen in Exhibit 16.1, students' concerns can be conceptualized as falling on a continuum, with one end anchored by "developmental" concerns and the other end by "remedial" concerns (Ender & Winston, 1982).

EXHIBIT 16.1. CONCEPTUALIZING STUDENTS' CONCERNS.

Range of Students' Concerns

Developmental Concerns	Unclear Concerns	Remedial Concerns
Characteristics or Cues	*Characteristics or Cues*	*Characteristics or Cues*
• Behavior or issues are predicted by developmental theory as appropriate to students' age, stage, or level.	• Problem appears to be a mixture of developmental and remedial concerns.	• Behavior is not consistent with developmental theory's projections for student of that stage, age, or educational level.
• Concern is directly or indirectly related to the present environment.	• Student is unable to identify source of problem or concern, which may be expressed as general dissatisfaction with life or the institution.	• Student is dysfunctional in meeting daily responsibilities.
• Problem is interpersonal or skill- or knowledge-oriented		• Problem is centered in past or basically unrelated to present environment and current experiences.
• Student is basically coping with the situation, though not to his or her satisfaction.	• Presenting problem is incongruent with level or intensity of emotion expressed or with nonverbal behavior.	• Concern is intrapersonal.
• Student is able and willing to initiate action.	• Student is unable to analyze own behavior realistically.	• Persistent pattern of self-defeating or self-destructive behavior is evident.
	• Student is unable to formulate realistic, coherent plans of action.	• Student indicates intention to do harm to self or others.
	• Student shows lack of motivation to address problems.	• Student reports persistent, chronic depression; anxiety; physical illness; pain; or discomfort or has experienced trauma.
	• Student blames others excessively.	• Student has highly unrealistic self-image or self-assessment.
	• Student pours out confused or rambling monologue.	

Source: Adapted from Ender & Winston (1982).

Developmental Concerns

Developmental concerns are the normal issues and problems encountered by basically effective people. They may be characterized by several of the following clues or characteristics:

1. *The problem is predicted by developmental theory as appropriate or expected for a student of a given age or educational level.* For instance, Shuronda, an entering freshman at a residential college, is homesick the first few days or weeks of the first term. She is experiencing appropriate feelings that are predicted by developmental theory and shared by many of her classmates.

2. *The problem is directly or indirectly related to the present environment.* The student has encountered a situation that requires new responses, and he or she is in the process of analyzing the situation and deciding upon or trying out new ways of coping or reacting. For example, Jacob, a sophomore who has not yet crystallized a decision about his academic specialization, is facing the college's requirement that he specify a major field of study. The environment has imposed a decision on him.

3. *The problem concerns interpersonal relationships or is caused by a skill or knowledge deficit.* Suppose Jill has difficulty mastering the content of a history course; her problem would be developmental in nature if it could be addressed by acquiring more information, spending more time on assignments, or acquiring new academic skills. Likewise, if the problem involves an interpersonal relationship (such as a marriage), it is not chronic, and it is centered around a particular issue or incident in the immediate or short-term past (perhaps a lack of time for proper housecleaning since resuming full-time study), then the concern would be classified as developmental.

4. *The student is basically coping with the situation, although not to his or her satisfaction.* Blocher (1987) describes coping as an individual's having control over large segments of his or her long-term transactions with his or her environment, although there may be a lack of satisfactory control over short-term transactions: "Behavior is purposeful and largely goal-oriented. . . . Problems and difficulties tend to be readily identifiable in terms of specific roles or relationships" (p. 155). For example, Juan is considering getting married, but his parents disapprove of his chosen mate and think he is too young. Juan can listen to his parents' concerns and appreciate their point of view while not allowing it to interfere with his meeting his academic demands or forcing him to terminate the relationship. Juan is torn between a desire to comply with his parents' wishes and a desire to be autonomous and to make his own decisions. While the situation is not comfortable,

Juan is able to cope as he searches for a solution. Juan's concern would be classi-fied as developmental. (Juan's concerns must also be understood within his spe-cific cultural context. Many Hispanic cultures emphasize the importance of maintaining close connections with one's family, which may mean that resisting parental wishes is more difficult for Juan than for a White student.)

5. *The student is able and willing to initiate action to deal with the problem.* The student recognizes the demands of her or his environment and is willing to face those demands by altering her or his behavior, seeking assistance from someone, or initiating a project on her or his own to deal with the situation. For example, Helen is having difficulty in an English course, even though she has used the same study techniques and routines she found effective in other English courses. She recognizes that she is not doing well and searches the environment for sources of help. A critical element that makes this a developmental concern is that she wants to take action; she is not attempting to deny the problem in the hope that it will disappear or seeking unproductive ways of reducing stress, such as cutting class.

Remedial Concerns

At the opposite end of the continuum from developmental concerns are remedial concerns. Characteristics or cues that help define or identify remedial concerns include the following:

1. *The student's behavior or reported feelings are inconsistent with the predictions of de-velopmental theory for a person of that age or educational experience.* For example, Bob, a graduate student, has been unable to establish a romantic relationship with any-one in either high school or college. Bob is not performing as developmental theory predicts for someone his age. His concerns are remedial in nature. (The same concerns encountered by a high school or college sophomore would proba-bly be regarded as developmental.)

2. *The student's behavior is basically dysfunctional, preventing her or him from perform-ing daily tasks.* Students who are unable to function well enough to eat regular meals, sleep at night, attend classes, and maintain personal hygiene are in a remedial con-dition. Often these dysfunctional behaviors have the obvious accompanying symp-tom (or cause) of excessive use of alcohol or other drugs. It is generally unwise, however, for an allied professional counselor to attempt a diagnosis of the causes of dysfunctional behavior patterns.

3. *The problem is centered in the past or is basically unrelated to the student's current en-vironment.* Students whose present unproductive behavior is an extension of past

dysfunctional behavior are operating in a remedial mode. For instance, Juanita's inability to establish close friendships predated her entry into college and is not a result of her college environment. Her problem is not simply having no close friends on campus this term; her problem establishing interpersonal relationships has a long history and is evidence of a persistent pattern of ineffective or self-defeating behavior.

4.   *The student reports persistent chronic depression, anxiety, illness, pain, or other discomfort that does not seem to have a medical explanation.* Students who hold highly unrealistic self-images or self-assessments often act in an erratic or alienating fashion that may be the result of developmental deficiencies or mental illness. Likewise, students who are frequently involved in acrimonious or hostile interactions (sometimes even physical assaults) with peers are operating in a remedial mode. Students who are addicted to alcohol or other drugs or who experience eating disorders such as bulimia or anorexia are dealing with remedial concerns that require the assistance of professionals skilled in the treatment of those specific illnesses. Students who have been attacked, sexually molested, or experienced other highly traumatic events generally require professional psychological services. These behaviors or events often cause significant disruption of the developmental pattern typical for most college students.

5.   *The student has a problem that is basically intrapersonal in nature.* A problem involving deep-seated internal conflicts that interfere with a student's ability to be purposeful in her or his behavior or to find personal satisfaction in any activity is indicative of a remedial condition. For example, long-standing feelings of inferiority, low self-esteem, and anxiety attacks fall into this category. Treatment of these kinds of problems are generally lengthy and require intensive therapy by highly skilled professionals.

6.   *The student reports an intention to harm others physically or threatens suicide.* These behaviors fall at the extreme remedial end of the continuum of concerns. Bernard and Bernard (1985) suggest a number of indicators that identify students with an increased likelihood of attempting suicide:

- A member of the student's family has attempted suicide.
- The student has made previous suicide attempts.
- The student has experienced the loss of a parent through death, divorce, or separation. Suicide is more likely if the loss led to destabilization of the family.
- The student reports feelings of being a burden, being useless, or being hopeless.
- The student has given away prized possessions or put her or his personal affairs in order. These behaviors are indicators of a suicidal orientation and are especially important if they occur after the loss of a loved one, a pet, or a job.
- The student has suffered a prolonged state of agitated depression.

Unclear Concerns

Many student concerns do not obviously fall at the extremes of the continuum; that is, they are not easily classified as developmental or remedial. When allied professional counselors listen to students talk about their concerns or problems, they typically hear a mixture of both remedial and developmental concerns and considerable confusion and ambiguity. Evidence that alerts the helper that a student's concerns are unclear include the following:

1. *The student is unable to identify the source of his or her concern.* That is, the student expresses a vague or pervasive dissatisfaction with life or the total educational experience, without providing any specifics.

2. *There is a lack of congruence between the presenting problem and the intensity of the student's emotions or nonverbal behavior.* For example, a student may complain about making a poor grade on a minor test while behaving in a highly emotionally disturbed manner—an obvious incongruence exists between the real importance of the concern and the level of emotion expressed.

3. *The student seems unable to analyze his or her own behavior realistically.* For example, Frank may complain about hallmates' being unfriendly, while he rejects invitations from hallmates to eat in the dining room or to engage in informal bull sessions. He is verbalizing one thing while behaving in a contrary fashion.

4. *The student shows a lack of motivation to address concerns or is unable to formulate realistic plans of action.* The student talks about his or her problems, but when encouraged to try various approaches to dealing with them, he or she seems reluctant to take action or makes excuses to justify inaction.

5. *The student blames others excessively.* That is, whatever the issue, the student finds that the responsibility belongs to someone else; it is never his or her own fault.

6. *The student cannot seem to get focused.* One of the most frequently encountered clues that a student's concerns are unclear (both to himself or herself and to the helper as well) are seemingly confused and rambling monologues that pour out a mass of issues, concerns, problems, fears, and seemingly irrelevant facts, accompanied by a relatively high level of emotion.

Assessing Students' Concerns

The allied professional counselor needs to assess the nature of students' concerns in order to formulate an appropriate response or plan of action. Blocher (1966) has cautioned, however, that assessment or diagnosis is most effective when it is continuous and tentative. Assessments must be frequently checked, revalidated, and revised as necessary. Blocher warns counselors to always view their assessments as hypothetical and therefore tentative. If the assessment of the student's concerns remains fixed and new observations are shut out, the counselor's responses may become increasingly inappropriate and can lead to premature termination of the relationship or inappropriate (unhelpful) action by the counselor.

Gazda et al. (1995) suggest that students come to helpers or counselors for four basic reasons: to request information, to request an appropriate action, to request an inappropriate action (or interaction), or for understanding and involvement.

The first, a request for information, is relatively simple. The helper provides the requested information or tells the student where it is available. The second request, for an appropriate action, is also relatively straightforward. The helper does what is requested. These two requests can be presented in less straightforward ways, however. For instance, students are sometimes embarrassed that they do not know something. Rather than simply ask for information, they hint around the subject in the hope that the helper will volunteer the information. The same is true of a request for action; students sometimes describe their needs to the helper rather than simply requesting assistance. For example, Kisha walks into her residence hall's office and begins talking about waiting for her roommate to return with her key to their room. She is describing her need to get into her room, in the hope that the helper will volunteer to unlock her door without her having to ask (and possibly be turned down or called irresponsible).

Sometimes students make a request for an inappropriate action. This may take a number of forms, from requests that the helper excuse them from a college requirement, overlook a rule, or solve their problems for them ("Please tell my mother the college requires me to stay here this weekend"). Helpers must discriminate between appropriate and inappropriate requests. When they encounter inappropriate requests, helpers must tactfully explain why the request is not appropriate while reassuring the student that the helper cares about her or his welfare. Refusal to do what is requested should not be equated with rejection of the person making the request. This distinction needs to be communicated clearly to the student, not just implied.

Finally, students often seek out allied professional counselors with requests for understanding and involvement. Sometimes this is explicit ("I have a problem that is really bothering me. Will you help me?"). More often, though, students approach their important concerns gradually, testing the helper's receptiveness and skill with "decoy" issues as they move closer to voicing their real concerns. For example, students often bring a "safe" problem to an allied professional helper, such as a simple request for information, as a means of establishing contact with the staff member and gauging his or her openness to helping, trustworthiness, and competence as a counselor. If they become convinced that the potential helper can handle their real issues, they then reveal their more significant concerns. The helper must first earn the right to be of assistance. The helper earns that right by communicating a willingness to become involved in the student's problems, by listening carefully to both the content of the student's "safe" issue and the tone of its communication, and by demonstrating an understanding and appreciation of the student's situation and perspectives.

Counseling Interventions

Once the allied professional counselor and the student have explored the student's concerns, the time arrives for action. Exhibit 16.2 summarizes possible actions that may be initiated, depending upon the assessed nature of the student's concerns and the skills and knowledge of the counselor or adviser.

EXHIBIT 16.2. CONCEPTUALIZING ADVISING AND COUNSELING INTERVENTIONS.

Range of Advising and Counseling Interventions

If Concern Is Developmental	If Nature of Concern Is Unclear	If Concern Is Remedial
• Assist in self-exploration.	• Act as a sounding board as a means of facilitating exploration of the concern.	• Show concern and willingness to listen.
• Explore alternatives.		• Explore alternatives for addressing concern.
• Assist in identifying desired goals.	• Respond to student in ways that communicate empathy, respect, genuineness, and concern.	• Describe available resources for dealing with concern.
• Assist in devising a plan of action to accomplish goals.		• Offer information and assistance in initiating contact with appropriate referral source.
• Identify resources and services.	• Encourage active problem solving.	
• Provide information.	• Confront student about incongruence between behavior or talk and actions.	• Offer encouragement and support.
• Teach specific strategies or techniques.		• If there appears to be danger to self or others, take extraordinary measures to assure that student receives assistance from appropriate professionals.
• Refer to established program especially designed to address issue.	• Decide whether concerns are basically developmental or remedial in nature and proceed appropriately.	
• Provide encouragement, reassurance, and support.		
• Provide positive feedback.		

Source: Adapted from Ender & Winston (1982).

If the student's concerns are basically developmental in nature, then the counselor should be able to offer a variety of helpful interventions. These include further self-exploration or exploration of the problem; identification of possible goals and alternative means of addressing them; identification of resources available on the campus or in the community; provision of information or identification of information sources on the campus; referral to agencies that have programs already established to address the student's concerns; providing encouragement, reassurance, and support; and teaching specific skills or strategies, which might range from simple study techniques to time-management strategies, goal-setting procedures, stress-reduction (relaxation) techniques, or social skills. These interventions may be offered informally, one-on-one, or through programs, such as intentionally structured groups (Winston, Bonney, Miller, & Dagley, 1988).

If the student's concerns are unclear, the allied professional counselor needs to act as a sounding board as a means of facilitating further exploration. This is done primarily by showing the student empathy, respect, and genuineness and demonstrating a commitment to helping the student clarify his or her situation. Encouraging the student to become active in the problem-solving process, expressing reassurance, and confronting incongruence (but only after a firm, trusting relationship has been established) may be appropriate strategies for helping the student clarify his or her issues and associated feelings. If applied with patience and sincerity, these techniques usually allow both the student and the helper to determine the nature of the concern—whether developmental or remedial. If the concern is developmental, the counselor may then adopt one or more of the interventions described above. If it is remedial in nature, the counselor has the responsibility to assist the student in contacting a campus or community agency that has the necessary resources and expertise. Once an assessment has revealed that a student's concerns are basically remedial in nature, the student should be assisted in getting help, not just told to "go see Dr. X" or "call Office Y for an appointment."

Career Counseling

Some student affairs professionals, for various reasons, have come to view career counseling as being fundamentally different from personal counseling. This is an artificial distinction that can lead to unfortunate consequences for those seeking help. The same counseling skills are required in dealing with career concerns as in addressing other areas of life. Another misconception sometimes associated with career counseling is the use of assessment instruments. Career counseling is seen primarily as the process of administering inventories to students and interpreting the results. This has led to the conception among some students that all that is required in making a career decision is to "take a test and find out what I'm supposed to be." As a consequence of this misinformed folklore, students often become disillusioned with their institution and its student affairs staff's ability or willingness to provide assistance.

Another danger in trying to separate career and personal counseling is the fact that one of the "safest" (and most socially acceptable among student peers) presenting problems for students is career indecision. If counselors fail to be sensitive to a student's total span of concerns, they may not allow the student to bring up issues that are emotionally more threatening to him or her. To assume that career decisions are in some way inherently different from other life decisions is to misunderstand both the content and the process of career development counseling.

As Super (1992) illustrates through the "arch of career determinates" (see Figure 16.2), career development—which is a lifelong process, not a single event—affects and is affected by the whole person and his or her environment. This model incorporates the biological bases of personality and physiology; specific aspects of the student's personality, such as needs, values, interests, intelligence, aptitudes, and special abilities; and the student's environment, including economic conditions, the social structure of the student's community, labor market demands for different occupations, and the student's family, school, and peer group. Super explains the arch this way:

> The arch at the top of the model is conceptually, as it is architecturally, the final product of the two columns. In it, the . . . interaction of the person and the environment help to shape the arch, first in the Developmental Stages (childhood and adolescence unlabelled at the left, adulthood and old age at the right, to suggest progression through the life span. . . .) The Self (the Person) and his or her Role Self-Concepts are the culminating products of the interaction of the person and of the environment: these are concepts of self as family member, as pupil and student, as athlete, as friend, as worker, etc. (Super, 1992, pp. 40–41)

As pointed out in Chapter Ten, students are called upon to achieve several developmental tasks during the "traditional" college years. The most important of these tasks include recognizing and accepting the need to make career decisions, becoming aware of interests and abilities, obtaining information about the world of work and how their personal interests and abilities relate to occupations, identifying possible fields and level of work consistent with their interests and abilities, and selecting and following through with educational programs that can lead to satisfying careers. For older students who are returning to college, these same developmental issues must be confronted. They generally have more life experiences to draw upon and a greater knowledge of the world of work than their

FIGURE 16.2. SUPER'S ARCH OF CAREER DETERMINANTS.

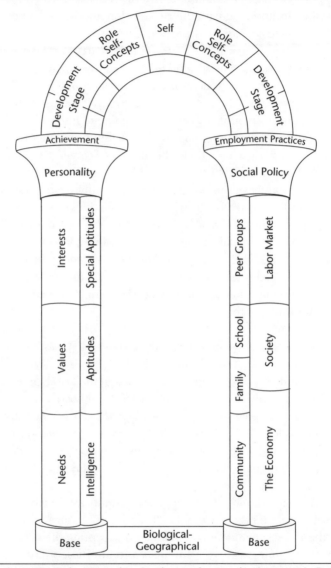

Source: D. E. Super. Toward a comprehensive theory of career development. In D. H. Montross, C. J. Shinkman, & Associates, *Career development: Theory and practice* (1992, pp. 35–64). Courtesy of Charles C Thomas, Publisher, Springfield, IL.

younger classmates, however. On the other hand, older students often feel compelled to complete their academic programs in the shortest period of time, which may preclude them from making careful and accurate assessments of their interests and abilities or from pursuing academic fields that do not seem to lead directly to post-college jobs.

Kinnier and Krumboltz (1984) suggest that there are six major obstacles to career fulfillment, and that the role of career counseling is to assist people in overcoming them. The obstacles are as follows:

- People acquire inaccurate information or maladaptive beliefs about themselves and the world. They often operate under presuppositions they have never examined.
- People are uncertain about their own priorities. They feel unclear or conflicted about what they really want to value.
- People are unaware of their own abilities and interests and how their skills and preferences are related to the occupational structure of society.
- Although a wealth of occupational information is available, people find it difficult to ask pertinent questions, to motivate themselves to find answers, to penetrate the overwhelming mass of material, and to distinguish biased information from facts.
- People generally do not have a systematic method for making career-related decisions. They often make decisions haphazardly.
- People find that obtaining a job is a lonely, frustrating task for which they are ill prepared (p. 311).

All of these obstacles fall at the developmental end of the continuum, and therefore they are issues that all student affairs professionals and academic advisers should be able to address. Rayman (1993) asserts that "a reasonable goal for the undergraduate curriculum might be sufficient self-understanding to provide a sense of direction and purpose in life" (p. 14). If this is accepted, then there is no question that all student affairs practitioners and academic advisers should possess the basic knowledge and skills needed to assist students in developing these important aspects of their lives. Almost all students can benefit from assistance in this area; consequently, no career services center can carry the responsibility alone. Much broader institutional involvement is required.

The use of personality, interests, and abilities inventories can help students get a better, more organized picture of themselves. It must be stressed, however, that they are not essential to career exploration. The danger is that students (and in some cases counselors) come to view these inventories as career counseling in and of themselves. These kinds of instruments only provide information—almost always information that the student already knows but may not have placed into a career context. The important task is to help the student integrate the information in a way that is useful for making career decisions and developing plans of action. Computer programs designed to bring together the various kinds of information generally needed in making career decisions are perhaps a step in the right direction, but many, if not most, students will benefit from additional exploration and opportunities to reflect about their decisions with a person who possesses good counseling skills.

Academic Advising

Many of the skills and competencies required of allied professional counselors are also needed by academic advisers, if the academic advising process is seen as consisting of more than completing class schedules and other administrative forms. Academic advising has received renewed attention since the 1980s, due in large measure to the increasing need to address student retention issues and the increasingly multicultural nature of many campuses. Academic advising is the single most frequently used strategy to increase student retention (Beal & Noel, 1980; Crockett, 1978, 1985; Forrest, 1985). Anderson (1985) has argued that one of the most powerful positive influences on student persistence in college is individual attention. He asserts that this attention can be expressed by helping students do the following:

- Identify and clarify their purposes for attending college
- Affirm themselves as persons who possess the potential to be successful
- Deal with anxiety and patterns of self-defeating behavior
- Find reinforcement of their determination to persist

Given the current organizational structures and political realities on most campuses, the academic advising process seems to be the only existing structure available to address these goals in a large-scale, systematic way.

Academic advising is "owned" by the academic sector in most institutions (especially four-year colleges and universities). Habley (1993) found that on the vast majority of the campuses he surveyed, academic advising is provided by faculty members. These faculty academic advisers were not critically selected (or not selected at all—everyone advised!), they received minimal (or no) training, and they were not systematically evaluated. Good performance generally went unrecognized and unrewarded. There continues to be some movement toward creating advising centers on campus (predominantly at public institutions) staffed totally, or in part, by personnel with educational preparation and experience as student development specialists. But there is a truism about academic advising that must be considered: no one but students cares about academic advising until someone shows an interest in making changes.

Nevertheless, academic advising can and should be viewed as a potent intervention for positively influencing students' educational and personal development (Ender, Winston, & Miller, 1982, 1984; Walsh, 1979). This kind of advising is sometimes called "developmental academic advising" to distinguish it from the mechanical, clerkish activities presently identified as academic advising on many campuses. Developmental academic advising is defined as "a systematic process based on a close student-adviser relationship intended to aid students in achieving educational, career, and personal goals through the utilization of the full range of institutional and community resources. It both stimulates and supports students in their quest for an enriched quality of life. . . . Developmental advising relationships focus on identifying and accomplishing life goals, acquiring skills and attitudes that promote intellectual and personal growth, and sharing concerns for each other and for the academic community" (Ender, Winston, & Miller, 1984, pp. 18–19). The goals of developmental academic advising are indistinguishable from the goals of most progressive student affairs divisions. For these goals to be realized, however, active collaboration between academic affairs and student affairs is required; neither can accomplish these goals alone (Frost, 1991; Grites, 1979; Winston, Grites, Miller, & Ender, 1984).

Ender, Winston, and Miller (1984) proposed seven conditions or principles essential to the process of developmental academic advising:

- Advising is a continuous process, with an accumulation of personal contacts that have a synergistic effect.
- Advising must concern itself with quality-of-life issues; the adviser's responsibility includes attention to the student's total experience in the institution.
- Advising is goal-related; that is, the advising process should include identification of academic, career, and personal goals as they relate to the college environment.
- Advising requires the establishment of a caring relationship. The adviser has the primary responsibility for initiating this relationship—good academic advising is intrusive.
- Advisers are models for students.
- Advising is a focal point for the integration of the services and expertise of both academic and student affairs professionals.
- Advisers should encourage students to utilize the full range of resources, services, and learning opportunities available within their institution.

As Creamer and Creamer (1994) conceptualize the developmental advising process, three distinct activities are involved: defining the task, identifying outcomes, and promoting development. The task of developmental academic advising is to communicate to students a vision of the purpose of higher education through the use of "interactive teaching, counseling, and administrative strategies" that assist students in achieving specific learning, developmental, career, and life goals (p. 19). Reasonable expectations for the outcomes of developmental advising include "setting career and life goals, building self-insight and esteem, broadening interests, establishing meaningful interpersonal relationships, clarifying personal values and styles of life, and enhancing critical thinking and reasoning" (p. 20). Advisers must be proactive in their interactions with students if they want to promote students' individual development. For instance, to help students broaden their interests, advisers might encourage students to interview successful people about their nonwork activities or to participate in new activities and events (for example, attending an opera, joining a volunteer service organization, or seeking an appointment to a faculty governance committee).

Unfortunately, on many campuses the focus is often on who provides advising (and therefore who has control of it) rather than on what goes on in advising or how effectively it addresses the needs and concerns of students. Some advocates of developmental advising have met resistance from academicians who charge that they are attempting to turn advising into counseling or psychotherapy. This is untrue (or at least it should be). Academic advising is not and should not be viewed as "counseling," although as argued previously, effective academic advisers are called upon to use counseling skills and techniques in their interactions with students.

Minimum Skills and Knowledge Required of Counselors and Advisers

If we change our focus from who advises and look instead at the skills, knowledge, and competencies developmental advisers need, there is considerable overlap with those needed by allied professional counselors. Identified below are the minimum skills and knowledge that both allied professional counselors and academic advisers need.

Counselors and advisers need a clear understanding of their institution's philosophy and mission and should be able to articulate it to students. Advisers and counselors should educate students about the opportunities available in the collegiate environment and should promote the ideal of an educated person. They have the responsibility to encourage and assist students in making personal meaning of their educational experiences.

Both counselors and advisers need a working knowledge of college student development theories. They need to understand both themselves and the students they work with as developing persons (Thomas & Chickering, 1984). They must know what is theoretically expected of a person of a particular age and educational experience. It is particularly important that counselors and advisers be able to classify behavior patterns within a theoretical framework.

Advisers and counselors need to understand the student population they work with. As Wright (1987) has pointed out, most theories of student development have not taken adequate notice of the environments many minority students come from and the unique forces that influence their development. Likewise, many theorists—for example, Gilligan (1982), Straub and Rodgers (1986), Straub (1987), Chickering and Reisser (1993), Baxter Magolda (1992), Josselson (1992), and Belenky, Clinchy, Goldberger, and Tarule (1986)—have demonstrated that women have a unique perspective and their development is not identical to that of men. Chickering and Havighurst (1981), Schlossberg (1984, 1989), and Schlossberg, Lynch, and Chickering (1989) have pointed out the importance of understanding the returning adult student as well. These differences need to be understood by counselors and advisers alike.

Students have a right to expect both counselors and advisers to be knowledgeable about the institution's rules, regulations, and policies. From a student's point of view, the only thing worse than not knowing something is being given incorrect information. Even in small institutions, remaining informed and current is a task that requires constant attention. Conscious effort must be directed at seeking out information; it is very easy to assume that nothing outside of one's own department changes.

Advisers and allied professional counselors should not be expected to be measurement experts. They do need to have a command of informal assessment techniques, though, to help them make decisions about whether to address a student's concern directly or make a referral. They should also be intelligent users of standardized assessment information. For example, advisers should understand and be able to interpret for students academic measures such as SAT and ACT scores and scores on any other achievement or placement tests used by their institution.

Both advisers and counselors need to understand the basics of creating a helping relationship, as described previously. Most professionals cannot predict or choose when they will be called upon to be a helper; opportunities are presented daily.

Counselors and advisers can provide valuable services by helping students identify their needs, offering support in addressing them, and making effective referrals to the appropriate campus or community services or programs. Most institutions have many potentially effective programs to assist students that are underutilized because students are simply unaware of them or are reluctant to contact them due to misconceptions about their services or resources or fear of being stigmatized ("only dumb or sick people go there").

Counselors and advisers need a repertoire of interventions appropriate to their functions. Advisers should be able to assist students who are having nonchronic problems managing their time, choosing a major, or employing effective study techniques, for example. Counselors should be able to help students overcome nonchronic problems related to stress and anxiety, for example, or interpersonal relationships with peers, parents, and authority figures. Both counselors and advisers need to be knowledgeable about the career development process and skilled in helping students initiate activities that can lead to satisfying academic and career decisions.

Ethical Issues and Factors That Affect the Helping Relationship

As Marylu McEwen pointed out in Chapter Eight, many current developmental theories display a White male bias, either from using White males as research subjects or from inadvertently incorporating a White male perspective in interpretations of data. As student bodies have become more diverse, the student affairs profession has become more aware of different perspectives on development. McEwen's chapter on new perspectives (Chapter Ten) discusses numerous factors that can significantly influence the course of student development. Of particular importance are the factors of gender, ethnicity, age, and sexual orientation.

Student affairs practitioners and academic advisers who act as counselors outside of designated counseling, career, and mental health centers on campus encounter several troubling, practical ethical problems. Particularly important are issues related to confidentiality and determination of competence. The American College Personnel Association's "Statement of Ethical Principles and Standards" (1993, p. 91) specifies that students should be informed about the limits placed on confidentiality. A problem often arises, however, in the way students approach staff for help—they often initially present a problem that does not appear to have confidentiality implications. But as discussed above, once a relationship is established, students sometimes make radical, unanticipated shifts in the content of their concerns, placing the student affairs practitioner in a vulnerable position. For example, the student may acknowledge having violated institutional rules (or even committed a serious criminal act) that the staff member has been charged by the institution to enforce.

Another major ethical issue centers around the helper's competence. It is not uncommon for lonely, socially isolated students to "latch on" to a staff member, especially in residence halls, and consume many hours talking about their feelings of alienation, rejection, and isolation. They often resist initiating action to change their situation and refuse referral to other agencies. The allied professional counselor or academic adviser may feel that such a student has a definite remedial concern and that his or her counseling competence is not adequate to address the student's problems. But what is the staff member to do when the student refuses referrals and continues to "hang around" the staff member's office or living quarters?

Academic advisers who also teach often encounter thorny ethical issues. For example, in the course of advising a student on academic matters, an adviser may learn of the student's personal problems or certain academic irregularities; this can cause conflict for the adviser when he or she is called upon as a teacher to evaluate that student's work. Adviser-teachers may become caught in such a conflict of roles before they can take action to avoid it. Similar problems can be encountered by student affairs practitioners who teach courses to the student paraprofessionals they supervise.

These problems do not have simple answers. Staff members who have frequent and informal daily contact with students (especially in residence halls, student organizations, student unions, or academic classes and advising sessions) should make a point of specifying in group presentations the limits to the confidentiality students can expect and the scope of actions and responsibilities that are relevant to the particular roles they play. Allied professional counselors and advisers should seek consultation with mental health professionals and with their supervisors when they encounter problems. Alerting students to the limits of action and confidentiality inherent in their professional position is an important first step. This ideal is often difficult to realize, however, given the pressures of time and the peripatetic way students often choose to initiate counseling relationships.

Conclusion

Despite the fact that the student affairs field requires specialized education, has minimum standards for entry, and is recognized as a specialty in higher education, we will have difficulty defending it as a profession unless we can demonstrate that student affairs practitioners contribute directly to the education and personal enrichment of students. Well-developed skills and extensive knowledge in counseling and advising are essential tools in student affairs professionals' repertoire of responses and interventions, no matter what their primary position or responsibilities.

These skills require development and constant attention. Although some people possess "natural helping skills," they are seldom sufficient to adequately meet the myriad legitimate concerns college students face today. Students have a right to expect expert assistance and support in addressing these concerns. Only through extensive formal education or training and supervised practice followed by periodic evaluation and feedback can student affairs professionals hope to maintain effective counseling and advising skills and keep current on innovations and new information.

References

American College Personnel Association. (1993). Statement of ethical principles and standards. *Journal of College Student Development, 34*, 89–92.

Anderson, E. C. (1985). Forces influencing student persistence and achievement. In L. Noel, R. Levitz, D. Saluri, & Associates, *Increasing student retention: Effective programs and practices for reducing the dropout rate* (pp. 44–61). San Francisco: Jossey-Bass.

Anthony, W. A., & Vitalo, R. L. (1982). Human resource development model. In E. K. Marshall, P. D. Kurtz, & Associates, *Interpersonal helping skills: A guide to training methods, programs, and resources* (pp. 59–92). San Francisco: Jossey-Bass.

Baxter Magolda, M. B. (1992). *Knowing and reasoning in college: Gender-related patterns in students' intellectual development.* San Francisco: Jossey-Bass.

Beal, P. E., & Noel, L. (1980). *What works in student retention.* Iowa City, IA: American College Testing Program.

Belenky, M. F., Clinchy, B. M., Goldberger, N. R., & Tarule, J. M. (1986). *Women's ways of knowing: The development of self, voice, and mind.* New York: Basic Books.

Bernard, M. L., & Bernard, M. L. (1985). Suicide on campus: Response to the problem. In E. S. Zinner (Ed.), *Coping with death on campus* (New Directions for Student Services No. 31, pp. 69–83). San Francisco: Jossey-Bass.

Blake, R. R., Mouton, J. S., & Williams, M. S. (1981). *The academic administrator grid: A guide to developing effective management teams.* San Francisco: Jossey-Bass.

Blocher, D. H. (1966). *Developmental counseling.* New York: Ronald Press.

Blocher, D. H. (1987). *The professional counselor.* New York: Macmillan.

Block, P. (1987). *The empowered manager: Positive political skills at work.* San Francisco: Jossey-Bass.

Branner, L. M., & Shostrom, E. L. (1982). *Therapeutic psychology: Fundamentals of counseling and psychotherapy* (4th ed.). Englewood Cliffs, NJ: Prentice Hall.

Carkhuff, R. R. (1969). *Helping and human relations: A primer for lay and professional helpers* (2 vols.). New York: Holt, Rinehart and Winston.

Chickering, A. W., & Havighurst, R. J. (1981). The life cycle. In A. W. Chickering & Associates, *The modern American college: Responding to the new realities of diverse students and a changing society.* San Francisco: Jossey-Bass.

Chickering, A. W., & Reisser, L. (1993). *Education and identity* (2nd ed.). San Francisco: Jossey-Bass.

Corey, G. (1991). *Theory and practice in counseling and psychotherapy* (4th ed.). Monterey, CA: Brooks/Cole.

Creamer, D. G., & Creamer, E. G. (1994). Practicing developmental advising: Theoretical contexts and functional application. *NACADA Journal, 14*(2), 17–24.

Crockett, D. S. (1978). Academic advising: Cornerstone of student retention. In L. Noel (Ed.), *Reducing the dropout rate* (New Directions for Student Services No. 3, pp. 29–35). San Francisco: Jossey-Bass.

Crockett, D. S. (1985). Academic advising. In L. Noel, R. Levitz, D. Saluri, & Associates, *Increasing student retention: Effective programs and practices for reducing the dropout rate* (pp. 244–263). San Francisco: Jossey-Bass.

Delworth, U., & Aulepp, L. (1976). *Training manual for paraprofessionals and allied professionals programs.* Boulder, CO: Western Interstate Commission for Higher Education.

Egan, G. (1990). *The skilled helper: A systematic approach to effective helping* (4th ed.). Monterey, CA: Brooks/Cole.

Ender, S. C., & Winston, R. B., Jr. (1982). Training allied professional academic advisers. In R. B. Winston, Jr., S. C. Ender, & T. K. Miller (Eds.), *Developmental approaches to academic advising* (New Directions for Student Services No. 17, pp. 85–103). San Francisco: Jossey-Bass.

Ender, S. C., Winston, R. B., Jr., & Miller, T. K. (1982). Academic advising as student development. In R. B. Winston, Jr., S. C. Ender, & T. K. Miller (Eds.), *Developmental approaches to academic advising* (New Directions for Student Services No. 17, pp. 3–18). San Francisco: Jossey-Bass.

Ender, S. C., Winston, R. B., Jr., & Miller, T. K. (1984). Academic advising reconsidered. In R. B. Winston, Jr., T. K. Miller, S. C. Ender, T. J. Grites, & Associates, *Developmental academic advising: Addressing students' educational, career, and personal needs* (pp. 3–34). San Francisco: Jossey-Bass.

Forrest, A. (1985). Creating conditions for student and institutional success. In L. Noel, R. Levitz, D. Saluri, & Associates, *Increasing student retention: Effective programs and practices for reducing the dropout rate* (pp. 62–77). San Francisco: Jossey-Bass.

Frost, S. H. (1991). *Academic advising for student success: A system of shared responsibility.* Washington, DC: Clearinghouse on Higher Education and Association for the Study of Higher Education.

Gazda, G. M., Asbury, F. R., Balzer, F. J., Childers, W. C., Phelps, R. E., & Walters, R. P. (1995). *Human relations development: A manual for educators* (5th ed.). Boston: Allyn & Bacon.

Gilligan, C. (1982). *In a different voice: Psychological theory and women's development.* Cambridge, MA: Harvard University Press.

Grites, T. J. (1979). *Academic advising: Getting us through the eighties.* Washington, DC: American Association for Higher Education, Educational Resource Information Center (AAHE-ERIC).

Habley, W. R. (1993). *Fulfilling the promise?: Final report, ACT fourth national survey of academic advising.* Iowa City, IA: American College Testing Program.

Hersey, P., & Blanchard, K. H. (1993). *Management of organizational behavior: Utilizing human resources* (4th ed.). Englewood Cliffs, NJ: Prentice Hall.

Ivey, A. E., & Authier, J. (Eds.). (1978). *Microcounseling: Innovations in interviewing, counseling, psychotherapy, and psychoeducation* (2nd ed.). Springfield, IL: Thomas.

Josselson, R. (1992). *The space between us: Exploring the dimensions of human relationships.* San Francisco: Jossey-Bass.

Kasdorf, J., & Gustafson, K. (1978). Research related to microtraining. In A. E. Ivey & J. Authier (Eds.), *Microcounseling: Innovations in interviewing, counseling, psychotherapy, and psychoeducation* (2nd ed., pp. 323–376). Springfield, IL: Thomas.

Kinnier, R. T., & Krumboltz, J. D. (1984). Procedures for successful career counseling. In N. C. Gysbers & Associates, *Designing careers: Counseling to enhance education, work, and leisure* (pp. 307–335). San Francisco: Jossey-Bass.

Lambert, M. J. (1982). Relations of helping skills to treatment outcome. In E. K. Marshall, P. D. Kurtz, & Associates, *Interpersonal helping skills: A guide to training methods, programs, and resources* (pp. 26–58). San Francisco: Jossey-Bass.

Rayman, J. R. (1993). Contemporary career services: Theory defines practices. In J. R. Rayman (Ed.), *The changing role of career services* (New Directions for Student Services No. 62, pp. 3–21). San Francisco: Jossey-Bass.

Rogers, C. R. (1957). The necessary and sufficient conditions of therapeutic personality change. *Journal of Consulting Psychology, 21,* 95–103.

Rogers, C. R. (1961). *On becoming a person.* Boston: Houghton Mifflin.

Rogers, C. R. (1967). *Person to person: The problem of being human.* New York: Pocket Books.

Schlossberg, N. K. (1984). *Counseling adults in transition.* New York: Springer.

Schlossberg, N. K. (1989). *Overwhelmed: Coping with life's ups and downs.* Lexington, MA: Lexington Books.

Schlossberg, N. K., Lynch, A. Q., & Chickering, A. W. (1989). *Improving higher education environments for adults: Responsive programs and services from entry to departure.* San Francisco: Jossey-Bass.

Straub, C. A. (1987). Women's development of autonomy and Chickering's theory. *Journal of College Student Personnel, 28,* 198–205.

Straub, C. A., & Rodgers, R. F. (1986). An exploration of Chickering's theory and women's development. *Journal of College Student Personnel, 27,* 216–224.

Super, D. E. (1992). Toward a comprehensive theory of career development. In D. H. Montross, C. J. Shinkman, & Associates, *Career development: Theory and practice* (pp. 35–64). Springfield, IL: Thomas.

Thomas, R. E., & Chickering, A. W. (1984). Foundations for academic advising. In R. B. Winston, Jr., T. K. Miller, S. C. Ender, T. J. Grites, & Associates, *Developmental academic advising: Addressing students' educational, career, and personal needs* (pp. 89–118). San Francisco: Jossey-Bass.

Walsh, E. M. (1979). Revitalizing academic advisement. *Personnel and Guidance Journal, 57,* 446–449.

Williamson, E. G. (1939). *How to counsel students: A manual of techniques for clinical counselors.* New York: McGraw-Hill.

Winston, R. B., Jr., Bonney, W. C., Miller, T. K., & Dagley, J. C. (1988). *Promoting student development through intentionally structured groups: Principles, techniques, and applications.* San Francisco: Jossey-Bass.

Winston, R. B., Jr., Grites, T. J., Miller, T. K., & Ender, S. C. (1984). Improving academic advising. In R. B. Winston, Jr., T. K. Miller, S. C. Ender, T. J. Grites, & Associates, *Developmental academic advising: Addressing students' educational, career, and personal needs* (pp. 538–550). San Francisco: Jossey-Bass.

Wrenn, C. G. (1951). *Student personnel work in college: With emphasis on counseling and group experiences.* New York: Ronald Press.

Wright, D. J. (1987). Minority students: Developmental beginnings. In D. J. Wright (Ed.), *Responding to the needs of today's minority students* (New Directions for Student Services No. 38, pp. 5–22). San Francisco: Jossey-Bass.

CHAPTER SEVENTEEN

CONSULTATION AND MEDIATION

Clyde A. Crego

The idea that student affairs practitioners can and should play multiple professional roles has received increasing attention in recent years. While multiple roles have long been a core element of the profession, student affairs specialists have traditionally been restricted to roles such as organizational adviser, career planner, mental health counselor, and judicial affairs officer. As the profession has become more sophisticated, however, campus personnel have acknowledged that a wider array of student needs may be met when student affairs professionals expand into new arenas, including consultation and mediation.

This chapter describes new roles for the student affairs professional that involve the systematic use of consultation and mediation skills and processes. Improving student environments through mediation and consultation promotes organizational health and removes roadblocks to effective functioning for both individuals and groups (Caplan, Caplan, & Erchul, in press). Consultation, conflict resolution, and mediation all represent important skill areas that student affairs professionals should acquire to significantly expand the scope and influence of their work. Three types of consultation are discussed here: expert, process, and collaborative. Mediation is both a process and a skill; mediation skills are presented here for use in limited situations. Conflict resolution is addressed in the descriptions of both consultation and mediation. Examples of both consultation and mediation are given, and issues concerning the development of specific skills are addressed.

Consultation is a specialized professional service, typically provided by experts who offer specific knowledge and advice to groups and individuals or employ special processes to assist groups in problem solving, program development, or organizational development. Consultants are not usually members of the same organization as the people they serve, but in the higher education setting they may in fact be peers or colleagues with different areas of responsibility and expertise (Gallessich, 1982). Consultation has sometimes been described as an "indirect" service, insofar as it frequently has an impact on third parties with whom the consultant has no contact.

Conflict resolution refers to the use of specific techniques by an outside professional employed to assist individuals or groups settle disputes that are not easily resolved independently. Mediation refers to the formal use of certain conflict resolution techniques. An outside mediator follows established, step-by-step procedures to guide disputants toward a settlement or a reduction in their conflict.

The Need for Expanded Roles

Increasingly, colleges and universities are engaging in the kind of organizational development that requires the intervention of human services specialists in order to enhance the functioning of their various constituents and improve their effectiveness in dealing with diverse other organizations. Today's complex collegiate culture ensures that the multiple academic interests of divergent groups will occasionally come into conflict at the personal or group level. Sometimes units hoping to creatively expand their programming are blocked by organizational or bureaucratic constraints. Student affairs professionals are increasingly seen as the best-equipped actors on campus to address such issues.

Evolving Roles for the Student Affairs Professional

Student affairs staff possess knowledge about students and student life that is difficult to apply across the campus environment in an organized or sustained fashion. This is often due to a lack of organizational processes for sharing knowledge in ways that can enhance problem solving, understanding of critical issues, program development, and skill development. Too often, professionals are timid about extending their knowledge or skills to others on campus, or they may resist doing so in order to retain unique functions that they perceive to be theirs alone. For example, counseling was often regarded in the past to be the province only of highly trained mental health professionals. Paraprofessional training programs developed in the 1960s and 1970s "gave away" a great deal of these professionals' knowledge and skills; as a result, counseling services are now available on a much wider scale on American campuses. Paraprofessional training programs were developed utilizing a consultation model and team approach; they are an early example of a highly organized, planned approach to expanding campus services (D'Andrea & Salovey, 1983). The concept of promoting human welfare by training others was described in the major work of Miller (1969).

As stated, organizational intervention approaches have been increasingly applied to various campus conflicts, including both intergroup and intragroup disputes. Conflict resolution skills and mediation skills are often combined with or embedded within consultation approaches. These skills have proven effective on college campuses (Crego, 1990; Gallessich, 1982). As other authors in this text have noted, current concerns over campus climate demand that student affairs professionals possess the necessary skills to readily address multiple problems, such as those that may occur when increased diversity on campus leads to clashes between various individuals or groups.

Student development theory and research, as well as hands-on experience with college students who have learned to solve problems before they escalate, have combined to create a strong interest in preventive approaches to conflict resolution. College students have long been seen to benefit from programs that take a preventive approach. Consultation with faculty, staff, and student groups can provide a framework for identifying problems early on; such consultation has been shown to be highly effective at blocking problems and providing the target group with skills for use in future problem solving. A highly refined model of primary prevention is offered by Caplan, Caplan, and Erchul (1994).

Historically, formal consultation on college campuses was offered by innovative counseling centers. Most of this consultation was in the area of mental health, on a case-by-case basis. The highly innovative, foundational work of Gerald Caplan (1970) provided much of the framework for these efforts. Organizational intervention approaches were tried much later, using models such as Schein's (1989) process consultation approach. Academic degree programs have historically offered insufficient training in consultation and mediation skills outside the discipline of industrial psychology. Nonetheless, developments in other areas, such as program development, campus ecology, and strategic planning, have created avenues for applied consultation on campus, resulting in the development of campus-based consulting techniques based on sound academic and professional practices (Keller, 1983; Morrill, Hurst, & Oetting, 1980; Oetting, 1980).

Increasingly, student needs are understood to interact with complex social and organizational systems that shape, limit, or enhance student development and learning. As noted in Chapter Twelve, the environmental perspectives in the work of Banning (1989; Banning & Kaiser, 1974), Conyne (1975, 1979), and Caplan and Caplan (1992) have had a significant impact on the field of student development in general and counseling psychology in particular. Applications of such approaches to understanding human behavior in complex human and institutional systems have yielded remarkable insights into the causes of student stress, for instance, and in designing programs to reduce it. The seminal work of Huebner (1979) provides an excellent example of this type of approach, which relies on consultation for proposing changes based on environmental assessments and campus redesign.

Consultation as a professional practice derives not only from the highly developed work of mental health counseling but also from the fields of systems applications and organizational development, which include personal development in their various models. Systems-oriented student development theorists who effectively test and apply their theories clearly understand this, whether they employ "personal fit" models of organizational dynamics or other models (Hurst, 1987). Conflict and other interpersonal differences that lend themselves to mediation illustrate some of these dynamics at the personal level.

Thus student affairs professionals' opportunity to have a wider impact across campus domains has grown due to their developing roles in areas such as consultation and mediation. In addition to specific training in consultation and mediation, skills needed by student affairs professionals include knowledge acquisition and knowledge application skills, basic counseling skills, program development skills, program evaluation skills, and critical thinking skills. For the serious student of consultation, knowledge about the principles of organizational development should be acquired. For the serious student of mediation, specific knowledge about the stages of mediation is essential, in addition to techniques for guiding clients toward convergent problem solving.

Consultation

There are various different models of consultation; they vary in their usefulness for student affairs staff and in the degree of training and experience needed to employ them effectively. Organizational development consultation, for instance, requires formal training in specific skills and knowledge areas, including assessment. The most salient models employed in campus-based consultation are the expert consultation model, the process consultation model, and the collaborative consultation model (which often includes elements of both the expert and the process models).

Substantive Approaches to Consultation

In addition to mental health consultation (Caplan, 1970; Gallessich, 1982), the types of consultations traditionally conducted by student affairs professionals typically include educational, research, and program development approaches. Educational approaches may be based on prior consultation and may involve the delivery of psychoeducational information to groups at the request of student government officers. Research consultation tracks student needs, characteristics, or behavior patterns based on studies conducted by institutional researchers. Program development approaches involve student affairs professionals in the design of specialized learning programs or student life programs, such as special programs for adult learners with disabilities, that require the input and involvement of a spectrum of campus personnel.

Distinguishing characteristics of the student affairs professional's role as a consultant most often include either specialized expertise or unique process consultation skills. Student affairs professionals provide specialized expertise when they apply their professional knowledge or use the resources of their office to solve a problem or provide desired information (for example, informing faculty advisers about the high school preparation patterns of newly admitted students). Process consultation provides a framework for training campus personnel in problem analysis and problem solving and for helping them use their own resources to benefit from such training (Schein, 1988). This section expands upon these traditional consulting roles.

Expert Consultation

Providing expert knowledge to persons who need and can benefit from it in their work with students is often accomplished via a consultative relationship. The role of the expert consultant requires the ability to address how consultees will best assimilate and employ such knowledge. Principles of knowledge acquisition and knowledge application come into play here and must be understood by the student affairs professional entering into an expert consultant role with campus colleagues. For example, test officers who accumulate vast arrays of data for specific academic departments frequently must abandon their consultant role when they fail to introduce a process for helping concerned faculty or academic administrators learn how to interpret the data or decide how to implement needed changes (such as program adjustments). Expert consultation involves learning a set of skills that will help consultees use both the process and the product of the consultation.

Providing research or technical assistance to campus personnel responsible for planning campus programs has been the most prominent use of the expert model of consultation by student affairs professionals.

The expert model also requires (1) knowledge of good teaching principles, for use in presenting information or advice to groups or individuals; (2) the ability to assess how information is being received; and (3) assessment skills, to be used when a problem analysis is sought from consultees. For instance, a faculty development office wishing to help faculty and academic administrators deal with disruptive students may seek expert consultation from the campus judicial affairs office. Effective consultation would require that an appraisal be made about what input is most needed by that office, what form the input should take, and what processes should be developed to permit continuing consultation (for example, after a faculty development workshop in which faculty learn how to confront disruptive students).

Collaborative Consultation

One of the most effective forms of consultation used by student affairs professionals is consultation based on collaboration (Caplan, Caplan & Erchul, 1994). Collaborative consultation usually involves using both the process and the expert models of consultation, in addition to a unique, team-based model that is particularly appropriate for campus-based consultation.

Unlike traditional models of consultation, in which the consultant typically comes from outside the organization, campus-based consultation usually employs members of the same organization. In a hierarchical organization consultees are often not free to accept or reject the internal consultant's advice, as they are in the external expert model of consultation. In the collaborative approach, the specialist-collaborator is an active team member; he or she is held jointly accountable for the outcomes of the consultation and assists in making the administrative changes necessary to implement the suggested improvements. This approach is somewhat suggestive of the campus "change teams" concept described by Schlossberg, Lynch, and Chickering (1989). Frequently, programming within student affairs involves the formation of a consultative team approach for designing and implementing new initiatives such as mentor programs for targeted undergraduate students.

At a time when unbounded (cross-departmental) relationships between various members of the college or university community may yield the most effective, if not creative, programs to deal with the extraordinary changes occurring in higher education, it appears that mutual consultation approaches based on a high degree of planned collaboration have great potential. The traditional boundaries between departments, institutional divisions (such as academic affairs versus student affairs), and roles (such as counselor, psychologist, career counselor, and residence hall counselor) often promote roadblocks that frustrate changes in institutional practices—changes that might otherwise yield new programs for enhancing student life and academic success or strengthen existing programs. Campus units that do not understand or cooperate with a collaborative approach or that do not know how to utilize consultation or expert assistance may unintentionally expose students to conflict with other parts of the institution. For instance, residence life programs that operate in total isolation from the remainder of student affairs may actually cause harm to student program recipients (Caplan, Caplan, & Erchul, 1994).

Unlike other forms of consultation, in which the consultant typically does not interact with students directly (direct services), the collaborative approach may involve both direct and indirect services.. As an example, career center staff consulting with residence life staff to develop residence hall–based career exploration activities may also function as direct providers in the delivery and subsequent evaluation of those activities as part of the collaboration.

Collaborative consultation also acknowledges role and possible status differences within an organization and the possibility of a hierarchical relationship (Caplan, Caplan, & Erchul, 1994). Collaborative consultation arrangements assume voluntary participation but permit the possibility of forced participation. The director of a collaborating unit in student affairs may require certain staff to participate in a team-based planning group that is designing a campuswide disaster-response plan; the plan would become operational in a campus disaster such as an earthquake.

In the collaborative model, consultees are less free to reject consultant advice. Consultants are viewed as specialists when they are selected for a collaborative consultation team, and they are usually deferred to as experts. Nevertheless, all team members share responsibility for the outcome of plans developed in collaborative consultations.

The choice of consultation model is important. Student affairs professionals possess knowledge about student life, student characteristics, student needs, and student behavior that can be invaluable in the planning or modification of campus programs. Frequently a consulting expert in student affairs is approached for information or advice without being informed of what the information will be used for. When asked to provide expert consultations, including diagnostic advice on how to improve a program, it is tempting to simply respond to each request without clarifying the factors that have prompted the call for aid. Consulting professionals in this situation may want to inquire into the reasons for the consultation and ask how the information, advice, or input will be used; whom it will affect and for how long; and how the changes that result will be monitored. Based upon the answers to these questions, the expert consultant may want to redefine the nature of the consulting relationship; perhaps a more collaborative role is warranted. Since almost all consulting provided by student affairs professionals is delivered in-house, shifting to a collaborative role is often warranted, especially when the consultant is able to successfully move the consultee toward a shared-venture approach. Many process consultations and collaborative consultations begin in this way.

Consider the following example of shifting consultation models. A health services office seeks information from the campus counseling center about referring suicidal and HIV-positive clients for professional counseling. In beginning to discuss the question, consulting counseling staff ask questions to determine what prompted the request. It is learned that the incidence of student disclosure of these problems to campus physicians has suddenly increased; physicians are expressing a strong concern that changes in student stress levels and sexual practices may have precipitated the rise. The discussion moves to a shared dialogue regarding mutual, interdepartmental observations of student behavior. Suggestions are made by all concerned to seek additional input, such as from the women's center. Some beginning mutual problem solving has occurred concerning how to educate students about early problem identification; this leads to a redefinition of the consulting relationship. Deliberate reexamination of how each group could best use the other to deal with what appears to be issues of common concern results in the development of a risk-assessment team to monitor these issues and develop new prevention programs in health education. It is often vital for administrators to be informed of such redefinitions of consulting relationships, especially if new programming results or new, quasi-permanent collaborative teams are developed to address issues not easily handled by single-service units alone.

Process Consultation

A third approach to campus-based consultation involves the use of Schein's process consultation model (1988). In process consultation the consultant helps his or her clients identify and improve the processes at work within their respective groups. Such processes may enhance or impede the group's work, goal achievement, or general functioning. Patterns of group effectiveness and ineffectiveness can often be identified and modified by group members themselves. Thus, consultees diagnose and intervene in their own processes.

Process consultants do not engage in what Schein terms the "doctor role," the typical stance of the expert consultant, who provides information or a diagnosis in order to "fix" a problem (Schein, 1988). While process consultants may assume an expert role at specific junctures in the consulting process, they mainly seek to help consultees diagnose and correct their own problems. According to Schein (1985), human systems develop their own cultures, and organizational members ultimately know best whether a given solution will work in their organization's culture.

Student affairs staff frequently employ elements of process consultation when helping student groups address their own problems or functions. Student affairs personnel are often very good observers of group processes, able to point out patterns of group functioning to group members they are working with. Attending to how group members utilize feedback to improve their problem-solving capabilities will help the novice process consultant learn to effectively employ this role of observer and occasional intervener in group processes.

Normally, advanced training in consultation techniques and procedures and organizational development is required to be able to perform effective process consultation (Crego, 1985). Some campus psychologists have had such training, or they use similar skills learned in their psychological training. Failure to understand various aspects of organizational dynamics that are usually confronted when using this approach can lead to difficulty. Staff that wish to learn process consultation skills can import outside trainers or attend specialized training programs.

There are some limited examples of campus mental health specialists trained in process consultation and organizational development who have become internal consultants to top university executives. Most often they are used to provide consultation to troubled units, such as departments that are attempting to diagnose and remedy their own problems. (This is an example of unbounded consultation, or consultation that crosses divisional lines within an organization.) Dysfunctional academic departments often have a very negative effect on their students, faculty, and staff, and they may become a chronic source of stress for the university administration. Process consultation will often help alleviate difficulties when the use of outside expert consultation has not, perhaps due to the high value academic personnel place on autonomy and program control.

A side benefit of process consultation is related to the fact that universities and colleges appear to be highly focused on strategic planning today, in response to uncertain future enrollment and dwindling budgets (Keller, 1983; Levine, 1989). But as Schein (1991) points out, "very little attention is given to the interpersonal and group processes by which strategy is implemented" (p. 17). The success or failure of strategic planning may depend in part, or completely, on an institution's ability to first recognize and then deal directly with such interpersonal and group process issues. Thus strategic planning meetings involving many campus participants can be significantly aided by the use of process consultation.

Process consultation can play an invaluable role for those student affairs personnel trained and motivated to use it. Clearly, when valued by administrators with specific units they are responsible for and who have encountered some functional difficulties with them that they are unable to circumvent without outside help, the process consultant may lend some assistance in making a diagnostic appraisal concerning the nature and dimension of the difficulty. Most often this occurs by first consulting individually with those responsible for the program to determine their analysis of the problem and to decide who will participate in the consultation. Establishing a plan for how the consultant will operate within the unit is warranted at this time, as is determining what kinds of expectations unit members may have for the use of an outside campus-based consultant. The goal is to help the unit come to its own aid; the consultant should help the group select self-study mechanisms and develop its own ideas about how and when to make suitable changes. The consultant may interview all unit members individually before developing a plan for working with the group as a whole. The consultant should agree to work with the unit for a specified amount of time, at regular established intervals, and in complete confidence. If the consultant was approached initially by the administration, it should be made clear to the unit that it will be a confidential intervention if the process consultation method is used. There are occasions when previously troubled units that have been successful in improving their functioning will ask the consultant to inform high-level administrators of their success. The consultant is free to agree or not agree to such a request.

Frequently, student organizations are distressed by what they regard as unresolvable conflicts blocking their forward progress. For example, an organization that has historically served the needs of most of its members quite well suffers a crisis over its organizational leadership. Newly elected leaders wish to seriously modify the group's goals for the coming academic year, without having sought support for these changes from the group's members. The group begins to experience considerable conflict about this change in direction and about how to deal with the perceived arbitrary decisions of the new leaders. Considerable divisiveness develops. The organization's student affairs adviser asks a colleague in student affairs to provide process consultation to help the group get past this impasse.

The process consultant, after learning about the dimensions of the conflict through interviews, draws upon various tools to work with the group. After sharing an appraisal of what is blocking the group's forward progress, the consultant offers ideas on developing a format for working through the interpersonal and organizational conflicts driving the dispute. Personal ambitions, ideas about how leaders should make decisions, and concern about the utility of various group processes all appear to be issues. Agreement to deal with the issues one at a time in an articulated, process-oriented, conflict-resolving format is achieved early. The consultant meets with the members over a three-month period. The consultant uses several techniques, including consensus-building methods, aimed at ensuring that all members have a stake in the outcome. Rules are established at the outset to cease certain divisive tactics and to work on all aspects of the problem within the established time frames. A focused organizational identity is achieved and agreed to, the organization's goals are formally agreed to, and interpersonal disputes are reduced.

In the above example, process consultation was employed both for conflict resolution and to move the group toward taking responsibility for solving its own problems. Previously the group had no means of processing major changes. Attempts to make changes were ineffective, because no vehicle existed to permit all members to participate. The use of a process consultation model shifted the responsibility for making changes to the entire membership.

Schein (1991) makes the point that most diagnosis occurs during the intervention itself: one must act on the system in order to reveal some of its characteristics. Schein further states that process consultation involves building a relationship with consultees through systematic, nonjudgmental inquiry; helping the consultee think in diagnostic terms; stimulating the consultee to generate problem-solving actions; and confronting the consultee with hypotheses and alternatives generated by the consultant.

Process consultation requires a high-level capacity to develop conflict-resolving routines (as well as other functions); it represents the most effective way for the in-house consultant to develop conflict-reduction assignments in an organizational culture that must be understood before intervention can fully occur (Schein, 1990). It should be made clear that mediation is a much more circumscribed technique that does not lend itself to the consulting role. Mediation plays a special, narrowly defined role that can be effective only when the affected parties agree to use it.

Campus Ecology: A Special Use of Consultation

Campus ecology theorists agree that much of the stress college students experience on campus is environmentally induced rather than resulting from a "poor adjustment" of individuals to a "bad" environment (Morrill & Banning, 1973). These innovative specialists most often use a formal type of evaluative consultation to help campuses determine changeable sources of student stress caused by dysfunctional or inappropriately negative external (outside the person) factors (Hurst & Morrill, 1980). This pacesetting ecology model caused much excitement among student affairs professionals in the 1970s and early 1980s due to its implications for producing a greatly broadened perspective on student cultures and behavior and for defining new modes of intervention that would ultimately lead to prevention programming. Nonetheless, the model soon became known as difficult to apply. The assessment techniques were highly time-consuming, and many personnel who attempted to employ the model did not have a consultation model available that permitted the necessary degree of campus participation in both ecosystem appraisal and application of the results in program redesign.

In order to reintroduce one of the most innovative methods for designing student affairs programming to come along in the past forty years, a collaborative model of consultation for campus ecosystems work is sorely needed. While ecosystem model creators clearly understood the need for the use of effective consultation at all stages of ecosystems analysis and program design, workers who have attempted to use the model often fail to place primary emphasis on the process of consultation, focusing instead on environmental assessment. Student affairs professionals interested in applying campus ecology theory to the study of student needs would be well advised to form campus change teams that can educate themselves in both ecosystems model employment and collaborative consultation approaches. This would help to ensure adequate stakeholder involvement in both the assessment and intervention phases of the model. The opportunity for involving the full spectrum of campus roles in collaborative change teams is limitless; the tasks are intellectually challenging and engaging; and the product is most frequently creative.

The Process of Change

It is very difficult to introduce change into the highly institutionalized practices of higher education. Student affairs personnel have a basic orientation toward change that can be useful in systems consultation. An institution's readiness for change is seldom confronted by program developers, outreach strategists, and institutional research specialists (Backer, 1991). Consultation may afford the only means by which change can be effectively introduced to highly institutionalized campus environments and subenvironments. Schein (1979) asserts that "the reason so many change efforts run into resistance or outright failure is usually directly traceable to their not providing an effective unfreezing process before attempting a change induction" (p. 144). Thus student affairs professionals attempting to induce change through program development, process consultation, collaborative consultation, expert consultation, ecosystems analysis, or administrative dictate would be well served to use techniques that embrace the institutional change process, rather than generating programs that are not designed to fit with established campus subcultures. As simple a task as interpreting a student's behavior for a concerned professor (case consultation) demands that the conveyor of the information consider how the information is going to be used. In such a situation the consultant may wish to assume some responsibility for guiding the professor on how the information should be used.

Mediation and Dispute Resolution

A unique means of engaging in a helping role as a student affairs professional involves adopting the role of mediator. When appropriately and successfully employed, mediation can serve as a dynamic and respected means for confronting campus disputes in an orderly, agreed-upon fashion. A student affairs professional serving as a mediator can employ techniques that will benefit all parties concerned in a dispute or conflict.

While many campuses do not provide mediation services to assist parties in dispute or in conflict with one another, there is clearly an increase in the number of campuses that provide formal services explicitly designed for this purpose. Mediation is an extension of negotiation. It involves the intervention of an outside party who is neutral, acceptable, and has no authority in relation to the conflict at hand or to the parties involved. Decision making is in the hands of the parties participating in the process. Mediation is voluntary, and it is usually provided or sought when parties can no longer resolve a dispute by themselves. Campus student affairs professionals frequently encounter disputes that are suitable for mediation, such as disputes between student groups, roommates, students and faculty members, or staff members within departments or divisions. Administrations in colleges and universities have been slow to recognize the value of formal mediation until recently; rather, much mediation on campus is initiated by personnel who are themselves interested in providing such a service. For example, student affairs professionals interested in or charged with the issue of campus climate have become proactive, on occasion, in developing campus mediation services. Increasing campus diversity, accompanied by an increased feeling of responsibility on the part of campus personnel for managing conflict and disputes that sometimes arise from it, has stimulated interest on some campuses in providing formal mediation. At the informal level, student affairs staff frequently find themselves in situations in which they may be able to utilize mediation skills to help resolve differences between motivated parties.

The field of mediation has grown considerably over the past ten years. Authors such as Moore (1986, 1987) have stimulated training programs in mediation skills for various types of professionals and have developed a respected literature on the topic. Experts in mediation have become increasingly interested in sharing their experience by promoting the development of mediation skills in other professionals (Moore, 1987). It is estimated that approximately fifty campuses now offer some sort of formal mediation, available to any level of campus personnel and involving varying degrees of training and participation on the part of student affairs professionals. Principles of sound mediation practice apply to both formal and informal interventions.

Mediators often assume a variety of neutral roles: the opener of communication channels; the process facilitator; the legitimizer, who helps parties recognize the rights of others in negotiation; the resource expander, who helps link parties to outside resources; the problem explorer; and the facilitator of dispute resolution (Moore, 1987).

Effective mediators analyze the nature of the dispute, its history, its extent, and the perceived or stated motivation of the parties for resolving it. A plan is then developed that details the steps mediation will follow for the specific case under review. Student affairs professionals conducting mediation—including informal mediation—need adequate background information, an agreement between the parties to submit to the mediation process, and an ability to establish ground rules to be adhered to by all parties during the mediation itself. A length of time, with outside and minimal limits, should also be agreed to by all parties in advance. Many novice mediators, while well intentioned, attempt mediation in one session. For example, a student affairs assistant dean offers to mediate between two minority student organizations in dispute over campus dance programming priorities. The assistant dean is pressed for time and pressures the group to process their issues and feelings within a two-hour time period. The assistant dean is surprised to observe that more emotional catharsis and scapegoating occurs during this meeting than movement toward a solution. Failure to understand that there are two types of mediation processes (conciliation and problem solving) frequently results in failure and increased frustration, if not an escalated dispute. Another problem is that the assistant dean's cultural background is quite different from that of the disputants. Particularly in situations such as this, adequate time must be allowed to listen to and understand both the content and the complexity of the conflict. Making a full assessment by asking appropriate questions to gain understanding is an entirely appropriate technique to facilitate the establishment of a suitable mediation process.

The timing issues in dispute resolution work are very important to recognize and require a thoughtful plan for intervention (Castrey & Castrey, 1987). The senior student affairs officer may ask campus parties to submit to mediation to be conducted by the campus judicial affairs officer. If the administrator fails to prepare the group, which may feel that it is required to submit to mediation, it is likely that untimely intervention will result in confusion and possible failure. Mediators must be aware of both when and how to initiate intervention in the form of mediation. Just sitting down and talking with all parties to a conflict is not mediation. Simply asking the parties to present their own side and state what they want or need to achieve resolution is insufficient.

In some instances a conflict will not disappear, but mediation can provide the parties with new ways of managing it. For instance, a student affairs professional may be called on to mediate disputes between parties who have highly varied cultural backgrounds that clash over certain issues, such as the process for allocating the student activity fee. A goal of mediation in such cases may be simply to help the parties achieve a way to disagree openly. The parties remain in conflict, but they learn to respect each other's differences in approach, as opposed to engaging in name-calling and "dirty tricks" such as taking out ads in the student newspaper accusing their opponent of ill deeds or intentions. Mediators need to be able to help parties establish realistic, achievable goals that will reduce, if not eliminate, their conflict.

Students enter college with varying degrees of exposure to healthy, effective ways for persons to be in conflict with one another. Families sometimes offer their children little or no assistance or experience in how to resolve conflict. Adults sometimes mistakenly assume that other adults, including college students, have the internal and interpersonal skills to resolve conflicts. When conflict occurs among parties who lack such experience, behavior often emerges that reveals random attempts to deal with the conflict that are actually counterproductive. Sometimes people are accused of not wanting to resolve a conflict, when they simply do not know how. Often mediators must take an educative role in these circumstances, teaching students useful ways to both approach and resolve conflict, at a level that permits substantial improvement in interpersonal relations. It should be noted that conflict is a normal part of living. It can be a healthy process, clarifying differences and providing a focus for problem solving. Teaching students how to handle conflict with civility and how to use effective conflict-resolving techniques will help them deal with conflict throughout their lives.

Mediators employ two very distinct processes for moving parties through the phases of the mediation process—the conciliation process and the joint problem-solving process (Wildau, 1987). Conciliation is aimed at creating an environment for discussion wherein negotiation can work. It usually involves reducing irrational fears, improving communication channels between parties, and correcting perceptions (Wildau, 1987). While conciliation is more a psychological process, joint problem solving is a series of tasks that produces real results by setting agendas, generating and evaluating settlement options, uncovering hidden agendas, and initially defining issues (Wildau, 1987). Many novice mediators fail to differentiate between these two processes and attempt goal setting before preparing parties for the process of attempting to achieve real solutions. For example, a student life professional who has agreed to mediate a dispute between two student groups asks the groups to mutually establish an agenda for negotiation. Even though it is clear that the dispute involves serious communication problems between the two groups and strong misperceptions about each group's agenda, the mediator's request requires the groups to engage in a process that depends for its success upon the very issues—communication and trust—that have created the dispute. Skipping the conciliation phase dooms this mediation attempt to failure and strengthens the perception of each group that the conflict cannot be resolved. Sometimes a situation like this can be saved by quickly reestablishing a more suitable process, often with outside expert consultation, to enable group members (and possibly outside observers interested in the outcome) to more adequately work through a designed mediation process.

Clearly, mediation requires training and consultative support. Many campus communities and state court systems offer training in mediation skills, as do some university extension services. Interested student affairs professionals may also contact the National Association for Mediation in Higher Education at the University of Massachusetts for assistance in seeking professional development in this area.

Ethics in Consultation and Mediation

Until recently, the potential ethical problems involved in conducting consultation and mediation were largely ignored (Crego, 1985; Robinson & Gross, 1985). Major issues analyzed by Robinson and Gross (1985) include education and training of consultants, difficulties in client identification, consultant versus client needs and values, and respect for client rights. They successfully argue that the lack of a defined set of ethical guidelines for consultation and mediation does not preclude practitioners from employing sound ethical principles culled from their respective professional backgrounds. They argue more strongly for the development of specialized ethical principles for situations in which consultation or mediation processes can affect a wide range of individuals. A major and highly legitimate concern of these authors has to do with the so-called indirect effects of consultation and mediation. The influence within their organization of individuals who have participated in mediation or consultation may be altered or changed in some way as a direct result of their participation in these processes. Consultants and mediators all too frequently ignore giving adequate attention to the impact their work may have on unseen others in the environments affected by the participants to the consultation or mediation process. These issues should be examined by professionals engaged in consultation and mediation and explored with clients at the end of the consultation or mediation process in the course of discussing how the results of the process will be employed. As presented in Chapter Six, familiarization with a professional organization's principles of ethics concerning working with individuals and groups is essential for understanding and learning to recognize potential ethical problems. Ideally, all student affairs professionals should be trained in ethical decision making (Crego, 1985).

Skills and Competencies Required for Effective Consultation and Mediation

In addition to the skills acquired in various in-service or continuing education programs on consultation and mediation, the student affairs professional might want to develop the following competencies: trust and rapport building, organizational diagnosis, dealing with process, resource utilization, managing change tasks, and building the capacity to continue (Saxl, Miles, & Lieberman, 1989). Training programs that deal with the development of both consulting skills and skills in introducing and managing change within educational environments do exist, such as those operated by the Association for Supervision and Curriculum Development in Alexandria, Virginia. Student affairs professionals typically have both organizational skills and interpersonal skills and are thus perhaps the most prepared campus professionals to provide unbounded consultation services. This implies a change in role for many and a new perception of student affairs professionals on the part of campus colleagues. The founders of the field of consultation faced the same challenges in the professional environments in which they first functioned. Given the pressures for managing change that will confront higher education in the next decade, it is an optimal time to expand one's role and skill base.

Conclusion

The expanding role of student affairs professionals is consistent with the movement in some universities and colleges for integrating the role of student affairs into academic planning and program development. Increased collaborative efforts that maximize the integration of student affairs professionals' unique skills and knowledge base into the life of their institutions clearly improve the educational environment for students and reduce the potential for some environments to become roadblocks to learning. Consultation is an effective way to create highly collaborative, unbounded problem-solving or program-development enterprises that address the significantly changing environment of higher education. Training is available in role-expansion skills such as consultation and mediation for the interested student affairs professional. Student affairs professionals skilled in consultation in particular have been perceived recently by educational administrators interested in the dynamics of the educational environment as having a significant role to play in helping integrate the work of student affairs personnel with that of the faculty and other administrators. Improvement in higher education may come to depend on a few campus personnel that have the capacity to foster processes that enhance planning, problem solving, and innovation. Student affairs professionals are uniquely suited to acquire expertise as campus consultants and mediation specialists.

References

Backer, T. E. (1991). Knowledge utilization: The third wave. *Knowledge: Creation, Diffusion, Utilization, 12*, 225–240.

Banning, J. H. (1989). Creating a climate for successful student development: The campus ecology manager role. In U. Delworth, G. Hanson, & Associates, *Student services: A handbook for the profession* (2nd ed., pp. 304–322). San Francisco: Jossey-Bass.

Banning, J. H., & Kaiser, L. (1974). An ecological perspective and model for campus design. *Personnel and Guidance Journal, 52*, 370–375.

Caplan, G. (1970). *The theory and practice of mental health consultation.* New York: Basic Books.

Caplan, G., & Caplan, R. B. (1992). *Mental health consultation and collaboration.* San Francisco: Jossey-Bass.

Caplan, G., Caplan, R. B., & Erchul, W. P. (1994). Caplanian mental health consultation: Historical background and current status. *Consulting Psychology Journal: Practice and Research, 46*, 2–12.

Caplan, G., Caplan, R. B., & Erchul, W. P. (in press). A contemporary view of mental health consultation: Comments on "Types of mental health consultation" by Gerald Caplan. *Journal of Educational and Psychological Consultation.*

Castrey, R. T., & Castrey, B. P. (1987). Timing: A mediator's best friend. *Mediation Quarterly,* 15–20.

Conyne, R. K. (1975). Environmental assessment: Mapping for counselor action. *Personnel and Guidance Journal, 54*, 151–154.

Conyne, R. K. (1979). The campus environment as client: A new direction for college counselors. *Journal of College Student Personnel, 20*, 437–442.

Crego, C. A. (1985). Ethics: The need for improved consultation training. *Counseling Psychologist, 13*, 473–476.

Crego, C. A. (1990). Campus-based consultation. In N. J. Garfield & B. Collison (Eds.), *Working with people: Careers in counseling and human development* (pp. 49–59). Alexandria, VA: American Counseling Association.

D'Andrea, V., & Salovey, P. (1983). *Peer counseling: Skills and perspectives.* Palo Alto, CA: Science and Behavior Books for Higher Education.

Gallessich, J. (1982). *The profession and practice of consultation: A handbook for consultants, trainers of consultants, and consumers of consultation services.* San Francisco: Jossey-Bass.

Huebner, L. A. (1979). Emergent issues of theory and practice. In L. A. Huebner (Ed.), *Redesigning campus environments* (New Directions for Student Services No. 8, pp. 1–21). San Francisco: Jossey-Bass.

Hurst, J. C. (1987). Student development and campus ecology: A rapprochement. *NASPA Journal, 25,* 5–18.

Hurst, J. C., & Morrill, W. H. (1980). Student/environmental development as the conceptional foundation for student affairs. In W. H. Morrill, J. C. Hurst, & E. R. Oetting (Eds.), *Dimensions of intervention for student development* (pp. 3–13). New York: Wiley.

Keller, G. (1983). *Academic strategy: The management revolution in American higher education.* Baltimore: Johns Hopkins University Press.

Levine, A., & Associates. (1989). *Shaping higher education's future: Demographic realities and opportunities, 1990–2000.* San Francisco: Jossey-Bass.

Miller, G. A. (1969). Psychology as a means of promoting human welfare. *American Psychologist, 24,* 1063–1075.

Moore, C. W. (1986). *The mediation process: Political strategies for resolving conflict.* San Francisco: Jossey-Bass.

Moore, C. W. (Ed.). (1987). Practical strategies for the phases of mediation. *Mediation Quarterly,* 1–2.

Morrill, W. H., & Banning, J. H. (1973). *Counseling outreach: A survey of practices.* Boulder, CO: Western Interstate Commission.

Morrill, W. H., Hurst, J. C., & Oetting, E. R.(1980). A conceptual model of intervention strategies. In W. H. Morrill, J. C. Hurst, & E. R. Oetting (Eds.), *Dimensions of intervention for student development* (pp. 85–95). New York: Wiley.

Oetting, E. R. (1980). A guide to program evaluation. In W. H. Morrill, J. C. Hurst, & E. R. Oetting (Eds.), *Dimensions of intervention for student development* (pp. 143–174). New York: Wiley.

Robinson, S. E., & Gross, D. R. (1985). Ethics of consultation: The Canterville ghost. *Counseling Psychologist, 13,* 444–465.

Saxl, E. R., Miles, M. B., & Lieberman, A. (1989). *Participant's manual: Assisting change in education.* Alexandria, VA: Association for Supervision and Curriculum Development.

Schein, E. H. (1979). Personal change through interpersonal relationships. In W. Bennis, J. Van Maanen, E. H. Schein, & F. I. Steele (Eds.), *Essays in interpersonal dynamics* (pp. 129–162). Homewood, IL: Dorsey.

Schein, E. H. (1985). *Organizational culture and leadership.* San Francisco: Jossey-Bass.

Schein, E. H. (1988). *Process consultation* (Vol. 1). Reading, MA: Addison-Wesley.

Schein, E. H. (1989). Process consultation as a general model of helping. *Consulting Psychology Bulletin, 41,* 3–15.

Schein, E. H. (1990). Organizational culture. *American Psychologist, 45,* 109–119.

Schein, E. H. (1991). The role of process consultation in the creation and implementation of strategy. *Consulting Psychology Bulletin, 43,* 16–18.

Schlossberg, N. K., Lynch, A. Q., & Chickering, A. W. (1989). *Improving higher education environments for adults: Responsive programs and services from entry to departure.* San Francisco: Jossey-Bass.

Wildau, S. (1987). Transitions: Moving parties between stages. *Mediation Quarterly,* 3–14.

CHAPTER EIGHTEEN

MULTICULTURALISM

Donna M. Talbot

With the promise of changing demographics (Bennett, 1986; Kuh, 1990; Schuster & Van Dyne, 1985), a shrinking global community resulting in higher numbers of international students (Pedersen, 1991), growing numbers of gay and lesbian students willing to "come out" within the college environment (Evans & Wall, 1991), and increasing numbers of nontraditional students (Schlossberg, Lynch, & Chickering, 1989), it has never been a more exciting or challenging time to work in higher education. Many have suggested that the student affairs profession will need to assume a leadership role in helping institutions bridge the gap between old skills and paradigms and the new tools necessary to effectively meet the needs of changing student populations. The journey toward multiculturalism and the development of these tools is the focus of this chapter.

Three models for individual and organizational multicultural development are presented in this chapter. Applications and implications of the models are explored using examples from college campuses. The effect of privilege and oppression on higher education is discussed. Finally, resources and references are shared for use in further personal and professional multicultural development.

The Journey Toward Multiculturalism

One of the greatest obstacles to discussing diversity and multiculturalism is the lack of common definitions to clarify the concepts involved. Perhaps this is grounded in people's fear of looking ignorant, insensitive, or exclusionary. Yet, how can we know where we are trying to go if we do not know where the journey can take us? With the analogy of a journey in mind, this chapter outlines the maps, landmarks, detours, and hazards along the road to multiculturalism. The maps are the theoretical and practice models developed for achieving multiculturalism. The landmarks are the developmental phases and tasks presented by the theoretical models and the techniques and tools that promote multicultural development. The detours are represented by short breaks or plateaus in growth, retreats from uncomfortable or unfamiliar situations, and smoke screens that stop individuals and organizations from clearly seeing the necessary steps for moving toward multiculturalism. Finally, the hazards are represented by overt and covert challenges to diversity and the costs associated with greater sensitivity to oppression and diversity. The journey toward multiculturalism is fraught with detours and hazards; however, having a well-drawn and usable map and recognizing the landmarks along the way will help make the journey a successful one.

Beliefs, Assumptions, and Definitions

Certain beliefs and assumptions serve as the foundation for the concepts presented in this chapter. First, the terms *diversity* and *multiculturalism* are related, but they are not completely interchangeable. *Diversity* is a structure that includes the tangible presence of individuals representing a variety of different attributes and characteristics, including culture, ethnicity, sexual orientation, and other physical and social variables. According to Pusch and Hoopes (as cited in Pusch, 1979), *multiculturalism* is a state of being in which an individual feels comfortable and communicates effectively with people from any culture, in any situation, because she or he has developed the necessary knowledge and skills to do so. In other words, the multicultural person has mastered the process of continually learning about culture, quickly and effectively, so that he or she can adapt to a variety of different cultural settings with minimal discomfort. An assumption embedded in this definition should not be overlooked nor taken for granted—it assumes that the journey toward multiculturalism is an ongoing, developmental process that can be learned. Multiculturalism is not an inherent characteristic of any individual, no matter his or her race, ethnicity, or gender; rather, it is based on an individual's ability and openness to learn. It is also understood, however, that while an individual's ethnicity or culture does not determine his or her ability to strive for multiculturalism, it does impact the individual's worldview, which shapes how that person perceives culture and ethnicity. Similarly, a *multicultural organization* "is one that is genuinely committed to diverse representation of its membership; is sensitive to maintaining an open, supportive and responsive environment; is working toward and purposefully including elements of diverse cultures in its ongoing operations; and . . . is authentic in its response to issues confronting it" (Strong, 1986, as quoted in Barr & Strong, 1988, p. 85). This definition incorporates the concepts of both diversity and multiculturalism.

Another belief that pervades this chapter is that while *ethnicity* refers to racial or national characteristics determined by birth, *culture* is much broader and more inclusive. Hoopes and Pusch (1979) define it as follows: "*Culture* . . . includes values, beliefs, linguistic expression, patterns of thinking, behavioral norms, and styles of communication which a group of people has developed to assure its survival in a particular physical and human environment. . . . Culture is the response of a group of human beings to the valid and particular needs of its members" (p. 3).

Using this definition, the vast array of populations filling campus communities can be incorporated into a multicultural environment: Asians, Jews, men, Latinos, Gays, Muslims, women, various international populations, older students, Whites, and so on. While it is important to recognize all cultures that influence the campus environment and the work of student affairs professionals, it is also important to recognize that not all cultures have been incorporated into higher education equally; some are still struggling to be recognized and heard in institutions today. These definitions and the models shared in this chapter recognize that in U.S. society, both historically and to a large degree today, there is a "dominant, powerful" group or culture that has privileges others do not. Typically and historically, that powerful group has been ascribed the following attributes: White, male, heterosexual, middle- to upper-class socioeconomic status, and able-bodied.

Models of Multicultural Development

There are several models that outline the changes an individual or organization must make in order to move toward a more inclusive or multicultural framework. These models are the maps an individual or organization follows on their journey toward multiculturalism. Presented here are just three of those different models, varied in complexity and scope.

Development of Intercultural Sensitivity

Milton Bennett (1986) describes a model he calls the Development of Intercultural Sensitivity. The focus of this model is the individual's ability to achieve sensitivity to differences by passing through a continuum from lack of experience and low tolerance to increased experience and appreciation for diversity. The six stages in this continuum are as follows:

1. *Denial* occurs when there is physical and/or social isolation that prohibits any contact with significant cultural differences. The individual remains in complete ethnocentrism, where his or her own worldview is unchallenged and is central to all reality.

2. *Defense* involves the recognition of differences. This recognition represents a threat to the individual's view of the world. Typical responses in this stage include denigration of difference and assumption of cultural superiority.

3. *Minimization* is characterized by the attitude that "basically, all humans are alike." This is an attempt to trivialize any differences that exist, stressing only cultural similarities.

4. *Acceptance* is divided into two phases. In the first phase there is recognition and acceptance of behavioral differences; in the second phase there is recognition and acceptance of differences in fundamental cultural values. This stage marks the shift from ethnocentrism to ethnorelativism.

5. *Adaptation* is based on the acceptance of difference as a relative process. The individual develops the ability to empathize with a person of a different culture in a particular, immediate situation.

6. *Integration* involves the evaluation of events and situations in a cultural context. Adler describes an individual in this stage as "a person who is always in the process of becoming a part of and apart from a given cultural context" (Adler, 1977, quoted in Bennett, 1986, p. 186).

Pedersen's Multicultural Development Model

Paul Pedersen's Multicultural Development model (1988), which comes out of the counseling literature, is an educational model rather than a medical model (that is, it is based on the assumption that the audience is healthy and normal and has an interest in becoming more multiculturally aware). The three stages of Pedersen's model are awareness, knowledge, and skill. Unlike other multicultural theorists, Pedersen focuses on three broad areas that need to be developed in an individual. Awareness represents the affective domain; knowledge represents the cognitive domain; and skill represents the behavioral domain. Fundamental to this model is the belief that by teaching multicultural development an individual will increase his or her repertoire of beliefs, knowledge, and behaviors for use in a variety of situations. The stages in Pedersen's model can be summarized as follows:

1. *Awareness.* In this stage an individual must learn accurate and appropriate attitudes, opinions, and assumptions about cultures. This includes awareness of oneself as a cultural being and one's own culture in relation to others. This may be difficult for White people because they often see themselves as "having no culture." The White culture is usually used as the yardstick

by which other cultures are compared; however, it is rarely ever defined or examined.

2. *Knowledge*. At this stage an individual acquires information or comprehension of different cultures and cultural beliefs. This represents the integration of cognition and beliefs.

3. *Skill*. At this stage the individual learns to translate beliefs and knowledge into action. The individual learns how to interact appropriately and effectively with persons from other cultures. Individuals in this stage learn to identify appropriate actions that will allow them to be accepted by persons from different cultures.

The Cultural Environment Transitions Model

Manning and Coleman-Boatwright (1991) have developed the Cultural Environment Transitions (CET) model, which defines a process by which people can move institutions toward achieving the goal of multiculturalism. While the process is chronological, Manning and Coleman-Boatwright clearly indicate that it is not necessarily contiguous. The model is not meant to be a way of explaining, predicting, or controlling the environment, but like the other models, it serves as a map or guide for people in institutions to follow as they journey toward multiculturalism. In the CET model, indicators are presented for characterizing an institution's openness and willingness to recognize its struggle with diversity issues. The indicators measure different stages in the journey toward multiculturalism (see Exhibit 18.1), labeled as Monocultural, Awareness with Inability to Change, Height of the Conflict, Institutional Rebirth Reflects Multicultural Goals, and Multicultural. Manning and Coleman-Boatwright describe the steps in their model as "steep 90 percent angles that community members must scale. The plateaus are not flat but can be viewed metaphorically like the rolling deck of a ship: slippery, difficult to traverse, and often treacherous" (p. 37). The initiatives presented in the upper half of the table are examples of actions that correspond with specific developmental steps or plateaus. As the initiatives and indicators progress, the institution moves from a one-culture paradigm to an organization that operates from and embraces multiple perspectives.

Commonalities Across Models

Some commonalities exist across the models presented. Each assumes that the individual or organization has a desire to move toward multiculturalism; there must be a willingness to learn and to begin the journey. The models also assume that there is a dominant culture with dominant norms. All emphasize that some level of self-awareness and awareness of others must be achieved and monitored. In the CET model, professionals within the institution must be aware of the indicators in

EXHIBIT 18.1. CULTURAL ENVIRONMENT TRANSITIONS MODEL.

INITIATIVES

Student programs based on culture
Outreach by minority staff
"Revolving door" for students of color
Family programs to build support
Multicultural mentors and support systems
Differences made explicit (e.g., incorporated into roommate contract)

Integrated staffs with limited support and understanding
Training focuses on awareness of differences
Offices of multicultural affairs established

Training focuses on internal "self" and racism
Effective staff recruitment invitations and reputation

Staff interventions change ways of operating
Change in disciplinary structure to reflect multiple perspectives

Training focuses on different "ways of knowing"
Training focuses on trust and changing modes of power and control

Upper administration makes verbal commitment to diversity but lacks knowledge to change

INSTITUTIONAL REBIRTH REFLECTS MULTICULTURAL GOALS

MULTICULTURAL

Advent of cultural centers
Minority members conduct training
Efforts result in guilt, denial, anger, and blaming of victim
Student awards chosen to respect students of color
Affirmative action hiring appointments

AWARENESS WITH INABILITY TO CHANGE
Avoidance of overly racist language
Black History Month, Hispanic Awareness Week, and sporadic programs

HEIGHT OF THE CONFLICT

Students of color initiate efforts to gain power
Backlash within community
Cries of "reverse discrimination"
Brawls and fighting
Call for men's centers

"Switching" by other than minority groups
Art, architecture, and campus symbols represent many cultures
Multiethnic foods served in dining halls and snack bars
Cultural center populated by all

Multiple learning and presentation styles

Integrated student groups

Power and authority equitably shared

Change in language of majority culture

Organizational structure more flexible and reflective of multiple styles of management

MONOCULTURAL
Segregated social activities and friendships
Racial slurs, newsletters, and flyers
Western civilization and other monocultural courses as requirements
"Pioneer" students join organizations, RA staffs, and student leadership

Isolated student leaders are spokespeople for everything

Staff and students predominantly associate with own group
Black English and Spanish spoken privately

INDICATORS

Note: From "Student Affairs Initiatives Toward a Multicultural University," by K. Manning & P. Coleman-Boatwright, 1991, *Journal of College Student Development, 32*, p. 370. Copyright 1991 by American College Personnel Association. Reprinted with permission.

order to develop appropriate initiatives. For each of these models, there is an initial introduction of difference that begins the developmental process. This contact with difference can be accidental, or it can be planned.

The stages, components, or phases of these models are not meant to be seen as having distinct, rigid boundaries. As is true for most student development theories, individuals may revisit, retreat, or stagnate as they progress through the stages. Stages or phases may overlap as an individual moves from one to another. Also, individuals usually do not journey toward multiculturalism by embracing all cultural groups at once; they may need to take several journeys, adding new groups each time. For example, under Pedersen's Multicultural Development model, it is possible that an individual could still be in the awareness stage (struggling with himself or herself as a cultural being) while transitioning into the knowledge stage (beginning to gather information about White identity development). Another alternative is that an individual may have reached the action or skill stage in the journey with regard to African Americans but may still be at the beginning of the awareness stage with regard to gays, lesbians, and bisexuals. Some of this will depend on many external factors, not the least of which is contact with particular populations.

Other similar developmental models that can be used are the Intercultural Learning Process (Hoopes, 1979; Jefferson, 1986), the Cultural Broker model (Stage & Manning, 1993), or the Multicultural Organization Development model (Pope, 1993). Before beginning a long journey, it is important to feel comfortable and confident with the map that will guide it. Therefore, in the journey toward multiculturalism it is important to find a strong model that can be understood and that seems to fit. While each model seems to have an endpoint or final stage, in reality the journey toward multiculturalism is never-ending. Cultures evolve and change constantly; therefore, the need to learn and adapt to the new and changing populations on campuses is continuous.

The Role of Privilege and Oppression in Education

It would be difficult to address multiculturalism and training without touching upon the topic of oppression. Oppression is an interesting phenomenon: one person or group of people maintains overwhelming power over another person or group of people. One of the goals of oppression is to maintain the status quo, to allow one person or group to stay in power. Some educators (Freire, 1970; Manning, 1994) believe that the pedagogical base of the U.S. educational system is oppressive in nature. Outside of experiential education and Montessori training, the traditional educational system in the United States is designed to make individuals conform. Children are taught not to speak unless spoken to; the teacher talks and the student listens; the teacher chooses, and forces his or her choices upon the students; the students are empty vessels waiting to be filled with knowledge by their teachers (Freire, 1970). This type of educational system is hierarchical and does not foster creative, critical thinking. It assumes that students have no knowledge to share and the teacher has no knowledge to gain. In this type of system, the responsibility for educating rests with the teacher; communication is one-way.

The new "pedagogy for liberation" emphasizes the need for all participants to be active and responsible both for educating and being educated. To benefit from this model, all participants must be aware, informed, and open to others' ideas. This is achieved through honest dialogue and exchange of ideas from a variety of perspectives (Manning, 1994). This redefinition of education as dialogical rather than hierarchical helps diminish the oppressor-oppressed relationship between teacher and student. The new roles created are that of teacher-student and student-teacher (Freire, 1970). This ideology fits nicely with the models for multicultural development.

Many experts in cross-cultural and intercultural training (Corvin & Wiggins, 1989; Sabnani, Ponterotto, & Borodovsky, 1991; Sue & Sue, 1990) believe that individuals (especially Whites) must engage in self-exploration and antiracism training. This training must expose individuals to the racist, sexist, heterosexist system that exists in the United States and the privileges that are associated with being a member of the dominant group. Accepting these privileges, whether or not one actively protects them, helps to maintain the system. This is an uncomfortable thought for most well-meaning individuals who do not see themselves as privileged. Peggy McIntosh (1989, 1992) writes about the ordinary, everyday ways in which Whites experience privileges denied people of color. These include, but are not limited to, being able to rent an apartment anywhere one can afford it without fear of being turned away for unknown reasons; being able to go shopping without being followed or harassed by the store detective or manager; being able to easily purchase cards, posters, greeting cards, dolls, and other toys featuring people of one's own race; and never being asked to speak for one's entire race. While any one such incident does not by itself define the balance of power in society, the totality of such events repeated on a daily basis reinforces the belief or perception that one group is preferable to others.

Applications of the Models

Consider the following fictional students:

Jenny is a first-generation Asian American college student in her first year. She arrives on campus knowing very little about what to expect from college life; however, she and her parents are sure that Jenny will be a doctor. Although Jenny was born in the United States, she speaks English with an accent; when she speaks to her parents, she always speaks in their native tongue.

Kelby is a junior in college. He is African American and has recently identified himself as gay. Kelby is a psychology major, he plays several intramural sports, and he loves to dance. This year, for the first time since going to college, Kelby has become involved in a number of activist student organizations, including the Gay, Lesbian, and Bisexual Alliance and the Pan-African Power student group.

Thomas is an RA at Anywhere University (which Jenny and Kelby attend). He is White, twenty years old, and from a rural, homogeneous community. Anywhere University (AU) has a moderately sized, growing multicultural population.

Jenny, Kelby, and Thomas could easily be students on any campus in the United States. However, how such students are perceived (and consequently how they are treated) may vary greatly, depending on the level of multiculturalism attained by the student affairs professionals who work with them and the level of commitment to diversity exhibited by the university they attend. How they interact with each other may also depend on their level of development toward multiculturalism and their level of minority or White identity development (see Chapter Ten) (Atkinson, Morten, & Sue, 1979; Helms, 1990). Examples of this and particular situations involving Jenny, Kelby, and Thomas are explored below.

As noted, applying the multicultural development models can be complex. Consider each of our three students, using the multicultural development models as a guide or map for understanding their behavior. Having achieved the status of RA, it would be hard to imagine that Thomas would be in the denial stage of the Intercultural Sensitivity model (Bennett, 1986), at least with respect to ethnic minorities. At this point in his college career, Thomas has probably been exposed to students from different ethnic backgrounds; thus his worldview has been challenged, and he has been forced to begin his journey with the acknowledgment that cultural differences exist. But due to the nature of the "invisible minority" (Fassinger, 1991), Thomas may not knowingly have come into contact with gay men, lesbians, or bisexuals; thus his journey regarding this population may not yet have begun.

If he were in the minimization stage of development, Thomas might look at Kelby and Jenny as if they were just "two other human beings," claiming he is "color-blind" and "gender-blind." He would trivialize the cultural differences that separate him from Jenny and Kelby, eliminating any chance of intercultural understanding in the process. In this stage, Thomas would not be able to see that his behaviors could be interpreted as racist. Simple interactions or discussions with Jenny and Kelby that emphasize the cultural differences that exist around topics like holidays or religious beliefs might begin to push Thomas out of the minimization stage; visiting and celebrating Kwanza or Chinese New Year with Kelby's or Jenny's family would challenge Thomas's basic beliefs that people are all alike despite their different cultural and ethnic backgrounds.

If Thomas continues to move along the continuum, he will begin to see Kelby and Jenny as cultural beings different from himself. In the acceptance stage, these differences are perceived as necessary and fundamental, but they are not evaluated. That is to say, at this stage, Thomas would not label some differences as good and others as bad. He will not begin the process of sorting through and selecting cultural beliefs, practices, and values from a variety of cultures until later in the journey.

If Thomas reaches the integration stage, he will begin to see his interactions with Jenny and Kelby in a cultural context. He will attempt to evaluate his own behaviors from Jenny's and Kelby's cultural perspective as well as his own; decisions about his behavior will be made incorporating all of these viewpoints.

Under Pedersen's Multicultural Development model, Thomas would be encouraged to explore his own culture (White culture) and its impact on how he works with individuals who are different from himself; he would probably begin to read about White racial identity development (Helms, 1990) as he moves toward the knowledge stage. Meanwhile, Thomas would watch how other White people behave and begin to notice similarities, as well as differences, in other ethnic groups. In the knowledge stage, Thomas would seek out information to help him understand the different cultures he comes into contact with. He would probably study the Minority Identity Development model (Atkinson, Morten, & Sue, 1979) and the Homosexual Identity Development model (Cass, 1979), as well as studying specific historical and cultural information about African Americans, Asian Americans, and gays, lesbians, and bisexuals. This would be Thomas's attempt to acquire knowledge about his residents' potential developmental issues and experiences on campus and in society.

Finally, in the skill stage of Pedersen's model, Thomas would apply his new awareness and knowledge. This might include attending gay rights meetings or discussions of African American or Asian American history. Thomas might plan and facilitate a program for his hall that addresses racial tensions on campus. Depending on his relationship with Jenny or Kelby, he might engage in discussions with them about their experiences as ethnic minorities on campus. (Given the characteristics of Kelby and Jenny described above and taking into account minority identity development, it is more likely that Kelby would be able to engage in these discussions than Jenny.)

Now, applying the CET model, imagine Thomas attends an institution that is at the Monocultural stage. In such an institution he would probably not be expected to plan culturally sensitive programming; in fact, he would likely receive subtle messages to stay away from such "difficult topics." If the institution were at the Height of the Conflict stage, Thomas might be too busy responding to racial conflicts and challenges for power on his floor to be able to complete much programming at all. When an institution displays multicultural indicators (the final stage in the CET model; see Exhibit 18.1), a commitment to diversity is visible. Symbols and structures around campus reflect many cultures. In this case, Thomas would have a diverse group of colleagues (other RAs and supervisors) with whom he could work to produce multicultural programs. All students would have a voice in framing the organizational structure; diversity would be embedded in all programming. For example, posters for a couples' communication workshop would portray gay, heterosexual, and lesbian couples, and the faces would reflect a variety of ethnic populations.

These snapshots of Thomas, Jenny, and Kelby at Anywhere University are helpful, but they do not answer several important questions: What tools or techniques are used to move an individual or organization along these models of multicultural development? What are some available resources to use during the journey? What prevents an individual or organization from developing multiculturalism?

Developing Competencies

Once an individual or organization has decided to take the journey toward multiculturalism, the initial focus is on awareness of others and self. Sue and Sue (1990) emphasize the importance of self-awareness: an individual who is unaware of his or her own cultural values is like a cup with a hole. Without knowledge of the hole, the liquid inside leaks out onto the owner, the floor, and anything else it touches. This is also true of the unaware student affairs professional, whose own cultural values will leak out and spill over everyone they contact.

For many individuals, the natural tendency is to make learning multiculturalism a cognitive process, because this is familiar and relatively nonthreatening (Sue et al., 1982). Naturally, the cognitive or academic component of the journey must be addressed. There are many resources available that relate to student affairs and various diverse populations. For example, there are publications (Atkinson & Hackett, 1988; Gilligan, 1982) that address issues and needs of nonethnic

American minority populations (women, people with disabilities, the elderly); these materials define the populations and discuss their inclusion in the term *minority*. There has been a steady increase in understanding of lesbian, gay, and bisexual issues by student affairs professionals (Croteau & Lark, 1995; Croteau & von Destinon, 1994) as well as students (D'Augelli, 1991; Evans & Wall, 1991; Fassinger, 1991). Similarly, there has been a growth in student affairs and related publications that address the development, needs, and experiences of ethnic minorities (Cheatham & Associates, 1991; Fleming, 1984; McEwen, Roper, Bryant, & Langa, 1990; Reynolds & Pope, 1991; Takaki, 1989). Finally, recent publications have addressed the training, skills, knowledge, and experience needed for helping professionals to understand themselves as cultural beings and to work effectively with diverse populations (Helms, 1992; McEwen & Roper, 1994; Parker, 1988; Sue & Sue, 1990; Talbot, in press). These are just a few of the key resources readily available to student affairs professionals in their journey to understand multiculturalism. Still, each of the models outlined earlier indicate a need for development beyond the cognitive arena if true multiculturalism is to be obtained.

Once individuals have become self-aware, become aware of cultures different from their own, and acquired knowledge about those cultures, it is time for them to experience difference. The goal is to provide stimulation on affective and behavioral levels as well as the cognitive level. Individuals should explore their openness, comfort, and discomfort with difference. Recognizing that there will be some discomfort and learning to understand and manage it is an important component of multicultural development.

Tools and Techniques

One tool for moving beyond the cognitive arena is Parker's Multicultural Action Plan (1988). This three-stage plan parallels the multicultural development process. The first stage is observation, in which the individual (the "armchair observer") is exposed to cultural differences from a "safe distance." The second stage is investigation, in which the individual (the "objective detective") gathers information about himself or herself and others from a closer distance. The information is processed, evaluated, and incorporated into the individual's way of perceiving the world. Finally, the third stage is transformation, in which the individual (the "transforming participant") is prepared for immersion by awareness and knowledge gained from the earlier stages. The contact in this plan is expected to be close and intense. Along with the plan's three stages, there needs to be a forum or mechanism for the individual to process his or her experiences. This is an excellent tool for the classroom or for staff development.

Some simple training techniques that have been very effective in helping individuals move along the multicultural continuum include the following: bringing in panels of culturally diverse individuals, attending events in which the individual is in the minority (perhaps for the first time), simulation exercises such as *BaFa BaFa* (Shirts, 1977) and *Star Power* (1993), role playing for a day (for example, being mobility impaired or blind for a day), and being asked to represent a different voice (Belenky, Clinchy, Goldberger, & Tarule, 1986).

During a recent semesterlong introductory student affairs course, students were asked to take on the voice of a population other than their own (such as gay, lesbian, or bisexual; people of color; disabled people; or international students). Each student was asked to consider that perspective as they did their reading and speak from that voice in class discussions. After getting over their initial fear of representing the voice inaccurately (especially with students from the represented groups in class), students reported feeling challenged, angry, and frustrated with the absence of their voice in the literature and the lack of services on campus that sensitively addressed their needs. Students reported feeling alienated, at times, by the profession they intended to enter. This led to some constructive discussions about how they might be more inclusive in their practices as student affairs professionals. This is just one example of the benefits of experiential activities in the classroom.

Language

For the most part this chapter has focused on the "big picture." It has discussed societal and educational dilemmas, institutional interventions, multicultural models and their applications, and scholarly resources for understanding culture and cultural differences. These concepts and issues can all seem somewhat distant and larger than any one individual. It must be remembered that continuing the journey toward multiculturalism and maintaining ground already gained in this struggle is a day-to-day activity. Language plays a large role in this aspect of the battle: language can be used to maintain power differentials and the status quo, or it can be used to challenge others to think. When college-age males are referred to as "young men" and college-age females are referred to as "girls," a power differential is maintained: men have higher status than girls. When race becomes a discussion about "us" and "them," segregated thinking is perpetuated. When the only legitimate coupling acknowledged in language and written documents is husband and wife, the status quo of heterosexist thinking is maintained. Finally, when outdated and inappropriate terms like *Oriental* are used to refer to all peoples of Asian descent, the wholeness and development of entire ethnic groups are denied. These are just a few examples of the power of misused language. It takes vigilance to constantly monitor one's daily language. Like culture and fashion, language is dynamic. Terms that were appropriate yesterday are not appropriate today; language that is correct today may not be acceptable tomorrow. Effective student affairs professionals should not use outdated, inappropriate language regarding diversity. Sensitivity to language issues in written materials is addressed thoroughly in numerous publications, including the American Psychological Association's (1994) publication manual (pp. 46–53).

Walking Our Talk

As part of a national study evaluating the level of diversity training taking place in student affairs master's degree programs (Talbot, in press), students interviewed mentioned "walking our talk" as a recurring theme. Though students were told by faculty that diversity and multiculturalism were very important, they did not always feel as if these words were matched with deeds. Students indicated that diversity was addressed sporadically at best in student affairs graduate programs, usually focusing on African Americans, women, and nontraditional students. Other diverse groups were rarely addressed. Students also watched faculty to see if diversity played an important role in faculty's personal and professional lives outside the classroom; generally this did not seem to be the case. This inconsistency disturbed most graduate students. They wanted faculty and student affairs practitioners to "walk their talk" regarding their commitment to multiculturalism and diversity.

Maintaining a consistent and vigilant commitment to diversity is challenging; the roadblocks and hazards are many. It is not uncommon to be labeled "politically correct" if you speak out on issues of diversity. At one point in the multicultural movement, "politically correct" was a positive appellation used to describe individuals making an effort to use appropriate language, challenge closed-mindedness, and learn new behaviors, knowledge, and skills. Along the way this expression was coopted by opponents of diversity, and its meaning seemed to shift. Now "politically correct" is used to describe someone who is overzealous about diversity but does not necessarily really believe in it. This backlash against multiculturalism and outspokenness on the issues, manifested by this turnaround in the use of the expression "politically correct," indicates that the challenge is being heard. People often put up smoke screens to cloud the issues when they fear that change is in the air and they are not ready for change. From my perspective, being labeled "politically correct," however it is used, is preferable to being seen as ignorant and insensitive to diversity. The only proper response to someone labeling you as "politically correct" is to say, "Thank you for recognizing my efforts."

Other roadblocks that keep individuals from completing their journey toward multiculturalism are the fear of saying the wrong thing, the fear of not being sufficiently knowledgeable about the topic, and the fear of looking foolish. These fears must be addressed; they will not disappear on their own. In fact, they may occasionally be well founded. If you choose to take this journey, you will make mistakes. You will step on toes, and you will reveal a lack of knowledge. This is to be expected. But if handled genuinely and respectfully, most people will overlook these shortcomings and recognize your efforts more than your mistakes.

Conclusion

The complexity of the issues involved in achieving multiculturalism are evident. Equally evident is the need to gain competency in this area in order to be an effective student affairs professional. Though the journey toward multiculturalism is fraught with roadblocks and hazards, maps (multicultural development models) and landmarks (tools and techniques, stages of development) exist to guide the trip. The biggest step, which must start with each individual and organization, is the decision to begin the journey in the first place.

References

American Psychological Association. (1994). *Publication manual of the American Psychological Association* (4th ed.). Washington, DC: Author.

Atkinson, D. R., & Hackett, G. (Eds.). (1988). *Counseling non-ethnic American minorities.* Springfield, IL: Thomas.

Atkinson, D. R., Morten, G., & Sue, D. (1979). *Counseling American minorities: A cross-cultural perspective.* Dubuque, IA: Brown.

Barr, D. J., & Strong, L. J. (1988). Embracing multiculturalism: The existing contradictions. *NASPA Journal, 26,* 85–90.

Belenky, M. F., Clinchy, B. M., Goldberger, N. R., & Tarule, J. M. (1986). *Women's ways of knowing: The development of self, voice, and mind.* New York: Basic Books.

Bennett, M. J. (1986). A developmental approach to training for intercultural sensitivity. *International Journal of Intercultural Relations, 10*(2), 179–196.

Cass, V. C. (1979). Homosexual identity formation: A theoretical model. *Journal of Homosexuality, 4,* 219–235.

Cheatham, H. E., & Associates. (1991). *Cultural pluralism on campus.* Alexandria, VA: American College Personnel Association.

Corvin, S. A., & Wiggins, F. (1989). An antiracism model for White professionals. *Journal of Multicultural Counseling and Development, 17,* 105–114.

Croteau, J. M., & Lark, J. S. (1995). On being lesbian, gay, or bisexual in student affairs: A national survey of experiences on the job. *NASPA Journal, 32,* 189–197.

Croteau, J. M., & von Destinon, M. (1994). A national survey of job search experiences of lesbian, gay, and bisexual student affairs professionals. *Journal of College Student Development, 35*, 40–45.

D'Augelli, A. R. (1991). Gay men in college: Identity processes and adaptations. *Journal of College Student Development, 32*, 140–146.

Evans, N. J., & Wall, V. A. (1991). *Beyond tolerance: Gays, lesbians, and bisexuals on campus.* Alexandria, VA: American College Personnel Association.

Fassinger, R. E. (1991). The hidden minority: Issues and challenges in working with lesbian women and gay men. *Counseling Psychologist, 19*, 157–176.

Fleming, J. (1984). *Blacks in college: A comparative study of students' success in Black and White institutions.* San Francisco: Jossey-Bass.

Freire, P. (1970). *Pedagogy of the oppressed.* New York: Continuum.

Gilligan, C. (1982). *In a different voice.* Cambridge, MA: Harvard University Press.

Helms, J. E. (1990). Toward a model of White racial identity development. In J. E. Helms (Ed.), *Black and White racial identity: Theory, research, and practice* (pp. 49–66). New York: Greenwood Press.

Helms, J. E. (1992). *A race is a nice thing to have.* Topeka, KS: Content Communications.

Hoopes, D. S. (1979). Intercultural communication concepts and the psychology of intercultural experience. In M. D. Pusch (Ed.), *Multicultural education: A cross-cultural training approach* (pp. 11–38). La Grange Park, IL: Intercultural Network.

Hoopes, D. S., & Pusch, M. D. (1979). Definitions of terms. In M. D. Pusch (Ed.), *Multicultural education: A cross-cultural training approach* (pp. 2–8). La Grange Park, IL: Intercultural Network.

Jefferson, F. C. (1986). Training develops multicultural awareness. *Bulletin of the Association of College Unions-International, 54*, 12–16.

Kuh, G. D. (1990). The demographic juggernaut. In M. J. Barr, M. L. Upcraft, & Associates, *New futures for student affairs: Building a vision for professional leadership and practice* (pp. 71–97). San Francisco: Jossey-Bass.

Manning, K. (1994). Liberation theology and student affairs. *Journal of College Student Development, 35*, 94–97.

Manning, K., & Coleman-Boatwright, P. (1991). Student affairs initiatives toward a multicultural university. *Journal of College Student Development, 32*, 367–374.

McEwen, M. K., & Roper, L. D. (1994). Interracial experiences, knowledge, and skills of master's degree students in graduate programs in student affairs. *Journal of College Student Development, 35*, 81–87.

McEwen, M. K., Roper, L. D., Bryant, D. R., & Langa, M. J. (1990). Incorporating the development of African-American students into psychosocial theories of student development. *Journal of Student Development, 31*, 429–436.

McIntosh, P. M. (1989, July-August). White privilege: Unpacking the invisible knapsack. *Peace and Freedom*, 10–12.

McIntosh, P. M. (1992). *White privilege and male privilege: A personal account of coming to correspondences through work in women's studies* (Working Paper No. 189). Wellesley, MA: Wellesley College Center for Research on Women.

Parker, W. M. (1988). *Consciousness-raising: A primer for multicultural counseling.* Springfield, IL: Thomas.

Pedersen, P. (1988). *Handbook for developing multicultural awareness.* Alexandria, VA: American Association of Counseling and Development.

Pedersen, P. B. (1991). Counseling international students. *Counseling Psychologist, 19,* 10–58.

Pope, R. L. (1993). Multicultural-organization development in student affairs: An introduction. *Journal of College Student Development, 34,* 201–205.

Pusch, M. D. (Ed.). (1979). *Multicultural education: A cross-cultural training approach.* La Grange Park, IL: Intercultural Network.

Reynolds, A. L., & Pope, R. L. (1991). The complexities of diversity: Exploring multiple oppressions. *Journal of Counseling and Development, 70,* 175–180.

Sabnani, H. B., Ponterotto, J. G., & Borodovsky, L. G. (1991). White racial identity development and cross-cultural counselor training: A stage model. *Counseling Psychologist, 19,* 76–102.

Schlossberg, N. K., Lynch, A. Q., & Chickering, A. W. (1989). *Improving higher education environments for adults: Responsive programs and services from entry to departure.* San Francisco: Jossey-Bass.

Schuster, M. R., & Van Dyne, S. R. (1985). Placing women in the liberal arts: Stages of curricular transformation. *Harvard Educational Review, 54,* 413–428.

Shirts, G. (1977). *BaFa BaFa: A cross culture simulation* [Simulation exercise]. Del Mar, CA: Simulation Training Systems.

Stage, F., & Manning, K. (1993). *Enhancing the multicultural campus environment: A cultural brokering approach* (New Directions in Student Services No. 60). San Francisco: Jossey-Bass.

Star Power [Simulation exercise]. (1993). Del Mar, CA: Simulation Training Systems.

Sue, D., Bernie, J., Doreen, A., Weinberg, L., Pedersen, P. B., Smith, E., & Vasquez-Nuttal, E. (1982). Position paper: Cross-cultural counseling competencies. *Counseling Psychologist, 10,* 45–52.

Sue, D. W., & Sue, D. (1990). *Counseling the culturally different* (2nd ed.). New York: Wiley.

Takaki, R. (1989). *Strangers from a different shore: A story of Asian Americans.* New York: Penguin.

Talbot, D. M. (in press). Master's students' perspectives on their graduate education regarding issues of diversity. *NASPA Journal.*

CHAPTER NINETEEN

PROGRAM DEVELOPMENT AND GROUP ADVISING

Michael J. Cuyjet

One of the major characteristics that sets student affairs professionals apart from their counterparts in business and their colleagues on the teaching faculty at their college or university is their ability to "program"—to plan and implement activities and events for the education, development, or satisfaction of a particular constituency. Styles (1985) indicates a belief "that the chief function of student services is to plan programs that facilitate psychological maturity" (p. 197). Whatever the intended purpose, proficiency in successful program development is among the more essential skills required of those in the student affairs milieu.

Student affairs professionals often call upon students to assume a similar role in delivering programs to the campus community; therefore they must be able to train students in these critical program development skills. As advisers to student organizations, their members, and their leaders, student affairs educators need to be competent programmers, and they need to be able to effectively transfer these abilities to the students who come to them for advice and mentoring.

This chapter examines a number of definitions of program development and some of the theoretical bases for promoting it. It also presents a number of program development models, closely examining one of them as a prototype for a wide variety of program development endeavors. Finally, it explores some of the roles and relationships incumbent in serving as advisers to student organizations, particularly those that provide programs to the campus.

Programming Defined

Barr and Keating (1985) define a program as "a theoretically based plan, under which action is taken toward a goal within the context of institutions of higher education" (p. 3). This appears to be one of the most widely accepted descriptions of a program (Andreas, 1993; Morrill, 1989). Barr and Keating's definition calls for the congruent inclusion of three components—the context, the goal, and the plan. This is, in effect, a quick formula for successful program development.

The general context for programming is the higher education community in the United States; the specific context is the unique characteristics and circumstances of the institution at which programming occurs. Student service programming generally has one of three goals: providing essential services, teaching life management skills, and providing opportunities for students to integrate knowledge gained in curricular and cocurricular settings (Barr & Keating, 1985, p. 5). Finally, the plan itself consists of two elements: the planning techniques and the end result of the process. As we will see in the models presented later in this chapter, successful program planning accounts for all of these components.

The issue of congruence among these components is equally important. Program planners may be influenced by their interests, their training, or their job responsibilities to focus more on one or two of these components. Imagine, for example, the diverse perspectives among members of a committee organizing the activities for Greek Week. The Greek adviser may be interested in identifying program goals that support the academic mission of the institution rather than a strictly social agenda. The interfraternity council representative may focus heavily on the plan, anxious to see that all anticipated activities are included. The dean of students may concentrate her concern on the contextual issue of the local community's reaction to the event and the effect on student groups that will not be participating in it. Keating (1985) describes this concern over context as a common pitfall in program planning and indicates that although the planner who overreacts to context may be politically astute, programs ruled primarily by contextual concerns often lack integrity and may be difficult to carry through.

As this example illustrates, the term *program* in college and university contexts is often used in a limited way, to refer only to social or recreational events. But the goals mentioned above are broad and cannot be accomplished through social activities alone. Service delivery, educational opportunities, and interactive intellectual events are also part of programming. Thus when referring to programs in a broad sense, as this chapter does, it is helpful to apply the three-part definition of programs offered by Barr and Cuyjet (1991): first, a program can refer to organized administrative units' delivery of specific activities or services; second, it can mean a series of planned interventions developed for a defined target population or to meet a specific goal; or third, it can cover one-time activities with a planned target and purpose.

Theoretical Bases

It is not difficult to find a theoretical basis for programming—both programming that provides services directly to students and programming designed to involve students in cocurricular activities. Hurst and Jacobson (1985) support the importance of "a theoretical/conceptual foundation for program development" (p. 123).

Furthermore, Barr and Keating (1985) indicate that the first underlying assumption of any program development effort is "the ability of the student services practitioner to understand and apply a variety of theories to the task of program development" (p. 3). Since several previous chapters in this book have specifically explored a variety of theories related to students and their environment, only cursory explorations of those principles will be made here.

Student Development Theory

The literature on student development theory is an important reference for professionals engaged in program development. Student affairs practitioners can draw upon a wide range of human development and organizational theory as they plan and implement programs. An awareness of Erikson's (1968) stages of identity development is useful for campus activities programmers who plan events that involve some measure of social intimacy. Health educators might consider Chickering's developmental vectors (Chickering & Reisser, 1993) in determining the appropriateness of a sophomore workshop on sexual intimacy. Perry's (1970) stages of intellectual and ethical development would be useful in assessing the readiness of residence hall students for activities intended to augment their ability to interact with one another in the halls. Kohlberg's (1984) theory of moral development and Gilligan's (1993) postulates, based on that theory, about the differences between women and men might be helpful to the adviser of a joint fraternity-sorority social infractions board. See Chapters Nine and Ten for a more in-depth review of these important theories.

One caution is in order: as noted in Chapters Nine and Ten, most of the theories generally included under this heading were developed by observations of middle-class, American-born, Caucasian students. Just as Gilligan's work demonstrated that a theory based on one segment of the population (men) is not necessarily applicable to another segment (women), programmers must determine if a similar lack of fit is possible for the groups they are working with, particularly if they consist of students with ethnic identities other than European American.

Environment Theory

Another set of theoretical perspectives examines the relationship between individuals and their environment. Known as interactionism or campus ecology, these draw on theoretical and empirical work from several intellectual traditions (Huebner, 1989). Among the campus ecology literature appear a number of constructs that merit the attention of campus program planners, including environment, interaction, transaction, and congruence or incongruence. For the program planner, probably the most significant among the various concepts of ecological development is the principle of altering the environment to fit the student, instead of expecting the student to adapt to fit the environment. See Chapter Twelve for an examination of the theories and models related to interactions between individuals and their environment.

Since much of the programming on campus is designed for students in groups, the reader would benefit from perusing some of the literature on group development theory. Tuckman's (1965) four-stage model—forming, storming, norming, performing—is considered a classic and is reflected in more recent models by Winston, Bonney, Miller, and Dagley (1988) and Johnson and Johnson (1991). An understanding of organizational theory can also be of assistance to program planners. In Chapter Thirteen, George Kuh describes the conventional and post-conventional "windows," or theoretical constructs and models, used to examine the behavior of individuals and groups in complex organizations.

Involvement Theory

There is one theoretical foundation that provides such a clear rationale for college and university program development that it merits specific mention here. Astin's (1984) student involvement theory argues that any particular curriculum, to achieve its intended outcomes, must "elicit sufficient student effort to bring about the desired learning and development" (p. 301). He defines student involvement as "the amount of physical and psychological energy that the student devotes to the academic experience" (p. 297). Astin suggests that the most precious institutional resource may be student time, and "the extent to which students can achieve particular developmental goals is a direct function of the time and effort they devote to activities designed to produce these gains" (p. 301). In other words, this developmental theory identifies the time and the psychic and physical energy students invest in campus events and activities as the direct link between the developmental goals of the institution and the programs its staff—particularly its student affairs staff—plan and implement. One important consideration to remember is that Astin's theory is based on a much broader definition of "involvement" than simply joining extracurricular activities or club events. He describes the highly involved student as "one who, for example, devotes considerable energy to studying, spends much time on campus, participates actively in student organizations, and interacts frequently with faculty members and other students" (p. 297).

Program Development Models

A number of useful program planning models have been developed which can be of assistance to those designing and implementing services, interventions, and activities on campus. The "cube" model, originally developed by Morrill, Oetting, and Hurst (1974) to display three dimensions of counselor functioning, examined the relationship between the target, purpose, and methods of an intervention. A modification and reapplication of the cube by Hurst and Jacobson (1985) resulted in a valuable tool for defining, describing, and interrelating these three dimensions specifically for program development (see Figure 19.1). The elements included in the updated model's "purposes of intervention" are taken from Drum's (1980) seven dimensions of student development: cognitive structures, aesthetic development, identity formation, physical health, moral reasoning, interpersonal relatedness, and social perspective. These provide a comprehensive set of values that can serve as the basis for a wide range of student support programs. The revised model expands upon the original's "targets of intervention" by adding several components of environment and ecology theory. It also adds administrative and resource management as a fourth method of intervention.

A model designed by Aulepp and Delworth (1976) focuses on the design and manipulation of environments as a major method of shaping student behavior. Commonly called the "ecomapping model" because of its emphasis on the campus ecology, this model includes seven steps: selecting institutional values, translating those values into goals, designing environments to match the goals, creating an environment fit for students, measuring students' perceptions, monitoring students' behavior, and feeding data back into the design. One important aspect of this model is that its steps are interdependent, so the process can begin at any step. Thus, on a campus that has already engaged in ecomapping, a particular intervention may begin at step five (Banning, 1989). Ecomapping can occur on three levels: macrodesign, which involves the entire campus community; microdesign, which identifies a target population; and life space design, which seeks to understand individual students' relationship to the campus environment (Styles, 1985).

FIGURE 19.1. THEORETICAL AND CONCEPTUAL FOUNDATIONS FOR PROGRAM DEVELOPMENT.

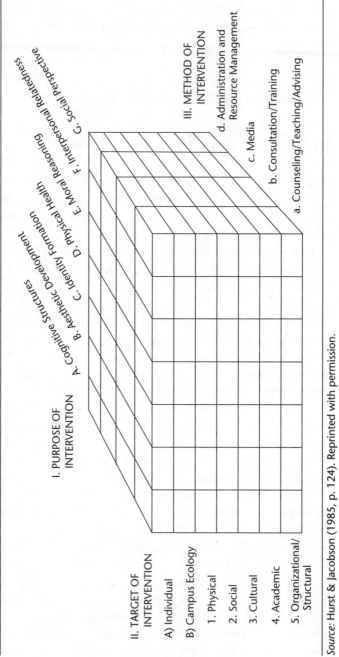

Source: Hurst & Jacobson (1985, p. 124). Reprinted with permission.

A somewhat more general model—one that presents a method for developing both the goal of a program and a plan for implementing it—is the linear model of Moore and Delworth (1976). This model proceeds through five stages:

1. *Initiating the program.* This stage consists of germinating the idea, assembling a planning team, assessing needs, resources, and constraints, identifying alternative targets and purposes, and selecting a program.
2. *Planning program goals, objectives, delivery systems, and evaluation.* This stage includes selecting goals and objectives, designing training methods or delivery systems, planning intervention methods, and planning for evaluation.
3. *Pilot program.* This stage involves circulating publicity, implementing a pilot program, and assessing it.
4. *Program implementation.* This stage repeats the pilot procedures in a full-scale program.
5. *Program refinement.* This stage consists of refining training procedures, training trainers, planning for continued evaluation, and offering a regular schedule for the program.

These brief descriptions of earlier models depict a sort of progression from the original cube model to counseling interventions, concerns regarding environmental impact, and finally a more generally applicable model. Continuing that evolution, Barr and Cuyjet (1991) proposed a six-step approach to program planning that places a greater emphasis on environmental assessment and on setting goals for target populations. Such considerations are crucial for today's programmers, who must design programs that satisfy an ever-widening diversity of student needs and interests. An adaptation of Barr and Cuyjet's six-step model is described below:

Step 1: Assessment

Current operations. Determine what activities and programs are already in place and serving the community's needs.

Student characteristics. Carefully analyze the demographic characteristics of the student community, taking notice of smaller, nonmainstream groups.

Needs. Use both obtrusive measures (asking students to supply information for program ideas) and unobtrusive measures (such as consulting other student affairs staff, faculty, community leaders with ties to the campus, and database information).

Institutional environment. Consider the institutional mission, history, and political climate and the views of significant campus decision makers.

Resources. Determine the availability and skill levels of the staff you would like to use; anticipated costs, potential funding sources, and availability of money; available resources such as space, furnishing, equipment, commodities, and services.

Past programming. Examine what has been tried before, and determine why past programs succeeded or failed.

Step 2: Goal Setting

Target population. Identify whom the program is intended for, and take steps accordingly to be appropriately inclusive or restrictive in your planning.

Desired outcomes. Be clear about what you expect to accomplish and what you do *not* plan to achieve. Indicate for whom and under what conditions outcomes should occur.

Objectives. Since broad-based goals are difficult to evaluate, set specific, measurable objectives that can be used to determine how successful the program is.

Step 3: Planning

Planning team. Establish a small but effective working group with a broad range of skills that is able to function as a team. The team must include members of the target population or others affected by the program, particularly if the target is not a mainstream group.

Approach. Consider what developmental theory indicates about the target population, how the group learns, what media are available, what delivery system will be most effective, and whether to use convergent thinking to focus the planning group or a divergent approach to consider different learning styles among the target population.

Initial extent of program. Determine the initial scope of the program—either a full program package, a limited program to which components can be added later, or a pilot program.

Training. Compare staff skills and abilities against the tasks to be performed to determine what training is required. Provide the necessary information and resources, including training of trainers if appropriate.

Time line. Determine a target date and work backward to establish a realistic, week-by-week activity plan.

Budget. Determine the actual fiscal resources necessary to complete the program, including all costs for personnel, materials, space, marketing, telecommunications, postage, food, transportation, and equipment.

Step 4: Implementation

Responsibilities. Delegate tasks and responsibilities, identifying clear lines of accountability, reporting relationships, and deadlines.

Publicity. Catch the target group's attention and make them want to seek more information. Use a variety of media, and collaborate with faculty who teach marketing and advertising. Involve members of the target group in designing the campaign.

Location. Locate the program in a barrier-free, highly visible, high-traffic facility. Pay attention to lighting (for safety), parking, building aesthetics, and proximity to related programs. If the program consists of a series of events, try to use a consistent place, day, and time.

Timing. Plan the program to complement other, related programs. Select a day, date, and time most conducive to the target population's needs and circumstances. Avoid conflicting with major traditional activities, academic events like final exams, or religious holy days or other special events observed by different members of the campus community.

Equipment. Be certain adequate amounts of all needed materials are on hand and in good working order. If a trained technician is required to operate a device, be sure to schedule that person. Provide for the proper removal of any leftover items.

Evaluation. Collect evaluative responses from participants. Solicit both process evaluations, on how well the planning and implementation went, and product evaluations, on the elements contained in the program itself. Use a variety of media for evaluation: face-to-face interviews, written forms, telephone calls, suggestion cards.

Step 5: Postassessment

Analysis. Review evaluation data and relate the information to program goals, objectives, and anticipated outcomes. Prepare these data in a report applicable to future programs.

Recognition and rewards. Identify individuals and groups who contributed significantly to the program's success, including program planners, participants, and peripheral sponsors, and publicly acknowledge and celebrate their roles.

Unexpected outcomes. Identify activities or events that were not part of the original plan, and determine whether they impeded or enhanced the program.

Fiscal evaluation. Determine how well actual expenses matched anticipated costs for each program component. Identify unusual factors that may account for any discrepancies. Decide if alternative methods of delivery would have been less expensive. If it is useful, document the cost per student, cost per transaction, or cost to the institution for each service provided.

Programmers' reactions. Collect evaluative data from program planners, including suggestions for potential changes. Ask about both process and product.

Ecological impact. Make sure the program's success did not come at the expense of some element of the campus environment. Determine the program's impact on the campus community as a whole, on other programs, on physical space and its use, on nontargeted segments of the population, and on the institution's mission and goals.

Community building. View the program in terms of its effect on efforts to develop positive relationships among all segments of the campus community and with the larger community surrounding the campus.

Program modifications. Use all evaluation data to identify suggestions for program modifications. Make appropriate recommendations; even small changes can often bring a program closer to its stated goals and objectives.

Step 6: Administrative Decision Making

Future plans. After examining all the information compiled in the postassessment step, decide on one of three actions for the future: modification, abandonment, or continuation. Continuation decisions should specify a definite period of time and include provisions for a built-in review. The decision to modify should also include a scheduled review at a specific later date.

This model provides the programmer with a useful tool for planning and implementing services, events, and activities on campus. But there is much more to programming than program structure. As indicated in Step 5, a program's ecological impact and its effects on enhancing community building are critical considerations in the complex campus societies of today.

Although any of the models described here can be useful in developing a variety of campus programs, particular attention is focused on this final model because it is both comprehensive and versatile. Such versatility is essential for today's programmer, who must consider a number of significant societal and cultural factors in the process of bringing a program to fruition. It is for good reason that analysis of target population demographics is among the first tasks in the model's assessment step. Most failures to provide services, interventions, or activities for all of the diverse populations on campus are a result of omission rather than intentional neglect. Campus officials who fail to fully understand the wide range of cultural identities that must be considered in the early stages of program development are often made aware of their negligence rather dramatically at the end of the implementation stage or while conducting postassessment evaluations.

For example, imagine your campus has a large number of part-time students who must take classes in the evening when other family members are available to provide child care. As the assistant director of career services, you are not aware of these students; you schedule a series of workshops on resume writing and job search skills during the noon hour, to accommodate commuter students. The outcry from the young mothers who attend in the evening takes you by surprise. While an absence of malice in such an oversight can be appreciated, it does not make it any less painful to those who feel slighted. As described by Donna Talbot in Chapter Eighteen, competency in recognizing and appreciating diversity and multicultural dimensions on campus is an essential programming skill. Chapter Four also provides a useful agenda for developing sensitivity to the needs of diverse campus populations.

The impact of programming on programmers is another important variable in this process, especially when program development is part of the educational experience of students assisting in or assuming program development responsibilities. This form of involvement has tremendous potential for the development of leadership skills, as explored by Judy Rogers in Chapter Fourteen.

Program Advising

A considerable amount of a typical campus's programming is done by students. As such, this program development constitutes an extension of the institution's educational activities, what Boatman and Shellogg (1989) describe as "teaching in a non-classroom setting" (p. 2). Several earlier chapters have examined various types of interaction between student affairs staff and students: advising (Chapter Sixteen), consultation (Chapter Seventeen), and teaching (Chapter Fifteen). In the same way that faculty are critical to the education that occurs in the classroom, student programming and student organization advisers can be important catalysts for learning that occurs through program development and implementation, outside the classroom. Hence, an examination of the roles, relationships, and responsibilities of student affairs advisers is significant to this discussion of program development.

Roles and Responsibilities

Although a number of writers (Averill, 1993; Boersig, 1993; Clement & Rickard, 1992; Emmett, 1983; Lorenz & Shipton, 1984; McKaig & Policello, 1984;

Sandeen, 1991) have addressed the subject of the adviser's role, many of them refer to Bloland's (1967) description as a good, comprehensive foundation. Bloland identifies three major areas of the adviser's role:

1. *Maintenance functions* are those activities that serve simply to maintain the student organization and keep it out of difficulty. Examples of maintenance are providing continuity with the history and traditions of past years, preventing the group from breaking the college's rules, and arbitrating intragroup disputes.
2. *Group growth functions* are those activities that improve the operation and effectiveness of the group and help it progress toward achieving its goals. These include coaching group officers in the principles of good organizational and administrative practice, teaching the elements of effective group operation, developing procedures and plans for action, and keeping the group focused on its goals.
3. *Program content functions* stimulate the intelligence and ability of the student participants and help them plan activities that will contribute to their own intellectual development while enriching campus life. In the area of program content, the student affairs adviser assumes a genuinely educational function that can parallel, complement, or supplement the formal curricular offerings of the college. Among these functions are introducing new program ideas with an intellectual flavor, providing opportunities for the practice of skills acquired in the classroom, pointing out new perspectives and directions, and supplying expert knowledge and the insights of experience.

Boersig (1993) groups these roles into six categories: educator and trainer, resource person, source of continuity, fiscal agent, confidant and counselor, and group dynamics and conflict mediator. Sandeen (1991) simply says the adviser must be a leader, a manager, a mediator, and an educator.

Bloland also describes a number of responsibilities advisers are likely to have. Among the general responsibilities are teaching or coaching, consulting on programs, providing continuity, counseling individual students, interpreting policy, supervising, and meeting emergencies. Possible specific responsibilities include providing financial supervision, sponsoring social activities, attending all organization meetings, monitoring scholastic eligibility, maintaining organizational records, and knowing institutional requirements.

Advising Relationships

It is critical to focus on the development of the relationship between advisers and groups in order to maximize their effective interaction. According to Golden and

Schwartz (1994), the adviser must view ethics, integrity, honesty, commitment, and caring as essential elements of a good relationship. Floerchinger (1992) offers five basic elements for developing good student-adviser relationships: shared responsibility for relationship building; open, direct communication; recognition of faculty and staff members' additional commitments; a focus on human value systems and individual styles of interaction; and attention to the process of growth and development.

Formal training for advisers is an excellent medium for building these relationships. Such a program provides an opportunity for the campus activities office or the dean of students office to provide tangible support for organizational well-being. It also provides a uniform structure for interactions between students and staff and a forum for them to discuss their responsibilities as members of the campus community. If formal training is not feasible, or if a supplement to such training is desired, activities staff can provide these additional supports for effective utilization of advisers: prepare an adviser notebook, guide, or contract; make sure the adviser receives copies of any and all correspondence sent to students; offer leadership training for the group members; offer institutional assistance in skill building, recruitment and retention of advisers, and facilitating interaction among advisers; provide incentives to faculty and staff to serve in these capacities; offer adviser training on specific student development issues; maintain a library of recent and pertinent information; and provide money to supplement faculty activities (Floerchinger, 1992). See Chapter Fifteen for a thorough examination of training procedures.

Advising Styles

In 1983, Allen theorized that three environmental factors can drastically affect an adviser's freedom to choose a style: the university's expectations of the adviser and the program; the students' expectations of the adviser and the program; and the level of the students' development. During the 1980s, student activities professionals began applying Hersey and Blanchard's (1988) situational leadership model to shape the advising role in the context of the development of student organization leaders. Allen (1983) and McKaig and Policello (1984) both presented models in which students progress through four stages of development: infancy, adolescence, young adulthood, and maturity. Advisers are expected to have four styles that correspond to the developmental maturity of the students they advise: director, teacher-director, adviser-teacher, and consultant.

McKaig and Policello (1984) also developed the following formula for determining effective advising style: EAS = A, G, C. In this model, an effective advising style (EAS) is determined by considering the adviser (A), evaluating his or her skill at performing advising functions and using available resources; the group (G), including its purpose, history, status, and work; and the context (C), including institutional expectations for the group and institutional policies regarding extracurricular activities.

In her more recent writings, Allen (1990) suggests that advising may follow "the underlying principles of complex dynamic systems" (p. 58). Allen recommends an emergent advising paradigm that shifts from linear to nonlinear thinking and updates "our definition of personal and professional competence" (p. 61). But such useful models notwithstanding, style is, ultimately, a personal choice. Perhaps that is the best advice for the potential adviser—adopt a style that works for you, reflects your outlook, and optimizes your ability to develop and maintain comfortable relationships with your advisees. Remember that a successful advising style is not static. As Boersig (1993) states, the successful adviser "will need to adjust his/her style and adapt to the student" (p. 13).

Staff or Faculty Advisers

One of the major factors affecting the extent to which student group advisers can assume one or more of these roles is the extent of their other responsibilities to the institution. Advisers generally come from one of two groups on campus— student affairs staff and faculty. For those in the former group, attention to students' needs and activities is a primary responsibility; therefore they can devote considerable effort and resources to a number of different advising roles. The clearest example is the staff of the campus activities or student activities office, whose primary role is to provide advice, consultation, partnership, leadership, and technical assistance to student organization leaders and programming groups.

The second group, advisers from the faculty, have a somewhat less convenient passage to the ranks of student advising in that student group advising is not among the faculty's primary responsibilities of teaching and conducting research. At some institutions, with the exception of academic advising to their department's majors, student advising is not even considered part of faculty members' service obligation. Thus the benefits of serving students in this manner are extrinsic to the faculty reward system. Fortunately this absence of direct compensation does not deter many faculty members, who volunteer their time and energy in a wide spectrum of advising relationships with students. Moreover, as Astin (1984) notes in discussing his involvement theory, "finding ways to encourage greater student involvement with faculty (and vice versa) could be a highly productive activity on most college campuses" (p. 304). Student involvement and interaction with faculty are considered determining factors in students' satisfaction, intellectual and personal development, and persistence (Floerchinger, 1992).

Rewards

In those cases where a faculty member does not receive recognition from his or her department or college for serving as an adviser to a student group, it is doubly important for the group to provide public recognition of the faculty member's service. As much as advisers, whether faculty or staff, are willing to give of themselves in support of a group, the group bears a responsibility to offer some tangible benefit to the adviser for his or her efforts. Framed certificates or plaques are common forms of recognition, but a letter extolling the adviser's contributions sent to the adviser's immediate supervisor may be a more poignant reward. Emmett (1983) suggests that student organizations endeavor to acquire a formal letter of appointment from the institution's president or chancellor as an official recognition of the faculty member's contribution to the campus community. Floerchinger (1992) adds that rewarding the volunteer efforts of advisers should be mandatory. Of course, saying "thank you" is irreplaceable as a means of enhancing the group's relationship with its adviser.

In addition to a need to feel appreciated, most faculty will also eventually lose interest if not made to feel needed. As described above, there are numerous potential, meaningful aspects to an adviser's role. It is incumbent upon the organization to discover not only those roles that maximize the adviser's capabilities but also those in which he or she is most likely to find personal satisfaction at being of service to the group.

Advice to Advisers

Finally, there are several issues that advisers on most campuses probably need to address in order to do the best advising job possible as well as protect themselves from awkward situations or personal liability:

1. *Determine the nature of your role.* The institution's expectations are a significant influence on how advisers perform, as well as a determinant in whether they assume an advisory role at all. Does the school want its advisers to be student advocates or agents of the institution? Advisers must learn exactly what these expectations are, and campus activities personnel can help teach them.

2. *Anticipate controversial situations.* Occasionally an adviser must resolve a dilemma created by a proposed group activity or event. The event may threaten the institution's mission (for example, a pro-choice rally at a Catholic college). Students may propose an event that includes some illegal activity, like serving alcohol to minors. Programs involving guest speakers who may be offensive to some portion of the campus community, films with explicit sex or violence, and entertainers

perceived to be inappropriate role models for younger students are other examples of dilemmas that advisers will want to help their advisees negotiate satisfactorily.

3. *Advocate for inclusion and diversity.* Use your own resources and all others available to you to sensitize group members to different perceptions, attitudes, and cultural characteristics. For example, help students understand that an event that excludes all nonwhite students, even if unintentionally, is hurtful to the group and to others outside the group and is probably also in violation of the school's equal opportunity policy. Group members may also need the adviser's help to understand the nuances and possible consequences of seemingly minor actions—for example, recruitment practices, membership requirements, or meeting times and locations that restrict participation.

4. *Assess the liabilities of participation.* The adviser needs to understand the liabilities involved in assuming an advisory role. These include not only legal liability (see Chapter Seven) but also personal sacrifice in terms of time that could otherwise be spent on class preparation or research, administrative responsibilities, family, or even personal leisure. While the rewards of advising can be great, it is important to understand the costs involved, too.

5. *Do your homework.* To deal with potential problems, advisers need a functional knowledge of the institution's mission, its major policies, its code of conduct, the political climate on campus, and local ordinances and laws. More importantly, a well-prepared adviser has good common sense and the willingness to use it for the good of the group and the institution.

Conclusion

Program planning and development are critical functions in American colleges and universities. Staff who possess skills that enable them to provide quality services, interventions, and activities for the cocurricular life of their campus make a significant contribution to higher education. This chapter has defined program development and examined a number of theoretical bases for promoting it on campus as part of the educational process.

Program planners need good theoretical models to assist them in designing and implementing activities and services. This chapter examined a number of such models and presented one as most useful for a wide range of program development options. Related issues, such as concern for the needs of diverse populations and cultural identities, were also explored.

Since one significant role of program development staff is to assist students in learning program planning as part of their academic experience, the major elements of student group advising were also examined here. The important roles and responsibilities incumbent in this advising function were reviewed. Enhancing the relationship between advisers and their advisees was discussed, along with how advisers can adopt different styles to work more effectively with students. The differences between faculty advisers and staff advisers was noted, as was the importance of providing advisers with appropriate rewards for the time and effort they devote to these tasks. Lastly, a number of other issues were examined that advisers need to address in order to adequately serve in this important, but often underrated, role.

References

Allen, K. E. (1983). Choosing the effective advising style. *Campus Activities Programming, 16*(1), 34–37.

Allen, K. E. (1990). Making sense out of chaos: Leading and living in dynamic systems. *Campus Activities Programming, 23,* 56–63.

Andreas, R. E. (1993). Program planning. In M. J. Barr & Associates, *The handbook of student affairs administration* (pp. 199–215). San Francisco: Jossey-Bass.

Astin, A. W. (1984). Student involvement: A developmental theory for higher education. *Journal of College Student Personnel, 25,* 297–308.

Aulepp, L., & Delworth, U. (1976). *Training manual for an ecosystem model.* Boulder, CO: Western Interstate Commission for Higher Education.

Averill, V. (1993). Responsibilities of being an RHA advisor. In N. W. Dunkel & C. L. Spencer (Eds.), *Advice for advisors: The development of an effective residence hall association* (pp. 19–26). Columbus, OH: Association of College and University Housing Officers—International.

Banning, J. H. (1989). Creating a climate for successful student development: The campus ecology manager role. In U. Delworth, G. R. Hanson, & Associates, *Student services: A handbook for the profession* (2nd ed., pp. 304–322). San Francisco: Jossey-Bass.

Barr, M. J., & Cuyjet, M. J. (1991). Program development and implementation. In T. K. Miller, R. B. Winston, Jr., & Associates, *Administration and leadership in student affairs* (pp. 706–739). Muncie, IN: Accelerated Development.

Barr, M. J., & Keating, L. A. (1985). Introduction: Elements of program development. In M. J. Barr, L. A. Keating, & Associates, *Developing effective student service programs: Systematic approaches for practitioners* (pp. 1–14). San Francisco: Jossey-Bass.

Bloland, P. A. (1967). *Student group advising in higher education* (Student Personnel Series No. 8). Washington, DC: American Personnel and Guidance Association.

Boatman, S., & Shellogg, K. (1989, February). *The student organization adviser role: Perceptions of officers and advisers.* Paper presented at the national convention of the National Association for Campus Activities, Nashville, TN.

Boersig, P. (1993). The first advising position. In N. W. Dunkel & C. L. Spencer (Eds.), *Advice for advisors: The development of an effective residence hall association* (pp. 9–18). Columbus, OH: Association of College and University Housing Officers—International.

Chickering, A. W., & Reisser, L. (1993). *Education and identity* (2nd ed.). San Francisco: Jossey-Bass.

Clement, L. M., & Rickard, S. T. (1992). *Effective leadership in student services: Voices from the field.* San Francisco: Jossey-Bass.

Drum, D. J. (1980). Understanding student development. In W. H. Morrill, J. C. Hurst, & E. R. Oetting (Eds.), *Dimensions of intervention for student development* (pp. 14–38). New York: Wiley.

Emmett, M. A. (1983). Enlisting faculty advisors. *Campus Activities Programming, 16*(5), 31–35.

Erikson, E. H. (1968). *Identity: Youth and crisis.* New York: Norton.

Floerchinger, D. (1992). Enhancing the role of student organization advisors in building a positive campus community. *Campus Activities Programming, 26*(6), 39–46.

Gilligan, C. (1993). *In a different voice: Psychological theory and women's development.* Cambridge, MA: Harvard University Press.

Golden, D. C., & Schwartz, H. L. (1994). Building an ethical and effective relationship with student government leaders. In M. C. Terrell & M. J. Cuyjet (Eds.), *Developing student government leadership* (New Directions for Student Services No. 66, pp. 19–30). San Francisco: Jossey-Bass.

Hersey, P., & Blanchard, K. H. (1988). *Management of organizational behavior: Utilizing human resources* (5th ed.). Englewood Cliffs, NJ: Prentice Hall.

Huebner, L. A. (1989). Interaction of student and campus. In U. Delworth, G. R. Hanson, & Associates, *Student services: A handbook for the profession* (2nd ed., pp. 165–208). San Francisco: Jossey-Bass.

Hurst, J. C., & Jacobson, J. K. (1985). Theories underlying students' needs for programs. In M. J. Barr, L. A. Keating, & Associates, *Developing effective student service programs: Systematic approaches for practitioners* (pp. 113–136). San Francisco: Jossey-Bass.

Johnson, D. W., & Johnson, F. P. (1991). *Joining together: Group theory and group skills* (4th ed.). Englewood Cliffs, NJ: Prentice Hall.

Keating, L. A. (1985). Common pitfalls in program planning. In M. J. Barr, L. A. Keating, & Associates, *Developing effective student service programs: Systematic approaches for practitioners* (pp. 275–297). San Francisco: Jossey-Bass.

Kohlberg, L. (1984). *Essays on moral development: Vol. 2. The psychology of moral development: The nature and validity of moral stages.* New York: Harper & Row.

Lorenz, N., & Shipton, W. (1984). A practical approach to group advising and problem solving. In J. H. Schuh (Ed.), *A handbook for student group advisors* (pp. 71–88). Alexandria, VA: American College Personnel Association.

McKaig, R., & Policello, S. (1984). Group advising—defined, described and examined. In J. H. Schuh (Ed.), *A handbook for student group advisors* (pp. 45–70). Alexandria, VA: American College Personnel Association.

Moore, M., & Delworth, U. (1976). *Training manual for student service program development.* Boulder, CO: Western Interstate Commission for Higher Education.

Morrill, W. H. (1989). Program development. In U. Delworth, G. R. Hanson, & Associates, *Student services: A handbook for the profession* (2nd ed., pp. 420–439). San Francisco: Jossey-Bass.

Morrill, W. H., Oetting, E. R., & Hurst, J. C. (1974). Dimensions of intervention for student development. *Personnel and Guidance Journal, 52,* 354–359.

Perry, W. G., Jr. (1970). *Forms of intellectual and ethical development in the college years.* New York: Holt, Rinehart and Winston.

Sandeen, A. (1991). *The chief student affairs officer: Leader, manager, mediator, educator.* San Francisco: Jossey-Bass.

Styles, M. H. (1985). Effective models of systematic program planning. In M. J. Barr, L. A. Keating, & Associates, *Developing effective student service programs: Systematic approaches for practitioners* (pp. 181–211). San Francisco: Jossey-Bass.

Tuckman, B. W. (1965). Developmental sequence in small groups. *Psychology Bulletin, 63,* 384–399.

Winston, R. B., Jr., Bonney, W. C., Miller, T. K., & Dagley, J. C. (1988). *Promoting student development through intentionally structured groups: Principles, techniques, and applications.* San Francisco: Jossey-Bass.

CHAPTER TWENTY

ASSESSMENT, EVALUATION, AND RESEARCH

T. Dary Erwin

How should ideas about college students' needs and the programs that serve them be formed and shaped? Should the practices of the profession be guided by intuition, logic, traditions, the political climate, or something else? Far too often, the missing ingredient in student affairs is credible information to guide practice. Information from research, assessment, and evaluation should be used to augment decisions based on tradition and politics. Assessment and evaluation, whether used to advance the profession's research base or to shed light on the effectiveness of local educational programs and services, provide a reality check to aid in understanding what happens to students while they are in college.

This chapter explains the role of information in decision-making processes concerning students and programs. The definitions and purposes of research, assessment, and evaluation are presented along with some key terms and concepts, qualitative and quantitative perspectives, and analytical and reporting strategies for the new student affairs professional. The chapter is intended as an introduction to research methodology and applied assessment practice (see Delworth & Hanson, 1989).

Rationale and Public Policy

The value of a college education has increasingly been questioned, particularly during the past ten years. A variety of reports conclude that the goals of higher education are often murky, the methods of measuring its quality are suspect, and its impact on students is mixed (Association of American Colleges, 1985; Mercer, 1994; Wingspread Group on Higher Education, 1994). Whatever the doubt or criticism, questions about the value of college remain in constituents' minds and are reflected in the lessening proportion of state budgets allocated to higher education. Public higher education has received 4.6 percent less of state budgets since 1982 (Kristin, 1992). In addition, accreditation agencies and the peer review system have come under fire for lack of rigor and absence of quality outcomes (Education Commission of the States, 1994). A series of national goals for education were delineated for college students, with proposed national tests in critical thinking, communication skills, and problem solving (Corrallo, 1991). Although the full effect of these acts is uncertain, governance of higher education is clearly shifting away from the academy.

The role of student affairs within higher education is also under closer scrutiny, and the profession is being pressed to change. According to the latest financial reports, student affairs divisions have borne greater cuts than academic affairs divisions (El-Khawas, 1994). Moreover, the recent conservative movement in the United States questions colleges' goal of educating students in areas of personal and social development, claiming that "social engineering" of students' attitudes are politically motivated and narrowly focused. Inside the profession of student affairs, concerns about quality are evident in revisions to statements of professional ethics to include statements like this: "Evaluate programs, services, and organizational structures regularly and systematically to assure conformity to published standards and guidelines. Evaluations should be conducted using rigorous evaluation methods and principles, and the results should be made available to appropriate institutional personnel" (American College Personnel Association, 1993, p. 92).

Whatever the source or reason, professionals need to document the educational effectiveness of the programs and services they provide or for which they are responsible. This process of documentation is one that can no longer be assigned to other people or totally relegated to offices outside student affairs. Each of us should be able to supply evidence about the usefulness of our programs and services—for our own use, for administrative use, or for use by external officials and the public. The more that graduates of programs of student development and higher education know about statistics and models of evaluation and measurement, the more informed decisions will be about students and the profession (Erwin, 1990, 1993).

What Are Assessment, Evaluation, and Research?

Assessment is the "systematic basis for making inferences about the learning and development of students" (Erwin, 1991, p. 15). It is a process for defining, measuring, collecting, analyzing, and using information to enrich the educational experience of students. Evaluation includes assessment but may also be concerned with measuring staff performance and the quality of noneducational programs and facilities. For example, assessment might be concerned with increasing students' flexibility and open-mindedness, while evaluation might focus on efficient processing of admissions applications. Assessment focuses on the primary mission of the institution—educating students. Assessment is a prime vehicle for addressing current questions about the nature and quality of the undergraduate curriculum. Evaluation is concerned with the overall value of education and with efficient operations of the institution. While evaluation includes assessment of educational practices, it also addresses the quality of noneducational institutional functions and facilities (such as financial aid processing, physical plant facilities, and campus parking). Assessment is student-oriented, asking whether students benefit or are changed in their learning and development. Evaluation may be either student- or resource-oriented. At most institutions, student affairs is concerned with both assessment and evaluation.

Research deals with advancing the professional knowledge of the higher education community. Although assessment is primarily concerned with a single institution, research findings may be generalizable to several institutions. Research is concerned both with forming new theories and conceptual approaches and with confirming or refuting existing theories and educational practices. Assessment, on the other hand, is primarily concerned with the confirmation or refutation of approaches. For example, Belenky, Clinchy, Goldberger, and Tarule (1986) put forth new theories, based on their research, about how women make decisions. Assessment might be concerned with how an adult women's reentry program is related to her identity development at a particular institution.

Historically, the focus of assessment began with basic skills, moved to undergraduate major or concentration programs, then to general education, and finally to the education-related activities of student affairs. Of course, overlap is typical. For example, oral communication skills may play a part in several of the areas.

The purposes of assessment and evaluation are important to establish early on, because the purposes often dictate the formality and rigor of the methods and study design (see Table 20.1).

Much of the time, program improvement is the primary reason for conducting assessments and evaluations. Educators or administrators use the findings to make improvements in the program. For example, if a study finds that roommate pairs who are at similar developmental levels mature faster and do better in school, roommate assignments might be structured accordingly (Erwin, 1984). Student affairs professionals and counselors have long provided feedback from tests to improve the lives of individual students. Given the economic and political

TABLE 20.1. PURPOSES OF ASSESSMENT.

	Formative (Improvement)	Summative (Accountability)
Students	needs	certification
Program	modifications	funding

climate of higher education today, it is wise to consider collecting and using information for accountability or summative purposes in offices and divisions of student affairs. In terms of accountability, test results demonstrate whether students have progressed to a higher educational level; they also determine whether programs receive funding. In general, studies used for purposes of accountability are more formal, planned studies, in which the quality (reliability and validity) of the methodology and research design are closely scrutinized.

What Should Be Studied?

The first step in most assessments of programs or services is to decide what should be accomplished in terms of educating the student. Program objectives and goals should specify the knowledge students will learn, the competencies necessary for success, and the expected developmental outcomes. For example, students will be able to describe and apply the steps for negotiating contracts with the student activities programming board (knowledge); students will maintain self-confidence when among people from another culture; students will demonstrate small-group interpersonal communication skills in identifying issues and problems, soliciting member points of view, reaching consensus, and implementing actions (competencies). Simply listing goal areas such as "intellectual skills" or "personal development" is insufficient for describing to outside audiences what student affairs is about. In addition, specifically defined purposes serve as guides in gathering information about quality. Other examples of objectives for student affairs can be found in Erwin, Scott, and Menard (1991).

As part of the assessment process, it is important to focus on what students are expected to learn, develop, or do rather than a description of the program or service. To offer an alcohol and substance abuse workshop, for instance, does not state the purpose for students. Many upper-level administrators and funding sources prefer clear purposes and objectives, which in turn help define student affairs work on campus.

Several other terms need to be defined here because of their frequent use in accreditation and other external reviews. In particular, accreditation agencies have criticized colleges and universities for substituting *inputs*—descriptions of facilities and services, measures of the scholastic ability of entering students, resource expenditures, and such—for measures of learning and development. William Bennett, former U.S. secretary of education, spoke forcefully of the misguided emphasis on inputs such as entering scholastic ability measures or amount of resources as measures of student learning. The number of library books or type of facilities at an institution are considered indirect inputs into the educational process. Students' participation in programs is also an input into the process of learning and development. *Outputs* are simplistic measures of the products of an institution, such as graduation and retention rates. Institutions are typically required to report outputs in the state and national review processes. Outputs can be easily misinterpreted, and they are really only indirect measures of quality. On the other hand, *outcomes* represent the actual results of education—what students have learned or developed. They are direct measures of quality. Developmental outcomes may be reported as basic skills, such as writing and mathematics; general education, such as knowledge in biological science and the arts; general intellectual skills, such as inductive reasoning; or personal development, such as in interpersonal relationships and identity. Occasionally outcomes are used as substitutes for objectives—assessment results are the actual outcomes, whether they meet the objectives or not.

As noted above, evaluation and research may have different purposes. In evaluation studies, goals may be unknown or not clearly stated. Some evaluation studies seek simply to understand more about current practices or to provide general enlightenment of program goals, without a stated purpose. Research, on the other hand, generally relies on a hypothesis or statement about the relationships between events or variables as a starting point. (Most professional journals require such statements for research papers.) If possible, the hypothesis is verified through an experiment to "determine the presence or absence of a difference, relationship, or treatment effect" (Yaremko, Harari, Harrison, and Lynn, 1986, p. 96) or through naturalistic observation (Guba & Lincoln, 1981). In many educational and social science applications, experiments are often not feasible or ethical because random assignment of students to treatment groups would be necessary.

Studies of educational impact—whether assessment, evaluation, or research—are usually concerned with measuring various aspects of the campus environment in addition to student outcomes. Why and how do some students learn or develop? The aspects of the campus environment that these studies measure include the strategies by which knowledge, skills, and development are learned and improved. These strategies are typically components of campus programs or services.

Evaluation generally focuses on the efficiency and effectiveness of campus environments. Improvements or changes in students come about through their interaction with these environments. As discussed in Chapter Twelve, *environment* refers to more than physical environments (such as residence halls). Environments can also be social (peer groups), organizational (institutional policies), fiscal (type of financial aid), or instructional (use of technology versus lectures) (Banning, 1994; Micek & Arney, 1974). Any of these environments may have an impact on student learning and development. When conceptualized as an intervention, environments can be measured as a discrete or categorical variable (such as participation or nonparticipation in a leadership training program) or as a continuous variable (such as the student union subtest on the College Student Experiences Questionnaire) (Pace, 1984). In planning assessment studies, it is wise to collect environmental data in conjunction with educational outcomes. The process of studying student learning and development together with campus environments is discussed further in the following section on analytical approaches.

Methods of Inquiry and Analysis

The conventional approach to research, evaluation, and assessment is to use either a qualitative or quantitative methodology, or both. Although these two paradigms are often characterized as antithetical and mutually exclusive (Smith & Heshusius, 1986), it is perhaps more useful to conceive of each as offering practical tools of inquiry and analysis for particular situations. The following sections describe qualitative and quantitative perspectives and some of their strengths and weaknesses. See also Borg and Gall (1989) for more complete descriptions.

Qualitative Methodologies

The qualitative perspective is a "tradition that depends on watching people in their own territory and interacting with them in their own language, on their own terms" (Kirk & Miller, 1986, p. 9). Qualitative inquiries are also called naturalistic inquiries or ethnographies and are traditionally identified with sociology, cultural anthropology, political science, and education. They usually involve field inquiries into the process of meaning-making, using people in natural settings (Creswell, 1994; Sherman & Webb, 1988). From the qualitative perspective, the "data" are people's interpretations of what happened to them in a given situation, such as within an organization or institution. The purpose of such studies is discovery or understanding, not generalizability across groups or settings. Self-descriptions are not related to constructs and are not generalizable to other times (such as another semester) or other contexts (such as another institution). Qualitative methods also include life history, phenomenology, and grounded theory (Creswell, 1994).

Superficial definitions of methodologies associate only words with qualitative projects and only numbers with quantitative projects. Technically, qualitative observation indicates the presence or absence of something (Kennedy, 1991), while quantitative observation involves measuring the degree of some feature or attribute (Kirk & Miller, 1986, p. 9). Neither characterization is entirely true, however.

Consider the two typical questions of inquiry: "What is happening out there?" and "Are these specific things happening out there?" The first question involves *discovery* about the unknown, with no preconceived notions of understanding. In the second question, certain beliefs or expectations are stated up front, with a desire for *confirmation*. Usually the qualitative perspective deals with the first question and the quantitative deals with the second. Research and evaluation deal with questions of discovery and confirmation, and assessment deals primarily with confirmation. For instance, research is concerned with formulating and testing theories and ideas. Assessment most frequently seeks to verify that educational goals and objectives are being met in a funded program: "Am I getting my money's worth?" In practice, qualitative approaches often precede quantitative approaches. Ideas, patterns, and theories are often gleaned from field exercises in qualitative research and become hypotheses for verification or greater generalization in quantitative research. Moreover, much predominantly quantitative research begins with open-ended, unstructured approaches to inquiry built in to the methodology and design. For example, in addition to relying on special education literature, Olney (1994) interviewed a variety of college students about their special needs (such as learning disabilities) before constructing her self-advocacy scale.

From the qualitative perspective, the researcher or evaluator is the primary instrument for data collection and analysis. The researcher or evaluator physically visits the setting and observes or records behavior through observation of participants, interviews, open-ended questionnaires, and existing documents (Creswell, 1994; Payne, 1994). These social interactions are recorded in field notes, audiotapes, or videotapes for later analysis. The process is open-ended and focuses on collecting exhaustive details, from which abstractions and working theories are formulated. Typically a qualitative study will have hundreds of pages of transcribed material and archival documents for later coding.

A qualitative analysis typically seeks to uncover "what is in the data rather than beginning with a theory or hypothesis to test" (Payne, 1994, p. 135). Categories or themes are initially identified through content analysis (Guba & Lincoln, 1981), analytical induction, or comparative analysis (Strauss, 1987). Though the focus is narrative-based, frequency counts, and proportions of categories or time may also be used to describe the materials and conversations.

One of these analysis schemes is content analysis, a systematic process for identifying and categorizing characteristics of messages (Holsti, 1969; Erwin,

1991). Definitions of categories, rules for categorizing, the representativeness of the categories, and the relationships among categories are critical components of this technique. Miles and Huberman (1984) suggest coding or categorizing the material by descriptive, interpretative, or explanatory types. Bogdan and Biklen (1982) advise this sorting scheme:

1. *Acts:* single actions in fleeting situations, typically consuming only a few seconds, minutes, or hours
2. *Activities:* repeated actions in settings of longer duration—days, weeks, months—that require significant subject involvement
3. *Meanings:* the verbal productions of participants that define and direct their actions
4. *Participation:* subjects' holistic involvement in or adaptation to a situation or setting under study
5. *Relationships:* interrelationships among several persons (considered simultaneously)
6. *Settings:* the entire setting under study, conceived as the unit of analysis

Content categories necessarily evolve over the course of a study as examinations of the transcribed material and documents reveal various connections and an overall theoretical shape to the endeavor.

In one example from my own research (Erwin & Delworth, 1982), students who retook my environmental identity scale (EIS) assessment during their freshman year were also administered an environmental referent. Environmental referents (Aulepp & Delworth, 1976) are open-ended questions about a student's perception of what is happening in his or her environment. One question asked, "What events or experiences at the university might have made you feel more or less confident in yourself?" The question was linked to confidence, because confidence is an EIS subscale. Content analysis grouped student responses into two categories: "conversations" and "other people."

As with quantitative analysis, several mistakes can occur in the application of qualitative studies (Borg & Gall, 1989). The responsibility of the qualitative investigator is heavy, because the data collection and analysis is all done through this single person's perspective. "Qualitative research issues of instrument validity and reliability ride largely on the skills of the researcher . . . more or less fallibly" (Miles & Huberman, 1984, p. 46). For any analysis, it is vital to disclose investigator bias, the effect of sampling procedures on how people were interviewed and documents selected, the number of site visits, and the coding scheme used.

One of the better-known examples in which an investigation was questioned concerned Freeman's (1983) revisionist challenge of Margaret Mead's (1928) study of Samoan culture. Freeman claimed that Mead was led to erroneous conclusions because of her unfamiliarity with the Samoan language and culture. "For instance, well-meant teasing by adolescent informants may have led to her mistaken theories of adolescent free love in Samoa" (Miles & Huberman, 1984, p. 48). Consequently, many evaluation studies in student affairs are conducted by people close to the program under review, such as the program or service provider. Objectivity of the investigator is, of course, a major concern.

A second possible pitfall of the qualitative process is participants' varying perspectives and interpretations of reality. For example, a participant's interpretation of a given experience is affected by his or her life experience and ability to remember. Also, participants vary in what they choose to share with investigators (Payne, 1994). For more information about qualitative research, see the references in this section and the September 1991 issue of the *Journal of College Student Development*.

Quantitative Methodologies

Although it predates the qualitative process, the quantitative process, also called logical positivism, seeks to reduce the qualitative process's weaknesses of possible investigator bias and low applicability of findings. The quantitative process devotes greater attention to measuring constructs for use across settings. Statistical procedures are also more heavily utilized, to compensate for other factors that may unduly influence the findings. The numbers, however, serve only as guides in the interpretation process, which culminates in a narrative description and generalization.

The quantitative perspective is characterized by a more independent instrumentation and design process. Known investigation, method, and participation or nonparticipation biases and error are singled out and compensated for to the extent possible. Quantitative studies are more structured and are planned a priori, or before the study is carried out, to focus on specific hypotheses or theories. In the physical sciences, experiments are planned for pursuit of cause and effect. In the social sciences and higher education, quasi-experiments are more commonplace. Some principles of the design process are covered later in the chapter.

Measurement and statistical techniques play a central role in quantitative methods. Tried-and-true techniques to ensure reliability, consistency, and validity offer a long-standing tradition for guidance. Whenever a method for measuring a given learning or development construct is selected or designed, it is critical that evidence of its reliability and validity be evaluated. Reliability coefficients range from 0 to 1.0, with higher values indicating more consistent measurement. If the method is to be used to provide feedback to individual students, reliability estimates should be in the high .70s or above, particularly for summative evaluation purposes. When using a method for studying group impact, such as a group of students' participation in a student affairs program, the reliability can be lower, say .60 and above. In quantitative studies, rater bias is a particular concern. Higher interrater reliability coefficients indicate that raters are observing students in a consistent, fair, and equitable manner.

Validity is represented by an accumulation of evidence that the method is worthy of a particular application. A test is not valid per se; validity rests with the test user. Determining the validity of a test is an inductive process that considers the following: adequate content representation of the learning, skill, or developmental construct; prior verification of the test taker's perspective (through interviewing); agreement or correlation with methods of similar constructs; and expected differentiation among groups such as prior student affairs interventions (Messick, 1989).

The social implication of any measurement method is also a part of determining validity. Student affairs professionals should guard against the use of any method that adversely impacts any group of people, even though other evidence of validity exists. Advanced techniques exist for analyzing bias at the test-item level (Berk, 1982). Similarly, reliability and validity issues are also a concern for qualitative investigators. See Kirk and Miller (1986) for examples of techniques. Additional explanations of reliability and validity may be found in Erwin (1991) for the quantitative perspective.

Quantitative approaches obtain measurements of human behavior through either selective response or constructed response formats. Selective response formats include multiple choice tests and surveys. Constructed response formats elicit behaviors of student performance, products, processes, or traits through available (naturalistic) or construed prompts. Examples include the evaluation of constructed response data through checklists or rating scales. A checklist is composed of observable behaviors indicative of a successful performance, product, process, or trait. These behaviors are either present or not present in the student. For example, one item on an oral communication scale might be "speaker displays direct eye contact with the audience."

A rating scale also consists of a series of student characteristics, but it displays a continuum of observable behaviors, from poor to good, rather than just indicating the presence or absence of a behavior. For example, consider the following sample item from a rating scale designed to measure interpersonal communication skills in small groups.

Rate student's ability to work in a group setting:

1. Works well in the group setting, offers and takes suggestions, talks freely and openly with others, promotes group harmony, concentrates on group goals, gives relevant contributions, and is sensitive and responsible.

2. Fairly strong in group interactions but shows some tendency to fluctuate in participation. At times may be withdrawn and quiet, on other occasions may become hostile and argumentative.

3. Is argumentative and disagreeable in interactions. May be late for meetings or not show interest when other group members are talking.

4. Seems intimidated by group situations, does not participate actively, usually withdrawn and quiet.

In selective and constructed formats, the test, survey, checklist, or rating scale is generally selected or designed *before* the study. In assessment, methods are based on the questions or expected educational objectives. As mentioned earlier, a primary difference between qualitative and quantitative perspectives is the purpose of the study. In the quantitative approach, specific hypotheses or expectations are established, and confirmation of these expectations is of primary interest. This practice is particularly prominent in the assessment process, in which educational objectives are the stated purpose for student affairs programs. As stated previously, these educational objectives describe the student knowledge, skill, or development acquisition attributable to environmental program or service interventions.

Some sources for quantitatively based methods are the Internet (for example, seek ERIC, then the ETS test locator service); the University of Tennessee Clearinghouse of Higher Education instruments (Smith, Bradley, & Draper, 1993; Smith, Draper, & Bradley, 1993); Robinson and Shaver (1973); Hood (1986); Rubin, Palmgreen, and Sypher (1994) for communication tests; and Snyder-Nepo (1994) for leadership scales. Regarding instrument design, consult Fink and Kosecoff (1985) and Fowler (1988) for surveys and Gable and Wolf (1993) for general affective scale design strategies.

Essentially, three primary analytical strategies are used in assessment and research and in some evaluation studies: group comparison, change over time, and criteria-based comparison. Group comparison is characterized by comparing student learning or development across certain groups defined by, for example, certain campus environments or levels of involvement. For example, would a student's identity development be higher if he or she were a campus leader, an officeholder in a student organization, an active participant, or a nonparticipant? A more fundamental assessment comparison would ask whether students learn or develop more if they participate versus if they do not participate in a student affairs program or activity. This question is perhaps the most critical question for administrators and funding sources. Do students derive a benefit from the program or service? Differences in outcomes among different environmental interventions do not prove impact, but they do offer positive evidence of worth.

Groups can also be compared according to the kind of intervention. Examples of assessment targets based on interventions include the differential impact of financial aid (impact on students of loans, scholarships, work-study programs, or internships), types of instruction (multimedia classrooms versus traditional lecture approaches), residential life (students in living-learning centers, Greek housing, on-campus or off-campus housing), and career services (students who participate in a career development class versus similar students who do not participate). In these examples, student groups would be compared based on some aspect of learning or development. Students who are well served by the environmental intervention being assessed should score or rate higher on average than students who do not participate in the student affairs program or service. Note that some of these groups are configured by naturally occurring events, such as type of financial aid, while others involve direct student affairs intervention. The ways of categorizing possible environmental categories are limited only by one's imagination.

When comparing students who participated in a program or service with students who did not participate, preexisting differences among students can influence the outcome measure. For instance, students who volunteer to participate in a student affairs program may already display higher learning and developmental outcomes than students who do not chose to participate. An erroneous conclusion may be drawn that participating students are better on average after the intervention, when they were in fact already better before the intervention. Planning to ensure the comparability of the control group is sometimes necessary. In traditional scientific experiments, subjects are randomly assigned to groups, but this is usually not feasible or ethical in education. Statistical procedures such as analysis of covariance remove the influence of extraneous factors (such as age) to an extent (Pascarella & Terenzini, 1991). Oetting and Cole (1978) discuss strategies such as using students who are wait-listed for a program as the control group in the program's assessment (because, unlike nonparticipants, these students would have the same motivation and interest for participating in the program as the students who actually did participate). Usual statistical techniques for analyzing group comparisons include the *t*-test, analysis of variance, and multivariate analysis of variance.

A second analytical strategy typical in assessment and research studies monitors students' change over time. These studies are also referred to as longitudinal-design studies. Pretest and posttest is one example. For example, students are measured at freshman matriculation and then retested at the end of their sophomore and/or senior years. Different development theorists hypothesize either steady constant increases (called linear change) or various rises and retreats over the undergraduate years. Students can also be assessed before and after a student affairs intervention. Cross-sectional designs study different student cohorts (for example, separate groups of freshmen, sophomores, juniors, and seniors). By using the same students, a longitudinal design controls for other factors that may cause changes in students' learning and development aside from the intervention or some aspect of the campus environment. Few longitudinal studies are conducted because of the length of time needed to obtain results, the difficulty in tracking students over time, and student attrition. For these reasons, good longitudinal studies are highly valued in student affairs research and assessment. Trends over time are always of inherent interest and represent some of the most prized findings in research.

Assessment and research studies occasionally combine group comparison and change-over-time strategies. That is, two cohorts of students are followed longitudinally: one student group participates in an environmental intervention such as a student affairs program or instructional sequence and the other student group does not. Do the two groups change over time at the same rate, or do the students who participated in the educational program develop at a greater rate? Common statistical techniques include single-subject designs, time-series analysis, and causal modeling.

A third analytical strategy is called criterion-based analysis: how many students reached a desired level of learning, competency, or development? The desired level is set by the educator and designates the expected learning or development after the environmental intervention. This strategy is used more commonly with learning interventions, to set passing scores, for example, or to rate the amount of knowledge learned or skills displayed. For instance, Carter and Olney (1994) reported on student cadets who assist campus safety officers in the performance of their duties. The students underwent training before being released to work; an assessment measuring the trainees' knowledge of conflict resolution and referral techniques was used to ensure that they were ready to begin their duties. See Erwin (1991) for several ways of establishing competency. Desired standards can also be established in the program development stage by selecting a particular stage from a developmental theory that the programmers want students to meet after participating in the program. This selected stage would represent the desired level of functioning or reasoning for program participants.

Qualitative and quantitative models can share the same purpose of representing what is occurring with students (in terms of learning, development, and so on) as a result of a given event (such as participation in a program). They also share the goal of using several methods to arrive at this understanding. Quantitative approaches use a multimethod approach (Campbell & Fiske, 1959), while qualitative approaches call it a triangulation of methods (Denzin, 1978). Both paradigms present problems related to the bias of methods and investigators. Although many writers favor one or the other paradigm, student affairs practitioners usually amalgamate the two approaches. (See Herriott and Firestone [1983] for combining quantitative and qualitative strategies.) When researchers have little idea what to study or how to design a measurement tool, a qualitative design is the place to start. When a clear idea exists of what is expected of students, designing a study to confirm these expectations through quantitative data is very enlightening. A beginning student of student affairs would do well to learn about both paradigms.

Using and Reporting Information

Utilizing the information gained from an evaluation study remains a constant challenge. For various reasons, findings from investigators often languish in written reports. If negative findings occur, a certain defensiveness prohibits their acceptance by program directors. Including program providers in every phase of the evaluation or assessment (or having them conduct the study themselves) is useful. Also, many studies do not lead to administrative action; some studies just tap student attitudes that are interesting but not helpful for student affairs administrators. Actively involving stakeholders in the selection of a study's methods and design are crucial at the beginning stages to prevent inertia at the end of the study. Just measuring the learning or development of students may not be sufficient. Studying alternative aspects of the related environment may suggest what works and what does not work. Moreover, responsible leaders who will act on evidence of program ineffectiveness are vital if studies are to have any impact; however, vice presidents of student affairs represent just one audience.

New student affairs professionals would be wise to consider the audience of their assessment and research studies. Journal editors and readers are one audience, of course. Professionals who deliver programs and services are another typical audience, as are one's own colleagues and students. Enhanced accountability has brought other concerned audiences to review the work of the profession. Presidents, vice presidents of academic and business affairs, state officials, federal officials, accreditors, the public, parents, and students are asking more direct (and more complex) questions. Student affairs personnel who may ask questions about programs, services, and various details of student affairs interventions include admissions staff, who may ask about the worth and fairness of student selection procedures; student activities professionals, who may inquire into the educational purposes and values of programs; financial aid personnel, who may be curious about high loan-default rates; career service personnel, who may ask about the high numbers of undecided students; and counseling, residence life, and health services professionals, who may wonder about the value of on-campus services compared to off-campus, privatized services. All of these and other problems demand increased information to help make the case for the funding of student affairs professionals as educators. See Woodard (1993) for additional challenges related to budgets and student affairs.

Conclusion

Collecting information about program and service effectiveness will become more commonplace in the future. External audiences will continue to scrutinize the worth of the methods and the uses of the evaluative information. The outside world will expect us to continue improving programs, using the information about quality that we gather or interpret. In addition, the evaluation process itself, including the constructs of the methods used, communicate what students affairs is about. Remember that assessment came about, in part, because of the absence of evaluative systems and the consequent lack of credibility of information used to assess performance. Mere descriptions of programs and services do not reflect what benefits students, and inputs and outputs are at best indirect measures of quality. Even satisfaction surveys about services are limited in what they really say about student experiences. Student affairs professionals who know about assessment and evaluation techniques and strategies are more marketable and more valuable to their institution than those who do not.

Student affairs professionals are collaborating on more and more projects with academic affairs personnel, as evidenced by efforts to restructure student affairs divisions and move them closer to academic affairs, by a renewed emphasis on learning by student affairs professionals, and by joint academic affairs–student affairs assessment projects. For instance, some assessment programs have faculty and student affairs staff collaborate on general education areas such as aesthetic development, wellness, and oral communication skills.

New student affairs professionals can also make a profound impact on the field by becoming involved in research. In fact, the future of the profession rests largely on developing new theories of student learning and development, designing new methods to measure these theories, and implementing new interventions to apply them. Research is a tool for formulating and confirming the new knowledge that will sustain the field into the twenty-first century. The desire to conduct research reveals an intellectual curiosity to try something new or test a better way. Information, systematically collected and analyzed, shapes new ideas and new practices. Future leaders who guide the field of student affairs will have this intellectual curiosity and will feel comfortable sharing the information they acquire with students, colleagues, and external constituents. The immense changes coming to higher education require professionals who can accept these challenges. Are you willing, and will you be prepared?

References

American College Personnel Association. (1993). Statement of ethical principles and standards. *Journal of College Student Development, 34,* 89–93.

Association of American Colleges. (1985). *Integrity in the college curriculum: A report to the academic community.* Washington, DC: Author.

Aulepp, L., & Delworth, U. (1976). *Training manual for an ecosystem model.* Boulder, CO: Western Interstate Commission for Higher Education.

Banning, J. H. (1994). Use of nonverbal cues of the physical environment in campus consultation. *Campus Ecologist, 11,* 1–3.

Belenky, M. F., Clinchy, B. M., Goldberger, N. R., & Tarule, J. M. (1986). *Women's ways of knowing: The development of self, voice, and mind.* New York: Basic Books.

Berk, R. A. (Ed.). (1982). *Handbook of methods for detecting test bias.* Baltimore: Johns Hopkins University Press.

Bogdan, R. C., & Biklen, S. K. (1982). *Qualitative research in education.* Boston: Allyn & Bacon.

Borg, W. R., & Gall, M. D. (1989). *Educational research.* New York: Longman.

Campbell, D. T., & Fiske, D. W. (1959). Convergent and discriminant validation by the multi-trait-multimethods matrix. *Psychological Bulletin, 56,* 81–105.

Carter, T., & Olney, C. A. (1994). *Assessing the professional development of student police cadets.* Paper presented at the Eighth Annual Virginia Assessment Conference, Virginia Beach.

Corrallo, S. (1991). Critical concerns in assessing selected higher-order thinking and communication skills of college graduates. *Assessment Update, 3*(6), 5–6.

Creswell, J. R. (1994). *Research design: Qualitative and quantitative approaches.* Newbury Park, CA: Sage.

Delworth, U., & Hanson, G. R. (1989). Future directions: A vision of student services. In U. Delworth, G. R. Hanson, & Associates, *Student services: A handbook for the profession* (2nd ed.). San Francisco: Jossey-Bass.

Denzin, N. K. (1978). *The research act.* New York: McGraw-Hill.

Education Commission of the States. (1994). *Quality assurance in undergraduate education: What the public expects* [Report from a Wingspread Conference]. Denver, CO: Author.

El-Khawas, E. (1994). *Campus trends.* Washington, DC: American Council on Education.

Erwin, T. D. (1984). The influence of roommate assignments upon students' maturity. *Research in Higher Education, 19,* 451–459.

Erwin, T. D. (1990). Student outcome assessment: An institutional perspective. In D. G. Creamer (Ed.), *College student development: Theory and practice for the 1990s* (pp. 217–228). Alexandria, VA: American College Personnel Association.

Erwin, T. D. (1991). *Assessing student learning and development: A guide to the principles, goals, and methods of determining college outcomes.* San Francisco: Jossey-Bass.

Erwin, T. D. (1993). Outcomes assessment. In M. J. Barr & Associates, *The handbook of student affairs administration* (pp. 230–241). San Francisco: Jossey-Bass.

Erwin, T. D., & Delworth, U. (1982). Formulating environmental constructs that affect students' identity. *NASPA Journal, 20,* 47–55.

Erwin, T. D., Scott, R. L., & Menard, A. J. (1991). Student outcome assessment in student affairs. In T. K. Miller, R. B. Winston, Jr., & Associates, *Administration and leadership in student affairs.* Muncie, IN: Accelerated Development.

Fink, A., & Kosecoff, J. (1985). *How to conduct surveys: A step-by-step guide.* Newbury Park, CA: Sage.

Fowler, F. J., Jr. (1988). *Survey research methods.* Newbury Park, CA: Sage.

Freeman, D. (1983). *Margaret Mead and Samoa: The making and unmaking of an anthropological myth.* Cambridge, MA: Harvard University Press.

Gable, R. K., & Wolf, M. B. (1993). *Instrument development in the affective domain* (2nd ed.). Boston: Kluwer-Nijhoff.

Guba, E. G., & Lincoln, Y. S. (1981). *Effective evaluation: Improving the usefulness of evaluation results through responsive and naturalistic approaches.* San Francisco: Jossey-Bass.

Herriott, R. E., & Firestone, W. W. (1983). Multisite qualitative policy research: Optimizing description and generalizability. *Educational Researcher, 12*(2), 14–19.

Holsti, O. R. (1969). *Content analysis for the social sciences and humanities.* Reading, MA: Addison-Wesley.

Hood, A. G. (Ed.). (1986). *The Iowa student development inventories.* Iowa City, IA: HiTech Press.

Kennedy, J. J. (1991). *Analyzing qualitative data: Log-linear analysis for behavioral research.* New York: Praeger.

Kirk, J., & Miller, M. L. (1986). *Reliability and validity in qualitative research.* Newbury Park, CA: Sage.

Kristin, K. (1992). *Current funds revenues and expenditures of institutions of higher education: Fiscal years 1982–1990* (National Center for Education Statistics Report No. 92–041). Washington, DC: U.S. Department of Education.

Mead, M. (1928). *Coming of age in Samoa.* Magnolia, MA: Smith.

Mercer, J. (1994, July 13). State group to focus on college quality. *Chronicle of Higher Education,* p. A20.

Messick, S. (1989). Meaning and values in test validation: The science and ethics of assessment. *Educational Researcher, 18,* 5–11.

Micek, S. S., & Arney, W. R. (1974). *Inventory of institutional environment variables and measures.* Boulder, CO: National Center for Higher Education Management Systems.

Miles, M. B., & Huberman, A. M. (1984). *Qualitative data analysis: A sourcebook of new methods.* Newbury Park, CA: Sage.

Oetting, E. R., & Cole, C. W. (1978). *Method, design, and implementation of evaluation.* In G. R. Hansen (Ed.), *Evaluating program effectiveness* (New Directions for Student Services No. 1, pp. 35–56). San Francisco: Jossey-Bass.

Olney, C. A. (1994). *Assessment of student affairs programs.* Workshop presented at the eighth annual Virginia Assessment Group conference, Virginia Beach.

Pace, C. R. (1984). *Measuring the quality of college student experiences.* Los Angeles: Higher Education Research Institute, University of California.

Pascarella, E. T., & Terenzini, P. T. (1991). *How college affects students: Findings from twenty years of research.* San Francisco: Jossey-Bass.

Payne, D. A. (1994). *Designing educational project and program evaluation: A practical overview based on research and experience.* Boston: Kluwer.

Robinson, J. P., & Shaver, P. R. (1973). *Measures of social psychological attitudes.* Ann Arbor: University of Michigan Press.

Rubin, R. B., Palmgreen, P., & Sypher, H. E. (Eds.). (1994). *Communication research measures: A sourcebook.* New York: Guilford Press.

Sherman, R. R., & Webb, R. B. (Eds.). (1988). *Qualitative research in education: Focus and methods.* New York: Falmer Press.

Smith, J. K., & Heshusius, L. (1986). Closing down the conversation: The end of the quantitative-qualitative debate among educational inquirers. *Educational Researcher, 15,* 4–12.

Smith, M. K., Bradley, J. L., & Draper, G. F. (1993). *Student services and student development assessment instruments and institutional effectiveness assessment instruments.* Knoxville, University of Tennessee: Clearinghouse for Higher Education Assessment Instruments.

Smith, M. K., Draper, G. G., & Bradley, J. L. (1993). *Affective assessment annotated bibliography.* Knoxville, University of Tennessee: Clearinghouse for Higher Education Assessment Instruments.

Snyder-Nepo, N. (1994). *Leadership assessment: A critique of common instruments* (National Clearinghouse for Leadership Program Leadership Paper No. 4). College Park: University of Maryland.

Strauss, A. L. (1987). *Qualitative analysis for social scientists.* New York: Cambridge University Press.

Wingspread Group on Higher Education. (1994). *An American imperative: Higher expectations for higher education.* Racine, WI: Johnson Foundation.

Woodard, D. B., Jr. (1993). Budgeting and fiscal management. In M. J. Barr & Associates, *The handbook of student affairs administration* (pp. 242–259). San Francisco: Jossey-Bass.

Yaremko, R. M., Harari, H., Harrison, R. C., & Lynn, E. (1986). *Handbook of research and quantitative methods in psychology: For students and professionals.* Hillsdale, NJ: Erlbaum.

PART FIVE

ORGANIZING AND MANAGING PROGRAMS AND SERVICES

Since the last edition of this text, the stewardship of our universities and colleges has come under close, if not intense, scrutiny by the public, legislative bodies, and governing boards. The public has challenged our institutions of higher education to improve the quality of the undergraduate experience and reduce the time required to graduate. Continuing financial constraints and demands for measurable outcomes have sparked major restructuring efforts at most colleges and universities. The restructuring movement is not simply the result of an imperative to become more "efficient" or "leaner and meaner"; rather, the push has been to fundamentally reorganize our institutions to focus them on student learning and on serving an expanding and increasingly diverse population of students. How student

affairs professionals' organize activities and functions to meet this objective, and how they acquire the requisite knowledge base to do so, is the topic of this section.

Chapter Twenty-One, by Arthur Sandeen, provides an overview of management models with an emphasis on decision making and communication within an academic context. The various functions of student affairs are briefly described, organizational options are presented, standards of practice are reviewed, and trends and issues related to educational organizations are discussed. In addition, examples of organizational arrangements at three different institutions are illustrated.

Planning and budgeting activities are powerful forces in the current restructuring environment. Most institutions have moved away from conventional models of planning to inclusive approaches that are more responsive to the contextual needs of the organization and more realistic concerning future financial resources. In Chapter Twenty-Two, John Schuh presents selected issues in planning and defines various approaches to the budgeting process. He concludes with a realistic discussion of contemporary budget issues facing student affairs officers today.

Nothing has changed so dramatically since the last edition of this book as the use of technology in higher education. The pace of technological change is so rapid that by the time this edition is printed, there will likely be new advances in software and hardware that were not in existence when Larry Benedict penned his discussion of technology in Chapter Twenty-Three. The purpose of his chapter is to present an overview of current and emerging technology and how it is being used in the workplace. The first part of the chapter is devoted to technology and learning—distance learning, learning and the Internet, other computer-based learning sources, and the implications of technology for learning today and tomorrow. The second half of the chapter explores how technology can help stu-

dent affairs practitioners improve their job performance and service to students. He concludes with a discussion of the uses of information systems.

Probably the area that challenges the student affairs practitioner the most is human resources. Chapter Twenty-Four, by Jon Dalton, is an excellent primer on selecting, hiring, developing, supervising, and evaluating professional, clerical, and student staff. He begins the chapter by establishing a framework of goals for human resource management and examining the core values that support such goals. He then discusses the importance of developing core competencies and individual talents and concludes with a discussion of the practical tasks of human resource management and advice to the practitioner.

The concepts, strategies, and advice provided in these chapters serve as a wonderful framework for practitioners to examine and evaluate their approach to the administration of programs and services. There are no fixed formulas but rather a blend of models and experiences that can be used depending on the setting. We are slowly coming to understand that success is built more on responsiveness to the context than on the use of some acclaimed, universal formula.

CHAPTER TWENTY-ONE

ORGANIZATION, FUNCTIONS, AND STANDARDS OF PRACTICE

Arthur Sandeen

When LeBaron Russell Briggs was appointed dean at Harvard in 1890, he became a one-person student affairs staff! With no job description, no organizational chart, and no set of professional standards to guide him, he learned to be a dean by listening to the students and helping them with their problems. His colleagues at other institutions, such as Marion Talbot at the University of Chicago and Stanley Coulter at Purdue University, faced similar challenges. When they moved into their offices, they had to create their own organizations!

Although the student affairs profession is still quite young, its organization and functions are now well established, with accepted standards of practice, distinct professional associations, and several professional publications devoted to the field. In 1995, virtually all 3,600 U.S. colleges and universities provided student affairs programs in various forms.

Organization of Higher Education

The internal organization of a college or university is determined by the governing board. The senior executive officer, usually called the president or chancellor, is charged by the governing board with administering the institution in accordance with priorities established by the board. While there is no universal administrative model used by all institutions, most colleges and universities have designated senior officers, appointed by the president, for such major functions as academic affairs, business affairs, institutional advancement, and student affairs. At some institutions, depending upon their complexity and mission, there may also be senior officers for medical affairs and community relations.

The senior officer for student affairs may have the title of vice president, vice provost, associate provost, or dean of students. The responsibilities of the senior officer often vary from one campus to another, depending upon the problems facing the institution, the priorities of the president, the ability of the senior student affairs officer, or the traditions and history of the institution. The senior student affairs officer often reports directly to the president, but in some cases he or she reports to the provost or the senior academic affairs officer. It is rare for all of the student affairs functions described in this chapter to fall under the direct administrative direction of the student affairs division at any given institution; at most institutions, some of the functions are administered by other departments. For example, admissions and registration may be part of academic affairs at some colleges; financial aid may be responsible to the business affairs division; and career and placement services might be part of the development program.

While the organizational chart of a college or university often yields useful information about the institution, the basic functions that provide assistance and support to students often transcend formal organizational lines. It is very important for student affairs staff to understand that to accomplish their goals they must work in collaboration with their colleagues in academic affairs, business, and development. The relationship of the student affairs organization to the institutional organization as a whole is very important, but it is not as critical to the success of student affairs as the relationships, coalitions, and cooperative programs that can be developed. Student affairs does not become effective on a campus as a result of the power arrangements described on an organizational chart; it earns its role by successfully accomplishing tasks deemed important to the institution.

The student affairs program and organization should reflect the mission of the institution, its academic goals, and the characteristics and needs of the students. With the great diversity in American higher education in the types and sizes of institutions and in students' academic, economic, and personal backgrounds, there are wide variations in the delivery of student affairs functions (see Chapters Three and Four for detailed information on student and institutional diversity). Moreover, the student affairs functions offered by an institution may reflect the community in which it is located and the financial resources available to it. The National Association of Student Personnel Administrators (NASPA) and the American College Personnel Association (ACPA) have networks and commissions that support many of these functions with newsletters and conferences.

In this chapter, the various functions of student affairs are described, organizational options are presented, standards of practice are reviewed, and trends and issues related to organization are discussed. In addition, examples of organizational arrangements at three different institutions are examined.

Functions of Student Affairs

Despite considerable variations in the style and extent of services, the following student affairs functions are usually found at most U.S. colleges and universities.

Admissions and Recruitment

These services inform prospective students about the institution and its programs and solicit, accept, and screen applicants. Usually students are admitted in accordance with policies established by the faculty, the president, the governing board, or the state legislature. Admissions offices maintain active communications with high schools, community colleges, community agencies, alumni groups, professional testing associations, parents, and others interested in the institution's admissions requirements. In many cases admissions offices target specific groups of students and actively recruit them because of their personal background, academic talents, or other abilities. Admissions offices frequently perform a centralized function for the entire institution, although this service might be decentralized at some institutions (especially large research universities with many graduate programs and professional schools). Establishing equity in admissions practices, determining admissions' relationship to financial aid, and clarifying ethical practices remain key issues in this area.

The National Association of College Admissions Counselors (NACAC) is the major professional association for admissions officers. The *Journal of College Admissions* and the *College Board Review* are the most frequently read professional publications.

Orientation

Orientation (also called new student programs) is the process of helping students learn the history, traditions, educational programs, academic requirements, and student life of the institution.

Programs may last one or two days, or they may extend throughout the first year. Orientation programs used to focus almost exclusively on such matters as registration, finances, and housing, but in recent years they have become much more extensive, involving parents, community leaders, faculty, and student leaders. The emphasis on many campuses is now upon student development, and there is active interest in enhancing the first-year experiences of students. Linking orientation to the academic program and deciding the actual content of orientation programs are major issues that will be addressed in the future.

The National Orientation Directors Association (NODA) is the professional association for this area of student affairs. The *Journal of the Freshman Year Experience* is the major publication.

Registration

In American colleges and universities, the office of the registrar is charged with keeping the official academic records of current and former students. This office also usually conducts the process by which students enroll for their academic courses and publishes the official schedules of courses for the institution. The registrar's office is sometimes linked administratively with admissions and, in some cases, with orientation or student financial aid. Issues that are likely to demand the attention of registrars in the future are how technology can best serve institutions and students and the legal status of student records.

The American Association of Collegiate Registrars and Admissions Officers (AACRAO) is the major professional association for this area. *College and University* is the publication most often read by professionals concerned with registration.

Financial Aid

Most colleges and universities provide a financial aid office to help students with their educational expenses. This student support is composed of grants, loans, scholarships, and student employment. The staff in student financial aid offices work closely with government agencies, banks, loan guarantee agencies, parents, corporate and individual donors, and, of course, student aid recipients. In addition to assessing student financial needs and making decisions about student aid packages, student financial aid staff also assist students with their personal financial planning while in college. On some campuses, the student financial aid office is linked administratively with admissions, retention, and registration. Issues abound in the financial aid arena, including heavy loan dependency of students, linking financial aid to the college's academic goals, and privatization of services.

The National Association of Student Financial Aid Administrators (NASFAA) is the major professional organization in this area. The *NASFAA Newsletter* is the most frequently read publication.

Academic Advising and Support Services

Especially at larger universities, special offices have been established to assist students in making decisions about their course of study. Often, staff specifically trained for this responsibility are hired for tasks that were traditionally assumed by faculty members. At most smaller institutions, the majority of academic advising is still carried out in this manner. The academic advising office often also includes special academic support services to address the needs of students who may need learning assistance, such as in math or writing. This office may be responsible to academic affairs or to student affairs, and it may be administratively linked with the counseling center, the orientation program, or a retention office. Finding adequate resources for advising, coordinating advising with the teaching program, and linking advising to recruitment and retention efforts will remain key issues in this area.

The National Academic Advising Association (NACADA) is the major professional organization for academic advisers. The *NACADA Journal* is the publication with the greatest visibility in this field.

International Student Services

With large numbers of international students in the United States, most colleges and universities have established special offices to meet their needs. These offices help international students with travel, orientation, financial aid, registration, housing, counseling, and (especially) successful adjustment to the campus and community. In many cases international student services offices are responsible for study abroad programs, foreign visitors, and the many international student organizations that exist on most campuses. At some institutions this office may be part of academic affairs or an international programs division; but regardless of where the service is located administratively, student affairs has a major role in its success. Issues likely to be addressed in this area include financial support and tuition, relations with U.S. students, and changing immigration policies.

The National Association of Foreign Student Advisers (NAFSA) is the major professional organization in this area. The *NAFSA Newsletter* is the most frequently read publication.

College Unions and Student Activities Offices

On most U.S. campuses, a college union serves as a center for students, faculty, staff, alumni, student organizations, and their various activities. This office is usually responsible for developing and supervising activities that complement the educational programs and aims of the institution. On some campuses there is a student activities office separate from the college union. Student activities usually advance the political, social, religious, academic, and recreational interests of students, and they are often linked to leadership and community service programs. Depending on the institution, there may be efforts to coordinate parts of the student activities program with the curriculum, especially the general education core curriculum. The student activities office may have responsibility for fraternities and sororities, student publications, and outdoor programming. Funding, user fees, privatization, and the relationship of student activities to the academic program are issues that are likely to be considered in the future.

The major professional organizations in this area are the Association of College Unions International (ACUI) and the National Association of Campus Activities (NACA). The most frequently read publications are the *ACUI Bulletin* and *Campus Activity Programming*.

Counseling Services ✓

American colleges and universities make a substantial effort to help students with their personal development and everyday problems. This is usually accomplished through a counseling service office. Staffed with professionals trained and in some cases licensed to provide assistance to students, this office usually includes mental health and psychological services. Many counseling services now engage in outreach activities with other campus offices, such as residence life and academic departments, and with various community agencies. The counseling office may also provide services to persons in crisis. It may be part of the student health service, an independent office within student affairs, or attached to a medical center. Issues that will affect the future of counseling centers include privatization, third-party payments from insurance companies, and licensing and accreditation.

The major professional associations serving the interests of counseling centers are the Division of Counseling Psychology of the American Psychological Association (APA), the American Counseling Association (ACA), and the Association of University and College Counseling Center Directors (AUCCCD). The principal publications in this area are the *Journal of Counseling Psychology,* the *Journal of Counseling and Development,* and *Counseling Psychologist*.

Career Development ✓

For many years, this service was known as "the placement office," as its primary function was considered to be to help students obtain jobs after graduation. Now the purposes of this student affairs office include helping students learn about their own interests and skills and developing plans that fit students' career and personal needs. Staff work closely with students, faculty, corporations, and community and government agencies to discover opportunities. The career development program often includes an emphasis on career planning, assessment, cooperative education, internships, placement, and alumni support. The office is sometimes part of academic affairs or the development program, but most frequently it is administratively placed under student affairs. On some large campuses career development services are decentralized into each of the major academic units, especially the professional colleges. Technological developments, privatization, and corporate support represent issues that will demand the attention of career development leaders in the future.

Major professional associations are the College Placement Council (CPC) and the National Career Development Association (NCDA). The most frequently read publications in this area are the *Journal of Career Planning and Employment*, the *CPC Annual*, and the *Career Development Quarterly*.

Residence Life

While not all U.S. colleges and universities provide residential programs for their students, a very substantial number of them do. This office is expected to provide a healthy, clean, safe, and educationally supportive living environment that complements the academic mission of the institution. The office may have responsibility for the financial management and maintenance of residence halls as well as student room assignments, student programming, and support services. Many residential life offices also assume responsibility for residence hall food service operations, whether they are self-operated or contracted out. Planning and supervising new construction may be part of the office's responsibilities as well. Administratively, residence life services may be partly or entirely linked to business affairs or academic affairs, depending on the purposes of the overall program. Most residence life offices, however, are part of the student affairs organization. Facility renovation and enhancement, availability of resources, and privatization are issues that will be actively discussed by residence life professionals in the future.

The major professional association in this area is the Association of College and University Housing Officers—International (ACUHO-I). The leading publications are the *Journal of College and University Student Housing* and the *ACUHO-I Talking Stick*.

Services for Students with Disabilities

Most colleges and universities provide a special service charged with improving the success of students with disabilities and students with special learning problems. This office also works to improve physical conditions and understanding on the campus and in the community. The office often finds itself in an advocacy role, serving as a catalyst in discussions of academic policies and procedures that affect students with disabilities. It may be part of academic affairs, the affirmative action office, or a facilities planning office. Most frequently it is administratively placed within student affairs. Legal clarifications of federal laws, financial support from colleges, and services for learning disabled students are issues that will be debated in the future.

The major professional organization is the Association on Higher Education and Disability (AHEAD). The principal professional publication is the *Journal of Postsecondary Education and Disability.*

Intercollegiate Athletics

Student affairs divisions often have responsibility for directing programs in intercollegiate athletics. These programs provide opportunities for students to participate in athletic competition with students at other institutions in a variety of sports. Intercollegiate athletics programs address issues of sportsmanship, training, nutrition, safety, gender equity, financial support, and institutional representation. Programs at smaller colleges may encourage broad student participation, while programs at some larger institutions may depend upon revenues from one or two sports and thus concentrate on recruiting highly sought after athletes. Establishing gender equity, ensuring financial health, and integrating athletes into mainstream campus life will be issues discussed in the future.

The major professional organizations in this area are the National Collegiate Athletic Association (NCAA) and the National Association of Intercollegiate Athletics (NAIA). The most frequently read publications are the *NCAA Manual* and the *NCAA News.*

Child-Care Services

Many colleges and universities provide child-care services to enable students with young children to pursue an education. These services, often subsidized by student fees, make it possible for students to attend classes and participate in college programs while their children are in child care. Student affairs divisions often initiate child-care programs, and they usually work closely with academic departments and community agencies in conducting them. In some cases the student affairs division contracts this service out to an off-campus agency. In some institutions the child-care program is part of a laboratory school or early childhood education program. Financial support, user fees, equity, and safety will continue to be key issues discussed by professionals in this area in the future.

The major professional association in this area is the National Association for the Education of Young Children (NAEYC); its major publication is *Early Childhood News.*

Student Health Services ✓

Most colleges and universities provide some form of health care for their students, whether directly through a service on campus or in conjunction with a community agency or hospital. The purposes of student health services are to provide medical assistance to students who are ill or injured, to encourage good health, and to help prevent illnesses or injuries. Health service staff often extend their work to campus residences, and they usually work closely with community health organizations. An increased emphasis on wellness has effectively linked health centers to many other campus programs, especially fitness centers and recreation programs. On some campuses coverage extends to faculty and staff in addition to students. Where the campus has an academic medical center, the student health service may be linked administratively to the medical school or the research hospital. On some campuses student health services are contracted out to a local health provider. Financial support, extent of services, privatization, and the impact of U.S. health care reform are major issues that will be discussed in the future.

The major professional association in this area is the American College Health Association (ACHA), and the primary publication is the *ACHA Journal.*

Food Services

Whether the campus is residential or commuter in nature, some form of food service program usually exists for students, employees, and visitors. Food service programs vary greatly, with some colleges providing only vending machines and snack bars and others serving full meals daily to thousands of students in many locations. Some institutions also have extensive catering needs for formal and special events. While many colleges and universities operate their own food services, a significant number contract for these services with private companies. Student affairs divisions are often responsible for the food service program and sometimes share this responsibility with another administrative division of the institution. Nutrition, finances, and privatization are issues that will demand the attention of professionals in this area in the future.

The National Association of College and University Food Services (NACUFS) is the professional organization in this area. Their publication is *Newswave.*

Dean of Students

This office, which often has responsibility for several of the functions listed in this section, has traditionally carried with it the expectation of helping to establish and enforce the community standards of the institution. The primary educational role within student affairs is assumed by the dean of students and is expressed most frequently through policy, links with academic departments, and campus leadership. At some colleges the dean of students has assumed the rather undefined but significant role of "conscience of the campus." This office responds to the general concerns of students, faculty, staff, parents, and community members and also organizes and directs the institution's responses to student crises.

The National Association of Student Personnel Administrators (NASPA) and the American College Personnel Association (ACPA) are the major professional associations for deans of students. The major publications are the *NASPA Journal* and the *Journal of College Student Development*.

Community Service and Leadership Programs

While most colleges and universities do not have a formal office dedicated to community service and leadership development, a large number are now conducting such programs, usually from other existing student affairs departments. Students are encouraged to participate in a variety of community service programs or service learning activities connected to their academic course work. Frequent cooperation with community organizations and agencies is necessary in this area. While sometimes organized separately, programs designed to teach and encourage leadership development are often part of such efforts. Future legislation, campus financial support, and integration with academic programs are future issues likely to be debated in this area.

The National Campus Compact and the Campus Outreach Opportunity League are major organizations offering support in this area. Among many publications, the *Compact News* is the most recognized. The Corporation for National Community Service, which includes Americorps, is a federally funded program that supports these efforts. The National Clearinghouse for Leadership Programs and the *Journal of Leadership Studies* are additional resources.

Student Judicial Affairs

To ensure that the academic integrity and behavioral standards of the institution are maintained, colleges and universities have established student judicial affairs offices to develop, interpret, and enforce campus rules and regulations. On many campuses these duties are assumed by the dean of students, but on others a separate office has been created to emphasize the importance of this function. Student judicial offices conduct student hearings, publish rules and regulations that define procedures and student rights, and encourage student learning through direct participation in the judicial system. This office has extensive contact with faculty as well as with police, community service agencies, and attorneys. It is likely that such issues as legal challenges to jurisdiction and increased violence will demand the attention of professionals in this area in the future.

The Association of Student Judicial Affairs (ASJA) is the professional organization in this area, and their publication is the *ASJA Newsletter.* Other publications of interest are *Synthesis,* the *Journal of College and University Law,* and *The College Student and the Courts.*

Student Recreation and Fitness Programs

Student recreation and fitness programs promote good health, teach physical skills, and encourage positive social interaction. This highly popular service has grown rapidly in recent years, leading to the construction of extensive new facilities. In addition to intramural and informal activities, many sports clubs also provide opportunities for students to compete outside the official intercollegiate program. Outdoor adventures and trips are also offered, and they are sometimes linked with teaching programs. On many campuses as many as 90 percent of students are participants in recreation and fitness programs. Funding of facilities, user fees, and privatization represent issues that will be debated in the future.

The National Intramural-Recreational Sports Association (NIRSA) is the professional association in this area. The major publication is the *NIRSA Journal.*

Student Religious Programs

While there is wide variation in the approach colleges and universities take to student religious programs, most campuses provide opportunities for religious groups to interact with their students. At public colleges the religious program may consist of a designated staff liaison and an association of off-campus religious centers; at some private colleges there are full-time staff who plan and develop religious programs and activities for students. Where student religious programs do exist, they are usually part of the student affairs organization. Issues likely to emerge in this area are use of campus facilities and support from activities funds.

Several denominational groups provide professional support for religious advisers. At the current time there is no single national association that represents all student religious advisers.

Special Student Populations

Many campuses have offices to address the special needs of women and minority students. While the major focus may be on the needs of racial and ethnic minorities, these offices might also advise gay, lesbian, and bisexual students; religious minorities; and women. In some cases this office is called the multicultural student services office and may include responsibility for ethnic and cultural centers and events. On campuses where there is not a separate office for these purposes, special efforts are usually made to respond to the educational and social concerns of these student populations. The purpose of such efforts are to help these students become successful at their college and to assist faculty, students, and staff in becoming more knowledgeable about their needs. The future of affirmative action programs; competition among various ethnic, gender, and minority groups for resources; and future funding of federal support programs are issues that will demand the attention of professionals in this area.

There are many professional associations representing the various interests and priorities within minority student programs. Among them are the National Association for Equal Opportunity (NAFEO), the National Association of Student Affairs Professionals (NASAP), and the National Council of Educational Opportunity Associations (NCEOA). Each association has a variety of professional publications.

Commuter Student Services

Commuter students may represent a small percentage of the student body or the majority of students at a college. Recognizing that students who commute to campus may have special needs, many colleges and universities have established offices within student affairs that provide services to them and act as their advocates. Often commuter students are employed off campus and attend classes at times when some services are not in operation. Safety, parking, equal access, recreation, food service, and participation in student life are some of the concerns of commuter student services offices.

The major professional organization in this area is the National Clearinghouse for Commuter Programs (NCCP). Their publication is the *Commuter*.

Program Research and Evaluation

Most student affairs divisions do not have adequate resources to establish a separate office dedicated to research and evaluation of campus programs and services; however, most student affairs divisions do assess their programs, conduct studies of their students, and review student reactions to campus services. These efforts may be undertaken by student affairs staff themselves, in cooperation with state and national testing agencies, or by faculty. Where an institutional research and evaluation office does exist, student affairs staff may work directly with its personnel to carry out the studies and assessments it needs. The information gained from such studies is considered critical to student affairs staff in planning and improving services and programs. Key issues of concern are likely to be continuing institutional support and establishing effective links with the teaching program.

The American Educational Research Association (AERA) is the leading professional organization in this area. Their publication is the *AERA Journal.*

Additional Functions

Depending on the size and type of institution, such functions as veteran's affairs, outreach programs, testing, speech and hearing clinics, transfer centers, and legal services may be offered. In many cases, of course, these functions are provided in conjunction with other, more general offices on campus.

Organizing Student Affairs Functions

How institutions organize their various student affairs functions depends on such factors as the educational purpose of the programs and services offered, the size of the institution, the nature of the student body, the nature of the external community, and the relationship of student affairs with other institutional functions. These factors are discussed in this section and elaborated on in the following section with examples from the student affairs activities at Lafayette College, Broward Community College, and North Carolina State University.

Educational Purpose

With over 3,500 colleges and universities in the United States, there is a great deal of diversity in their educational goals. These may emphasize liberal arts, vocational preparation, professional education, religious enlightenment, social reconstruction, military training, personal enrichment, or artistic and creative development. Student affairs programs vary along with these educational purposes, of course, since their primary role is to support the academic mission of the institution.

A liberal arts college whose primary focus is on academic scholarship is likely to organize its student affairs functions in ways that closely involve faculty. The boundaries between academic and student affairs are usually less clear at these colleges than at colleges that stress professional or career preparation. Indeed, academic departments at liberal arts colleges may assume some traditional student affairs functions such as academic advising, orientation, and career development. At institutions that view the classroom and laboratory as the exclusive domain of education, there is likely to be a sharper separation between student affairs functions and academic programs. Moreover, the student affairs functions may be organized into relatively independent units themselves, with less participation from faculty in policy making and programming.

Nature of the Student Body

Apart from educational purpose, no other factor is more important in deciding how student affairs functions ought to be organized than the nature of the student body. The student affairs organization should reflect the social, financial, academic, and cultural needs of the students. A college with first-generation students from lower socioeconomic backgrounds will likely place a strong emphasis on recruitment, academic support, financial aid, and career development and will organize these services to maximize their visibility and access. A college that attracts traditional-age, academically talented students from upper-middle-class backgrounds may be more likely to emphasize student activities and leadership programs, service learning, and study abroad programs. A college with older, part-time students who mostly work full time is likely to emphasize such services as child care, financial aid, commuter services, and counseling.

Size of Institution

At smaller colleges, the organizational structure of student affairs divisions may not include separate departments for specialized functions, as staff assume several roles in assisting students. At some community colleges and larger institutions, size alone may dictate that extensive, separate departments, especially in such areas as registration, financial aid, and housing, be established. When such large and relatively autonomous departments exist, the distance between student affairs and other campus programs can easily increase.

External Community

A college in an isolated, rural setting may need to offer certain services that colleges in large cities can choose to forego, especially in the areas of student health services, counseling, child care, recreation, and housing. Community colleges, of course, adapt virtually the entire institution to the needs of their surrounding community. Students services at these colleges often emphasize hands-on outreach programs located directly in areas where students live or work.

Relationship to Other Institutional Functions

How a student affairs division is organized also depends on its relationship with academic affairs, business services, development, and the president. At large institutions with academic health programs and professional schools, the structure of student affairs may be affected as well. On some campuses the academic affairs office and business services office assume responsibility for some student affairs functions, and development offices may do so as well. Professional colleges on large campuses may have extensive and sometimes separate student services. All of these arrangements can change with the appointment of a new president, provost, or other administrative officer. No matter how the various student affairs functions are organized, student affairs leaders usually understand that it is beneficial to integrate their efforts with other major units on campus, working to blur administrative boundaries and improve quality of service through cooperation and collaboration.

Three Institutional Examples

Broward Community College

This institution was founded in 1960 and now enrolls more than fifty-five thousand students on its four campuses in Fort Lauderdale, Davie, Coconut Creek, and Pembroke Pines, Florida. Students are enrolled in a large variety of programs, many of which lead to an associate of arts or associate of science degree; about 35 percent of BCC students plan to transfer to a four-year college or university. Each of the four campuses is closely associated with its community, and cooperation with business, government, health, and service agencies is reflected in all its programs.

The vice president for student affairs at Broward Community College has served in this position for twenty-seven years. As the senior student affairs officer, the vice president is responsible for all student affairs functions on the four campuses. There is a principal student affairs officer on each of the four campuses. These officers report to their branch campus provost, and the vice president coordinates overall policy. The vice president has responsibility for all policy matters, staff development, accountability, facilities management, outcomes assessment, and resource development. In addition, the vice president serves as the director of the intercollegiate athletics program.

The student affairs organization at Broward Community College includes six major departments: student financial services, the registrar and enrollment management, student services and evaluation, student life, academic intervention services, and outreach. Each department is led by a director, who reports to the vice president. Among the many program responsibilities assumed by these departments are veterans' affairs, student employment, grant development and administration, disability services, international student programs, transfer evaluation, graduation, intramural sports, entertainment and special events, and precollegiate programs. There is a special emphasis on community service, with large numbers of BCC students participating in local schools and government and community agencies.

Reflecting on the student affairs organization, the vice president indicates that

> we try to put as much responsibility as possible on the people who are the closest to the students in terms of decision making, and while we sometimes get some creative decisions from one campus that are not consistent with another, it generally works better in terms of student outcomes than a more traditional, highly centralized operation. In terms of the future, I think we have to become much more customer service–oriented, less bureaucratic, and more creative. We will need a lot more staff development in order to effectively serve and retain our students. The new students are shoppers and much more conscious of bureaucracies that run them around stumps! (G. Young, personal communication, November 10, 1994)

Lafayette College

Lafayette College, located in Easton, Pennsylvania, and founded in 1826, is a liberal arts and engineering institution with an enrollment of two thousand students. The current dean of students has served as the senior student affairs officer at Lafayette for twenty-eight years. The dean reports to the president of the college and is responsible for intercollegiate athletics, health services, international student services, the food service program, the counseling center, student residences, student activities, the office of the chaplain, and cultural programs, including the art gallery and the theater program. Two other senior officers, the provost and the dean of the college, have responsibility for academic advising, admissions, student financial aid, career planning and placement, and the registrar's office. The dean of students also serves as the secretary of the board of trustees' committee on athletics and student affairs.

The dean emphasizes that Lafayette's organization depends on who happens to be in a given place at a given time; he has tried to find ways of providing increased opportunities for certain staff to grow and develop, and this has at times influenced the way functions have been aligned. The staff works hard to establish close working relationships with faculty. Faculty are involved in all student affairs programs and have a significant influence on policy. The dean's daily contact with the provost, the vice president for development, and the vice president for business makes it very important for them to be well informed about student affairs issues and priorities and for the dean to be well informed about their issues and problems as well. The dean has worked for four presidents in his years at Lafayette, and he emphasizes the importance of understanding the president's priorities and of helping presidents achieve their goals. While the organizational structure of Lafayette's student affairs function has not changed greatly in many years, the dean has made adjustments based upon the goals of particular presidents, especially in the areas of athletics, cultural programs, and student behavior. The dean expressed caution that

> personal friendships can sometimes result in awkward problems within the organization, especially at a small college. Relationships with others members of a senior staff become dependent upon so many different variables. The dismissal of a fraternity angers the vice president for development; of course, he is pleased with a league championship and football victory over an arch rival. The vice president for finance really does not want to see students about changes in the meal plan but is pleased when the director of student residence manages to squeeze in a few extra bodies into the residence halls. Ironically, the senior staff seems to come together best when operating under adverse conditions. When all is well and we have the opportunity to run off in our different directions, the glass sometimes breaks. (H. Kissiah, personal communication, November 29, 1994)

North Carolina State University

Located in Raleigh, North Carolina, this institution was founded in 1887 and now enrolls 27,500 students in a great variety of undergraduate, graduate, and professional programs. North Carolina State University is a land grant institution and an active member of the National Association of State Universities and Land Grant Colleges. The current vice chancellor for student affairs has served in this position for the past ten years. The vice chancellor has held a variety of positions within student affairs at the same institution since 1971 and was appointed vice chancellor in 1985. The vice chancellor reports to the university provost and works directly with the vice chancellors for business, academic affairs, and advancement.

The student affairs organization at North Carolina State includes three associate vice chancellors. One has responsibility for honors and scholars programs; one oversees support services such as counseling, financial aid, health services, and registration; and one directs cultural and arts programs for theater, music, dance, crafts, and the visual arts. The student affairs division is also responsible for all Reserve Officer Training Corps (ROTC) programs, university dining services, student development, and student housing. The directors of these four programs report directly to the vice chancellor.

North Carolina State's student affairs organization reflects the institution's large size and also its strong traditional commitment to the performing and creative arts. Holding responsibility for these highly visible programs within student affairs requires close cooperation and collaboration with academic departments and other campus agencies. While the vice chancellor is actively involved in the entire student affairs organization, the decision to have three associate vice chancellors to oversee major components of this large division has resulted in better-quality programs in each of the departments, due to the personal time and attention that the associate vice chancellors can give to their needs. This arrangement has also enabled the vice chancellor to participate more fully in senior management decisions at the university.

The vice chancellor states that

> our student affairs organization obviously includes some components that might seem unusual when compared with some other institutions, such as theater and ROTC. However, part of our mission is to encourage students to develop their leadership skills and their appreciation of the creative and performing arts, and we are very proud to have a major role in these efforts. Two of my biggest challenges within our organization are to make sure that people are communicating effectively with each other and to bring all these diverse interests we represent into a coherent, unified student affairs division. Our institution has had remarkable stability in its administrative structure; however, when new chancellors have been appointed, we have changed both our organization and some of our focus to meet the priorities of the chancellor. (T. Stafford, personal communication, December 16, 1994)

Standards of Practice

The major professional associations in student affairs (NASPA and the ACPA) have published statements designed to help institutions and their individual members achieve high professional standards. These statements can serve as effective guidelines as institutions develop student affairs organizations and as they consider the ways in which they will deliver various services. NASPA's *Standards of Professional Practice* (1983) addresses seventeen standards, including agreement with institutional goals, conflict of interest, confidentiality of records, hiring practices, performance evaluation, and professional development. The ACPA's *Statement of Ethical Principles and Standards* (1993) emphasizes the ethical obligations of student affairs professionals. Both of these statements are used by institutions and individuals to maximize the effectiveness of student affairs organizations. See Chapter Six for additional information on student affairs standards.

In 1979, in response to the American Council on Education's Advisory Committee on Self-Regulation Initiatives and the encouragement of the Council on Postsecondary Accreditation, twenty-two student affairs professional associations came together to form the Council for the Advancement of Standards for Student Services/Development Programs. (The name was later changed to the Council for Advancement of Standards in Higher Education; the council is generally referred to as simply the CAS.) The council's statement of professional standards and guidelines (Miller, 1986) has had a very significant impact on student affairs organizations on U.S. campuses. The goals of the CAS are to establish professional standards for student affairs, to help institutions and professionals use these standards for program evaluation and accreditation, and to establish a system of regular review of the standards to keep pace with changes in the field (Yerian, 1988). The CAS developed the *Self-Assessment Guide* (Council for the Advancement of Standards for Student Services/Development Programs, 1988), which provides a detailed system of self-evaluation for student affairs programs. This guide has proven very effective in helping institutions upgrade their student affairs organizations and improve the quality of their services and staff.

Trends and Issues Related to Organization

Student affairs organizations have continued to develop new services and programs as the needs of students and institutions have expanded. There are an estimated fifty thousand student affairs staff in higher education today (Bloland, Stamatakos, & Rogers, 1994), and various services are now routinely provided that would not even have been imagined when the field began one hundred years ago. Student affairs leaders face many new challenges in the nineties that will result in new priorities and changes within student affairs organizations. The following issues, while certainly not exhaustive, are presented as major organizational concerns student affairs leaders face.

Diminishing Financial Support

Whether private or public, most institutions of higher education are scrutinizing their entire budget more rigorously than ever before. The emphasis is on creating lean, efficient organizations that stress increased productivity. This drive to cut back on administrative costs is occurring at a time when demands for increased and more rapid services are on the rise. This situation has forced student affairs leaders to become more entrepreneurial in their financial management practices in order to maintain their current level of services or to enhance them. No longer can student affairs leaders simply look to their institution for financial support for needed services. Like most of their academic counterparts on campus, they are expected to create or raise financial resources themselves. As a result, many student affairs organizations have created fundraising positions in conjunction with their campus development offices for the purpose of supporting specific programs and services. Other approaches include parental fundraising, designated student services fees, student user fees, and direct support from corporations and foundations, especially those that conduct business with the institution.

This diminution of direct, institutional financial support is not specific to student affairs programs and services. It is happening in all areas of higher education, and the trend is likely to continue. It is changing the way student affairs leaders do their jobs, and it will certainly affect the kinds of persons hired by institutions to lead student affairs organizations in the future.

Privatization of Services

As institutions think of ways to conserve their resources and improve the quality of their services, increased attention is being paid to contracting out services to private companies. This practice, common for years in large corporations but relatively new to higher education, is referred to in the public sector and in education as "privatization." Bookstores, food services, housing facilities, and child-care services are now often contracted out by colleges and universities to save money, increase income, and improve the quality of service. There are now companies available to take over financial aid, counseling, placement, and student health operations for institutions. This trend is likely to grow as college leaders and board members look for solutions to increasing costs and ways to satisfy student and parent demands for quality and efficiency. When a private company claims it can provide better services for lower costs, most institutional leaders feel they have an obligation to listen!

The privatization issue has caused some student affairs leaders to look closely at their organization and focus more clearly on matters such as quality, staff effort, and student satisfaction. The best student affairs leaders view privatization not as a threat to their organization but as healthy competition that can produce better results and higher-quality services. Student affairs leaders are obligated to provide the best student services they can for their institution. If they can meet this goal most effectively by contracting with private companies, then they should choose this option.

Accountability, Assessment, and Liability

In the 1990s, the emphasis in organizational management is on results. Student affairs leaders are making changes in their organizations that reflect this emphasis. To justify continued support for a service or program, student affairs leaders are now expected to provide assessment and evaluative information to indicate what the actual benefits are. This trend will continue as all institutional programs and services come under greater scrutiny by students, administrators, parents, legislators, and governing board members. Some student affairs organizations have responded by creating a special position responsible for assessing quality, evaluating programs, and measuring student reactions to campus services. Others have made assessment a requirement of each department within the institution. The results of these assessments are used for program planning and budgetary allocations.

With litigation increasing in all areas of American life, colleges and universities now face liability concerns that would have been unimaginable thirty years ago. This has resulted in greatly increased legal costs for institutions, greater caution in sponsoring certain kinds of activities, and much tighter controls over policy-making processes. Student affairs organizations have been influenced significantly by this concern for liability in housing, financial aid, student activities, health service, child care, counseling, and athletics. At some institutions these concerns have caused student affairs leaders to at the same time distance the college or university from student organizations and programs or exert much greater centralized control over their activities.

Technology

Rapid advances in communications, information processing, and computer technology have changed the way colleges and universities conduct their affairs. These advances have also changed the expectations of students and others for efficient, rapid services and around-the-clock access to information. When students and their parents can talk with the college president via electronic mail at any time, and when students have on-line access to data services throughout the world, old-line, top-down, bureaucratic organizational structures are unlikely to be viewed as effective.

For student affairs, technological advances have meant greatly improved communication with students, free and easy access to information, improved services, and the blurring of departmental boundaries. Greater contact and cooperation between institutional departments has brought student affairs professionals closer to their colleagues in academic and business affairs. With advances in technology, students have more control of their own learning and can participate more fully in the affairs and policy-making decisions of their colleges. This should change the ways colleges relate to their students and make them more open to participation by everyone. Student affairs leaders will benefit by looking beyond their formal organizational structures to the real experiences of their students in cyberspace—the revolution in communications is just beginning!

Community Service and Leadership

Among the most encouraging campus developments in recent years is the surge of interest in community service. With new federal and state initiatives to support such activity, most colleges and universities are encouraging their students to participate in voluntary community service programs or have developed service-related learning activities of their own. Student affairs offices have often taken the lead in developing community service programs on campus, and these programs have brought student affairs organizations into regular contact with academic departments, community agencies, and governmental offices. These efforts are often coordinated with student leadership and multicultural programs, as institutions have found that community service activities offer ideal settings for students to learn to work together. As a result, where community service programs become well established, former departmental barriers begin to disappear, resulting in many cooperative programs between student affairs and academic affairs.

Proliferation of Functions

Ironically, one of student affairs' greatest strengths may reveal one its most serious weaknesses—specialization has produced higher quality, but it may have splintered the field. In the past twenty-five years, student affairs functions have become highly professionalized and specialized. As a result, the quality of staff and effectiveness of services have improved substantially. Moreover, each of these specialized areas within student affairs has developed its own national association, complete with conferences and professional publications. But this increased specialization has sometimes led to multiple "fiefdoms" within organizations, poor communication across departments, and confusion among students. With such proliferation, it is difficult to maintain a coherent, unified organization; this balkanization within student affairs is a serious concern of leaders in the field today. As specialized services develop their own accreditation mechanisms, they may become insulated and unresponsive. Adapting services to the actual needs of institutions may become more difficult. The most effective student affairs organizations will find ways to encourage the creativity necessary for specialized services while insisting on a coherent, unified approach to their work with students.

Conclusion

Student affairs organizations are still evolving and will continue to adapt to the changing needs of students and institutions. There is no fixed administrative model that fits every college or university, and an organizational structure that has been in place for many years at one institution may change as well. The principles represented by the professional standards of practice provide excellent guidelines to student affairs leaders who are charged with delivering high-quality programs and services to students. Instead of beginning with a fixed administrative structure, institutions can use the standards as a basis for providing high-quality services to their students. With student affairs staff becoming more specialized and sophisticated, the quality of services and programs will likely increase. As a result, leaders in the profession will be challenged to develop organizational structures that integrate these diverse services and ensure that effective collaboration with other institutional programs occurs. Student affairs is still a young profession; its place within an institution's organizational structure is not set in concrete. The main task for student affairs leaders is to develop and deliver effective services for students that fit the needs of the individual institution.

References

American College Personnel Association. (1993). *Statement of ethical principles and standards.* Alexandria, VA: Author.

Bloland, P. A., Stamatakos, L. C., & Rogers, R. R. (1994). *Reform in student affairs.* Greensboro, NC: ERIC Counseling and Student Services Clearinghouse, 1994.

Council for the Advancement of Standards for Student Services/Development Programs. (1988). *Self-assessment guide.* College Park, MD: Author.

Miller, T. K. (1986). *CAS standards and guidelines for student services/development programs.* College Park, MD: Consortium of Student Affairs Professional Organizations.

National Association of Student Personnel Administrators. (1983). *Standards of professional practice.* Washington, DC: Author.

Rentz, A. L., & Saddlemire, G. L. (1988). *Student affairs functions in higher education.* Springfield, IL: Thomas.

Yerian, J. M. (1988). *Putting the CAS standards to work.* College Park, MD: Council for the Advancement of Standards for Student Services/Development Programs.

CHAPTER TWENTY-TWO

PLANNING AND FINANCE

John H. Schuh

A few years ago, I observed that "this is not a pleasant time to be responsible for financing institutions of higher education" (Schuh, 1990, p. 1). If any improvements have occurred in the financial circumstances of higher education since then, the changes have been only marginally positive. For example, a recent survey reported in the *Chronicle of Higher Education* (1994) revealed that 23 percent of the respondents indicated having a midyear budget cut in 1993–94, and only 36 percent rated their financial condition as "good or excellent" (p. 44).

Higher education, in part because of increasing costs, is suffering from an erosion of public confidence: "The withdrawal of public support for higher education can only accelerate as students, parents, and taxpayers come to understand that they paid for an expensive education without receiving fair value in return" (Wingspread Group, 1993, p. 2). Woodard (1993), citing Zemsky and Massey, observes that "most colleges and universities have utilized a cost-plus pricing strategy rather than one of growth by substitution" (p. 243). He concludes that this approach results in a bloated administration and misplaced faculty priorities. Woodard recommends that institutions "establish a philosophy that emphasizes accountability and a reshaped mission tied to future budget realities" (p. 243).

Thus, the fiscal environment in which the student affairs profession finds itself is challenging at best (Schuh, 1993). Williamson and Mamarchev (1990), citing Meyerson, point to six forces that have contributed to the decline of direct institutional support for student affairs: competition for institutional resources, shifting institutional priorities, declining external resources, a shift to community services, rising student consumerism, and the inability of student affairs personnel to evaluate themselves. They conclude that "it is surprising that most student affairs divisions proceed with 'business as usual'" (p. 200). One way for student affairs officers to deal with their financial challenges is to develop the best planning and budgeting skills possible.

This chapter addresses selected issues in planning and defines various approaches to the budgeting process. Specifically, it provides basic answers to the following questions:

1. What is strategic planning, and what are the elements in the strategic planning process?
2. What are the most common approaches to budgeting in higher education, and what are the advantages and disadvantages of these approaches?
3. What are the differences between cash accounting and accrual accounting, and how are these approaches utilized in higher education?
4. How does one prepare a unit budget?
5. What are some current budgeting issues facing student affairs officers?

Planning Approaches

Over the past several decades, various approaches to planning that were initiated and developed by business and government have been assimilated by institutions of higher education. Many of the more notable models are easily recognizable by catchy acronyms: PPBS (Planning, Programming, and Budgeting Systems), MBO (Management by Objectives), PERT (Program Evaluation Review Technique), and MIS (Management Information Systems) (Baldridge & Okimi, 1982). These approaches represent both theory and practice, and no single planning model predominates among the over 3,700 institutions of higher education in the United States. Nevertheless, institutions of higher education are taking planning seriously. For example, a recent report by El-Khawas (1994) indicates that a wide variety of significant actions have been taken by institutions of higher education to reorganize and restructure their programs and administrative activities. (Also see George Kuh's discussion of organizational theory in Chapter Thirteen. Planning and theory are closely linked.)

Bregman and Moffett (1991) assert that strategic planning, "a process of continuous adaptation to a changing environment" (Meyerson & Johnson, 1993, p. 77) that is drawn from the business world, can be quite useful in the higher education setting. They observe that "strategic planning for business is driven by competition in the private sector and the need to plan wisely, allocating resources in the best interest of the company" (Bregman & Moffett, 1991, p. 43). Strategic planning, in their view, is tied to the "survival of an organization and its attempt to realize its goals, strengths and the wisest use of resources" (citing Morrell, 1986).

The success or failure of planning in student affairs depends in part on perceptions and attitudes about the nature of the planning process. Moreover, the attitudes and behavior of the senior student affairs officer (SSAO) and other top-level staff play a key role in the successful execution of planning. Bean (1983) suggests that "many chief student affairs officers believe that they can plan rationally, despite evidence to the contrary" (p. 41). He indicates that plans are influenced more by subjective than objective knowledge. If the SSAO and other staff assume that planning will follow a logical, rational process, a likely consequence is disillusionment and disappointment. Accordingly, student affairs administrators need to better understand and appreciate subjective aspects of planning.

In the early 1980s, strategic planning was the latest trend in higher education. In 1983, the readers of *Change* magazine selected *Academic Strategy: The Management Revolution in American Higher Education* (Keller, 1983) as the best book about higher education of the previous two years. Ern (1993) observes that strategic planning is more than just a trendy topic, however, and that planning is an absolutely essential activity in student affairs: "Without the benefit of an intermediate to long-range planning activity by each unit, a chance to be accountable for what student affairs does and to clarify its importance to the institutional mission is lost" (p. 442). Meyerson and Johnson (1993) agree by indicating that "although strategic planning by business organizations falls in and out of favor, it is critical to the future health of higher education, where few commonly accepted performance measures are set by the market" (p. 77).

The distinction between strategic planning and conventional planning has been summarized by Baldridge and Okimi (1982). Strategic planning emphasizes linking organizational mission to external market conditions, shortening the long-range perspective of traditional planning, and focusing outside the organization with an open-systems perspective (in contrast to the internal focus of closed systems). Strategic decision making is an art and a science. Planners must interpret qualitative data based on experience, intuition, trial and error, hunches, and value judgments. The planning process is viewed in terms of a stream of decisions leading toward the best course rather than a single, "right" plan. Because it involves art and intuition as well as science and rationality, metaphors and analogies are useful tools for capturing planning's essence. For example, in describing how strategic planning differs from conventional planning, Baldridge and Okimi (1982) suggest that leaders must learn to think less like desk-bound planners at headquarters and more like field commanders.

The Planning Process

The usual elements of the planning process have been identified by various authors (Clugston, 1986; Cope, 1981; Keller, 1983; Kotler & Murphy, 1981; Pillinger & Kraack, 1980). These elements include examining critical trends in the environment and assessing threats and opportunities, assessing institutional strengths and weaknesses, determining strategic directions based on the institutional mission and assessments of opportunities and strengths, establishing program priorities, and reallocating resources from low-priority to high-priority programs. Following is an example strategic planing process based on the elements listed above and an adaptation of the models developed by Ern (1993) and Meyerson and Johnson (1993).

1. *Initiating the planning process.* This first step involves assembling a planning team, identifying work assignments, and developing a timetable. As is the case with any activity of this sort, identifying the various constituencies affected by the plan is crucial. Moreover, making sure team members have the necessary skills, commitment, and time to devote to the process is essential to its success.

2. *Review the institution's mission statement.* The importance of mission statements cannot be overlooked. As Lyons (1993) observes, "The most important factor that determines the shape and substance of student affairs is the mission of the institution" (p. 14). In the course of developing a strategic plan for student affairs, reviewing the mission statement will serve as a useful reminder of what the institution is about and what it aspires to achieve.

3. *Develop plans for each unit.* Each unit within the division of student affairs should have a set of plans that support and complement the goals of the overall division. For example, the division might have the goal of improving access to the institution for members of historically disadvantaged groups. Supporting this goal would include aggressive recruitment of such students by the admissions staff, special financial aid packages from the financial aid office, and ongoing mentoring programs for the students. The division's goals ought to be prioritized and each unit's plans developed accordingly.

4. *Assess the environment.* During this step both the external and internal environment are reviewed, and assumptions about each are identified. External environmental factors might include the priorities of the governing board or state legislature, and internal factors could include the strengths and weaknesses of staff.

The information gleaned from environmental scanning provides snapshots of the threats to and opportunities for the student affairs division and the institution as a whole. Institutional and student affairs officers continuously assessing external environments are like air traffic controllers observing blips on a radar screen. Student affairs professionals must continuously monitor social, economic, political, and technological trends in their environment. The threats and opportunities represented by changing environmental conditions create challenges that require a vigorous response.

Assessing the internal environment includes assessing the strengths and weaknesses of the student affairs division. Assessment of academic departments typically involves comparisons of research productivity and other measures with peer departments at other institutions. Although student affairs departments need to identify exemplary programs at peer institutions, their primary focus should be on responding to the threats and opportunities that affect their own institution's mission. Campuswide issues that transcend departmental boundaries, such as the quality of student life or enrollment management, will increasingly be priority concerns for student affairs administrators. The process of determining strengths and weaknesses inevitably involves asking questions about what is done, why it is done, and how well it is done, as well as investigating how services are organized and funded. Moreover, who asks the questions will largely determine the credibility and impact of the assessment. Involving students and faculty in the process adds noise to the proceedings but provides perspectives other than those of student affairs professionals.

5. *Develop a vision for success.* If the student affairs division were working at maximum capacity, what would it look like? What would its activities be? How would students be served? What kind of impact on students would the division have? Asking questions like these contributes to developing a hypothetical view of what the division might become. The division probably will not realize this vision to its full potential, but this step is nevertheless a useful exercise.

6. *Review preliminary plans.* This review should be conducted in the context of the student affairs vision and the assessments of the internal and external environments. Individual unit plans should be reviewed, as well as the overall plan for the division. Remember that the unit plans and the overall divisional plan will be developed simultaneously but separately. The relationship between the plans should be symbiotic and complementary; that is, they should support one another, and success for one will help ensure success for the others.

7. *Identify alternatives and determine a final plan.* A variety of potential plans may emerge based on different environmental assessments and different aspects of the student affairs vision. At this time, selecting the plan that will work best given the mission of the institution and the vision for student affairs is important. For example, if one goal for the division is to improve the institution's retention rate, one approach might be to enroll more students of higher academic ability. That approach has certain implications for admissions and financial aid. Another approach might be to improve tutoring and other support programs. If both approaches

cannot be implemented, a choice has to be made. Consequently, resources available to implement each aspect of the plan need to be identified. Rarely will enough resources be available to do everything that is desired.

Determining Program Viability

At times programs will have to be cut, and decisions will have to be made concerning which programs should be continued and which should be eliminated or scaled back. Pillinger and Kraack (1980) identified the following criteria for use in making such decisions:

- *Essentiality.* Is the function essential or peripheral to the university's or the student affairs division's mission? Recall the observation from Jim Lyons quoted above. The institution's mission statement shapes student affairs. Accordingly, the functions of student affairs ought to, at a minimum, complement and support the institution's mission statement.

- *Quality.* Does the program or service consistently maintain a high standard of excellence? This standard may be measured by peer ratings, faculty recognition, student evaluation, program contributions to knowledge or practice, and so on.

- *Availability.* To what degree is the function available outside the student affairs unit or the university? Increasingly, when services are provided outside student affairs or the institution they will not be duplicated. Among targets for this kind of questioning are food services, bookstores, housing, and health services.

- *Need or demand.* What is the student, institutional, and societal demand for this function? Need or demand may be measured by the number of students or staff served by a program or service, the number of student visits to a particular office, the work load of program staff, and so on. To what degree does the function meet current and future projections of need or demand? Is there a legal or public mandate for the function?

- *Efficiency.* How effective is the program at providing the most service for the least money? Could the function be performed appropriately with fewer resources? This analysis may involve comparing units of services produced to resources used.

- *Outcomes.* One other criterion needs to be added to Pillinger and Kraack's list—the influence on students. The effect of a program or activity on students is best measured through a process called outcomes assessment. As Upcraft and Schuh (1996) assert, "Outcome assessment is the most valid way of demonstrating the effectiveness of student services, programs, and facilities" (in press). Programs with a demonstrable positive influence on students should be continued; those that do not benefit students are candidates for restructuring or removal.

Developing Action Steps and Implementing the Plan

After the strategic plan has been finalized, it is time to put it into action. Action steps for implementing the plan are determined at this point. A timetable is developed to ensure the work is completed on a timely basis. No matter how widespread consultations with other institutional actors have been, the plan will generate resistance. Some of the people affected will feel they have not been involved in the planning process, or they may not like the plan. Getting people to accept the plan and begin work toward implementing it will require deliberate, ongoing effort. Simply assuming people will accept the plan because you say they should is an exercise in wishful thinking.

Evaluating the Plan

The final step is to review the plan and its effect on institutional personnel and programs. Is the vision for student affairs emerging as a result of the plan's implementation? Are student affairs services and programs successfully supporting the vision? What midcourse changes need to be made? For example, if one goal was to improve retention and the strategy chosen for achieving it was an enhanced tutoring program, are students who participated earning better grades and being retained at a higher rate? If not, why not? Is the training program for the tutors adequate? What adjustments should be made in recruiting tutors? Such questions would have to be addressed if the program were not successful.

Campuswide Planning Efforts

Because strategic planning requires a wide perspective and the authority to make decisions, most of the senior leaders of an institution will likely be involved in the process. The SSAO represents the division of student affairs at the top level of institutional leadership and must be an active participant in institutionwide strategic planning. The potential for adverse outcomes requires strong leadership from the SSAO. Also, if the SSAO and other student affairs staff fail to participate fully in planning and to assertively promote the interests of the division and of students, student affairs may be perceived as peripheral to the central mission of the institution. As a result, staff may feel and act like second-class citizens, staff morale may decline, service to students may be negatively affected, and the student affairs division may even break up or lose functions through privatization.

Planning Problems

Meyerson and Johnson (1993) have identified a variety of impediments to planning, including the autonomous nature of departmental operations, the political environment in which decisions are made, the loose organization of institutions of higher education, and their systemic resistance to change. They conclude that "strategic planning is not a panacea. . . . Strategic planning may help an organization avoid major mistakes or make incremental changes that benefit it over the long term" (p. 89). More importantly, they identify three factors critical to the success of strategic decision making in higher education: "consensus, leadership, and the management of the process of change" (p. 89). Linking planning to budgeting is one way to ensure long-term success. The next section describes a variety of approaches to budgeting and suggests several strategies for improving the budgeting process.

Budgeting

Budgeting is the process by which resources are allocated to support programs, services, activities, and learning opportunities. A budget maps out a plan for utilizing available resources to make sure that program and educational objectives can be attained. Budgeting is an absolutely essential activity in higher education, and it is crucial to the success of student affairs units.

Budgeting in the university setting is a hybrid of the budgeting processes found in business, government, and charitable organizations (Said, 1974). In the public sector, budgeting focuses on control: "Budgets are created to hold expenses within limits and to avoid a deficit" (Sherwood & Best, 1975, p. 395). Spending prescriptions and accountability are stressed. Increasingly, the effects of spending on higher education are of interest to governmental agencies and bodies: "As financial constraints have tightened, legislators and others responsible for providing public higher education with resources have become anxious to have evidence of the return on their investment" (Ewell, 1985, p. 1).

Budgeting Approaches

Several budgeting approaches are introduced in this section, including line-item, incremental, program, and cost-center budgeting. Most institutions of higher education utilize one or a combination of these approaches. Two other budgeting approaches, formula and zero-base budgeting, are not discussed since they appear to be employed less commonly than in previous years. Readers seeking more information about these approaches should consult Woodard (1993).

Line-Item Budgeting

As Douglas (1991) explains, line-item budgets are commonly used "when overall development of any program or activity initially requires the enumeration of various components" (p. 629). This type of budget can be defined as a "financial plan of estimated expenditures expressed in terms of the kinds and quantities of objects to be purchased and the estimated revenues needed to finance them during a specified period, usually one year" (Bubanakis, 1976, p. 9). This is the simplest approach to budgeting (Muston, 1980).

The real purpose of a line-item budget is to make sure that expenditures and revenues are brought into balance at the end of each fiscal year. As Bubanakis (1976) points out, this form of budgeting provides excellent control over resources, makes sure that funds are utilized for the purposes originally intended, and protects fiscal resources.

Bubanakis also contends that this budgeting approach has a number of disadvantages. First, it orients managers toward increasing what is already being done rather than toward raising fundamental questions concerning what the institution should be doing. Second, line-item budgets do not encourage long-range planning. Third, line-item budgets encourage competition for funds. Departments attempt to obtain as large a resource allocation as possible, regardless of whether the resources are well spent or duplicated by another department.

Why, then, are line-item budgets so common? For one thing, they are easy to understand. It does not take much of an accounting background to understand the concepts underlying line-item budgets. Second, they are easy to construct. Third, for those who are interested in amassing resources, this approach facilitates that end. New resources are added to a department's budget whenever possible, perhaps without serious questions being raised about the programs and activities the department provides.

Incremental Budgeting

Incremental budgeting "is based on the previous year's allocation, and the budget is adjusted based on guidelines provided by the budget office" (Woodard, 1993, p. 247). This type of budget is often used in combination with line-item budgeting. Put simply, this approach takes the previous year's budget and makes a percentage or incremental change in it. For example, the total amount of money allocated to salaries is increased by 3 percent, or funding for supplies is cut by 2 percent. In the end, budget managers adjust their budgets accordingly, and the work of budgeting is accomplished. Douglas (1991) observes that this approach works well in institutions that have similar budgets throughout their divisions and departments.

Incremental budgeting has some disadvantages. Perhaps foremost among them is that it "does not force the institution to examine priorities in a way that encourages reallocation, reductions, and elimination of programs" (Woodard, 1993, p. 247). Moreover, it makes the assumption that all aspects of a budget category can be increased or decreased at the same rate, which may not be the case. For example, annual increases in the cost of employee health insurance premiums may be much greater than annual increases in employee life insurance programs. Remember that strategic planning challenges an institution to develop a vision of what it might become, and thus it may require striking changes in organization and programs. Incremental budgeting does not lend itself well to making major changes in an institution's educational program and services.

Program Budgeting

Program budgeting is not a new concept (Muston, 1980). According to Steiss (1972), a program is a "group of interdependent, closely related services or activities which possess or contribute to a common objective or set of allied objectives" (p. 157). Program budgeting consists of five tasks: identifying goals, analyzing current programs, developing a multiyear plan, analyzing and selecting alternative programs, and evaluating the programs.

Douglas's (1991) appraisal of program budgeting is that it allows the overall cost associated with a program to be examined. Novick (1973) suggests that program budgeting provides for a formal, systematic method of improving decisions concerning resource allocation. Finally, program budgeting provides clear, basic information for planners and managers who must choose between various alternatives. Once the choices are made between alternatives, detailed planning can begin. For the most part, program budgeting is less concerned with specific details than is line-item budgeting. It provides a big-picture approach to budgeting and planning and identifies the path and direction of programming for the next several budget cycles.

Cost-Center Budgeting

The final budgeting approach discussed here is cost-center budgeting. Finney (1994) defines a cost center as "a unit of an organization for which costs are budgeted and collected, implying measurable characteristics of performance and responsibility" (p. 174). "Cost-centered budgeting," says Woodard (1993), "is based on the principle that every unit or department pays its own way" (p. 249). Each unit is treated in much the same way as auxiliary services are treated under most other budgeting systems. They are expected to generate enough revenue (including from charges to other departments) to cover their expenses. Lee and Van Horn (1983) point out that this approach works best with self-contained units, such as a hospital or athletic department. It is more difficult for units that support the activities of the entire campus, such as the registrar's office.

Accounting Methods

Depending on the kinds of accounts a student affairs office manages, at least two different forms of accounting—cash or accrual—may be used.

Cash accounting is defined as a form of bookkeeping in which "revenue, expense, and balance sheet items are recorded when cash is paid or received" (Finney, 1994, p. 174). Accrual accounting is a system in which "revenue is recorded when earned and balance sheet account charges are recorded when commitments are made" (p. 173), regardless of when funds are actually received or disbursed. Accrual accounting is designed to provide a more satisfactory means of comparing revenues and other credits with expenses and other debits in a given accounting period (Meisinger & Dubeck, 1986, p. 123).

What are the implications of different accounting approaches for student affairs budget managers? Cash accounting, sometimes referred to as fund accounting, is typically used for accounts supported by the institution's general fund (supplied by tuition and state revenues for a state-assisted institution). The accounting process may include encumbrances (commitments for expenditures), but it is not for the most part dramatically different from balancing a checkbook. Funds are deposited in the account on a routine basis, at the beginning of the fiscal year or, at some schools, more often. Expenses are deducted on a monthly basis, and the account manager must make sure that expenditures do not exceed budgeted amounts. When cash accounting is coupled with line-item budgeting, the purpose becomes obvious. Budgets are protected and overdrafts avoided. The quality of spending is not an important issue in this approach; the real concern is to make sure the budget is balanced at the end of the fiscal year.

On the other hand, when accrual accounting is used—as it frequently is for programs and services funded without state revenues or tuition dollars (such as student housing, the bookstore, or the student union)—the manager has to make sure

revenue projections are realistic and expenditures are kept within the revenue level realized. This form of accounting is more complicated than cash accounting—just because revenues appear on a budget statement, it does not follow that 100 percent of that amount will actually be collected. In fact, accrual accounting forces the budget manager to approach the budgeting cycle more like a manager of a for-profit business. Delving into the subtleties and nuances of accounting practices is beyond the scope of this chapter; however, budget managers in institutions of higher education must understand the distinctions between cash and accrual accounting and realize that the accrual basis, while it provides a more accurate financial picture, also has additional risks.

Preparing Budgets

Budgeting in higher education can be very accommodating. Fincher (1986) observes that "the budgeting process in institutions of higher education is successful because it has many accommodating features. Within hours after the arrival of a new fiscal year, budgeting-in-amendment begins" (p. 76). (That is, changes to the adopted budget for the fiscal year begin almost as soon as the budget goes into effect.) Remember this as we discuss the process of preparing a budget for a discrete department within a student affairs division. Much of what is described hereafter is based on Robins's excellent discussion on unit budgeting (1986) and reflects a combination of the features of line-item and incremental budgeting.

Budget forms are distributed by the institution's budget office to department heads, usually during the spring. These forms, along with guidelines concerning percentage adjustments to salaries and supplies, provide the basis for the department head's work. The guidelines often provide an acceptable range for salary increases and guidance on how supply budgets may be amended for the next year. Salary guidelines also might indicate whether salary adjustments should include awards for meritorious service. In some instances merit must be recognized. In other cases, merit awards may be added to the basic cost-of-living increase.

The materials provided by the budget office address many of the following expense categories: personal services, which includes salaries and wages; supplies, which may be called operating expenses; capital, which includes equipment purchases; fringe benefits, which includes such items as retirement, insurance, and Social Security costs; and travel expenses. Different institutions organize these categories in different ways, but all these items are typically found in the budget preparation material. The information supplied for personal services tends to be quite detailed; such information as position number, rank or grade, percentage of time

worked, and length of appointment, along with current salary information, may be provided for every position. The unit head's job is to apply the budgetary guidelines to the various categories of the budget.

Guidance is usually provided for this task. The budget office prepares estimates for the next fiscal year for the cost of such items as postage, telephone rental, office supplies, and the like. The unit head must merely apply the necessary adjustments to the budget items within these categories. In the area of salaries, as mentioned earlier, cost-of-living and merit increases may be recommended for each salary grade. Merit increases should be linked to performance reviews; if they are not, the unit head will have a difficult time explaining to the unit's employees why some of them received larger increases than others. Merit increases should not be awarded unless unequal increases can be validly justified.

After completing the unit budget, the unit head forwards the budget material to the division head for review. This review examines such factors as compliance with the guidelines prepared by the budget office, internal consistency, and compatibility with budgetary plans prepared by other unit heads. The division head has to be concerned with all of the same issues as the unit heads, but he or she also needs to make sure that the budget plans fit nicely with one another. If one department consistently receives larger increases (or smaller decreases) than other units, the division head will have to explain why, not only to his or her supervisor but also to disgruntled employees. When the division head completes work on the budget, it is forwarded through normal channels for review by appropriate campus offices.

Pembroke (1985) points out that student affairs officers are often perceived to have limited expertise in their ability to prepare and manage a budget. He suggests five budget preparation principles designed to assist the student affairs officer: knowing the budget guidelines, knowing what is possible, observing deadlines, helping to forecast potential problems, and reexamining the division's mission. These five principles provide a good basis for developing unit budgets. They will keep the budget officer in good standing with the campus budget office.

Woodard (1993) offers some additional budgeting suggestions, including identifying measurable outcomes for services or programs, determining if savings resulting from eliminating units are real or illusory, and ensuring that health, safety, and ethical standards are protected. For example, if an institution downsizes one unit and assigns a number of its activities to another unit that does not have adequate staff or expertise to take on the additional responsibilities, the institution is only fooling itself. Funds might be saved, but students will be poorly served. Little good will result. The reader is referred to Woodard (1993, 1995) for additional discussions of the budget development process.

Budgeting for Auxiliary Services

Building a budget for an auxiliary service, such as student housing or the student union, incorporates some of the principles described above but includes several additional features. Normally, auxiliaries use more of a zero-based budgeting approach than units funded primarily by the general fund. Auxiliaries must review such additional factors as changes in debt service, utilities, and institutional overhead charges.

Once an auxiliary services budget is developed, consultation is sought with appropriate student groups. In fact, the auxiliary may even have a budget committee that includes students. Student endorsement is sought for budgets that include increases in charges to students, such as increased room and board charges or student union fees. This process can take weeks or months. In some states, such as Indiana and Kansas, approval of room and board rates by the state's governing board is scheduled much earlier in the academic calendar than changes in other fees or tuition. The budget manager may have to forecast costs as far out as eighteen months or more. This requires great skill and good luck, because an intervening external variable, such as an oil embargo or crop failure, can have a major negative impact on the auxiliary service's budget.

Auxiliary unit heads should heed the same advice given for other unit heads regarding personnel expenditures. The director of the student union cannot give employees 6 percent raises, even if the money is available, if the average increase for all staff at the institution is 4 percent. Nor can fringe benefits be adjusted differently, such as providing a better retirement package for auxiliary unit staff or more vacation days. Auxiliaries generally function within the budgeting framework of their institution, even if they must generate virtually all of their operating revenue.

Trends in Finance and Budgeting

Downsizing

One unpleasant aspect of budgeting in the past few years has been dealing with institutional mandates to downsize many operations. Downsizing refers to eliminating positions or, in some cases, entire units. Downsizing results from institutions' simply not having a sufficient revenue stream to support all the activities and services they would like to provide. When funding sources are insufficient, hard choices have to be made. Determining which essential programs and services need to be provided and which can be eliminated is an exercise that senior leaders and department heads are forced to undertake. Downsizing will likely result in fundamental changes in programs and services and many unhappy staff, faculty, and students. Involving students and faculty in the process is crucial. In many ways the process, if time permits, will resemble the strategic planning process described earlier in this chapter. One approach to downsizing is outsourcing, described next.

Outsourcing or Privatization

One strategy related to downsizing—outsourcing or privatization—involves entering into contracts with enterprises outside the institution to provide services that have become quite expensive for the institution to offer itself. Food service operations, for example, have been outsourced for years. One institution went from losing about $100,000 per year when the college operated its own food service to an annual rebate from a contractor of $168,000 (Angrisani, 1994). Although such savings are not always the case, outsourcing represents one attractive scenario for senior administrators looking for ways to cut expenditures.

As an example of the kinds of activities that are being privatized, the University of Delaware outsourced the following activities in the past several years: food service, laundry facilities, computer networking, personal computer maintenance, mainframe computer maintenance, the university pharmacy, and energy conservation efforts (Roselle, 1994). While not all institutions choose to move in the direction of privatizing services, this option may be considered as a way of decreasing expenditures and eliminating the headaches associated with some aspects of institutional management.

One should not assume that outsourcing is a panacea, however. When a unit such as a bookstore is outsourced, employees can be affected. Private companies may not have similar pay scales or fringe benefit packages as institutions of higher education. Even if the employees do not lose their jobs in an outsourcing arrangement, there is an excellent chance that their total compensation will be reduced. This presents quite an ethical dilemma for the student affairs officer faced with solving a budgetary problem. Outsourcing may be the only solution, but it does not come without cost. See Chapter Twenty-One for further information on privatization.

Increasing Revenues

While outsourcing and downsizing are used to reduce costs, two recent trends have emerged in higher education to help raise additional revenues. One is to apply substantial overhead charges to auxiliary units for services provided by general administrative units on campus, such as purchasing, accounting, security, and the like. Auxiliaries are expected to pay their way without subsidies from the campus general fund. At some institutions, contributions from auxiliaries actually exceed the value of the services provided by the institution. Situations exist where some units, such as health services, are charged rent for the space they occupy in a campus building. In other circumstances, charges are assessed for custodial and maintenance services without the auxiliary's being given the option of hiring its own staff or contracting with a private firm. The consequence of levying overhead charges is that additional funds are provided for other needs on campus, such as faculty salaries, library support, and other activities charged to an institution's general fund.

Another option is to charge students dedicated fees or activity fees for student affairs units. These might include a special fee to pay the debt on student affairs buildings (such as the student union) or a dedicated health services or counseling fee. These fees reduce the pressure on the general fund and allow the institution to take the political position that tuition increases have been slowed. Quite obviously, dedicated, mandatory fees represent additional costs to students. Whether the trend of charging additional fees to students will continue or even accelerate in the future is unknown. Given the lack of fiscal health in higher education over the past decade, more fees quite possibly will be charged to students.

Conclusion

Student affairs officers must possess strong planning and budgeting skills. Financial pressure on student affairs units will continue to rise in the future. States are running short of funds, and the federal government cannot be looked to as a dependable source. Student fees will likely increase at a faster rate than tuition, and the use of downsizing and outsourcing will increase. Given this unpleasant scenario, student affairs managers and leaders have no choice but to acquire excellent planning and budgeting skills or face dire consequences.

This chapter examined some of the more salient issues related to these topics. Planning and budgeting are central activities in the contemporary financial environment of higher education. Refer to the reference list below for additional sources of information about these topics and for guidance in developing the appropriate skills. A high level of expertise will serve all student affairs officers well, helping them develop programs that provide learning opportunities for students while simultaneously meeting the administrative and organizational needs of their institution.

References

Angrisani, C. (1994). Students' needs dictate contract decision. *On-Campus Hospitality, 16*(4), 22–26.

Baldridge, J. V., & Okimi, H. P. (1982). Strategic planning in higher education. *American Association for Higher Education Bulletin, 35*(6), 15–18.

Bean, J. P. (1983). Planning as a self-fulfilling prophecy. In G. D. Kuh (Ed.), *Understanding student affairs organizations* (New Directions for Student Services No. 23, pp. 39–50). San Francisco: Jossey-Bass.

Bregman, N. J., & Moffett, M. R. (1991). Funding reality within higher education: Can universities cope? In R. R. Sims & S. J. Sims (Eds.), *Managing institutions of higher education into the 21st century* (pp. 31–48). New York: Greenwood Press.

Bubanakis, M. (1976). *Budgets.* Westport, CT: Greenwood Press.

Chronicle of Higher Education. (1994, September 1). (Almanac Issue).

Clugston, R. M. (1986, February). *Strategic planning in an organized anarchy: The emperor's new clothes.* Paper presented at the annual meeting of Association for the Study of Higher Education, San Antonio, TX.

Cope, R. (1981). Environmental assessments for strategic planning. In N. Poulton (Ed.), *Evaluation of management and planning systems* (New Directions for Institutional Research No. 31, pp. 5–15). San Francisco: Jossey-Bass.

Douglas, D. O. (1991). Fiscal resource management: Background and relevance for student affairs. In T. K. Miller, R. B. Winston, Jr., & Associates, *Administration and leadership in student affairs* (pp. 615–641). Muncie, IN: Accelerated Development.

El-Khawas, E. (1994). *Restructuring initiatives in public higher education: Institutional response to financial constraints* (ACE Research Brief No. 8). Washington, DC: American Council on Education.

Ern, E. H. (1993). Managing resources strategically. In M. J. Barr & Associates, *The handbook of student affairs administration* (pp. 439–454). San Francisco: Jossey-Bass.

Ewell, P. T. (1985). [Editor's notes]. In Author (Ed.), *Assessing educational outcomes* (New Directions for Institutional Research No. 47, pp. 1–5). San Francisco: Jossey-Bass, 1985.

Fincher, C. (1986). Budgeting myths and fictions. In L. L. Leslie & R. E. Anderson (Eds.), *ASHE reader on finance in higher education* (pp. 73–86). Lexington, MA: Ginn.

Finney, R. G. (1994). *Basics of budgeting.* New York: AMACOM.

Keller, G. (1983). *Academic strategy: The management revolution in American higher education.* Baltimore: Johns Hopkins University Press.

Kotler, P., & Murphy, P. (1981). Strategic planning for higher education. *Journal of Higher Education, 52,* 470–489.

Lee, S. M., & Van Horn, J. C. (1983). *Academic administration.* Lincoln: University of Nebraska Press.

Lyons, J. W. (1993). The importance of institutional mission. In M. J. Barr & Associates, *The handbook of student affairs administration* (pp. 3–15). San Francisco: Jossey-Bass.

Meisinger, R. J., Jr., & Dubeck, L. W. (1986). Fund accounting. In L. L. Leslie & R. E. Anderson (Eds.), *ASHE reader on finance in higher education* (pp. 119–150). Lexington, MA: Ginn.

Meyerson, J. W., & Johnson, S. L. (1993). Planning for strategic decision making. In R. T. Ingram & Associates, *Governing public colleges and universities: A handbook for trustees, chief executives, and other campus leaders* (pp. 77–90). San Francisco: Jossey-Bass.

Muston, R. A. (1980). Resource allocation and program budgeting. In C. H. Foxley (Ed.), *Applying management techniques* (New Directions for Student Services No. 9, pp. 79–92). San Francisco: Jossey-Bass.

Novick, D. (1973). *Current practice in program budgeting.* London: Heinemann.

Pembroke, W. J. (1985). Fiscal constraints on program development. In M. J. Barr, L. A. Keating, & Associates, *Developing effective student services programs: Systematic approaches for practitioners* (pp. 83–107). San Francisco: Jossey-Bass.

Pillinger, B. B., & Kraack, T. A. (1980). Long range planning: A key to effective management. *NASPA Journal, 18,* 2–7.

Robins, G. B. (1986). Understanding the college budget. In L. L. Leslie & R. E. Anderson (Eds.), *ASHE reader on finance in higher education* (pp. 28–56). Lexington, MA: Ginn.

Roselle, D. P. (1994). *A retrospective view: Management of the University of Delaware since 1990.* Unpublished manuscript, University of Delaware, Newark.

Said, K. E. (1974). *A budget model for an institution of higher education.* Unpublished manuscript, University of Texas, Austin.

Schuh, J. H. (1990). Current fiscal and budgetary perspectives. In Author (Ed.), *Financial management for student affairs administrators* (pp. 1–19). Alexandria, VA: American College Personnel Association.

Schuh, J. H. (1993). Fiscal pressures on higher education and student affairs. In M. J. Barr & Associates (Eds.), *The handbook of student affairs administration* (pp. 49–68). San Francisco: Jossey-Bass.

Sherwood, F. P., & Best, W. H. (1975). The local administrator as budgeter. In R. T. Golembiewski & J. Robin (Eds.), *Public budgeting and finance* (pp. 386–396). Itasca, IL: Peacock.

Steiss, A. W. (1972). *Public budgeting and management.* Lexington, MA: Heath.

Upcraft, M. L., & Schuh, J. H. (1996). *Assessment for student affairs practitioners.* San Francisco: Jossey-Bass.

Williamson, M. L., & Mamarchev, H. L. (1990). A systems approach to financial management for student affairs. *NASPA Journal, 27,* 199–205.

Wingspread Group on Higher Education. (1993). *An American imperative: Higher expectations for higher education.* Racine, WI: Johnson Foundation.

Woodard, D. B., Jr. (1993). Budgeting and fiscal management. In M. J. Barr & Associates, *The handbook of student affairs administration* (pp. 242–259). San Francisco: Jossey-Bass.

Woodard, D. B., Jr. (Ed.). (1995). *Budgeting as a tool for policy in student affairs* (New Directions for Student Services No. 70). San Francisco: Jossey-Bass.

CHAPTER TWENTY-THREE

TECHNOLOGY AND INFORMATION SYSTEMS

Larry G. Benedict

This chapter provides an overview of current and emerging technology in higher education. The rapidly changing nature of technology, combined with a student population increasingly diverse in age, geographic location, physical abilities, and technological sophistication, provide both challenges and opportunities for the student affairs professional. This chapter considers the new possibilities for practice brought by these changes and raises cautions and concerns as well. Finally, it focuses on the use of technology and information systems for planning and evaluation.

The impact of technology on education is changing so rapidly that by the time this chapter is published, some of the information in it will be outdated. New services and new software will be available that haven't even been invented yet, some of the ways we do business will be different, and lingering questions about the implications of technological change for student affairs practitioners will loom larger and larger. In fact, questions will be raised that haven't even been asked yet.

Technology and Learning

One of the areas in which technology currently has a major impact on higher education is the question of how, where, and when student learning takes place.

This is a subject not just of interest to the student affairs practitioner but of vital importance to the entire academy, since many of these changes directly affect how, where, and when student services are provided. Hence the practitioner needs to be aware of such trends and monitor them as they develop in order to understand and prepare for the impact of such change on his or her practice.

Distance Learning

When most people think of the process of higher education, they usually think of a group of students sitting together in a specific place, at a specific time, and for a specified duration of time, usually a semester of fourteen or fifteen weeks. This image often includes a faculty member presenting information to the students, usually in a lecture format. Indeed, for most of the past five hundred years, a college or university education has changed little from this description. With the advent of new technologies in the last two decades, however, this form of education has been gradually giving way to something radically different.

Imagine a class of students who never meet face to face with one another or the professor; whose homes are spread throughout the country; who communicate through computers, fax machines, and videotapes; and who register for classes, pay their tuition, submit their homework, and receive their grades without leaving home. Impossible? Not at all. In fact, this describes one form of distance learning, as it has come to be known, in use today. Distance learning in various forms is a rapidly growing phenomena.

There are several models that illustrate how dramatically traditional higher education has begun to change. The Education Network of Maine (Blumenstyk, 1994; University of Maine, 1992) is a comprehensive, interactive television (ITV) system that allows students in any part of the state to take courses offered at any of the state college campuses without having to go to those campuses. Live classes are broadcast to numerous sites throughout the state, and audio connections back to the broadcast site allow students to interact with the instructor. Classes are also videotaped so students can access them whenever they choose. Computer conferencing, fax machines, and voice mail are used to augment the broadcasts and tapes. It is possible for students to take a single course or even earn their degree without ever having to go to the campus where the instruction originates. However, students do have to be physically present at one of the receiving sites to receive most of the instruction.

Phoenix University (Stecklow, 1994) is a private, for-profit business school with an on-line educational program that allows students all over the country to complete their degree without ever going to Phoenix. A home computer is all that is needed.

In between these two prototypes are other variations on the theme. The Mind Extension University (Waldron, 1994) combines the traditional with the nontraditional. This consortium of twenty-five universities from around the country allows students who have finished two years of college work to complete their degree off campus through the use of technology. Courses are televised, as in Maine, and can also be seen on videotape. Course materials are mailed or faxed to students, and students mail or fax their papers back to the university. Students use E-mail or an 800 number to communicate with faculty. Degrees are awarded by one of the participating universities.

Another new venture, Virtual Online University (Jacobson, 1994) is currently being planned. This university will exist entirely on-line. Initially it plans to offer classes through computer conferencing. All students in a class and the instructor will be connected at the same time and interact on-line, allowing each to read what the others send. The planners see their primary target audience as disabled students, former dropouts, and other nontraditional students.

Students report several advantages to distance learning. It is flexible, individualized, self-paced in terms of completing degree requirements, and doesn't require a specific geographic location. Disadvantages include a sense of isolation or loneliness and missing the classroom interaction. Some students, though, find they get more attention through E-mail with their peers and faculty than they did in traditional classes, especially large ones.

There are also some disadvantages from the faculty perspective. When the academic process is conducted only at a distance, there are perhaps more concerns about academic integrity. Is plagiarism a greater problem in distance learning? Is student interaction on the Internet as meaningful and substantive as face-to-face interaction in a classroom? What about oral presentation skills and public speaking skills? How does a faculty member write a recommendation for a student she has never seen? These are just some of the challenging questions posed by this new technology.

Regardless of what traditional academics might think of it, distance learning is becoming widespread. With increasingly sophisticated hardware and software, distance learning is expected to grow exponentially. One noted educator, Arthur Levine, has even been quoted (Pavela, 1994a) as saying that by the year 2050 there will be no need for college classrooms as we now know them (although he does concede that liberal arts colleges and research universities will survive).

There may be some practitioners at more traditional colleges and universities who feel that distance learning is only suitable for community colleges or slightly kooky "techies," who might well profit from something like Virtual Online University. You shouldn't be surprised, however, to find that the college or university where you get your next job has distance learning options already in place or is at least exploring the possibilities.

Learning and the Internet

In an article titled "9 Ways Going On-Line Can Change Your Life" (Kennelly, 1994), the following example of one use of technology in education is given: "When high school junior and aspiring journalist Lindsay Wohl set out to do a term paper on Australian media tycoon Rupert Murdoch, she ignored the school library. She posted messages on on-line bulletin boards on the media, Australia, and the press, asking people who'd worked for Murdoch or one of his properties for some insight. She was quickly swamped with E-mail from people all over the globe hoping to get their two cents in about the pugnacious empire builder. Lindsay amazed her teacher by gathering so much timely, detailed information so quickly" (p. 9). Lindsay used two aspects of the Internet to help her do her research: bulletin boards and E-mail. (I used both of these tools as well as two others—Telnet and Gopher—in preparing this chapter.)

One can imagine the Internet as one vast, international network of computers. Accessing and using the Internet is exciting, challenging, and full of potential. Frankel (1994) asserts that "at one level, it's like having a highly efficient telephone and telegraph service, with both private and party lines. At another, it's like flying an information spaceship and docking at other computers to copy lists and texts and pictures and computer programs. And yet at another level, it can feel like an untethered walk in space to visit other travelers—thrilling, disorienting, unreal. It's not, yet, an easy trip" (p. 36).

This chapter is not about how to use the Internet, but there are some excellent resources available to help you learn. In particular, see Goodrich (1994), Krol (1994), Levine and Baroudi (1993), and Moneta (1994). In addition, the journal *Syllabus,* which is specifically about education and the Internet, and the magazine *Internet World* provide useful and timely information.

The Internet is beginning to change how students and staff learn, literally opening up a whole new world of learning, with attendant advantages and disadvantages. Even in traditional classroom settings, faculty are beginning to use the Internet to enhance learning: posting syllabi, reading assignments, and homework assignments; receiving homework assignments; having "office hours" on-line; setting up tutorial groups and discussion groups on-line; and providing one-on-one tutorials for individual students. These applications, however, are really only electronic enhancements of traditional teaching tools.

An even more exciting development is the high-tech, multimedia term paper. Such projects "can now include such things as campaign commercials, recordings of poetry readings, articles from 100-year-old magazines, and full-color movies of developing chicken embryos" (De Loughry, 1994e, p. A23). This is an example of how technology is changing the nature of academic work.

Pavela (1994b) writes that the Internet will not only facilitate new ways of learning but also encourage new voices, since anyone with access to a computer can participate, reduce alienation and create a sense of community, protect freedom of expression, foster public debate and involvement, and even promote international understanding.

He also notes a downside to all of this. The Internet could lead to a whole new wasteland, not just in terms of vacuous content but also in wasted time. With the advent of new tools like Mosaic and Netscape, "cruising the Internet" for hours has become easy and seductive. Pavela also warns that it is easy to become overwhelmed by the sheer amount of material available and that the Internet has the potential to undermine students' capacity for critical and scientific thinking. Weakened local communities may also result, since cyberspace communities may "divert energy from the equally important task of building the kinds of friendships that make local communities work" (p. 412).

With the Internet here to stay, its impact on education is inescapable. The ways in which it will be used to enhance learning are just beginning to be explored. The options seem to be limited only by one's own creativity and imagination.

On-Line Journals and Newspapers

These electronic publications are an offshoot of the distance learning movement and the Internet. The only things keeping them from experiencing a dramatic explosion are the problems of protecting copyrights and securing profits for publishers. However, the rapidly advancing technology is forcing publishers and libraries to confront these issues. De Loughry (1994a) describes Project Muse, one of the first electronic publishing efforts. Through Project Muse, the Johns Hopkins University Press publishes several of its journals electronically, making them available on the Internet. A number of other university presses are beginning to do the same or are planning to do so soon.

More than just university presses are beginning to publish on-line. Project EASI, described below (Coombs & Cartwright, 1994), publishes *Information Technology and Disabilities,* a quarterly journal, on-line. The *Chronicle of Higher Education* is available on the Internet as well. Strangelove and Kovacs (1993) have written a directory of electronic journals. Dozens of journals, both popular and professional, are beginning to appear on-line.

Many newspapers and magazines are now available on-line. Likewise, many college student newspapers have been made available on-line, and the numbers of both seem to be increasing rapidly. The trend is quite clear: more and more publications are going to be available to students on-line. As with so many other things, the Internet is going to change the way we and our students learn.

Commercial On-Line Services

So far this discussion has focused on "free" access to the Internet via college and university servers. There are, however, a number of rapidly growing commercial on-line services that offer access to the Internet. America Online, CompuServe, Delphi, and Prodigy are among the more familiar names in this business.

These companies provide a wide variety of services: financial, entertainment, sports, educational programming, games, and business services. In an attempt to expand their subscription bases, they have also begun to develop specific services for the college market. America Online, for example, is establishing College Online for professors and students to participate in class-related discussions, find out about relevant research at other universities, participate in tutorial sessions, and perhaps even talk with authors of textbooks (De Loughry, 1994b).

Many computer-literate students arriving on campus have experience with such services. Students are becoming increasingly sophisticated, educated consumers on the information superhighway, and they will expect a high level of computer access and service on their college campus.

Implications of New Technologies

Student Learning

Several implications of new technology for student learning were indicated in the section above on distance learning. In addition, students can now access libraries worldwide, communicate with faculty and other specialists on selected topics, and identify like-minded individuals all over the world—all without leaving their room. The high-tech term paper provides a new vehicle for showcasing new skills and integrating varied perspectives. In short, the Internet is going to allow students to take more control of their learning than they have ever had before.

Community

For some practitioners, this technology raises more than the question of how to provide services in new and different ways. For some, the "technouniversity" of the future poses a real threat to one of the most important functions of student affairs professionals on campus—namely, developing a sense of community. In a recent discussion on the Internet, concerns were raised about the rush to technology's undermining a sense of community and fostering instead an ever-greater emphasis on the individual. André Auger, a member of the Listserv Stu-Dev, wrote that "the planned 'technouniversity' seems to exacerbate the trend toward individualism and minimize occasions for face-to-face human importance that alone can create a sense of the urgency, importance, and validity of community" (personal communication, December 13, 1994).

Another subscriber responded that this is an important concern to raise, but what we should be asking, perhaps, is, "How do we provide challenge and support to students living on the Information Superhighway, not the campus quadrangle?" (A. Hall, personal communication, December 14, 1994).

Some would argue that the notion of community expressed by Auger has not existed on college campuses or even in the nation as a whole for some time. Steven Case, founder of America Online, is one of those individuals. He states that the goal of his company is "to build a strong sense of community" (E. Schwartz, 1994, p. 10F). Case goes on to say, "I think people have a thirst for community. Interactive technology is not the be-all and end-all. But in a small way a service like AOL can help bring people together to discuss issues they care about" (p. 10F). Others have made similar points (see Pavela, 1994b).

Indeed, developing a sense of community remains a central tenet of our profession. A challenge for the future will be to balance "high tech" with "high touch" and to seek ways in which technology can complement the services the profession provides rather than replace them. (See the section on student services below for some examples.)

The Practitioner as Learner

What are some of the other implications of technology for how the student affairs professional does his job? And what is the practitioner's responsibility for becoming knowledgeable about technology?

At the very least, it is every practitioner's responsibility to become computer literate. But what is computer literacy? Simply knowing how to use word processing programs is not the answer. In the future, computer literacy will mean being able to access the Internet and whatever it evolves into; knowing how to use E-mail and listservs to converse with colleagues, researchers in the field, and students and staff; working with campus technicians to improve student services, whether registration and financial aid, room assignment, or career planning and preparation; organizing on-line discussion groups for freshmen, resident assistants, or other groups; and setting up and managing computer networks for women's groups, gay and lesbian groups, minority groups, and so on.

How does one become computer literate? One way is to use the many texts and self-help guides that are appearing in bookstores in ever-increasing numbers

(Krol, 1994). A second way is through newspapers, magazines, journals, and newsletters, which are becoming the most effective way to keep up with this fast-changing field. The *Chronicle of Higher Education* now includes a section on information and technology, as does *Change* magazine. As noted above, the journals *Syllabus* and *Internet World* are excellent resources. Newsletters published by professional organizations like NASPA and NAWE are another source of up-to-date information.

Computer workshops offered through the computer center, the library, or the continuing education department are other options. Topics often include basic computer use, introduction to the Internet, and navigating the Internet.

Asking colleagues who seem to have good computer skills is an obvious way to gain these skills yourself. Perhaps even better, the work study student in your office may very well be the most knowledgeable and helpful individual in this area.

Subscribing to one of the many different student affairs–related newsgroups (discussion groups) on the Internet to monitor current happenings is another strategy. Determining which groups exist is not always easy. Two recent on-line tools have been developed to help: *Listservs for Student Affairs* (Brown, 1994) and *Internet Resources for Student Affairs* (Shinn, 1994). By the time this chapter is published there will be Internet discussion groups for most of the areas of student affairs, and doubtless there will be other new Internet resources as well.

There are some campuses—perhaps many—where staff computers are not connected to the university's Internet server. For staff members who find themselves in this situation, there are several strategies to pursue. First, check the computer center; its computers are probably connected to the Internet. A second possibility is the library (after all, access to libraries was one of the first Internet applications). Third, if access is not available in these places, buy a computer and modem and subscribe to a commercial on-line service.

This may seem overwhelming to the staff person who has had little or no experience with computers or the Internet. To some it may seem like a whole other world. More than a few staff probably feel bewildered and perhaps even left behind on the information superhighway. But as one novice noted, "There is no reason to fear that the Internet jet has taken off without you; it's a work in progress. There is every reason to prepare the young to ride it somewhere" (Frankel, 1994, p. 36).

And there is every reason to prepare ourselves, as student affairs practitioners, to ride along as well. The point is to take the responsibility to become knowledgeable and begin to develop competency in this field, because it will be a core competency in the next century. The practitioner who has not developed it will not be as effective and productive as he or she needs to be and in fact will not be able to respond to changing student needs.

Technology and Student Services

Clearly, the advent of new technology is changing the way students pursue their education. Technology, for the most part, has not and probably will not entirely replace the traditional college setting, but "business as usual" for colleges and universities is changing rapidly. College administrators must be aware of these changes and lead the way. As Baier (1994) writes, "For the remainder of the twentieth century it will be necessary for all student affairs organizations that have not already done so to actively engage themselves in the broad scale computerization of their programs, services, and administrative functions. . . . To accomplish this, most student affairs professionals will need to acquire and/or increase their technological literacy level as well as their comfort level with using advanced technologies in their daily activities" (p. 16).

Given the new developments in learning and technology, where do the student affairs profession and individual student affairs practitioners fit into this picture? If many students don't come to campus at all and those who do spend much of their time on computers and faxes, how does the practitioner deliver services? In fact, what services need to be delivered at all?

Imagine an entirely different scenario for students: *Tap a few keys on your home computer and take a "virtual tour" of a college or university you are interested in, seeing its buildings, looking at its library holdings, or checking out the gym. Complete an admissions application form and send it electronically to the college of your choice. Arrive on campus and choose your roommate through your computer account. Sign up for courses while sitting in your room, eating a pizza that's just been delivered in response to your fax and paid for with your college ID card. Wondering about the status of your financial aid at 2:00 A.M.? A quick call to your university's interactive voice mail system reassures you. Complete your resume on your computer and E-mail it to an on-line national job clearance and placement center.* The university of the future? No, not entirely. Many campuses have witnessed significant technological advances in various student services during the last twenty years or so, and while your campus may not have all or even any of the services and applications just described, each of them is currently available at colleges and universities around the country.

The recent work of Baier and Strong (1994) details many technological advances in a number of student service areas: academic advising, financial aid, international student services, housing, counseling, teaching-learning programs, career planning and placement, student life and activities, recreation, health services, and the office of the senior student affairs officer. Examples from these and other areas illustrate just how rapidly student services are changing on some college campuses.

The ubiquitous student ID card is probably as much a college tradition as the fight song or freshmen orientation. Most readers will imagine a plastic-coated, wallet-size card, probably with a photo on it. Except for the possible addition of a black magnetic strip on the back, little about the student ID card has changed in the last thirty years. Now imagine a card that is used not only for such traditional functions as library and dining hall access but also as a debit card for use in copy, laundry, and vending machines; the campus bookstore; and even off-campus retail outlets, from the local convenience store to the local mall. Furthermore, the card is networked with a phone company or carrier for use as a calling card, with a banking system for use as an ATM card, and with Visa or MasterCard as a charge card. All of these functions are accommodated with one card.

Some universities have already adopted such a card. Florida State University (Norwood, 1994) seems to be at the forefront in such multiple-use technology. Officials there also talk of replacing the magnetic strip on their ID card with a computer chip, allowing even greater flexibility. The benefits to both the students and the university are considerable.

Students at the University of Southern Maine (Lau, 1994) can access their academic records or financial aid status twenty-four hours a day. Students simply make a phone call to the campus interactive voice system. Students at the University of Maryland, College Park, can similarly access their account at the bursar's office twenty-four hours a day. Many university offices are now accessible around the clock due to new technologies (S. Komives, personal communication, September 21, 1994).

Technology and Students with Disabilities

Dramatic changes over the last few years have expanded access and services for students with disabilities. Clearly, many of the technological innovations cited previously—distance learning, E-mail, fax machines—will benefit students with physical disabilities.

Many specific applications for students with disabilities are characterized as "assistive computer technology" (Brown, 1993) or "adaptive technology" (Castorina, 1994). Computer speech recognition systems allow people with cerebral palsy to operate a computer: "Simply by talking, they can operate the computer and connected devices, dictate letters, run spreadsheets, access databases, use electronic mail, and gain access to the world of information" (Coombs & Cartwright, 1994, p. 43). One-handed keyboards and scanners that can process text into braille output are two other emerging technologies with dramatic implications for enhancing learning and services for students with disabilities.

A number of assistive technologies exist for students with learning disabilities. Programs that review texts auditorially and automated text correction programs are two examples. Having tests available on-line allows students to take them at their own pace. Indeed, the whole learning environment is rapidly becoming more accessible to students with disabilities: "By employing a combination of adaptations, including word prediction programs, real-time spelling checkers, screen-reading systems, and advanced speech synthesizers, we can create a writing environment that is multisensory" (Brown, 1993, pp. 96–97).

Project EASI (Equal Access to Software and Information) (Castorina, 1994; Coombs & Cartwright, 1994), is "dedicated to assisting higher education in developing computer support services for people with disabilities" (Coombs & Cartwright, 1994, p. 43). In addition to its electronic journal, *Information Technology and Disabilities*, Project EASI maintains an on-line discussion group.

The Internet and Changing Student Services

Enhancing student learning and providing services for distance learners are only two areas in which the Internet is being used in student affairs. The technology not only presents student affairs practitioners with challenges to their current way of providing services, it also opens up whole new avenues for students to pursue services themselves.

As part of its orientation program, the University of Colorado, Boulder, has established FYE-NET, a local E-mail network for freshmen to converse with one another. Students have used it to seek social connections (for example, for partners for concerts or skating), to hold discussions about favorite bands, to organize study groups, and to ask for needed resources (Conklin, 1994; I. Honey, personal communication, September 30, 1994).

The Massachusetts Institute of Technology uses an E-mail system to provide freshmen with residence hall assignments. Their students also use E-mail to see which other students might want to order a pizza or to find out where that night's parties might be (Weise, 1994).

Students at the State University of New York, Plattsburgh, who are concerned about their health can access Nutrient Network, a software program loaded on a computer in the dining hall. A student enters what he plans to eat and the program generates a breakdown on the meal's nutrition: calories, protein, fat, cholesterol, and so on (De Loughry, 1994c). Dartmouth used its E-mail system to administer health surveys to all its students following the outbreak of an illness on campus ("Link Sought in Sickness at 2 Colleges," 1994).

At the Rochester Institute of Technology (RIT), students can seek advice from the counseling center using E-mail. RIT has an E-mail network for students, similar to FYE-NET, on which senior student affairs staff are logged in. This system facilitates rapid communication on emerging issues, providing rumor control and improved communication between staff and students.

The dean of student affairs at Johns Hopkins University provides his E-mail address to the student body and especially encourages student leaders to use it regularly. Students get quick and easy access, have their questions answered, and make the dean aware of developing issues on campus. Communication is improved and small problems are handled expeditiously. Rather than making the dean seem more remote or isolated from students, quite the opposite has resulted; it is usually easier, more convenient, and faster to swap E-mail messages with the "electronic dean" than to get an appointment to see him in person. And all of this has occurred without an overwhelming number of daily messages.

Ethical Problems with the Internet

Certain ethical problems arise from what technology allows. Increasing use of the Internet has created some new and challenging problems: on-line sexual harassment ("'Cybersexism' Raises New Issues to Deal With" 1994; Peterson, 1994); unwanted or threatening E-mail; "electronic stalking"; racial harassment of students and faculty through E-mail and in newsgroups and other electronic forums; using stolen passwords to send hate mail ("Hate Messages on E-mail," 1994), threats, or intentionally misleading statements; sending and receiving pornography (De Loughry, 1994d; J. Schwartz, 1994a, 1994b); and reading other people's E-mail.

Cocooning, or spending an inordinate amount of time in one's room using the Internet (sometimes to the detriment of one's academic performance), is a phenomenon now seen on some campuses. Increased obsessive behavior is also seen—for example, constantly checking one's E-mail to see if any new messages have arrived. It is likely that other such behavioral problems will arise in the future.

These examples have emerged during the writing of this chapter. Again, by the time this is published, many other problems will have developed. The point is to monitor such developments and ensure that your campus and student affairs division are prepared to deal with the consequences of such developments. For example, does your campus have policies and procedures in place to deal with sexual or racial harassment on-line? Has it adopted any "censorship" policies, and have such policies been reviewed by university counsel in light of First Amendment rights? Are procedures in place to protect the confidentiality of students in cyberspace? Does the campus have a clear statement of student rights and responsibilities regarding use of campus computers? Does the campus judicial code reflect these issues?

The University of Delaware has responded to some of these issues by requiring all new students to pass an "electronic community citizenship examination" in order to gain access to the university's computers. Students are first given a booklet covering such topics as abuse and misuse of the system, password protection, and their responsibilities when using on-line services. Using this test as a prerequisite to accessing the computer ensures that students have at least read about these issues ("New Students . . . ," 1994).

Peterson (1994) lists five recommendations universities should adopt in this area:

1. Review current codes of conduct to ensure that computer misuse will result in disciplinary action.
2. Do not adopt computer discipline codes like "hate speech" codes, since they won't work and have been declared unconstitutional.
3. Develop a set of procedures for handling complaints of harassment.
4. Educate the campus community about these issues and procedures.
5. Educate the community about responsible use of computers.

At least two recent works have appeared that begin to help the campus administrator address such questions and concerns. First is the *Bill of Rights and Responsibilities for Electronic Learners* ("New Technology, Old Problems," 1994). Produced by the American Association of Higher Education, this has been developed to help college administrators avoid legal complications arising from issues of censorship, plagiarism, and harassment. (It is available on-line from Frank W. Connolly at FRANK@america.edu).

The second is *Rights and Responsibilities of Participants in Networked Communities* (Denning & Lin, 1994). This book includes chapters on free speech, electronic vandalism, intellectual property rights, and privacy, among others. One clear implication for the student affairs practitioner is that all of this will require consulting with legal counsel and being vigilant about such things as abuse of computer services and systems, sexual harassment on the Internet, stalking of students, and distribution of pornographic materials. Being prepared to respond to crises that might emerge over the Internet, such as a threatened suicide or a rash of electronic hate mail, is another requirement.

Possibly all of the social problems that administrators have faced on campus in the last two decades may now be faced anew in this brave new world of cyberspace. Preparing to meet these changes ethically and legally, as well as administratively, is a growing challenge for the campus administrator.

Data-Based Decision Making

This chapter has looked at many implications of changing technology for the student affairs practitioner. It has noted that technology is changing the nature of how we do business, how "high tech" can complement the "high touch" nature of the profession, and how it offers both opportunities and challenges.

The new technologies described above can provide useful information for the practitioner. A related theme is the use of information systems that already exist on campus to provide useful data to help improve planning and decision making in routine operations. Just as technology can help us improve our job performance and service to students, so too will the use of adequate data improve our daily decision making, whether for programming, planning, or evaluation.

Graduate school preparation and on-the-job experience are important for developing the skills needed to be an effective practitioner. These experiences need to be constantly informed by the routine use of high-quality data: "The ability to use information effectively has become a critical element of student affairs work as we enter the last decade of this century" (Madson, Benedict & Weitzer, 1989, p. 513). This concept can be labeled "data-based decision making."

Rather than becoming overwhelmed by yet more jargon, one needs to get beyond it (just as with Internet jargon) to see the possibilities. Some technical jargon and phraseology is unavoidable. One needs to understand broadly what an information system is. Madson, Benedict, and Weitzer (1989) provide this definition: "a means of collecting and storing data that are reliable, valid, and readily available. An effective information system therefore includes processes for collecting and storing data, means of ensuring the reliability and validity of the data, and procedures for ensuring that the data are available in a useful, comprehensive form when needed by decision makers" (p. 513).

As a practitioner, then, one must be able to identify such systems on and off campus, as appropriate, and know how to access them. Next, one must understand who a student affairs decision maker is. Benedict (1991) writes that "Student Affairs staff do not usually view themselves as researchers, planners, or decision makers. . . . As they practice delivering service to students, caring for students, supporting students, enhancing student development, and managing the cocurricular experience, student affairs staff continually, almost unconsciously, make decisions" (pp. 26–27). In essence, then, each student affairs staff person is a decision maker.

Depending upon the nature of the decision one wants or needs to make, different information systems can be accessed to provide valuable data. Knowing where such systems exist and how to access the information they contain is an important skill for the student affairs practitioner. In the absence of any existing system or database, the practitioner needs to be able to gather information herself (see Chapter Twenty).

There are many sources of data available on a college campus. Most campuses have an office of institutional research (IR) or a research and planning office that houses information on student enrollment, characteristics, and demographics. Many institutions participate in the ACE/CIRP study of entering freshmen, which profiles a number of demographic variables as well as attitudinal information. Such data may be housed in the admissions office, enrollment office, or the IR office. Some campuses even have a student affairs research office, which would also be logical place to start (Malaney, 1993). These kinds of data are useful not only for understanding the student body but also as a basis for program planning. A program or series might be designed based on the attitudes of the entering freshmen class, for example.

Other common sources of data are the national organizations to which most colleges and universities belong, such as the National Association of State Universities and Land Grant Colleges (NASULGC) and the Consortium on Financing Higher Education (COFHE). Each of these organizations gathers data about its member institutions, including data on their student body. These data are often available through the campus offices mentioned above or from the organizations themselves.

Many offices within student affairs also routinely gather information on student attitudes, needs, and concerns. If a staff person is interested in health and wellness issues and wants information to help develop programming in this area, the college health service may have information on the kinds of problems students are reporting, the kinds of diagnoses being made, and trends of different occurrences over the years. Based on such data, programs could be developed on eating disorders, safer sex practices, or sound nutrition. Conversely, such data could be used to evaluate a current program (in other words, by looking at such data as an outcomes assessment). For example, after a series of safer sex workshops on campus, does the number of condoms distributed by health services increase? This is perhaps a simplistic indicator, but the point is that campus services are repositories of data that can be used for planning and evaluation. Using data on your institution's own students will help focus your programming and make it more effective.

The campus counseling center is another likely source of useful data. What are the most common problems being brought to the center by students? Are the problems different for men and women? Graduates and undergraduates? Such data might form the basis for establishing a support program for female graduate students, for example, or for students who have lost a family member.

The housing office, orientation program, and residential life office are all likely sources. The student activities office probably has data on what kinds of programs have worked well in the past with specific types of students. They may have gathered evaluative data or conducted a needs assessment on programming as well.

Academic departments are also possible sources. Psychology and sociology departments, for example, often conduct surveys of students. There are numerous locations on campus where information is gathered or stored (Benedict, 1991; Erwin, 1991; Kuh, 1991; Madson, Benedict & Weitzer, 1989). The effective practitioner will scout these out as he does his program planning and evaluations. Often a simple phone call to one of these offices will yield the desired results.

There will be numerous times when needed information is not available. In such cases, the practitioner needs to become a researcher. One research vehicle that has become increasingly popular in higher education is the use of focus groups (Kaase and Harshbarger, 1993). A focus group is a small group of six to twelve students, led by a trained facilitator who guides discussion on selected topics. A focus group session typically lasts for 90 to 120 minutes. Focus groups are used to assess the attitudes, opinions, and needs of students; the results are used in planning and programming. For example, if a staff person wants to start a new coffeehouse, what kind of programming would be most appropriate? What kinds of food should be offered? The questions that could be posed are almost endless. Focus groups are a fast and relatively convenient research tool.

Polls and surveys are well-established techniques that are very effective for gathering information for use in planning (Erwin, 1991; Malaney, 1993). These methods tend to be more costly in terms of time and resources, but when they are conducted properly they yield excellent results. Often there are resources available to help in conducting surveys. For example, knowing that the psychology department routinely conducts surveys on campus, one might approach the faculty about incorporating some of one's data needs into the next survey. The same is true of the office of institutional research and any of the student affairs offices.

The goal in conducting research is to improve the way you do your job and hence to improve services to students. While at first glance it might seem to be an overwhelming task, it need not be, as this section has tried to demonstrate.

Conclusion

This chapter has provided an overview of current and emerging technology in higher education, emphasizing how it impacts or will impact the work of the student affairs practitioner. It has sought to raise as many questions as answers in the mind of the reader. In a field that is changing so rapidly and dramatically, writing a chapter that will remain topical for several years is quite a challenge, if not impossible. Hence I have tried to present the information to the reader as a challenge itself. For the reader, much of this may seem daunting; however, understanding and using technology and information systems is a critical part of the daily work of the student affairs practitioner, and it will become even more important in the future. Perhaps the best advice is echoed by the common expression "Just do it." Get started, and begin to develop expertise. Start creating and implementing new and creative applications of technology on your college campus. Such expertise will enhance your practice significantly and even add a new dimension of fun. Just do it.

References

Baier, J. L. (1994). Assessing and enhancing technological competencies of staff. In J. L. Baier & T. S. Strong (Eds.), *Technology in student affairs: Issues, applications, and trends* (pp. 15–26). Lanham, MD: University Press of America.

Baier, J. L., & Strong, T. S. (Eds.). (1994). *Technology in student affairs: Issues, applications, and trends.* Lanham, MD: University Press of America.

Benedict, L. G. (1991). In search of the lost chord: Applying research to planning and decision making. In K. J. Beeler & D. E. Hunter (Eds.), *Puzzles and pieces in Wonderland: The promise and practice of student affairs research* (pp. 18–34). Washington, DC: National Association of Student Personnel Administrators.

Blumenstyk, G. (1994, February 14). Networks to the rescue? *Chronicle of Higher Education,* p. A21.

Brown, C. (1993). Assistive computer technology: Opening new doorways. In S. Kroeger & J. Schuck (Eds.), *Responding to disability issues in student affairs* (New Directions for Student Services No. 64, pp. 89–102). San Francisco: Jossey-Bass.

Brown, S. (1994). Listservs for student affairs. [Machine-readable data file]. Available: Gopher://gopher.uconn.edu. Waterbury: University of Connecticut, Office of Student Affairs [Producer].

Castorina, C. (1994, March-April). Project EASI: Spreading the word about adaptive technology. *Change,* 45–47.

Conklin, A. R. (1994). Electronic mail network helps new students adjust. *National On-Campus Report, 22*(17), 1.

Coombs, N., & Cartwright, G. P. (1994, March-April). Project EASI: Equal access to software and information. *Change,* 42–44.

"Cybersexism" raises new issue to deal with: Computer messages vs. free speech. (1994). *About Women on Campus, 4*(1), 1–2.

De Loughry, T. J. (1994a, March 9). Journals via computer. *Chronicle of Higher Education,* pp. A25–A26.

De Loughry, T. J. (1994b, September, 7). 2 companies plan electronic services for academe. *Wall Street Journal,* p. 35.

De Loughry, T. J. (1994c, October 5). Computer offers SUNY students the skinny on the content of their dining-hall meal. *Chronicle of Higher Education,* p. A26.

De Loughry, T. J. (1994d, November 16). Carnegie Mellon eliminates 3 bulletin boards with sexual themes from its computer system. *Chronicle of Higher Education,* pp. A22, A24.

De Loughry, T. J. (1994e, December 7). Term papers go high tech. *Chronicle of Higher Education,* pp. A23, A25.

Denning, D. E., & Lin, H. S. (Eds.). (1994). *Rights and responsibilities of participants in networked communities.* Washington, DC: National Press Academy.

Erwin, T. D. (1991). *Assessing student learning and development: A guide to the principles, goals, and methods of determining college outcomes.* San Francisco: Jossey-Bass.

Frankel, M. (1994, November 13). Liftoff. *New York Times Magazine,* pp. 36, 38.

Goodrich, T. (1994). Mining the Internet: Tools for access and navigation. *Syllabus, 8*(3), 17–22.

Hate messages on e-mail. (1994, October 19). *Washington Post,* p. A5.

Jacobson, R. L. (1994, November 16). Scholars plan a "virtual university," offering courses exclusively on the Internet. *Chronicle of Higher Education,* p. A20.

Kaase, K. J., & Harshbarger, D. B. (1993). Applying focus groups in student affairs assessment. *NASPA Journal, 30*(4), 284–289.

Kennelly, J. (1994, September). 9 ways going on-line can change your life. *Fast Forward*, 8–13.

Krol, E. (1994). *The whole Internet* (2nd ed.). Sebastopol, CA: O'Reilly & Associates.

Kuh, G. D. (1991). Rethinking research in student affairs. In K. J. Beeler & D. E. Hunter (Eds.), *Puzzles and pieces in Wonderland: The promise and practice of student affairs research* (pp. 55–79). Washington, DC: National Association of Student Personnel Administrators.

Lau, E. (1994, October 7). Voice of USM carries instant data for callers. *Portland Press Herald*, p. 15A.

Levine, J. R., & Baroudi, C. (1993). *The Internet for dummies*. San Mateo, CA: IDG Books Worldwide.

Link sought in sickness at 2 colleges. (1994, December 9). *New York Times*, p. A20.

Madson, D. L., Benedict, L. G., & Weitzer, W. H. (1989). Using information systems for decision making and planning. In U. Delworth, G. R. Hanson, & Associates, *Student services: A handbook for the profession* (2nd ed., pp. 513–532). San Francisco: Jossey-Bass.

Malaney, G. D. (1993). A comprehensive students affairs research office. *NASPA Journal, 30*(3), 182–189.

Moneta, L. (1994). Internet 101. *NASPA Region II Newsletter, 15*(1), 5–6.

New students at the University of Delaware have one extra test to take this year. (1994, October 19). *Chronicle of Higher Education*, p. A36.

New technology, old problems. (1994). *NASPA Forum, 15*(4), 1, 4.

Norwood, B. R. (1994, Spring). Evolution of smart-card technology development at Florida State University. *Cause/Effect*, 34–46.

Pavela, G. (1994a). Arthur Levine on higher education in transition. *Synthesis, 5*(4), pp. 400–401, 414–416.

Pavela, G. (1994b). What Internet means. *Synthesis, 5*(4), 397–399, 412–413.

Peterson, R. (1994). Harassment by electronic mail. *Synthesis, 5*(4), 402–403, 416.

Schwartz, E. (1994, October 9). Linking the information superhighway to main street. *New York Times*, p. 10F.

Schwartz, J. (1994a, November 6). Carnegie Mellon University is banning sex—on its computer network. *Washington Post*, p. A26.

Schwartz, J. (1994b, November 9). University reverses on-line ban. *Washington Post*, p. A13.

Shinn, D. D. (1994). Internet resources for student affairs professionals. [Machine-readable data file]. Available: Gopher://gopher.siu.edu/. Carbondale, IL: Southern Illinois University, Office of the Vice-President for Student Affairs [Producer].

Stecklow, S. (1994, September 12). Virtual U. at Phoenix University: Class can be anywhere—even in cyberspace. *Wall Street Journal*, pp. 1, A10.

Strangelove, M., & Kovacs, D. (1993). *Directory of electronic journals, newsletters, and academic discussion lists*. Washington, DC: Association of Research Libraries.

University of Maine. (1992, August). The Education Network of Maine Progress Report, 1988–1992. Augusta: Author.

Waldron, T. W. (1994, June 19). No place like home to earn college degree. *Baltimore Sun*, pp. B1–B2.

Weise, E. (1994, September 30). On campus, students tune in, sign on. *Baltimore Sun*, p. D4.

CHAPTER TWENTY-FOUR

MANAGING HUMAN RESOURCES

Jon C. Dalton

One of the most challenging and rewarding aspects of student affairs administration is the leadership and management of staff. While few student affairs staff enter the profession to become managers, almost every advancement in leadership requires greater skills in human resource management. To be successful as a leader in the profession, one must understand the nature of student affairs organizations as well as how to effectively manage their staff and resources. This is especially important in this time of institutional restructuring and downsizing, in which great emphasis is placed on efficiency and productivity.

This chapter begins with a framework of goals for human resource management and examines the core values that support those goals. Building upon this conceptual framework, the chapter then examines the importance of developing core competencies and individual talents. The second half of the chapter focuses on the practical tasks of human resource management: recruitment, supervision, staff development, and addressing specific problems.

Human Resource Management Today

So many changes have occurred in the field of human resource management that a quick overview of recent developments may be useful. Until late in the twentieth century, many of our beliefs about organizations and human resource management were shaped by the effort to apply science and rational thinking to human organizations (see Chapter Thirteen). Such thinking led to bureaucratic models of organization that emphasized division of labor, specialization of roles, hierarchies of authority, and an elaborate system of rules and laws that governed relationships and processes.

This approach to organizational structure stressed chains of command, delegation of authority, and unity of command. It was believed that such an approach would maximize efficiency and enable leaders to order and predict outcomes. For much of the twentieth century, this bureaucratic model was the dominant approach in organizational and management theory.

The bureaucratic model had several problems, however. These became increasingly apparent during the 1970s and 1980s with the rise of a new global marketplace and various alternative management approaches. Employees did not always act in predictable ways; rules did not cover every situation; innovation could be stifled by ingrained, rigid regulations and procedures; and bureaucracies were often too cumbersome to respond to rapidly changing environments. As Seymour (1994) asserts, a paradigm shift became necessary in management philosophy and practice.

Consequently, new approaches to organizational and management theory developed, stressing a more decentralized, collaborative, and change-oriented approach. Concepts such as cross-training, boundary spanning, participatory decision making, and quality circles reflected a new emphasis on interactive processes and less organizational rigidity and hierarchy. The new theories also recognized modern pluralism, in which social relationships are much more complex and diverse and there is great concern for the creation and maintenance of communities. These changes helped form the current style of human resource management in student affairs, and they can help explain some of the new directions explored in this chapter.

A Conceptual Framework for Human Resource Management

Three essential tasks provide a broad conceptual framework for human resource management in student affairs:

1. *Helping employees master the specific competencies necessary for success in their assigned duties.* The primary obligation of student affairs human resource managers is to provide the means for every employee to be successful in performing his or her assigned duties. While some employees can "hit the ground running," most need some time and assistance to adjust to the specific requirements of their

position. Staff also need opportunities to enhance their skills and knowledge in order to perform their duties with greater expertise. Thus the first goal of human resource management is to ensure that employees are given the necessary support and resources to be successful in their job.

2. *Helping employees understand and cope—professionally and personally—with the culture and requirements of their work environment.* Few student affairs jobs are performed in isolated settings divorced from contact and interaction with other people and organizations. Student affairs work occurs within the context of a variety of higher education and community settings and thus requires some understanding of the broader work environment. Colleges and universities are unique settings with special traditions, practices, customs, values, and organizational structures and procedures. Moreover, the many departments and offices within a college or university have their own organizational culture and practices. Employees should understand both the larger institutional culture and the specific local cultures that constitute their own work environment.

3. *Helping employees engage in continual learning, professional development, and personal renewal.* Cone (1968) argues that organizational obsolescence occurs when staff lose the technical, interpersonal, and political skills necessary to perform their jobs. Student affairs positions are so demanding in terms of time and pressure that burnout and obsolescence are ever-present dangers. Thus individuals need opportunities for development and renewal to adapt to the changing circumstances of their lives and work environment. Employees who increase their knowledge and skills and grow professionally are much more likely to be effective in their work and relationships.

Lindquist (1981) points out that there is usually an important personal dimension to professional development, which cannot be overlooked. Personal concerns have a way of intruding into all domains. For example, staff members struggling with financial problems, children leaving home, or personal health problems will likely bring these concerns to their job, whether they intend to or not. The student affairs leader must recognize these hidden concerns and how such problems affect employee performance and relationships.

Productivity is ultimately a function of the vitality and energy employees bring to their work. Most of us can remember the enthusiasm we felt about our first job and the energy we poured into it. Such high energy and enthusiasm can be maintained if employees are given opportunities for personal renewal and development (Kay, 1974). Later in this chapter we will examine in more detail how to organize a comprehensive staff development program.

In summary, the goals of human resource management relate to three essential objectives:

The task: helping employees master the necessary job skills

The situation: helping employees thrive in the work culture and environment

The person: helping employees achieve personal and professional development and renewal

This conceptual framework is extremely useful in developing a practical and effective program for human resource management that is faithful to the purposes of student affairs work. Moreover, the three objectives outlined above are applicable to all employees—professionals, support staff, and student employees. (The best method for applying them will, of course, vary significantly with different groups of employees and within different institutional settings.)

The Place of Values in Human Resource Management

Every model of human resource management has explicit and implicit values. High-performing organizations function within a context of particular values (Kuh, 1983). Effective organizations communicate their values clearly and help employees identify with and support those values. Robert Young (1993; also see Chapter Five) identifies three philosophical schools of thought that have informed the values of the student affairs profession: rationalism, neohumanism, and pragmatism. Values are important in organizations because they help define how and why certain things should be done. Values are what bind organizations together and create a sense of common purpose (Pastin, 1991). So it is important to identify and briefly discuss the values essential to effective human resource management and development. These values are summed up in the following five statements:

1. *Employees are individuals with unique abilities and needs that transcend group characteristics.* One should not lose sight of employees' individuality, no matter how many employees one supervises nor how routine or common their duties. Every person brings something special and different to his or her job. Recognizing individuals' needs and valuing their personal contribution is very important to successful supervision and in building effective teams and organizations.

2. *Excellence in organizations requires a high level of regard for and utilization of the talents of organizational members.* Personnel costs are typically the greatest single budget item in student affairs organizations. Thus a student affairs organization's personnel represent its greatest financial investment. Unfortunately, employees are too often viewed merely as workers who provide specific and often narrowly defined service roles rather than as a rich source of talent that can serve the

organization in many ways. (We will examine the concept of talent development more fully later in the chapter.)

3. *Fairness and equal consideration in relationships with employees is the bedrock of human resource management.* This is one of those rules learned in kindergarten: be fair! Like most simple truths in life, it is easy to comprehend but very difficult to practice. Because employees are so different from one another (and some are more agreeable than others), leaders are often inclined to treat them differently. But the perception that a leader favors or gives preferential treatment to some employees on matters relating to job performance can be very damaging to the leader's effectiveness and to organizational excellence. Conversely, leaders who are perceived as fair can command great loyalty and even sacrifice from employees.

4. *The most powerful motivator of human development is personal challenge, which is created by high performance standards, feedback, and a clear reward structure.* As with student development, challenge is the key to employee growth and development. Individuals respond to expectations of high performance when they are challenged to do so and given consistent support and recognition by leaders.

5. *Effective organizations have identifiable shared values and beliefs that provide a common framework of purpose and meaning for employees.* The importance of a clear sense of organizational values has been repeatedly stressed in research on organizational development (Adams, 1984; Albanese, 1978; Kuh, 1983; Schein, 1988). Individuals' efforts are energized and focused when there is widespread agreement on organizational goals (Du Brin, 1978). For example, promoting the welfare of students is a central goal of student affairs organizations. Highly visible, shared goals such as this help integrate organizations by giving employees a clear sense of organizational values, clear objectives, and a sense of common purpose. An organization's core values should be clearly articulated by leaders and integrated into all aspects of the organization's activities.

Talent Development: Maximizing Human Potential

One of the most important changes in human resource management in recent years has been the recognition of the employee as a dynamic organizational participant whose talent and potential for productivity and innovation are often untapped. Jacoby, Astin, and Ayala (1987) describe talent development as a process of focusing on changes and improvement in employees' performance, starting when they are first hired by an organization. When a new staff member is hired, the organization is gaining an individual who can not only perform certain tasks but also potentially do many other things to further the organization's goals. When an individual's potential talents are ignored, both the individual and the organization lose. But when employees are viewed as individuals with diverse talents that can be tapped and developed, the benefits can be enormous.

Few job roles in higher education remain static. Rather, job responsibilities are constantly undergoing alterations to respond to changing circumstances and changing student populations. Employees are constantly changing in their knowledge and capabilities. Consequently, human resources must be viewed as dynamic and full of potential. Thus a primary task of the leader is to identify, develop, and channel the resource of employee talent in the midst of ever-changing circumstances. This task is particularly challenging today because of increasing diversity in the student affairs work force. Men and women from a variety of racial, ethnic, and cultural backgrounds are better represented in student affairs work than in the past, and this trend will continue in the future. Such human diversity provides a richer array of talent and resources; leaders must see the potential of such diversity and provide opportunities to tap what it offers.

Human development is a lifelong process. Thus it is important to provide for and facilitate employees' continuing development. Most individuals regard their career as a major focal point of their personal growth and development. And since employees want to succeed in their jobs, they particularly welcome opportunities that will both enhance their development and benefit their organization. Effective student affairs leaders look for ways to promote talent development so that employees have the opportunity to continue to grow and thereby achieve greater excellence in their work.

Some of the most important management strategies for promoting talent development include the following:

1. *Assess employees' basic skills and knowledge.* To utilize employees' talents, one must know what they are. Some information about employees' skills and talents is gained from resumes and interviews, but unfortunately many employee skills, interests, and abilities go unrecognized. Thus a basic assessment of employee skills and knowledge should be conducted at the time of hiring and then updated on a regular basis as part of the annual evaluation process. This assessment should also gather information on employees' attitudes, interests, and self-knowledge. Such information will help leaders understand the personality and personal perspectives of each employee—often very important factors in an employee's success or failure.

2. *Design specific learning and performance objectives.* Supervisors can encourage talent development by working with employees to design learning and performance objectives and then providing feedback on their accomplishments. For example, young staff members often have little experience in budget management and planning. Practical training in budget management can be designed—with

employee input—to help such employees enhance their basic knowledge and skills and to provide them with some personal mentoring and feedback. Such an approach helps identify promising areas for professional growth and achievement and serves as a powerful personal motivator.

3. *Focus on changes and improvement in employees' performance.* Too often, the focus in evaluations of employee performance is solely on correcting problems. The most effective way to correct failures is to help employees understand as clearly as possible what is expected of them and to provide specific directions on how to achieve the required level of performance. This is the mentoring role of supervision, which can be one of the most useful and rewarding roles of leadership.

4. *Recognize and reward achievement.* Recognizing and rewarding achievement are the most powerful motivators for developing employees' talents and performance (Sandeen, 1991). There are many ways to reward achievement in job performance, including salary increases, glowing performance evaluations, special assignments, expanded job responsibilities, verbal praise, and personal complimentary notes. All of these means of recognition and reward can be especially effective when combined within a consistent pattern of supervision. Bringing out the best in employees is directly related to the support and recognition they receive for their talents. Salary increases are certainly appreciated, but they are often less important than other forms of recognition for a job well done.

5. *Train employees for leadership.* One of the basic principles of talent development is to help employees maximize their skills and abilities for leadership. Leadership is more than excellent job performance. Leadership involves an understanding of problems and issues that go beyond one's own job description and a willingness to take responsibility for solving those problems even when there is no requirement or expectation to do so. Training employees for leadership is a powerful means of developing individual talent and strengthening organizations.

6. *Measure learning and development outcomes.* Supervisors are often unable to systematically document improvements in employee performance. Assessing development is a difficult task in any area of human development, and it is especially difficult in the workplace. The most effective supervisors work with employees to establish specific performance goals, identify the means for achieving those goals, and then evaluate whether employees actually achieve them.

Staff Development: Common Knowledge and Core Competencies

As Studs Terkel (1974) eloquently put it, "Most people have work that is too small for their spirits" (p. 175). Thus human development is an essential aspect of effective personnel management. It provides opportunities for training, motivating staff, developing teamwork, and enhancing organizational effectiveness. Deegan, Steele, and Thielen (1990) claim that staff development is the pillar of any system of management. Moreover, student affairs staff trained in human development theory are more likely to recognize the importance of ongoing personal development and to expect it from their leaders.

Development activities provide an essential bridge from employees' graduate education to their professional practice. Staff development programs help employees make the necessary personal transition from studying a profession to becoming a professional. Furthermore, staff development provides a baseline of content and skills training that ensures that employees without a degree in student affairs possess the necessary competencies to fulfill their job roles and responsibilities.

The dramatic impact of computer technology on our society is mirrored in the student affairs profession (see Chapter Twenty-Three). Hardly any area of student affairs has been unaffected by the computer revolution. Moreover, the pace of change, both in hardware and software, has been swift and dramatic, requiring staff to almost constantly upgrade their computer skills. Familiarity with general computer technology is important for all student affairs staff, as is competence in specific applications used by particular student affairs professionals. Thus staff development programs should include opportunities for employees to develop knowledge and skills in computer technologies used in student affairs settings.

An important contemporary staff development strategy is the promotion of team building and collaboration. Many new management theories stress the importance of employee involvement in quality circles or other small teams that promote an exchange of ideas and shared problem solving. (Some of the new constructs emerging in postconventional organizations are discussed by George Kuh in Chapter Thirteen.)

As Baier (1985) points out, the work of student affairs requires a wide variety of skills, including counseling, teaching, supervising, managing budgets, knowing group dynamics, and managing computer technology. Student affairs organizations are composed of individuals with very different professional training, experience, and job responsibilities. This great diversity of roles and specializations often makes it difficult to achieve a sense of common purpose and shared objectives within a student affairs organization.

Consequently, all staff should possess certain basic knowledge and competencies geared toward achieving the goals of the organization. Harry Canon (1985a) describes this as a remediation process, in which employees are provided a common ground of knowledge and core skills. Following are some of the most important aspects of this common ground:

1. *The nature and history of the institution.* Every employee should be familiar with the origin, traditions, and historic mission of the institution where they work. Such information helps staff understand and appreciate why the institution has its present form and practices and how their role fits into the institutional culture.

2. *The goals, policies, and procedures of the student affairs organization.* Every student affairs organization has certain policies and procedures that guide the organization and define its boundaries and standards of professional practice. Not only should employees be familiar with these organizational policies and procedures, they should also understand the rationale behind them. Some practices are required by law, some by state governing boards, some by institutions, and some by student affairs organizations themselves.

3. *A profile of the characteristics of students served.* Institutions of higher education differ widely in part because they serve very different student bodies. For example, students who attend predominantly undergraduate residential colleges generally have quite different characteristics than students who attend urban commuter institutions or community colleges. Thus the work of student affairs is shaped by the unique characteristics and needs of different student populations.

Not only do student characteristics differ by institutional type, they also change over time. Consequently, student affairs staff should be familiar with the profile of the student body they serve, including such information as basic demographics, educational aspirations, academic achievement, personal goals and values, prior activities and experiences, and current needs. Much information is usually available about students from the admission, testing, and matriculation processes. Sadly, student affairs staff do not always take full advantage of such information. (Chapter Twenty-Three provides a detailed discussion of various sources of information on and off campus.)

4. *Ethical standards of practice.* Every profession within higher education needs clear standards of right and wrong to guide its members in their work. Knowing the standards of one's profession and institution is an important prerequisite for ethical practice. It is particularly important for student affairs staff, since they are often the most visible role models on campus. As Harry Canon (1985b) suggested, student affairs staff serve as the conscience of the campus.

"Right" and "wrong" in professional practice are defined by the ethical standards established by professional organizations and individual colleges and universities. In addition, many areas of ethical conduct are defined by law and social mores. Student affairs practice includes some special ethical standards and obligations. One such standard in many student affairs organizations is that staff members do not have consenting sexual relationships with students. Student affairs staff need to understand and observe such standards in their work, and they must have the opportunity to examine them as a regular part of their professional preparation and practice.

5. *Basic communication skills.* While it may seem unnecessary to provide training in communication skills, student affairs staff do need ongoing opportunities for learning how to communicate effectively. There are two reasons for this. First, as has been discussed above, student affairs staff come from many disciplines and backgrounds. Consequently, they often have difficulty understanding one another's perspective and communication style.

Second, student affairs work is very often done in teams or small work groups, in which collaboration and interpersonal communication are essential. In such situations, being effective in one's job depends upon good listening skills, knowing how to give constructive feedback, and being able to interact effectively with colleagues and students. This is particularly important in highly diverse institutions.

6. *Leadership skills.* In every student affairs position, success depends to some degree on specific leadership competencies such as decision-making skills, the ability to organize and plan, a capacity to work effectively with others, and an ability to take the initiative. As mentioned above, some individuals have a special talent for leadership which can be enhanced through training and practice. But every staff member can be taught certain basic leadership skills and given opportunities to develop them. Encouraging leadership skills and helping staff see themselves as leaders are powerful tools for staff development and effective performance. (See Chapter Fourteen for a detailed discussion of leadership.)

7. *Time management skills.* A common dilemma for student affairs staff is how to manage all the demands of their job and live up to the numerous expectations placed upon them. When student affairs staff are unable to manage the heavy demands of their job, they either burn out and lose interest, become resentful, or simply look for another place to work. Sometimes they do all three. Student affairs work is by nature time-consuming, demanding, and sometimes hectic, because of the energy and needs of students and the busy pace of university life. Staff need to develop basic coping and time management skills so they can work effectively in such settings.

Finally, two highly individualized staff development activities should be mentioned. Mentoring and self-directed training can be effective techniques for staff development in some situations. In a mentoring relationship, a more experienced professional serves as a personal adviser and resource guide for a less experienced staff member. Self-directed training permits staff members to learn independently and focus on particular skills or knowledge that may be of special interest or relevance. Self-directed activities also enable individuals to study at their own pace while still participating in an organized educational program.

Staff development programs come in all shapes and sizes. Although there is not space in this chapter to describe each type in detail, the following list includes the most popular types:

- New staff orientation
- Workshops and seminars
- Newsletters and in-house communications
- Self-directed study
- Leaves of absence for formal academic course work
- Temporary staff assignments
- Interdepartmental staff exchanges
- Mentoring
- Team projects and group activities
- Combinations of the above (a "cafeteria approach")

Recruiting Staff: Tips on Finding the Best Employees

Any organization can only be as good as the individuals it employs. Hiring the most talented and capable employee for every job role in the organization is one of the most important functions of student affairs leaders. Although even the most effective search process cannot guarantee that the best candidate will always be hired, it will enhance the odds of generating the best possible pool of candidates.

Unfortunately, many excellent candidates are lost in job searches because of problems such as delays, miscommunication, the appearance of disorganization, lack of attention or enthusiasm, or a need for information. When competing for top candidates who may also be considering other job offers, any one of these problems can result in the loss of a good candidate. Consequently, staff recruitment must be organized and administered in a very efficient manner. An effective search consists of the following steps:

1. *Orient the search committee.* Every search committee member needs to be clear about the demands of the position and the kind of candidate being sought to fill it. Failure to orient the search committee is the single most common reason why search committees wind up disagreeing over final candidates. The supervisor responsible for the position to be filled should normally provide this orientation. He or she should be as specific as possible about the necessary qualifications and the most important responsibilities of the position. The committee should also clearly understand its role and authority in the search process.

2. *Draw up an accurate job description.* To conduct an effective search, a current and accurate job description must be available. Investing sufficient time and effort in clearly defining job duties and required qualifications will save the search committee and interviewers from wasted time and effort as they sort through the candidates for the job. Trying to hire the right candidate for a position with an

ill-defined job description is like trying to find an unfamiliar destination without a road map. You are never quite sure where you are going, and you often don't realize when you have arrived. The job description is the road map to hiring the best candidate. Without it there is sure to be confusion and disagreement.

3. *Follow job-posting guidelines.* Posting is the process of publicly advertising a vacant position and formally announcing that candidates are being sought. The public announcement is generally made only after the job description has been clearly defined and the search committee has been formed and oriented. Requirements and customs differ with respect to how posting is conducted; thus it is important to be clear about what your institution expects. Many institutions are required to follow specific guidelines in listing positions to comply with affirmative action and other state and federal regulations. The basic principle behind such guidelines is to ensure that a wide and diverse pool of qualified individuals are informed of the job vacancy and have an equal opportunity to compete for the position.

4. *Screen all job applicants.* All applicants' written credentials and supporting materials are reviewed to narrow the field of candidates down to a group of finalists. Those candidates who are not qualified for the position are eliminated, and the candidates with the strongest credentials and experience are identified.

5. *Interview the finalists.* The next step is to conduct personal interviews with the finalists to determine which are the most qualified. This is usually accomplished through campus visits, telephone calls, or other personal contacts designed to learn as much as possible about the candidates. Interviewing is in many respects the most crucial stage in the search process. Most candidates who advance to the interview stage are capable individuals who have demonstrated, at least on paper, that they can provide the leadership needed for the position. The purpose of the interview process is to determine which individual, if any, provides the best fit for the position. The interview process is also an important opportunity for candidates to assess whether the job is a good fit for themselves. Many things about a candidate cannot be determined solely through written credentials. A person's personality, communication skills, interpersonal skills, and leadership skills can best be determined through personal interaction in a series of structured interviews in which a variety of individuals can observe and evaluate the candidate.

6. *Make the hiring decision.* If the search process works well, the best choice is usually apparent. When there is clear agreement and enthusiasm about a single candidate who is judged to clearly excel, the hiring decision is a happy task. But when there is no clearly superior candidate, the hiring decision is a difficult one indeed. At this point the hiring official has the responsibility to weigh all the information and recommendations and determine who should be offered the job.

Before any job offer is officially made, it is very important to verify that final hiring authority has been secured. Some institutions, for example, require clearance from the affirmative action office before a job offer is extended. Job offers are generally not official until all necessary paperwork is complete and the institution's final hiring authority has given its written approval. It is important to recognize the distinction between authorization to search and authorization to hire.

Ultimately, unit supervisors are responsible for the candidate who is hired; consequently, they should make the final determination of which candidate provides the best fit for the position. In the event that the supervisor's decision differs substantially from the recommendations of the screening committee, the committee should be provided with an explanation of the decision.

Getting the Best out of Employees

Almost every employee wants to succeed and looks for ways to continue to grow and be successful. Often what employees need and look for in terms of supervision does not cost a great deal of money nor require a large investment of time. Most staff want simply to know that their work matters and that it makes a difference.

There are some effective ways to let staff know that what they do matters and makes a valuable contribution to the organization. The following strategies are especially effective in motivating employees to enhance their performance:

1. *Notice good work.* Nothing encourages good performance like noticing good work. Noticing good work can be as simple as a comment or complimentary note or as formal as pinning a medal on an employee. Good work should never go unnoticed. Noticing quality work is one of the most important roles of managers and one of the most powerful stimulants for promoting excellence.

2. *Maintain a personal touch.* Nothing kills incentive like the perception that one is simply a faceless member of an organization. Much of life is filled with the impersonal experiences of waiting in lines, fighting traffic, dealing with crowds and strangers, and so on. Supervisors who focus on individual employees, get to know them personally, and touch base with them occasionally on a personal level can develop strong loyalty and commitment from employees. These small efforts yield large performance dividends. Boyett and Conn (1992) claim that the heart of the new management style is to treat people as individuals so that they are motivated to be creative and make significant contributions.

3. *Interpret the meaning of employees' work.* Often employees perform roles or tasks that are so specialized or isolated that they have difficulty seeing how their efforts affect overall outcomes. Leaders can play a very important role in helping

employees see the larger context of their work and understand how it contributes to organizational outcomes.

4. *Communicate shared values.* As noted above, it is very important for employees to understand their work in the context of the organization's shared goals and values. Adams (1984) claims that effective organizations, like effective people, operate best as integrated wholes. Understanding the shared values of the organization helps individual staff members see their work in the context of a broader purpose and meaning. Leaders help motivate staff when they talk about the shared values of the organization and communicate their personal commitment to and support for those values.

5. *Communicate personal values.* Unfortunately, too many supervisors assume that they must keep their own personal values and beliefs private, since values are often subjective and contentious. It is impossible to mask them, however, since what a person values and believes always finds a way into his or her conduct and communications. Moreover, employees expect leaders to have convictions about the most important aspects of their work and human relationships, to articulate personal values, and to model them in their behavior.

Where Managers Fail

Some areas of human resource management are especially difficult "trouble spots" that merit some special discussion. Failure to recognize the following mistakes and handle them appropriately can result in serious personnel problems:

1. *Underestimating personnel issues.* Personnel issues can be highly deceiving. What appears to be a minor problem can mask a torment of feelings and complexity. Never underestimate an employee's problem. Treat every issue seriously until the nature of it is more fully known.

2. *Rewarding the wrong behavior.* It is a common failing of managers to "grease the squeaky wheel," to give in to persistent pressure or give the greatest attention to those who make the greatest noise. Pressure tactics used by some employees can make it difficult for leaders not to compromise, but rewarding the wrong behavior weakens a leader's credibility with all employees and sets him or her up for repeated failures.

3. *Pursuing the task without a vision.* Every employee needs to have a well-defined set of tasks; nothing is quite as frustrating on the job as an ill-defined assignment. Yet, every employee must also be able to see how their specific responsibilities fit into the mission and goals of the department and division. Seeing only the trees, without a guiding perspective on the forest, makes one's work

seem ultimately unsatisfying and unimportant. But a task imbued with a vision is powerful and energizing for the employee.

4. *Pursuing the vision without a task.* Hickman (1992) notes that charismatic leaders motivate organizations to action, but managers are necessary to run them. Some leaders set powerful visions for their organization but are ineffective at translating those visions into practical tasks for their staff. Consequently, when the emotion and energy of the vision wanes, there is little accomplished on an ongoing basis to sustain the vision. Managers fail when they create lofty goals but do not help employees translate those goals into practical and achievable tasks.

5. *Failing to see leadership as service.* Every leader is tempted by the power and influence of leadership. No matter how great or small the leadership role, there is a constant threat of self-importance. It is especially important in student affairs to maintain a service-oriented leadership style. When leaders keep a clear perspective on their role—as enablers of others—they seem better able to keep their personal needs in balance with the needs of others. Much of new management theory stresses the facilitating role of effective leaders.

6. *Ignoring your own advice.* One of the quickest and easiest ways to fail as a manager is to ignore your own advice. Leaders who consistently do themselves what they expect others to do provide a very powerful example for employees. No exceptions go unnoticed by employees, and repeated exceptions completely undermine a leader's moral authority. No leader should expect others to respect what they are not prepared to honor themselves.

Things That Go Bump in the Night

Some contemporary human resource problems in student affairs are so complex and intense that they are the source of many sleepless nights for student affairs leaders. Recognizing the following issues and preparing for them can help student affairs leaders negotiate this difficult terrain when the going gets really rough:

1. *Economic and organizational downsizing.* At some point every organization faces changes that threaten the status quo. In recent years, much of higher education has been going through a process of restructuring. (See Chapter Twenty-One for a thorough examination of organizational restructuring in higher education.) Such times are very threatening to employees and create special challenges for leaders. Employees need to understand what changes are taking place and why. The worst enemy of leadership in such situations is rumor. The perception that changes are occurring in an orderly and just manner is critical to employee morale and productivity. The most important tool of leadership in such tough times is a well-thought-out plan of action that incorporates the input of many staff and utilizes

an effective process of communication. Bad news is bad news, but it can be mini-mized through responsible and humane administration. Also, as increasing num-bers of colleges and universities choose to hire private firms to provide a variety of support services, leaders must adapt to working with contract employees.

2. *Sexual harassment.* Complaints about sexual harassment have become much more frequent in higher education in the 1990s. New laws prohibiting such con-duct have been enacted, and existing laws are more strongly enforced than in the past. Education and awareness regarding problems of sexual harassment have helped change social attitudes and empower individuals to take action against such mistreatment. Student affairs organizations must clearly prohibit such conduct, educate employees regarding procedures for redressing sexual harassment, and strongly administer sanctions when such behavior occurs.

3. *Discrimination and equal treatment.* Unlawful discrimination against individ-uals is not only illegal, it tears at the fabric of any organization. Discrimination de-humanizes individuals based on human characteristics over which they have no ultimate control. Student affairs leaders must be constantly vigilant, committed, and results-oriented with respect to this issue. As college students and the higher education work force become increasingly diverse, the incidence of illegal dis-crimination and unequal treatment is likely to increase. As with sexual harassment, the key management responsibilities are to clearly prohibit such conduct, to edu-cate employees regarding procedures for redressing it when it does occur, and to administer strong sanctions for all violations. An important prevention strategy is to institute an active education and awareness program that fosters appreciation of differences and socializes employees to embrace pluralism in the workplace.

For some issues related to discrimination, a clear legal or moral consensus is lacking—both in the workplace and in society at large—concerning how em-ployers should proceed. One such issue pertains to domestic partner relationships. Some colleges and universities provide housing, insurance, and other benefits to domestic partners of gay, lesbian, and bisexual employees; other institutions do not. If there are no institutional guidelines to follow nor a clear consensus on the proper course of action, student affairs leaders must determine the appropriate actions through a consideration of pertinent legal, ethical, and political variables. Such issues are often the most difficult test of leadership.

4. *When things fall apart: leadership and organizational change.* One of the eventu-alities of professional work is that sooner or later leaders and organizations change—often at the same time. Familiar patterns and practices are disrupted, and employees experience uncertainty about their role and livelihood. While such changes are often viewed with anxiety and fear, they almost always present an open-ing for new opportunities and directions. Staff are more likely to succeed during times of significant change if they maintain a positive outlook. Employees can help shape the direction of change by offering creative ideas and solutions to problems.

Learning to adjust to change and effectively utilize the change process are very important professional survival skills.

5. *When good people do bad things: dealing with individual failures.* All of us fail at some point in our career. When failure is the result of sheer negligence, ineptitude, or deception, it may be difficult to execute the necessary disciplinary action, but it is usually not difficult to determine that some corrective action is needed. Dealing with the failures of good employees is another situation. When a good employee fails, the task of responding to the failure is more complex. One temptation is to ignore the failure, because the employee so seldom fails; another is to overreact to the failure, because it is simply out of character for the employee. Both responses can hurt the employee's development and relationship with you, the supervisor. It is very important to openly acknowledge the failures of good employees but to do so in a way that also affirms their overall strengths and contributions.

Conclusion

In *Workplace 2000* (Boyett & Conn, 1992), the authors forecast a future in which technology, global competition, and consumer demands will increasingly require more flexible, creative, and team-oriented workplaces. These changes are already well under way in American business and industry, and they are increasingly common in American colleges and universities. It seems clear that the traditional, hierarchical student affairs organization, with its highly specialized service units and independent specialists, will move toward a flatter organizational structure characterized by much greater integration of roles and employee participation. Student affairs staff of the future will make greater use of technology to manage services, be more directly involved in a wider array of problem solving, and give greater priority to continual improvement in the quality of programs and services for students. These changes will require student affairs staff who are good communicators, who are flexible and innovative, who can work effectively in teams, and who are committed to continual learning.

Those who aspire to supervise student affairs staff in the future must be visionary leaders as well as practical managers. They must be able to articulate goals and motivate their staff to commit to them. They must model the values they espouse and be able to inspire their employees to actively participate in all aspects of the student affairs mission. Because of this orientation toward flexibility and change, there will be less certainty and stability in student affairs jobs in the future; the profession will be even more challenging and fulfilling, however, because of the greater involvement and commitment of staff.

In many respects, student affairs professionals are likely to respond quite readily to these developments. The boundary-spanning nature of their work and their historic emphasis on service, shared values, and participation will make it easier for them to thrive in this new environment. Hopefully this chapter has provided some practical strategies for increasing managers' effectiveness in working with those with whom they share a common mission—to serve students.

References

Adams, J. D. (1984). *Transforming work.* Alexandria, VA: Miles Reeve Press.

Albanese, R. (1978). *Managing toward accountability for performance.* Homewood, IL: Irwin.

Baier, J. L. (1985). Recruiting and training competent staff. In M. J. Barr, L. A. Keating, & Associates, *Developing effective student service programs: Systematic approaches for practitioners.* San Francisco: Jossey-Bass.

Boyett, J. H., & Conn, H. P. (1992). *Workplace 2000: The revolution reshaping American business.* New York: Penguin.

Canon, H. J. (1985a). Developing staff potential. In U. Delworth, G. R. Hanson, & Associates, *Student services: A handbook for the profession* (pp. 439–455). San Francisco: Jossey-Bass.

Canon, H. J. (1985b). Guiding standards and principles. In U. Delworth, G. R. Hanson, & Associates, *Student services: A handbook for the profession* (pp. 57–79). San Francisco: Jossey-Bass.

Cone L. M., Jr. (1968). *Toward a management theory of managerial obsolescence: An empirical and theoretical study.* Unpublished doctoral dissertation, New York University.

Deegan, W. L., Steele, B. H., & Thielen, T.B. (1990). *Translating theory into practice: Implications of Japanese management theory for student personnel administrators* (NASPA Monograph Series No. 3). Washington, DC: National Association of Student Personnel Administrators.

Du Brin, A. J. (1978). *Fundamentals of organizational behavior.* New York: Pegasus Press.

Hickman, C. R. (1992). *Mind of a manager, soul of a leader.* New York: Wiley.

Jacoby, M. A., Astin, A. W., & Ayala, F. (1987). *College student outcomes assessment* (ASHE-ERIC Higher Education Report No. 7). Washington, DC: Association for the Study of Higher Education.

Kay, E. (1974). *The crisis in middle management.* New York: American Management Associates.

Kuh, G. D. (Ed.). (1983). *Understanding student affairs organizations* (New Directions for Student Services No. 23). San Francisco: Jossey-Bass.

Lindquist, J. (1981). Professional development. In A. W. Chickering & Associates, *The modern American college: Responding to the new realities of diverse students and a changing society* (pp. 730–747). San Francisco: Jossey-Bass.

Pastin, M. (1991). *The hard problems of management: Gaining the ethics edge.* San Francisco: Jossey-Bass.

Sandeen, A. (1991). *The chief student affairs officer: Leader, manager, mediator, educator.* San Francisco: Jossey-Bass.

Schein, E. H. (1988). *Organizational culture and leadership.* San Francisco: Jossey-Bass.

Seymour, D. (1994). *Total quality management on campus: Is it worth the effort?* (New Directions for Student Services No. 86). San Francisco: Jossey-Bass.

Terkel, S. (1974). *Working.* New York: Pantheon Books.

Young, R. B. (1993). *Identifying and implementing the essential values of the profession* (New Directions for Student Services No. 61). San Francisco: Jossey-Bass.

PART SIX

LAYING NEW FOUNDATIONS FOR THE FUTURE

Parts One through Five have presented an extensive scholarly review of the field of student affairs—its history and contemporary context, guiding values and philosophy, ethical and legal foundations, theoretical underpinnings, core competencies, and administrative structures. Each day, student affairs professionals apply this knowledge base to solve students' problems and help them succeed. We stay current with the literature and research in the field by attending workshops and conferences, reading books, consulting professional journals, and discussing commissioned reports with our colleagues. It may seem at times that we suffer from "time famine," that it is impossible to devote the necessary time to read and understand the literature and research that informs our practice. It must be stressed, however,

that these sources of professional development are critical to maintaining a fresh perspective and developing creative approaches to meeting the challenges of our job. Thus this final section addresses how the research and literature in the field informs our practice and the likely future directions of the profession.

Much has been written on the outcomes of higher education; this literature requires careful analysis to assess what is useful and under what conditions. In Chapter Twenty-Five, Leonard Baird provides an insightful discussion of research on student outcomes, framed around the following four reconceptualizations: students are viewed as active and diverse rather than as a monolithic group; the college environment is viewed as a collection of evolving environments rather than a static and homogeneous milieu;

student outcomes are seen as individually chosen rather than institutionally determined; and multiple pathways to understanding student outcomes are presented as alternatives to the dominant, positivistic approach. Baird concludes with a very strong agenda for future research, based on his reconceptualized paradigm.

In Chapter Twenty-Six, the editors focus on the student affairs practitioner's professional identity, using this perspective as a springboard to discussing the profession's future directions. The nineties have been the decade of institutional restructuring, resulting in organizations and professional roles that are more in tune with and responsive to their social context. It has been a time to refocus on undergraduate education—especially on the interconnectedness of student learning and development; a time to make use of those institutional practices that we know foster learning, development, and success. It has been time to understand the powerful transforming nature of future changedrivers, such as the shifts in funding, multiculturalism, the redefinition of individual and social roles, technology, and globalization. These trends and changedrivers will influence the practice of student affairs well into the twenty-first century. This chapter concludes with a discussion of these issues and trends that will continue to shape and redefine the practice of student affairs.

CHAPTER TWENTY-FIVE

LEARNING FROM RESEARCH ON STUDENT OUTCOMES

Leonard L. Baird

The last few years have seen a vast amount of research on student outcomes, ranging from Pascarella and Terenzini's meta-analyses (1991) to Astin's massive multi-institutional longitudinal studies (1993) and examinations of specialized topics such as the influence of women's colleges and the academic careers of African Americans. Likewise, new theoretical explorations of intellectual development (especially as it relates to gender) have brought us new understanding into how students grow and learn. And finally, new research on the college environment has investigated such topics as the characteristics of involving colleges and the unique needs of important groups of students, especially disabled students. This new research and thinking has important consequences for the theory and practice of student affairs, today and into the future. This chapter attempts to describe those consequences in terms of four reconceptualizations of traditional viewpoints. These reconceptualizations are outlined below.

The first reconceptualization discards the traditional view of students as a monolithic group in favor of a new appreciation of students as active and diverse individuals. Students are increasingly seen as responsible actors who shape their own experience and choose the outcomes *they* value. They are also increasingly regarded as a diverse group, not only in terms of demographics (gender, age, ethnicity) but also in terms of personal characteristics (learning styles, psychosocial development, individual abilities).

The second reconceptualization moves from a view of college environments as static and universal milieus to a concept of multiple environments that can best be understood by the different interactions they demand. Some environments foster academic achievement, some personal development, and some a sense of community.

The third reconceptualization is from outcomes as institutionally chosen and social to outcomes as individually chosen and personal. Students bring their own agenda to campus, and it affects their choices and behaviors as much or more than the institution's plans for them. Increasingly, outcomes are seen less in terms of individual benefit and more in terms of social or community benefit. The search for viable, humane communities in our colleges and in our society is one example.

The fourth reconceptualization concerns our ways of knowing. The study of student outcomes (and, indeed, the student affairs profession in general) has been dominated by a psychological and positivistic approach for many years. But a variety of alternative pathways to understanding student outcomes is leading to a richer account of how students are influenced by the colleges they attend as well as by their other experiences.

Each of these reconceptualizations has consequences for student affairs and the ways we work with students. The possibilities and limitations these consequences suggest for professional practice are outlined below. The goal is to help new professionals begin their work with a deeper understanding of how colleges interact with students, and thus provide them with a greater understanding of appropriate actions.

The Growing Interest in Student Outcomes

Student affairs professionals, like most other professionals in higher education, are being called upon to pay greater attention to defining, assessing, and demonstrating students' progress toward academic and developmental outcomes. Although these goals have been discussed in much the same terms for more than a quarter of a century (for example, see Hartnett, 1971; Lawrence, Weathersby, & Patterson, 1970), they have increased salience in recent times because of the changing fiscal and political environment in higher education. Legislatures, boards of trustees, the public, and accrediting agencies are asking for evidence that their investment in higher education has been worthwhile. This evidence is generally provided by measuring what happens to students as a result of their college experience (for histories of the student outcomes movement, see Borden & Bottrill, 1994; Cave, Hanney, & Kogan, 1991).

Thus student affairs professionals are involved not only in defining outcomes but also in using outcomes for assessment, evaluation, and research. (Assessment, evaluation, and research techniques are discussed in detail in Chapter Twenty.) Although many of the outcomes that constituent groups are concerned with involve basic progress (time to degree completion, placement in the work force, passing rates on licensing exams), other outcomes involve learning and personal development (Buchanan, 1993; Cooms & Gehring, 1994). As Garland and Grace (1993) point out, these latter outcomes are especially important to student affairs professionals, since they are held accountable for students' personal development and increasingly play a large role in students' cognitive development as well. The domains of affective and character development have become almost the sole province of student affairs professionals; as Bloland (1991) has noted, these are "forms of education that faculty neither understand nor respect" (p. 32). Thus the combination of public pressure for evidence of academic achievement and the traditional concern of student affairs with students' affective development means that student affairs professionals are often called upon to assume wide responsibility for a considerable range of outcomes. Furthermore, as the people who are usually most knowledgeable about campus climate, student affairs professionals play a critical role in "creating a culture where assessment improves learning" (Loacker & Mentkowski, 1993, p. 5). Finally, with their knowledge of student development theory, student affairs professionals can provide an anchor for the identification and assessment of student outcomes.

Reconceptualizing Students

When we look at old movies that portray college students, a common picture emerges: college students are young; they major in liberal arts; they attend school full time; they are supported by their parents; and they are concerned with ideas as well as with success. Students are also portrayed as white, middle class, and supportive of mainstream assumptions about the meaning of education. (The main character is also usually male.) This stereotypical conception of college students has permeated much of the thinking of academics as well; thus when faculty and administrators interact with students, they sometimes make assumptions that are far removed from reality. This may result in a "chilly climate" for students who don't fit preconceived notions, to borrow Hall & Sandler's (1984) term.

The inaccuracy of these stereotypes has been pointed out by many authors who have reflected on the changing demographics in our educational system (see Chapter Four). For example, Sagaria and Johnsrud (1991) discuss the increasing number of minority students on our campuses and the challenges they represent to traditional practice. Carter and Merkowitz (1993) provide information related to the status of minority students and institutional responses to them. The cultural diversity in our society also presents challenges to our institutions of higher education (Stage & Manning, 1992). Even greater challenges may be presented by the increasing numbers of international students and recent immigrants in American colleges and universities. As Stewart (1993) points out, immigrants and the children of recent immigrants create potential crises as well as opportunities for colleges and universities.

The age of college students has also changed. Students over twenty-five years of age now make up more than a third of all college students nationally, and on many campuses they represent the majority of students. Likewise, the assumption that students attend school full time has been increasingly eroded. If present trends continue, the majority of students will attend part time in the near future. Women now represent the majority of all college students (National Center for Education Statistics, 1995), and projections suggest even larger numbers of women in college in the future. As various critics have pointed out, the increasing presence of women on campus presents a challenge to colleges and universities dominated by a male-oriented culture (for example, see Hackman, 1992; Kuk, 1990; Pearson, Shavlik, & Touchton, 1989). Finally, many more students with disabilities attended college in the last decade (Henderson, 1992). Obviously, disabled students' physical needs challenge those who plan and manage the physical environment on campus; in addition, their psychological and social needs present a challenge to the concerned student affairs professional (Kroeger & Schuck, 1993). Altogether, these demographic changes in U.S. college students mean that our institutions need to reexamine their traditional practices, their traditional definitions of outcomes, and their assumptions about the relationship between their practices and the outcomes they desire for students.

Students have not only changed in demographic terms; they have also mirrored changes in the general culture. As discussed by Garland and Grace (1993), students increasingly report severe financial pressures, poor academic preparation for college, drug and alcohol abuse, and risky sexual practices. At the same time, entering students are more likely to be interested in ecological and social issues, if not traditional politics (Astin, 1994). The mixture of vocationalism, materialism, concern for the environment, and commitment to social justice seen on campus today indicates that students represent a complex mosaic of attitudes and values that are not simple to summarize. The possibility, emphasized in the popular press, that students are also uninspired, alienated, and irresponsible makes any uniform understanding of students even more difficult (Howe & Strauss, 1993). Likewise, the increasing pace of technological advances, which are usually adopted most eagerly by the younger segments of society, is altering our society in ways that may be difficult to quantify. Thus, "college students" cannot be thought of without recognizing a diversity that matches that of a multicultural and rapidly changing society. The most important consequence of all this for colleges is that the concept of a college education now has multiple meanings for students; thus the outcomes educators are concerned with must be equally diverse.

Further, as King (1994) has pointed out, numerous recent attempts to understand the different forms of development among multiple groups of students, particularly those from minority ethnic and cultural backgrounds, has led to the realization that there are multiple paths of development that do not always lead to the same place. In addition, detailed attempts to understand the complexity of areas that were once thought to be uniform have led to additional recognition of diversity. For example, elaborations of Erikson's conception of identity have resulted in the development of separate models for sexual identity, cultural or ethnic identity, female identity, and ethical identity (King, 1994). An important consequence of these concepts is that rather different outcomes are appropriate for different groups of students. Thus a single model for defining and assessing outcomes is not only unwise but also, in the strictest sense, unfeasible.

To have an authentic assessment of outcomes, we need to understand how institutional goals interact with student goals. Students pursue a great variety of paths to reach the goals or outcome they aspire to achieve. Students' widely varying learning styles (Claxton & Murrell, 1987) and their preference for active, collaborative learning are often ignored by faculty (Bonwell & Eison, 1991; Johnson, Johnson & Smith, 1991). This point is elaborated in the following sections, which reach related conclusions in our reconceptualizations of the college environment, outcomes, and students' basic ways of knowing.

Reconceptualizing Campus Environments

The college environment has traditionally been seen to possess stable traits, such as size or "emphasis on scholarship," that are different from student characteristics and that characterize institutions as a whole (Baird, 1988). (See Chapter Twelve for a rich discussion of the college environment.) Thus, the college environment was thought of in static terms, as monolithic. The main task for researchers was to identify the environmental dimensions that separate different colleges in meaningful ways. Of the myriad ways in which campuses may differ, those most often identified as systematic differences with the potential to affect students' experiences were summarized by Baird (1990). These include "the following dimensions of an institution's climate: friendliness or cohesiveness of the student culture, warmth or quality of faculty-student relations, flexibility and freedom versus rigidity and control of the academic and other programs, overall rigor of academic standards, emphasis on personal expression and creativity, emphasis on research versus concern for undergraduate learning, importance of fun and big-time sports, and sense of a shared identity or mission. These are all important aspects of the psychological climate as perceived by respondents in many studies" (p. 39).

As plausible as these dimensions are, research that has attempted to relate them to student change has been disappointing (Astin, 1993; Pascarella & Terenzini, 1991). For example, institutional prestige has been found to have few effects, once students' initial characteristics are taken into account (Terenzini & Pascarella, 1994). One explanation offered for these meager results is that they have been neglectful of theory (Baird, 1988). But when theories that are used to help explain students' cognitive and affective development are examined, few deal with the environment to any extensive degree (Rodgers, 1991). Further, those theories that do deal with the environment have been criticized for being so complex or general that they do not lead to useful distinctions or implementations (Huebner & Lawson, 1990).

Researchers have consequently rethought the assumption that the characteristics of colleges can be identified by means of statistical differentiation, or that studies of college characteristics should be based on psychological theories oriented toward the individual. Thus, researchers have turned to sociological approaches to the college environment (Weidman, 1989). Increasingly, studies have emphasized the importance of students' interactions with their institution and the institution's aggregate values, norms, and behavior (Pascarella & Terenzini, 1991). The greater attention given these more conceptual kinds of variables has also led to a greater recognition of the cultural approach to environments (see Tierney, 1990). Colleges are increasingly seen as coherent, if complex, wholes rather than summations of unconnected characteristics.

But even a cultural approach to environment can characterize institutions in static terms, offering the student an externally defined set of stimuli and pressures. In contrast, the kinds of theories described as "impact models" by Pascarella and Terenzini (1991) emphasize students' *interactions* with the environment. There have been several attempts to analyze the nature of these interactions. The work of Spady (1991), who emphasized the importance of students' social integration with their environment, led Tinto (1975) to develop a model of student interaction that describes its impact on student retention. The model describes how students enter the college environment with a particular background and set of characteristics that help determine their initial commitment to their educational goals and their institution. This commitment is increased or decreased by the extent to which students are integrated into the academic and social environment of their institution. Tinto's work, and the simultaneous use of statistical methods to test his ideas, led Pascarella (1985), among others, to propose more general impact models that apply to more criteria than retention and include two classes of variables missing from Tinto's model—institutional characteristics and the level of student effort (Davis & Murrell, 1993). Institutions with various characteristics are seen as varying in the degree to which they provide enabling situations and stimuli for student change and achievement. The key change in the models, however, is in the concept of student effort or involvement.

The empirical evidence suggests that integration and involvement have consistent effects. As summarized by Davis and Murrell (1993), the evidence about integration is impressive: "student-faculty interaction and academic integration exert a direct and important effect on persistence, intellectual and academic outcomes, and institutional loyalty. Peer relations appear to be important in enhancing persistence and personal development" (p. 58). "Involvement" has wide meaning and equally wide-ranging effects, but as Davis and Murrell emphasize, three areas stand out:

> Involvement with other students, with faculty, and with work. . . . Student-faculty contact is correlated with student satisfaction, college GPA, graduation, and enrollment in graduate school. Such interaction, even after controlling for most individual student differences, is positively associated with intellectual and personal growth. . . . The involvement of students with one another around social and academic topics promotes a wide range of positive outcomes, even after controlling for many individual and institutional differences. When students help one another on class projects, discuss assignments, participate in social organizations, or simply socialize with different kinds of people, good things follow. Students who are socially involved also make gains in general knowledge and intellectual skills and tend to be more satisfied with the college experience. . . . There are some kinds of involvement, especially those which take students away from their studies or isolate them from the campus environment, that appear to have a negative effect on college outcomes.

> Astin (1993) reports that the single largest negative effect on degree completion is holding a full-time or part-time job off campus. Working has a negative effect on other outcomes too, such as GPA, growth in cultural awareness, college satisfaction, and willingness to re-enroll in college. (pp. 59–60)

These results, combined with extensive analyses of Pace's College Student Experiences Questionnaire (1993), led Davis and Murrell (1993) to call for student responsibility, by which students recognize their own role in making the most of their education. Other research, most notably that of Kuh, Schuh, and Whitt

(1991), has shown that institutional culture and climate play a large role in determining whether students are positively involved with their college. Such factors as a clear and consistent mission and philosophy, symbolic actions that celebrate interaction and involvement, events that socialize students to core institutional values, programs and physical spaces that promote interaction, and a variety of other policies and practices all promote involvement. One key factor is respect and celebration of differences among students. This research suggests the power (and therefore the responsibility) of the institution to promote a culture that promotes involvement among all students. Another implication of the research on student integration, involvement, and effort is that students make their own environments based on their interactions with their institution. Thus, the college environment is constructed by a process of psychological and social negotiation between the institution and its students. The potential consequences of this idea are discussed in the concluding section.

Reconceptualizing Outcomes

For many years, outcomes were described with grandiose rhetoric like that found in college catalogs. In more recent times there have been attempts to make the goals of a college education more specific and, importantly, better related to specific educational programs. Dressell (1976) summarized the logic:

> If students are expected to develop a degree of independence in pursuit of learning, reach a satisfactory level of skill in communication, demonstrate sensitivity to their own values and those of their associates, become capable of collaborating with peers in defining and resolving problems, be able to recognize the relevance of their increasing knowledge to the current scene, and seek continually for insightful understanding and organization of their total educational experience, . . . outcomes must be specifically stated. In addition, they must be made explicit in relation to learning experiences and by providing opportunities for demonstration of the developing behavior and for evaluation of it. Content, subject matter, and behavior are interrelated and must be so construed by teachers, students, and evaluators. This requires an interrelated trinity of conceptual statements defining the objectives of operational statements, indicating how the behavior is to be evoked and appraised, and providing standards for deciding whether progress is evident and whether accomplishment is finally satisfactory. (p. 303)

Summarizing the thinking since Dressell's work, Winston and Miller (1994) found some commonality in outcome taxonomies across writers and groups as diverse as Howard Bowen (1977) and the Southern Association of Colleges and Schools (1992). According to Winston and Miller, eight "developmental themes" run through these taxonomies: academic development, cultural development, emotional development, intellectual development, moral development, physical development, development of purpose, and social-interpersonal development. Like Dressell, Winston and Miller emphasized the importance of making developmental goals specific, of linking them to specific curricular and cocurricular programs and developing methods for assessment that can be used to evaluate students' progress toward achieving these goals. As these authors suggest, the logic, the assessment methods, and even the goals themselves have remained much the same for many years. Indeed, as Pace (1993) suggests, there were many imaginative and diverse attempts to assess student movement toward desired outcomes in the 1930s.

How have these long-dormant concepts changed in recent times? Perhaps the most important change is in the nature of the goals, as opposed to their content. As both Winston and Miller (1994) and Seybert (1994) have suggested, colleges can reach general agreement on outcomes; however, outcomes have traditionally been thought of in individualistic terms and, paradoxically, as defined by the institution. There is a growing recognition of the importance of community-oriented outcomes and, again paradoxically, student individuality. The basic approach was to emphasize individual achievement in terms of "independence, self-reliance, self-motivation, personal responsibility, and other personal traits" (King, 1994, p. 414). The constellation of values that these outcomes reflect are deeply embedded in our culture (Boyer, 1987; Noddings, 1984). The consequence is that outcomes are thought of as involving individual success, to be assessed by individual measures and evaluated only in terms of individual achievement. Ironically, these outcomes have been regarded as so obvious that there has apparently been no effort to consider individual students' definition of them. Thus institutions have considered themselves as the natural and appropriate source of outcome goals. The college outlines student goals, defines their meaning for students, and decides on ways to assess student progress toward meeting them.

In contrast, it has been argued that the emerging society of the twenty-first century will require a set of skills and attitudes that are much more community-oriented and will be needed in both the workplace and in private life (Power, Higgins, & Kohlberg, 1989). As summarized by King (1994), these attributes include "interdependence and altruism, creating just and caring communities, showing compassion and respect . . . being productive, responsible, honest and compassionate members of many communities," and knowing that "being part of a community requires some degree of involvement and positive identification, and demonstrating that making individual sacrifices is sometimes necessary for the good of the community" (p. 414). Thus, an emerging paradigm shift in our society may be from individualistic to community-oriented goals. Although the outcomes trends that such goals suggest are not widely recognized in most assessment schemes, they are part of many conceptions of liberal education (for example, see Heath, 1968; Oakley, 1992). Indeed, there has been much discussion among college presidents and administrators in recent years of the need to foster a sense of community in higher education.

One of the implications of a sense of community is respect both for individuals' personal goals and for their needs as members of various groups and subgroups (Jones, 1990). This perspective is important to many specific groups of students now entering higher education in increasing numbers. As King (1994) points out, this "perspective is found among Asian/Pacific Americans, American Indians, African Americans, and Hispanic Americans, whose cultural experiences and values offer many insights for fostering community values on college campuses, as well as for preparing students to live and work effectively in a multicultural society" (p. 416). Thus, the stance for colleges and universities increasingly will be to work with students in defining their own goals as they consider their personal needs and plans and the definitions and outcomes of the institution. This process will involve a negotiation between student and institutional definitions of outcomes. An emerging role for student affairs professionals is to serve as negotiators or brokers between colleges and students so that both may make progress toward the goals they desire. The student affairs professional may then not only help students clarify what they desire from their collegiate experience but also help institutions develop a strategy for merging their desired outcomes with those of each student. The result should be a procedure that will appropriately recognize the needs of students and simultaneously reflect the responsibility of the institution to meet its stated goals. Individualized goals call for an equally individualized assessment and evaluation procedure that will provide evidence of students' progress toward attaining their personal goals and those of the institution. This would represent a major shift from the practice of defining outcomes solely in terms of the institution's desires to one where the student is recognized as a partner in defining the meaning of his or her education (Stark, 1991; Stark, Shaw & Lowther, 1989). This approach has already been recommended for working with the increasing number of adults on our campuses (for example, see Schlossberg, Lynch, & Chickering, 1989).

The change in focus from individualistic to community-oriented outcomes necessitates a similar shift in our conception of the college experience. That is, as we emphasize community-oriented outcomes, we must also emphasize community-oriented processes. The educational approaches that match community-oriented outcomes are different from the traditional, individualistic approach. Not surprisingly, they emphasize collaboration, cooperation, and interaction. A movement toward these ideals can be seen in the concept of learning communities

(Kuh, 1993; Smith, 1993; Tinto, Goodsell-Love, & Russo, 1993). The orientations of learning communities, as contrasted to traditional communities, are summarized by Smith (1993) and shown in Exhibit 25.1.

Clearly, the outcomes emphasized in learning communities focus on students' definitions of their goals as well as on institutional definitions. Learning communities attempt to help students and institutions collaborate in making progress toward achieving their respective desired outcomes. One of the additional positive consequences of working toward the outcomes needed for learning communities is that students obtain skills needed for citizenship in our society. As listed by Morse (1989), these include an attitude of thoughtfully considering problems and issues and the ability to apply methods of logical reasoning and inquiry. Thus an emphasis on learning communities can be quite consistent with the traditional goals of a liberal education; and a major potential task for student affairs professionals is to help colleges become learning communities.

EXHIBIT 25.1. ORIENTATIONS OF TRADITIONAL EDUCATION AND LEARNING COMMUNITY REFORM EFFORTS.

Traditional Orientations	Learning Community Reform Efforts
• Curricula built around disciplines	• Interdisciplinary foci
• Meaning seen as something that is individually constructed	• Meaning seen as socially constructed, through collaborative learning
• Competitive learning environment	• Cooperative learning environment
• Predominantly passive modes of learning	• Active learning, experiential encounters
• Stresses objective nature of knowledge, rationalizes value of knowledge	• Admits subjective and value-laden nature neutrality of knowledge
• Emphasizes "procedural" and "separate" knowing	• Encourages "connected" and "constructed" knowing
• Focus more on the nature of the curriculum than on who is in the classroom	• Increasing focus on who is in the classroom
• Educational delivery system in discrete courses	• Delivery system organized around larger packages of time and credit programs
• Change happens through individual action	• Change through collaboration
• Hierarchical leadership	• Collaborative leadership

Source: Smith (1993). Reprinted with permission.

Whatever the conception of outcomes, student affairs professionals should recognize the difficulties in defining and assessing them (Ewell, 1994). The technical problems are succinctly described by Banta and Associates (1993): "The issues of comparability, relevance, reliability, and sensitivity to change are but a few of the measurement problems that educators face in attempting to provide the evidence of learning and satisfaction that will serve the purposes of accountability and of improvement. . . . Indeed, student outcomes are so complex and multifaceted that we may never be able to derive simple linear cause-effect relationships between what the faculty and staff put into the college experience and what students take away" (p. 362).

Reconceptualizing Ways of Knowing

For many years, thinking and research about college students has been dominated by psychological paradigms and positivistic assumptions about the nature of evidence, especially the view that quantitative data was necessary for knowledge (King, 1994; Strange, 1994). As suggested earlier, other theoretical perspectives have begun to illuminate the work of student affairs professionals, particularly impact theories (see Chapter Eight). At the same time, a whole constellation of new qualitative methods and approaches to research and understanding have developed that emphasize interpretation and the social construction of reality (Lincoln, 1989). As outlined by Glesne and Peshkin (1992), the contrasting predispositions of the quantitative and qualitative approaches are shown in Exhibit 25.2.

The range of qualitative methods is extremely broad (Denzin & Lincoln, 1994), and qualitative researchers do not necessarily agree (for example, see Eisner & Peshkin, 1990), so it is fair to say that the approaches and their epistemologies will be debated for some time to come (see Miller & Fredericks, 1994, for a discussion of these epistemological debates). The most important points for student affairs, however, are that there are multiple ways to gain understandings of students, institutions, and the work of student affairs professionals themselves, and that our definitions of what is important are constructed by our interactions with others. Our models for the ways institutions influence students are likewise constructed by our interactions and contexts. Finally, our conception of what constitutes evidence of our impact on students—and thus the processes available to us to influence students—can be much richer and diverse. (The rich insights of Belenky, Clinchy, Goldberger, & Tarule, 1986, and Baxter Magolda, 1992, are helpful in this effort.)

The implications of these multiple approaches to evidence and the view that we construct our views of issues are discussed in the next section.

EXHIBIT 25.2. PREDISPOSITIONS OF QUANTITATIVE AND QUALITATIVE MODES OF INQUIRY.

Quantitative Mode	Qualitative Mode
Assumptions	
Social facts have an objective reality	Reality is socially constructed
Primacy of method	Primacy of subject matter
Variables can be identified and relationships measured	Variables are complex, interwoven, and difficult to measure
Etic (outsider's point of view)	Emic (insider's point of view)
Purpose	
Generalizability	Contextualization
Prediction	Interpretation
Causal explanations	Understanding actors' perspectives
Approach	
Begins with hypotheses and theories	Ends with hypotheses and grounded theory
Manipulation and control	Emergence and portrayal
Uses formal instruments	Researcher as instrument
Experimentation	Naturalistic
Deductive	Inductive
Component analysis	Searches for patterns
Seeks consensus, the norm	Seeks pluralism, complexity
Reduces data to numerical indices	Makes minor use of numerical indices
Abstract language in write-up	Descriptive write-up
Researcher Role	
Detachment and impartiality	Personal involvement and partiality
Objective portrayal	Empathic understanding

Source: Becoming Quantitative Researchers by Corrine Glesne and Alan Peshkin. Copyright © 1992 by Longman Publishers. Reprinted with permission.

Implications for Student Affairs Practice

The perspectives drawn from the research described above have numerous implications for student affairs professionals. Although the research is often complex, and an understanding of the web of interrelated influences on any outcome can become difficult to achieve, the findings do form a distinct pattern.

First, the diversity in students' cultural backgrounds, personal characteristics, approaches to learning, and developmental status leads to a wide variety in student educational goals. Further, the ways in which students can most effectively attain their goals also vary. Clearly, the extent to which students' goals mesh with those of their institution can have a powerful effect on what they learn and the ways they grow. The extent to which institutions help students integrate their goals with those of the institution also has a powerful impact. This implies that institutions must also change to meet the needs of the student. That is, progress toward academic and social integration, to use the terms used in the impact models, is a mutual process. Also, the extent to which institutional goals emphasize students' personal development and individuation influences student change. This process may be quite difficult for institutions committed to research. Student affairs professionals have particularly large challenges in such institutions.

Thus, because of the differences in students' characteristics and goals, the ways in which students change and interact with their environment are critical. Environments that lead to greater involvement and integration have been shown to be more effective than those that do not. Likewise, students play a large role in creating the environment they inhabit. Therefore, students bear a responsibility for the educations they attain. Colleges that respect and encourage students' individuality *and* responsibility for their own careers are not only more effective but are more satisfying places to study and teach (Kuh, Schuh, & Whitt, 1991).

When we apply the approach of respect for students' individuality and responsibility to college outcomes, we see the importance of including personal development as well as intellectual outcomes (Winston & Miller, 1994). Research suggests that these kinds of outcomes are most affected by involvement with peers and faculty (Astin, 1993; Pascarella & Terenzini, 1991). Likewise, the most effective way to increase positive involvement is to create a college culture that promotes involvement (that is, to create learning communities).

Finally, the changes in our ways of knowing suggest that our conception of what is important is based on our interactions with others. Once again, we are led to the idea that when students become co-creators of their education, they will consider their experiences to be authentic.

The consequences for student affairs professionals of these reconceptualizations are numerous. If the argument put forward in this chapter is correct, the implication is that student affairs professionals should attempt to create learning communities that encourage student involvement and engagement. They should do this by creating the conditions for an active student life, which includes serving as negotiators between students and the institution so that students can become co-creators of their educational outcomes. These outcomes should include goals for personal development and recognition of students' individuality, based as much or more on their approach to thinking and learning as on their background. The end result will be a culture of responsibility and mutual respect. To promote learning and development, institutions need to place the responsibility for students' education in students' own hands; at the same time, institutions have a responsibility to help students learn how to handle this responsibility. The best way to create such mutual responsibility is to create a culture that promotes the process of negotiating individual and institutional goals. Such a culture necessarily involves mutual respect.

Any such program of culture creation needs to pay special attention to the "nontraditional" students described at the beginning of this chapter. For many students, college is not the most important force in their lives. One goal should be to find ways to encourage positive involvement among all students, wherever that involvement takes place. Students who are supported at home or by external community members should be encouraged to reinforce these positive involvements. Involvement with the college should add to, not compete with, outside involvements. Another task for student affairs professionals is to create a culture where students can sort out their own commitments and find ways to integrate them synergistically.

This altered role for student affairs professionals means that they need to be as concerned with (and proficient at) shaping culture as they are with working with individual students (Hamilton, 1994; Spitzberg & Thorndike, 1992). Also, they must often be the advocates for students' point of view, since students have relatively little power on most campuses. As Silverman (1980) asserts, "Our uniqueness as student personnel workers rests on our ability to fashion significant educational environments, using the resources, values, norms, and opportunities of the variety of constituencies on our campuses. To the extent that we are successful in our innovative work, we will be respected, not because of position, but as a result of the impacts we have on campus life. Truly, student personnel workers have the opportunities to be central figures for campus improvement in an era when resources must be perceived as newly combined rather than as new" (p. 12).

These conceptions are similar to those of the "learning organization," a concept promoted by Peter Senge (1990) and widely discussed in the corporate arena. Lewis (1994) summarizes Senge's thought:

> According to Senge, the goal should be to build an organization where people from all levels are continually learning how to learn together. The key to that learning is a sense of connection between the individual's concerns and those of the greater whole. The real leaders of the organization are those who are not only open learners to themselves but are also able to inspire in others the confidence and the will to work collectively in creating new answers as well as new issues. The people in a learning organization who emerge as leaders, therefore, are not necessarily those in positions of formal authority. (p. 6)

Thus student affairs professionals can play a powerful, if unorthodox, role in their institution's life. As co-creators and maintainers of a culture of responsibility and respect, they can become the leaders of the emerging campuses of the new millennium.

Directions for Future Research

Although it is hazardous to project into the future, the reconceptualizations discussed in this chapter suggest some areas where more work is needed. Each reconceptualization suggests further work in theory, methods, and practice. It may be helpful to consider each reconceptualization in turn.

Students

The increased diversity of students presents challenges to traditional, monolithic conceptions of student development. One theoretical question is whether multiple models of development are needed or whether existing models are so robust that they can encompass this diversity. If traditional models are to be used, how do they need to be altered? If multiple models are needed, on what personal qualities should they be based—age, cohort, gender, ethnicity, social class, or cultural background? Should they be "grand theories" concerned with the total person or "midlevel theories" to be used on particular aspects of development, such as ethnic or racial identity or adaptation to academic material? A major methodological challenge lies in finding methods to assess either reworked traditional models or new models. Research on developing such methods and assessing the development of diverse groups of students is greatly needed. A major challenge for professional practice lies in finding ways to work with diverse kinds of students and ways to engage part-time, commuter, and older students with the life of the campus.

Environments

A much better theoretical basis is needed for understanding how environments are formed, sustained, and changed. Student affairs professionals might look to sociological theories based on conflict, exchange, or interactionist approaches (Turner, Beeghley, & Powers, 1995). These approaches are used extensively in sociological studies, on a wide variety of topics. Another methodological concern is the quality of the measures used to assess the nature of the colleges students attend, students' experiences within those colleges, and—perhaps most important—how students interact with and are affected by their college and experiences. Pace's College Student Experiences Questionnaire (1993) provides an excellent beginning toward mapping and measuring how students interact with their institution, but much more work is needed, both conceptually and technically (Baird, 1988). In general, we need to pay much closer attention to measurement issues.

A set of pragmatic issues concerns how to influence the formation, sustenance, and change of environments and cultures. The very diversity of student bodies today creates challenges for the formation of new campus cultures. On the other hand, the forces of tradition and entropy make changing an existing campus culture difficult. Both areas need to be addressed in the years ahead.

Outcomes

A major challenge for outcomes theory lies in explicating the place of community in defining outcomes. Combining individually chosen outcomes within a community framework requires the reworking of philosophical ideas and psychological and sociological theory. This shift in thinking is mirrored in the challenge of assessing individually chosen outcomes and identifying and providing evidence on the development of communities. How can communities of learning really be created and sustained? How can the entropy and resistance of those segments of a campus that are committed to traditional ways of doing things be overcome?

Ways of Knowing

The changes in our ways of knowing reflect those made in many disciplines. There are extremely lively discussions of the philosophical and conceptual bases of our approach to knowledge and understanding. Although student affairs professionals may join in these discussions only occasionally, they should nevertheless be aware of the issues and implications for their work (for example, see Bloland, in press). The challenge for research in student affairs is to find qualitative approaches that are reliable and valid yet flexible and responsive to changing conditions and multiple perspectives. Perhaps the clearest practical implication for student affairs lies in the definition of professional knowledge. The journals and other forms of discourse within the field need to be receptive to newer approaches and incorporate them into the structure of what we "know."

Conclusion

In all of this, the people on campus—students, faculty, staff, and student affairs professionals—need to seek ways to come together as well as respect and affirm their differences. As Nevitt Sanford (1962) wrote, over thirty years ago, that differentiation is an

> essential feature of development, in a college or in an individual. But it increases the necessity of integration, which must keep pace, if fragmentation is not to be

the final outcome. One basis for unity in the college could be its concerted attempt to find rational solutions to its educational problems. Here at least is something that all teachers can discuss together; here is an intellectual inquiry in which all can take part. The more the college becomes diversified and the more it finds integration in this kind of intellectual cooperation, the more will it do to make its students as complex and as a whole as they are capable of becoming. (p. 1033)

References

Astin, A. W. (1993). *What matters in college: Four critical years revisited.* San Francisco: Jossey-Bass.

Astin, A. W. (1994). *The American freshman: National norms for fall 1994.* Los Angeles: University of California, Higher Education Research Institute.

Baird, L. L. (1988). The college environment revisited: A review of research and theory. In J. C. Smart (Ed.), *Higher education: Handbook for theory and research* (Vol. 4, pp. 1–52). New York: Agathon Press.

Baird, L. L. (1990). Campus climate: Using surveys of policy and understanding. In W. G. Tierney (Ed.), *Assessing academic climates and cultures* (New Directions for Institutional Research No. 68, pp. 35–46). San Francisco: Jossey-Bass.

Banta, T. W., & Associates. (1993). *Making a difference: Outcomes of a decade of assessment in higher education.* San Francisco: Jossey-Bass.

Baxter Magolda, M. B. (1992). *Knowing and reasoning in college: Gender-related patterns in students' intellectual development.* San Francisco: Jossey-Bass.

Belenky, M. F., Clinchy, B. M., Goldberger, N. R., & Tarule, J. M. (1986). *Women's ways of knowing: The development of self, voice, and mind.* New York: Basic Books.

Bloland, P. A. (1991). Key academic values and issues. In P. L. Moore (Ed.), *Managing the political dimension of student affairs.* (New Directions for Student Services No. 55, pp. 27–42). San Francisco: Jossey-Bass.

Bloland, P. A. (in press). Postmodernism and higher education. *Journal of Higher Education.*

Bonwell, C. C., & Eison, J. A. (1991). *Active learning: Creating excitement in the classroom.* Washington, DC: Association for the Study of Higher Education.

Borden, V. M. H., & Bottrill, K. V. (1994). Performance indicators: History, definitions, and methods. In V. M. H. Borden & T. W. Banta (Eds.), *Performance indicators: Guides for strategic decision making* (New Directions for Institutional Research No. 82, pp. 5–22). San Francisco: Jossey-Bass.

Bowen, H. R. (1977). *Investment in learning.* San Francisco: Jossey-Bass.

Boyer, E. L. (1987). *College: The undergraduate experience in America.* New York: Harper & Row.

Buchanan, E. T. (1993). The changing role of government in higher education. In M. J. Barr & Associates, *The handbook of student affairs administration* (pp. 493–508). San Francisco: Jossey-Bass.

Carter, D., & Merkowitz, D. R. (1993). *Annual status report on minorities in higher education.* Washington, DC: American Council on Education.

Cave, M., Hanney, S., & Kogan, M. (1991). *The use of performance indicators in higher education: A critical analysis of developing practice* (2nd ed.). London: Kingsley.

Claxton, C. S., & Murrell, P. H. (1987). *Learning styles: Implications for improving educational practices* (ASHE-ERIC Higher Education Report No. 4). Washington, DC: Association for the Study of Higher Education.

Cooms, M. D., & Gehring, D. D. (Eds.). (1994). *The impact of the federal government on student affairs* (New Directions for Student Services No. 68). San Francisco: Jossey-Bass.

Davis, T. M., & Murrell, P. H. (1993). *Turning teaching into learning: The role of student responsibility in the collegiate experience* (ASHE-ERIC Higher Education Report No. 8). Washington, DC: George Washington University.

Denzin, N. K., & Lincoln, Y. S. (Eds.). (1994). *Handbook of qualitative research*. Newbury Park, CA: Sage.

Dressell, P. L. (1976). *Handbook of academic evaluation: Assessing institutional effectiveness, student progress, and professional performance for decision making in higher education*. San Francisco: Jossey-Bass.

Eisner, E., & Peshkin, A. (Eds.). (1990). *Qualitative inquiry in education: The continuing debate*. New York: Teachers College Press.

Ewell, P. T. (1994, November-December). A matter of integrity: Accountability and the future of self-regulation. *Change*, pp. 25–29.

Garland, P. H., & Grace, T. W. (1993). *New perspectives for student affairs professionals: Evolving realities, responsibilities and roles*. Washington, DC: Association for the Study of Higher Education.

Glesne, C., & Peshkin, A. (1992). *Becoming qualitative researchers*. White Plains, NY: Longman.

Hackman, J. D. (1992). What's going on in higher education? Is it time for a change? *Review of Higher Education, 16,* 10–16.

Hall, R., & Sandler, B. (1984). *The classroom climate: A chilly one for women?* Washington, DC: Project on the Status and Education of Women, Association of American Colleges.

Hamilton, S. J. (1994). Freedom transformed: Toward a developmental model for the construction of collaborative learning environments. In K. Bosworth & S. J. Hamilton (Eds.), *Collaborative learning: Underlying processes and effective techniques* (pp. 93–102). San Francisco: Jossey-Bass.

Hartnett, R. T. (1971). *Accountability in higher education: A consideration of some of the problems of assessing college impacts*. New York: College Entrance Examination Board.

Heath, D. (1968.) *Growing up in college*. San Francisco: Jossey-Bass.

Henderson, C. (1992). *College freshman with disabilities: A statistical profile*. Washington, DC: American Council on Education.

Howe, N., & Strauss, B. (1993). *13th gen: Abort, retry, ignore, fail?* New York: Vintage Books.

Huebner, L. A., & Lawson, J. M. (1990). Understanding and assessing college environments. In D. Creamer & Associates (Eds.), *College development theory and practice for the 1990s* (pp. 54–63). Alexandria, VA: American College Personnel Association.

Johnson, D. W., Johnson, R. T., & Smith, K. A. (1991). *Cooperative learning: Increasing college faculty instructional productivity*. Washington, DC: Association for the Study of Higher Education.

Jones, W. T. (1990). Perspectives on ethnicity. In L. V. Moore (Ed.), *Evolving theoretical perspectives on students* (New Directions for Student Services No. 51, pp. 59–72). San Francisco: Jossey-Bass.

King, P. M. (1994). Theories of college student development: Sequences and consequences. *Journal of College Student Development, 35,* 413–421.

Kroeger, S., & Schuck, J. (Eds.). (1993). *Responding to disability issues in student affairs* (New Directions for Student Services No. 64). San Francisco: Jossey-Bass.

Kuh, G. D., Schuh, J. H., Whitt, E. J., & Associates. (1991). *Involving colleges: Successful approaches to fostering student learning and development outside the classroom.* San Francisco: Jossey-Bass.

Kuk, L. (1990). Perspectives on gender differences. In L. V. Moore (Ed.), *Evolving theoretical perspectives on students* (New Directions for Student Services No. 51, pp. 25–36). San Francisco: Jossey-Bass.

Lawrence, B., Weathersby, G., & Patterson, V. W. (Eds.). (1970). *The outputs of higher education: Their identification, measurement, and evaluation.* Boulder, CO: Western Interstate Commission for Higher Education.

Lewis, P. H. (1994). Creating a culture of leadership. In S. A. McDude & P. H. Lewis (Eds.), *Developing administrative excellence: Creating a culture of leadership* (pp. 5–10). San Francisco: Jossey-Bass.

Lincoln, Y. S. (1989). Trouble in the land: The paradigm revolution in the academic disciplines. In J. C. Smart (Ed.), *Higher education: Handbook of theory and research* (Vol. 5, pp. 52–133). New York: Agathon Press.

Loacker, G., & Mentkowski, M. (1993). Creating a culture where assessment improves learning. In T. W. Banta & Associates, *Making a difference: Outcomes of a decade of assessment in higher education* (pp. 5–74). San Francisco: Jossey-Bass.

Miller, S. I., & Fredericks, M. (1994). *Qualitative research methods: Social epistemology and practical inquiry.* New York: Lang.

National Center for Education Statistics. (1995). *Digest of education statistics.* Washington, DC: U.S. Department of Health and Human Services.

Noddings, N. (1984). *Caring: A feminine approach to ethics and moral education.* Berkeley: University of California Press.

Oakley, F. (1992). *Community of learning: The American college and the liberal arts tradition.* New York: Oxford University Press.

Pace, C. R. (1993). [Foreword]. In T. W. Banta & Associates, *Making a difference: Outcomes of a decade of assessment in higher education.* San Francisco: Jossey-Bass.

Pascarella, E. T. (1985). College environmental influences on learning and cognitive development: A critical review and synthesis. In J. C. Smart (Ed.), *Higher education: Handbook of theory and research* (Vol. 1, pp. 1–62). New York: Agathon Press.

Pascarella, E. T., & Terenzini, P. T. (1991). *How college affects students: Findings and insights from twenty years of research.* San Francisco: Jossey-Bass.

Pearson, C. S., Shavlik, D. L., & Touchton, J. G. (Eds.). (1989). *Educating the majority: Women challenge tradition in higher education.* New York: Macmillan.

Power, F. C., Higgins, A., & Kohlberg, L. (1989). *Lawrence Kohlberg's approach to moral education.* New York: Columbia University Press.

Rodgers, R. F. (1991). Using theory in practice in student affairs. In T. K. Miller, R. B. Watson, Jr., & Associates (Eds.), *Administration and leadership in student affairs: Actualizing student development in higher education* (pp. 203–255). Muncie, IN: Accelerated Development.

Sagaria, M. A., & Johnsrud, L. K. (1991). Recruiting, advancing, and retaining minorities in student affairs: Moving from rhetoric to results. *NASPA Journal, 28,* 5–20.

Sanford, N. (1962). Research and policy in higher education. In N. Sanford (Ed.), *The American college: A psychological and social interpretation of the higher learning* (pp. 1009–1034). New York: Wiley.

Schlossberg, N. K., Lynch, A. Q., & Chickering, A. W. (1989). *Improving higher education environments for adults: Responsive programs and services from entry to departure.* San Francisco: Jossey-Bass.

Senge, P. M. (1990). *The fifth discipline: The art and practice of the learning organization.* New York: Doubleday.

Seybert, J. A. (1994). Assessment from a national perspective: Where are we, really? In T. H. Bers & M. L. Mittler (Eds.), *Assessment and testing: Myths and realities* (New Directions for Community Colleges No. 88). San Francisco: Jossey-Bass.

Silverman, R. J. (1980). The student personnel worker as leading-edge leader. *NASPA Journal, 18,* 10–15.

Smith, B. L. (1993, Fall). Creating learning communities. *Liberal Education,* 32–39.

Southern Association of Colleges and Schools. (1992). *Criteria for accreditation: Commission on colleges, 1992–1993 edition.* Decatur, GA: Author.

Spady, W. (1991). Dropouts from higher education: Toward an empirical model. *Interchange, 2*(3), 38–62.

Spitzberg, I. J., Jr., & Thorndike, V. V. (1992). *Creating community on college campuses.* Albany: State University of New York Press.

Stage, F. K., & Manning, K. (1992). *Enhancing the multicultural campus environment: A cultural brokering approach.* San Francisco: Jossey-Bass.

Stark, J. S. (1991). *Student goals exploration user's manual: Institutional research guide.* Ann Arbor: University of Michigan Press.

Stark, J. S., Shaw, K. M., & Lowther, M. A. (1989). *Student goals for college and courses: A missing link in assessing and improving academic achievement.* Washington, DC: Association for the Study of Higher Education.

Stewart, D. W. (1993). *Immigration and higher education: The crisis and the opportunities.* New York: Lexington Books.

Strange, C. C. (1994). Student development: The evolution history and status of an essential idea. *Journal of College Student Development, 35,* 399–412.

Terenzini, P. T., & Pascarella, L. T. (1994). Living with myths: Undergraduate education in America. *Change, 26,* 28–32.

Tierney, W. G. (Ed.). (1990). *Assessing academic climates and cultures* (New Directions for Institutional Research No. 68). San Francisco: Jossey-Bass.

Tinto, V. (1975). Dropouts from higher education: A theoretical synthesis of recent research. *Review of Educational Research, 45,* 89–125.

Turner, J. H., Beeghley, L., & Powers, C. H. (1995). *The emergence of sociological theory* (3rd ed.). Belmont, CA: Wadsworth.

Weidman, J. (1989). Undergraduate socialization: A conceptual approach. In J. C. Smart (Ed.), *Higher education: Handbook of theory and research* (Vol. 5, pp. 289–322). New York: Agathon Press.

Winston, R. B., Jr., & Miller, T. K. (1994). A model for assessing developmental outcomes related to student affairs programs and services. *NASPA Journal, 30*(1), 2–19.

CHAPTER TWENTY-SIX

BUILDING ON THE PAST, SHAPING THE FUTURE

Susan R. Komives and Dudley B. Woodard, Jr.

One can hardly pick up an educational journal or magazine today that does not contain an article or lead story on the condition of higher education, advice on what steps are necessary to remedy its woes, or a clarion call for it to shape solutions to the dilemmas and paradoxes that face the country and the world. Opportunities for higher education to contribute to significant societal and scientific change have never been more apparent, and the pressure to perform in a more timely and cost-effective manner has never been so strong.

The last three generations of American college students have witnessed or contributed to (1) student protests, quieted by materialistic interests and the stirrings of a national consciousness, (2) a loss of public confidence in education (including higher education) and the resultant calls for educational reform and performance-based outcomes, (3) increased competition for enrollment and continued financial constraints, (4) tension on campus between individual rights and community responsibilities challenging new views of competitiveness and cooperation, and (5) profound and encouraging demographic change. On the eve of the twenty-first century, these factors continue to influence the restructuring of higher education in the United States.

As George Kuh stated in Chapter Thirteen and Judy Rogers reiterated in Chapter Fourteen, these rapidly changing times require a paradigm shift away from conventional concepts about teaching and learning, how educational systems are organized to deliver learning and developmental outcomes, and the roles of faculty and student affairs professionals. In *Sustaining Excellence in the 21st Century*, Katz and West (1992) describe a new administrative vision for higher education: "The vision represents a significant departure from existing cultural norms, structures, behaviors, and systems. In particular, it suggests the need for more widespread delegation of authority, rewards for employee risk-taking and initiative, an enhanced emphasis on service and quality, and increased reliance on the campus technological infrastructure and architecture" (p. 8). Meanwhile, Garland and Grace (1993) describe the emerging role of the student affairs practitioner as a campus integrator: "a role that is more central and critical to the achievement of other institutional goals and seeks greater integration of other roles and activities" (p. 103). Bob Shaffer (1993), Indiana University's longtime dean of students and dean emeritus, admonishes us to respond to these new challenges with creativity, flexibility, and ingenuity; otherwise, he asserts, we may end up wallowing in self-pity and battling to protect our boundaries. Student affairs professionals must assertively help to shape the new forms that higher education will take in the future and advocate changes to enhance student learning and development. This chapter looks briefly at the professional perspective of student affairs, challenges the profession to transform itself, and offers a glance into the crystal ball to discover trends and issues that will demand our attention and benefit from our involvement in the future.

Professional Identity and Historical Perspectives

Erikson (1968) proposed that individuals need to look to their "conceptual ancestors" to help them define and understand their identity. Perhaps people can discover their professional identity in the same manner. Who are the conceptual ancestors of student affairs from the past three hundred years? You have been introduced to them throughout this book. In Chapters Two and Five, Elizabeth Nuss and Robert Young described some of the pioneer deans of men and women, the seminal professional statements in the field, and several professional organizations that provided structure and direction to the emerging profession of student affairs. The 1937 and 1949 *Student Personnel Point of View* (American Council on Education, 1994a, 1994b) and the guidelines published by the Council for Advancement Standards in Higher Education have had an enormous shaping influence on our profession.

The doctrine of in loco parentis was the guiding philosophy of early student affairs professionals; although it is no longer legally viable, it is still visible in the ethic of care that permeates the field. Barr (1988) describes how the law dramatically redefined students' relationship with their institution, especially the 1967 Joint Statement on Rights and Freedoms of Students and federal statutes

such as Titles VI and IX of the Civil Rights Act and Section 504 of the Rehabilitation Act. Marylu McEwen (Chapters Eight and Ten), Nancy Evans (Chapter Nine), Patricia King (Chapter Eleven), and Carney Strange (Chapter Twelve)
all discussed the profound influence of the student development movement that
began in the 1960s, and Leonard Baird (Chapter Twenty-Five) chronicled the
attendant research and theory on the influence of the college environment on student outcomes. These theories and research efforts have led to a deeper understanding of student development, the interactive relationship between students
and the collegiate environment, and the outcomes of the undergraduate experience. The events, concepts, and individuals briefly mentioned above represent a
sampling of the richness and diversity of our conceptual ancestors. They sym-
bolize Erikson's (1968) epigenetic principle—the many facets of student personnel work that have emerged to form the functioning whole we call student affairs.

Transformation of the Profession

The history and development of the student affairs profession has been both rapid
and controversial. Student affairs functions exist on all campuses and have enjoyed
significant growth during the last three decades. During this same time, however, the identity of the profession has been at times heatedly debated, ranging
from discussions as to whether or not the field is truly a profession to debates about
professional accreditation, certification, and licensing. The field is in the process
of becoming a credible profession, anchored in an identifiable philosophy based
on guiding principles, a rich and diverse literature, a recognized body of theory
(much of it based on research performed in the last twenty-five years), practice
guided by ethical principles, and energetic professional associations working on
behalf of both students and student affairs professionals. We are engaged in what
Young (1994) calls the profession's "laying stone on sacred stone" (p. 7).

A Philosophy Based on Guiding Principles

The principles of the profession have withstood the test of time and guided us
through substantial change (Woodard, 1990). Individuals like Thomas Arkle Clark,
appointed dean of men at the University of Illinois in 1901, and Evelyn Wright
Allen, appointed dean of women at Stanford in 1910, were pioneers in the emerging profession then known as student personnel work. For these two ground-
breaking professionals there was no coherent institutional philosophy or purpose
to guide their work. Clark said, "I had no specific duties, no specific authority,
no precedence either to guide me or to handicap me. . . . My only chart was that
of the action of the Board of Trustees which said I was to interest myself in the
individual student" (Fley, 1979, p. 37). Thus these professionals were left to decide

for themselves how to handle the student service functions of their time. They, along with many others, helped shaped the events that led up to the 1937 *Student Personnel Point of View*. This pioneering document gave the profession its soul. Its second paragraph expands on the many aspects of student development that continue to deserve the attention of professionals in higher education: "This philosophy imposes upon educational institutions the obligation to consider the student as a whole—the student's intellectual capacity and achievement, emotional make-up, physical condition, social relationships, vocational aptitudes and skills, as well as moral and religious values, economic resources, aesthetic appreciation" (American Council on Education, 1937/1994a, p. 68). Thus an overriding goal of the profession has always been to further the development of the student as an individual. This guiding principle and others identified by Elizabeth Nuss (Chapter Two) and Robert Young (Chapter Five) have been reaffirmed throughout the history of student affairs. Even if the politics of some foundational statements and professional projects were controversial at the time, the core of their content affirmed the professional values and philosophies of student affairs and the impact of our work on the student experience.

In addition to the *Student Personnel Point of View*, the field has been immensely shaped by such thoughtful pieces as the following:

- *Student Development Services in Postsecondary Education,* by the Council of Student Personnel Associations (1975/1994)
- *A Perspective on Student Affairs,* by the National Association of Student Personnel Administrators (1987)
- Various foundation- and association-sponsored studies, such as *Campus Life: In Search of Community* (Carnegie Foundation for the Advancement of Teaching, 1990) and *College: The Undergraduate Experience in America* (Boyer, 1987)
- The National Institute of Education's report *Involvement in Learning* (Study Group on the Condition of Excellence in American Higher Education, 1984) and the 1967 and 1992 versions of the joint statement on student rights and freedoms
- Pivotal early projects such as Tomorrow's Higher Education, which resulted in such pieces as Brown's *Student Development in Tomorrow's Higher Education: A Return to the Academy* (1972) and Miller and Prince's *Future of Student Affairs* (1976)
- Recent works such as *The Student Learning Imperative* (American College Personnel Association, 1994) and *Reasonable Expectations,* commissioned by the National Association of Student Personnel Administrators (Kuh, Lyons, Miller, & Trow, 1995)
- Reports of various research projects, including *Involving Colleges* (Kuh, Schuh, Whitt, & Associates, 1991), *What Matters in College* (Astin, 1993), and *How College Affects Students* (Pascarella & Terenzini, 1991), which was so ably summarized by Leonard Baird in Chapter Twenty-Five.

These works speak to the importance of focusing on student development and student learning; emphasizing student rights; encouraging students to take responsibility for their own learning and personal development; affirming the uniqueness, worth, and dignity of all students; respecting others regardless of individual differences such as race, gender, or beliefs; and supporting the creation and maintenance of a caring and collaborative community based upon common purposes. These goals embody the enduring principles of our profession, principles that have transcended generations to become what Jung (1923) called our "collective conscience."

A Rich and Diverse Literature

Research and scholarship in the field of student affairs has come into its own during the last twenty-five years. The sheer volume of published research and books written on matters pertaining to the profession is quite impressive. A review of Pascarella and Terenzini's book *How College Affects Students* (1991) attests to the amount of research undertaken since the publishing of Feldman and Newcomb's book *The Impact of College on Students* (1969). Books like Rentz's *Students Affairs: A Profession's Heritage* (1994); Astin's *What Matters in College* (1993); Miller, Winston, and Mendenhall's *Administration and Leadership in Student Affairs* (1983); Barr, Upcraft, and Associates' *New Futures for Student Affairs* (1990); the Jossey-Bass New Directions in Student Services series; and the expanded number of generalist and professional journals related to student affairs attest to the field's explosive growth. Numerous research grants and nationally funded projects over the past twenty-five years have produced a rich and varied body of research and scholarship in student affairs, both from student affairs practitioners and from teaching professionals.

We must acknowledge that not all of our literature and published research is of equal quality, and not all of what is useful finds its way into practice. We are encouraged that our field is now concentrating on needed critiques of its professional practices, promoted by the almost simultaneous publication of such reform-minded works as Bloland, Stamatakos, and Rogers's *Reform in Student Affairs* (1994) and the series of five articles in Caple's capstone issue of the *Journal of College Student Development* (1994), led by Strange's piece "Student Development: The Evolution and Status of an Essential Idea" (1994). Informed critique will serve to enhance and advance our work in the twenty-first century.

A Growing Body of Theory

Our understanding of student development has been advanced by a growing body of theory on student learning and retention, allowing us to respond confidently to the rapidly changing world of higher education. Early student development theory and retention models were unidimensional in their approach. As many authors in this book have explained (see Chapters Eight through Eleven), they were skewed toward a traditional-age, White, male perspective, both in their initial conception and because of the subjects used in studies to validate them. But since the 1960s and 1970s, the paradigm of student development has been stretched and reframed. Researchers and theorists have helped us understand multiple views of student development, including the notions that retention is not about integration into the dominant culture and that dominant modes of teaching do not connect with all learners.

Informed Practice

Over the past twenty-five years, student affairs professionals have been outspoken advocates of civil rights, student rights, and inclusive campus practices. They have often functioned as the moral conscience of the campus. Sometimes this has brought criticism of their being too "politically correct." A more accurate description is that student affairs professionals are "educationally correct," dedicated to upholding the principle of inclusion for all students. Student affairs divisions are proudly the most diverse units on campus, reflecting the principles of the profession in their hiring policies; not all campus environments achieve this match between intentions and results. These principles are reflected in other aspects of student affairs work as well; student affairs professionals have consistently promoted and used authentic and ethical processes in our daily practice as we advocate for students.

Professional Organizations

The growth, strength, and contributions of the many national student affairs organizations has been amazing. These professional associations have produced statements of ethical practice, sponsored research, and advanced continued professional development through national, regional, and local conferences and special workshops and institutes. Student affairs associations have published a significant amount of literature, often on neglected topics such as fiscal management; gay, lesbian, and bisexual student issues; and the needs of international students. Interassociation collaboration is laudable and perhaps best evidenced by the Council for the Advancement of Standards. Current work on quality assurance continues to raise important issues regarding preparation and practice (Creamer et al., 1992). Various student affairs organizations have also assumed national leadership roles on such issues as financial aid, student right-to-know acts, campus safety and violence prevention, community service, and drug and substance abuse programming.

The Transformative Sum of the Parts

Pat Cross (1991) helps us think about the future of higher education when she states that "the problems we face now call for a new lens, new way of looking at issues, a paradigm shift" (p. 9). Her thesis is that we need to move beyond unidimensional and multidimensional perspectives, toward a transformational view of higher education. In Stage 1, or unidimensional thinking, theories, events, and practice are shaped "by a single dominant culture or paradigm, and frequently the alternatives are not even visible" (p. 10). This stage is best illustrated by the once-common belief that college was for the education and training of the sons of the privileged, to prepare them to become national political and industrial leaders. Thus colleges and universities were once dedicated to perpetuating the power structure of society by "reproducing" those in positions of power. Many students were so unwelcome in traditional institutions that parallel systems were created for their education (see Chapter Three). The tremendous increases in enrollment after World War II began to stretch various paradigms; individuals began to view human behavior and social systems through multiple lenses as a result of the increased numbers of women and minority students attending college. Values and beliefs were no longer shaped by a single dominant culture; new perceptions were introduced, and alternatives became visible.

The weakness of multidimensional, or Stage 2, thinking is that "while there is recognition that multiple perspectives are richer, more inclusive, and more productive than unidimensional models, the new dimensions are simply added to the old; they aren't integrated to form a new vision" (Cross, 1991, p. 10). Cross concluded that to achieve transformational, or Stage 3, thinking, we need to stop using an identifiable number of distinct cultures and ethnic groups as a proxy for social progress: "We are after transformed attitudes that recognize group differences, to be sure, but that also value individual difference" (p. 11).

The number of colleges and universities undergoing restructuring in the 1990s illustrates that higher education is undergoing a remarkable transformation. In a report in the journal *Research Briefs* (1994b) on restructuring, El-Khawas reports that over two-thirds of the country's public colleges and universities have taken steps to redirect their operations and programs during the past few years. This change has been driven largely by changing social and financial conditions and the country's changing demographics. Also, new social and organizational theories are replacing logical positivism. The outcome will likely be Cross's Stage 3—the transformation of the whole "so that it is something more than the sum of many separate and distinctive cultures" (1991, pp. 10–11). This transformation will fuel our discussion of the vision of the profession's future.

Studying the Future

Forecasting the future and analyzing trends are risky ventures. With this caveat in mind, we now venture into a discussion of societal and campus trends influencing higher education and the student affairs profession.

Societal Trends

Among the many trend analysts and forecasters in the United States, the United Way's Strategic Institute (United Way of America, 1989) has a strong track record for correctly identifying those issues that will have a strong influence on the nation's human and social systems. In 1989, institute analysts identified nine forces they called "changedrivers"—profound influences upon our shared experience" (p. 1). Each of these forces has direct and indirect implications for higher education. Each could be described in great detail. Space is lacking, however, so instead we present here a brief summary of each force and leave it to the reader to determine which are applicable to their own particular campus or professional activities.

1. *Maturation of the U.S. population.* The average age of Americans is increasing. The graying of America has implications for careers in health services, geriatrics, adult care programs, continuing education, leisure education, and teleconferencing. In addition, more services will be provided by retired professionals to the campus community.

2. *A mosaic society.* Americans are increasingly diverse, and a broadened base of diverse Americans is seeking higher educational experiences. The development of diversity and the need for services for diverse students has been gaining the attention of student affairs professionals for two decades and continues to deserve attention. Campuses have only recently developed strategies to cultivate multicultural awareness in members of the dominant culture. Curriculum transformation is essential in all fields so as adequately to address diverse needs and views on campus. The challenge is to develop a common purpose and a sense of community within the mosaic campus.

3. *Redefinition of individual and social roles.* As the public sector substantially tightens its fiscal belt and reexamines social service programs that have been in place for decades, we are seeing a similar reexamination of what Americans should expect from their institutions of higher education. American colleges and universities have been asking themselves what they must do differently. As a result, self-help groups now abound on campus, support groups provide expertise that was only available in the past from professionals, and community service has become a

meaningful way for institutions to help themselves and span boundaries that might have blocked needed resources in the past.

4. *An information-based economy.* Our postindustrial world is increasingly based in cyberspace. Our information-based economy has the potential to welcome both women and men because it is based on intellectual activity. We must address the gender imbalance on the Internet, however (most users are currently male), and the fact that computer access is generally limited to those with a certain level of income. Universities should teach and expect computer literacy of all students, faculty, and staff. Campus information systems need to be easily and equally accessible.

5. *Globalization.* Satellite communications and other technology bring distant wars, earthquakes, and political upheaval into our living rooms. Our interdependence is unquestioned, and students need to learn cross-cultural skills to understand and function alongside those with differing expectations and values. U.S. college programs and services must have international links. Too often we rely on limited study abroad programs, available only to the privileged, to address this need.

6. *Personal and environmental health.* The environmental movement is a growing cultural norm. More Americans are willing to make the connection between their personal behavior (e.g., smoking, drunk driving) and risks to their own health and the health of the ecosystem. Campuses must follow, modeling new environmental practices. These policies should be applied consistently and across the board. Automobile speed limits and policies on smoke-free buildings do not apply just to students or any other single group. We should support similar policy reforms in such areas as alcohol abuse and campus immunizations.

7. *Economic restructuring.* Our system of taxation and issues regarding the emerging global economy are leading to new views on national and personal financial health. Campus finances and students' ability to finance their education are equally affected. As mentioned earlier, reorganization and restructuring are taking place on most campuses, resulting in profound and fundamental changes in organizational structures and academic and support programs. Restructuring involves increased scrutiny of programs, reorganizing administrative units, cutting budgets of some units and tightening procedures for monitoring expenditures, increased fundraising, and reorganizing academic and student services units (El-Khawas, 1994b). There will be continued competition for federal and state dollars from K–12 education, health care, law enforcement, and corrections.

8. *Redefinitions of family and home.* Single-parent families, extended families, and domestic-partner arrangements have distinct needs that are not addressed by programs and services designed around the traditional family model. Further, things that used to be done only in the home, like caring for children, are now done externally, and things that used to be done externally, like seeing a movie,

shopping, banking, and attending college, can now be done at home. Issues involving children and their education need attention and research from college scholars. The families of adult students need to be involved, and various services need to be offered for them.

9. *Rebirth of social activism.* Renewed civic activism to address school violence, youth crime, drugs, unethical business practices, and environmental safety is evidence of an increasingly concerned citizenry. More students engage in protest during high school today than at the height of the college student protest era of the 1960s and 1970s. Protest and citizen involvement are accepted practices, even in the most conservative sectors of society. The willingness to get involved and make a difference signals a new move toward civic leadership, community service, and involvement.

Issues Challenging Higher Education

Various professional associations in higher education have identified their agenda for the twenty-first century. These associations have focused on such persistent issues as transfer student articulation, school-college relations, restructuring faculty work, and access and equity in the face of changing practices in affirmative action and changes in financial aid programs. They focus on outcomes accountability and emergent issues such as decaying infrastructures, minority enrollments in graduate and professional education, and distance learning. Changing financial conditions, expanding technology, changing demographics, and the conflict between a renewed emphasis on teaching and an increased faculty work load have special implications for student affairs professionals.

Most observers agree that the financial condition of higher education will not improve. Higher education is moving into a new era of permanently diminished financial support (Breneman, 1993). In a report by the Association of Governing Boards of Universities and Colleges (1992), the major conclusion on the financial condition of higher education was that "no matter what level of public confidence is assumed, resources per student for higher education can increase only if the economy grows robustly over the next 30 years. No matter how high public confidence rises, resources per student will decline if economic growth is nonexistent. . . . Higher education cannot expect to enjoy the same growth in resources that occurred in the [1980s]. In the short term, the economic recession and continuing criticism of higher education will limit resource growth" (pp. 8–9). Continued financial constraints will force institutions to constantly rethink their mission and make hard choices among competing programs. Institutions will have to continue their efforts to find ongoing ways to reduce or hold the line on operating expenses, stabilize their budgets, and reallocate their resources to high-priority programs. Many institutions have pursued effective strategic planning initiatives to increase their flexibility in responding to growing internal and external financial pressures.

Technology will play an increasingly important role in how services are delivered and how learning occurs. As Larry Benedict noted in Chapter Twenty-Three, more institutions will take advantage of distance learning, and more students will use computers in a variety of settings to receive and process information. Classrooms may be used more for discussion groups, while video and computers are used to provide much of the instruction. Virtual reality may reduce the need for demonstration laboratories, and libraries will become communication centers. Technology is costly and can create a great disadvantage for institutions that cannot afford it. For all of the benefits of technology and the intriguing possibilities of surfing the Internet, higher education must develop responses to such downside issues as student cocooning and ethical and legal challenges to campus electronic discussion groups.

Changing demographics will continue to influence how we think about education and what we must do to meet the needs of a changing population. Enrollment pressure will vary, and fewer new markets will develop. Multicultural awareness will transcend the movement to validate individual differences that began in the 1980s and early 1990s. Within-group and between-group similarities will be emphasized to help build effective learning communities. Although technological change has dominated the end of the twentieth century, futurists contend that "the most exciting breakthroughs of the 21st century will occur not because of technology, but because of an expanding concept of what it means to be human" (Naisbitt & Aburdene, 1990, p. 16). Higher education must lead the way by emphasizing such issues as biomedical ethics, the search for common purpose, and the framing of new expectations of community.

The 1990s trend toward a stronger focus on undergraduate teaching and learning will affect faculty work loads, tenure and promotion policies, and institutions' commitment to the success and persistence of new students. Although encouraging, this trend is fraught with tensions as accountability mechanisms lag behind changing role expectations. But a new generation of faculty and staff will rediscover the central role of the academy—educating students. This trend will likely result in greater interdisciplinary courses and integrative seminars.

Influencing Student Affairs Practice

Whether in 1976, 1986, 1996, 2006, or 2016, there have always been and always will be issues and problems in any professional work. Issues change in form and nature, but they are a reality of personal and organizational life. Professionals must continually monitor their environment to identify the trends and changing conditions influencing higher education and the student experience. The negative influences that push us outside our comfort zone and force us to rethink what we do or why we do it are easily identified; nevertheless, it is hard not to be resistant, entrenched, and defensive about some aspects of change. Often, identifying positive changes in practice can be equally stressful, but it must be remembered that these changes represent opportunities to build new paths.

The following trends and issues are examples of the challenges and opportunities facing us as we move into the twenty-first century. On some campuses these issues may have already been addressed or resolved; on others they may not have appeared yet. We encourage student affairs professionals to read widely, track trends that may become issues in their state or on their campus, and build coalitions to seek understanding and ways to resolve these issues locally.

Student Trends and Issues

Student affairs professionals must lead their campus in understanding the changing needs of students. Specifically, student affairs staff need to identify generational trends that will affect traditional-age students, set new priorities indicated by changing demographics, and help students prepare for a complex world.

1. *Generational trends and shifts.* The generation that will enter early adulthood at the turn of the century will enroll in our graduate and undergraduate programs well into the first quarter of the twenty-first century. Strauss and Howe (1991) describe this period as a time when "boomer and 13er cultures will move into self-contained camps: loud, moralizing aggressors on the older side and atomized, pleasure-seeking victims on the younger—a vindictive age polarization America has not witnessed since the Roaring Twenties. The elder Silent will express dismay at growing signs of tribalism, nativism, social intolerance, and just plain meanness. Boomers will voice exasperation over the ineffective leadership of their next-elders and fury at the help-myself nihilism of their next-juniors" (pp. 380–381). The so-called millennial generation, also tagged the "civic generation," will come of age during a time when the nation is moving close to a secular crisis. If Strauss and Howe's forecast is accurate, then who will your students be? What will your campus climate be like? What will be the pressing social and economic issues of the day? Place yourself in this fast-approaching period. How can you best prepare yourself to be an effective professional and change agent during a period of U.S. history that may be quite bumpy and difficult?

2. *Shifting emphases.* The changing demographics and social issues of the twenty-first century will redefine how student affairs practitioners set their priorities.

The needs of unique groups of students—including students with disabilities, underprepared students, and returning students seeking a career change—will lead to new student affairs specialties. Campuses can no longer frame all or even most services for traditional-age, residential students but must reshape their services and programs to meet the needs of graduate students, commuters, adult learners, part-time students, and distance learners. Dysfunctional behavior such as harassment and violence toward others will be addressed with focused counseling, educational interventions, and new institutional policies. Financial difficulties will slow time to graduation as more and more students will need to work in order to afford their education. Institutions will have to adjust their course offerings accordingly, which may slow progress for all students. In addition, funding sources for programs and services will come under greater scrutiny, and programs will be held strictly accountable for their outcomes.

3. *Societal demands and conditions.* Issues surrounding poverty, juvenile delinquency, high secondary-school dropout rates, racism, violence, substance abuse, hunger, high-tech genetics, the national debt, and environmental problems like groundwater depletion and air pollution will challenge students in the late 1990s and continue to be with us into the twenty-first century. These issues will influence how students think about their future. How will colleges and universities help students understand and grapple with these social issues? The idea of an "ivory tower" is clearly anachronistic; college students must be involved in the real world, bringing these issues to the classroom and into the agendas of student organizations. The student affairs practitioner will be asked to design seminars and symposia to discuss these issues and make them relevant to students' education and future plans. Moreover, practitioners will be asked to encourage and help prepare a new generation of leaders. This does not imply the skill development commonly referred to as "leadership training" but rather a heterarchic model based on influence through vision, accomplishment through collaboration, and advancement through courage and commitment.

Campus Trends and Issues

Campuses are facing numerous challenges today, including decaying infrastructures, disputes over employee work loads and benefits, rapid curriculum development, and increased calls for faculty and staff accountability. Colleges and universities are under increasing pressure to enhance their learning environment, lead with technology, create and nurture a campus community, creatively fund student affairs services and programs, and deal comfortably with continuing paradoxes and dilemmas. Several campus issues deserve focused attention.

1.   *Enhancing learning environments.* Academic and support service departmental boundaries will be less distinct in the future, as Garland and Grace (1993) have suggested. Student affairs professionals of the twenty-first century will work closely with faculty to develop a learning environment that addresses different learning styles and approaches to learning. Student affairs professionals will be expected to be knowledgeable about who students are in terms of characteristics, values, and academic preparation. They will also need to know how to help faculty use this knowledge in designing improved learning environments. The student affairs professional will become the campus expert in assessing student outcomes and will translate outcome data for faculty. Student affairs professionals will be expected to teach more core, leadership, and developmental courses. Student affairs staff must become experts at identifying the developmental and learning experiences inherent in student employment, community service, cooperative education, and other forms of experiential learning and link those to students' academic experience.

2.   *Creating and leading with technology.* Technology will play an important part in shaping the emerging role of the twenty-first century student affairs practitioner. Computer literacy is not enough. Many practitioners will be expected to know how to harness technology to design learning environments and meet the service needs of students. For example, students will increasingly enroll in interactive classes and perform such tasks as paying their bills or checking their graduation status without leaving their residence hall, apartment, or home. Who will design, support, and troubleshoot for these systems? A posting on the Internet from a colleague in Canada asks, "Will there still be a role in the techno-university of the future for a 'residential campus' with its emphasis on helping young adults develop into whole persons? What can we learn from the 30 to 40 years of theory on cognitive, psychosocial, and moral development about how traditional age students might be helped or hindered in their development in the new 'virtual' university? How do we manage to continue to 'humanize' the young adults who will access the university of the 21st century?" (A. Auger, personal communication, 1994). These questions need rigorous discussion so that we do not replace our community soul with a motherboard!

3.   *Creating and nurturing the campus community.* The balkanization of campuses into units that rarely communicate has reduced many campuses to silos of antagonism. Effective change will require coalitions of stakeholders working creatively to share human, fiscal, and other resources. Student affairs staff are positioned in the connective junctures of campus life—serving students, faculty, and the broader community. Our process skills will be essential in forming new leadership structures, work teams, and other flexible systems. Students are perhaps the ultimate

boundary spanners, daily experiencing a variety of milieus: the classroom, the bursar's office, a job at the front desk in the student union, soccer practice, and so on. Creating community is a process of building commitment to the whole among all the parts. Student affairs staff play an important role in creating the rituals, symbols, and other cultural interventions that bring people together. Connecting people should be a priority for all student affairs offices, through funding, programming, and personal commitments.

4. *Funding student affairs services and programs.* The conventional wisdom is that the best tactic to secure funding into the twenty-first century is to opt for modest growth at best. This reality will continue to force institutions to look at alternative sources of revenue. In a national survey conducted by the American Council on Education, "half of all institutions have recently reorganized their student services offices. . . . Almost as many have set new fees for student services" (El-Khawas, 1994a, p. 1). Major issues will include how much to privatize and what fees to charge students for services currently funded from state or other sources. A restructuring of student affairs based on privatization will result in a very different campus community and a changed relationship between students and their institution. How would you characterize this new relationship? What are the benefits and trade-offs? Unless institutions remain firm in their commitment to programs and services essential to the education and personal development of students, a possible outcome of outsourcing and fee charges is the consumer demand model. In other words, the consumer decides what is important, and the campus character is largely shaped by the consumer's priorities. An array of private service providers, such as learning support centers, wellness programs, and residential communities, may constitute a new growth industry on campus.

5. *Dealing comfortably with continuing practices and dilemmas.* The rapid pace of change today means organizations are no longer just faced with solving problems—they must deal with dilemmas and paradoxes. Many issues have equally reasoned principles and values on opposing sides. For example, campuses are faced with valuing both freedom of speech and campus civility, promoting individuality and community, and advancing research while respecting animal rights (Barr & Golseth, 1990). Campus personnel need to value diverse perspectives and make decisions within the scope of the college mission, purpose, and culture. The trend toward quick fixes in our society, exemplified by its ever-faster computers, TV remote controls, ready divorces, and disposable products, creates a challenge for decision makers who need time, patience, and long attention spans in order to resolve difficult campus dilemmas. (On the other hand, an increased willingness to move quickly to resolve important issues could be quite beneficial to the world of academic administration, which is infamous for its interminable meetings.)

Issues Within the Profession

Student affairs professionals and related professional associations must focus on several issues in the near future that will benefit from their collective attention. Issues like privatization of services, the renewed emphasis on learning and other developmental outcomes, quality assurance for professional competence, and the need to build broader coalitions in the higher education community all have implications for professional leadership.

1. *Privatization.* Art Sandeen and John Schuh discussed this trend in Chapters Twenty-One and Twenty-Two. Higher education must acknowledge the trend toward privatization of functions such as graduate housing, student unions, health centers, and, to a lesser extent, personal and career counseling. Institutions will have students contract with private enterprises for these services to reduce institutional liability and the day-to-day issues and problems generated by these services. Student affairs administrators will need extensive new skills in contract management to ensure that private service providers communicate as necessary with campus personnel, and they will need to design requests for proposals that result in inclusive and equitable services. Student affairs staff may find new employment possibilities with these private service providers, or they may become entrepreneurs and offer these services themselves. Implications for professional associations include the inclusion of professionals employed by such providers, who currently feel unwelcome at best in professional meetings and professional settings. Boundary spanning will mean that we must collaborate in new ways with such contract services.

2. *Emphasis on learning and other developmental outcomes.* Because of the renewed focus on student learning and performance-based outcomes, student affairs professionals will be called upon to handle new responsibilities associated with these objectives. Student affairs professionals will be needed in these areas because of their knowledge about students and student development theory and because of their skill at designing environments that facilitate individual growth and learning. Links with such programs as new student experience interventions (for example, first-year courses), living-learning centers, experiential learning, and service applications of traditional courses can all lead to new partnerships. Student affairs professionals must move beyond mere lip service about the importance of measuring outcomes and learn both how to assess outcomes and how to apply the results to student affairs programs. As Dary Erwin highlights in Chapter Twenty, in addition to measuring quantifiable outcomes, such assessments may employ a multidimensional approach, using portfolios, focus groups, and other interpretive research methods.

3. *Quality assurance.* Student affairs professionals will continue to be expected to stay current with literature and research in the future. They will likely be required to take continuing education courses to maintain an active professional status. Some type of quality assurance program may be adopted by the major student affairs organizations to guide practitioners' continuing education. The growing cultural norm will be one of active learners' keeping themselves updated on developments in the field. Professional associations, consortia, and staff development programs will need to develop new and innovative methods for this continuing education through the use of technology and collaborative learning.

4. *Building broader coalitions.* Further, student affairs associations must initiate and form coalitions within the higher education community to seek a stronger voice in governmental affairs and to bring the best of collaborative thinking to campus-based issues. Our associations do not own issues of student development, student learning, or campus community. We share those issues and their solutions with other communities. We have only minimal connections with such groups as the American Council on Education; the American Association of Higher Education should build and develop those links. We need to reach out to the Council of Graduate Schools, various equal employment opportunity organizations, the National Society for Experiential Education, and such student groups as the National Association of Graduate and Professional Students and the Coalition of Graduate Employee Unions. We must also tend our own garden and foster closer communication and shared activity between such organizations as the American Council of Personnel Administrators, the National Association of Student Personnel Administrators, the National Association of Student Affairs Professionals, and the National Association for Women in Education.

Conclusion

These future trends are challenging, exciting, frightening, and demanding. Effective student affairs professionals will be those who are realistic but hopeful about approaching seemingly unsolvable problems. A can-do attitude is essential in working with others toward change. Newspapers report that Americans are now living in the "key of D" (Oldenburg, 1990), obsessed with "daily dread, doom, defeat, despair, depression, denial, decay, debt, distrust, drugs, danger, dysfunction, divisiveness, darkness, dearth, doubt, disgust, and generally deep doo-doo" (p. C5). Sadly, this may reflect the life experience of some Americans, but it is not the relevant frame or professional philosophy for those who will be the active leaders of tomorrow. We must rewrite the score for the 1990s in the "key of C," valuing change, choices, candor, capabilities, compassion, courage, catalysts, cooperation, collaboration, compromise, consensus, conflict, controversy, chaos, connectedness, cohesiveness, and community.

Student affairs professionals must practice individual renewal, and they must promote ethical work practices that encourage organizational renewal as well. This means learning to be adaptable, being enthusiastic but realistic, and modeling the highest ethical standards—with students and among colleagues. Professionals must be skilled at reframing issues and problems and viewing challenges from perspectives other than their own. Flexibility will be an essential skill in the future. Student affairs professionals must have the ability to engage in paradigm shifts in their thinking. They must be open to doing business very differently; they cannot afford to rigidly adhere to old ways and conventional models.

Student affairs staff must practice professional empowerment—they must claim a significant place in the life of their institution and exert considerable influence on how its students are educated. Emphasizing the potential contributions of all staff—from the newest professional to the most experienced sage—will help to span boundaries, lower barriers, and focus significant talent on addressing numerous institutional issues. The great deterrent to empowering staff in organizational settings is control. We must be increasingly aware in these times of rapid change that "the dominant principle of organization has shifted, from management in order to control an enterprise to leadership in order to bring out the best in people and respond quickly to change" (Naisbitt & Aburdene, 1990, p. 218).

We hope that by reading this book you have developed a kinship with our conceptual ancestors and made connections with the enduring principles that have guided our profession throughout this century. We hope you have become better acquainted with the theory and research that has strengthened our knowledge base and provided student affairs practitioners with invaluable guidance. We encourage you to think about the competencies discussed in Part Four, which you will need to function effectively and to become a change agent in the new world of higher education.

References

American College Personnel Association. (1994). *The student learning imperative: Implications for student affairs.* Alexandria, VA: Author.

American Council on Education. (1994a). The student personnel point of view. In A. L. Rentz (Ed.), *Student affairs: A profession's heritage* (American College Personnel Association Media Publication No. 40, 2nd ed., pp. 66–77). Lanham, MD: University Press of America. (Original work published 1937)

American Council on Education. (1994b). The student personnel point of view. In A. L. Rentz (Ed.), *Student affairs: A profession's heritage* (American College Personnel Association Media Publication No. 40, 2nd ed., pp. 108–123). Lanham, MD: University Press of America. (Original work published 1949)

Association of Governing Boards of Universities and Colleges. (1992). *Trustees and troubled times in higher education.* Washington, DC: Author.

Astin, A. W. (1993). *What matters in college: Four critical years revisited.* San Francisco: Jossey-Bass.

Barr, M. J., & Associates. (1988). *Student services and the law: A handbook for practitioners.* San Francisco: Jossey-Bass.

Barr, M. J., & Golseth, M. B. (1990). Managing change in a paradoxical environment. In M. J. Barr, M. L. Upcraft, & Associates, *New futures for student affairs: Building a vision for professional leadership and practice* (pp. 201–216). San Francisco: Jossey-Bass.

Barr, M. J., Upcraft, M. L., & Associates. (1990). *New futures for student affairs: Building a vision for professional leadership and practice.* San Francisco: Jossey-Bass.

Bloland, P. A., Stamatakos, L. C., & Rogers, R. R. (1994). *Reform in student affairs: A critique of student development.* Greensboro, NC: ERIC Counseling and Student Services Clearinghouse.

Boyer, E. (1987). *College: The undergraduate experience in America.* New York: Harper & Row.

Breneman, R. (1993). *Higher education: On a collision course with new realities* (AGB Occasional Paper No. 22). Washington, DC: Association of Governing Boards of Universities and Colleges.

Brown, R. (1972). *Student development in tomorrow's higher education: A return to the academy.* Alexandria, VA: American College Personnel Association.

Caple, R. B. (Ed.). (1994). [Entire issue]. *Journal of College Student Development, 35.*

Carnegie Foundation for the Advancement of Teaching. (1990). *Campus life: In search of community.* Princeton, NJ: Princeton University Press.

Council of Student Personnel Associations. (1994). Student development services in postsecondary education. In A. L. Rentz (Ed.), *Student affairs: A profession's heritage* (American College Personnel Association Media Publication No. 40, 2nd ed., pp. 390–401). Lanham, MD: University Press of America. (Original work published 1975)

Creamer, D., Winston, R. B., Jr., Schuh, J. H., Gehring, D. D., McEwen, M. K., Forney, D. S., Carpenter, D. S., & Woodard, D. B. (1992). *Quality assurance in college student affairs: A proposal for action by professional associations.* Report prepared for the American College of Personnel Administrators and the National Association of Student Personnel Administrators.

Cross, K. P. (1991). Reflections, predictions, and paradigm shifts. *AAHE Bulletin, 43*(9), 9–12.

El-Khawas, E. (1994a). *Campus trends, 1994.* Washington, DC: American Council on Education.

El-Khawas, E. (1994b). Restructuring initiative in public higher education: Institutional response for financial constraints. *Research Briefs 5*(8), 1–8.

Erikson, E. H. (1968). *Youth and crisis.* New York: Norton.

Feldman, K. A., & Newcomb, T. M. (1969). *The impact of college on students.* San Francisco: Jossey-Bass.

Fley, J. (1979). Student personnel pioneers: Those who developed our profession. *NASPA Journal, 7*(1), 23–39.

Garland, P. H., & Grace, T. W. (1993). *New perspectives for student affairs professionals: Evoking realities, responsibilities, and roles* (ASHE-ERIC Higher Education Report No. 7). Washington, DC: ERIC Clearinghouse on Higher Education.

Jung, C. G. (1923). Psychological types. In *The collected works of C. G. Jung* (R. C. Hull, Trans.) (Vol. 6). New York: Bollingen Foundation.

Katz, R. N., & West, R. P. (1992). *Sustaining excellence in the 21st century: A vision and strategies for college and university administration.* Boulder, CO: CAUSE.

Kuh, G. D., Lyons, J., Miller, T. K., & Trow, J. (1995). *Reasonable expectations.* Washington, DC: National Association of Student Personnel Administrators.

Kuh, G. D., Schuh, J. H., Whitt, E. J., & Associates. (1991). *Involving colleges: Successful approaches to fostering student learning and development outside the classroom.* San Francisco: Jossey-Bass.

Miller, T. K., & Prince, J. (1976). *The future of student affairs.* San Francisco: Jossey-Bass.

Miller, T. K., Winston, R. B., Jr., & Mendenhall, W. R. (1983). *Administration and leadership in student affairs.* Muncie, IN: Accelerated Development.

Naisbitt, J., & Aburdene, P. (1990). *Megatrends 2000: Ten new directions for the 1990s.* New York: Morrow.

National Association of Student Personnel Administrators. (1987). *A perspective on student affairs.* Washington, DC: Author.

National Association of Student Personnel Administrators. (1992). *Student rights and freedoms: Joint statement on the rights and freedoms of students.* Washington, DC: Author.

Oldenburg, D. (1990, February 1). What's in store for the 1990s? Upside, downside and in between. *Washington Post,* p. C-5.

Pascarella, E. J., & Terenzini, P. T. (1991). *How college affects students: Findings and insights from twenty years of research.* San Francisco: Jossey-Bass.

Rentz, A. L. (1994). *Student affairs: A profession's heritage* (American College Personnel Association Media Publication No. 40, 2nd ed.). Lanham, MD: University Press of America.

Shaffer, R. H. (1993). Whither student personnel work from 1968 to 2018? A 1993 retrospective. *NASPA Journal, 30,* 162–168.

Strange, C. (1994). Student development: The evolution and status of an essential idea. *Journal of College Student Development, 35,* 399–412.

Strauss, W., & Howe, N. (1991). *Generations.* New York: Morrow.

Study Group on the Condition of Excellence in American Higher Education. (1984). *Involvement in learning: Realizing the potential of American higher education.* Washington, DC: National Institute of Education.

United Way of America. (1989). *What lies ahead: Countdown to the 21st century.* Alexandria, VA: Author.

Woodard, D. B., Jr. (1990). *Tenacious tenets of an involving learning environment.* Paper presented at the annual Region IV-East meeting of the National Association of Student Personnel Administrators, Pheasant Run, IL.

Young, J. H. (1994). Laying stone on sacred stone: An educational foundation for the future. *Educational Record 75*(1), 7–12.

RESOURCES

NASPA'S STANDARDS OF PROFESSIONAL PRACTICE

The National Association of Student Personnel Administrators (NASPA) is an organization of colleges, universities, agencies, and professional educators whose members are committed to providing services and education that enhance student growth and development. The association seeks to promote student personnel work as a profession which requires personal integrity, belief in the dignity and worth of individuals, respect for individual differences and diversity, a commitment to service, and dedication to the development of individuals and the college community through education. NASPA supports student personnel work by providing opportunities for its members to expand knowledge and skills through professional education and experience. The following standards were endorsed by NASPA at the December 1990 board of directors meeting in Washington, DC.

1. *Professional Services.* Members of NASPA fulfill the responsibilities of their position by supporting the educational interests, rights, and welfare of students in accordance with the mission of the employing institution.

Source: National Association of Student Personnel Administrators (1993). NASPA standard of professional practice. 1993–94 Member Handbook. Washington, D.C.: National Association of Student Personnel Administrators. Reprinted with permission.

2. *Agreement with Institutional Mission and Goals.* Members who accept employment with an educational institution subscribe to the general mission and goals of the institution.

3. *Management of Institutional Resources.* Members seek to advance the welfare of the employing institution through accountability for the proper use of institutional funds, personnel, equipment, and other resources. Members inform appropriate officials of conditions which may be potentially disruptive or damaging to the institution's mission, personnel, and property.

4. *Employment Relationship.* Members honor employment relationships. Members do not commence new duties or obligations at another institution under a new contractual agreement until termination of an existing contract, unless otherwise agreed to by the member and the member's current and new supervisors. Members adhere to professional practices in securing positions and employment relationships.

5. *Conflict of Interest.* Members recognize their obligation to the employing institution and seek to avoid private interests, obligations, and transactions which are in conflict of interest or give the appearance of impropriety. Members clearly distinguish between statements and actions which represent their own personal views and those which represent their employing institution when important to do so.

6. *Legal Authority.* Members respect and acknowledge all lawful authority. Members refrain from conduct involving dishonesty, fraud, deceit, and misrepresentation or unlawful discrimination. NASPA recognizes that legal issues are often ambiguous, and members should seek the advice of counsel as appropriate. Members demonstrate concern for the legal, social codes and moral expectations of the communities in which they live and work even when the dictates of one's conscience may require behavior as a private citizen which is not in keeping with these codes/expectations.

7. *Equal Consideration and Treatment of Others.* Members execute professional responsibilities with fairness and impartiality and show equal consideration to individuals regardless of status or position. Members respect individuality and promote an appreciation of human diversity in higher education. In keeping with the mission of their respective institution and remaining cognizant of federal, state, and local laws, they do not discriminate on the basis of race, religion, creed, gender, age, national origin, sexual orientation, or physical disability. Members do not engage in or tolerate harassment in any form and should exercise professional judgment in entering into intimate relationships with those for whom they have any supervisory, evaluative, or instructional responsibility.

8. *Student Behavior.* Members demonstrate and promote responsible behavior and support actions that enhance personal growth and development of stu-

dents. Members foster conditions designed to ensure a student's acceptance of responsibility for his/her own behavior. Members inform and educate students as to sanctions or constraints on student behavior which may result from violations of law or institutional policies.

9. *Integrity of Information and Research.* Members ensure that all information conveyed to others is accurate and in appropriate context. In their research and publications, members conduct and report research studies to assure accurate interpretation of findings, and they adhere to accepted professional standards of academic integrity.

10. *Confidentiality.* Members ensure that confidentiality is maintained with respect to all privileged communications and to educational and professional records considered confidential. They inform all parties of the nature and/or limits of confidentiality. Members share information only in accordance with institutional policies and relevant statutes when given the informed consent or when required to prevent personal harm to themselves or others.

11. *Research Involving Human Subjects.* Members are aware of and take responsibility for all pertinent ethical principles and institutional requirements when planning any research activity dealing with human subjects. (See *Ethical Principles in the Conduct of Research with Human Participants,* Washington, DC: American Psychological Association, 1982.)

12. *Representation of Professional Competence.* Members at all times represent accurately their professional credentials, competencies, and limitations and act to correct any misrepresentations of these qualifications by others. Members make proper referrals to appropriate professionals when the member's professional competence does not meet the task or issue in question.

13. *Selection and Promotion Practices.* Members support nondiscriminatory, fair employment practices by appropriately publicizing staff vacancies, selection criteria, deadlines, and promotion criteria in accordance with the spirit and intent of equal opportunity policies and established legal guidelines and institutional policies.

14. *References.* Members, when serving as a reference, provide accurate and complete information about candidates, including both relevant strengths and limitations of a professional and personal nature.

15. *Job Definitions and Performance Evaluation.* Members clearly define with subordinates and supervisors job responsibilities and decision-making procedures, mutual expectations, accountability procedures, and evaluation criteria.

16. *Campus Community.* Members promote a sense of community among all areas of the campus by working cooperatively with students, faculty, staff, and others outside the institution to address the common goals of student learning and development. Members foster a climate of collegiality and mutual respect in their work relationships.

17. *Professional Development.* Members have an obligation to continue personal professional growth and to contribute to the development of the profession by enhancing personal knowledge and skills, sharing ideas and information, improving professional practices, conducting and reporting research, and participating in association activities. Members promote and facilitate the professional growth of staff and they emphasize ethical standards in professional preparation and development programs.

18. *Assessment.* Members regularly and systematically assess organizational structures, programs, and services to determine whether the development goals and needs of students are being met and to assure conformity to published standards and guidelines such as those of the Council for the Advancement of Standards for Student Services/Development Programs (CAS). Members collect data which include responses from students and other significant constituencies and make assessment results available to appropriate institutional officials for the purpose of revising and improving program goals and implementation.

RESOURCE B

ACPA'S STATEMENT OF ETHICAL PRINCIPLES AND STANDARDS

American College Personnel Association
Standing Committee on Ethics

Preamble

The American College Personnel Association (ACPA) is an association whose members are dedicated to enhancing the worth, dignity, potential, and unique-ness of each individual within post-secondary educational institutions and thus to the service of society. ACPA members are committed to contributing to the comprehensive education of the student, protecting human rights, advancing knowledge of student growth and development, and promoting the effective-ness of institutional programs, services, and organizational units. As a means of supporting these commitments, members of ACPA subscribe to the following principles and standards of ethical conduct. Acceptance of membership in ACPA signifies that the member agrees to adhere to the provisions of this statement.

This statement is designed to address issues particularly relevant to college student affairs practice. Persons charged with duties in various functional areas of higher education are also encouraged to consult ethical standards specific to their professional responsibilities.

As revised and approved by ACPA Executive Council, November 1992. American College Person-nel Association (1993). Statement of ethical principles and standards. *Journal of College Student Development, 34*, 89–92. Reprinted with permission of American College Personnel Association.

Use of This Statement

The principal purpose of this statement is to assist student affairs professionals in regulating their own behavior by sensitizing them to potential ethical problems and by providing standards useful in daily practice. Observance of ethical behavior also benefits fellow professionals and students due to the effects of modeling. Self-regulation is the most effective and preferred means of assuring ethical behavior. If, however, a professional observes conduct by a fellow professional that seems contrary to the provisions of this document, several courses of action are available.

- *Initiate a private conference.* Because unethical conduct often is due to a lack of awareness or understanding of ethical standards, a private conference with the professional(s) about the conduct in question is an important initial line of action. This conference, if pursued in a spirit of collegiality and sincerity, often may resolve the ethical concern and promote future ethical conduct.
- *Pursue institutional remedies.* If private consultation does not produce the desired results, institutional channels for resolving alleged ethical improprieties may be pursued. All student affairs divisions should have a widely-publicized process for addressing allegations of ethical misconduct.
- *Contact ACPA Ethics Committee.* If the ACPA member is unsure about whether a particular activity or practice falls under the provisions of this statement, the Ethics Committee may be contacted in writing. The member should describe in reasonable detail (omitting data that would identify the person[s] as much as possible) the potentially unethical conduct or practices and the circumstances surrounding the situation. Members of the Committee or others in the Association will provide the member with a summary of opinions regarding the ethical appropriateness of the conduct or practice in question. Because these opinions are based on limited information, no specific situation or action will be judged "unethical." The responses rendered by the Committee are advisory only and are not an official statement on behalf of ACPA.
- *Request consultation from ACPA Ethics Committee.* If the institution wants further assistance in resolving the controversy, an institutional representative may request on-campus consultation. Provided all parties to the controversy agree, a team of consultants selected by the Ethics Committee will visit the campus at the institution's expense to hear the allegations and to review the facts and circumstances. The team will advise institutional leadership on possible actions consistent with both the content and spirit of the ACPA Statement of Ethical Principles and Standards. Compliance with recommendations is voluntary. No sanctions will be imposed by ACPA. Institutional leaders remain responsible

for assuring ethical conduct and practice. The consultation team will maintain confidentiality surrounding the process to the extent possible.

- *Submit complaint to ACPA Ethics Committee.* If the alleged misconduct may be a violation of the ACPA Ethical Principles and Standards, the person charged is a member of ACPA and the institutional process is unavailable or produces unsatisfactory results, then proceedings against the individual(s) may be brought to the ACPA Ethics Committee for review. Details regarding the procedures may be obtained by contacting the Executive Director at ACPA Headquarters.

Ethical Principles

No statement of ethical standards can anticipate all situations that have ethical implications. When student affairs professionals are presented with dilemmas that are not explicitly addressed herein, five ethical principles may be used in conjunction with the four enumerated standards (Professional Responsibility and Competence, Student Learning and Development, Responsibility to the Institution, and Responsibility to Society) to assist in making decisions and determining appropriate courses of action.

Ethical principles should guide the behaviors of professionals in everyday practice. Principles, however, are not just guidelines for reaction when something goes wrong or when a complaint is raised. Adhering to ethical principles also calls for action. These principles include the following.

- *Act to benefit others.* Service to humanity is the basic tenet underlying student affairs practice. Hence, student affairs professionals exist to (a) promote healthy social, physical, academic, moral, cognitive, career, and personality development of students; (b) bring a developmental perspective to the institution's total educational process and learning environment; (c) contribute to the effective functioning of the institution; and (d) provide programs and services consistent with this principle.
- *Promote justice.* Student affairs professionals are committed to assuring fundamental fairness for all individuals within the academic community. In pursuit of this goal, the principles of impartiality, equity, and reciprocity (treating others as one would desire to be treated) are basic. When there are greater needs than resources available or when the interests of constituencies conflict, justice requires honest consideration of all claims and requests and equitable (not necessarily equal) distribution of goods and services. A crucial aspect of promoting justice is demonstrating an appreciation for human differences and opposing intolerance and bigotry concerning these differences. Important human differences include,

but are not limited to, characteristics such as age, culture, ethnicity, gender, disabling condition, race, religion, or sexual/affectional orientation.

- *Respect autonomy.* Student affairs professionals respect and promote individual autonomy and privacy. Students' freedom of choice and action are not restricted unless their actions significantly interfere with the welfare of others or the accomplishment of the institution's mission.
- *Be faithful.* Student affairs professionals are truthful, honor agreements, and are trustworthy in the performance of their duties.
- *Do no harm.* Student affairs professionals do not engage in activities that cause either physical or psychological damage to others. In addition to their personal actions, student affairs professionals are especially vigilant to assure that the institutional policies do not: (a) hinder students' opportunities to benefit from the learning experiences available in the environment; (b) threaten individuals' self-worth, dignity, or safety; or (c) discriminate unjustly or illegally.

Ethical Standards

Four ethical standards related to primary constituencies with whom student affairs professionals work—fellow professionals, students, educational institutions, and society—are specified.

1. *Professional Responsibility and Competence.* Student affairs professionals are responsible for promoting students' learning and development, enhancing the understanding of student life, and advancing the profession and its ideals. They possess the knowledge, skills, emotional stability, and maturity to discharge responsibilities as administrators, advisors, consultants, counselors, programmers, researchers, and teachers. High levels of professional competence are expected in the performance of their duties and responsibilities. They ultimately are responsible for the consequences of their actions or inaction.

As ACPA members, student affairs professionals will:

1.1. Adopt a professional lifestyle characterized by use of sound theoretical principles and a personal value system congruent with the basic tenets of the profession.

1.2. Contribute to the development of the profession (e.g., recruiting students to the profession, serving professional organizations, educating new professionals, improving professional practices, and conducting and reporting research).

1.3. Maintain and enhance professional effectiveness by improving skills and acquiring new knowledge.

1.4. Monitor their personal and professional functioning and effectiveness and seek assistance from appropriate professionals as needed.

1.5. Represent their professional credentials, competencies, and limitations accurately and correct any misrepresentations of these qualifications by others.

1.6. Establish fees for professional services after consideration of the ability of the recipient to pay. They will provide some services, including professional development activities for colleagues, for little or no remuneration.

1.7. Refrain from attitudes or actions that impinge on colleagues' dignity, moral code, privacy, worth, professional functioning, and/or personal growth.

1.8. Abstain from sexual harassment.

1.9. Abstain from sexual intimacies with colleagues or with staff for whom they have supervisory, evaluative, or instructional responsibility.

1.10. Refrain from using their positions to seek unjustified personal gains, sexual favors, unfair advantages, or unearned goods and services not normally accorded those in such positions.

1.11. Inform students of the nature and/or limits of confidentiality. They will share information about the students only in accordance with institutional policies and applicable laws, when given their permission, or when required to prevent personal harm to themselves or others.

1.12. Use records and electronically stored information only to accomplish legitimate, institutional purposes and to benefit students.

1.13. Define job responsibilities, decision-making procedures, mutual expectations, accountability procedures, and evaluation criteria with subordinates and supervisors.

1.14. Acknowledge contributions by others to program development, program implementation, evaluations, and reports.

1.15. Assure that participation by staff in planned activities that emphasize self-disclosure or other relatively intimate or personal involvement is voluntary and that the leader(s) of such activities do not have administrative, supervisory, or evaluative authority over participants.

1.16. Adhere to professional practices in securing positions: (a) represent education and experiences accurately; (b) respond to offers promptly; (c) accept only those positions they intend to assume; (d) advise current employer and all institutions at which applications are pending immediately when they sign a contract; and (e) inform their employers at least thirty days before leaving a position.

1.17. Gain approval of research plans involving human subjects from the institutional committee with oversight responsibility prior to initiation of the study. In the absence of such a committee, they will seek to create procedures to protect the rights and assure the safety of research participants.

1.18. Conduct and report research studies accurately. They will not engage in fraudulent research nor will they distort or misrepresent their data or deliberately bias their results.

1.19. Cite previous works on a topic when writing or when speaking to professional audiences.

1.20. Acknowledge major contributions to research projects and professional writings through joint authorships with the principal contributor listed first. They will acknowledge minor technical or professional contributions in notes or introductory statements.

1.21. Not demand co-authorship of publications when their involvement was ancillary or unduly pressure others for joint authorship.

1.22. Share original research data with qualified others upon request.

1.23. Communicate the results of any research judged to be of value to other professionals and not withhold results reflecting unfavorably on specific institutions, programs, services, or prevailing opinion.

1.24. Submit manuscripts for consideration to only one journal at a time. They will not seek to publish previously published or accepted-for-publication materials in other media or publications without first informing all editors and/or publishers concerned. They will make appropriate references in the text and receive permission to use if copyrights are involved.

1.25. Support professional preparation program efforts by providing assistantships, practica, field placements, and consultation to students and faculty.

As ACPA members, preparation program faculty will:

1.26. Inform prospective graduate students of program expectations, predominant theoretical orientations, skills needed for successful completion, and employment of recent graduates.

1.27. Assure that required experiences involving self-disclosure are communicated to prospective graduate students. When the program offers experiences that emphasize self-disclosure or other relatively intimate or personal involvement (e.g., group or individual counseling or growth groups), professionals must not have current or anticipated administrative, supervisory, or evaluative authority over participants.

1.28. Provide graduate students with a broad knowledge base consisting of theory, research, and practice.

1.29. Inform graduate students of the ethical responsibilities and standards of the profession.

1.30. Assess all relevant competencies and interpersonal functioning of students throughout the program, communicate these assessments to students, and take appropriate corrective actions including dismissal when warranted.

1.31. Assure that field supervisors are qualified to provide supervision to graduate students and are informed of their ethical responsibilities in this role.

2. *Student Learning and Development.* Student development is an essential purpose of higher education, and the pursuit of this aim is a major responsibility of student affairs. Development is complex and includes cognitive, physical, moral, social, career, spiritual, personality, and educational dimensions. Professionals must be sensitive to the variety of backgrounds, cultures, and personal characteristics evident in the student population and use appropriate theoretical perspectives to identify learning opportunities and to reduce barriers that inhibit development.

As ACPA members, student affairs professionals will:

2.1. Treat students as individuals who possess dignity, worth, and the ability to be self-directed.

2.2. Avoid dual relationships with students (e.g., counselor/employer, supervisor/best friend, or faculty/sexual partner) that may involve incompatible roles and conflicting responsibilities.

2.3. Abstain from sexual harassment.

2.4. Abstain from sexual intimacies with clients or with students for whom they have supervisory, evaluative, or instructional responsibility.

2.5. Inform students of the conditions under which they may receive assistance and the limits of confidentiality when the counseling relationship is initiated.

2.6. Avoid entering or continuing helping relationships if benefits to students are unlikely. They will refer students to appropriate specialists and recognize that if the referral is declined, they are not obligated to continue the relationship.

2.7. Inform students about the purpose of assessment and make explicit the planned use of results prior to assessment.

2.8. Provide appropriate information to students prior to and following the use of any assessment procedure to place results in proper perspective with other relevant factors (e.g., socioeconomic, ethnic, cultural, and gender related experiences).

2.9. Confront students regarding issues, attitudes, and behaviors that have ethical implications.

3. *Responsibility to the Institution.* Institutions of higher education provide the context for student affairs practice. Institutional mission, policies, organizational structure, and culture, combined with individual judgment and professional standards, define and delimit the nature and extent of practice. Student affairs professionals share responsibility with other members of the academic community

for fulfilling the institutional mission. Responsibility to promote the development of individual students and to support the institution's policies and interests require that professionals balance competing demands.

As ACPA members, student affairs professionals will:

3.1. Contribute to their institution by supporting its mission, goals, and policies.

3.2. Seek resolution when they and their institution encounter substantial disagreements concerning professional or personal values. Resolution may require sustained efforts to modify institutional policies and practices or result in voluntary termination of employment.

3.3. Recognize that conflicts among students, colleagues, or the institution should be resolved without diminishing appropriate obligations to any party involved.

3.4. Assure that information provided about the institution is factual and accurate.

3.5. Inform appropriate officials of conditions that may be disruptive or damaging to their institution.

3.6. Inform supervisors of conditions or practices that may restrict institutional or professional effectiveness.

3.7. Recognize their fiduciary responsibility to the institution. They will assure that funds for which they have oversight are expended following established procedures and in ways that optimize value, are accounted for properly, and contribute to the accomplishment of the institution's mission. They also will assure equipment, facilities, personnel, and other resources are used to promote the welfare of the institution and students.

3.8. Restrict their private interests, obligations, and transactions in ways to minimize conflicts of interest or the appearance of conflicts of interest. They will identify their personal views and actions as private citizens from those expressed or undertaken as institutional representatives.

3.9. Collaborate and share professional expertise with members of the academic community.

3.10. Evaluate programs, services, and organizational structures regularly and systematically to assure conformity to published standards and guidelines. Evaluations should be conducted using rigorous evaluation methods and principles, and the results should be made available to appropriate institutional personnel.

3.11. Evaluate job performance of subordinates regularly and recommend appropriate actions to enhance professional development and improve performance.

3.12. Provide fair and honest assessments of colleagues' job performance.

3.13. Seek evaluations of their job performance and/or services they provide.

3.14. Provide training to student affairs search and screening committee members who are unfamiliar with the profession.

3.15. Disseminate information that accurately describes the responsibilities of position vacancies, required qualifications, and the institution.

3.16. Follow a published interview and selection process that periodically notifies applicants of their status.

4. *Responsibility to Society.* Student affairs professionals, both as citizens and practitioners, have a responsibility to contribute to the improvement of the communities in which they live and work. They respect individuality and recognize that worth is not diminished by characteristics such as age, culture, ethnicity, gender, disabling condition, race, religion, or sexual/affectional orientation. Student affairs professionals work to protect human rights and promote an appreciation of human diversity in higher education.

As ACPA members, student affairs professionals will:

4.1. Assist students in becoming productive and responsible citizens.

4.2. Demonstrate concern for the welfare of all students and work for constructive change on behalf of students.

4.3. Not discriminate on the basis of age, culture, ethnicity, gender, disabling condition, race, religion, or sexual/affectional orientation. They will work to modify discriminatory practices.

4.4. Demonstrate regard for social codes and moral expectations of the communities in which they live and work. They will recognize that violations of accepted moral and legal standards may involve their clients, students, or colleagues in damaging the personal conflicts and may impugn the integrity of the profession, their own reputations, and that of the employing institution.

4.5. Report to the appropriate authority any condition that is likely to harm their clients and/or others.

ACPA'S POLICIES AND PROCEDURES FOR PROCESSING COMPLAINTS OF ETHICAL VIOLATIONS

American College Personnel Association Standing Committee on Ethics

Section A: General

1. The American College Personnel Association (ACPA) is an association whose members are dedicated to enhancing the worth, dignity, potential, and uniqueness of each individual within post-secondary educational institutions and thus to the service of society. ACPA members are committed to contributing to the comprehensive education of the student, protecting human rights, advancing knowledge of student growth and development, and promoting the effectiveness of institutional programs, services, and organizational units. As a means of supporting these commitments, members of ACPA subscribe to the Statement of Ethical Principles and Standards. Acceptance of membership in ACPA signifies that the member agrees to adhere to the provisions of this Statement.
2. The purpose of this document is to facilitate the work of the Ethics Committee by specifying the procedures for processing cases of alleged violations of the Statement of Ethical Principles and Standards, codifying options for sanctioning members, and stating appeal procedures.

Approved by the ACPA Executive Council, November 7, 1992. American College Personnel Association (1993). Policies and procedures for processing complaints of ethical violations. *Journal of College Student Development, 34*, 93–97. Reprinted with permission of American College Personnel Association.

Section B: Ethics Committee Members

1. The Ethics Committee is a standing committee of ACPA. The Committee consists of twelve (12) members. Four (4) members are appointed annually, serving for three (3) year terms. The members shall consist of two (2) representatives of the commissions, two (2) representatives of the state divisions, two (2) representatives of the Executive Council and six (6) at large members. All members shall be chosen by the ACPA President in consultation with the Chair of the Ethics Committee. The Ethics Committee will be guided by all the standard procedures of ACPA including the Affirmative Action Policy, in conducting its business.
2. The Chair of the Ethics Committee is appointed biannually by the ACPA President-Elect and serves a term of two (2) years as Chair. The Chair must have served on the Ethics Committee for at least one (1) year subsequent to the formation of ACPA as an independent organization.

Section C: Role and Function

1. The role of the Ethics Committee is to assist in the resolution of conflicts among members of ACPA. The Committee also is responsible for:
   A. educating the membership as to the Statement of Ethical Principles and Standards;
   B. periodically reviewing and recommending changes in the Statement of Ethical Principles and Standards of ACPA as well as the Policies and Procedures for Processing Complaints of Ethical Violations;
   C. receiving and processing complaints of alleged violations of the Statement of Ethical Principles and Standards; and
   D. receiving and processing questions.
2. The Ethics Committee itself will not initiate any ethical violation charges against an ACPA member. The Ethics Committee will allow non-members to bring allegations of unethical conduct to the attention of the Ethics Committee. The Ethics Committee has the authority to determine if the charges have merit and to respond to charges which are determined to have merit.
3. In processing complaints about alleged ethical misconduct, the Ethics Committee will compile a factual account of the dispute in question and make the best possible recommendation for the resolution of the case. The Ethics Committee, in the imposition of sanctions or discipline, shall do so only for cause, shall only take the degree of disciplinary action that is reason-

able, shall utilize these procedures with objectivity and fairness, and in general shall act only to further the interests and objectives of ACPA and its membership.

4. All formal allegations of ethical misconduct will be reviewed by a Hearing Panel. Hearing Panels shall consist of five (5) members chosen by the Chair. In addition, the Chair will serve on all Hearing Panels as presiding officer and a non-voting member. Members of the Ethics Committee who have a personal interest in any case will be excluded from serving on the panel which hears the case. The findings of all Hearing Panels are understood to represent the Ethics Committee as a whole.

5. The Chair of the Ethics Committee and/or any ACPA Executive Director (or his/her designee) may consult with ACPA legal counsel at any time.

Section D: Responsibilities of Committee Members

1. The members of the Ethics Committee must be conscious that their position is extremely important and sensitive and that their decisions involve the rights of many individuals, the reputation of the student affairs profession, and the careers of the members. The Committee members have an obligation to act in an unbiased manner, to work expeditiously, to safeguard the confidentiality of the Committee's activities, and to follow procedures that protect the rights of individuals involved.

Section E: Responsibilities of the Chair

1. In addition to the above guidelines for members of the Ethics Committee, the Chair, in conjunction with Headquarters staff and Hearing Panels, has the responsibilities of:

   A. receiving (via Headquarters) complaints that have been certified for membership status of the accused;

   B. notifying the complainant and the accused of receipt of the case;

   C. notifying the members of the Ethics Committee of the case;

   D. presiding over the meetings of the Committee;

   E. preparing and sending (by certified mail) communications to the complainant and accused member on the recommendations and decisions of the Committee; and

   F. arranging for legal advice with assistance and financial approval of the ACPA Executive Director.

Section F: Complaints

1. All correspondence, records, and activities of the Ethics Committee will remain confidential.
2. The Ethics Committee will not act on anonymous complaints nor will it act on complaints known to be currently under civil or criminal investigation.
3. The Ethics Committee will act only on those cases where the accused is a current member of ACPA or was a member of ACPA at the time of the alleged violation.

Section G: Submitting Complaints— Procedures for ACPA Members

1. The procedures for submission of complaints to the Ethics Committee are as follows:
   A. If feasible, the complainant should discuss with utmost confidentiality the nature of the complaint with a colleague to see if he/she views the situation as an ethical violation.
   B. Whenever feasible, the complainant is to approach the accused directly to discuss and resolve the complaint.
   C. In cases where a resolution is not forthcoming at the personal level, the complainant shall prepare a formal written statement of the complaint and shall submit it to the Ethics Committee. Action or consideration by the Ethics Committee may not be initiated until this requirement is satisfied.
   D. Formal written complaints must include a statement indicating the behavior(s) that constituted the alleged violation(s), the date(s) of the alleged violation(s), and the Standard(s) which the person making the charges believes has (have) been violated. The written statement must also contain the accused member's full name and complete address. Any relevant supporting documentation may be included with the complaint.
   E. All complaints that are directed to the Ethics Committee should be mailed to the Ethics Committee, c/o The ACPA Executive Director, One Dupont Circle, Suite 360-A, Washington, DC 20036–1110. The envelope must be marked **"CONFIDENTIAL."** This procedure is necessary to ensure the confidentiality of the person submitting the complaint and the person accused in the complaint.

Section H: Submitting Complaints— Procedures for Non-ACPA Members

1. The Ethics Committee will permit a non-ACPA member to bring allegations of unethical conduct to the attention of the Ethics Committee. Ordinarily this non-member will be a colleague, student, or client of an ACPA member who believes that the ACPA member has acted unethically.
2. In such cases, the complainant shall contact the ACPA Executive Director (or his/her designee) and outline, in writing, those behaviors he/she feels were unethical in nature.
3. The Executive Director will forward to the complainant the Statement of Ethical Principles and Standards and the Policies and Procedures for Processing Complaints of Ethical Violations. Complainant will follow the procedures outlined in Section G1 C and D above. The Ethics Committee has the authority to determine if the charges have merit and to respond to charges which are determined to have merit.

Section I: Processing Complaints

1. When complaints are received at Headquarters, the ACPA Executive Director (or his/her designee) shall: (a) check on the membership status of the accused, (b) acknowledge receipt of the complaint within ten (10) working days after it is received at Headquarters, and (c) consult with the Chair of the Ethics Committee within ten (10) working days after the complaint is received in Headquarters to determine whether it is appropriate to proceed with the complaint. If the Director (or his/her designee) and Chair determine it is inappropriate to proceed, the complainant shall be so notified. If the Director (or his/her designee) and Chair determine it is appropriate to proceed with the complaint, they will identify which Standard(s) are applicable to the alleged violation. A formal statement containing the Standard(s) that were allegedly violated will be forwarded to the complainant for his/her signature. This signed statement will then become a part of the formal complaint.
2. Once the formal complaint has been compiled (as indicated above), the Chair of the Ethics Committee shall do the following:
    A. Direct a letter to the accused member informing the member of accusations lodged against him/her, including copies of all materials submitted

by the complainant, asking for a response, and request that relevant information be submitted to the Chair within thirty (30) working days, and

    B. Inform the complainant in writing that the accused member has been notified of the charges.

3. The accused is under no duty to respond to the allegations, but the Ethics Committee will not be obligated to delay or postpone its review of the case unless the accused so requests, with good cause, in advance. Failure of the accused to respond should not be viewed by the Ethics Committee as sufficient grounds for taking disciplinary action.

4. The Chair will choose five (5) members of the Ethics Committee to serve as the Hearing Panel for the case.

5. Once the Chair has received the accused member's response or the thirty (30) days have elapsed, the Chair shall forward to the members of the Hearing Panel legal counsel's opinion (if applicable), staff verification of membership status, allegations, and responses, and direct the Hearing Panel to review the case and make recommendations for its disposition within 90 days of receipt of the case.

6. The Ethics Committee Chair may ask the President of ACPA to appoint an investigating committee at the local or state level to gather and submit relevant information concerning the case to the Hearing Panel.

Section J: Available Options

1. After reviewing the information forwarded by the Chair, the Hearing Panel has the authority to:

    A. dismiss the charges, find that no violation has occurred or that the allegation is frivolous, and dismiss the complaint; or

    B. find that the practice(s) in which the member engaged that is (are) subject of the complaint, is (are) unethical, notify the accused of this determination, and request the member to voluntarily cease and desist in the practice(s) without impositions of further sanctions; or

    C. find that the practice(s) in which the member engaged, that is (are) the subject of the complaint, is (are) unethical, notify the accused of this determination, and impose sanctions.

Section K: Appropriate Sanctions

1. The Hearing Panel may consider extenuating circumstances before deciding on the penalty to be imposed. If the Hearing Panel finds that the accused

has violated the Statement of Ethical Principles and Standards and decides to impose sanctions, the Hearing Panel may take any of the following actions:

A. issue a reprimand with recommendations for corrective action, subject to review by the Hearing Panel; or

B. place the member on probation for a specified period of time subject to review by the Hearing Panel; or

C. suspend eligibility for membership in ACPA for a specified period of time, subject to review by the Hearing Panel; or

D. expel the member from ACPA permanently.

Section L: Consequences of Sanctions

1. Neither a reprimand nor probation carry with it a loss of membership rights or privileges.

2. A suspended member forfeits the rights and privileges of membership only for the period of his/her suspension.

3. In the event a member is expelled from ACPA membership, he/she shall lose all rights and privileges of membership in ACPA and its divisions permanently. The expelled member shall not be entitled to a refund of dues already paid.

4. If the member is suspended or expelled, and after any right to appeal has been exhausted, the Ethics Committee will notify any appropriate licensing board(s) of the disciplined member's status with ACPA. Notice also will be given to the ACPA State Divisions of which the disciplined party is a member, the complainant, and other organizations appropriate given the member's professional affiliations. Such notice shall only state the sanctions imposed and the sections of the Statement of Ethical Principles and Standards that were violated. Further elaboration shall not be disclosed.

5. Should a member resign from ACPA or fail to renew his/her membership after a complaint has been brought against him/her and before the Hearing Panel has completed its deliberations, that member is considered to have been expelled from ACPA for failure to respond to an allegation of ethical misconduct under consideration by the Ethics Committee.

6. Annually the Ethics Committee will publish a list of all suspended and expelled members in an official publication.

Section M: Hearings

1. At the discretion of the Hearing Panel, a hearing may be conducted when the results of the Hearing Panel's preliminary determination indicate that

additional information is needed. The Chair shall schedule a formal hearing on the case and notify both the complainant and the accused of their right to attend.

Section N: Hearing Procedures

1. Purposes of Hearings. The purposes for which hearings shall be conducted are: (a) to determine whether a breach of the Statement of Ethical Principles and Standards has occurred, and (b) if so, to determine what disciplinary action should be taken by ACPA. If a hearing is held, no disciplinary action will be taken by ACPA until after the accused member has been given reasonable notice of the hearing and the specific charges raised against him/her and has had the opportunity to be heard and to present evidence in his/her behalf. The hearings will be formally conducted. The Hearing Panel will be guided in its deliberations by principles of basic fairness and professionalism and will keep its deliberations as confidential as possible, except as provided herein.

2. Notice. At least forty-five (45) working days before the hearing, the accused member should be advised in writing of the time and place of the hearing and of the charges involved. Notice shall be given either personally or by certified or registered mail and shall be signed by the Committee Chair. The notice should be addressed to the accused member at his/her address as it appears in the membership records of ACPA. The notice should include a brief statement of the complaints lodged against him/her and should be supported by the evidence. The accused is under no duty to respond to the notice, but the Hearing Panel will not be obligated to delay or postpone its hearing unless the accused so requests in writing, with good cause, in advance. Failure of the accused to appear at the hearing should not be viewed by the Hearing Panel as sufficient grounds for taking disciplinary action.

3. Conduct of the Hearing.

   A. Accommodations. The Hearing Panel shall provide a private room in which to conduct the meetings and no observers shall be permitted. The location of the hearing shall be determined at the discretion of the Committee taking into consideration the convenience of the Committee and the parties involved.

   B. Presiding Officer. The Chair of the Ethics Committee shall preside over the hearing and deliberations of the Hearing Panel. In the event the Chair or any other member of the Hearing Panel has a personal interest in the case, he/she shall withdraw from the hearing and deliberations and shall not participate therein. The Hearing Panel shall select from among its members a presiding officer for any case in which the Chair has excused him/herself. At the conclusion of the hearing and deliberation of the Hearing Panel, the Chair shall promptly notify the accused and complainant of the Hearing Panel's decision in writing.

C. Record. A record of the hearing shall be made and preserved, together with any documents presented as evidence, at Headquarters for a period of three (3) years following the hearing decision. The record may consist of a summary of testimony received or a verbatim transcript at the discretion of the Hearing Panel.

D. Right to Counsel. The parties shall be entitled to have counsel present to advise them throughout the hearing but the counsel may not participate beyond advising. Legal Counsel for ACPA may also be present at the hearing to advise the Hearing Panel and may respond only to questions of procedure.

E. Witnesses. Either party shall have the right to call witnesses to substantiate his/her version of the case. The Hearing Panel shall also have the right to call witnesses it believes may provide further insight into the matter before the Hearing Panel. Witnesses shall not be present during the hearings except when they are called upon to testify. The presiding officer shall allow questions to be asked of any witness by the opposition or members of the Hearing Panel and shall ensure that questions and testimony are relevant to the issues in the case. The presiding officer has the right to determine when sufficient information has been heard, may limit witnesses, and determine when to stop testimony. Witnesses shall be excused upon completion of their testimony. All expenses associated with witness or counsel on behalf of the parties shall be borne by the respective parties.

F. Presentation of Evidence.

1. The presiding officer shall present the charge(s) made against the accused and briefly describe the evidence supporting the charge(s).

2. The complainant or a member of the Hearing Panel shall then present the case against the accused. Witnesses who can substantiate the case shall testify and answer questions of the accused and the Hearing Panel.

3. If the accused has exercised the right to be present at the hearing, he/she shall be called upon last to present any evidence which refutes the charges against him/her. This includes the presentation of witnesses as in Subsection E above. The accused member has the right to refuse to make a statement in his/her behalf. The accused will not be found guilty simply for refusing to testify. Once the accused chooses to

testify, however, he/she may be questioned by members of the Hearing Panel or the complainant.

4. The Hearing Panel will endeavor to conclude the hearing expeditiously.

5. The accused has the right to be present at all times during the hearing and to challenge all of the evidence presented against him/her.

G. Evidence. The Hearing Panel is not a court of law and is not required to observe the rules of evidence that apply in the trial of lawsuits. Consequently, evidence that would be inadmissible in a court of law may, at the Hearing Panel's discretion, be admissible at the hearing if it is relevant to the case and probative on a relevant issue. The Hearing Panel will not receive evidence or testimony for the purpose of supporting any charge that was not set forth in the notice of the hearing or that is not relevant to the issues of the case.

4. Burden of Proof. The burden of proving a violation of the Statement of Ethical Principles and Standards is on the complainant and/or the Hearing Panel. It is not up to the accused to prove his/her innocence of any wrongdoing. Although the charge(s) need not be proved "beyond a reasonable doubt," the Hearing Panel will not find the accused guilty in the absence of substantial and credible evidence to sustain the charge(s).

5. Deliberation of the Hearing Panel. After the hearing is completed, the Hearing Panel shall meet in a closed session to review the evidence presented and reach a conclusion. The Hearing Panel shall be the sole trier of fact and shall weigh the evidence presented and judge the credibility of the witnesses. The act of a majority of the members of the Hearing Panel shall be the decision of the Hearing Panel.

6. Decision of the Hearing Panel. The Hearing Panel will first resolve the issue of the guilt or innocence of the accused. Applying the burden of proof in paragraph 4 above, the Hearing Panel will vote by secret ballot, unless the members of the Hearing Panel consent to an oral vote. In the event a majority of the members of the Hearing Panel do not find the accused guilty, the charges shall be dismissed and the parties notified. If the Hearing Panel finds the accused has violated the Statement of Ethical Principles and Standards, it must then determine what sanctions to impose in accord with Section K.

Section O: Appeal Procedures

1. Appeals will be heard only in such cases wherein the appellant presents new evidence which would have affected the outcome of the original hearing or can demonstrate that a procedural error has occurred which can be shown to have had an adverse effect on the outcome.

A. The Appeals Committee will be composed of three (3) people: the past President, a member of the Ethics Committee who did not serve on the Hearing Panel, and another member of the Executive Committee chosen by the current President in consultation with the Chair of the Ethics Committee. ACPA Counsel and the Executive Director shall be available as consultants to the Appeals Committee.

B. The appeal with supporting documentation must be made in writing within sixty (60) working days by certified mail to the ACPA Executive Director and indicate the basis upon which it is made. If the member requires a time extension, he/she must request it in writing by certified mail within thirty (30) working days of receiving the decision by the Ethics Committee. The extension will consist of ninety (90) working days beginning from that request.

C. The Appeals Committee shall review all materials considered by the Ethics Committee.

D. Within thirty (30) working days of this appeal, the members on the Appeals Committee shall submit to the President of ACPA a written statement giving their opinion regarding the decision of the Hearing Panel.

E. Within fifteen (15) working days of receiving this opinion, the President of ACPA will reach a decision based on the considered opinions of the Appeals Committee from the following alternatives:
   1. support the decision of the Hearing Panel, or
   2. reverse the decision of the Hearing Panel.
3. The parties to the appeal shall be advised of the action in writing.

Section P: Records

1. Records of the Ethics Committee and the Appeals Committee shall remain at Headquarters and be confidential except for use by the Ethics Committee.

NAME INDEX

SUBJECT INDEX

595